Practices of Looking

Practices of Looking

An Introduction to Visual Culture

Second Edition

Marita Sturken and Lisa Cartwright

New York Oxford
OXFORD UNIVERSITY PRESS
2009

Oxford University Press, Inc., publishes works that further
Oxford University's objective of excellence
in research, scholarship, and education.

Oxford New York
Auckland Cape Town Dar es Salaam Hong Kong Karachi
Kuala Lumpur Madrid Melbourne Mexico City Nairobi
New Delhi Shanghai Taipei Toronto

With offices in
Argentina Austria Brazil Chile Czech Republic France Greece
Guatemala Hungary Italy Japan Poland Portugal Singapore
South Korea Switzerland Thailand Turkey Ukraine Vietnam

Published by Oxford University Press, Inc.
198 Madison Avenue, New York, New York 10016

www.oup.com

Library of Congress Cataloging-in-Publication Data

Sturken, Marita
Practices of looking : an introduction to visual culture / Marita Sturken and Lisa Cartwright.—2nd ed.
p. cm.
ISBN 978-0-19-531440-3
1. Art and society. 2. Culture. 3. Visual perception. 4. Visual communication. 5. Popular culture. 6. Communication and culture. I. Cartwright, Lisa, II. Title.
N72.S6S78 2009
701'.03—dc22 2008042118

9 8 7 6 5 4 3 2 1

Printed in the United States of America
on acid-free paper

contents

acknowledgments

We are grateful to many colleagues and students whose input has deeply informed this second edition of *Practices of Looking*. Our heartfelt thanks to those who offered advice and pointed criticisms, to our many anonymous readers, and to Sarah Banet-Weiser, Elspeth Brown, Hatim El-Hibri, Nitin Govil, Wendy Kozol, Nicholas Mirzoeff, Scott Selberg, and Ira Wagman. Heidi Solander was amazingly, impressively skilled in pulling together and tracking down the many images, and Kari Hensley did stellar research for us on images and generously lent her MA thesis analysis of images of the Iraq war. David Benin and Carolyn Kane helped with early research. Our students have provided crucial feedback and steered us toward many useful examples. Our thanks to the many artists who allowed us to reproduce their work.

At Oxford University Press, we have benefited immensely from the enthusiastic support and unerring patience of Peter Labella, truly a dream editor. Chelsea Gilmore was amazingly efficient in helping to keep the book on track, and Josh Hawkins and Brian Black have guided its production with great skill. We thank Carol Petro and Kathleen Lynch for their excellent work on, respectively, the layout and cover design for this Second Edition. We also thank the reviewers: David Blumkrantz, California State University, Northridge; Elspeth Brown, University of Toronto; Cynthia Chris, College of Staten Island, City University of New York; Michael Coventry, Georgetown University; James Elkins, Art Institute of Chicago; Bernard L. Herman, University of Delaware; Louis Kaplan, University of Toronto; Marina Levina, University of California, Berkeley; Briana L. Martino, Simmons College; Lisa Mills-Brown, University of Central Florida; Monica Pombo, Appalachian State University; Drew Tiene, Kent State University; Gregory Turner-Rahman, University of idaho.

Dana Polan provided steady support to an extraordinary degree. We thank Lori Boatright for her expert help and support in guiding us through practical and intellectual aspects of image property law covered in this edition and for her practical assistance with images and image rights along the way. Brian Goldfarb gave many suggestions and helped with new concepts and issues to be included in this edition, as well as with images; we thank him for this help. Nilo Goldfarb steered us to pop surrealism and many of the ideas about animation and new media included in this edition, and we thank him for his ideas and corrections to our new sections. To Sabina Goldfarb we are grateful for making us aware of the importance of new programming and the latest in youth media culture.

introduction

Is it possible in the early twenty-first century to distinguish between social realities and the media forms that represent them? From North American and European urban centers such as Los Angeles and Paris to transborder locations such as the frontier between Hong Kong and South China, digital images and imaging technologies increasingly facilitate cultural expression, communication, and everyday social interaction. Images and the screens that frame them seem every day to be more complexly saturated with text, detailed pictures, and color, to offer more information faster, and to call us to look more routinely than ever before. The social worlds most of us inhabit are filled with things designed to be seen or to be used in ways that involve looking. Every conceivable surface, from our car dashboards to our telephones, seems to hold potential as a site on which to put a visual screen.

We negotiate the world through visual culture, whether we are sighted or have low vision that requires adaptive or assistive technologies, and whether we live in urban spaces saturated with surfaces covered in advertisements and signs or remote places in which we depend on our screens to connect with "the world." Our lives are increasingly dominated by the visual and by communication technologies (both wired and wireless) that allow for the global circulation of ideas, information, and politics. Ideas and information circulate globally in visual forms, and images play a central role in political conflict and meaning. We are thus at a moment in history in which the visual matters more than ever, as representation, as information, as politics, as provocation, as forms of play and entertainment, and as both a connecting force and a source of conflict around the world.

Practices of Looking provides an overview of a range of theories about how we engage in looking in everyday ways, how we understand a wide array of visual media, and how we use images to express ourselves, to communicate, to experience pleasure, to feel, and to learn. The term "visual culture" encompasses many media forms ranging from fine art to popular film and television to advertising to visual data in fields such as the sciences, law, and medicine. This book explores the following questions: What does it mean to study these diverse forms together? How do shared understandings of these various forms of visual culture emerge? How does meaning circulate through diverse visual forms, and how has the visual impacted our societies? We feel that it is important to consider visual culture as a complex and richly varied whole for an important reason: when we have an experience with a particular visual medium, we draw on associations with other media and other areas of our lives informed by visual images. For example, when we watch a television show, the meanings and pleasure we derive from it might be drawn, consciously or unconsciously, from associations with things we have seen in movies, works of art, or advertisements. The experience of viewing a medical ultrasound image might evoke emotions or meanings more typically associated with viewing photographs. Playing video games is connected to watching films, and the practice of circulating digital images via e-mail and the World Wide Web borrows from practices of image exchange through photograph albums and slide shows. Our visual experiences do not take place in isolation; they are enriched by memories and images from many different aspects of our lives.

Despite this cross-fertilization of visual forms, our cultures tend to rank different areas of visual culture according to systems of supposed quality and importance. For many decades, colleges and universities offered courses on the fine arts but did not consider popular media such as movies and television to be worthy of serious academic study. Today, in contrast, many art historians include photography, computer animation, mixed media, installation, and performance art among the practices they study. At the same time other fields, some of them new, have taken up a broader range of media forms. Since the 1950s, scholars in the field of communication have written important studies of radio, television, print media, and now the Internet. The disciplines of cinema, television, and media studies, which were instituted in the 1960s and 1970s, have helped us to consider how movies, television programs, and the Web have contributed to changes in culture over the course of this century. These fields have established the value of studying popular forms of visual media. The field of science and technology studies has encouraged the study of visual technologies and the use of images in areas outside the arts and entertainment, such as the sciences, law, and medicine. Cultural studies, an interdisciplinary field that emerged in the late 1970s, has offered many ways of thinking about the study of both popular culture and the seemingly mundane uses of images in our daily lives. One of the aims of cultural studies is to provide viewers, citizens, and consumers with the tools to gain a better understanding of how visual media help us make sense of our society. Looking at images across disciplines can help us to think about the interrelatedness of different kinds of visual media. In the course of reading this book, the reader will encounter ideas drawn from cultural studies, cinema and media studies, communication, art history, sociology, science studies, and anthropology.

What is visual culture? Culture has been famously characterized by theorist Raymond Williams as one of the most complex words in the English language. It is an elaborate concept, the meaning of which has changed over time.[1] Traditionally, culture was equated with the "fine" arts: classic works of painting, literature, music, and philosophy. The philosopher Matthew Arnold defined culture in the eighteenth century as the "best that has been thought and said" in a society, something reserved for an elite, educated, discerning audience.[2] If one uses the term this way, a famous work by Michelangelo or a composition by Mozart would represent the epitome of culture. Culture is something cultivated in people through exposure to and education about quality. The idea of "high" culture formerly was implicit in definitions of culture, followed by the notion that culture can be separated into the categories of high (fine art, classical painting, literature) and low (television, popular novels, comic books). As we explore further in chapter 2, high versus low was the traditional way of framing discussions about culture through most of the twentieth century, with high culture widely regarded as quality culture and low culture as its debased counterpart.

The term *culture*, in what is known as the "anthropological definition," refers to a "whole way of life," meaning a broad range of activities geared toward classifying and communicating symbolically within a society. Popular music, print media, art, and literature are some of the classificatory systems and symbolic means of expression and communication through which humans organize their lives. So too are sports, cooking, driving, relationships, and kinship. This definition, which emphasizes culture as sets of everyday and pervasive activities, allows for an understanding of mass and popular forms of classification, expression, and communication as legitimate aspects of culture.

In this book, we are defining *visual culture* as the shared practices of a group, community, or society through which meanings are made out of the visual, aural, and textual world of representations and the ways that looking practices are engaged in symbolic and communicative activities. Here, we are indebted to the foundational ideas of twentieth-century British theorist Raymond Williams and the work of British cultural studies scholar Stuart Hall. Williams and Hall both have argued that culture is not so much a set of things (television shows or paintings, for example) as a set of processes or practices through which individuals and groups come to make sense of things, including their own identities within and even against or outside the group. Culture is produced through complex networks of talking, gesturing, looking, and acting, through which meanings are exchanged between members of a society or group. Objects such as images and media texts come into play in this network of exchange not as static entities traded or consumed but as active agents that draw us to look and to feel or speak in particular ways. Hall states, "It is the participants in a culture who give meaning to people, objects, and events. . . . It is by our use of things, and what we say, think and feel about them—how we represent them—that we give them a meaning."[3] We take this concept a step further by asserting that just as we humans give meaning to objects, so too do the objects we create, gaze on, and use for communication or simply for pleasure have the power to give meaning to us as well in the dynamic interaction of social networks. The exchange of meaning and value between people, on the one hand, and the objects and technologies in their worlds, on the other, is interactive and dynamic. This means that artifacts such as images and imaging technologies have politics and agency.

It is important to keep in mind that in any group that shares a culture (or set of processes through which meaning is made), there is always a range of meanings and interpretations "floating about," so to speak, with regard to any given issue or object at any given time. Culture is a process, not a fixed set of practices or interpretations. For example, three different viewers of the same advertisement who share a general view of the world may differently interpret the ad's meaning based on their respective experiences and knowledge. These people may share the same culture but still subject the image to different interpretive processes. These viewers may then talk about their responses, influencing one another's subsequent views. Some viewers might argue more convincingly than others; some might be regarded as having more authority than others. In the end, meanings are produced not in the minds of individual viewers so much as through a process of negotiation among individuals within a particular culture and between individuals and the artifacts, images, technologies, and texts created by themselves and others. Interpretations, then, are as effective as the visual artifacts (such as advertisements or films), industries, and producers that generate them in influencing a culture's or a group's shared worldview. Our use of the term *culture* throughout this book emphasizes this understanding of culture as a fluid and interactive process—a process grounded in multimodal and multisensory social practices, not solely in images, texts, or interpretations.

Practices of Looking is concerned with those aspects of culture that are manifested in visual form or that are organized in a way that invites looking—paintings, drawings, prints, photographs, film, television, video, digital images, animation, graphic novels and comic books, popular culture, news images, entertainment, advertising, images as legal evidence, and science images. We feel that visual culture is something that should be understood in an analytical way, not only by art historians and other "image specialists" but also by all of us who increasingly encounter a startling array of images and invitations to look in our daily lives. At the same time, many theorists of visual culture have argued that foregrounding the visual in visual culture does not mean separating images from writing, speech, language, or others modes of representation and experience. Images often are integrated with written words or sounds, as in much contemporary art and in the history of advertising. Our goal is to set out some of the theories that can help us to understand how images function in a broader cultural sphere and how looking practices inform our lives beyond our perception of images per se.

This book, in its first edition, took as its distant inspiration John Berger's classic book, *Ways of Seeing*. Published in 1972, *Ways of Seeing* was a model for the examination of images and their meanings across such disciplinary boundaries as media studies and art history. Berger's work was groundbreaking in bringing together a range of theories, from Walter Benjamin's concept of mechanical reproduction to Marxist theory, in order to examine images from the history of art and advertising. We pay homage to many of the strategies of that book in updating such an approach to visual culture in the contemporary theoretical and media context. The terrain of images and their trajectories has become significantly more complex since Berger wrote his book, as have the theoretical concepts that we use as tools. Technological changes have made possible the movements of images throughout the globe at much greater speed. The economic context of postindustrial capitalism has enabled a blurring of many previously understood boundaries between cultural and social realms such as art, news, and commodity culture. The mix of styles in postmodernism has aided in producing a context of image circulation and cross-referencing that prompts this kind of interdisciplinary approach.

The approaches of *Practices of Looking* can thus be understood in several different ways. One approach is to use theories to study images themselves and their meanings as texts. This is a primary, yet not the only, approach to understanding the dynamics of looking. It allows us to examine what images tell us about the cultures in which they are produced. A second approach is to look at the modes of responding to visuality, as represented in studies of spectators or audiences and their psychological and social patterns of looking. In this approach, the emphasis shifts from images and their meanings to viewers' practices of looking and the various and specific ways people regard, use, and interpret images. Some of these approaches concern theorizing an idealized viewer, such as the cinematic spectator; others involve considering what actual viewers do with popular culture texts through studies of reception. A third approach considers how media images, texts, and programs move from one social arena to another and circulate in and across cultures, which is especially relevant in light of the escalation of globalization since the mid-twentieth century. This approach looks at the institutional frameworks that regulate and sometimes limit the circulation of images, as well as the ways in which images change meaning in different cultural contexts. In these approaches, this book offers a set of tools, some drawn from the critical theory of the late twentieth century, that can be used in deciphering and re-deploying visual media, and to analyze how and why we have come to rely so heavily on visual forms to make meaning in almost all aspects of our lives.

By the beginning of the 1990s, scholars working on the theory of visual culture had become aware that critical theory was in a crisis. *Critical theory* refers to a set of models or systematic frameworks developed in the late twentieth century across fields including sociology, literature, linguistics, and philosophy to describe, explain, and critique phenomena or experience in the world. Critical theorists drew from structuralism, phenomenology, Marxism, feminism, and psychoanalysis, approaches well represented in this book. Theory was seen to be in crisis by the end of that century because the writing associated with it was not providing the kind of explanatory power or impetus to social change desired by many of its authors. Critiquing something does not necessarily change it, nor does it describe social conditions adequately. Some postmodern theorists, many of whom rejected the term *theory* itself, began to propose ways of writing and thinking about culture that did not have the same coherence or unity of approach but that, rather, allowed for movement and change beyond what had been imaginable within the framework of current social conditions.

Practices of Looking shares with these postmodern writers the idea that theory, and getting theory exactly right, cannot in itself provide adequate understanding and impetus to change. We therefore set forth a plurality of theories in this book, some older and some more recent, as a kind of toolbox for critical thinking and for action with regard to how we look and how we make and use things in the realm of the visual in our everyday worlds. There is no single method or approach that we advocate in this book. Rather, we offer here a range of concepts through which one might pursue ideas to arrive at new ways of engaging with the visual in the social worlds in which we interact.

We therefore encourage you to use this book interactively with other texts and other media in your everyday lives. Go out in the world to museums, community centers, and consumer environments and look at the ways visuality comes into play. Look at how looking practices are enacted around you. When you go to your clinic for health care, notice how and when looking and visual representation come into play in your course of treatment. Notice how and when looking is off limits. Do not just read the news; watch the news with full attention to how it is composed, framed, and edited. Watch others watching the news. Try to discern not only what is shown but also what news is *not* shown. Studying visual culture is not only about seeing what is shown. It is also about seeing *how* things are shown and seeing what we are *not* shown, what we do not see—either because we do not have sight ability, because something is restricted from view, or because we do not have the means for understanding and coming to terms with what is right before our eyes.

Practices of Looking is organized into ten chapters that address cultural ways of looking in relationship to knowledge and power, considering visual culture across various media and cultural spheres. Chapter 1, "Images, Power, and Politics," introduces many of the themes of the book, such as the concept of representation, the role of photography, the relationship of images to ideology, the basic concept of semiotics, and the ways in which we make meaning from and award value to images. It is one of the central tenets of this book that meaning does not reside within images but is produced at the moment that they are consumed by and circulate among viewers. Thus chapter 2, "Viewers Make Meaning," focuses on the ways that viewers produce meaning from images, discusses the concept of ideology in more depth, and explores the complex dynamics of appropriation, incorporation, and cultural production in contemporary image culture. In chapter 3, "Modernity: Spectatorship, Power, and Knowledge," we step back to examine the foundational aspects of modernity and theories of power and spectatorship. This chapter explores the concept of the modern subject, as well as the concept of the gaze, in both psychoanalytic theory and theories of power. Here we examine the ways that images can be used as elements of discourse, institutional power, and categorization.

Chapters 4 and 5 map out theories of images throughout the history of representation and situate them in relation to contemporary image culture. Chapter 4 is the most art historical of the chapters. "Realism and Perspective: From Renaissance Painting to Digital Media" explores the history of realism in representation and maps out the history of technologies of seeing, such as perspective, from the Renaissance to contemporary image practices and game culture. This chapter analyzes the concept of realism in art from Egyptian art to photography to digital image culture in relation to the development of perspective and challenges to perspective's dominance in image conventions. Chapter 5, "Visual Technologies, Image Reproduction, and the Copy," takes a similar historical approach to the history of visual technologies, such as the development of photography and cinema, and concepts of reproduction that have dominated visual analysis. We also examine the political and legal issues raised by image reproduction from the nineteenth century to digital image culture. Chapter 5 includes discussion of images and intellectual property, an issue of increasing importance in the twenty-first century era of digital reproducibility.

In chapter 6, "The Media in Everyday Life," we turn to the history of concepts of mass media, tracing critiques of the media throughout the twentieth century and concepts of propaganda and the public sphere. This chapter addresses how the Web and digital media have dramatically changed the forms and institutions of the media to the extent that the term *mass media* has lost its currency. We examine concepts of the democratic potential of media, media flows, and national and global media events. Chapter 7, "Advertising, Consumer Cultures, and Desire," focuses on the role of the visual in the development of and social impact of consumer culture. This chapter discusses theories of ideology and semiotics as tools for understanding the strategies used in advertising images and examines the marketing of coolness and the reconfiguring of consumer culture it has entailed.

In chapter 8, "Postmodernism, Indie Media, and Popular Culture," we look at the central concepts of postmodern theory and at a range of styles in contemporary art, popular culture, and advertising that can be seen as postmodern. We discuss postmodern strategies of reflexivity, pastiche, parody, and the politics of postmodernism as a philosophical concept. Chapter 9, "Scientific Looking, Looking at Science" returns to many of the concepts of photographic truth discussed earlier in the book to look at the relationship of images to evidence and the role of images in science. This chapter begins with the history of how science has been depicted as a form of theater and analyzes the politics of imaging the body's interior, the meanings created by new medical imaging technologies, and the marketing of science in pharmaceutical ads. The final chapter, chapter 10, "The Global Flow of Visual Culture," looks at the ways in which images travel in the contemporary context of globalization. This chapter examines the role that images have played in the concept of the global, how popular culture has become increasingly global in its circulation and content, and the impact of globalization on art production and exhibition. It looks at the conditions within and across societies in a globalizing economy in which the distribution of visual technologies is remarkably wide ranging but radically uneven. The book concludes with an extensive glossary of many terms used in the book.

Practices of Looking aims to engage with a broad range of issues of visual culture by examining how images gain meaning in many cultural arenas, from art and commerce to science and the law; how they travel through different cultural arenas and in distinct cultures; and how they are an integral and important aspect of our lives. Culture matters, and images matter, to how we live our lives in relation to others and the politics of meaning in the world today.

Notes

1. Raymond Williams, *Keywords: A Vocabulary of Culture and Society*, rev. ed., 87 (New York: Oxford University Press, 1983).
2. Matthew Arnold, *Culture and Anarchy*, 6 (Cambridge: Cambridge University Press, 1932).
3. Stuart Hall, "Introduction," in *Representation: Cultural Representations and Signifying Practices*, ed. Stuart Hall, 3 (Thousand Oaks, Calif.: Sage, 1997).

Further Reading

Berger, John. *Ways of Seeing*. London: Penguin, 1972.

Bryson, Norman, Michael Ann Holly, and Keith Moxey, eds. *Visual Culture: Images and Interpretations*. Middletown, Conn.: Wesleyan University Press, 1994.

Elkins, James. *The Object Stares Back: On the Nature of Seeing*. New York: Harcourt, 1997.

———. *The Domain of Images*. Ithaca, N.Y.: Cornell University Press, 2001.

Evans, Jessica, and Stuart Hall, eds. *Visual Culture: The Reader*. Thousand Oaks, Calif.: Sage, 1999.

Goldfarb, Brian. *Visual Pedagogy: Media Cultures in and Beyond the Classroom*. Durham, N.C.: Duke University Press, 2002.

Hall, Stuart, ed. *Representation: Cultural Representations and Signifying Practices*. Thousand Oaks, Calif.: Sage, 1997.

Holly, Michael Ann, and Keith Moxey, eds. *Art History, Aesthetics, Visual Studies*. New Haven: Yale University Press/Clark Art Institute, 2002.

Howells, Richard. *Visual Culture*. Cambridge: Polity Press, 2003.

Jenks, Chris, ed. *Visual Culture*. New York: Routledge, 1995.

Jones, Amelia, ed. *The Feminism and Visual Culture Reader*. New York: Routledge, 2003.

Lester, Paul Martin. *Visual Communication: Images with Messages*. 4th ed. Belmont, Calif.: Thomson/Wadsworth, 2006.

Mirzoeff, Nicholas, ed. *The Visual Culture Reader*. 2nd ed. New York: Routledge, 2002.

———. *An Introduction to Visual Culture*. New York: Routledge, 1999.

Mitchell, W. J. T. *Picture Theory*. Chicago: University of Chicago Press, 1994.

———. *What Do Pictures Want?: The Lives and Loves of Images*. Chicago: University of Chicago Press, 2005.

Nakamura, Lisa. *Digitizing Race: Visual Cultures of the Internet*. Minneapolis: University of Minnesota Press, 2007.

Rose, Gillian. *Visual Methodologies: An Introduction to the Interpretation of Visual Materials*. 2nd ed. Thousand Oaks, Calif.: Sage, 2007.

Schwartz, Vanessa R., and Jeannene M. Przyblyski. *The Nineteenth-Century Visual Culture Reader*. New York: Routledge, 2004.

Staniszewski, Mary Anne. *Believing is Seeing: Creating the Culture of Art*. New York: Penguin, 1995.

chapter **one**

Images, Power, and Politics

Every day, we engage in practices of looking to make sense of the world. To those of us who are blind or have low vision, seeing and visuality are no less important than they are to those of us who are sighted, because the everyday world is so strongly organized around visual and spatial cues that take seeing for granted. Looking is a social practice, whether we do it by choice or compliance. Through looking, and through touching and hearing as means of navigating space organized around the sense of sight, we negotiate our social relationships and meanings.

Like other practices, looking involves relationships of power. To willfully look or not is to exercise choice and compliance and to influence whether and how others look. To be made to look, to try to get someone else to look at you or at something you want to be noticed, or to engage in an exchange of looks entails a play of power. Looking can be easy or difficult, pleasurable or unpleasant, harmless or dangerous. Conscious and unconscious aspects of looking intersect. We engage in practices of looking to communicate, to influence, and to be influenced. Even when we choose not to look, or when we look away, these are activities that have meaning within the economy of looking.

We live in cultures that are increasingly permeated by visual images with a variety of purposes and intended effects. These images can produce in us a wide array of emotions and responses. We invest the visual artifacts and images we create and encounter on a daily basis with significant power—for instance, the power to conjure an absent person, the power to calm or incite to action, the power to persuade or mystify, the power to remember. A single image can serve a multitude of purposes, appear in a range of settings, and mean different things to different people.

This image of women and schoolchildren looking at a murder scene in the street dramatically draws our attention to practices of looking. The photograph was taken by Weegee, a self-taught photographer of the mid-twentieth century whose real name was Arthur Fellig. The name *Weegee* is a play on the board game called Ouija, because he showed up at crime scenes so quickly that it was joked he must have supernatural psychic powers. He was known for his hard-core depictions of crime and violence in the streets of New York. Weegee listened to a police radio he kept in his car in order to arrive at crime scenes quickly, then, while onlookers watched, he would develop the photographs he took in the trunk of his car, which was set up as a portable darkroom.

"A woman relative cried . . . but neighborhood dead-end kids enjoyed the show when a small-time racketeer was shot and killed," states the caption accompanying this image, titled "The First Murder," in Weegee's 1945 publication *Naked New York*.[1] On the facing page is displayed a photograph of what the children saw: the

FIG. 1.1
Weegee (Arthur Felig), *The First Murder*, before 1945

dead body of a gangster. In *The First Murder*, Weegee calls attention to both the act of looking at the forbidden scene and the capacity of the still camera to capture heightened fleeting emotion. The children are gawking at the murder scene with morbid fascination, ignoring the bawling relative. As viewers, we look with equal fascination on the scene, catching the children in the act of looking, their eyes wide with shock and wonder. We also witness the woman crying. Her eyes are closed, as if to shut out the sight of her dead relative. Near her another woman, the only other adult in the photograph, lowers her eyes, averting her look in the face of something awful. This is an adult practice that serves as a counterpoint to the children's bold first look at murder to which the title draws our attention.

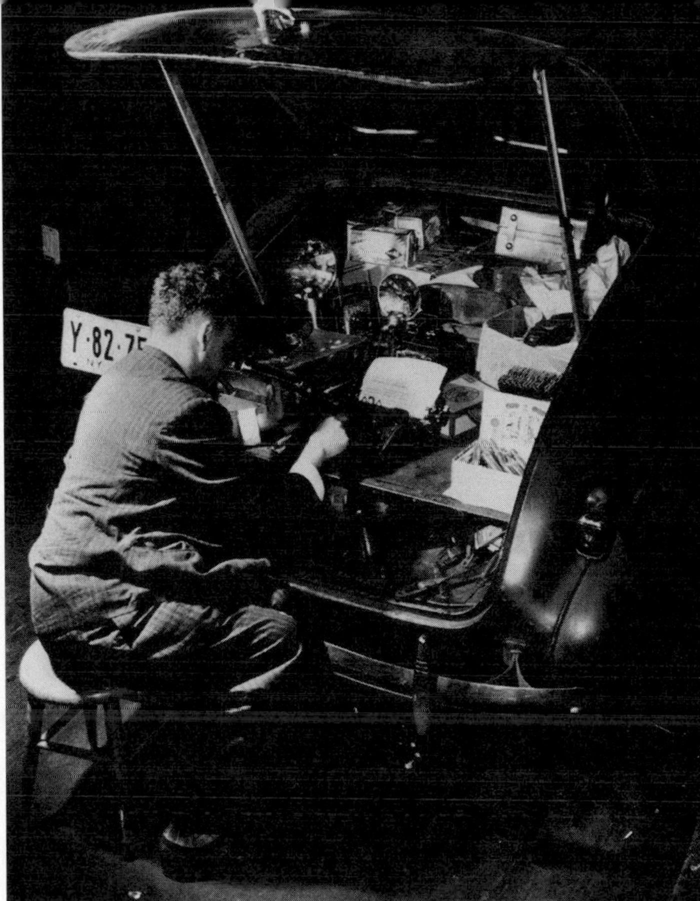

FIG. 1.2
Weegee working in the trunk of his Chevrolet, 1942

The role of images in providing views of violence, and of voyeurism and fascination with violence, is countered by a history of using images to expose the devastating aspects of violence. One particularly graphic historical example of this use of images was the wide circulation of an image of Emmett Till, a boy who was murdered during the beginning of the civil rights movement in the United States. Till, a 14-year-old young black man from Chicago, was visiting relatives in a small Mississippi town in August 1955. In the context of the strict codes of Jim Crow segregation, he allegedly whistled at a white woman. In retaliation for this act, he was kidnapped by white men, tortured (his eye gouged out), beaten, and shot through the head, then thrown into the Tallahatchie River with a gin mill tied to his neck with barbed wire. Till's mother, recognizing the power of visual evidence, insisted on holding an open-casket funeral. She allowed his corpse to be photographed so everyone could see the gruesome evidence of violence exacted upon her son. The highly publicized funeral, which brought 50,000 mourners, and the graphic photograph of Till's brutalized body (fig. 1.3), which was published in *Jet* magazine, were major catalysts of the nascent civil rights movement. This image showed in shockingly graphic detail the violence that was enacted on a young black man for allegedly whistling at a white woman. It represented the violent oppression of blacks in the time period. In this image, the power of the photograph to provide evidence of violence and injustice is coupled with the photograph's power to shock and horrify.

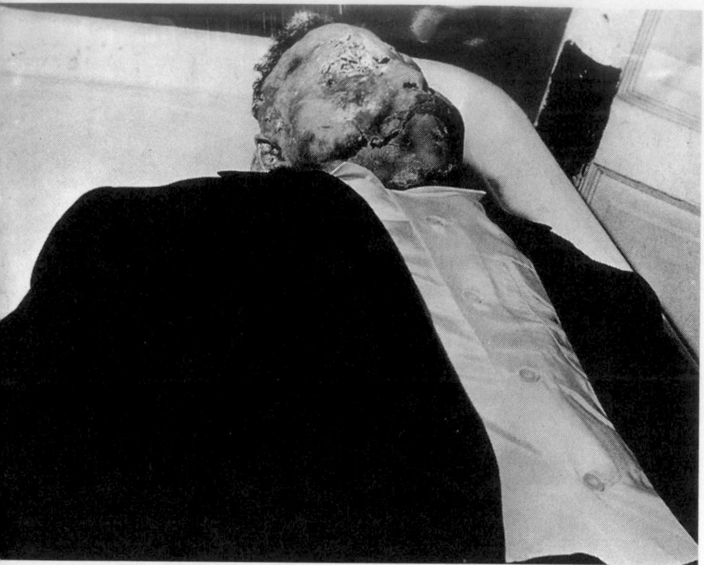

FIG. 1.3
Photograph of Emmett Till's brutalized body in his casket, 1955

Representation

Representation refers to the use of language and images to create meaning about the world around us. We use words to understand, describe, and define the world as we see it, and we also use images this way. This process takes place through systems such as language that are structured according to rules and conventions. A language has a set of rules about how to express and interpret meaning. So do the systems of representation used in painting, drawing, photography, cinema, television, and digital media. Although these systems of representation are not languages, they are in some ways *like* language systems and therefore can be analyzed through methods borrowed from linguistics and semiotics.

Throughout history, debates about representation have considered whether representations reflect the world as it is, mirroring it back to us through mimesis or imitation, or whether we construct the world and its meaning through representations. In this book, we argue that we make meaning of the material world through understanding objects and entities in their specific cultural contexts. This process of understanding the meaning of things in context takes place in part through our use of written, gestural, spoken, or drawn representations. The material world has meaning and can be "seen" by us only through representations. The world is not simply reflected back to us through representations that stand in for things by copying their appearance. We construct the meaning of things through the process of representing them. Although the concept of mimesis has a long history, today it is no longer accepted that representations are mere copies of things as they are or as the person who created them believes they ought to be.

The distinction between the idea of reflection, or mimesis, and representation as a construction of the material world can be difficult to make. The still life, for instance, has been a favored genre of artists for many centuries. One might surmise that the still life is motivated by the desire to reflect, rather than make meaning of, material objects as they appear in the world. In this still life, painted in 1765 by French painter Henri-Horace Roland de la Porte, an array of food and drink is carefully arranged on a table and painted with attention to each minute detail. The objects, such as the fruit, the bowl and cup, and the wooden tabletop, are rendered with close attention to light and detail. They seem so lifelike that one imagines one could touch them. Yet, is this image simply a reflection of this particular scene,

FIG. 1.4
Henri-Horace Roland de la Porte, *Still Life*, c. 1765

rendered with skill by the artist? Is it simply a mimetic copy of a scene, painted for the sake of showing us what was there? Roland de la Porte was a student of Jean-Batiste-Siméone Chardin, a French painter who was fascinated with the style of the seventeen-century Dutch painters, who developed techniques of pictorial realism more than a century before the advent of photography. The seventeenth- and eighteenth-century still life ranged from paintings that were straightforwardly representational to those that were deeply symbolic. This painting includes many symbols of rustic peasant life. It invokes a way of living even without the presence of human figures. Elements such as food and drink convey philosophical as well as symbolic meanings, such as the transience of earthly life through the ephemeral materiality of basic, humble foods. The fresh fruits and wildflowers evoke earthy flavors and aromas. The crumbs of cheese and the half-filled carafe conjure the presence of someone who has eaten this simple meal.

In 2003, artist Marion Peck produced this painting, *Still Life with Dralas*, in the style of the Roland de la Porte still life. *Drala* is a term used in Buddhism to refer to energy in matter and the universe. Peck, a contemporary pop surrealist painter, interprets Roland de la Porte's still life to contain a kind of anthropomorphic energy in the rendering of the fruit and the dishes and glassware, which she brings to life with comic little faces. The painting holds an abundance of looks. Each tiny grape contains an eyeball. The conventions of painting used in the eighteenth-century work are understood to convey realism according to the terms of that era. In Peck's contemporary painting, the genre of the still life is subject to a kind of reflexive interpretation that humorously animates and makes literal its meanings, emphasizing possible metaphysical values

FIG. 1.5
Marion Peck, *Still Life With Dralas*, 2003

FIG. 1.6
René Magritte, *The Treachery of Images (This is Not a Pipe) [La Trahison des images (Ceci n'est pas une pipe)]*, 1928–29

contained in the original painting's symbolism. Here, we want to note that that these paintings produce meanings through the ways that they are composed and rendered, and not just in the choices of objects depicted.

We learn the rules and conventions of the systems of representation within a given culture. Many artists have attempted to defy those conventions, to break the rules of various systems of representation, and to push the boundaries of definitions of representation. This painting, by the Belgian Surrealist artist René Magritte,

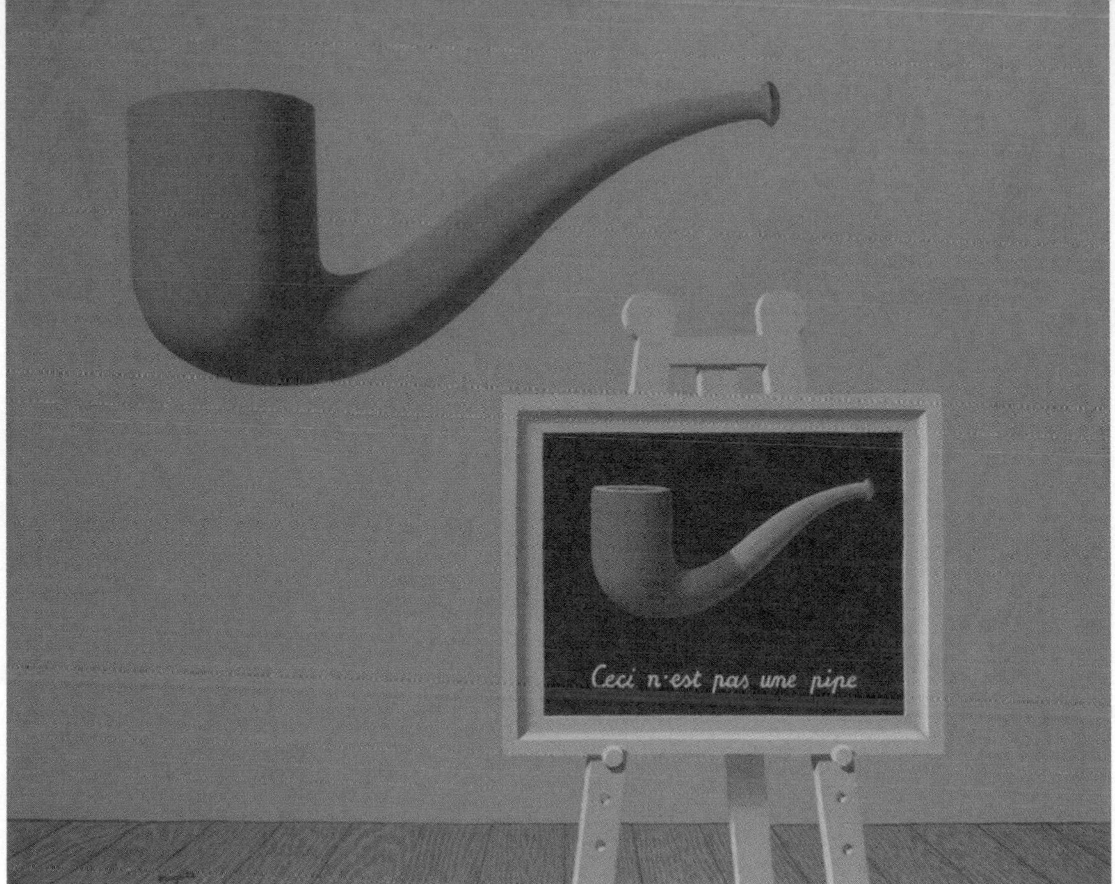

FIG. 1.7
René Magritte, *Les Deux Mysteres (The Two Mysteries)*, 1966

comments on the process of representation. Entitled *The Treachery of Images* (1928–1929), the painting depicts a pipe with the line in French, "This is not a pipe." One could argue, on the one hand, that Magritte is making a joke, that of course it is an image of a pipe that he has created. However, he is also pointing to the relationship between words and things, as this is not a pipe itself but rather the representation of a pipe; it is a painting rather than the material object itself. Magritte produced a series of paintings and drawings on this theme, including *The Two Mysteries* (1966), a painting in which a pipe is rendered ambiguously as floating in space either behind, in front of, or just above a painting of a pipe, with the same witty subscript, propped on an easel. Here, we have two pipes—or rather, two drawings of the same pipe—or a painting of a pipe and a painting of a painting of a pipe and a subscript identifying it. French philosopher Michel Foucault elaborated on Magritte's ideas by exploring these images' implied commentary about the relationship between words and things and the complex relationship between the drawing, the paintings, their words, and their referent (the pipe).[2] One could not pick up and smoke this pipe. So Magritte can be seen to be pointing out something so obvious as to render the written message absurd. He highlights the very act of labeling as something we should think about, drawing our attention to the word "pipe" and the limits of its function in representing the object, as well as the limits of the drawing in representing the pipe. Magritte asks us to consider how labels and images produce meaning yet cannot fully invoke the experience of the object. Negations, Foucault explains, multiply, and the layers of representation pile on one another to the point of incoherence. As we stop to examine the process of representation in this series by Magritte, we can see how the most banal and everyday, sensible uses of representation can so easily fall apart, can be simply silly. In many of his other visual works, Magritte demonstrated that between words and objects one may create new relations and meanings through juxtaposition and changing contexts.

Magritte's painting is famous. Many artists have played off of it. The cartoon artist Scott McCloud, in his book *Understanding Comics*, uses Magritte's *Treachery of Images* to explain the concept of representation in the vocabulary of comics, noting that the reproduction of the painting in his book is a printed copy of a drawing of a painting of a pipe, and following this with a hilarious series of pictograms of icons such as the American flag, a stop sign, and a smiley face, all drawn with disclaimers attached (this is not America, this is not law, this is not a face). The digital theorist Talan Memmott, in a work of digital media called *The Brotherhood of the Bent Billiard*, offers a "hypermediated art historical fiction" about Magritte's *Treachery* and the generations of textual and visual interpretations it spawned. Book One of *The Brotherhood* traces the development of the pipe as an emblem from its first appearance in a painting of 1926 to the famous works reproduced here. In Memmott's piece, Magritte's image play with meaning and representation is the impetus for the production of a reauthored narrative of Magritte that is an opportunity for considering meaning and representation in the era of digital imaging. Memmott describes his work as a "narrative hack" of the complex system of allegories and symbols built up over Magritte's career, referred to as his "symbolic calculus."[3] As these examples all make clear, today we are surrounded by images that play with representation, unmasking our initial assumptions and inviting us to experience layers of meanings beyond the obvious or the apparent real or true meaning.

The Myth of Photographic Truth

Throughout its history, photography has been associated with realism. But the creation of an image through a camera lens always involves some degree of subjective choice through selection, framing, and personalization. It is true that some types of image recording seem to take place without human intervention. In surveillance videos, for instance, no one stands behind the lens to determine what and how any particular event should be shot. Yet even in surveillance video, someone has programmed the camera to record a particular part of a space and to frame that space in a particular way. In the case of many automatic video and still-photography cameras designed for the consumer market, aesthetic choices such as focus and framing are made as if by the camera itself, yet in fact the designers of these cameras also made decisions based on social and aesthetic norms and standards concerning elements such as depth of focus and color. These selections are invisible to the user—they are black-boxed, relieving the photographer of the need to make various formal decisions. It remains the photographer who frames and takes the image, not the camera itself. Yet, despite the subjective aspects of the act of taking a picture, the aura of machine objectivity clings to mechanical and electronic images. All camera-generated images, be they photographic, cinematic, electronic, or digital, bear the cultural legacy of still photography, which historically has been regarded as a more objective practice than, say, painting or drawing. This combination of the subjective and the objective is a central tension in our regard of camera-generated images.

Photography, the technique in which light rays reflecting off objects pass through a lens and register an imprint on a medium such as silver halide film (or, in the case of digital photography, a digital chip), was developed in Europe during the mid-nineteenth century, when concepts of positivist science held sway. Positivism, a philosophy that emerged in the mid-nineteenth century, holds that scientific knowledge is the only authentic knowledge and concerns itself with truths about the world. In positivism, the individual actions of the scientist came to be viewed as a liability in the process of performing and reproducing experiments, as it was thought that the scientist's own subjective actions might influence the outcome or skew the objectivity of the experiment. Hence, in positivism, machines were regarded as more reliable than unaided human sensory perception or the hand of the artist in the production of empirical evidence. Photography seemed to suit the positivist way of thinking because it is a method of producing representations through a mechanical recording device (the camera) rather than the scientist's subjective eye and hand (using pencil to sketch a view on paper, for example). In the context of positivism, the photographic camera could be understood as a scientific tool for registering reality more accurately.

Since the mid-nineteenth century, there have been many arguments for and against the idea that photographs are objective renderings of the real world that provide unbiased truth. Some advocates of photography held that cameras render the world in a perspective that is detached from a subjective, particular human viewpoint because the conventions of the image are for the most part built into the apparatus. Others emphasized the role of the photographer in the subjective process of choosing, composing, lighting, and framing scenes. These debates have taken on new intensity with the introduction of digital imaging processes. A photograph is often perceived to be an unmediated copy of the real world, a trace of reality skimmed off the very surface of life, and evidence of the real. Photographs have been used to prove that someone was alive at a particular time and place in history. For instance, after the Holocaust, some survivors sent photographs to their families from whom they had long been separated as an affirmation that they were alive.

The French theorist Roland Barthes famously noted that the photograph, unlike a drawing, offers an unprecedented conjunction between what is here now (the image) and what was there then (the referent, or object, thing, or place).[4] This conjunction relies on a myth of photographic truth. When a photograph is introduced as documentary evidence in a courtroom, it is often presented as if it were incontrovertible proof that an event took place in a particular way and in a particular place. As such, it is perceived to speak the truth in a direct way. Barthes used the term *studium* to describe this truth function of the photograph. The order of the studium also refers to the photograph's ability to invoke a distanced appreciation for what the image holds. At the same time, the truth-value of photography has been the focus of skepticism and debate, in contexts such as courtrooms, about the different "truths" that images can tell and the limits of the image as evidence. That is why we refer to photographic truth as a myth. The contestation of truth in photographs has come into question with special urgency with the more increasing use since the 1990s of digital editing software, which allows photographs to be manipulated with much greater ease than ever before. Barthes referred to photographic truth as myth not because he felt that photographs do not tell the truth but because he regarded truth as always culturally inflected, never pure and uninfluenced by contextual factors. For Barthes, there is no singular truth to be identified outside the myths or ideologies of cultural expression.

Photographs are also objects in which we invest deep emotional content. They are one of the primary means through which we remember events, conjure up the presence of an absent person, and experience longing for someone we have lost or someone we desire but whom we have never seen or met. They are crucial to what we remember, but they can also enable us to forget those things that were not photographed. Photographs are objects that channel affect in ways that often seem magical. Roland Barthes once wrote that photographs always indicate a kind of mortality, evoking death in the moments in which they seem to stop time.[5] Barthes coined the use of the term *punctum* to characterize the affective element of those certain photographs that pierce one's heart with feeling. The meaning of photographs can thus be seen as somewhat paradoxical in that they can be emotional objects through the punctum, or the emotionally piercing quality, yet they can also, through the effect of the studium, serve as banal traces of the real, documentary evidence of something that simply *has happened*. Photographic meaning derives precisely from this paradoxical combination of affective and magical qualities and the photograph's cultural status as cold proof. Artist and theorist Allan Sekula proposes: "photographs achieve semantic status as fetish objects *and* as documents. The photograph is imagined to have, depending on its context, a power that is primarily affective or a power that is primarily informative. Both powers reside in the mythical truth-value of the photograph."[6]

It is an additional paradox of photography that, although we know that images can be ambiguous and are easily manipulated or altered, particularly with the help of digital technology, much of the power of photography still lies in the shared belief that photographs are objective or truthful records of events. Our awareness of the subjective nature of imaging is in constant tension with the legacy of objectivity that clings to the cameras and machines that produce images today, even as the increasing availability of digital imaging software makes the alteration of photographs both easy and widespread.

The images created by cameras can be simultaneously informative and expressive. This photograph was taken by Robert Frank while he was traveling around the United States from 1955 to 1957 on two Guggenheim fellowships awarded to him to document American life at every strata. Eighty-three photographs selected from 687 rolls of film (more than 20,000 photographs) he took over two years were published as *The Americans*, a photographic essay with an introduction by the Beat poet Jack

FIG. 1.8
Robert Frank, *Trolley—New Orleans*, 1955. © Robert Frank, from *The Americans*

Kerouac.[7] The photograph reproduced here documents passengers on a segregated city trolley in New Orleans—a white matron looking suspicious, a white boy in his Sunday best, a black man looking mournful. As a factual piece of evidence about the past, it records a particular moment in time in the racially segregated American South of the 1950s. Yet, at the same time, this photograph, titled *Trolley—New Orleans* (1955), does more than document these particular facts. For some viewers, this image is moving insofar as it connotes a culture on the precipice of momentous change, evoking powerful emotions about the history of segregation and the racial divide in America encapsulated in this chance look into the windows of a passing trolley. The picture was taken just as laws, policies, and social mores concerning segregation began to undergo radical changes in response to civil rights activism and, in particular, to the United States Supreme Court's 1954 *Brown v. Board of Education* ruling against segregation and the Montgomery bus boycott of 1955–1956, which followed Rosa Parks's famous refusal to move to the back of the bus (a few months after the publication of the Emmett Till image we discussed earlier). In Frank's photograph, the faces of the passengers each look outward with different expressions, responding in different ways to their lives, their journey. It is as if the trolley itself represents the passage of history, and the expressive faces of each passenger frozen in a fleeting moment of transit here foreshadow the ways in which each one will confront and perform his or her place in the history that will ensue. The trolley riders seem to be held for one frozen, pivotal moment within the vehicle, a group of strangers thrown together to journey down the same road that would become so crucial to American history, just as the civil rights era in the South brought together strangers in a political journey toward major social change.

Thus this photograph is valuable both as an empirical document of what has been and as an expressive, symbolic vehicle of what was at that moment and what would soon be. The power of the image derives not only from its status as photographic evidence of this exact moment in time but also from its powerful evocation of the personal and political struggles of the era that encompasses this moment. The photograph thus has the capacity both to present evidence and to evoke a magical or mythical quality that moves us beyond specific empirical truths.

In *Trolley—New Orleans*, as in all images, we can discern multiple levels of meaning. Roland Barthes uses the terms *denotative* and *connotative* to describe different kinds and levels of meaning produced at the same time and for the same viewers in the same photograph. An image can denote certain apparent truths, providing documentary evidence of objective circumstances. The denotative meaning of the image refers to its literal, explicit meaning. The same photograph may connote less explicit, more culturally specific associations and meanings. Connotative meanings are informed by the cultural and historical contexts of the image and its viewers' lived, felt knowledge of those circumstances—all that the image means to them personally and socially. As we noted, this Robert Frank photograph denotes a group of passengers on a trolley. Yet clearly its meaning is broader than this simple description. This image connotes a collective journey of life and race relations in the American South in the 1950s. A viewer's cultural and historical knowledge that 1955 is the same year in which the Montgomery bus boycotts took place and that the photograph was taken shortly after the *Brown v. Board of Education* desegregation ruling potentially contributes to the photograph's connotative messages. The dividing line between what an image denotes and what it connotes can be ambiguous, and connotative meanings can change with changes in social context and over time. It can be argued that all meanings and messages are culturally informed—that there is no such thing as a purely denotative image. The two concepts, denotation and connotation, can be useful, however, because they help us to think about the ways in which images both function narrowly to signify literal, denoted meanings and also go beyond that to connote culturally and contextually specific meanings.

We have been discussing the myth of photographic truth. Roland Barthes used the term *myth* in a slightly different way to refer to the cultural values and beliefs that are expressed through connotation. For Barthes, myth is the hidden set of rules and conventions through which meanings, which are specific to certain groups, are made to seem universal and given for a whole society. Myth thus allows the connotative meaning of a particular thing or image to appear to be denotative, literal, or natural. For instance, Barthes argued that a French advertisement for a particular brand of Italian sauce and pasta is not simply presenting a product but is engaging in, as well as helping to produce, a myth or stereotype about Italian culture—the concept of "Italianicity."[8] This connoted message, wrote Barthes, is not for Italians but is specifically for a French audience, for whom the advertisement fosters a particular romanticized sense of what constitutes true Italian culture. Similarly, one could argue that contemporary representations of beauty (ultra-thin bodies, for example) promote the idea that certain body types and shapes are universally regarded as attractive. These standards constitute a myth in Barthes's terms (what some feminist critics have described as the feminine beauty myth) because they are historically and culturally constructed, not given or "natural." We all "know" this body to be the standard of beauty when we see it, not because it is simply naturally true that such bodies are objectively more beautiful than other types but because the connotative message has become so widely incorporated as to seem obvious and natural. In this way, denotative meanings can help to feed the production of connotative meaning, and connotative meanings can become more explicit and generic.

Barthes's concepts of myth and connotation are particularly useful in examining notions of photographic truth. Context influences our expectations and uses of images with respect to their truth-value. We do not, for example, bring the same expectations about the representation of truth to advertisements or film images that we view in a movie theater that we do to newspaper photographs or television news images. Significant differences among these forms include their relationship to time—does the image document something happening now, as television sometimes does, or is the event past?—and their ability to be widely reproduced. Whereas conventional photographs and films need to be developed and printed before they can be viewed and reproduced, the electronic nature of television images means that they are instantly viewable and can be transmitted around the world live, and the immediate realization of digital images makes them instantly available. Liveness and immediacy can contribute to the truth-value of an image. As moving images, cinematic and television images are combined with sound and music in narrative arrangements. Their meaning often lies in the sense we make of the sequence of images as they compose an overall story and the relationship of the image to sound, which we understand as having been produced and designed. We know better than to look for empirical evidence in fiction film images.

Similarly, the cultural meanings of and expectations about computer and digital images are different from those of conventional photographs. Because digital computer images can easily be made to look like conventional analog photographs, people who produce them sometimes play with the conventions of photographic realism. For example, an image generated exclusively by computer graphics software can be made to appear to be a photograph of actual objects, places, or people, when in fact it is a simulation, that is, it does not represent something in the real world. There is no expectation, in digital imaging, of the camera "having been there" to document something that really happened, which we see here and now in the image. Digital simulations of photographs imitate photographs of real phenomena using mathematical formulas translated into visual coordinates that approximate

FIG. 1.9
Nancy Burson, *First Beauty Composite: Bette Davis, Audrey Hepburn, Grace Kelly, Sophia Loren, and Marilyn Monroe* and *Second Beauty Composite: Jane Fonda, Jacqueline Bisset, Diane Keaton, Brooke Shields, and Meryl Streep*, 1982

photographic conventions of space. The difference resides in the fact that the process of producing a digital image does not require that the referent (the actual object, person, or place) is present or even that the referent exists. In addition, digital imaging software programs can be used to modify or rearrange the elements of a "realistic" photograph, erasing elements or introducing features that were not really there at the time of the picture's taking or suggesting events that in fact did not happen—such as staging a diplomatic handshake by combining photographs taken of two world leaders at different times and places or morphing the faces of famous women into a composite of conventions of beauty, as the photographer and artist Nancy Burson has done. In this 1982 image, Burson used early digital technologies to make a composite of images of Bette Davis, Audrey Hepburn, Sophia Loren, Grace Kelly, and Marilyn Monroe, famous beauties of the 1950s, juxtaposed with a composite of stars of the 1980s (Jane Fonda, Jacqueline Bisset, Diane Keaton, Brooke Shields, and Meryl Streep). Together these two images evoke the idea that different looks are favored and become the standard in different eras. Moreover, there is no one ideal beauty. Rather, our standards derive from a range of types. Yet certain notions of beauty are standardized, such as whiteness, symmetry, and full lips. Widespread use of digital imaging technologies since the 1990s has dramatically altered the status of the photograph relative to truth claims, particularly in the news media. Digital imaging thus can be said to have partially eroded the public's trust in the camera image as evidence, even as the truth-value of the photograph clings to digital images. The meaning of an image and our expectations of that image are thus tied to the technology through which it is produced, even if that technology has undergone radical change, as photography has since the 1990s. We discuss this issue further in chapter 5.

Images and Ideology

To explore the meaning of images is to recognize that they are produced within dynamics of social power and ideology. Ideologies are systems of belief that exist within all cultures. Images are an important means through which ideologies are produced and onto which ideologies are projected. When people think of ideologies, they often think in terms of propaganda—the crude process of using false representations to lure people into holding beliefs that may compromise their own interests. This understanding of ideology assumes that to act ideologically is to act out of ignorance. In this particular sense, the term *ideology* carries a pejorative cast. However, ideology has come to be understood as a much more pervasive, mundane process in which we all engage and about which we are all for the most part aware, in some way or other. In this book, we define ideologies as the broad but indispensable shared sets of values and beliefs through which individuals live out their complex relations in a range of social networks. Ideologies are widely varied and intersect at all levels of all cultures, from religions to politics to choices in fashion. Our ideologies are diverse and ubiquitous; they inform our everyday lives in often subtle and barely noticeable forms. One could say that ideology is the means by which certain values—such as individual freedom, progress, and the importance of home—are made to seem like natural, inevitable aspects of everyday life. Ideology is manifested in widely shared social assumptions not only about the way things are but also about the way things should be. Images and media representations are some of the forms through which we engage or enlist others to share certain views or not, to hold certain values or not.

Practices of looking are intimately tied to ideology. The image culture in which we live is an arena of diverse and often conflicting ideologies. Images are elements of contemporary advertising and consumer culture through which assumptions about beauty, desire, glamour, and social value are both constructed and lived. Film and television are media through which we see reinforced certain familiar ideological constructions such as the value of romantic love, the norm of heterosexuality, nationalism, or traditional concepts of good and evil. The most important aspect of ideologies in the modernist period was that they appeared to be natural or given, rather than part of a system of belief that a culture produces in order to function in a particular way. Ideologies were thus, like Barthes's concept of myth, connotations that appear to be natural. As we move forward through the postmodern period, the idea that media representations naturalize ideologies becomes displaced by the idea that images are on par with and at play with naturalized ideologies. In an era of media saturation, images do not naturalize ideas as models of experience so much as they serve as parallel entities with experience.

Visual culture is thus not just a representation of ideologies and power relations but is integral to them. Ideologies are produced and affirmed through the social institutions that characterize a given society, such as the family, education, medicine, the law, the government, and the entertainment industry, among others. Ideologies permeate the world of entertainment. They also permeate the more mundane and everyday realms of life that we do not usually associate with the word *culture*: science, education, medicine, law. All are deeply informed by the ideologies of the particular social institutions as they intersect with ideologies of a given culture's religious and cultural realms. Though we tend to think of images in association with culture and the arts, all of these everyday institutions and areas of life use images. Images are used, for example, for the categorization and classification of peoples for identification, as evidence of disease in medical screening and diagnosis, and as courtroom evidence. Shortly after photography was developed in Europe in the early nineteenth century, private citizens began hiring photographers to make individual and family portraits. Portraits often marked important moments such as births, marriages, and even deaths (the funerary portrait was a popular convention). One widespread early use of photography was to incorporate the image into a *carte de visite*, or visiting card. These small cards were used by many middle- and upper-class people in European-American societies as calling cards featuring photographic portraits of themselves. In addition, in the late nineteenth century there was a craze of purchasing carte de visites of well-known people, such as the British royal family. This practice signaled the role that photographic images would play in the construction of celebrity throughout the twentieth century. This carte de visite of U.S. General George Custer, which was taken in the 1860s, shows Custer's image and signature, with the salutation "Truly Yours." On the reverse side is the name of the photo studio. Thus in the carte de visite, the photographic portrait, sometimes accompanied by a signature, was a means to affirm individuality, and it demonstrated one of the ways that photography was integrated into bourgeois life and its values in the nineteenth century. Sekula writes that photography developed quickly into a medium that functioned both honorifically (for example, in the case of portraiture) and repressively (in the case of the use of photography for the cataloging of citizens, police photographs, and the use of photographs to discern qualities such as pathology or deviance in human subjects).[9]

FIG. 1.10
Carte de visite of George Armstrong Custer, 1860s

Photographs were widely regarded from the beginning as tools of science and of public surveillance. Astronomers spoke of using photographic film to mark the movements of the stars. Photographs were used in hospitals, mental institutions, and prisons to record and study populations, in hopes that they could be classified and tracked over time. Indeed, in rapidly growing urban industrial centers, photographs quickly became an important way for police and public health officials to monitor urban populations perceived to be growing not only in numbers but also in rates of crime and social deviance.

What is the legacy of this use of images as a means of managing and controlling populations today? Portrait images, like fingerprints, are frequently used as personal identification—on passports, driver's licenses, credit cards, and identification cards in schools, in the welfare system, and in many other social institutions. Photographs are a primary medium of evidence in the criminal justice system. We are accustomed to the fact that most stores, banks, and public places are outfitted with surveillance cameras. Our daily lives are tracked not only through our credit records but also through camera records of our movements. On a typical day of work, errands, and leisure, the activities of people in cities are recorded, often unbeknownst to them, by surveillance cameras. Often these images stay within the realm of identification and surveillance, where they go unnoticed by most of us, and are stored unviewed. But sometimes their venues change and they circulate in the public realm, where they acquire new meanings.

FIG. 1.11
Newsweek, June 27, 1994

This happened in 1994, when the former football star O. J. Simpson was arrested as a suspect in a notorious murder case. Simpson's image had previously appeared only in sports media, advertising, and celebrity news media. He was rendered a different kind of public figure when his portrait, in the form of his police mug shot, was published on the covers of *Time* and *Newsweek* magazines. The mug shot is a common use of photography in the criminal justice system. Information about all arrested people, whether they are convicted or not, is entered into the system in the form of personal data, fingerprints, photographs and sometimes even DNA samples. The conventions of the mug shot were presumably familiar to most people who saw the covers of *Time* and *Newsweek*. The conventions of framing and composition alone connote to viewers a sense of the subject's deviance and guilt, regardless of who is thus framed; the image format has the power to suggest the photographic subject's guilt. Simpson's mug shot seemed to be no different from any other in this regard.

Whereas *Newsweek* used the mug shot as it had been initially photographed, *Time* heightened the contrast and darkened Simpson's skin tone in its use of this image on the magazine's cover, reputedly for "aesthetic" reasons. Interestingly, *Time* magazine's publishers do not allow this cover to be reproduced (we reproduce the *Newsweek* version here). What ideological assumptions might be said to underlie these uses of the same image? Critics charged that *Time* was following the historical convention of using darker skin tones to connote evil and to imply guilt. For instance, in motion pictures made during the first half of the twentieth century, when black and Latino performers appeared, they were most often cast in the roles of villains. This convention tied into the lingering ideologies of nineteenth-century racial science, in which it was proposed that certain bodily forms and attributes, including darker shades of skin, indicated a predisposition toward social deviance. Though this view was contested in the twentieth century, darker skin tones nonetheless continued to be used as literary, theatrical, and cinematic symbols of evil (as they have been for centuries). Hollywood studios even developed special makeup to darken the skin tones of Anglo, European, and light-skinned black and Latino performers to emphasize a character's evil nature. In this broader context, the darkening of Simpson's skin tone cannot be seen as a purely arbitrary or aesthetic choice but rather an ideological one. Although the magazine cover designers may not have intended to evoke this history of media representations, we live in a culture in which the association of dark tones with evil and the stereotype of black men as criminals still circulate. In addition, because of the codes of the mug shot, it could be said that by simply taking Simpson's image out of the context of the police file and placing it in the public eye, *Time* and *Newsweek* influenced the public to see Simpson as a criminal even before he had been placed on trial. In 1995, the announcement of the verdict in which Simpson was acquitted by a jury was reportedly watched by more than half of the U.S. population (he was later found liable in a civil trial).

As this example shows, the meaning of images can change dramatically when those images change social contexts. Today, the contexts in which images circulate have become infinitely more complex than they were even in the mid-twentieth century. Digital images taken on cell phones are e-mailed to websites, video shot by people of their daily lives is easily uploaded to Web media sites, Web cameras track people's lives and display them directly on websites, and photographs and videos of private moments can circulate rapidly on the Web and via e-mail, all then potentially seen by millions. This means that any given image or video clip might be displayed in a short period of time in many very different contexts, each of which might give it different inflections and meanings. It also means, to the dismay of many politicians and celebrities, that once images are set loose in these image distribution networks, they cannot be fully retrieved or regulated. The legal regulation of this circulation of images through copyright and fair use laws is an issue we consider in chapter 5.

How We Negotiate the Meaning of Images

We use many tools to interpret images and create meanings with them, and we often use these tools of looking automatically, without giving them much thought. Images are produced according to social and aesthetic conventions. Conventions are like road signs: we must learn their codes for them to make sense, and the codes we learn become second nature. Company logos operate according to this principle of instant recognition, counting on the fact that the denotative meaning (the swoosh equals Nike) will slide into connotative meanings (the swoosh means quality, coolness) that will boost sales. We decode images by interpreting clues pointing to intended, unintended, and even merely suggested meanings. These clues may be formal elements such as color, shades of black and white, tone, contrast, composition, depth, perspective, and style of address to the viewer. As we saw in the case of the tonal rendering of O. J. Simpson's mug shot, seemingly neutral elements such as tone and color can take on cultural meanings. We also interpret images according to their socio-historical contexts. For example, we may consider when and where the image was made and displayed or the social context in which it is presented. Just as Simpson's mug shot took on new meanings when taken out of police records and reproduced on the cover of popular magazines, so an image appearing as a work of art in a museum takes on quite a different meaning when it is reproduced in an advertisement. We are trained to read for cultural codes such as aspects of the image that signify gendered, racial, or class-specific meanings.

Thus image codes change meaning in different contexts. For instance, the representation of smiles has meant many things throughout history. The *Mona Lisa*, for instance, is famous in part for her smile, which is understood to be enigmatic, hiding some kind of secret. The "smiley face" that emerged in the 1960s has largely been understood as a symbol of happiness. This symbol, which proliferated on buttons and T-shirts, also inspired the common emoticon practice of using punctuation in e-mail to signify a smile :-). Yet what a smile means depends on context. Is the little blond boy in *The First Murder* smiling or grimacing, and how does the context help us to determine the meaning of his expression? Chinese artist Yue Minjun creates paintings that evoke "symbolic smiles" and that make reference to the images and sculptures of laughing Buddha and comment with irony on the smile as a mask. The smiles in Minjun's paintings seem to rise from anxiety, stretched across faces in painful caricature, connoting the irony, folly, and artificial sincerity of everyday life. We can infer these connotations from his painting titled *BUTTERFLY* (fig. 1.13), with its exaggeration of the smiles, the distorted faces, the horned heads, the strange and naked red bodies, here juxtaposed with colorful butterflies. Yet we can also learn more about those connotations by finding out about the artist, whose work is considered to be part of a Chinese art movement of cynical realism, and references to both modern and traditional China and the legacy of the laughing Buddha. Whereas the Buddha is laughing in contentment, Minjun's figures seem to be smiling in agony. These are very different smiles from the smiley face or the smile of the *Mona Lisa*.

FIG. 1.12
Smiley face

Our discussion of the differing meaning of smiles draws from the concepts of semiotics. Every time we interpret an image around us (to understand what it signifies), whether consciously or not, we are using the tools of semiotics to understand its signification, or meaning. The principles of semiotics were formulated by the American logician, scientist, and philosopher Charles Sanders Peirce in the late nineteenth century and the Swiss linguist Ferdinand de Saussure in the early twentieth century. Both proposed important linguistic theories that were adapted in the middle of the twentieth century for use in image analysis. Saussure's writing, however, has had the

FIG. 1.13
Yue Minjun, *BUTTERFLY*, 2007

most influence on the theories of structuralism that inform the ways of analyzing visual culture discussed in this book. Language, according to Saussure, is like a game of chess. It depends on conventions and codes for its meanings. At the same time, Saussure argued, the relationship between a word (or the sound of that word when spoken) and things in the world is arbitrary and relative, not fixed. For example, the words *dog* in English, *chien* in French, and *hund* in German all refer to the same kind of animal; hence the relationship between the words and the animal itself is dictated by the conventions of language rather than by some natural connection. It was central to Saussure's theory that meanings change according to context and to the rules of language.

Charles Sanders Peirce (whose name is pronounced "purse") introduced the idea of a science of signs shortly before Saussure. Peirce believed that language and thought are processes of sign interpretation. For Peirce, meaning resides not in the initial perception of a sign or representation of an object but in the interpretation of the perception and subsequent action based on that perception. Every thought is a sign without meaning until a subsequent thought (what he called an interpretant) allows for its interpretation. For example, we perceive an octagonal red sign with the letters STOP inscribed. The meaning lies in the interpretation of the sign and subsequent action (we stop).

Saussure's ideas about language were adapted by theorists, from Barthes to film theorists, for use in the interpretation of visual representational systems. Peirce's concepts have been used for visual analysis as well. In applying semiotics to film, theorists emphasized that film involves a set of rules or codes that function in some ways like a language. There have been many revisions of the application of semiotics to images, but it nonetheless remains an important method of visual analysis. We choose to concentrate in this book on the model of semiotics introduced by Barthes (as we discussed earlier) and based on Saussure, because this system offers a clear and direct way to understand the relationship between visual representations and meaning.

In Barthes's model, in addition to the two levels of meaning of denotation and connotation, there is the sign, which is composed of the signifier—a sound, written word, or image—and the signified, which is the concept evoked by that word or image. In the familiar smiley face icon, the smile is the signifier, and happiness is the signified. In the Minjun painting reproduced here, the smile is the signifier, and anxiety is the signified. The image (or word) and its meaning together (the signifier and signified together) form the *sign*.

Image/sound/word = Signifier
Meaning = Signified

For Saussure, *signifier* is the entity that represents, and *sign* is the combination of the signifier and what it means. As we have seen with these two different images of smiles, an image or word can have many meanings and constitute many signs in Saussure's use of that term. The production of a sign is dependent on social, historical, and cultural context. It is also dependent on the context in which the image is presented (in a museum gallery or a magazine, for instance) and on the viewers who interpret it. We live in a world of signs, and it is the labor of our interpretation that makes the signifier-signified relationship fluid and active in the production of signs and meaning.

Often the meaning of an image is predominantly derived from the objects within the frame. For instance, old Marlboro advertisements are well known for their equation of this cigarette brand with masculinity: Marlboro (signifier) + masculinity (signified) = Marlboro as masculinity (sign). The cowboy is featured on horseback or just relaxing with a smoke, surrounded by natural beauty evocative of the unspoiled American West. These advertisements connote rugged individualism and life on the American frontier, when men were "real" men. The Marlboro Man embodies a romantic ideal of freedom that stands in contrast to the more confined lives of most everyday working people. It is testimony to the power of these ads to create the sign of Marlboro as masculinity (and the Marlboro Man as connoting a lost ideal of masculinity) that many contemporary Marlboro ads dispense with the cowboy altogether and simply show the landscape, in which this man exists by implication. This ad campaign also testifies to the ways in which objects can become gendered through advertising. It is a little-known fact that Marlboro was marketed as a "feminine" cigarette (with lipstick-red-tipped filters) until the 1950s, when the Marlboro Man made his first appearance. Indeed, the Marlboro Man has long been appropriated as a camp icon in gay male culture. In 1999, the well-known huge Marlboro Man billboard on Sunset Strip in Hollywood was taken down and replaced by an antismoking billboard that mocked this icon of buff masculinity. The Marlboro Man has been invoked in many antismoking ads to create new signs for smoking, such as Marlboro Man = loss of virility or smoking = disease, as this antismoking ad does.

Our understanding of the Marlboro ad and its spoof is dependent on our knowledge that cowboys are disappearing from the American landscape, that they are cultural symbols of a particular ideology of American expansionism and the frontier that began to fade with urban industrialization and modernization. We bring to these images cultural knowledge of the changing role of men and the recognition that it indicates a fading stereotype of masculine virility. Clearly, our interpretation of images often depends on historical context and the viewers' cultural knowledge—the conventions the images use or play off of, the other images they refer to, and the familiar figures and symbols they include. As conventions, signs can be a kind of shorthand language for viewers of images, and we are often incited to feel that the relationship between a signifier and signified is "natural." For instance, we are so accustomed to identifying a rose with the concept of romantic love and a dove with peace that it is difficult to recognize that their relationship is constructed rather than natural. We can see how Barthes's model can be useful in examining how images construct meanings. Moreover, the very fact that the sign is divided into a signifier and a signified allows us to see that a variety of images can convey many different meanings.

Peirce worked with a somewhat different model in which the sign (which for him is the word or image, not the relationship between word or image and object) is distinguished not only from the interpreted meaning (the interpretant) but also from the object itself. Peirce's

FIG. 1.14
Anti-smoking ad

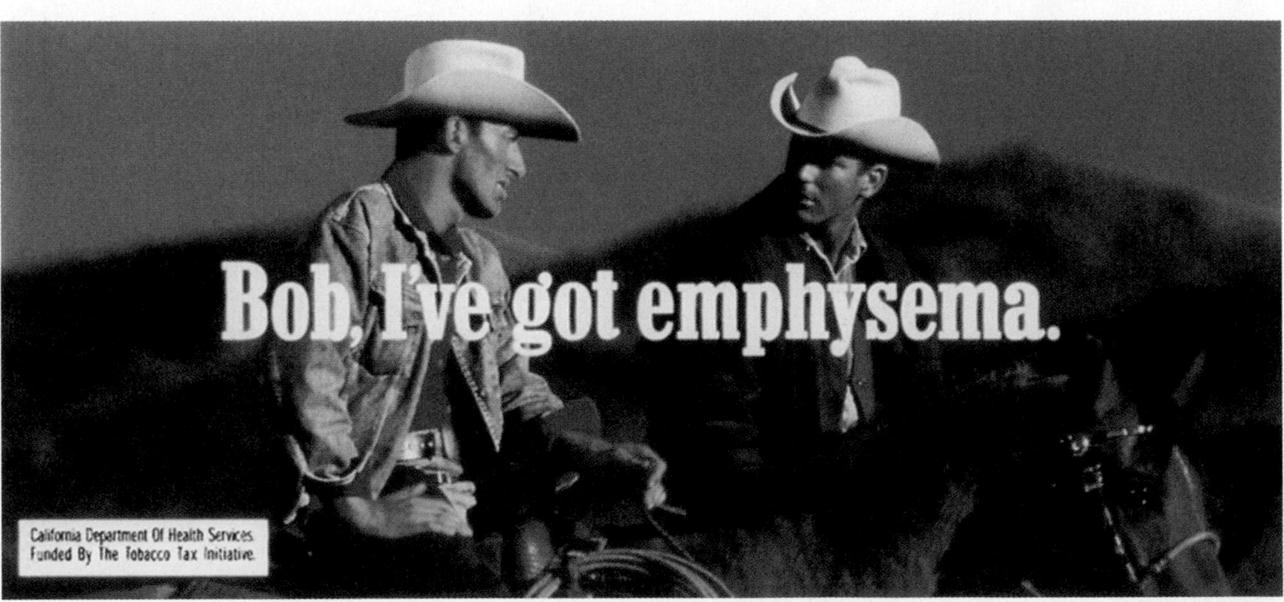

Bob, I've got emphysema.
California Department Of Health Services
Funded By The Tobacco Tax Initiative

FIG. 1.15
Marjane Satrapi, frames from *Persepolis*, 2003

work has been important for looking at images because of the distinctions that he makes between different kinds of signs and their relationship to the real. Peirce described three kinds of signs or representations: iconic, indexical, and symbolic. In Peirce's definition, iconic signs resemble their object in some way. Many paintings and drawings are iconic, as are many comics, photographs, and film and television images.

We can see iconic signs at work in Marjane Satrapi's autobiographical graphic novel, *Persepolis*, which was the basis for a 2007 animated film. *Persepolis* is the story of Satrapi's growing up in Iran during the time of the Iranian Revolution. Her personal life is caught up in the violent changes in Iranian society. In this image, she depicts herself as a young girl who with her classmates has been obliged to wear a veil to school. The simplicity of Satrapi's style creates iconic signs of the young women and their veils—we know how to read these images, in Peirce's terms, because they resemble what they are representing. In stark black and white, the veils command visual attention within the frame. Satrapi uses visual repetition and framing to depict the homogenizing visual effect of the girls' veils, as well as to mark herself as an individual (in a separate frame). These strategies of framing, motif, and the flattening of space (here, the girls are situated against a blank background) are used to depict character and psychological states of mind. The girls' hands are all folded in unison, making clear how they must conform in the school environment (and by implication in the society). Yet their facial expressions establish from this first page that they are all responding in different ways (annoyance, dejection, compliance) to the demand that they wear the veil and conform.

The cultural meaning of the veil is highly complex. Its depiction as an artifact of oppression, as we see here in Satrapi's image, has been countered by a politics of appropriating the veil as a means of affirming one's Muslim identity in the Islamic diaspora. For instance, the Spirit21 blog (www.spirit21.co.uk) presented, in 2007, a series of cartoons that comment on the politics of the veil in Britain, where former Prime Minister Tony Blair and his wife Cherie had spoken out against the wearing of the veil in British streets, stating that it constituted a security matter. One cartoon shows Blair delivering a speech and offering to take a question from "the woman in the black veil" in an audience filled with women wearing identical black veils, invoking the more familiar image of a room full of men wearing the standard business uniform of the black suit. The veil is referenced here as icon not of oppression but of the new Muslim woman who participates in civic life and who publicly signifies her cultural identity through a uniform that connotes belonging and respect.

Unlike iconic signs in comics, which typically resemble their objects, symbolic signs, according to Peirce, bear no obvious relationship to their objects. Symbols are created through an arbitrary (one could say "unnatural") alliance of a particular object and a particular meaning. For example, languages are symbolic systems that use conventions to establish meaning. There is no natural link between the word *cat* and an actual cat; the convention in the English language gives the word its signification. Symbolic signs are inevitably more restricted in their capacity to convey meaning in that they refer to learned systems. Someone who does not speak English can probably recognize an image of a cat (an iconic sign), whereas the word *cat* (a symbolic sign) will have no obvious meaning.

It is Peirce's discussion of images as indexical that is most useful in visual culture study. Indexical signs as discussed by Peirce involve an "existential" relationship between the sign and the interpretant. This means that they have coexisted in the same place at some time. Peirce uses as examples the symptom of a disease, a pointing hand, and a weathervane. Fingerprints are indexical signs of a person, and photographs are also indexical signs that testify to the moment that the camera was in the presence of its subject. Indeed, although photographs are both iconic and indexical, their cultural meaning is derived in large part from their indexical meaning as a trace of the real.

The creation of signs semiotically is usually the result of a combination of factors in an image,

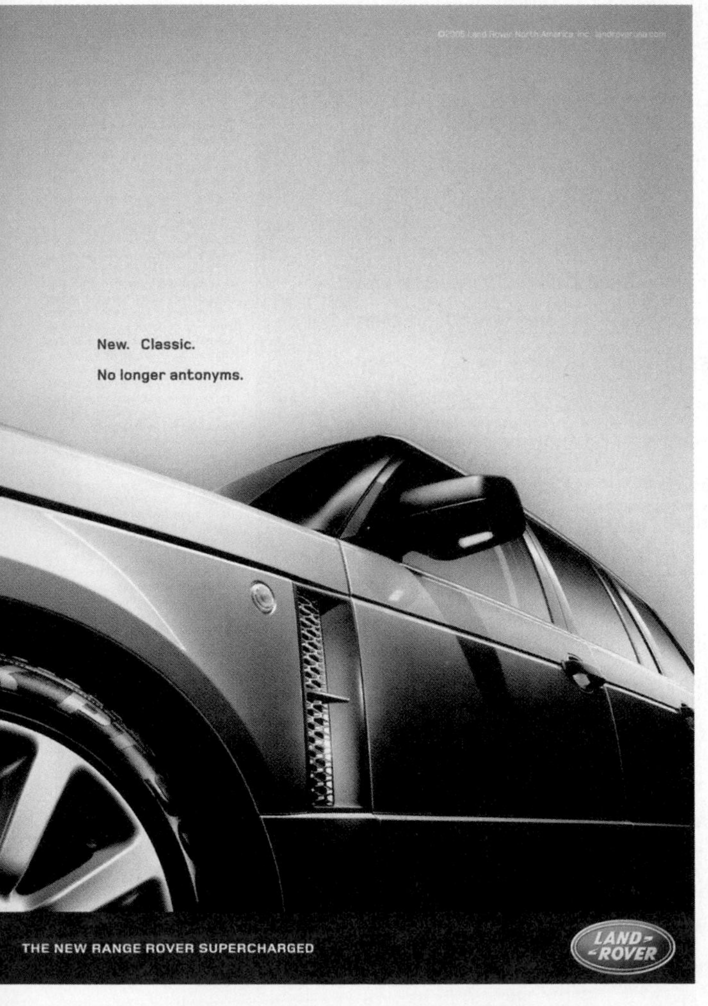

New. Classic.
No longer antonyms.
THE NEW RANGE ROVER SUPERCHARGED
LAND ROVER

FIG. 1.16
Land Rover ad, 2007

and this means that meaning is often derived through the combination of text and image. This is particularly the case in advertising, public service advertising, and political posters, in which the combination of text and image can be used to direct the viewer's interpretation to a particular meaning through a kind of double take—the image first looks a certain way and then changes meaning with the addition of the text. It is important to the indexical meaning of most advertisements that they use photographs to construct their messages. In that photographs always carry with them the connotation of photographic truth yet are also a primary source of fantasy, they provide important dual meanings in many advertisements. However, text functions in ads to shape the commodity signs of the image, to rein in and limit the meaning of the image in some way. This Land Rover ad (fig. 1.16) uses text, which suggests that the car can be new as well as classic, to shape how viewer-consumers will see the image of the car itself. Other slogans could have guided the meaning of the image in other ways to consider the tank-like aspect of the car or its massive size. A parody of the ad could use text to play off this aspect of the car, pointing to the company's role as a military vehicle supplier. Contemporary advertising, with its complex combinations of words, photographs, drawing, sound, and television images, deploys all three kinds of signs designated by Peirce to construct selling messages, including not only indexical photographs and symbolic text but also iconic signs in the forms of drawings and graphs. It is important to keep in mind that Peirce's system allows us to see the cultural weight that is given to photographs—as indexical signs, as traces of the real, photographs are awarded a particular sense of authenticity in relation to other signs.

FIG. 1.17
Vincent van Gogh, *Irises*, 1889

The Value of Images

The work of detecting social, cultural, and historical meanings in images often happens without our being aware of the process and is part of the pleasure of looking at images. Some of the information we bring to reading images has to do with what we perceive their value to be in a culture at large. This raises the question: What gives an image social value? Images do not have value in and of themselves; they are awarded different kinds of value—monetary, social, and political—in particular social contexts.

In the art market, the value of a work of art is determined by economic and cultural factors, including collecting by art institutions such as museums and by private collectors. This painting of irises by Vincent van Gogh (fig. 1.17) achieved a new level of fame in 1991 when it was sold for an unprecedented price of $53.8 million to the Getty Museum in Los Angeles. Other paintings have since sold for even more extraordinary amounts. In 2006, the private sale of the American abstract expressionist Jackson Pollock's 1948 painting titled *No. 5* brought its seller $140 million. In each case, the painting in itself does not inherently contain or reveal its monetary value; rather, this is information we bring to an interpretation of it through such factors as changes in the art market and contemporary taste with regard to the style of a past period. Why was the Pollock worth so much money in 2006? Why was the van Gogh worth so much in 1991? Beliefs about a work's authenticity and uniqueness, as well as about its aesthetic style, contribute to its value. The social mythology that surrounds a work of art or its artist can also contribute to its value. Van Gogh's *Irises* is considered authentic because it has been proven that it is an original work by van Gogh, not a copy, though the market for his work has been fraught with counterfeits. Van Gogh's work is valued because it is believed to be among the best examples of the innovative modern painting style of impressionism, which was adapted by van Gogh in a more expressionist approach during the late nineteenth century. The myths that surround van Gogh's life and work also contribute to the value of his works. Most of us know that van Gogh was often unhappy and mentally unstable, that he cut off his ear, and that he committed suicide. We may know more about his life than we know about the technical and aesthetic judgments made by art historians about his work. We may also be aware that Pollock drank and died at age forty-four in a tragic crash while driving under the influence and that he painted his most famous works by walking around huge canvases, dripping paint from a can and brush in gestures that resulted in abstract, nonfigurative globs and lines. Although some of it is extraneous to the artwork itself, this biographical information contributes to the work's value—partly insofar as it plays into the stereotype or myth of the creative artist as a sensitive figure whose artistic talent is not taught but rather is a "natural" form of creativity that can border on madness and is released in the graphic form of the painting.

The van Gogh gains its economic value in part through cultural determinations concerning what society judges to be important in assessing works of art. It is regarded as authentic because it bears the artist's signature and has been verified by art historians who pay close attention to authentication of the work of this artist because he was posthumously subject to a major case of forgery. The press surrounding the forgeries and their discovery heightened the reputation of the artist and made his works even more valuable. The artist has international fame and notoriety that go beyond the work itself to include not only his personality and life history but also the life of his works as they are bought, sold, copied illicitly, and legally reproduced in books and videos. Finally, van Gogh's technique is regarded as unique and superior among other works of the period. Part of our recognition of its value has to do simply with its stature within institutions such as museums, art history classes, and art auctions. One way that value is communicated is through the mechanisms of art display.

We sometimes know a work of art is important because it is encased in a gilded frame. This convention has become something of a joke, with everything from low brow art (a contemporary genre of painting that appropriates the aesthetics of 1950s, 1960s, and 1970s popular iconography) to advertising appropriating the gilded frame as an ironic reference to the object in the frame as (anything but) high culture. We might assume that a work of art is valuable simply because it is on display in a prestigious museum or is displayed in a special way, as is the case with the *Mona Lisa* by Leonardo da

FIG. 1.18
Mona Lisa on display in the Louvre

FIG. 1.19
Van Gogh's *Irises* on a coffee mug

Vinci, which is displayed in a climate-controlled room behind bulletproof glass to protect it from any potential vandals among the six million or so people who view it annually (vandals had doused the painting with acid and thrown a rock at it in 1956). Although the fine art object may be valued because it is unique, it may be valued also because it can be highly marketable as an item reproduced for popular consumption. For example, van Gogh's paintings have been reproduced endlessly on posters, postcards, coffee mugs and T-shirts. Ordinary consumers can own a copy of the highly valued originals. We discuss this aspect of image reproduction further in chapter 5.

As images are increasingly easy to generate and reproduce electronically, the values traditionally attributed to them have changed. In any given culture, we use different criteria to evaluate various media forms. Whereas we evaluate paintings according to the criteria of uniqueness, authenticity, and market values, we may award value to television news images, for instance, on the basis of their capacity to provide information and accessibility to important events. The value of a television news image lies in its capacity to be transmitted quickly and widely to a vast number of geographically dispersed television screens and that of the digital news image lies in it being instantly distributable to newspapers and websites.

Image Icons

This image of the lone student at Tiananmen Square has value as an icon of worldwide struggles for democracy precisely because of the meaning of this historical event and because many students lost their lives in the protests. Here, we use the term *icon* in a general sense, rather than in the specific sense used by Peirce that we discussed earlier. An icon is an image that refers to something outside of its individual components, something (or someone) that has great symbolic meaning for many people. Icons are often perceived to represent universal concepts, emotions, and meanings. Thus an image produced in a specific culture, time, and place might be interpreted as having broader meaning and the capacity to evoke similar responses across all cultures and in all viewers.

The television news image of the student protest at Tiananmen Square in Beijing in 1989 can be said to be a valuable image, although the criteria for its value have

FIG. 1.20
Tiananmen Square, Beijing, China, 1989

nothing to do with the art market or the monetary value of any particular print of this photograph. The value of this image is based in part on its capturing of a special moment (it depicts a key moment in an event during which media coverage was restricted) and the speed with which it was transmitted around the world to provide information about that event (at a historical moment when the Web did not yet exist as a forum for image circulation). Its value is also derived from its powerful depiction of the courage of one student before the machinery of military power. This photograph achieved worldwide recognition, becoming an *icon* of political struggles for freedom of expression. Whereas its denotative meaning is simply a young man standing before a tank, its connotative and iconic meaning is commonly understood to be the importance of individual actions in the face of injustice and the capacity of one individual to stand up to forces of power. This image thus has value not as

FIG. 1.21
Photograph of protestors at April 9, 2008 San Francisco protest against decision to hold Summer Olympics in Beijing

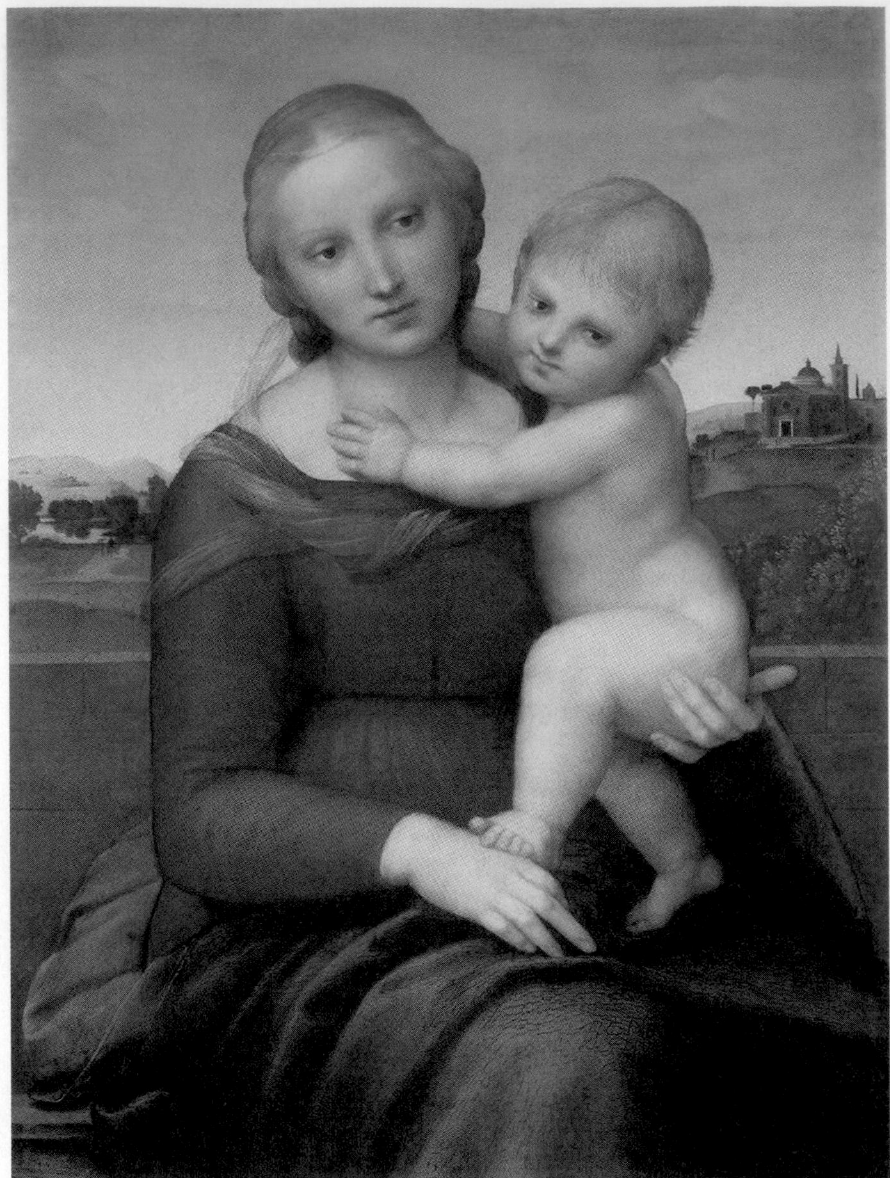

FIG. 1.22
Raphael, *The Small Cowper Madonna*, c. 1505

a singular image (once broadcast, it was not one image but millions of images on many different TV sets and newspapers, though it was censored in China) but through its speed of transmission, its informative value, and its political statement. We can say that it is culturally valuable because it makes a statement about human will and the potential of resistance, and as such it has become an icon. It is not incidental that the image achieves this iconic status through the depiction not of the many thousands of protestors at Tiananmen Square but through the image of one lone individual. As Robert Hariman and John Lucaites explain in *No Caption Needed*, the iconicity of the image derives in part from its simplicity, from the fact that the events seems to take place in a deserted public space (there is actually a crowd outside the frame) and that the image is viewed from a modernist perspective that affords a distance to the viewer.[10] They argue that the image of the lone individual potentially limits the political imagination within a liberal framework of individualism. The iconic status of the Tiananmen Square image has resulted in a broad array of remakes of the image.

FIG. 1.23
Joos van Cleve, *Virgin and Child*, c. 1525

The simplicity of the image of the protestor confronting tanks emerged in the protests against the oppression of Tibet in the months before the 2008 Summer Olympics in Beijing, in which a simple pictograph (in Peirce's terms, an iconic sign) of a tank and a civilian invokes the famous photograph of Tiananmen Square. Here, the protestors have effectively combined the iconic sign of the Olympic rings with the iconic sign of the tank and student to put their protest in historical context.

Image icons are experienced as if universal, but their meanings are always historically and contextually produced. Consider the example of the image of mother and child that is so ubiquitous in Western art. The iconography of the mother and child is widely believed to represent universal concepts of maternal emotion, the essential bond between a mother and her offspring, and the importance of motherhood throughout the world and human history. The sheer number of paintings with this theme throughout the history of art attests not simply to the centrality of the Madonna figure in Christianity but also to the idea that the bond between mother and

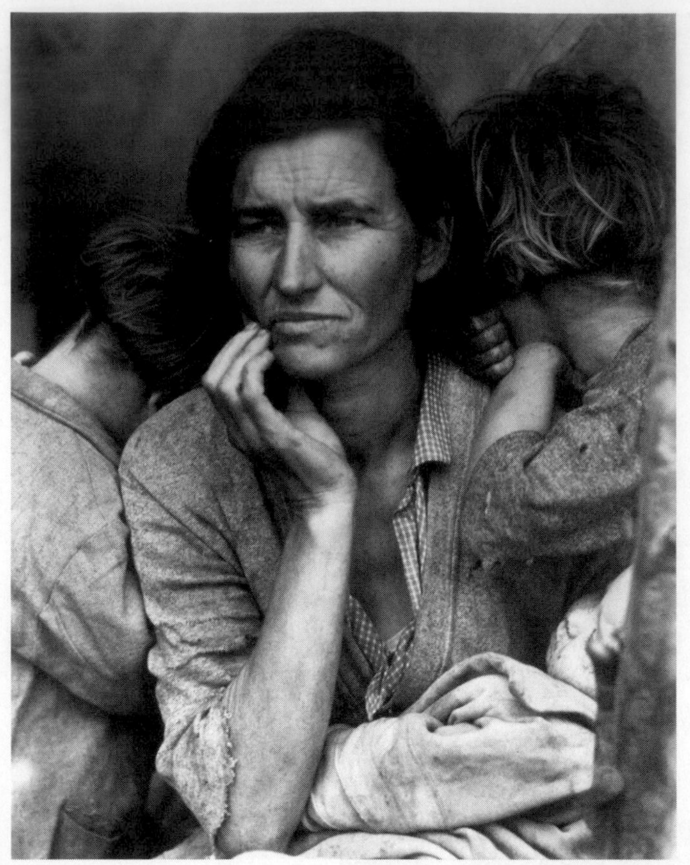

FIG. 1.24
Dorothea Lange, *Migrant Mother, Nipomo, California*, 1936

child represented in images like these is universal and natural, not culturally and historically specific and socially constructed.

To question the assumptions underpinning this concept of the universal would mean to look at the cultural, historical, and social meanings that are specific in these images. There is an increased understanding that these concepts of the universal were actually restricted to specific privileged groups. Icons do not represent individuals, nor do they represent universal values. Thus the mother and child motif present in these two paintings by Italian painter Raphael and Dutch painter Joos van Cleve can be read not as evidence of universal ideals of motherhood but as an indicator of specific cultural values of motherhood and the role of women in Western culture in the sixteenth century, particularly in Europe. In both paintings, there are particular image codes at work—both infants are depicted as naked with adult-like faces, and the woman's maternal figures are shapely in the conventions of sixteenth-century Europe. Whereas the Madonna of Raphael's painting looks out of the frame in an almost detached way, the van Cleve Madonna is nursing and reading, surrounded by an array of symbolic objects. Furthermore, these images situate these figures within particular cultural landscapes, Raphael's Madonna before an Italian landscape and van Cleve's before an elaborate Dutch vista. The closer we look at these two images, the more culturally and historically specific they appear.

It is in relationship to this tradition of Madonna and child paintings that more recent images of women and children gain meaning. For instance, this famous photograph, *Migrant Mother*, by Dorothea Lange depicts a woman, also apparently a mother, during the California migration of the 1930s. This photograph is regarded as an iconic image of the Great Depression in the United States. It is famous because it evokes both the despair and the perseverance of those who survived the hardships of that time. Yet the image gains much of its meaning from its implicit reference to the history of artistic depictions of women and their children, such as Madonna and child images, and its difference from them. This mother is anxious and distracted. Her children cling to her and burden her thin frame. She looks not at her children but outward as if toward her future—one seemingly with little promise. This image derives its meaning largely from a viewer's knowledge of the historical moment it represents. At the same time, it makes a statement about the complex role of motherhood that is informed by its place in the iconic tradition.

This photograph has historically specific meanings, yet in many ways its function as an icon allows it to have meanings that go beyond that historical moment. Lange took the image while working on a government documentation project funded by the Farm Security Administration. With other photographers, she produced an extraordinary archive of photographs of the Great Depression in the United States in the 1930s. Lange was one of a small number of women photographers who worked on the project, and the story of her taking of this image is legendary in the history of photography. She took five pictures of this woman and her children. The one reproduced here shows the family's surrounding context the least. Years later, researchers tracked down the woman depicted in the image, who was still living in relative poverty in California, not having benefited in the least from the wide dissemination of her image as an icon. It is the close framing of this image that allows it to emerge as not just an image of one mother with her children but as an icon of maternal devotion and perseverence.[11]

People themselves can be image icons. For example, Marilyn Monroe was a pop icon of the 1950s and 1960s, a star who was regarded as the embodiment of female glamour. Her wavy blond hair, open smile, and full figure were stereotypical components of an American

FIG. 1.25
Andy Warhol, *Marilyn Diptych*, 1962

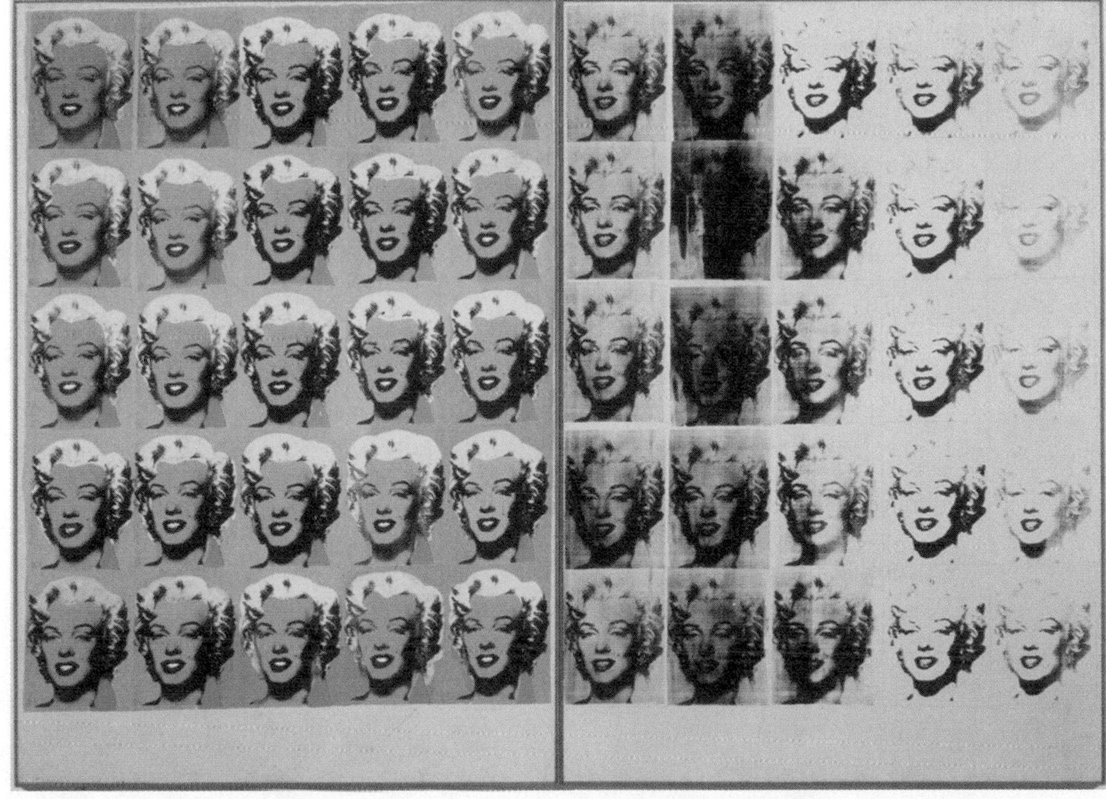

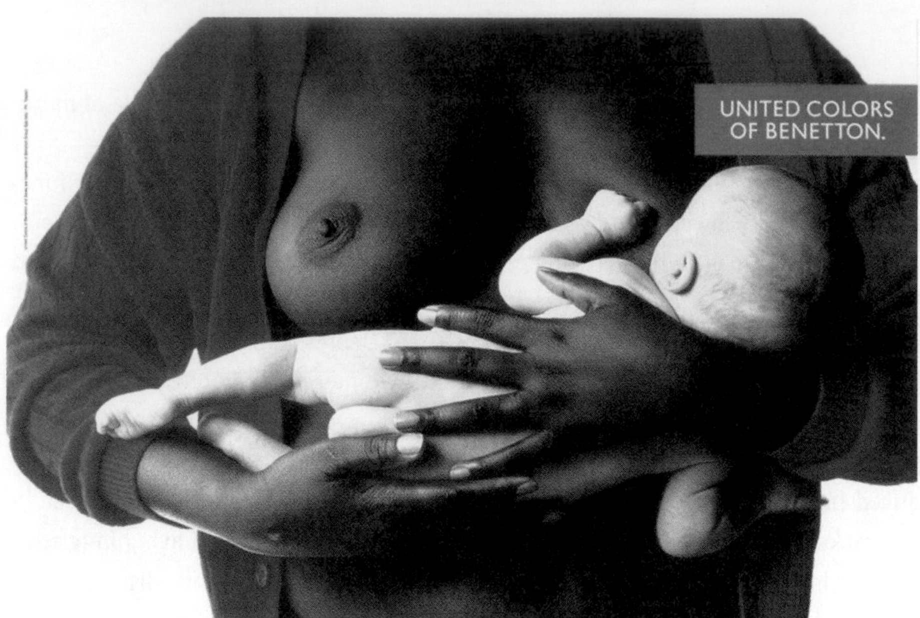

FIG. 1.26
Benetton ad, 1990s

beauty ideal. What counts as glamourous or sexy changes over time and across cultures, as Burson's beauty composites, which we discussed earlier, suggest. The preference for full-figured women was replaced in the late twentieth century by an idealization of the thin, athletic body. Pop artist Andy Warhol, who made works about postwar consumer culture, mass manufacture, and commercial reproduction, worked with an iconic photograph of Marilyn Monroe that was familiar to virtually the entire nation. He printed multiple versions of this same image in a colorful grid. This print, *Marilyn Diptych* (fig. 1.25), comments not only on the star's iconic status as a glamourous figure but also on the role of the star as media commodity—as a product of the entertainment industry. Marilyn the icon can be infinitely reproduced for mass consumption, thanks to the technologies of photography and commercial printing. Warhol's work emphasizes one of the most important aspects of contemporary imaging technologies: they offer us the capacity to reproduce images many times and in different contexts, thereby changing their meaning and altering their value—and that of the objects or people they represent—as commodities. In this work, the multiple images of Monroe emphasize that cultural icons can and must be mass distributed in order for the star herself to have mass appeal. These copies do not refer back to the original so much as they indicate the endless reproducibility of Monroe as a product to be consumed in many forms.

To call an image an icon raises the question of context. For whom is this image iconic and for whom is it not? These images of motherhood and of glamour are specific to particular cultures at particular moments in time. One could regard them as indicators of the cultural values attributed to women throughout history and the restrictive roles to which women have been relegated (mother or sex symbol, virgin or vamp). Images have divergent meanings in different cultural and historical contexts. When, for instance, Benetton produced this advertisement in the 1990s of a black woman nursing a white child, a range of interpretations were possible. This advertisement was published throughout Europe, but magazines in the United States refused to run it. The image can be understood in the history of images of mother and child, although its meaning is contingent on the viewer's assumption, on the basis of the contrast of their skin color, that this woman is not the child's biological mother but its caretaker. In the United States this image carried the troubling connotation of the history of slavery and the use of black women slaves as wet nurses to breast-feed the white children of slave owners. Thus the intended meaning of this image as an icon of an idealized interracial mother-child relationship is not easily conveyed in a context in which the image's meanings are overdetermined by historical factors. Similarly, the classical art history image of Madonna and child may not serve as an icon for motherhood in non-Christian cultures but rather as an example of specifically Western and particularly Christian beliefs.

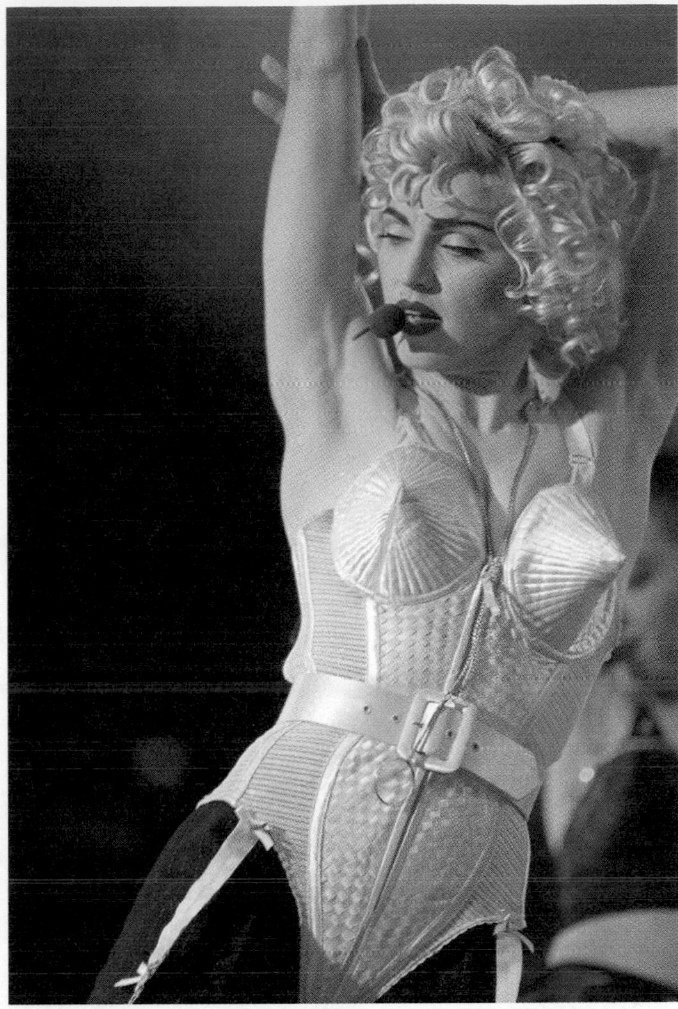

FIG. 1.27
Madonna on Blonde Ambition Tour, London, England, 1990

Pop star Madonna gained notoriety by combining and playing off of one another the religious iconography of the Madonna and the sexual iconography of Marilyn Monroe. Madonna borrowed and reworked the elements of both these cultural icons. At various points in her career, Madonna assumed Monroe's blonde hair color and 1940s clothing styles. In this image, we can see the 1990 incarnation of Madonna's Marilyn appropriation, here on her Blonde Ambition Tour, wearing a signature blonde wig and campy corset. Through these acts of cultural appropriation, Madonna acquired the power of these icons (of Madonna and Marilyn) while reflecting ironically on their meaning in the popular culture of the 1980s and 1990s.

In 2003, the San Francisco painter Isabel Samaras took the mother and child iconography into the realm of nonhuman species. In *Behold My Heart*, Samaras depicts a scene from the 1971 film *Escape from the Planet of the Apes*, in which Zira, the talking chimpanzee scientist who studied (and lobotomized, neutered, and spayed) humans in the 1968 film *Planet of the Apes*, cradles lovingly to her breast the child she will be forced to abandon after she is stigmatized and ostracized on the discovery of her experiments, sacrificing her own life for his survival. As in the 1525

FIG. 1.28
Isabel Samaras, *Behold My Heart*, 2003

Virgin and Child (fig. 1.23), a book sits open before the pair, and a backdrop of landscaped foliage reminiscent of backdrops in a Renaissance painting extends behind the curtain backdrop that frames them. Caesar, the baby monkey—who will grow up to become a revolutionary hero in later films of the series and is credited as being the first ape to say no to a human—fingers hieroglyphic-like markings on a leather plate strapped to his mother's cloaked bosom. The film series, widely regarded as a campy parable of racial oppression and resistance, is here invoked as a pop surrealist expression of the iconography of maternal relations. Here, the politics of species is a displaced site for articulating a critique of the politics of race in an age dominated by a revival of biological ways of understanding culture.

FIG. 1.29
Daniel Edwards, *Monument to Pro-Life: The Birth of Sean Preston*, 2006

Although parody and irony have appeared to be dominant modes of image production and interpretation in the late twentieth and early twenty-first centuries, they are not the only modes invoked in popular culture. Take the example of Britney Spears, yet another female performer who achieved the status of cultural icon at a young age. Spears is the eighth best-selling musical artist in American musical history. Having established herself as one of the most successful American female pop vocalists by the age of twenty in 2000, she put aside her career in 2005 to give birth to the first of her children, announcing that she would dedicate herself to her role as mother. In 2005, a New York gallery unveiled a sculpture by Daniel Edwards titled *Monument to Pro-Life*. It depicts Spears nude, her body splayed on a bearskin rug, belly pushed down and hips thrust upward to reveal the crowning skull of a child emerging from her pelvis. This image of the female pop star turned mother was directly reminiscent of the role that Madonna took on as a young pop star in the 1980s and 1990s. However, whereas Madonna's use of the referent of the virgin mother was highly ironic, parodic, and rife with appropriations of beauty codes and standards of bygone years, Britney's performance of motherhood (and Edwards' depiction of it) seemed to be without any intended irony. Both her decision to change roles and the appropriation of her by the pro-life movement seemed to be in earnest. The irony emerged later when, in 2007, Spears lost custody of her children in a trial that was closely paralleled by media stories revealing her heavy partying, drug use, and psychiatric treatment, and when, in 2008, her 16-year-old sister Jamie

Lynn Spears, star of Nickelodeon's *Zoey 101*, shocked millions of young fans by ending the season with a real-life pregnancy, then embracing life as a teen mom in rural Mississippi. The meanings of Britney Spears as a maternal figure change, then, with changing events that bring new connotations to older images. Although Britney's media coverage has characterized her life as fraught with ironies, Britney herself did not use irony as a political and creative tool, as did her predecessor, Madonna.

Britney images offered yet another level of meaning when fan Chris Crocker, an infamous figure on YouTube, appeared in an emotionally charged two-minute video self-production, demanding of his very large viewing audience (he has received upwards of ten million hits), with tears in his eyes, "how f***** dare anyone out there make fun of Britney after all she's been through?" Crocker, an established young gay YouTuber from Eastern Tennessee, lambasted the media for shamelessly making money from Britney's difficult life circumstances. Rather than critiquing Britney and everything she personifies, as an earlier generation of media-savvy youth might have done, Crocker attempted to protect her right to a public existence free of judgment and criticism. Does Crocker's response suggest that we have entered into a postcritical era of visual culture? It is interesting, as a postscript, to note that Crocker's career received a big boost with this defense of his idol, with invitations to appear on talk shows and even a well-known star of television and film (*Family Guy*'s Seth Green) posting his own YouTube send-up of the Crocker performance, replete with mascara and tears.

To chart this representation of mother and child from sixteenth-century painting to the performance of the Madonna by a pop star to the widely viewed homemade video of a fan posted on a website demonstrates many aspects of the complexity of contemporary visual culture and the codes and signs through which cultural meaning is produced. These codes build on one another, incorporating these historical legacies of image codes at the same time that they rework, play off, and recode them.

To interpret images is to examine the assumptions that we and others bring to them at different times and in different places and to decode the visual language that they "speak." All images contain layers of meaning that include their formal aspects, their cultural and sociohistorical references, the ways they make reference to the images that precede and surround them, and the contexts in which they are displayed. Reading and interpreting images is one way that we, as viewers, contribute to the process of assigning value to the culture in which we live. Practices of looking, then, are not passive acts of consumption. By looking at and engaging with images in the world, we influence the meanings and uses assigned to the images that fill our day-to-day lives. In the next chapter, we examine the many ways that viewers create meaning when they engage in looking.

Notes

1. Weegee [Arthur Fellig], *Naked City* (Cambridge, Mass: Da Capo, [1945] 2002).
2. See Michel Foucault, *This Is Not a Pipe*, with illustrations and letters by René Magritte, trans. and ed. James Harkness (Berkeley: University of California Press, 1983).
3. Talan Memmott, "RE: Authoring Magritte: *The Brotherhood of Bent Billiards*," in *Second Person: Role Playing and Story in Games and Playable Media*, ed. Pat Harrigan and Noah Wardrip-Fruin, 157–58 (Cambridge, Mass.: MIT Press, 2007).
4. Roland Barthes, *Camera Lucida: Reflections on Photography*, trans. Richard Howard, 85 (New York: Hill and Wang, 1981).
5. Barthes, *Camera Lucida*, 14–15.
6. Allan Sekula, "On The Invention of Photographic Meaning," in *Thinking Photography*, ed. Victor Burgin, 94 (London: Macmillan, 1982).
7. Robert Frank, *The Americans* (Millerton, N.Y.: Aperture, [1959] 1978).
8. Roland Barthes, "Rhetoric of the Image," from *Image Music Text*, trans. Stephen Heath, 34 (New York: Hill and Wang, 1977).
9. Allan Sekula, "The Body and the Archive," *October* 39 (Winter 1986), 6–7.
10. Robert Hariman and John Louis Lucaites, *No Caption Needed: Iconic Photographs, Public Culture, and Liberal Democracy* (Chicago: University of Chicago Press, 2007), chapter 7. See also their website, www.nocaptionneeded.com.
11. For an extensive overview of interpretations of the "Migrant Mother" image, see Hariman and Lucaites, *No Caption Needed*, 49–67; and Liz Wells, *Photography: A Critical Introduction*, 3rd ed., 37–48 (New York: Routledge, [1996] 2004).

Further Reading

Anderson, Kirsten, ed. *Pop Surrealism: The Rise of Underground Art*. San Francisco: Resistance Publishing/Last Gasp, 2004.

Barthes, Roland, *Mythologies*. Translated by Annette Lavers. New York: Hill and Wang, [1957] 1972.

———*Elements of Semiology*. Translated by Annette Lavers and Colin Smith. New York: Hill and Wang, 1967.

———"The Photographic Message" and "Rhetoric of the Image." In *Image Music Text*. Translated by Stephen Heath. New York: Hill and Wang, 1977.

———*Camera Lucida: Reflections on Photography*. Translated by Richard Howard. New York: Hill and Wang, 1981.

Berger, John. *Ways of Seeing*. New York: Penguin, 1972.

Bryson, Norman. *Looking at the Overlooked: Four Essays on Still Life Painting*. Cambridge, Mass.: Harvard University Press, 1990.

Burgin, Victor, ed. *Thinking Photography*. London: Macmillan, 1982.

Foucault, Michel. *This Is Not a Pipe*. With illustrations and letters by René Magritte. Translated and edited by James Harkness. Berkeley: University of California Press, 1983.

Hall, Stuart, ed. *Representation: Cultural Representations and Signifying Practices*. Thousand Oaks, Calif.: Sage, 1997.

Hariman, Robert, and John Louis Lucaites. *No Caption Needed: Iconic Photographs, Public Culture, and Liberal Democracy*. Chicago: University of Chicago Press, 2007.

Hawkes, Terence. *Structuralism and Semiotics*. Berkeley: University of California Press, 1977.

Hoopes, James, ed. *Peirce on Signs*. Chapel Hill: University of North Carolina Press, 1991.

Liszka, James Jakób. *A General Introduction to the Semiotics of Charles Sanders Peirce*. Bloomington: Indiana University Press, 1996.

McCloud, Scott. *Understanding Comics: The Invisible Art*. New York: Kitchen Sink/HarperPerennial, 1993.

Merrel, Floyd. *Semiosis in the Postmodern Age*. Toronto: University of Toronto Press, 1995.

———. *Peirce, Signs, and Meaning*. Toronto: University of Toronto Press, 1997.

Metz, Christian. *Film Language: A Semiotics of the Cinema*. Translated by Michael Taylor. Chicago: University of Chicago Press, [1974] 1991.

Mirzoeff, Nicholas. *An Introduction to Visual Culture*. New York: Routledge, 1999.

Mirzoeff, Nicholas, ed. *The Visual Culture Reader*. 2nd ed. New York: Routledge, [1998] 2002.

Rose, Gillian. *Visual Methodologies: An Introduction to the Interpretation of Visual Materials*. 2nd ed. Thousand Oaks, Calif.: Sage, 2007.

Satrapi, Marjane. *Persepolis*. New York: Pantheon, 2003.

de Saussure, Ferdinand. *Course in General Linguistics*. With contributions by Charles Bally. Translated by Roy Harris. Chicago: Open Court Publishing, [1915] 1988.

Schama, Simon. *The Embarrassment of Riches: An Interpretation of Dutch Culture in the Golden Age*. Berkeley: University of California Press, 1988.

Sebeck, Thomas A. *Signs: An Introduction to Semiotics*. Toronto: University of Toronto Press, 1995.

Sekula, Allan. "On the Invention of Photographic Meaning." In *Thinking Photography*. Edited by Victor Burgin. London: Macmillan, 1982, 84–109.

Silverman, Kaja. *The Subject of Semiotics*. New York: Oxford University Press, 1983.

Sontag, Susan. *On Photography*. New York: Delta, 1977.

Staniszewski, Mary Anne. *Believing Is Seeing: Creating the Culture of Art*. New York: Penguin, 1995.

Storey, John, ed. *Cultural Theory and Popular Culture: A Reader*. Athens: University of Georgia Press, 1998.

Wells, Liz, ed. *Photography: A Critical Introduction*. 3rd ed. New York: Routledge, [1996] 2004.

Wollen, Peter. *Signs and Meaning in the Cinema*. London: British Film Institute, 1969.

chapter **two**

Viewers Make Meaning

*I*mages generate meanings, yet the meanings of a work of art, a photograph, or a media text do not, strictly speaking, lie in the work itself, where they were placed by the producer waiting for viewers to find them. Rather, meanings are produced through the complex negotiations that make up the social process and practices through which we produce and interpret images. In the process of making, interpreting, and using images, meanings change. The production of meaning involves at least three elements besides the image itself and its producer: (1) the codes and conventions that structure the image and that cannot be separated from the content of the image; (2) the viewers and how they interpret or experience the image; and (3) the contexts in which an image is exhibited and viewed. Although we can say that images have what we call dominant or primary meanings, they are interpreted and used by viewers in ways that do not strictly conform to these meanings.

Throughout this book, we discuss the *viewer* more than the *audience*. A viewer is, in the most basic sense of the term, an individual who looks. An audience is a collective of lookers. In focusing on the viewer, we are concerned with the activity of the individual as a social category that emerges through practices of looking. Viewing involves a set of relational social practices. These practices occur not simply between individual human subjects who look and are looked at but among people, objects, and technologies in the world. Viewing, even for the individual subject, is a multimodal activity. The elements that come into play when we look may include not only images but also other images with which they are displayed or published, our own bodies, other bodies, built and natural objects and entities, and the institutions and social contexts in which we engage in looking. Viewing is a relational and social practice whether one looks in private or in public and whether the image is personal (a photograph of a loved one, for example), context-specific (a scientific image used as an information source in a laboratory), or public (a news photograph).

By looking at the *viewer*, we can understand certain aspects of practices of looking that cannot be captured by examining the concept of the audience, an entity into which producers hope to mold viewers as consumers.[1] The term *interpellation* is an important aspect of this point. To interpellate, in the traditional usage of this concept, is to interrupt a procedure in order to question someone or something formally, as in a legal or governmental setting (in a Parliamentary procedure, for example). The term was adapted by political and media theorists in the 1970s, who made the case that *images interpellate viewers*. They used this term, as we do, to describe the way that images and media texts seem to call out to us, catching our attention. Here, we draw on and move beyond the theories of French philosopher Louis Althusser, whose ideas theorists have drawn on to suggest that ideologies "hail" subjects and enlist them as their authors. Images hail viewers as individuals, even when each viewer knows that many people are looking at the same image—that the image was not intended "just for me" but reaches a wider audience. There is an interesting paradox inherent in this experience: for viewer interpellation by an image to be effective, the viewer must implicitly understand himself or herself as being a member of a social group that shares codes and conventions through which the image becomes meaningful. I may feel that an image apprehends or touches me personally, but it can do so only if I am a member of a group to whom its codes and conventions "speak," even if the image does not "say" the same thing to me as it does to someone else. I do not have to like or appreciate the dominant messages of the image to be interpellated by it or to understand that message. To be interpellated by an image, then, is to know that the image is meant for me to understand, even if I feel that my understanding is unique or goes against the grain of a meaning that seems to have been intended.

Advertising seeks, of course, to interpellate viewer-consumers in constructing them within the "you" of the ad. The codes and meanings of an advertisement, for example, might be entirely clear to me, even if I do not share or am opposed to the tastes and values it promotes and even if the ad tries to represent "people like me" in a manner that I feel is "not really me" or is offensive to me. This Olay ad interpellates the viewer with the promise of an idealized future self. The ad uses the "O" of "You" to target the model, who stands in for the consumer and whose transformation is promised. Here, the ad visualizes the "you" that is normally implied within image texts. The message of the image, even if not intended for me, nonetheless draws me in as a spectator, interpellating me, even though I know I am not the person for whom it was meant. Some images strongly interpellate viewers, some do not. But even if the primary or dominant message conveyed by the image is not, strictly speaking, "for me," my experience with the image may be personal in that there are various roles I may occupy in relationship to the image.

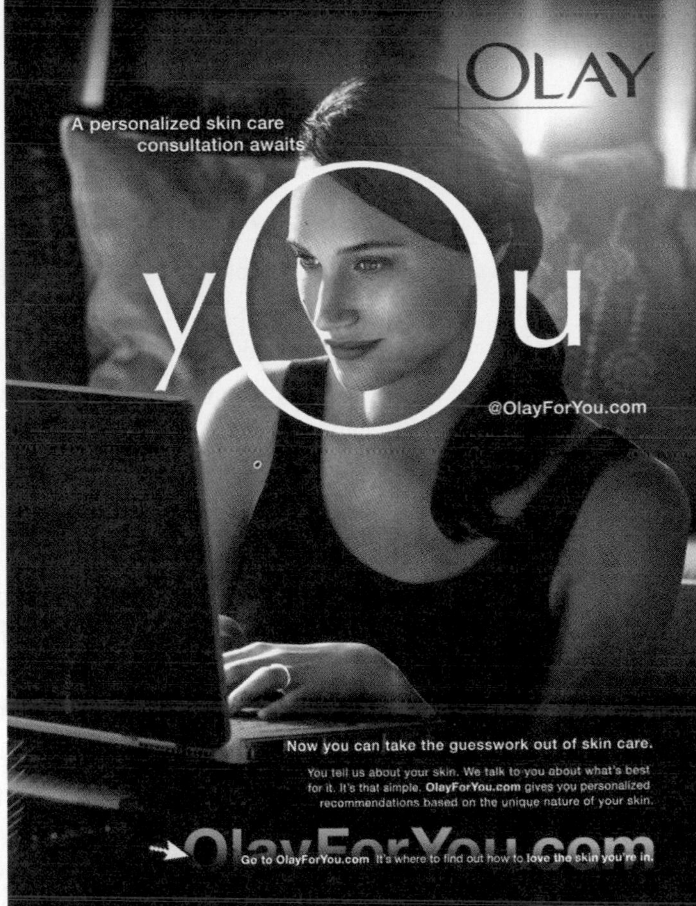

FIG. 2.1
Olay ad, 2008

In the process of interpellation we are describing, an image or media text can bring out in viewers an experience of being "hailed" in ways that do not always promote a sense of being exactly the subject for whom the message is intended. As John Ellis notes, the term *audience*, a unifying concept that is so important to media marketing experts, does not adequately capture this process. A viewer's direct and complete engagement with the image producers' intended messages may be the goal of the producer, but such an engagement is not really possible. Even the most personal images work this way. I may feel that a photograph of a loved one interpellates, or speaks, to me and only me, but it does so through the photographic codes and conventions of "the personal" that we use to convey such messages. Such photographs can use close-ups to give the sense that the photographed subject looks directly into the viewer's eyes and soul. Romantic photographs of stars coveted by fans use the same conventions and may hail viewers in the same way, inciting romantic fantasies of intimacy. I may be interpellated by such an image, recognizing romantic love as a dominant or intended message that others will "get" without having these feelings invoked in me personally but rather recognizing them as feelings others are likely to have (those who admire the star, for example). I may even feel disgust or contempt for the intended message. This would be another way of being interpellated by the image.

By focusing on the viewer (and not the audience) throughout this book, we are emphasizing the practices through which images and media texts reach out and touch audience members in ways that engender experiences of individual agency and interpretive autonomy, even in cases in which the image is widely viewed as a shared text with effective dominant meanings with which we may or may not fully engage. For some theorists, the effective delivery of dominant messages is "ideological" in the sense that "individual" felt experience with the image or text is thought to be a false feeling that producers aim to achieve in viewers through marketing strategies that figure out which codes and conventions will most effectively "reach" targeted audiences. In this view, to feel touched by a mass image is to harbor a mistaken understanding of oneself as the individual for whom that image's meaning is *personally* intended. The viewer, in this view, is duped by the image. We understand the process of interpellation to work differently from this. To be interpellated or touched in an individual way as a viewer is a common and all but unavoidable aspect of looking at images and media texts, public and private. But this aspect of practices of looking is neither insidious nor fully controlled by external forces such as advertisers or the media industry. Individual human agency and desire are not wholly controlled by the strategies of industry market experts, and dominant meanings are not the only or the most important ones that we experience. By considering viewers, not audiences, we can describe some of the many ways that viewers make meanings outside the boundaries of producers' intended messages and effects, even as viewers recognize those intended meanings.

Producers' Intended Meanings

Who produces images? The concept of the producer becomes complicated when we consider forms that involve multiple producers, as in the case of a major studio film production or the work of a collective of artists. In film parlance, a producer is a person who identifies financing and oversees the many jobs involved in a production. When the art collective Group Material displayed their public art throughout the streets and subways of New York City in the 1980s, the "producer" widely noted for generating this category or "brand" of work was the collective itself, and not the individual artists who designed each work. In advertising, the term *producer* could refer to the advertising agency, the lead designer, or the company whose product is represented in the ad. When we use the term *producer,* then, we may be referring to an individual maker (as in the case of one artist who produces a painting), a plurality of creative individuals unified by a shared set of aesthetic strategies of production design and display (the art collective or collaborators creating a work), or a corporate conglomerate engaged in different phases and aspects of an ad. The art collective RTMark plays up the anonymity of the individual artist in the manufacture of goods in postindustrial capitalism by presenting itself as an anonymous artist collective structured like a corporation and using corporate language and investment strategies to make a parodic critique of the mass visual culture of commodity production and branding.

French theorist Roland Barthes, in his classic 1967 essay on "The Death of the Author," was concerned with questions of authority and power between the individual author and readers.[2] We adapt his concept of the author's "death" to consider questions of authority and power as they are enacted between viewers and producers of images and media texts. According to Barthes, the text offers a multidimensional space that the reader deciphers or interprets. There is no ultimate authorial meaning for readers to uncover in the text. The approach to the image that we adopt throughout this book follows a similar logic. Although images and media texts may hold dominant meanings, it is the job of the critical reader not to simply point out dominant meanings for others to see but to show how these meanings are made. The text is also open to meanings and interpretations that exist alongside and even against these more obvious meanings. Barthes advocated for the work of a critical and analytical reader whose interpretive practices are grounded in the historical contexts and positions from which texts are always read, as a means of showing how the authority of the author as the primary producer of the literary text is in fact a myth. His point was, in part, that texts are produced in the act of reading them and that these acts are performed from the cultural and political perspectives of readers and never fully according to the intentions of the author or producer.

Barthes's idea of critical reading was adapted among critics and theorists writing about images as a means of advocating for critical viewing practices—that is, practices of looking that take into account the authority and power of the historically and culturally situated viewer in the production of meanings. This perspective was especially important at the moment in history at which Barthes wrote, which preceded the era of the 1980s and 1990s, when video and computer hardware and software became widely available to the broad public. Today it goes without saying that consumers can produce their own media images and texts, because the technology to self-produce or to copy and manipulate found images is so widely available. During the time that Barthes's essay first circulated, however, home video and digital production and editing programs were a futuristic fantasy. The idea of the consumer of images as the producer of meaning was quite radical and new in the 1960s and 1970s, but today it is an everyday reality.

The French philosopher Michel Foucault, in his 1979 essay, "What is an Author?," written in response to Barthes's "Death of the Author," argues that the concept of author did not always exist and will probably pass out of relevance but that it is not exactly dead.[3] Foucault uses the concept of an "author function" rather than an "author." We adapt this concept as a means of thinking about the producer function. The producer function is a set of beliefs that lead us to have certain expectations about a work with regard to the status of its producer. The function of the author or producer is linked to the idea that "someone" (an artist, a company) must stand behind any given image. Copyright law is based on the premise that ownership of creative expression can be traced to someone, whether that be an individual or a company that owns the rights to the work. The "producer function" concept helps us to understand that "authorship" derives not just from who created something but often from who owns the rights to something. When we speak of a Nike ad, for example, we attribute the producer function to Nike because the corporation, and not the actual creative director of the ad, is the entity that owns and appears to speak through the work.

Most if not all images have a meaning that is preferred by their producers. Advertisers, for example, conduct audience research to try to ensure that the meanings they want to convey about a particular product are the ones viewers will perceive when they encounter an advertisement for that product. Artists, graphic designers, filmmakers, and other image producers create images with the intent that we read them in a certain way. It is also the case that architects design buildings with the intent that people will engage with and utilize the spaces in particular ways.

Analyzing images and built spaces according to what we believe to be the intentions of their producers, however, is rarely a completely useful strategy. We usually have no way to know for certain what a producer, designer, or artist intended his or her image or structure to mean. Furthermore, knowing a producer's intentions often does not tell us much about the image, because intentions may not match up with what viewers actually take away from an image or text. People may experience an image or media text differently from how it is intended to be seen, either because they bring experiences and associations that were not anticipated by its producers or because the meanings they derive are informed by the context in which an image is seen. Context cannot fully be controlled by the producer. For example, we could say that the intentions of the creators of the many advertising images that are on display in an urban context may not necessarily coincide with the ways those images are seen by the many different viewers who encounter them. The visual clutter of the context alone of, say, a place like Times Square, may affect how viewers interpret these images, as may juxtapositions with other images. Similarly, a video that is uploaded onto YouTube will be instantly linked to many other videos,

FIG. 2.2
Times Square, New York, 2008

and how viewers see it can be influenced by the range of videos they see before and after it. Many contemporary images, such as advertisements and television images, are viewed in a huge variety of contexts, each of which may affect their meanings. As visual culture scholar Nicholas Mirzoeff writes, "intervisuality," or the interaction of a variety of modes of visuality, is a key aspect of visual culture; thus any experience of viewing may incorporate different media forms, networks of infrastructure and meaning, and intertextual meanings.[4] Importantly, viewers themselves bring cultural associations that will affect their individual interpretations of an image, as our discussion below will show. This does not mean that viewers wrongly or subjectively interpret images or that images are unsuccessful or fail to persuade viewers when intended and received meanings diverge. Rather, meanings are created in part when, where, and by whom images are consumed, and not only when, where, and by whom they are produced. Simply put, a producer may make an image or media text, but he or she is not in full control of the meanings that are subsequently made through the work.

Although it has always been the case that viewers make different meanings in different cultural contexts, the context of global cultural flows has made this even more true. For example, in 1998, film viewers in China had an unexpected and overwhelmingly positive response to *Titanic*, the 1997 movie directed by James Cameron. According to the *Encyclopaedia Britannica*, in its entry on "cultural globalization," scores of middle-aged Chinese viewers saw the film numerous times and were reduced to tears, prompting a lively street trade in facial tissue outside Shanghai theaters. Sales of posters and the soundtrack were strong, as were video sales, with an estimated 25 million pirated and 300,000 legitimate copies sold. *Titanic* was invested with meanings in China that did not match the meanings produced in the film by its Western viewers, and these meanings were not anticipated by the movie's producers. These meanings were produced by viewers who spontaneously used the text to share emotions about a difficult cultural transition. As the author of the *Britannica* entry writes, "*Titanic* served as a socially acceptable vehicle for the public expression of regret by a generation of aging Chinese revolutionaries who had devoted their lives to building a form of socialism that had long since disappeared."[5] We learn from this example that viewers may make meanings that are not intended or anticipated by its producers, and that viewers are active agents in the production of meaning. Some critics might argue that the movie's marketing to China simply expanded the U.S. movie industry's power and authority and is an example of a kind of cultural imperialism and market domination. The author of the *Encyclopedia Britannica* entry makes a different case: in fact, the production of meaning was very much in the hands of the viewers, who made the text their own.

Neither interpretation of the movie is more or less accurate than the other. An image creates meaning through its circulation among viewers. Hence, we can say that meanings are not inherent in images. Rather, meanings are the product of a complex social interaction among image, viewers, and context. Dominant meanings—the meanings that tend to predominate within a given culture—emerge out of this complex social interaction and may exist alongside alternative and even opposing meanings.

Aesthetics and Taste

All images are subject to judgments about their qualities (such as beauty or coolness) and their capacity to have an impact on viewers. The criteria used to interpret and give value to images depend on cultural codes, or shared concepts, concerning what makes an image pleasing or unpleasant, shocking or banal, interesting or boring. As we explained earlier, these qualities do not reside in the image or object but depend on the contexts in which it is viewed, on the codes that prevail in a society, and on the viewer who is making that judgment. All viewer interpretations involve two fundamental concepts of value—aesthetics and taste.

When we say that we appreciate something (a work of art, a photograph) for "aesthetic" reasons, we usually imply that the value of the work resides in the pleasure it brings us through its beauty, its style, or the creative and technical virtuosity that went into its production. Aesthetics has traditionally been associated with philosophy and the arts, and aesthetic objects have stood apart from utilitarian objects. In the twentieth century, the idea of aesthetics steadily moved away from the belief that beauty resides within a particular object or image. By the end of the century, it was widely accepted that aesthetic judgment about what we consider naturally beautiful or universally pleasing is in fact culturally determined. We no longer think of beauty as a universally shared set of qualities. Contemporary concepts of aesthetics emphasize the ways in which the criteria for what is beautiful and what is not are based on taste, which is not innate but rather culturally specific.

Taste, however, is not simply a matter of individual interpretation. Rather, taste is informed by experiences relating to one's class, cultural background, education, and other aspects of identity. This idea was popularized in the late twentieth century by the influential book by the sociologist and philosopher Pierre Bourdieu, *Distinction: A Social Critique of the Judgement of Taste* (1979), which captured the century's changed understanding of taste as something that is always connected to social identity and class status. Bourdieu provided a description of tastes and their origins in patterns of class distinction. Following from Bourdieu, when we speak of taste or say that someone "has taste" we are usually using culturally specific and class-based concepts. When we say that people have "good taste" we may mean that they participate and are educated in middle-class or upper-class notions of what is aesthetically pleasing, whether or not they actually inhabit these class positions. Or we may regard someone as having "good" taste when they have in common with us a particular aesthetic or style that we believe reflects some special, elite knowledge, such as participation in a market that trades in "quality," edgy, or elite products. Taste can be a marker of education and an awareness of elite cultural values, even if one's expression of taste is to stick one's nose up at what is deemed "good" taste. "Bad taste" is sometimes regarded as a product of ignorance of what is deemed "quality" or "tasteful" within a society. Embracing "bad" taste or "artless" taste, on the other hand, can also signify cultural belonging to an educated elite that stands in opposition to the dictates of taste. Taste, in this understanding, is something that can be learned through contact with culture. But it is also something that one can studiously defy. Taste can be exercised and displayed through patterns of consumption and display.

Notions of taste provide the basis for the idea of connoisseurship. The traditional image of a connoisseur evokes a "well-bred" person, a "gentleman" who possesses "good taste" and knows the difference between a good work of art and a bad one and who can afford the "quality" work over the shoddy reproduction. A connoisseur is considered to be more capable than others of passing judgment on the quality of cultural objects. Traditionally "good taste" has been associated with knowledge of "high" culture forms such as fine art, literature, and classical music. Yet what counts as good taste is more complex than this notion of taste suggests. The term *kitsch* formerly referred to images and objects that are trite, cheaply sentimental, and formulaic. Kitsch is associated with mass-produced objects that offer cheap or gaudy versions of classical beauty (plastic reproductions of crystal chandeliers, for example). Cheap tourist trinkets, gift cards embossed with seraphim, paintings on velvet—these are kitsch. Art critic Clement Greenberg wrote a famous essay in 1939, "Avant Garde and Kitsch," in which he argued that unlike avant garde art, kitsch is formulaic, offering cheap and inauthentic emotion to the uneducated masses.[6] In the 1980s the concept of kitsch was newly revived by postmodern artists, architects, and critics interested in defying the austere aesthetics and universalizing values of modern works of art and architecture. Embracing the lowbrow aesthetics of kitsch and the "bad" design elements of everyday mass culture became a means of defying modernism's tendency toward elite, "high quality" design. Kitsch objects also gained value precisely because they became recognized as iconic of a historical moment in which everyday life was saturated with cheesiness. Certain objects formerly deemed "tasteless" or just silly, the everyday artifacts of the everyday middle-class or working-class consumer, were given new value over time precisely because they had become iconic artifacts of a past era. The educated connoisseur can collect and display these now-valuable artifacts to demonstrate engagement in the culture of lowbrow aesthetics.

The lava lamp is an example of how kitsch can gain value in a second level of meaning. When it was first made in England in the postwar period, the lamp, in which wax floats in strange shapes in oil, was widely regarded as ugly. But in the 1960s, the weird Astro Lamp (in the American market dubbed the Lava Lite) meshed perfectly with the tastes of the psychedelic generation. The light then fell out of fashion again, tumbling back into the obscurity of bad taste such that even thrift shop collectors spurned it. However, with the broad resurgence of interest in 1960s music and visual and clothing styles in the 1990s, the lamp was back in vogue, to the delight of the company that bought out the original U.S. manufacturer after the

FIG. 2.3
Lava lamp

lamp fell out of favor during the 1980s. Now the original lamp goes for over $100 on eBay, and the copy sells for about $20 in retail stores. In contemporary taste cultures, the circulation of objects through categories of taste and the reclassification of objects according to new scales of value show us that hierarchies of taste and beauty are not fixed but are relative to historical and cultural interpretations.

The Most Wanted Paintings on the Web (1995), a Web work by Vitaly Komar and Alex Melamid, artists originally from the former Soviet Union who have worked in the United States since 1978, is an excellent project through which to examine questions about taste in an international context. The artists, who have worked in the medium of painting to parody and critique forms such as Soviet realism, commissioned a professional market survey in which people in the United States and Russia were asked about their recreational preferences, their politics and lifestyles, their knowledge of famous artists and historical figures, and their preferences for or reactions against paintings with angles, curves, brushstrokes, colors, sizes, themes, and styles. Komar and Melamid then tallied and computed the results of the survey, using their findings to arrive at a formula for the creation of paintings showing each country's most and least wanted image. Each painting represents a composite of the dominant answers from each group. These paintings were exhibited under the rubric of "The People's Choice." Both countries disliked abstract images and preferred calm landscapes in which were featured well-known figures. America's "most wanted" painting was calculated to be "dishwasher-sized" and to include a landscape, wild animals, and George Washington, whereas America's "most unwanted" painting was abstract with sharp angles and a thick textured surface.[7] The Russian most wanted painting displays Jesus in a landscape similar to that depicted in America's most wanted. Both paintings utilize a sort of pictorial realism associated with Soviet-era state-mandated form. Komar and Melamid expanded this project into a Web extravaganza for which groups in twelve countries were polled and their preferences analyzed to arrive at digitized renderings of composite paintings for each nation. This Web project is hosted by the Dia Center for the Arts and has as its primary sponsor the Chase Manhattan Bank, an institutional relationship that the artists no doubt find befitting of their ironic message. With a few exceptions, the results of this poll are remarkably consistent, with most countries preferring soft landscapes and pictorial realism over abstract, minimal compositions. Italy's most

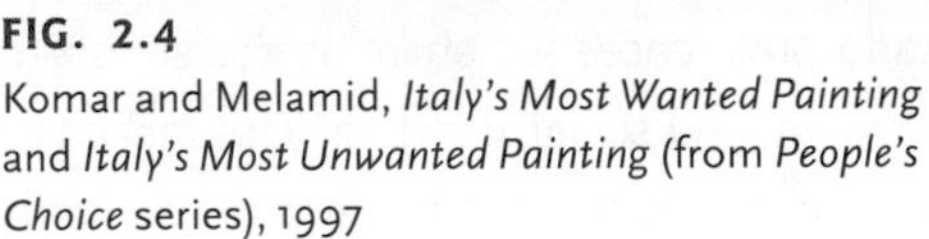

FIG. 2.4
Komar and Melamid, *Italy's Most Wanted Painting* and *Italy's Most Unwanted Painting* (from *People's Choice* series), 1997

wanted painting, pictured here, is, by contrast, more impressionistic, whereas Italy's most unwanted painting features a picture of Elvis and a nude male figure.

One of the chief points of this project is to make a joke about the degree to which the art market is not immune to consumer values and tastes; artists are not unresponsive to the vagaries of a mass public psychology of taste uninformed by the avant-garde aesthetics represented in some museums and galleries of modern art. In this project, decisions about the making of art are brought down to the level of the Nielsen television poll, turning the revered individual fine art painting into something tacky and generically pleasing. The project is also a pointed critique of the ways in which opinion polls and statistics about collective opinions carry so much weight in contemporary society and in the media, even as it uses those statistics to render its works. This art project posed the question about what art would look like if it were produced by audience ratings and opinion polls. Yet at the same time it is also a visual manifestation of just how shallow opinion polls can be in providing an image of the tastes of viewers, here made into a mockery of the conglomerate concept of "the people."

In *Distinction*, Bourdieu established through extensive survey research that taste is used by individuals to enhance their position within the social order and that distinction is the means through which they establish their taste as different from that of other, lower classes of people. This is not a matter of actual class position based on one's economic status but of cultural capital. "Taste classifies," Bourdieu famously wrote, "and it classifies the classifier. Social subjects, classified by their classifications, distinguish themselves by the distinctions they make, between the beautiful and the ugly, the distinguished and the vulgar, in which their position in the objective classifications is expressed or betrayed."[8] Bourdieu also concluded that taste is learned through exposure to social and cultural institutions that promote certain class-based assumptions about correct taste. So, for instance, institutions such as museums function not only to educate people about the history of art but also to instill in them a broader sense of what is tasteful and what is not, what is valuable and what is not, and what is "real" art and what is not. Through these institutions, people, regardless of their class position, learn to be "discriminating" viewers and consumers of images and objects. That is, they "learn" to rank images and objects according to a system of taste that is deeply steeped in class-based values. Even the collecting of objects "in bad taste" is steeped in elite class values, insofar as one must be educated in the meaning of everyday design and kitsch style to appreciate those aesthetics.

In Bourdieu's theory, all aspects of life are interconnected and unified in what he called a *habitus*—a set of dispositions and preferences we share as social subjects that are related to our class position, education, and social standing. This means that our taste in art is related to our tastes in music, food, fashion, furniture, movies, sports, and leisure activities and is in turn related to our profession, class status, and educational level. Taste may often work to the detriment of people of lower classes because it relegates objects and ways of seeing associated with their lifestyles as less worthy of attention and respect. What is more, the very things deemed tasteful—works of fine art, for example—are often off limits to most consumers.

These distinctions between different kinds of taste cultures have traditionally been understood as the difference between high and low culture. As we noted in the introduction, the most common definition of culture throughout history was the idea of the best of a given culture. However, this definition was highly class-based, with those cultural pursuits of the ruling class seen as high culture and the activities of the working class as low culture. Thus high culture has traditionally meant fine art, classical music, opera, and ballet. Low culture was a term used to refer to comic strips, television, and at least initially, the cinema. However, in the late twentieth century, this division of high and low was heavily criticized, not only because it affirms classist hierarchies but also because it is not an accurate measure of the relationship between the cultural forms people consume and the class positions they occupy. The distinction between fine art and popular culture has been consistently blurred in the art movements of the late twentieth century, from pop art to postmodernism. (We discuss this work in chapters 7 and 8.) In addition, as we have noted, the collection of certain kinds of cultural artifacts, such as kitsch, which are valued now precisely because they once were the expression of the everyday consumer's "bad" taste, blurs distinctions between high and low. Furthermore, analyses of B movies (and other cultural products such as popular romance novels) that were once regarded as low culture have emphasized the impact and value of contemporary popular culture among specific communities and individuals, who interpret these texts to strengthen their communities or to challenge oppression. Comic books and graphic novels, once considered to be for children or the uneducated, are now thought of as mainstream and cutting-edge cultural forms. Animated films are now one of the most popular and lucrative genres of popular film, aimed at all ages. It was once the case that universities did not study forms of popular culture—in British universities, for instance, even the study of the novel (as opposed to poetry) did not begin until the mid-twentieth century, because novels were considered lowbrow. The study of popular culture and visual culture in all its forms is now integral to university and high school curricula because of the now widespread belief that we cannot understand a culture without analyzing its production and consumption of all forms of culture, from high to low.

FIG. 2.5
Shepard Fairey, Obey Giant Logo

The model of analysis that Bourdieu used is class-stratified in ways that are specific to what he perceived to be a largely homogeneous native French population when he collected his survey data in the mid-1960s. Both the context in which he asked those questions—that of a postwar pre-May 1968 French society that was significantly class-stratified, with a highly class-based educational system—and the kinds of questions he asked of French bourgeois society are historically and culturally specific. His idea that categories of taste and distinction trickle down from the upper, educated to the lower, less educated classes does not account for the dynamics of taste and judgment in the evaluation of those valued cultural forms that began as the expression of a marginalized culture or class, such as jazz in the 1920s and hip-hop in the 1980s. In the case of forms such as these, taste and distinction can trickle up to more affluent, culturally dominant groups. The same can be said about the graffiti or street art of producers such as Jean-Michel Basquiat, whose graffiti was brought from the streets to the galleries in New York in the 1980s, or Shepard Fairey, the world-renowned street artist, founder of *Swindle* magazine, and designer of the loading screen for Guitar Hero II who stenciled and postered his André the Giant logo in urban public spaces in the 1980s. Fairey's Obey stickers and stencils were designed to get people to think about the messages of images on the street. Yet their meaning was often ambiguous, what Fairey calls an "experiment in phenomenology." His artwork is now copyrighted under the label "Obey Giant" and an offshoot clothing line for sale in mall skate stores alongside Vans, Diesel, and Stussy. Bourdieu's system does not help us to understand the particular patterns of minority, immigrant, or countercultural values and distinction—for example the patterns of taste and distinction among those who immigrated to France from Northern and Sub-Saharan Africa in the years following the demise of French colonialism. Our point is not only that cultural values and tastes may trickle up or may develop differently among members of a politically and culturally minoritized diaspora but also that cultural values and tastes are increasingly subject to movement in a variety of directions, as markets diversify in kind laterally, as well as to globalization. In today's culture, images and objects circulate within and across social strata, cultural categories, and geographical distances with speed and ease, such that youth cultures in Central Asia and North America may look very much alike in their clothing choices despite these groups being separated by geographic distances and political differences. The globalization of manga (Japanese comics) is an example of this phenomenon in which taste and distinction are forged in ways that do not strictly follow Bourdieu's observed patterns of class and cultural influence.

Collecting, Display, and Institutional Critique

As we noted in chapter 1, there are many ways in which the value of a work of art is determined in the art market. One of the key economic and cultural factors in the valuing of art is collecting by art institutions such as museums and by private collectors. Not only does this activity create a market for art, but it also creates a financial context in which work is expected to appreciate in value over time. The collecting of art for economic and cultural capital has a long history. This seventeenth-century painting by David Teniers of Archduke Leopold Wilhelm's collection was one of the first visual catalogings of an art collection. In this image, Teniers imagined the archduke standing among his many paintings as a means to both illustrate the collection and affirm the importance of the archduke's role as collector. The large scale of the painting, in which the figures seem diminutive, affirms the size of the collection. This painting thus functions as an actual catalogue of the archduke's collection, as an affirmation of his taste and role as a connoisseur, and as evidence of the value of his large collection. Ownership is a key factor in establishing value in art. Much of the value of art collections is established through the details of the provenance of artworks, such as the history of who has owned them and when they changed ownership—information that has little to do with the artist or the work's creation.

FIG. 2.6
David Teniers the Younger, *Archduke Leopold Wilhelm in his Picture Gallery in Brussels*, c. 1650–51

Collecting always involves the elements of hierarchy and value judgments. The cultural theorist James Clifford has written about how the practices of collecting and exhibiting art and artifacts contributed to the ways viewers make meaning. In a well-known essay on practices of collecting, "On Collecting Art and Culture," Clifford considers the fate of African tribal art, artifacts, and cultural practices when these items and practices are relocated to Western museums, archives, art markets, and discursive systems. He adapts the "semiotic square" (designed by A. J. Greimas) for the purpose of mapping the movement of art and cultural artifacts from one cultural context to another in relationship to changes in their classification and value. Clifford's map of the "art-culture system" allows us to see how the movement of objects through the collecting practices of museums, scholars, and connoisseurs effects transitions in the meaning and value of works from, for example, not-art (such as religious artifacts) to art or from authentic to inauthentic. Clifford describes the collecting process as a machine in which common works of everyday culture are given value as a commodity in the rarified fine art market, trading on the mystified aura of the work as "true" tribal religious artifact.

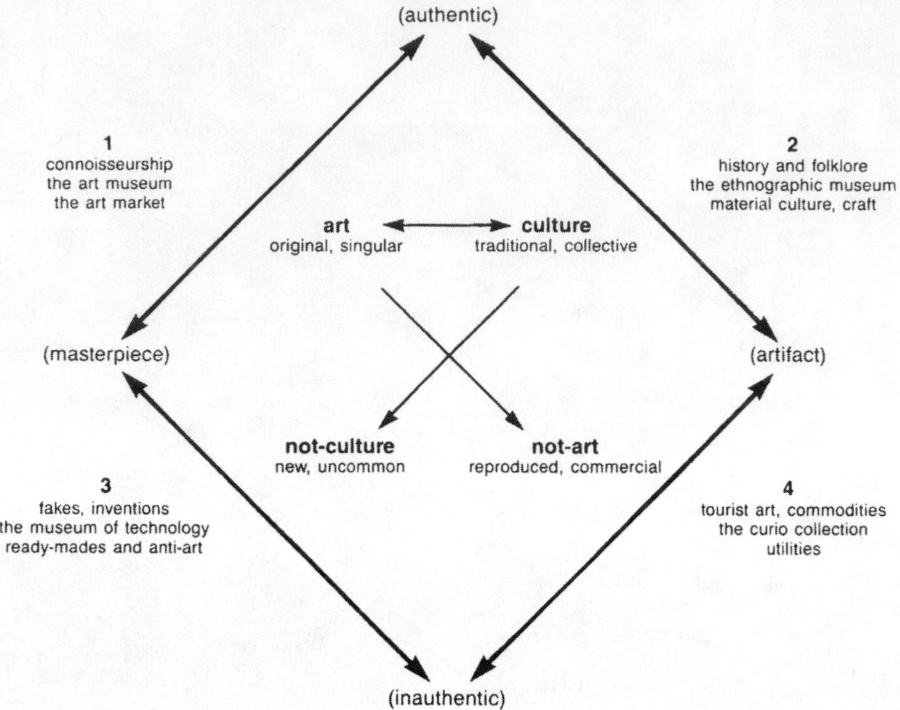

FIG. 2.7

The Art-Culture System © James Clifford, *The Predicament of Culture: Twentieth-Century Ethnography, Literature, and Art*, Harvard University Press, 1988

Although the context in which contemporary art is collected includes dealers, galleries, and art auction houses as the primary arbiters of taste and value, there is also a parallel set of collecting practices in cultural artifacts, the "culture" section of Clifford's chart. These collections are, as his chart indicates, primarily based on notions of cultural authenticity. In the early 1990s, the anthropologists Ilisa Barbash and Lucien Taylor followed Gabai Baaré, a West African merchant who trades in wood carvings produced by members of his village and surrounding communities. In their documentary, *In and Out of Africa* (1992), Barbash and Taylor reveal the complex role played by "insider" figures such as Baaré in the entry of "local" cultural art and artifact to the lucrative global art market. They reveal that Baaré and the artists who produce the reproductions of religious artifacts that he peddles to art galleries in New York's Soho and to tourist emporia alike are neither naïve nor beholden to the Western value system. They actively engage in the irony of a process in which they recognize that their mythification by Western consumers can bring profit. Their products have, since the era of colonialism, included iconic "Colon" figures, hand-carved parodies of the colonial authorities and the very connoisseurs who covet their "authentic" reproductions of religious iconography produced exclusively for the tourist and art trade market.

Practices of collecting are intricately tied up in practices of exhibition and the valuing of work that comes from display contexts. Thus works of art and cultural

FIG. 2.8
Thomas Struth, *Hermitage I, St. Petersburg*, 2005

artifacts are awarded value when they are purchased by museums and put on display within the institutions that represent art and culture, such as museums and galleries. In these institutional contexts, viewers can engage in a broad array of viewing practices, some in concert with institutional missions such as art pedagogy (by listening to commentaries on audio players offered for rent at the start of an exhibition, for instance) and some in defiance of them (as when we move quickly through an exhibition, skipping over many works within it, or make ironic or critical interpretations of the work on the basis of our taste, politics, or the cultural knowledge we bring to the show that is elided from the safe facts offered in the canned exhibition narrative).

Photographer Thomas Struth took a series of photographs of people viewing art in museums in order to capture the complexity of these kinds of art-viewing practices. These photographs, which are normally displayed within a museum or gallery, give a sense of the varied responses that ordinary people have to art. Struth took these photographs in some of the most famous museums around the world, capturing images of people gazing at, scrutinizing, and walking past famous works of art. In this image, visitors at the Hermitage Museum in St. Petersburg, Russia display a full range of responses to looking at art—turning away, listening to audio commentary without looking at the work, looking at it intently. Struth created these images with a large-format camera and displays them in the form of very large prints, effectively replicating the experience of the viewers they portray when they are exhibited in large museum spaces. These museum photographs give us a sense of the range of responses and expressions of taste that can be found in museums. They also convey, in part through their large size, the sense of presence of the large works of art on exhibition in these spaces. Struth has remarked on how art is fetishized by being exhibited in museums as great masterworks. He suggests that in this process they become dead objects, but that through viewers' interactions with these works they can regain some of their vitality.[9] At the same time, Struth's images point to the central role that museums play in designating which images and objects are of value in any given society by determining what it is that gets displayed and by creating the conditions (majestic, pristine, grandiose, or gritty) under which works of art are displayed. Our taste is influenced not only by what we are taught to seek out and appreciate but also by how those artworks and objects are publicly exhibited.

In the 1990s, the discipline of museum studies (or museology) became a location of vibrant intellectual critique among visual culture scholars and artists interested in challenging the role of the museum in shaping taste. The systems of value imposed by museums, they held, were a means of protecting, maintaining, and hiding ruling class interests in the art market. Some of these artists began to do work later described as a form of *institutional critique*. This concept draws on writings by Michel Foucault about the function of institutions, such as asylums and prisons, in the production of particular forms of knowledge and states of being. One of the tenets of institutional critique is that institutions historically have provided structures through which power could be enacted without force or explicit directives, but rather through more passive techniques such as education, the cultivation of taste, and the cultivation of daily routines. With this focus on the institution as a structure through which power is enacted in a banal way, social critics of art and artists concerned with dynamics of power in the art market turned to the museum as a site where viewers could be interpellated with messages that reflexively drew attention to the politics of the museum itself. Viewing practices, they realized, could be disrupted as a means of undercutting the smooth trickle of standards of taste from the institution down to the viewing public.

Institutional critique can be traced back to the Dadaist interventions of Marcel Duchamp, the French artist who challenged taste and aesthetics. In the 1910s, Duchamp took a jab at the veneration of art objects with his "readymades," gallery and museum displays composed of mundane everyday objects such as a bicycle wheel. In 1917 Duchamp contributed a urinal, titled *Fountain* and signed with the pseudonym R. Mutt, to a highly publicized painting exhibition he helped to organize. The exhibition's organizers were offended by the piece and its clear message about art's value, taste, and the practices of display; they threw it out of the show. Duchamp subsequently became the cause célèbre of Dada, a movement that reflexively poked fun at the conventions of high art and museum display conventions. Dada helped to inspire many movements in art that aimed to critique the art market and its valuing of art for collecting, including political art, guerrilla art, performance art and happenings, and other ephemeral kinds of art that could not be commodified in the form of valued objects.

Many of Duchamp's ideas about disrupting the art system were taken up starting in the 1960s by artists who attempted to examine museums as financial institutions

FIG. 2.9
Slave shackles displayed next to fine silver in *Mining the Museum: An Installation by Fred Wilson*, 1992–93, The Maryland Historical Society and The Contemporary, Baltimore

and arbiters of taste. In the late 1960s, the German artist Hans Haacke, working primarily in the United States, made a number of works that famously revived this strategy of leading the viewer to question the museum's role in shaping taste. Haacke's conceptual works included an exposé of the business connections of the trustees of the Guggenheim Museum, the intended site of this work's exhibition in 1971. Although this solo exhibition was canceled by the museum's director, many other of his works of institutional critique were displayed in museums around the world. In the 1990s, artists engaged in institutional critique interrupted viewing practices through strategies that included taking on the role of the curator and reordering or disrupting the logic of display as a means of making obvious, and thereby disrupting, the formerly invisible politics and policies of the institution. To prepare for the installation *Mining the Museum* (1992–1993), the American artist Fred Wilson spent a year in residence at the staid Maryland Historical Society getting to know their collections, their exhibition practices, and the community they served. He then "mined" the museum's collection, resurrecting pieces held in storage and organizing them in a series of juxtapositions with more conventional exhibition objects. With minimal labeling, these displays relied on juxtaposition to make their point about the politics of display, concealment, and assignation of meaning and value in which this museum had engaged. Slave shackles were resurrected from storage and placed alongside a silver tea service that had previously been on display. Wilson gave lectures and tours of his exhibition. By shifting his role from the traditional one of artist as producer to that of artist as curator and docent, Wilson was able to make an intervention in the hidden politics of a museum that had

FIG. 2.10
Fred Wilson, *Guarded View*, 1991

remained entrenched in traditional, "neutral" exhibition practices that included the showing of works of material value (the silver tea service) and the hiding of works that made visible the shameful and ugly aspects of Southern culture and politics.

In another work of institutional critique, *Guarded View* (1991), Wilson displays life-size headless statues of museum guards, forcing viewers to ponder directly those very institutional subjects who are rendered invisible by the dynamics of the gaze at work in the museum. Whereas many of the guards in U.S. art museums are black and Latino, most of the patrons are white. This installation foregrounded the issue of race in relation to labor and marketing practices of museums. These works of figurative sculpture disrupted conventions of viewing by forcing museumgoers to notice the human presence of living guards, the very figures we are likely to ignore when we focus intently on the artworks the museum has displayed for our appreciation and scrutiny. By displaying the "invisible" figure of the guard, Wilson brings to our attention the selectivity of our gaze, which readily excludes notice of these underpaid, low-level employees who have always been fully present in the visual field of the museum gallery.

Cultures of collecting and display have also been radically transformed by the emergence of online collecting and exhibition. Thus many people create online galleries for their own images on photographic websites, artists are increasingly exhibiting and selling their work online, and collecting takes place through such websites as eBay. The critique of institutional power in relation to display has thus been paralleled by the changes taking place in cultural production and technological access. In this sense, the roles of the expert, the author, and the amateur are constantly being disrupted and reconfigured in ways that form a direct lineage back to Duchamp and readymade culture.

Reading Images as Ideological Subjects

As we often accept the idea of good taste unquestioningly, taste can be seen as a logical extension of a culture's ideology. Societies function by naturalizing ideologies, making the complex production of meaning take place so smoothly that it is experienced as a "natural" system of value or belief. As a consequence, it is easier for us to recognize the production of meanings in other times and cultures as ideological than it is to see our own meanings as ideological. Most of the time, our dominant ideologies just look to us like common sense.

Much of the way that ideology is conceived today originates with its formulation in the theories of Karl Marx. Marxism is a theory that analyzes both the role of economics in the progress of history and the ways that capitalism works in terms of class relations. According to Marx, who wrote in the nineteenth century during the rise of industrialism and capitalism in the Western world, those who own the means of production are also in control of the ideas and viewpoints produced and circulated in a society's media venues. Thus, in Marx's terms, the dominant social classes that own or control the newspaper, television, film, and communication industries are able to control the content generated by these media forms. Marx's ideas, and the ideas that they inspired in subsequent theorists, can help us understand how we interpret images as ideological subjects. Marx thought of ideology as a kind of false consciousness that was spread by dominant powers among the masses, who are coerced by those in power to mindlessly buy into the belief systems that allow industrial capitalism to thrive. Marx's idea of false consciousness, which has since been rejected as too simplistic by most contemporary theorists, emphasized the ways that people who are oppressed by a particular economic system, such as capitalism, are encouraged to believe in it anyway. Many now view his concept of ideology as overly totalizing and too focused on a top-down notion of ideology.

There have been at least two significant alterations to the traditional Marxist definition of ideology that have shaped subsequent theories about media culture and looking practices. One change came in the 1960s from Louis Althusser, whom we discussed earlier in relation to the concept of interpellation. He insisted that ideology cannot be dismissed as a simple distortion of the realities of capitalism. Rather, he argued, "ideology represents the imaginary relationship of individuals to their real conditions of existence."[10] Althusser moved the term ideology away from its association with false consciousness. His intervention at the level of thinking of this "imaginary" relationship is crucial to changing concepts of ideology, as it brings in psychological (and psychoanalytic) concepts in understanding what motivates subjects to embrace particular values. For Althusser, ideology does not simply reflect the conditions of the world, whether falsely or not. Rather, it is the case that without ideology we would have no means of thinking about or experiencing that thing we call reality. Ideology is the necessary representational means through which we come to experience and make sense of reality.

Althusser's modifications to the term ideology are crucial to the study of visual culture because they emphasize the importance of representation (and hence images) to all aspects of social life, from the economic to the cultural. By the term *imaginary,* Althusser does not mean false or mistaken ideas. Rather, he draws from psychoanalysis to emphasize that ideology is a set of ideas and beliefs shaped through the unconscious in relationship to other social forces, such as the economy and institutions. By living in society, we live in ideology, and systems of representation are the vehicles of that ideology. Althusser's theories have been especially useful in film studies, in which they helped theorists to analyze how media texts invite people to recognize themselves and identify with a position of authority or omniscience while watching films.

Althusser's concepts of ideology have been influential, but they can be seen as disempowering as well. If we are always already defined as subjects and are interpellated to be who we are, then there is little hope for individuality or social change. In other words, the idea that we are already constructed as subjects does not allow us to feel that we have any agency in our lives. Althusser's concept of interpellation contains within it a restrictive sense of individual agency. Ideologies speak to us and in the process recruit us as "authors"; thus we become/are the subject that we are addressed as. In Althusser's terms, we are not so much unique individuals but rather are "always already" subjects—spoken by the ideological discourses into which we are born and in which are asked to find our place. This means that in his model, the different modalities of interpellation that we described at the beginning of this chapter would not be possible.

It is important for us to think in terms of ideologies, in the plural. The concept of a singular mass ideology makes it difficult to recognize how people in economically and socially disadvantaged positions really do challenge or resist dominant ideology. Long before Althusser, an Italian Marxist, Antonio Gramsci, had already introduced the concept of hegemony in place of the concept of domination in order to help us to think about this kind of resistance. Within visual studies, Gramsci's concept of hegemony has been useful among critics who want to emphasize the role of image consumers in influencing the meanings and uses of popular culture in ways that do not benefit the interests of producers and the media industry. Gramsci wrote mostly during the 1920s and 1930s in Italy, but his ideas became highly influential in the late twentieth century. There are two central aspects to Gramsci's definition of hegemony that concern us: that dominant ideologies are often presented as "common sense" and that dominant ideologies are in tension with other forces and constantly in flux.

The term *hegemony* emphasizes that power is not wielded by one class over another; rather, power is negotiated among all classes of people. Unlike domination, which is won by the ruling class through force, hegemony is enacted through the push and pull among all levels of a society. No single class of people "has" hegemony; rather, hegemony is a state or condition of a culture arrived at through negotiations

FIG. 2.11
Barbara Kruger, *Untitled (Your manias become science)*, 1981

over meanings, laws, and social relationships. Similarly, no one group of people ultimately "has" power; rather, power is a relationship within which classes of people struggle. One of the most important aspects of hegemony is that these relationships are constantly changing; hence dominant ideologies must constantly be reaffirmed in a culture precisely because people can work against them. This concept also allows counter-hegemonic forces, such as political movements or subversive cultural elements, to emerge and to question the status quo. The concept of hegemony and the related term *negotiation* allow us to acknowledge the role that people may play in challenging the status quo and effecting social change in ways that may not favor the interests of the marketplace.

How can Gramsci's concepts of hegemony and counter-hegemony help us to understand how people create and make meaning of images? In her work, the American artist Barbara Kruger takes "found" photographic images and adds text to give these images ironic meanings. In this example, created in 1981, Kruger took a well-known image of the atomic bomb, changing its meaning by adding text. The image of an atomic bomb indicates a broad set of ideologies, from the spectacle of high technology to anxiety about its tremendous capacity to destroy, that depend on the context in which the image is viewed. It could be argued that the bomb itself and images of it are indicative of a particular set of ideological assumptions that emerged from the Cold War about the rights of nations to build destructive weapons and the so-called need to create more and more destructive weapons in the name of protecting one's country. In the 1940s and 1950s, an image of the bomb was thus likely to uphold many ideas about the primacy of Western science and technology and the role of the United States and the Soviet Union as superpowers. Produced close to the end of the twentieth century, however, this image clearly criticizes the existence of nuclear weapons throughout the world.

Kruger used text in this image to comment on these ideological assumptions about Western science. Who is the "you" of this image? We could say that Kruger is speaking to those with power, perhaps those who helped to create the atomic bomb and those who approved it. But she is also speaking in a larger sense to the "you" of Western science and philosophy that allowed a maniacal idea (bombing people) to acquire the validation of rational science. In this work, the image is awarded new meaning through the bold, accusatory statement spread across it and the red frame placed around it. Here, the text dictates the meaning of the image and provokes the viewer, in often oblique ways, to look at it differently. Kruger's work functions as a counter-hegemonic statement about the dominant ideology of science.

It is important, when thinking about ideologies and how they function, to keep in mind the complicated interactions of powerful systems of belief and the things that very different kinds of viewers bring to their experiences. If we give too much weight to the idea of a dominant ideology, we risk portraying viewers as cultural dupes who can be "force fed" ideas and values. At the same time, if we overemphasize the potential array of interpretations viewers can make of any given image, we can make it seem as if all viewers have the power to interpret images any way they want and that these interpretations will be meaningful in their social world. In this perspective, we would lose any sense of dominant power and its attempt to organize our ways of looking. Meanings of images are created in a complex relationship among producer, viewer, image or text, and social context, and the negotiation of meaning is a key factor in that relationship. Because meanings are produced out of this relationship, there are limits to the interpretive agency of any one member of this group.

Encoding and Decoding

All images are encoded with meanings in their creation and production that is decoded by viewers. In a well-known essay titled "Encoding, Decoding," Stuart Hall has written that there are three positions that viewers can take as decoders of cultural images and artifacts:

1. Dominant-hegemonic reading. They can identify with the hegemonic position and receive the dominant message of an image or text (such as a television show) in an unquestioning manner.

2. Negotiated reading. They can negotiate an interpretation from the image and its dominant meanings.
3. Oppositional reading. Finally, they can take an oppositional position, either by completely disagreeing with the ideological position embodied in an image or rejecting it altogether (for example, by ignoring it).[11]

Viewers who take the dominant-hegemonic position can be said to decode images in a relatively passive manner. But it can be argued that few viewers actually consume images in this manner, because there is no mass culture that can satisfy all viewers' culturally specific experiences, memories, and desires. The second and third positions, negotiation and opposition, are more useful and deserve further explanation.

The term *negotiation* invokes the process of trade. We can think of it as a kind of bargaining over meaning that takes place among viewer, image, and context. We use the term negotiation in a metaphorical sense to say that we often "haggle" with the

FIG. 2.12
Australian Idol grand final winner Damien Leith (right) with hosts James Matherson (left) and Andrew G., Sydney Opera House, November 26, 2006

dominant meanings of an image when we interpret it. The process of deciphering an image always takes place at both the conscious and unconscious levels. It brings into play our own memories, knowledge, and cultural frameworks, as well as the image itself and the dominant meanings that cling to it. Interpretation is thus a mental process of acceptance and rejection of the meanings and associations that adhere to a given image through the force of dominant ideologies. In this process, viewers actively struggle with dominant meanings, allowing culturally and personally specific meanings to transform and even override the meanings imposed by producers and broader social forces. The term negotiation allows us to see how cultural interpretation is a struggle in which consumers are active meaning-makers and not merely passive recipients in the process of decoding images.

Let's consider how this might work with a particular product of popular culture, such as the *Idol* series. Originally begun as *Pop Idol* in Britain, the *Idol* television program now has versions in more than thirty countries, many of them designated nationally, such as *American Idol, Australian Idol, Deutschland such den Superstar* (Germany), and *Philippine Idol*. What would a dominant reading of the *Idol* series entail, considering that so many local versions exist? The ideological basis of the series, clearly an element in its enormous popularity, is the idea that ordinary people can rise to stardom and celebrity purely on the basis of their talent, which is sometimes presented as "natural" rather than acquired or learned. Watching the show is also about the pleasures (both generous and sadistic) in seeing people succeed, fail, and be subjected to often withering criticism from the panel of expert judges. In those versions of the series that are nationally coded, such as *Australian Idol*, the show also conveys a set of values about national identity, designating the winner as somehow emblematic of national values and taste. Versions, such as *American Idol*, that involve audience voting for contestants embody a set of ideological beliefs about democracy, encouraging the idea that voting in the show (which is usually done as a part of a product placement deal for a particular telephone service) is like voting in political elections. Finally, a dominant reading of the show would be that ordinary people have the same opportunities to be rewarded for their talent as those who have the advantages of wealth and social capital as means to building fame.

The *Idol* programs have been enormously popular and the source of much public discussion and debate. Most viewers watching these shows throughout the world interpret them not with an uncritical dominant reading but in a negotiated reading, agreeing with some elements of the shows' message and critiquing others. The decision in the 2008 season of *American Idol* to include Carly Smithson, the former recipient of a major record label contract under her former name (Carly Hennessy), in the roster of finalists was criticized by viewers who saw the show as a venue for undiscovered talent and not a place for an unsuccessful recording artist to get a second chance. As we discuss in chapter 7, *American Idol* has been ridiculed for its blatant product placement (large Coca-Cola glasses line the judges' table, labels facing the camera). A negotiated reading of the show might see the *Idol* shows as entertainment that offers an image of success that is blatantly obvious to viewers as fantasy, as constructed mythology. An oppositional reading of the shows might interpret reality television programming in general as a means for television industries to create cheap programming without having to pay the high fees of known performers and scriptwriters. Such an oppositional critique might also interpret the show as an example of the myth that everyone has equal opportunity to succeed, when in fact it is fundamental to the structure of capitalism that only a few achieve power, wealth, and fame.

Reception and the Audience

Of the three different modes of engagement with popular culture introduced by Stuart Hall (dominant-hegemonic, negotiated, and oppositional), the category of oppositional readings raises perhaps the most complicated set of questions. Hall's theory has been criticized for reducing what viewers do to three positions, when in fact the viewing practices of most viewers fall along a continuum of negotiated meanings. Nevertheless, it is important to ask: What does it mean to read a television show or a media image in an oppositional way? Does it make any difference that individual viewers may often read against the intended meaning of an image? The lone oppositional reading of a single viewer may mean nothing compared with the popularity of a particular cultural product on the basis of its dominant shared meanings. This consideration raises the important issue of power: Whose readings matter, and how and when do subjugated or minority readings come to matter? There are many ways in which negotiated and oppositional readings of popular culture demonstrate the complicated dance of power relations in contemporary societies, the tension of hegemonic and counter-hegemonic forces.

When we are considering viewer responses to cultural texts, we are looking at the question of reception. Reception theory has for the most part looked at the practices of individual viewers in interpreting and making meaning from watching and consuming cultural products. Entertainment and marketing industries gauge audience responses in many ways. Nielsen audience ratings have historically measured the number of viewers watching television shows (through viewing logs and electronic devices), although these practices are now largely questioned as television viewing has declined. Industries often expend significant amounts of money doing focus-group and marketing research to find out what viewer-consumers think of different shows, advertisements, and products. Marketing research uses an increasingly complex array of techniques, from surveys to consumer-viewer blogging and diaries to consumer-generated videos, as well as significant amounts of quantitative data about viewership and consumer purchases, to attempt to gauge viewer-consumer interest.

Scholarly reception studies differ from audience studies in that they focus on viewers, not audiences. Scholars who undertake reception studies typically rely on ethnographic methods, interviewing actual viewers to try to get a sense of the meaning they take away from a particular cultural product. For instance, in the 1980s, British researcher David Morley used Hall's model of encoding-decoding as a framework for focus group research to study viewers of the BBC television show *Nationwide*; Janice Radway studied women who read romance novels as a kind of "interpretive community" through interviews and participant observation; and Ien Ang used letters from viewers of *Dallas* to explore the meaning of the television show for Dutch viewers.[12]

Most viewer-consumers make meaning from cultural products by watching and interpreting them. Yet, particularly with the advent of a broad array of computer technologies, the Web, iPods, cell phone imaging, and the capacity to easily upload digital and video images to websites such as YouTube, many people have access to the technical means to produce images and cultural products. Nevertheless, the fact remains that the vast amount of cultural production and image production is done through the entertainment and business industries, which are also increasingly skilled in infiltrating amateur media and finding ways to profit from it. We discuss the cultural production of fans and viewers in the next section. Here, we attempt to make clear the complexity of that process of viewing and interpreting.

As we have noted, viewers are not simply passive recipients of the intended message of public images and cultural products such as films and television shows. They have a variety of means by which to engage with images and make meaning from them. This negotiation with popular culture is referred to as "the art of making do," a phrase that implies that although viewers may not be able to change the cultural products they observe, they can "make do" by interpreting, rejecting, or reconfiguring the cultural texts they see. An oppositional reading can take the form of dismissal or rejection—turning off the TV set, declaring boredom, or turning the page. But it can also take the form of making do with, or making a new use for, the objects and artifacts of a culture. As viewers, we can appropriate images and texts (films, television shows, news images, and advertisements), strategically altering their meanings to suit our purposes. As we explained earlier, however, meanings are determined through a complex negotiation among viewers, producers, texts, and contexts. Hence images themselves can be said to resist the oppositional readings that some viewers may wish to confer on them. In other words, meanings that oppose the dominant reading of an image may not "cling" to an image with the same tenacity as meanings that are more in line with dominant ideologies.

The kind of negotiation of meaning that goes on when viewers engage with images can thus be seen as a fluid and complex process. It is for this reason that Hall's tripartite formulation has since begun to seem too reductive and fixed. Reading and viewing can be seen as highly active and individual processes, even as readers and viewers do them within the confines of the dominant meanings of culture. This strategy was famously called *textual poaching* by French literary and cultural theorist Michel de Certeau. Textual poaching was described by de Certeau as inhabiting a text "like a rented apartment."[13] In other words, viewers of popular culture can "inhabit" that text by negotiating meanings through it and creating new cultural products in response to it, making it their own. De Certeau saw reading texts and images as a series of advances and retreats, of tactics and games, through which readers can fragment and reassemble texts with as simple a strategy as a television remote control.

De Certeau saw the relationship of readers/writers and producers/viewers as an ongoing struggle for possession of the text—a struggle over its meaning and potential meanings. This notion operates in opposition to the educational training that teaches readers to search for the author's intended meanings and to leave a text unmarked by their own fingerprints, so to speak. However, this is a process steeped in the unequal power relations that exist between those who produce dominant popular culture and those who consume it. De Certeau defined strategies as the means through which institutions exercise power and set up well-ordered systems that consumers must negotiate (the programming schedule of television, for instance), and he defined tactics as the "hit and run" acts of random engagement by viewers/consumers to usurp these systems, which might include everything from using a remote control to change the "text" of television to creating a website that analyzes a particular film or TV show. De Certeau examined in particular the kinds of tactics used by workers to feel just a small amount of agency during their working day—doing personal activities during work hours, for instance, or even engaging in low-level office sabotage by "helping" office machines to malfunction.

FIG. 2.13
Marlene Dietrich in *Morocco*, 1930

Reading and viewing are thus processes of give and take. One example of negotiated looking is the technique of reading lesbian or gay subtexts in movies that feature gender-bending (bending the traditional codes of gender roles and sexual norms) performances or same-sex friendships. Films starring Marlene Dietrich, a well-known film star of the 1920s and 1930s, for example, have a cult following among lesbian viewers interested in appropriating Dietrich's sometimes gender-bending performances for the underconsidered history of lesbian and gay film culture. In the 1930 film *Morocco*, Dietrich, who was an icon of glamour in her time, dresses in a man's tuxedo and kisses another woman. Her films have been widely noted as depictions that are open for interpretation within the terms of lesbian desire as a queer reading of the films as texts.

Another example of oppositional viewing is the affirmation of qualities within genres previously regarded as exploitative or insulting to a group. The blaxploitation "B movie" film genre, for example, has been widely noted for its negative representations of black culture during the 1970s, with such stereotypes as the black male stud, gangster, and pimp. Yet, more recently, this genre has been revived to emphasize the evidence these films provide of valuable aspects of black culture and talent during the 1970s. Not only did these films star black actors, but they also were the first to include soundtracks that featured black music (funk and soul). Pam Grier, the star of numerous prison dramas and blaxploitation films of the 1970s, such as the 1974 *Foxy Brown* (a film that preceded the contemporary rap performer of this name), reemerged in the cinema in the lead role of *Jackie Brown*, director Quentin Tarantino's 1997 homage to the blaxploitation genre. We can say, then, that this genre has been appropriated, its meanings strategically transformed to create an alternative view of representations of blackness in film.

These forms of making do and appropriation for political empowerment can also be found at the level of language. Social movements sometimes take terms that are derogatory and reuse them in empowering ways. This process is called *transcoding*. In the 1960s, the phrase "Black is beautiful" was used by the civil rights and black power movements as a means to reappropriate the term *black* and change its meaning from a negative to a positive one. Similarly, in recent decades, the term *queer*, which was traditionally used to insult gays, has been transcoded as a cultural identity to be embraced and proudly declared.

One of the terms that can help us to understand the kinds of signifying practices that people use to make sense of culture is *bricolage*. Bricolage is a mode of adaptation in which things (mostly commodities) are put to uses for which they were not intended and in ways that dislocate them from their normal or expected context. It derives from a French term used by anthropologist Claude Lévi-Strauss to mean "making do," or creatively making use of whatever materials are at hand, and it loosely translates to the idea of do-it-yourself culture. In the late 1970s, cultural theorist Dick Hebdige applied the term *bricolage* to the practices of youth subcultures such as punk, and the way they took ordinary commodities and gave them new stylistic meanings.[14] The use of household safety pins as a form of body decoration by punks in the 1970s is the iconic example of bricolage, in which a safety pin that would have previously signified a simple fastener became recoded as a form of body decoration that signaled a refusal to participate in mainstream (parent) culture and disdain for the norms of everyday consumer culture. Hebdige called these kinds of moves *signifying practices* in order to emphasize that they do not simply borrow commodities from their original context but rather give them new meanings, so that, in the terminology of semiotics, they create new signs.

The concept of bricolage and Hebdige's influential use of it focused on youth subcultures of the 1970s and 1980s and the kinds of fashion, music, and style statements they were making, mostly on the street. Hebdige defined a youth subculture as a group that distinguished itself from mainstream culture through various aspects of its style that are assembled by participants from various "found" items

FIG. 2.14
Punk "Irokese" haircuts, from *City Indians*, 1983

whose meanings are altered. Doc Martens, for example, were originally created in the 1940s as orthopedic shoes and sold in Britain in the 1960s as work boots, but they were appropriated to become key elements in various subcultures from the 1970s onward, such as punk, AIDS activism, neopunk, and grunge. The Carhart brand of denim clothing, also originating as blue-collar work gear, became popular among youths favoring the hip-hop look during the 1990s. Cultural theorist Angela McRobbie has examined the ways in which the "ragmarket" of used clothing, begun in the 1990s, has allowed young people to create new styles by mining styles of the past.[15] McRobbie argues that women have played a central role as both entrepreneurial street sellers and as consumers in fostering complex styles of retro fashion, the appropriation of work clothes, and the use of men's clothing, such as formal dress suits and long underwear (as leggings), to create styles that were then appropriated by mainstream fashion.

The subcultures that Hebdige and other theorists of that time were writing about were mostly white working-class male subcultures, and since that time, subculture style (and analyses of it) has undergone many transformations. For participants in fashion subcultures, the remaking of style through appropriation of historical objects and images can be a political statement about class, ethnic, and cultural identity. Many young people assert their defiance of mainstream culture specifically by developing styles that do not conform to the "good taste" of mainstream culture. Chicano "lowriders," for instance, enact style with their cars, which are named and decorated

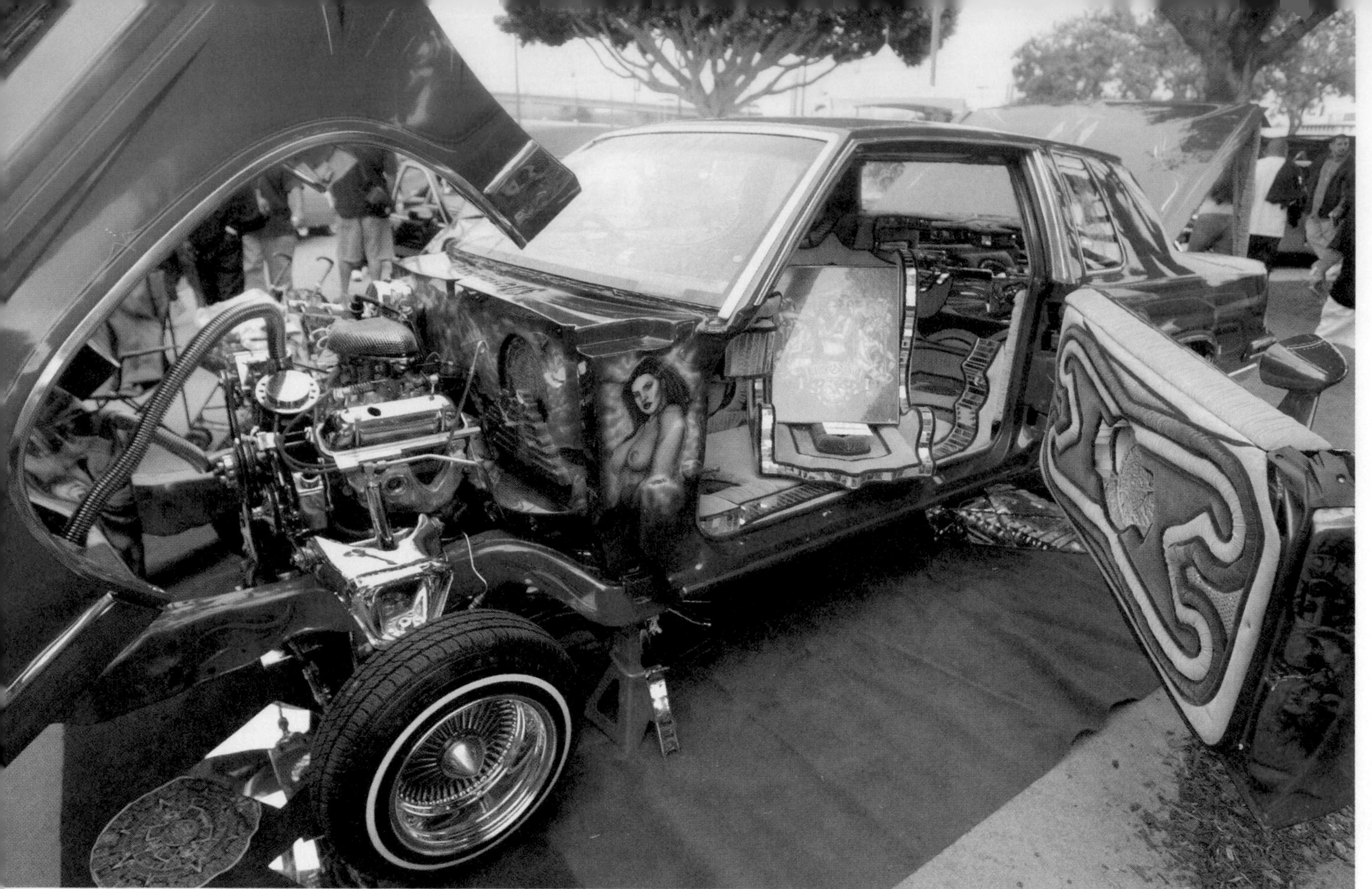

FIG. 2.15
Lowrider car at the 2003 Lowrider Experience, Los Angeles Sports Arena

with paintings of Mexican figures and history, remodeled to both rise up and drive slowly, and refashioned like living spaces. As cultural theorist George Lipsitz notes, the lowrider car defies utilitarianism; it is about cruising for display, codes of ethnic pride, and defying mainstream car culture. He writes, "Low riders are themselves masters of postmodern cultural manipulation. They juxtapose seemingly inappropriate realities—fast cars designed to go slowly, 'improvements' that flaunt their impracticality, like chandeliers instead of overhead lights. They encourage a bi-focal perspective—they are made to be watched but only after adjustments have been made to provide ironic and playful commentary on prevailing standard of automobile design."[16] In remaking these cars so that they defy their design functions and in painting their cars so that they are works of art incorporating meanings from Mexican culture, lowriders produce cultural and political statements in defiance of mainstream Anglo culture. The radical intervention of this culture can be seen in the ways that it has prompted the response of law enforcement, with the creation of laws in the United States that make it illegal to drive too slowly on certain roads after lowriders made it a regular Saturday-night activity to drive at minimal speeds (impeding traffic) down the main streets of certain towns and cities such as Los Angeles. Similarly, skateboard culture, which has at various times intersected with punk culture and hip-hop culture, is associated more broadly with youth and has produced an array of antiskating ordinances restricting its practice in certain locations or the use of metal barriers in public spaces to make it difficult to practice there.

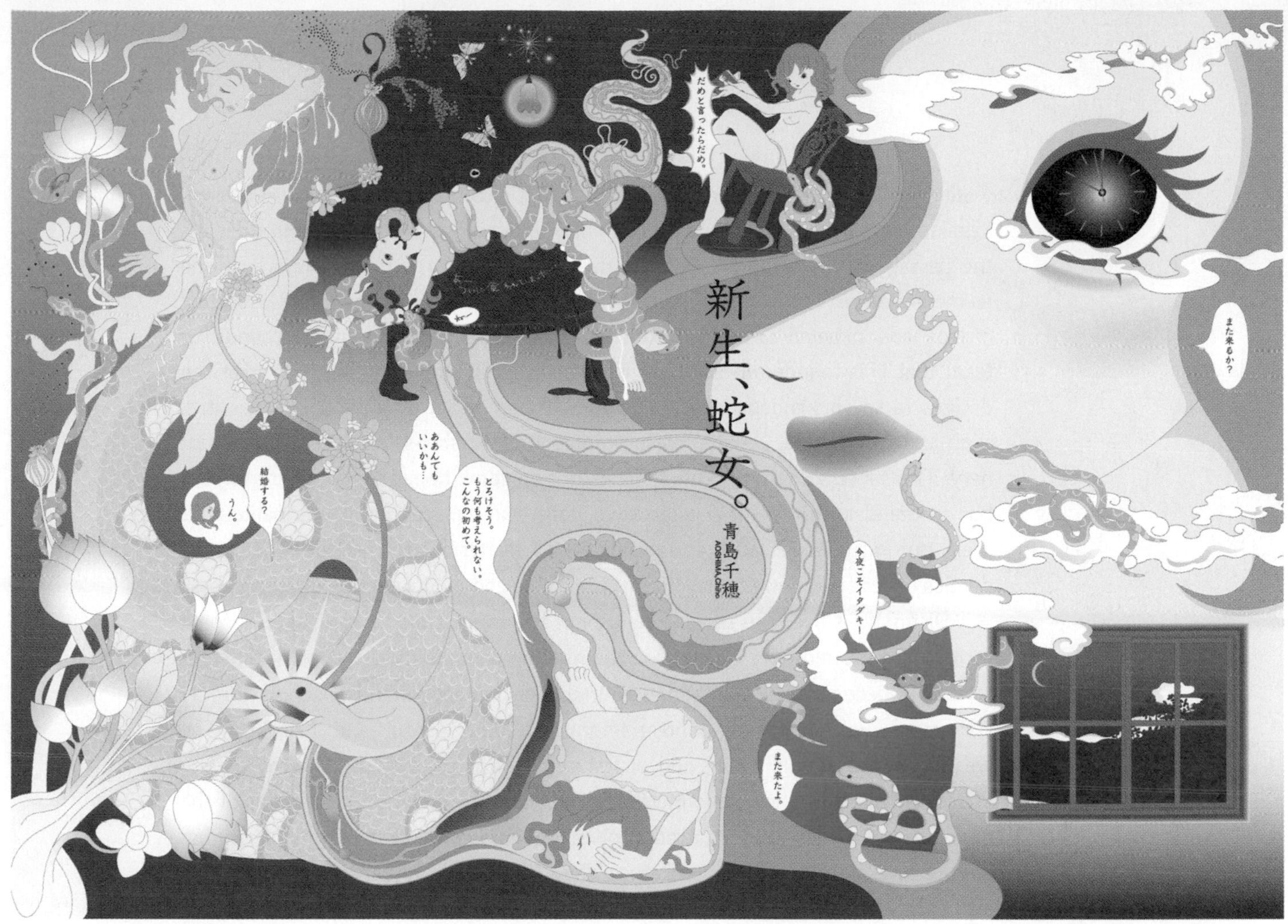

FIG. 2.16
Chiho Aoshima, *The Rebirth of a Snake-Woman*, 2001

In contemporary urban centers such as New York, Los Angeles, and London, much of fashion is seen as specifically ethnic in its significations, with the prominence of Latino and hip-hop subculture street fashion, such as low-slung chinos, do-rags, platform shoes, gold chains, skull-and-bones insignia, and hoodies filtering out to a range of youth consumers beyond the ethnic groups with which these styles were originally associated. Subculture style is evident not simply in fashion and hairstyles but also in styles of body marking, such as tattoos and piercings, that have become far more mainstream forms of self-expression in Western urban culture in the twenty-first century than they were in the twentieth. The rapid cooptation and marketing of styles signifying resistance makes the idea of individual expression through alternative clothing styles a complicated process for youths committed to independent expression and resistance to the mainstream values promoted through the clothing lines marketed to mall culture and chain stores.

At the same time, the early 2000s saw a notable upsurge of independent retailers specializing in youth-produced independent clothing and retail goods ranging from magazines and toys to housewares and beauty products. Giant Robot is a five-store chain of boutiques launched by *Giant Robot* magazine editors Eric Nakamura and Martin Wong in the late 1990s. It sells indie designer clothing, toys, fine art and art books in the genres of lowbrow, pop surrealism, and Tokyo pop—including the work of Dalek (aka James Marshall), Elizabeth McGrath, Yuko Marada, Marcel Dzama, Tabaimo, and Chiho Aoshima, whose print *The Rebirth of a Snake Woman* depicts the passage of a woman through the digestive tract of a python from which she reemerges anew. The store and magazine take their name from the Giant Robot era of Japanese animated cartoons. Poketo is a Los Angeles independent merchandising team that was founded in 2003 by Ted Vatakan and Angie Myung to market the designs of seventy independent contemporary pop artists on affordable necessities such as wallets, bags, T-shirts, plastic (notably dishwasher-safe) dishes, and stationery. The success of these ventures rests not on some hoped-for corporate buyout but on the identification of an alternative global and transcultural youth market that seeks out independent labels and products as a matter of personal aesthetics and a politics of consumption that favors small business and independent expression.

Distinctions between subculture fashion and mainstream fashion have become increasingly blurred—for instance, in the hip-hop community, a mixing of different styles has become quite common, with traditionally preppy brands, such as Tommy Hilfiger and Polo, becoming popular among hip-hop celebrities and their fans. The wearing of heavy gold chains and of fashions associated with the wealthy preppy classes by many hip-hop performers signified access to the goods and codes of the upper classes. These subcultures do not fit the model of working against consumer culture and mainstream value. Rather, they are complexly appropriative, buying into the system while creating codes of irony through exaggeration of scale that are intended to signify resistance to it. Many hip-hop stars have become fashion designers themselves, creating brands that market a range of styles that would otherwise be coded as upper-class fashion. It is too simple to say that these kinds of moves are "selling out." Rather, they form new kinds of negotiations over cultural forms and power. Such trends call into question simple hierarchies of taste: symbols of upper-class taste are appropriated by subcultures, and subculture styles gain taste and cultural capital and in turn become valuable to monied classes. These kinds of dynamics create new signs, in semiotic terms, for a critique of class status and knowledge. Not only does this demonstrate the degree to which traditional notions of class difference no longer hold in the same way today, but it also shows how cultural capital, in particular the knowledge of culture, has been dramatically reconfigured at a time when knowledge of hip-hop culture, for instance, might be valued across social strata just as knowledge of classical music might be. Cultural capital can trickle up as well as down.

Appropriation and Cultural Production

Thus far, we have been discussing the negotiated process of reading and viewing, yet the negotiation over the meaning of texts can also take the form of cultural production. There is a long history, for instance, of artists appropriating particular texts of art or popular culture in order to make a political statement; of fans of particular shows engaging with those shows by remaking the texts into new productions, and, increasingly in the context of Web media, of viewer-consumers actively engaging with advertising, popular culture, and news media images by remaking them into new kinds of texts with altered meanings. The term *appropriation* is traditionally defined as taking something for oneself without consent. Cultural appropriation is the process of "borrowing" and changing the meaning of cultural products, slogans, images, or elements of fashion.

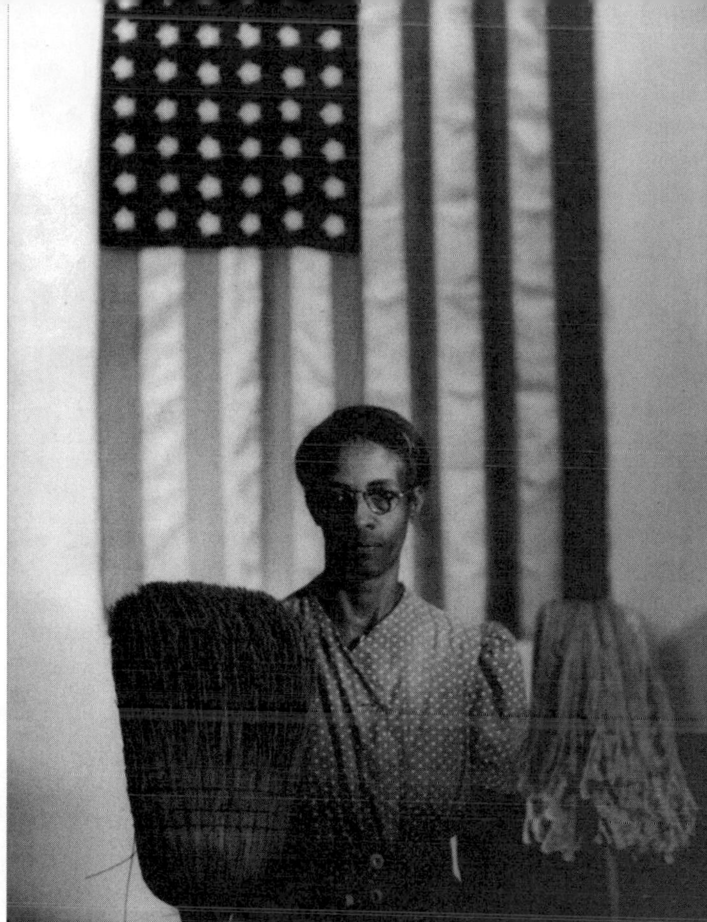

FIG. 2.17
Gordon Parks, *Ella Watson*, 1942

Cultural appropriation has been used quite effectively by artists seeking to make a statement that opposes the dominant ideology. Thus an image that appropriates a famous image can have a kind of doubled meaning, building on its reversal of the original that it remakes. This image by photographer Gordon Parks, *Ella Watson* (1942), makes a statement by referring to the well-known 1930 painting *American Gothic*, by Grant Wood, of an American farming couple standing holding a pitchfork before a classic wooden farmhouse. *American Gothic* has been the source of innumerable remakes, many of them humorous commentaries on changing social values in the United States. Parks's image, however, taken before the emergence of the civil rights movement, is a bitter commentary on the discrepancy between the codes of this black woman office cleaner, holding her broom and mop before an American flag, and the puritan codes of Americana in the *American Gothic* icon. Most important, by playing off the well-known codes of the *American Gothic* image, Parks pointed to the fact that not all Americans were included in its mythic image. As Steven Biel writes, Parks ensured that "the normative whiteness of the now iconic *American Gothic* did not go unrecognized and unchallenged."[17] It is precisely the strategy of appropriation that allows Parks's image to make this larger statement about social exclusion and inequality.

Strategies of appropriation have often been key to political art. A good example is the public art of Gran Fury, an art collective formed in 1987 (named after the Plymouth car then favored by undercover police) that produced posters, performances, installations, and videos alerting people to facts about AIDS and HIV that public health officials refused to publicize. One of their posters advertised a 1988 demonstration, a "kiss in" intended to publicly dispel the myth that kissing transmits the AIDS virus. The phrase "read my lips," which refers to the poster's image of two women about to kiss, was appropriated from a much-discussed slogan in the

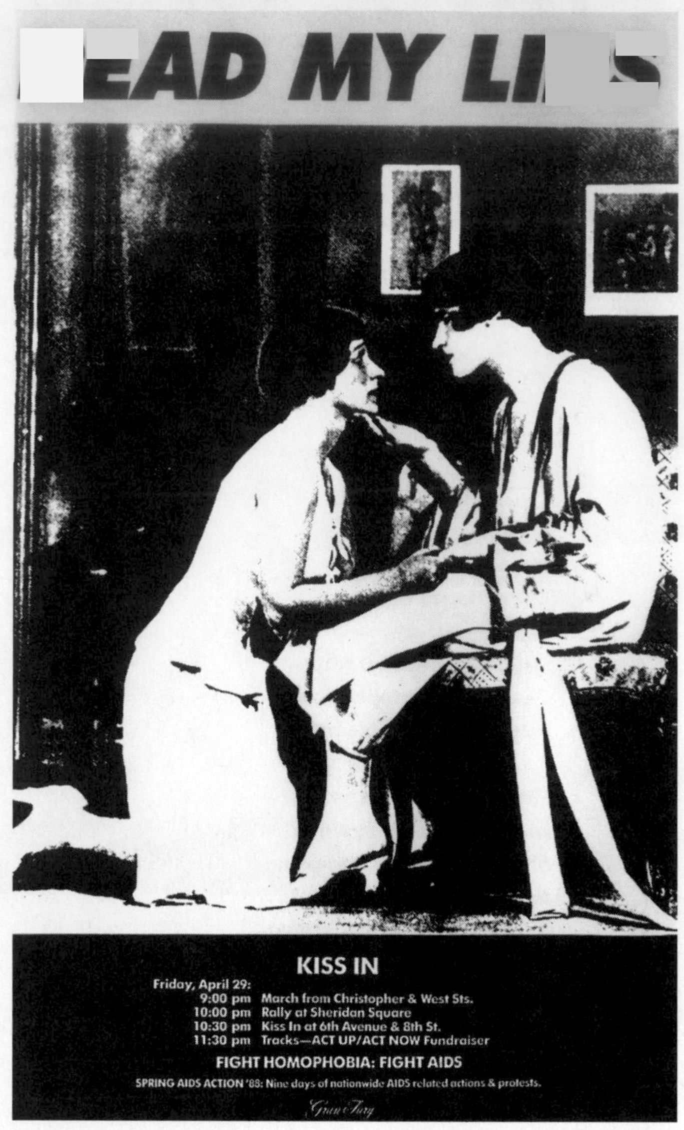

KISS IN
Friday, April 29:
9:00 pm March from Christopher & West Sts.
10:00 pm Rally at Sheridan Square
10:30 pm Kiss In at 6th Avenue & 8th St.
11:30 pm Tracks—ACT UP/ACT NOW Fundraiser
FIGHT HOMOPHOBIA: FIGHT AIDS
SPRING AIDS ACTION '88: Nine days of nationwide AIDS related actions & protests.
Gran Fury

FIG. 2.18
Gran Fury, *Read My Lips (girls)*, 1988

presidential campaign of President George H. W. Bush. His slogan was "read my lips, no new taxes." In "lifting" the phrase "read my lips" and placing it with images about homosexual contact, Gran Fury suggested that the phrase had meanings that Bush and his campaign advisors clearly did not intend. Gran Fury's appropriation gives the poster a biting political humor, making it both a playful twist of words and an accusation at the time against a president who was overtly homophobic and helped to lead a political denial of the seriousness of the AIDS epidemic that had tragic consequences.

These strategies of appropriation in art, which have been integral to various movements of modern art, also emerged as part of fan cultures in the 1980s and 1990s. Before the Web created a forum for the sharing of images and video, fan cultures of certain television shows and series would meet at conventions, rewrite episodes of the shows, and reedit (sometimes crudely on rudimentary video equipment) episodes to change their meaning.[18] Analysis of these fan cultures often used de Certeau's concepts of "textual poaching" to talk about how these viewers remade the shows in order both to change their meaning and to affirm their fan status (as viewers who are authoritative about the show, seeing themselves as more knowing than the producers themselves). Most famous of these 1980s fan cultures was the "slash fiction" culture of fans of the science fiction television series *Star Trek*, who would rewrite scenes from the show and reedit episodes of the show to depict a romantic and erotic relationship between the characters of Spock and Captain Kirk (the term "slash" connotes the combining of the two characters' names to indicate their pairing, as in Spock/Kirk). These fan cultures expanded into numerous other shows and strategies, though the rereading of screen relationships through new sexual desires is a primary theme. Analysis of this kind of cultural production saw them as emblematic of de Certeau's concept of "poaching" in that they "make do" with the original popular culture texts, yet use them to make new kinds of scenarios that depend on the original texts for their new meanings.

These kinds of fan productions signaled the beginning of what would become a much more significant cultural trend with the rise of Web media that allow Web users to create their own websites, use Web cameras to create streaming video, rework and remake television episodes, ads, and news images, and parody media and popular culture in general. Much of the vast array of cultural production by people who would have traditionally been thought of as "amateurs" is playful and humorous, with little social or political critique. These image cultures circulate largely though social networks in which people recommend videos to their friends via e-mail and social networking sites such as Facebook and in which Web media sites such as YouTube recommend videos to viewers. In these online contexts, users are increasingly deploying images (often uploading images daily from their cell phones) to define their public profiles and construct their identities. These social networks have also become primary resources and outlets for marketers, who are constantly creating new strategies to tap into them, and who use them to target networked, plugged-in youth consumers.

In many ways, the proliferation of digital (moving and still) images on the Web has replaced the role played by images in the street, such as the Gran Fury poster we discussed earlier. As people increasingly upload their personal images onto public websites, and use images to define themselves through their Web pages, and as search programs make finding certain kinds of images on the Web easy, the circulation of images on the Web has dramatically accelerated. Yet there remains a street culture of political art in some major cities, and this was clear when an artist or artist collective in New York, going by the pseudonym of Copper Greene waged a guerrilla campaign in 2004 by putting up numerous posters on the street and in the subways that used the well-known iPod campaign to comment on the then-recent revelations of the atrocities committed by U.S. soldiers in Iraq at the Abu Ghraib prison. Copper Greene (which took the pseudonym from the Pentagon code name for detainee operations in Iraq) managed in this campaign to create a new set of meanings with the most well-known of the Abu Ghraib images, that of a man standing hooded on a box with electrical wires attached to his hands (see fig. 6.17). Reportedly the man had been told that he would be shocked by electricity if he moved or lowered his arms.[19] The posters replaced the

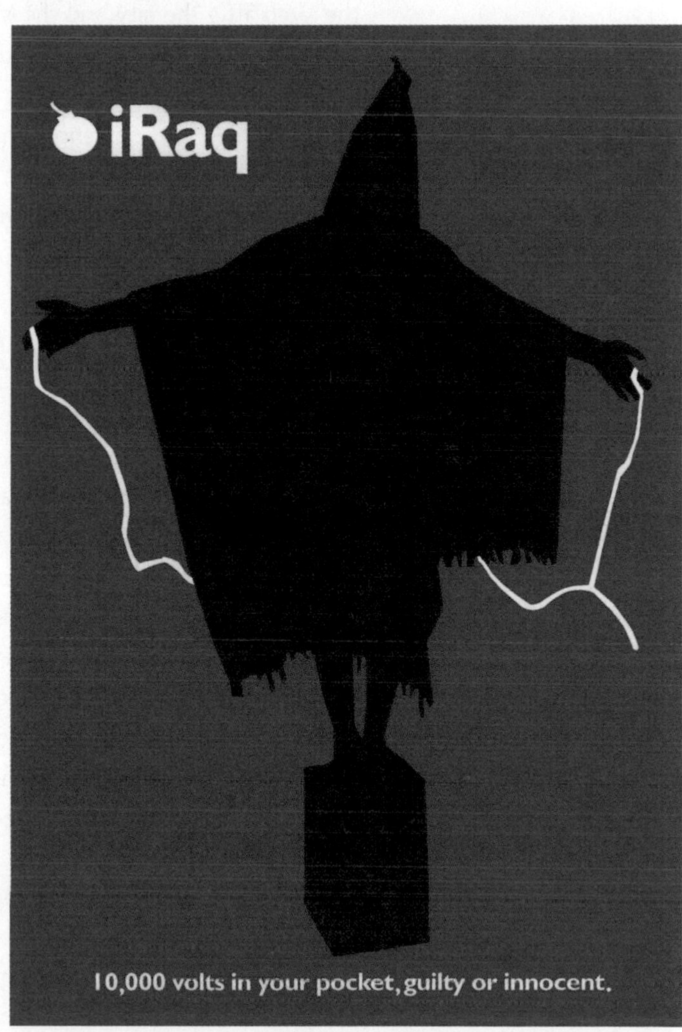

FIG. 2.19
Copper Greene, *iRaq: 10,000, volts in your pocket, guilty or innocent*, 2004.

iPod slogan "iPod: 10,000 songs in your pocket" with the tagline "iRaq: 10,000 volts in your pocket, guilty or innocent." In placing the posters near and within actual iPod ads, Copper Greene succeeded in subtly getting pedestrians to do double takes and in creating a critique not only of the use of torture in military prisons, but also of advertising culture and consumer culture in general. (We discuss the Abu Ghraib images more fully in chapter 6 and the iPod campaign and culture jams at more length in chapter 7.) Thus the meaning of the work is a demand not only to recognize the Abu Ghraib image as integral to the "home front" of the war but also to make connections between the culture of the Iraq war and consumer culture in the United States. The white wires of the iPod advertising campaign become the electric wires of torture to critique the way in which iPod culture (with headphones that shut us off from the surrounding environments) reflects an insular consumer culture, one that has allowed U.S. citizens to disavow the war and their complicity in it. Copper Greene's campaign affirms that the street remains a site of contested intents and meanings.

It is not incidental to the Copper Greene campaign that it had a second life on the Web after the city and the Metropolitan Transit Authority took down the posters. Photographs of the iRaq/iPod images, some of them showing it inserted into billboards of numerous iPod ads, circulated on the Web, and the poster was eventually included in an art book about the design of dissent.[20] The image thus continued to resonate on the "street" context of the Web, gaining a more global audience just as the Abu Ghraib images themselves circulated out of the control of any of the players in that incident in a very short time.

Reappropriation and Counter-Bricolage

Appropriation is not always an oppositional practice. The study of fan cultures has been critiqued precisely because it is often difficult to ascertain what counts as "resistant" when producers are at the ready to incorporate fan ideas into their product lines and shows. In an age when marketers are actively selling a broad range of brands as hip and cool, the appropriation of alternative cultures and subcultures by mainstream producers and fashion designers has never been more prevalent.[21] Since marketers began to borrow the concepts of the counterculture of the 1960s to sell products as youthful and hip, there has been a constant mining of youth cultures and marginal subcultures for mainstream fashion and other products. (We discuss aspects of the marketing of coolness at more length in chapter 7.) Most obviously, one of the consequences of these kinds of trends is that commodities that had been appropriated by subcultures through bricolage lose their political meaning when they are reappropriated and marketed to the mainstream. The vintage thrift store clothing fashions originally associated with oppositional youth culture were, in turn, reappropriated by the mainstream fashion industry, which capitalized on the market for inexpensive and widely available knockoffs of vintage fashions. Although Doc Martens work boots in the early 1990s might have signaled an association with AIDS activism or the values of neopunk culture, within a few years they had become respectable everyday shoes for a wide range of consumers, bearing no clear political significance beyond being somewhat fashionable. Their revival, along with other punk fashions, in the early 2000s may or may not invoke the legacy of the shoe as a symbol of activism, depending on the wearer's knowledge and interests.

This process of appropriation by mainstream marketers and producers has been termed "counter-bricolage" by Robert Goldman and Stephen Papson.[22] This process, by which the counter-hegemonic bricolage strategies of marginal cultures are reappropriated by mainstream designers and marketers and then parlayed into mainstream designs that signal "coolness," is thus counter to the intent of the bricolage strategy. Of course, as the example of hip-hop makes clear, appropriating strategies works back and forth to the point at which the distinction between the margins and the mainstream is increasingly unclear. For instance, the street style of wearing boxer shorts visibly above one's pants that emerged in the 1990s then produced a fashion trend for designer boxer shorts, in which Calvin Klein and other designers began marketing high-end designer boxer shorts. Calvin Klein marketed this new men's underwear in an ad campaign that borrowed codes from Greco-Roman images of men bonding in homosocial contexts. Similarly, designers use signifiers of hip culture, such as tattoos and body piercings, in fashion photos as a means of creating signs of coolness. In this Juicy Couture ad (fig. 2.20), tattoos, previously a signifier of countercultural status, are appropriated to signify being on the cutting edge of fashion—by a highly mass-marketed brand.

The marketing of the qualities of hipness and cool points to how the class-based categories of high and low culture have been rendered meaningless. The signifiers of youth street culture are marketed to middle- and upper-class consumers so they can look edgy. The signifiers of inner-city ethnic subcultures are marketed to white consumers with the promise of conferring hip insider status. Mainstream culture, through the processes of hegemony and counter-hegemony, is constantly mining the margins of culture for new sources of meaning—and new styles for making money. The culture industries are constantly establishing what is new style by mining the margins, and subcultures on the margins are always reinventing themselves by appropriating from mass culture and from other margins.

What are the consequences of this kind of cultural circulation of meaning? On one hand, we could see this as evidence of the complexity of cultural signs, the way that semiotic meaning can easily be remade, reworked, and reconfigured in new cultural contexts. Yet this also means that important ideals and concepts can become what are known as "free-floating" signifiers, floating through cultural domains with little grounded meaning. Take, for instance, the trend of fashion designers to use particular concepts as brand names, with the creation of brands such as "Theory" and "Ideology." Calling a clothing brand Ideology suggests a

FIG. 2.20
Juicy Couture ad, 2008

use of concept reflexively to draw our attention to the ways ideology draws us into consumption. But the fact that this message is used by a brand that successfully encourages consumption makes the message benign. Signifiers of cultural critique are emptied of their potential effects as agents of change when they are used by major brands themselves.

Cultural meaning is highly fluid and ever changing, the result of complex interactions among images, producers, cultural products, and readers/viewers/consumers. The meaning of images emerges through these processes of interpretation, engagement, and negotiation. Importantly, this means that culture is not a set of objects that are valued in some way but a set of processes through which meaning is constantly made and remade through the interactions of objects and peoples. We might look to new designers and business owners such as Nakamura and Wong, the entrepreneurs of the Giant Robot magazine and retail store chain, as offering a way of living one's life with everyday art and artifacts designed to intervene in the dynamics of consumption on a small scale for a globalized niche demographic of consumers. This can be seen as a way of making an intervention in the corporate politics of mass media production and in the art market politics of high-culture aesthetic reverence. If in the 1990s institutional critique was expressed in the form of artists such as Fred Wilson, who "mined the museum" to exhibit old work to make new meanings, in the 2000s creative producers such as Nakamura and Wong engage in a new iteration of institutional critique, changing the marketing of "good taste" by creating commercial venues that combine the popular magazine, the fine art gallery, the retail clothing store, the small book merchant, and the kitsch tchotchke shop into one emporium. In doing so, these new entrepreneurs challenge the worn dichotomies of high and low culture, of mainstream and resistant culture, of good and bad taste, making art into an affordable form of everyday consumption for everyday youth culture. They also give the corporate conglomerate a run for the money by turning synergy on its head, maximizing connections across forms and genres on a small and human scale. Their products engage youth in everyday ways in the ideal of being both producers and consumers of culture without apology and in practices of looking that are not reactively resistant but instead are actively productive of new cultural forms that resist corporate and institutional cooptation.

As this chapter has shown, we have moved beyond the moment of the death of the author heralded by Barthes into an era in which we might speak about the death of the producer. The new modes embraced by youth culture consumers are about networks, connections, and aggregation—using websites and social networking to link to their interests and friends, and blogs to create networks about their style choices and social concerns. The viewer or consumer has emerged as the locus of creative production, in the performative guise of the anonymous corporate investment manager, as the example of RTMark illustrates, as a curator who reorders art and artifact to make new meanings, and as the purveyor of small-market lifestyle art for everyday youth who cannot afford "high" art and would not even want it. Just as the identification of the locus of creative production of meaning was, for Barthes, relocated from writer to reader, so it was again relocated, in the late twentieth century, to the less glamorous work of the viewer as manager, marketer, and bricoleur of visual culture's products. The viewer who makes meaning does so not only through describing an experience with images but also through reordering, redisplaying, and reusing images in new and differently meaningful ways in the reordering of everyday life.

Notes

1. See John Ellis, "Channel 4: Working Notes," *Screen*, 24.6, (1983) 37–51, citation from page 49.
2. Roland Barthes, "The Death of the Author," in *Image, Music, Text*, trans. Stephen Heath, 142–48 (New York: Hill and Wang, 1978).

3. Michel Foucault, "What is an Author?" trans. Donald F. Bouchard and Sherry Simon, in *Language, Counter-Memory, Practice,* 124–27 (Ithaca, N. Y.: Cornell University Press, 1977).

4. Nicholas Mirzoeff, "The Subject of Visual Culture," in *The Visual Culture Reader,* 2nd ed., ed. Nicholas Mirzoeff, 3 (New York: Routledge, 2002).

5. *Encyclopaedia Britannica Online,* s.v. "Globalization, cultural," www.britannica.com/eb/article-225011 (accessed March 2008).

6. Clement Greenberg, "Avant-Garde and Kitsch," in *Clement Greenberg: The Collected Essays and Criticism,* Vol. I, *Perceptions and Judgments, 1939–1944,* ed. John O'Brian, 5–22 (Chicago: University of Chicago Press, [1939] 1986).

7. See JoAnn Wypijewski, ed., *Painting by Numbers: Komar and Melamid's Scientific Guide to Art,* 6–7 (New York: Farrar, Strauss, & Giroux, 1997).

8. Pierre Bourdieu, *Distinction: A Social Critique of the Judgement of Taste,* trans. Richard Nice, 6 (Cambridge, Mass.: Harvard University Press, 1984).

9. Phyllis Tuchman, "On Thomas Struth's 'Museum Photographs,'" *Artnet.com,* July 8, 2003.

10. Louis Althusser, "Ideology and Ideological State Apparatuses," in *Lenin and Philosophy and Other Essays,* trans. Ben Brewster, 162 (London: Monthly Review Press, 1971).

11. Stuart Hall, "Encoding, Decoding," in *The Cultural Studies Reader,* ed. Simon During, 90–103 (New York: Routledge, 1993).

12. David Morley, *The Nationwide Audience* (London: British Film Institute, 1980) and *Television, Audiences, and Cultural Studies* (New York: Routledge, 1992); Janice Radway, *Reading the Romance: Women, Patriarchy, and Popular Literature* (Chapel Hill: University of North Carolina Press, [1984] 1991; Ien Ang, *Watching* Dallas*: Soap Opera and the Melodramatic Imagination* (London: Methuen, 1985).

13. Michel de Certeau, *The Practice of Everyday Life,* trans. Steven Rendall, xxi (Berkeley: University of California Press, 1984).

14. Dick Hebdige, "From Culture to Hegemony," in *Subculture: The Meaning of Style,* 5–19 (New York: Routledge, 1979).

15. Angela McRobbie, "Second-Hand Dresses and the Role of the Ragmarket," in *Postmodernism and Popular Culture,* 135–54 (New York: Routledge, 1994).

16. George Lipsitz, "Cruising around the Historical Bloc," in *The Subcultures Reader,* ed. Ken Gelder and Sarah Thornton, 358 (New York: Routledge, 1997).

17. Steven Biel, *American Gothic: A Life of America's Most Famous Painting,* 115 (New York: Norton, 2005).

18. See, in particular, work by Henry Jenkins and Constance Penley on the television series *Star Trek:* Henry Jenkins, *Textual Poachers: Television Fans and Participatory Culture* (New York: Routledge, 1992); and Constance Penley, *NASA/Trek: Popular Science and Sex in America* (London: Verso, 1997).

19. Devin Zuber, "Flanerie at Ground Zero: Aesthetic Countermemories in Lower Manhattan," *American Quarterly* 58.2 (June 2006), 283–285.

20. Milton Glaser and Mirko Ilic, eds., *The Design of Dissent* (Gloucester, Mass.: Rockport Publishers, 2005).

21. See Thomas Frank, *The Conquest of Cool: Business Culture, Counterculture, and the Rise of Hip Consumerism* (Chicago: University of Chicago Press, 1998).

22. See Robert Goldman and Stephen Papson, "Levi's and the Knowing Wink," *Current Perspectives in Social Theory,* 11 (1991), 69–95; and Robert Goldman and Stephen Papson, *Sign Wars: The Cluttered Landscape of Advertising,* 257 (New York: Guilford, 1996).

Further Reading

Althusser, Louis. "Ideology and Ideological State Apparatuses." In *Lenin and Philosophy and Other Essays.* Translated by Ben Brewster, 127–86. London: Monthly Review Press, 1971.

Bad Object-Choices. *How Do I Look? Queer Film and Video.* Seattle, Wash.: Bay Press, 1991.

Barthes, Roland. "Death of the Author." In *Image, Music, Text.* Edited and translated by Stephen Heath, 142–48. New York: Hill and Wang, 1978.

———. *The Fashion System.* Translated by Matthew Ward and Richard Howard. Berkeley: University of California Press, 1990.

Bourdieu, Pierre. *Distinction: A Social Critique of the Judgement of Taste.* Translated by Richard Nice. Cambridge, Mass.: Harvard University Press, 1984.

Clifford, James. *The Predicament of Culture: Twentieth Century Ethnography, Literature and Art.* Cambridge, Mass.: Harvard University Press, 1983.

de Certeau, Michel. *The Practice of Everyday Life.* Translated by Steven Rendall. Berkeley: University of California Press, 1984.

Doty, Alexander. *Making Things Perfectly Queer: Interpreting Mass Culture.* Minneapolis: University of Minnesota Press, 1993.

Duncombe, Stephen, ed. *Cultural Resistance Reader.* London: Verso, 2002.

Eagleton, Terry, ed. *Ideology.* London: Longman Press, 1994.

Fiske, John. *Reading Popular Culture.* New York: Routledge, 1989.

Frank, Thomas. *The Conquest of Cool: Business Culture, Counterculture, and the Rise of Hip Consumerism.* Chicago: University of Chicago Press, 1998.

Foucault, Michel. "What Is an Author?" In *Language, Counter-Memory, Practice,* translated by Donald F. Bouchard and Sherry Simon, 124–27. Ithaca, N. Y.: Cornell University Press, 1977.

Golden, Thelma, ed. *Black Male: Representations of Masculinity in Contemporary American Art.* New York: Whitney Museum of American Art, 1994.

Goldman, Robert, and Stephen Papson. *Sign Wars: The Cluttered Landscape of Advertising.* New York: Guilford, 1996.

Gramsci, Antonio. *Selections from the Prison Notebooks.* Translated by Quintin Hoare and Geoffrey Nowell-Smith. New York: International Publishers and London: Lawrence & Wishart, 1971.

Hall, Stuart. "Encoding, Decoding." In *The Cultural Studies Reader.* Edited by Simon During, 90–103. New York: Routledge, 1993.

——— "The Problem of Ideology: Marxism Without Guarantees." In *Stuart Hall: Critical Dialogues in Cultural Studies.* Edited by Kuan-Hsing Chen and David Morley, 25–46. New York: Routledge, 1996.

——— "Gramsci's Relevance for the Study of Race and Ethnicity." In *Stuart Hall: Critical Dialogues in Cultural Studies.* Edited by Kuan-Hsing Chen and David Morley, 411–40. New York: Routledge, 1996.

Hebdige, Dick. *Subculture: The Meaning of Style.* New York: Routledge, 1979.

Jenkins, Henry. *Textual Poachers: Television Fans and Participatory Culture.* New York: Routledge, 1992.

Klinger, Barbara. *Beyond the Multiplex: Cinema, New Technologies, and the Home.* Berkeley: University of California Press, 2006.

Lipsitz, George. "Cruising around the Historical Bloc: Postmodernism and Popular Music in East Los Angeles." In *The Subcultures Reader.* Edited by Ken Gelder and Sarah Thornton, 350–59. New York: Routledge, 1997.

McRobbie, Angela. "Second-Hand Dresses and the Role of the Ragmarket." In *Postmodernism and Popular Culture,* 135–54. New York: Routledge, 1994.

McShine, Kynaston. *The Museum as Muse: Artists Reflect.* New York: Museum of Modern Art, 1999.

Nakamura, Lisa. *Digitizing Race: Visual Cultures of the Internet.* Minneapolis: University of Minnesota Press.

Penley, Constance. *NASA/TREK: Popular Science and Sex in America.* London: Verso, 1997.

Price, Sally. *Primitive Art in Civilized Places.* Chicago: University of Chicago, 1989.

Radway, Janice. *Reading the Romance: Women, Patriarchy, and Popular Culture.* Rev. ed. Chapel Hill: University of North Carolina Press, 1991.

Sconce, Jeffrey. "'Trashing' the Academy: Taste, Excess, and an Emerging Politics of Cinematic Style," *Screen,* 36.4 (Winter 1995), 371–93.

Vartanian, Ivan. *Drop Dead Cute.* San Francisco: Chronicle Books and Tokyo: Goliga Books, 2005. (A catalog of art of the 2000s by ten female painters and illustrators, some of whom were members of the Kaikai Kiki Art Collective of the Tokyo pop artist Takashi Murakami.)

chapter three

Modernity

Spectatorship, Power, and Knowledge

Just as images are both representations and producers of the ideologies of their time, they are also factors in the power relations between human subjects and between individuals and institutions. When we look at images, we look within a field that includes much more than just our own gaze and the image. This field includes, among other things, the medium through which we see the image (the screen of a movie, television, cell phone, or computer or a billboard or page in a newspaper or magazine) and the architectural, cultural, national, and institutional contexts in which we see the image. This field includes objects, technologies, and built and natural environments, as well as other people who are either present and looking with us (and we may also look at these people, and they at us) or those who we know or imagine to have looked before or to be looking simultaneously at the same image elsewhere, on a different screen.

Our other senses also come into play when we look at an image. Looking is rarely performed in total isolation from the activities of listening and feeling. The gallery in which we view a photograph may be cold and quiet; the bus on which we encounter an advertisement may be hot and noisy. If we are blind or have limited vision, we engage in this field of appearances and looking no less actively than would a sighted person, by using contextual information, as well as low- and high-tech assistive devices and techniques (glasses, listening, touching, Braille signage, canes, screen magnifiers, service dogs), to negotiate a social world that is increasingly organized around practices of looking and the faculty of sight. The concept of *spectatorship* allows us to talk about this broader context in which looking is enacted in an interactive, multimodal, and relational field.

We call this context in which looking practices are engaged the field of *the gaze*. In this chapter, we examine the modern power relations at work in the practices that make up the field of the gaze and the power relations at work in specific relationships of image *spectatorship*. The term *gaze*, in common usage, means, in its noun form, a look and, in its verb form, the act of looking. We, as human subjects, gaze on objects, places, and one another. The term *gaze* sometimes carries connotations of looking long and intently with affection, awe, wonder, or fascination. When we glance at an image our process of looking can be quick and fleeting, but when we gaze our look is sustained. The concept of the gaze has been used in specific ways by visual theorists to emphasize the embeddedness of the gaze of the individual viewer in a social and contextual field of looks, objects, and other sensory information. To gaze is to enter into a *relational* activity of looking. The concept of the gaze plays a central role in theories of looking and spectatorship in modernity, the historical, economic, and cultural context that saw the rise of industrialization, urbanization, and scientific rationalism over the past few centuries.

This chapter discusses modernity, spectatorship, and the gaze as interrelated phenomena through which the modern subject is visually constituted. In what follows, we make a distinction between different uses of the term *gaze* in spectatorship theory, some of which are based on the writings of the French psychoanalyst Jacques Lacan and others on the writings of the French philosopher Michel Foucault. We situate these concepts in relation to concepts of the human subject in modernity and the context of modern power. Before discussing spectatorship, power, and the gaze, however, it is necessary for us to explain how concepts of the human subject have evolved over time and in the context of modernity and how these concepts form the foundation for these theories of looking.

The Subject in Modernity

The individual is a concept that we do not take for granted in visual theory. Our goal is, in part, to ask *how* we come to experience the world as individual human subjects. Most important for us is the question of what role images and practices of looking play in the making of this entity, the human subject. There are a number of routes through which we can approach these questions. Some scholars choose to begin their explanation of the subject with seventeenth-century French philosopher René Descartes, a key figure of the Scientific Revolution who is widely known for his contributions to a rationalist philosophy that places man at the center of the universe, a concept that most of us take for granted today. Descartes was interested in using the sciences and mathematics to establish rational certainty about the world and nature. He emphasized the importance of techniques and instruments of objectivity (tools of measurement, for example) designed to shore up subjective perception in the production of knowledge about the world, and he believed that embodied sensory perception and empirical observation were not accurate means of knowing the world. For Descartes, the world becomes known when we accurately represent it in thought, not when we experience it through the senses and not when we imagine it in our mind's eye. Representation held an important place in the Cartesian understanding of the human subject. The Cartesian subject is constituted in part through an activity of thinking that involves spectatorship.

In the context of contemporary visual culture, the Cartesian notion of the subject is of relevance because it has functioned as a rationale justifying the political dominance of the modern liberal democracies in world politics. The philosophy of modernity was based on an ideal of the liberal human subject as a self-knowing, unified, and autonomous entity with individual human rights and freedoms. In modern thought, this subject was understood to be fully endowed with consciousness and a sense of itself as authentic and unique and as an autonomous source of action and meaning in the world. This concept of the subject was revised by a broad array of contemporary thinkers during the period of modernity.

Modernity is a term that scholars use to refer to the historical, cultural, political, and economic conditions related to the Enlightenment (an eighteenth-century philosophical movement); the rise of industrial society and scientific rationalism; and to the idea of controlling nature through technology, science, and rationalism. Modernity is associated with the belief that industrialization, human technological intervention in nature, mass democracy, and the introduction of a market economy are the hallmarks of social progress. Most historians would agree that these were largely eighteenth- and nineteenth-century phenomena. But the exact dates and conditions of modernity as a period are debated by historians. This is because not all countries became "modern" in this sense during the eighteenth and nineteenth centuries and because even those countries that did modernize in this way did not all embrace this same notion of "the modern." The French and American revolutions of the late eighteenth century are associated with the introduction of modernity because they marked the formation of republics based on explicitly modern political ideals such as liberal democracy and the inalienable rights of citizens to representation and self-determination. When we speak of the liberal human subject, we are usually referring to the individual as imagined through developments based on the Enlightenment and democratic political ideals introduced in these revolutions.

Not all countries embraced the same ideology of progress in the economy, technology, and military power. Whereas modernization was part of instituting a capitalist economy and a liberal democracy in the United States, for the Soviet Union modernization in the form of industrialization and technological advancement was tied to a Communist ethos of equal benefits and living conditions for all citizens. Imperial Europe played a role in instituting modernizing enterprises in its colonies, but typically in a top-down fashion. European systems of culture and knowledge were often instituted in the form of paternalistic benevolence in the colonies, with resources and industry ownership largely in the hands of European companies and not colonial subjects. These colonial strategies of modernization were justified by the Eurocentric belief that European practices and beliefs were objectively better (more advanced, more sanitary, more ethical, more modern) than the cultural practices and ways of knowing and living in the world that had been in place prior to colonization.

The conditions of modernity were the grounds for the emergence of modernism, a term that refers to a group of styles and movements in art, architecture, literature, and culture around the world dating from approximately the 1880s through the mid- to late 1900s. As we explain later, although the earliest writings about modernism characterized its movements as being based in Europe, later accounts stress the development of alternative modernities in colonial and postcolonial settings and in nations introducing industrial development later than did the Western European and North American countries. During modernity, it was taken as a given that industrial development was required to advance all of humankind toward a better way of living in the future.

We use the term *modern* in an everyday sense to mean present or recent times or to refer to contemporary views and fashions. In relation to art and culture, however, the term *modern* takes on a different set of meanings. German scholar Jürgen Habermas explains that the concept of the modern has been used over and over again by societies since as long ago as the late fifth century.[1] In Habermas's terms, the present culture sees itself as the product of a transition from old to new, modeling itself on a past era that is regarded as embodying timeless, classical principles. Renaissance artists, for example, revived and built on "classical" Greek standards of form and beauty.

The idea of being modern on the model of the classical changed, Habermas explains, with the Enlightenment, which was associated with a rejection of tradition and an embrace of the concept of reason. Enlightenment thinkers and practitioners emphasized rationality and the idea of achieving moral and social betterment through scientific progress. Science took on a new role in the arts and culture during the period of the Enlightenment, which was future-oriented rather than basing itself on a relation to the past.

Modernity reached its height in the nineteenth century and into the early twentieth century with the increased movement of populations from rural communities into cities and the escalation of industrial capitalism. It was characterized by the experience of upheaval and change, yet also by optimism and a belief in a better, more advanced future. The experience of modernity entailed increased urbanization, industrialization, and technological change linked to industrial capitalism and supported by an ideological faith in these changes as being integral to progress. Indeed, cities such as New York, Chicago, and Paris are often thought of as quintessentially modern, defined by architecture that captures the ethos of modernity by emphasizing mechanically inspired design and a use of high-tech materials such as metal and glass. Thus the architecture of the skyscraper is iconic of the new modern ethos, in which an embrace of industrial materials such as steel, modern technologies, and

FIG. 3.1
Times Square, New York City, c. 1927

the aesthetic of the machine resulted in towering buildings that dwarfed the newly arrived urban populace. The Chrysler Building in New York, which was built in 1930, is an icon of modernist Art Deco architectural and design styles. Art Deco is an ornate style of modernism that evokes a machine aesthetic and was originally conceived as functional design, called art moderne. Modern architecture was defined by this kind of engagement with the built environment, in which a functional approach to structuring space is combined with a formalist aesthetic that embraces technology, progress, and the new.

We can see modern ideals in much of the architecture of the early twentieth century that aims to master nature in its use of iron, steel, glass, and machine-like structures. A famous example of a modern structure, one that was never built, is sculptor and painter Vladimir Tatlin's *Monument to the Third International*, which was constructed in model form in 1919–20 (fig. 3.3). It was intended to be a 1,312-foot-high structure consisting of a metal spiral frame tilted at an angle, enclosing three glass structures (in the shape of a cylinder, a cone, and a cube) housing conference spaces. Like other early Soviet artists, Tatlin wanted to capture the vitality and dynamism of the latest engineering and architectural forms and technologies that the Soviet Union

FIG. 3.2
View of the Chrysler Building, New York, 1930

was eager to embrace in this time of transition. Tatlin and other artists saw the potential for representing structure and technology as the embodiment of the new Soviet process of restructuring society according to the theories of Marx and Lenin. All three units of the Monument were to revolve slowly at intervals, emphasizing dynamism and dialectical change, with rotating chambers meant to display political meaning in their form. The executive block on top, for instance, would turn once a day, whereas the lower chamber of the legislative council would rotate one degree every day, or a complete rotation every year. The tower was meant to embody the meanings of the word *revolution*. In its embrace of technology as an expression of the Soviet ethos and in its focus on form as an expression of cultural meaning, this work is emblematic of modernism.

Architectural form was key to the new experience of urban life, and new modern citizens and subjects needed new practices through which to engage the modern city. The figure of the *flâneur*, which we discuss at more length in chapter 7, helps us to better understand how people experienced the new modern city. A *flâneur* is a kind of urban dandy who strolls through a modern city (such as Paris), a space that is newly organized in modernity to encourage a mobile and specular (looking) relationship to urban space and the new consumer goods of mass manufacture displayed there. The *flâneur* observes urban life through the glass windows and reflective surfaces of the new city, amidst the visual spectacle of the many goods newly available for mass consumption thanks to the expansion of factories and a labor pool of workers in manufacture and industrial production.

FIG. 3.3
Vladimir Tatlin next to model of *Monument to the Third International*, 1919

In modernity, technological and social changes were viewed as both beneficial and imperative to progress. In the twenty-first century we are much more concerned about the environmental and social costs of technological advancement because we have seen the long-term impact of initiatives such as large-scale industrial development (overuse of natural resources, overproduction of emissions, and excessive industrial waste, for example). In the era of modernity, the effects of technology and commerce were not subject to this kind of criticism. Some critics, such as the nineteenth-century political economist and revolutionary Karl Marx, criticized industrial capitalism for the system's economic and physical exploitation and social alienation of workers. However, Marx's criticism was against the labor system instituted under capitalism, and not concerned with the overall consequences of industrial development.

The social malaise of the alienated individual who felt lost in the crowds and dehumanized by the industrialized life of the modern city came to characterize the era not only for the capitalist but also for the socialist worker. The urban experience of being lost in a crowd of strangers was thematized in nineteenth-century and early twentieth-century novels, poetry, and film by poets such as Charles Baudelaire and filmmakers such as King Vidor in *The Crowd* (1928). By the early twentieth century, radical political and technological change began to generate significant cultural anxiety. The breaking down of traditions allowed people to have a sense of infinite possibility yet also generated fears about the loss of the feeling of security and social connectedness that came with those traditions. Charlie Chaplin's 1936 film *Modern Times* is a well-known critique of the impact of modernity and industrialization on the body of the everyday man. Chaplin is swallowed up by the world of machines that surround him in modern industrial society, with its monotonous assembly-line labor practices. Chaplin, in his famous tramp characterization, attempts to retain his integrity as a human subject while working on a brutally fast assembly line as his body is entrapped by machines in a hilarious series of physical comedy gags.

The alienated worker, the liberal human subject, and the subject constituted through scientific inquiry and concepts of progress all are common to the period of modernity. Yet as philosopher of science Bruno Latour has argued, we have never been truly modern. The rational, self-knowing human subject understood to stand at

FIG. 3.4
Charlie Chaplin in *Modern Times*, 1936

the center of the world view associated with science and the Enlightenment never truly existed. The separation of man from nature, Latour argues, was never really achieved. We have inherited a world of hybrids, entities that combine human, technological, and object forms together (think of pacemakers and prosthetic devices or the ways in which we use computers as extensions of our senses). We live through associations between bodies, machines, nature, and inanimate objects and across biology, technology, culture, and science. Latour invites his readers to downplay the reductive thinking of modern binaries such as the nature-culture divide or the representation-real or man-machine distinctions. He suggests that we instead embrace the more complex concept of hybridity.[2]

Beginning in the nineteenth century, several influential modern thinkers challenged the concept of the autonomous, self-knowing subject. Sigmund Freud, the founder of psychoanalysis, wrote about the subject as an entity governed by the unconscious, the forces of which are held in check by consciousness. Freud postulated that we are not aware of the urges and desires that motivate us. This is a far cry from the model of the self-willed, self-knowing individual of the Enlightenment. Karl Marx wrote about class and the alienating effects of a capitalist economic system on laboring individuals in the late nineteenth century. He criticized the idea that human beings are self-determining individuals. Instead, he emphasized that we are collectively subject to, and produced as human subjects by, the forces of labor and capital. French philosopher Michel Foucault, in the twentieth century, argued that the human subject is constituted in modernity not through liberal human ideals but through the discourses of institutional life of the period. Foucault saw the subject as an entity produced within and through the discourses and institutional practices of the Enlightenment. Foucault's subject is never autonomous but is always constituted in relationships of power that are enacted through *discourse*.

Challenges, such as Foucault's, to the idea of the unitary subject ruled by conscious action can be thought of as part of the twentieth century's contribution to the destabilization of the concept of the subject. This destabilization is one of the chief characteristics of postmodern thought, which we discuss at length in chapter 8. One aspect of Foucault's thinking that gives some insight into the ways he challenged ideas about the individual is his reworking of Freud's theory of repression. Freud believed that we repress emotions, desires, taboo feelings, and anxieties unconsciously in order to keep them in check. Foucault proposed instead that repression does not result in leaving things unsaid or not acted on; rather, repression is productive of activities, speech, meanings, and sexualities.[3] Foucault argues that the repression of talk about sexuality during the Victorian period produced a particular discourse of sexuality in the late nineteenth century and the twentieth century that was about regulating and producing particular forms of sexual expression rather than fully repressing it. For Foucault, psychoanalysis is an institutional discourse through which the human subject is constituted and through which the human subject comes to apprehend itself. We discuss the concept of discourse at length in the following section.

Jacques Lacan, a psychoanalyst who developed some of Freud's ideas, also argued that the liberal human subject never really existed as such but was an ideal against which emerges a subject who is radically split at the very time that it comes into being. According to Lacan, who like Foucault wrote his most influential works in the period after World War II, the human subject becomes aware of itself and thus emerges as such not at birth but during a period of self-awareness and apparent autonomy that typically begins sometime between the ages of six and eighteen months. This period, which Lacan called the mirror phase, involves a process in which the infant gains motor skills adequate to venture away from the maternal body and in this process comes to understand itself, in a rudimentary way, as a unitary entity separate from that body. This process of the beginnings of ego emergence is schematized by Lacan in an account in which, in its first self-comprehending look into the mirror, the infant (mistakenly) sees itself as an independent and unitary subject apart from others in the world. Lacan emphasizes that this is a *mis*apprehension of self because at this developmental moment the infant is in fact still quite dependent and without highly developed motor coordination and skills. It sees, in fact, an Ideal-I, an ego ideal, and this encounter is traumatic, as the subject is constituted in a fundamental split between self and image, me and not-me. In Lacan's theory, the infant's relationship as a unitary ego to the world, understood as outside and other, is thus produced through a process in which the ego is split from its very inception. Apprehension of oneself apart from others is always achieved in a rupture that divides the self. As we discuss later, the mirror phase is an influential concept in psychoanalytic film theory. The concept of the human subject as self-knowing and autonomous thus has been systematically questioned by twentieth-century thinkers.

Spectatorship

Looking practices and the concept of the spectator are crucial to an understanding of the modern subject. As we noted, Lacan's concept of the unconscious chips away at the notion of a self-knowing subject, and the theories of psychoanalysis are crucial to understanding concepts of spectatorship and the gaze within the visual field of modernity. Whereas in everyday parlance the terms *viewer* and *spectator* are synonymous, in visual theory, the terms *spectator* (the individual who looks) and *spectatorship* (the practice of looking) have added meanings that derive specifically from film theory. Not only is the spectator's gaze constituted through a relationship between the subject who looks and other people, institutions, places, and objects in the world, but also the objects we contemplate may be described as the source of the look in the gaze. The film theorist Christian Metz wrote, "What fundamentally determines me is the look which is outside."[4] This means: "I" exist to myself only insofar as I can imagine myself in a field in which I appear in light of others (objects, people) who make me apparent to myself. This concept is drawn from Lacan, who wrote about the human subject as being constituted in part through the gaze, as well as from the theories of semiotics, derived from Saussure, which we discussed in chapter 2.

Not all writings in visual studies that use the terms *spectator* and *spectatorship* are steeped in psychoanalytic theory. Use of the term in visual studies, however, usually signals to readers an engagement with the field of study that developed out of psychoanalysis. The concepts of gaze and spectatorship remain important cornerstones of visual studies because they provide a set of terms and methods through which to consider some aspects of looking practices that the concept of the viewer does not really allow us to consider in depth. These are (1) the roles of the unconscious and desire in viewing practices; (2) the role of looking in the formation of the human subject as such; and (3) the ways that looking is always a relational activity and not simply a mental activity engaged in by someone who forms internal mental representations that stand for a passive image object "out there." Theories of the gaze and spectatorship are theories of address, rather than theories of reception in which methods are used to understand how actual viewers respond to a cultural text. When we study address, we consider the ways that an image or visual text invites certain responses from a particular category of viewer, such as a male or female viewer.[5] Both ways of examining images, through reception and through address, are incomplete in themselves. Together they can help us to understand what happens in the process of looking by taking into account both the conscious and unconscious levels of viewer experience.

The use of these concepts—the gaze, the spectator, and spectatorship—typically signals to the reader that the author does not take the concept of the individual or the person as a given. As we have discussed, the meaning of the individual human subject is not universal but is both historically and culturally contingent. Each era has its own way of making, or constituting, the meaning and experience of the human subject through its discourses. Discourse in Foucault's sense means not just spoken language but the broader variety of institutions and practices through which meaning is produced. In Foucault's terms, we cannot know what it means to be a human subject outside of the discursive practices through which subjective experience and representations of human subjectivity are enacted. Therefore, each era's concept of the human subject is different. The Enlightenment human subject is different from the human subject of modernity, and so forth.

Much of the theoretical work on spectators is concerned with how images and media texts contribute to the production of the human subject in its particular historical and cultural context—that is, how images give those who look at them a sense of themselves as individual human subjects in the world in a particular historical moment and cultural context. The image or visual appearance, in this sense, is not simply a representation or a medium of information. It is one of the elements in the broad network through which the subject is constituted (or made) in a given historical and cultural moment. A person who looks achieves a sense of himself or herself as an individual human subject, not only in his or her own eyes and in the eyes of others but also in a world of natural and cultural places, things, and technologies that together make up the field of the gaze.

As we will see, the process through which the subject is made to exist in the field of the gaze is quite complex. We do not just take into account context when we consider relationships of looking. Analysis of spectators and spectatorship also considers the role of unconscious thinking and feeling. The hallmark of theories of spectatorship and the gaze is attention to unconscious processes as they influence looking practices. It is very hard to study unconscious thoughts and feelings with clarity and certainty. In this aim, psychoanalysis was brought in to visual theory (from literary theory) in order to explain more fully the idea that the subject is constituted at an unconscious, as well as a conscious, level.

In chapter 2, we introduced the concept of interpellation. Viewing, we emphasized, is a multimodal activity that involves a range of active elements besides the individual who looks and the image at which he or she looks. The viewer, we explained, is interpellated—that is, hailed—by images in this field. We described interpellation as a process of interruption through which an individual viewer comes to recognize himself or herself as among the class or group of subjects for whom the image's message seems to be intended. Interpellation, in this sense, is less about creating a relationship between the viewer and the image alone than it is about situating the viewer in a field of meaning production (organized around looking practices) that involves recognition of oneself as a member of that world of meaning. This is what we mean when we describe *the gaze* as a field rather than an individual's act of looking.

Foucault provided a classic example of the gaze as being something enacted through a spatialized field in his discussion of *Las Meninas* (1656), one of the most analyzed paintings in the history of art. Painted by Diego Velázquez, the leading painter in the seventeenth-century Spanish court of King Philip IV, *Las Meninas* is composed in a manner that positions the spectator ambiguously. The painting is a depiction of a room within the king's palace in which several figures (the king's young daughter, her maid, a chaperone, other children and figures, a dog) interact. At the center of the composition is the daughter and, behind her, at the deepest space within the room, the composition is split. On one side appears a doorway beyond which is posed the artist Velázquez himself. He stands painting a large

FIG. 3.5
Diego Velázquez, *Las Meninas*, 1656

canvas of which we see only the back, while he looks in through the doorway at us and at the backs of the figures facing us in the foreground of the painting. Next to this open door, on the deepest plane of the room, is a mirror in which are reflected the upper bodies of the king and queen, their faces looking out, like that of Velázquez, at us and, presumably, on the scene we witness. The position of the mirror suggests that they in fact stand somewhere in front of this scene—if not in the same position we occupy as spectators, then somewhere in this vicinity. The placement of the king and queen before this scene and the organization of their viewpoint in relation to that of the spectator has been of great interest to writers, including Foucault. In his book *The Order of Things*, Foucault discusses the spectator in relationship not only to the royal couple but also to the looks of the painter and the child.[6] Our attention is extended across the field of the gazes constituted among these figures and our own gaze. It moves across the space represented in the painting, the implied off-canvas space occupied by the king and queen in the mirror, and the space of the gallery in which the spectator views the painting. (In fact, the painting was viewed for many years only by the king in his chambers, but Foucault imagined it to have hung in a museum or gallery.)

For Foucault, this painting challenges the verisimilitude of paintings during this period by introducing instability in a previously stable system of representation. This interpretation of the painting, though challenged by various art historians, remains an important demonstration of the ways in which the gaze can be distributed across different representations, subject positions, and lines of sight even in the case of one spectator's act of looking at one painting. Not only does it demonstrate how the gaze is always constituted through a relational field, but it also shows, quite literally, that the look of the spectator is always constituted in a field of looks, including "looks" that emanate from objects (such as the painting). The depiction of people who look (the artist, the king and queen) out of the painting and toward the position of the spectator makes literal the proposition that any image or object interpellates the human subject who looks at it with a look back—that is, a call, an appeal, or an address.

Discourse and Power

In modernity, the gaze is constituted through a relationship of subjects defined within and through the discourses of institutions. The modern state and political systems that are dependent on bureaucracies and social institutions to function are important aspects of modernity. In the nineteenth century, institutions increasingly used techniques of classification and archiving not only to count and regulate human subjects but also to keep them in line. In examining the practices of modern social institutions, Foucault created influential theoretical paradigms for thinking about how power works through benign institutional techniques and discourses.

Foucault's concept of discourse is helpful to understanding how power systems work to define how things are understood and spoken about (and, by implication, represented in images) in a given society. The term *discourse* is usually used to describe passages of writing or speech, the act of talking about something. Foucault used the term more specifically. Foucault was interested in the rules and practices that produce meaningful statements and regulate what can be spoken in different historical periods. By discourse he meant a group of statements that provide a means for talking (and a way of representing knowledge) about a particular topic at a particular historical moment. Hence discourse is a body of knowledge that both defines and limits what can be said about something. In Foucault's terms, one could talk about the discourses of law, medicine, criminality, religion, sexuality, technology, and so forth, in other words, broad social domains that define particular forms of knowledge and that change from any given time period and social context to another. There are no particular rules, though, saying we must use the term in a Foucaultian way, and people often use the term discourse when analyzing language and speech in general.

One of Foucault's topics of study for discourse was the concept of madness and the modern institutionalization of the idea of insanity. In the nineteenth century, psychiatry emerged as a science, medical definitions of madness were produced, and the insane asylum came into being. By comparison, during the Renaissance, madness was not considered to be a disease or an illness, and the mad were not excluded from the rest of society but rather were integrated into the fabric of small villages. They were considered to be under the influence of "folly"—a benign way of thinking—and sometimes seen as wise or revelatory, such as the idiot savant. With the emergence of modernity in the eighteenth and nineteenth century, as people moved increasingly into urban centers and the modern political state emerged, madness became medicalized, pathologized, and seen as a polluting factor that had to be removed from society. According to Foucault, madness is defined through the varying discourses of medicine, law, education, and so forth, and includes statements that give us a certain kind of knowledge about it; the rules that govern what can be said and thought about insanity at a particular moment; subjects who in some ways personify the discourse of madness—the paranoid schizophrenic, the criminally insane, the psychiatric patient, the therapist, the doctor; how the knowledge about madness acquires authority and is produced with a sense of the truth; the practices within institutions for dealing with these subjects, such as medical treatment for the insane; and the acknowledgement that a different discourse will arise at a later historical moment, supplanting the existing one, producing in turn a new concept of madness and new truths about it. This can be seen in the fact that certain concepts about the discourse of madness did not exist (and hence could not be spoken or represented) before they emerged in the discourse (the concept of the paranoid schizophrenic emerged in the mid-twentieth century, the idea of the criminally insane person first existed at the end of the nineteenth century but is now highly debated, the broad use of pharmaceutical drugs to treat new categories of mental disorder emerged in the late twentieth century). Hence, in this example, mental illness is not an objective fact that remains the same in different historical periods and in different cultures. It is only within particular discourses that it is made meaningful and intelligible. It is fundamental to Foucault's theory that discourses produce certain kinds of subjects and knowledge and that we occupy to varying degrees the subject positions defined within a broad array of discourses. Here, history provides a lens on the present: examining how discourses (and the values that underlie them) change over time allows us to look more critically at the discourses at work in our current social context.

Photography has been a central factor in the functioning of social discourses since the nineteenth century. When photography was invented in the early nineteenth century, its development coincided with the rise of the modern political state. Photography thus became an integral part of both scientific professions and the regulation of social behavior by bureaucratic institutions of the state. It is used in the law as evidence, in medicine to document pathologies and to identify a visual difference between the "normal" and "abnormal," and in the social sciences, such as anthropology and sociology, to enable the creation of the subject positions of the researcher (anthropologist) and the object of study (formerly defined as the "native"). The versatility of the photographic image thus spawned a broad array of image-making activities for the purpose of surveillance, regulation, and categorization. Photographs thus often function to establish difference. They are a medium through which that which is defined as *other* is posited as that which is not the norm or the primary subject. In chapter 9, we discuss the use of photography as a means of categorization and demarcation of the categories of normal and abnormal.

We can thus begin to see the complexity of the ways in which the gaze is integral to systems of power and ideas about knowledge. Three central concepts introduced by Foucault are useful for thinking about the relation of images and power: panopticism, power/knowledge, and biopower. Foucault's famous description in his book *Discipline and Punish* of the panopticon, a prison structure designed by the English philosopher and social reformer Jeremy Bentham, helped him to elaborate on the idea of an *inspecting gaze*.[7] Bentham's design was organized around a concentric building composed of rings of cells, at the center of which stood a guard tower. When positioned in the tower, the guard could see and hear activity in the prison cells (which were connected to the tower by listening channels), but the guard could not be seen by inmates. Observation ports were covered in blinds and carefully designed to block visual evidence from below of the presence or absence of the observer, making it possible for prisoners to imagine the presence of a guard when the tower was in fact unmanned. This concept of seeing without being seen and of imagining oneself being seen when in fact no human subject is looking is what Bentham had in mind when he described this as a plan for gaining power of mind over mind. Because prisoners would come to imagine themselves being seen by the guard, there was no need for an actual guard to be present to keep the community of prisoners under control. What mattered was the imagined spectator fixed in the mind of each inmate. Unlike the dungeon, which removed prisoners from sight yet afforded them some protection from scrutiny, the panopticon subjected prisoners to a relentless gaze. Imagining being watched thereby kept them in line. Foucault noted the fact that inmates of the panopticon internalized the figure of the imagined observer, modifying their behavior as subjects under surveillance even when in fact no one was watching.

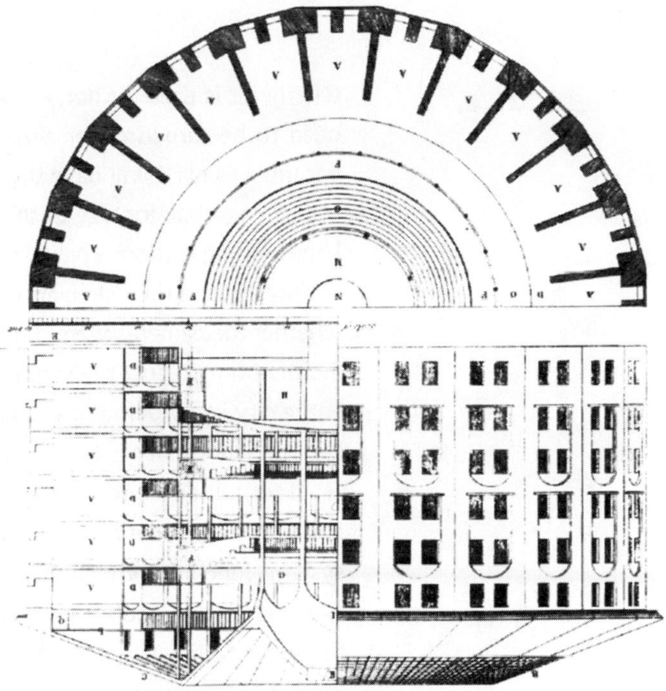

FIG. 3.6
The Panopticon Penitentiary

The concept of the panopticon is about how we participate in practices of self-regulation in response to systems of surveillance, whether they are in place or simply assumed to be in place. It is the case, of course, that camera surveillance has actually become a significant part of our everyday lives. We are subject to camera surveillance in stores, on elevators, in parking garages, and at cash machines, and we are accustomed to the surveillance of border controls, to identification checking, to passport monitoring, and so on. Photographic identification is prevalent in the criminal justice system, the legal system, and the bureaucracy of everyday life. Not only are photographic IDs now commonly demanded for monetary transactions and for entry into many public buildings, but also the systems that are used to identify individualness continue to expand, from photographs and fingerprints to DNA profiles and biometric fingerprinting and iris scanning in amusement parks, lunch lines, and airport security checkpoints.

We could easily say that the camera is used here as a form of intrusion and policing of our behavior. Most urban centers are now filled with surveillance cameras for such diverse purposes as reading license plates of cars violating traffic rules and capturing footage of criminal or terrorist acts. There were 4.2 million such cameras in Great Britain in 2006, approximately one for every fourteen people. However, if we use Foucault's concept of the panopticon, we would also have to recognize that the camera is merely a visible presence of the inspecting gaze that we imagine, whether it is there or not, visible to us or not. In other words, the camera does not need to be turned on or even in place for the inspecting gaze to exist; merely its potential to exist will have this effect. After the July 2005 London bombing, the police made public footage of the alleged bombers walking down the street and in the London tube station. These images made clear the extent of the camera surveillance in the city, and their circulation established the city as a site of constant monitoring, whether the cameras were functioning (or their footage being watched) at any given moment or not. Just the simple publication of these images served to affirm that the entire city is, by definition, a site in which all behavior is monitored, and all citizens self-regulate by necessity in response.

Foucault also wrote influentially about how modern societies are structured on a basic relationship of power/knowledge. Whereas monarchies and totalitarian political systems function through the overt exercise and display of punishment, such as public execution for the violation of laws, in modern societies power relations are structured to produce citizens who will actively participate in self-regulating behavior. Hence the function of power in modern political states is less visible. This means that citizens willingly obey laws, participate in social norms, and adhere to dominant social values. Modern societies function, Foucault argued, not through coercion but through cooperation. Foucault saw modern power not as a conspiracy among leaders or as authoritarian rule by particular individuals but as a system enacted among all strata of society and effective in normalizing bodies in order to maintain relations of dominance and subordination across these strata. Power relations, he argued, establish the criteria for what

FIG. 3.7
A closed circuit television (CCTV) camera in central London, 2006

FIG. 3.8
Image from CCTV footage of alleged bomber Ramzi Mohamed, shown to the jury of the July 7, 2005, London bombing trial

gets to count as knowledge in a given society, and knowledge systems in turn produce power relations.

Certain kinds of knowledge are validated in our society through social institutions such as the press, the medical profession, and education while other kinds of knowledge may be discredited because they do not carry the authority of institutional discourse. This means that the word of a journalist may be taken over that of the witness, that of the doctor over the patient, of the anthropologist over the people he or she is studying, of the police officer over the suspect, or of the teacher over the student. Although certainly one could argue that expertise may give more credence to those in the first category over the second, Foucault's work demonstrates that expert knowledge (and who has it) is a fundamental aspect of power relations. In Foucault's terms, we can see how the structure of a classroom itself sets up a particular power dynamic between teacher and students, getting students to internalize the oversight of the teacher so that discipline is enacted in a passive and self-regulating manner.

For Foucault, modern power is not something that negates and represses so much as it is a force that produces—it produces knowledge, and it produces particular kinds of citizens and subjects. Many of the relationships of power in the modern political state are exercised indirectly on and through the body, and this is what Foucault called *biopower*. He wrote that "the body is also directly involved in a political field; power relations have an immediate hold upon it; they invest it, mark it, train it, torture it, force it to carry out tasks, to perform ceremonies, to emit signs."[8] This means that the modern state has a vested interest in the maintenance and regulation of its citizens; in order to function properly, it needs citizens who are willing to work, to fight in wars, and to reproduce, and to have healthy and capable bodies to do so. Therefore the state actively manages, orders, and catalogues the properties of the body through social hygiene, public health, education, demography, census-taking, and regulating reproductive practices. Foucault argued that these institutional practices create knowledge of the body. They force the body to "emit signs," that is, to signify its relation to social norms. The body that is trained, exercised, and regulated was also captured in photographs through an array of social institutions. Beginning in the nineteenth century these institutions regulated the bodies of the citizens through public health, a burgeoning mental health field, and the emergence of the disciplines of exercise, gymnastics, and posture training (exemplified by learning to walk with books on one's head).

FIG. 3.9
Biopower in action: students at St. Thomas School, Sydney, Australia, 1931

Photographic images have been instrumental in the production of what Foucault called the docile bodies of the modern state—citizens who participate in the ideologies of the society through cooperation and a desire to fit in and conform. This happens in

the vast array of media and advertising images that produce homogeneous images for us of the perfect look, the perfect body, and the perfect pose. Because we as viewers of advertising images do not often think of the ways in which they are operating as ideological texts, these images have the power to affect our self-images. This means that the norms of beauty and aesthetics that these images present in standards that establish white and Anglo features as the desired look and thinness as the essential body type are part of the normalizing gaze that viewers turn on themselves.

The Gaze and the Other

The gaze, whether institutional or individual, thus helps to establish relationships of power. The act of looking is commonly regarded as awarding more power to the person who is looking than to the person who is the object of the look. The tradition of institutional photography, in which prisoners, mental patients, and people of various types were photographed and catalogued, can be related to the traditions of visual anthropology and travel photography, as well as to the tradition of painting peoples of so-called exotic locales. All function to varying degrees to represent codes of dominance and subjugation, difference and otherness.

The photograph is thus a central tool in establishing difference. In systems of representation, meaning is established through difference. Hence, throughout the history of representation and language, binary oppositions, such as man/woman, masculine/feminine, culture/nature, or white/black, have been used to organize meaning. We believe we know what culture is because we can identify its opposite (nature); thus difference is essential to its meaning. The theory of structuralism saw the world and its representations as organized by such binary oppositions. However, binary oppositions are reductive ways of viewing the complexity of difference, and, as philosopher Jacques Derrida has argued, all binary oppositions are encoded with values and concepts of power, superiority, and worth.[9] In addition, as Derrida and other poststructuralist scholars have argued, these categories of difference are themselves overlapping and not mutually exclusive. The category of the norm is always set up in opposition to that which is deemed abnormal or aberrant in some way, hence other. Thus binary oppositions designate the first category as unmarked (the "norm") and the second as marked, or other. The category of the feminine is marked and commonly understood as that which is not masculine (unmarked, most obviously in the way that the term "man" stands in for all humans), whereas in reality these distinctions are often blurred, and people can be understood to have aspects of both. The category of white is understood in European American contexts to be the primary category, whereas black (or brown, etc.) is understood as other to that category—what white is not. Hence the work of understanding how racism and sexism function and of how to understand difference in terms that do not replicate concepts of dominance and superiority must take place at the level of linguistic meaning, as well as social and cultural meaning.

FIG. 3.10
Guess ad, 1990s

The capacity of the photograph to establish both norms and otherness is highly evident in contemporary advertising, in which ads attach notions of exoticism to their products through images of places that are coded as distant and outside the world of consumption. In this Guess fashion ad, the implied locale of a rice paddy and the use of an Asian model give ordinary women's clothing a peasant quality. Here the hats worn typically by workers in rice paddies in order to shield their faces from the sun are recoded as signifiers of exoticism. We are not intended to think that these women are actually performing the labor of working in the rice paddies; rather, the paddy offers an exotic location in which highly paid models and expensive clothing can be put on display.

Some advertisements, such as this Safari ad (fig. 3.11), sell products by placing consumers in distant scenarios to conjure a nostalgic sense of being a colonial-era traveler. The ad invites the viewer/consumer to assume the role of the liberated traveler who moves through an unidentified exotic locale. The ad is arranged like a travelogue or scrapbook. The consumer is interpellated in these ads as a westerner who can buy an "authentic" exotic experience. Although these ads do not go so far as to sell the idea that the experience depicted will actually impute the culture to the consumer, they do encode products and consumable experiences with the aura of the exotic. The consumer is promised a virtually authentic experience as tourist in consuming the product.

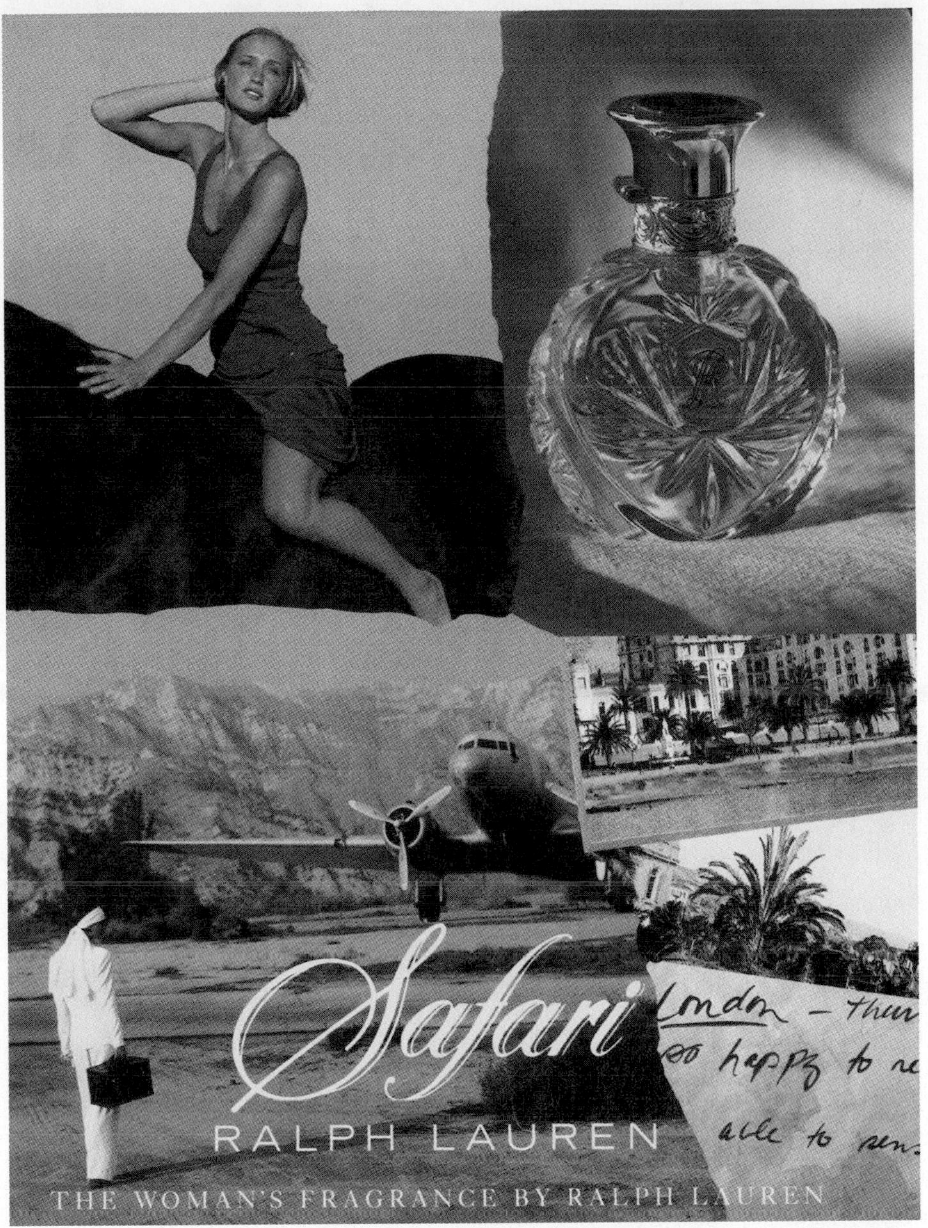

FIG. 3.11
Ralph Lauren Safari ad, 1990s

One of the primary binary oppositions that is reiterated (and debated) in contemporary representation today is that of the differences between Western and Eastern cultures. This difference formerly was captured in the terms Occidental and Oriental, with *Orientalism* describing the tendencies of westerners who have fetishized, mythologized, and feared the cultures, lands, and peoples of Asia and the Middle East. Photographs and other forms of representation are central elements in the production of Orientalism. Through photographs, literature, and film, Western cultures have attributed to Eastern and Middle Eastern cultures qualities such as exoticism and barbarism thereby establishing those cultures as foreign, strange, and other. Cultural theorist Edward Said emphasized that the Orient is not strictly a place(s) or culture(s) in itself, but rather a European cultural construction. Orientalism, he explained, is about "the Orient's special place in European Western experience. The Orient is not only adjacent to Europe; it is also the place of Europe's greatest and richest and oldest colonies, the

FIG. 3.12
Jean-Léon Gérôme, *The Bath*, c. 1880–1885

source of its civilizations and languages, its cultural contestant, and one of its deepest and most recurring images of the Other."[10]

Said argued that the concept of the Orient as other serves to establish Europe and the West as the norm. Orientalism creates a binary opposition between the West (the Occident) and the East (the Orient), with negative and fetishistic fantasies to the latter. Orientalism can be found not only in political policy but also in cultural representations, such as contemporary popular culture in which, for instance, films depict Arab men as terrorists and Asian women as highly sexualized. The representation of Muslims as fanatics or extremists or the representation of the Middle East as mysterious, unknowable, and sensual are examples of how Orientalism functions to reinforce cultural stereotypes that have their roots in the colonial era.

There is a long tradition of European painters imagining Arab countries as sites of mystery, and depicting, as in this painting by Jean Léon Gérôme, a secretive glimpse into forbidden sites. Gérôme created a number of Orientalist works in the late nineteenth century in the style of neoclassicism. Here the women are on display for the viewer, with the image marking a distinct racial difference between the demure white woman turned away from the camera and the black woman servant who

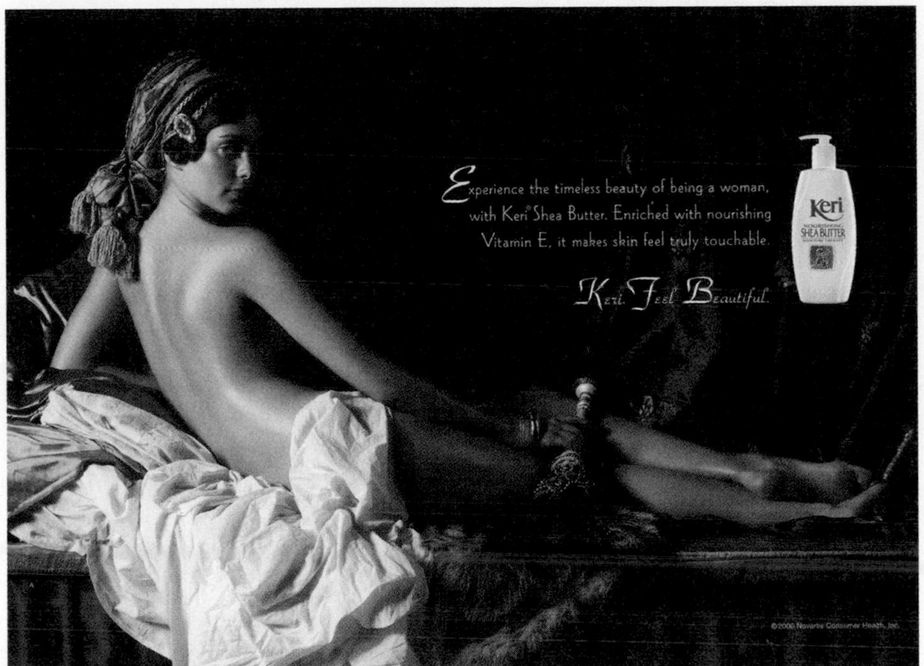

FIG. 3.13
Keri ad remake of Ingres, *La Grande Odalisque*, 2006

bathes her and is on full display for the viewer. Within the codes of the image, the black servant is fully available to the viewer, whereas the white woman, clearly a consumer of the exoticized locale of the bath, is shielded from our gaze.

We can trace the legacy of this kind of Orientalist image produced by French neoclassicist painters through a number of image contexts toward the present. In this 2006 advertisement for Keri lotion (fig. 3.13), we find an explicit reproduction of a well-known painting by the French artist Jean-August-Dominique

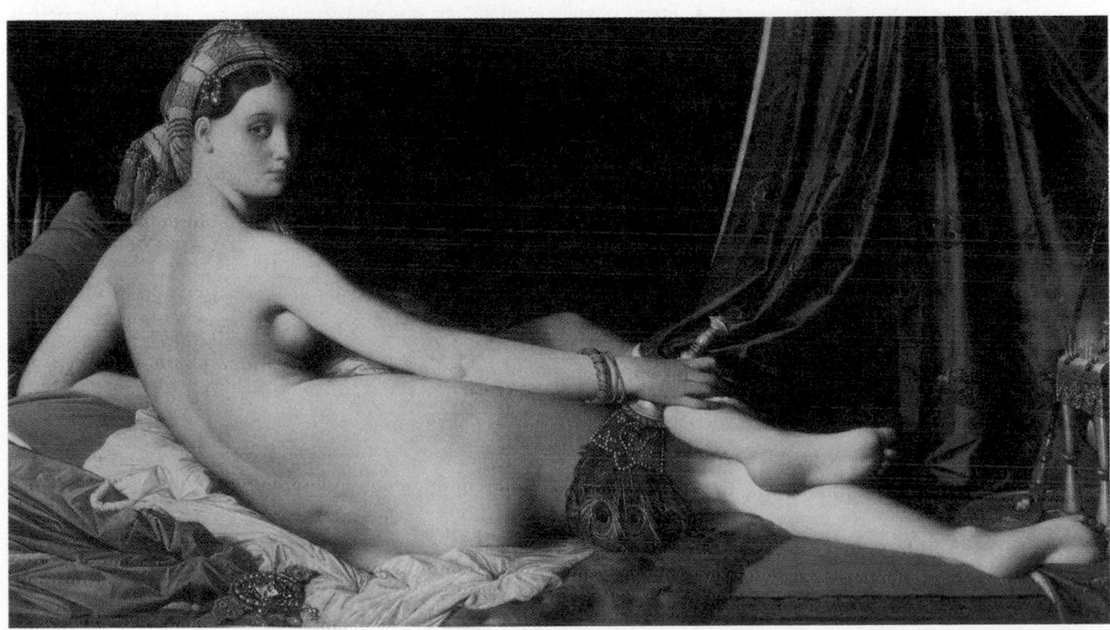

FIG. 3.14
Jean-Auguste-Dominique Ingres, *La Grande Odalisque*, 1814

Ingres (fig. 3.14). Such a close reproduction of the painting would suggest a decision on the part of the company to make unmistakable the reference to a specific work of art. This is not simply a case in which the conventions and themes of an artist or a style are copied nor a familiar exoticized pose, but rather there is a careful reproduction of enough particular elements of the original painting so as to make obvious the specific referent. The composition does not need to use text to let us know that *La Grande Odalisque*, painted by Ingres in 1814, is the original referenced here. The advertisers rely on the assumption that the painting has wide international recognition as a masterpiece in the history of art, a classic example of the female nude, even if most consumers might not be certain about details such as the name of the artist, the title of the work, the year it was painted, or where it hangs (in the Louvre). The painting is regarded as an important icon, a generic and seemingly timeless signifier of classical female beauty.

The Ingres painting was itself a reproduction of sorts. Ingres drew on iconography of the harem during the Ottoman Empire (1299–1922) that circulated in nineteenth-century European art and culture to render his own versions of the odalisque in Turkish harem life. An odalisque is a female slave, a virgin, who acted as chambermaid to the harem of the sultan in hopes of elevating herself to the status of the concubine. Although favored women of the harem played an important role in government during a notable period of the Ottoman Empire, the odalisque, situated at the bottom of the harem's hierarchy, was the most subjugated class of women in the imperial harem. Although Ingres painted a number of scenes invoking the Ottoman odalisque in harem and bath scenes. This painting of 1814, commissioned by the Queen of Naples (who was the sister of Napoleon Bonaparte), became the best known despite its initial mixed reception. The painting was displayed in French salons after its completion, where it gained a critical reception, because the queen lost her empire before the painting was finished and had to forgo ownership of the work.

In the book *The Colonial Harem*, Malek Alloula shows that the figure of the harem woman was invoked in France as a visual and literary icon of female sexual submission among painters and photographers enmeshed in the broader tradition of *Orientalism* in the arts and sciences.[11] Postcards, paintings, and literary works helped to spin fantasies about sexual pleasure and conquest in regions of North Africa, Asia, and the Middle East that were targets of European imperial conquest and trade expansion. In many of these photographs, the model is not an authentic member of a harem but a French woman posed by the photographer for the Orientalist-themed scene. This image, of "reclining Moorish women," is part of what Alloula calls the mode of "Oriental Sapphism," in which an eroticism is implied not only in the availability of the women's bodies to the viewer but also in the implication that they are objects of eroticism to each other.

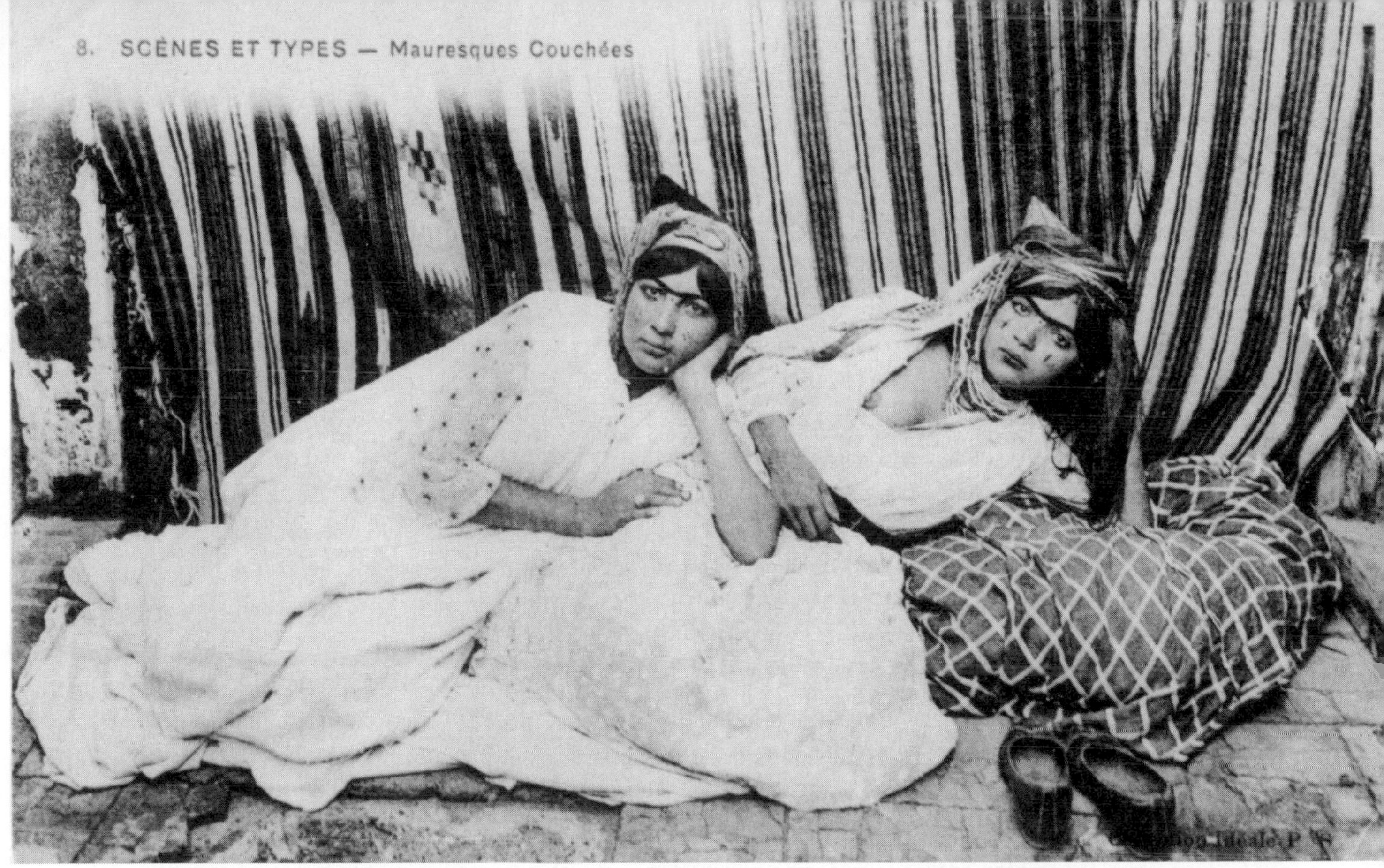

FIG. 3.15
Nineteenth-century postcard of "Reclining Moorish Women," from Malek Alloula, *The Colonial Harem*

In the Ottoman Empire, it was forbidden for a man to lay his eyes on another man's harem. The representation of the Turkish odalisque nude in her chambers as Ingres imagined her was a transgression of the moral codes of the context he invoked. Our point is not, however, that the depiction of harem women in painting must always be read as demeaning, objectifying, or wholly representative of a colonialist gaze. The politics of representation is always more complex than this passive-active model of representation suggests. Deborah Cherry and other contributors to the volume *Orientalism's Interlocutors* ask readers to be aware of the potential agency of the women in some of these cultural settings.[12] For example, some of the women who achieved social status through their role as the Sultan's favored members of the harem negotiated their own portraits by nineteenth-century British artists during the period of the Ottoman Empire known as the Reign of Women.

However, in each image, the original and its remake, the Orientalist gaze on the nude female body is what defines the image. In the Keri lotion advertisement, reference to Ingres's famous odalisque is obvious in the replication of the model's distinctively elongated spine, her back turned to face the camera and her head turned to meet the gaze of the camera. Framing and color choices, skin tone and quality, and even the styling of the model's hair, fabric draping, and accoutrements such as the peacock-feather fan held against the flesh of the thigh, are careful, closely matched variations on details in this well-known painting.

Ingres is widely recognized as a one of the last advocates of neoclassicism among French painters who had begun to turn to the new Romantic style before the radical shifts of modernism. His paintings are regarded for their revival of classical beauty ideals, captured in the rendering of the human form in pure, classic lines and smooth textures. In the painting, the model's skin, like her form, is rendered as if without flaw. Ingres was known for obsessively retouching his work in order to render the line and the texture of the skin in its ideal state, immaculate and perfect. By incorporating such an overt reference to this painting and hence to the neoclassical ideals of "timeless" bodily perfection it invokes, the makers of Keri lotion enhance their message that the use of their product will make the consumer's skin radiate the same idealized "timeless beauty of being a woman," a woman gazed on by the camera and the spectator, captured in Ingres's "timeless" masterpiece.

But it is interesting to note that Ingres's work was not universally regarded as the embodiment of classical beauty during his time. He was widely criticized for what was regarded at the time as his gothic distortions of the human form. His decision to add three vertebrae to the figure of the odalisque, for example, in order to achieve the elongated spine was disparaged for making the body appear abnormal. The figure of the odalisque takes on new meanings not just in Ingres's social and historical context, evoking the conventions of Orientalism and its exoticizing of Middle Eastern themes and women's bodies; with this copy this exoticizing tendency is carried over into our own era. It is significant that the beauty-product advertisement references a neoclassical painting and the meaning of timeless beauty in a digitally enhanced photographic montage that gives the image a contemporary, airbrushed feel. We might say the lotion offers skin that looks digitally airbrushed, an effect not unlike Ingres's famously smooth, translucent skin.

It is also worth noting the fact that although the French neoclassical fantasy that is the source of this icon concerns female sexuality during the Islamic Ottoman Empire, this advertisement appeared during the American and British "war on terror," in which Islamic peoples and culture have been invoked as the source of a political threat to the West. The gaze on the exoticized female figure is thus also invoked as a gaze on the other as a means of negating its threat. Ingres's appropriation of the odalisque figure as sexual icon bears significance in relationship to the context of European imperial expansion and colonial conquest. This advertisement, through reappropriating this same icon, places the odalisque in the contemporary context of its reception in the West. In France, England, and the United States, Islamic conventions of femininity, such as veiling and covering of the body, have been a subject of intense public political debate, fascination, misunderstanding, political harassment, and even derision.

Viewers of the Keri ad may take away the simple message that equates Keri lotion with classical beauty without ever thinking much at all about the historical referent and its meanings. Yet we are proposing that these historical references contribute to a naturalized mythology of ideals such as classical beauty. The values and meanings of signifiers reproduced in these generic codes have become so embedded in the culture as to seem *as if* they are natural and unmediated. We borrow here an early phrase of Roland Barthes's to suggest that this image performs *as if* it held a message (timeless beauty) without a code. Historical meanings are reproduced in the codes and conventions we use, whether producers intend these meanings to be there or not, and whether any given spectator explicitly notices them or not. To stay timeless, as if outside changing tastes and conventions, the codes of beauty must be reproduced over time. But in each reproduction, as we see here, these codes are rendered with differences such as context, framing, and media, making the message contemporary even as it carries the weight of natural fact and timeless truth.

It is significant that the odalisque and her remake are not only nude but also turn toward the spectator. As we discuss further, this is a convention of images of women throughout the history of art that has been reiterated in advertising. The nude exemplified by the Ingres painting invites the spectator, presumed to be male, to take possession of the image and the woman within it. This image convention was used by the Guerrilla Girls, a feminist activist art group, to make a point about how few women artists had their work in the collection of the renowned Metropolitan Museum of Art in New York. Here, the Ingres odalisque is invoked not to evoke associations with its "timeless" beauty but to question the equally "timeless" fact that women, as compared with men, have been disproportionately represented in museums of art not as artists but as subjects of works of art, often in states of undress. The exclusion of women painters

FIG. 3.16

Guerrilla Girls, *Do women have to be naked to get into the Met. Museum?*, 2005

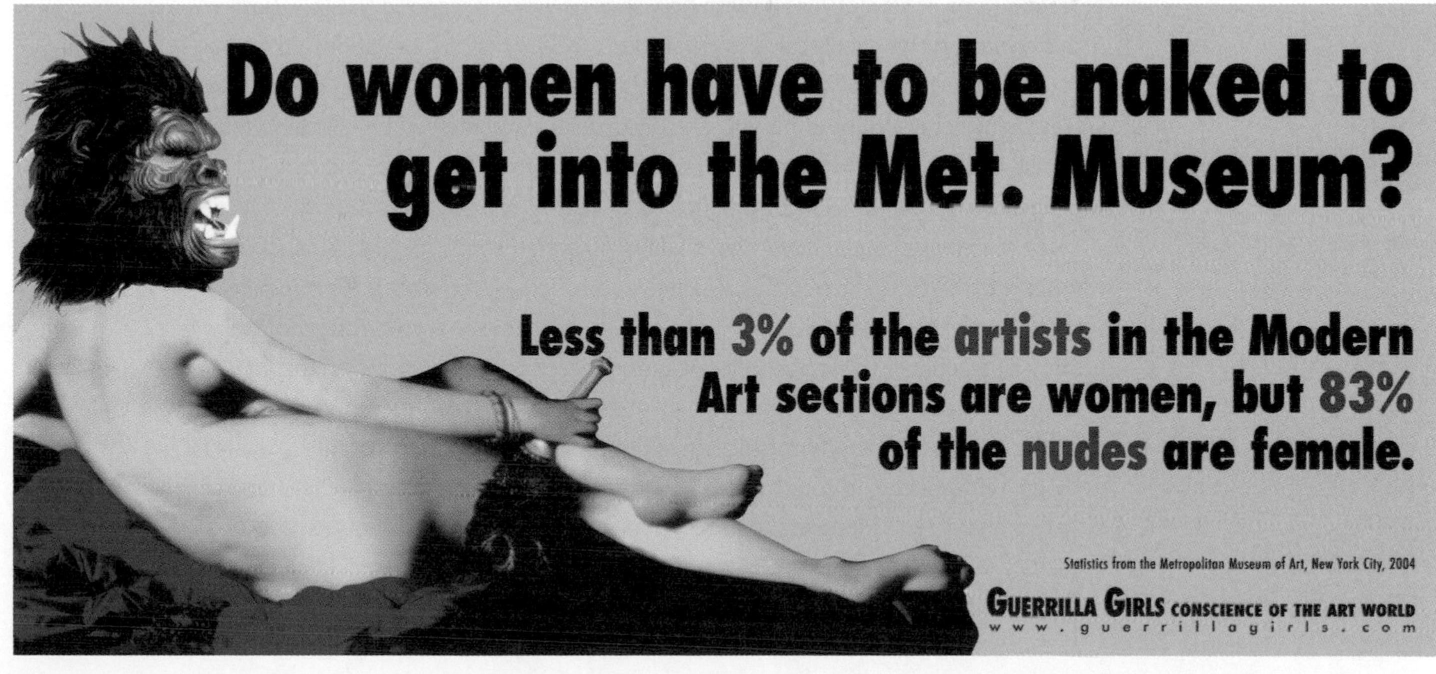
Do women have to be naked to get into the Met. Museum?
Less than 3% of the artists in the Modern Art sections are women, but 83% of the nudes are female.
Statistics from the Metropolitan Museum of Art, New York City, 2004
GUERRILLA GIRLS CONSCIENCE OF THE ART WORLD
www.guerrillagirls.com

from the institutions whose collecting and exhibition practices are key factors in establishing the value of works of art and cementing the reputations of particular artists as masters is the subject matter of this poster that appropriates Ingres's masterpiece, replacing the head of the woman with a gorilla mask, to pose the question: Do Women Have to be Naked to Get into the Metropolitan Museum of Art in New York? The Guerrilla Girls wear gorilla masks both to hide their identity and to play off the gorilla/guerrilla trope. It is notable that the Guerrilla Girls first did the survey for this poster in 1989, when the results showed that 5 percent of the artists were women and 85 percent of the nudes were female; in 2004 that number had actually gone down, with only 3 percent of the artists represented in the collection being women. In covering the face of the model, or odalisque, with the gorilla mask, these artist-activists are quite pointedly refusing to look back at the spectator.

The Gaze in Psychoanalysis

We have been discussing the relationship of the gaze to questions of institutional power, power/knowledge, and the other. Yet, as we noted at the beginning of this chapter, theories of the gaze derived from psychoanalysis also play an important role in understanding spectatorship and the unconscious processes that undergird the practices of looking. Theories of spectatorship have been central to an understanding of how the visual address of cinema accomplishes a particular set of relational meanings for spectators and give us the means to analyze the subject positions constructed for and offered to viewers by a given film text. Psychoanalytic film theory is not primarily concerned with individual viewers' acceptance or rejection of representations or stereotypes or with how specific viewers respond to films. Rather, in this approach the spectator is understood to be shaped, in a relationship of the gaze, within a network that includes the film text and its institutional context, as well as the spectator him- or herself. The unconscious and the symbolic activity that gives rise to representations, linking "personal" feelings to the world, are considered to be important components of that network.

The cinematic apparatus—the traditional social space of the cinema that includes a darkened theater, projector, film, and sound—is crucial to the experience of cinema spectatorship. Christian Metz and other theorists who wrote about film in the 1970s generally described the process of spectatorship as follows: the viewer suspends disbelief in the fictional world of the film and identifies not only with specific characters in the film but also, and more important, with the film's overall ideology. This occurs through identification with the position of the camera or with film characters. Identification with character or camera position puts into play fantasy structures (such as an imagined ideal family) that derive from the viewer's unconscious.

Film theorists Jean-Louis Baudry and Christian Metz drew an analogy between the early process of a child's ego construction described by Lacan in his account of the mirror phase and the experience of film viewing. As we noted, the mirror phase is an important step in infants' recognition of themselves as autonomous beings with the potential ability to control their body's negotiation of the world. The mirror phase provides infants with a sense of their existence as a separate body in relationship to another body, but it also provides a basis for alienation, since the process of image recognition involves a splitting between what they are physically capable of and what they see and imagine themselves to be (powerful, in control). There are two contradictory relationships here to the image—infants see that they and the image are the same, yet at the same time they see the image as an ideal (not the same). Hence the mirror phase offers an experience of self-recognition, but that experience is coupled with a kind of misrecognition and self-fragmentation. This framework can help us to understand the investment of tremendous power that viewers place in images and the reasons that we can so easily read images as a kind of ideal version of human subject relations. Importantly, Lacan's theory is not about the mirror as a reflection of the self but about the mirror as the constitutive element in the construction of the self. As theorist Jane Gallop writes, "Lacan posits that the mirror constructs the self, that the self as organized entity is actually an imitation of the cohesiveness of the mirror image."[13]

Part of the fascination with cinema, according to Baudry, is that the darkened theater and the conditions of watching a mirror-like screen invite the viewer to regress to a childlike state. The viewer undergoes a temporary loss of ego as he or she identifies with the powerful position of apprehending bodies on the screen, much as the infant apprehended the mirror image. The spectator's ego is built up through an illusory sense of owning the body on the film screen. It is important to emphasize that it is not the specific image of bodies on screen with which the viewer is thought to identify most significantly in this theory, but the cinematic apparatus. The idea that the viewer is in a regressive state is the aspect of psychoanalytic theory that has come under the most criticism, because it likens the spectator to an infant.

The concept of the unconscious is crucial to theories of cinematic spectatorship. As we have noted, one of the fundamental elements of psychoanalysis lies in its demonstration of the existence and mode of operation of unconscious mental processes. According to psychoanalytic theory, in order to function in our lives, we actively repress various desires, fears, memories, and fantasies. Hence, beneath our conscious, daily social interaction there exists a dynamic, active realm of forces of desire that is inaccessible to our rational and logical selves. The unconscious often motivates us in ways of which we are unaware and is active in representational activities such as dreaming. In this view, films are a little like externalized places for the activation of the kinds of memories and fantasies that typically work their way to the surface in dreams.

Lacan was the key theorist from whom film theorists began to understand the role of desire in creating subjects and to explain the powerful lure of film images in our culture. Lacan's concept of the gaze differs from Foucault's in that his gaze does not make the subject knowable to itself or to others. Rather, the gaze is part and parcel of a desire for completion of oneself through the other (the image in the mirror, the other person through whom the subject misrecognizes himself or herself). But this completion is never achieved. The image of self in the other allows the subject to forget the lack of autonomous selfhood revealed in one's own mirror image. For Lacan, the eye and the gaze are split; they engage, within the individual subject, in a process of seeking out others in hopes of obtaining the sense of self-certainty and completion in their look. This desired completion is imagined but never achieved precisely because it derives from a misapprehension or misrecognition (of self and other) which occurs in the early constitution of the ego.

In his later work on the gaze, Lacan emphasizes that the gaze is a property of the object and not the subject who looks. The gaze is a process in which the object functions to make the subject look, making the subject appear to himself or herself as lacking. We can understand this not only through objects—pictures that, like *Las Meninas*, depict a literal subject who looks—but also through the concept of interpellation, in which we may be hailed as if the message were "for me and only me" but never truly is "mine," is always potentially out of reach and potentially for others. This concept allows us to understand how the inanimate object can be an active player in processes of sexual desire. Not only can objects make us look, but they can also make us understand ourselves as subjects who *want* to look and who cannot help but look, even if we do not see ourselves as the one who the object hails—the one by whom the object is meant to be seen.

Lacan's formula for understanding the gaze and the look, with its representation of the rich network of living and inanimate actors who compose the field of the gaze, does help us to better understand an important component of this process that we have not yet discussed: the process of *identification*. An important area of scholarship on spectatorship has been devoted to understanding how we respond to images through identification with them, or with the figures or objects in them. In reacting to images of other human subjects, do we experience the person in the image or on the screen as an object of our desire—that is, do we identify with the apprehending look of the camera and admire the imaged human subject as an other whose image we might enjoy and consume in fantasies of touch and interaction? Or do we fantasize ourselves in the place of the person on the canvas or screen? Perhaps we are identifying with the body on the screen—for example, imagining ourselves wearing the same clothes or interacting in the same social world in which they appear. We will explore these issues of identification later in this chapter.

Gender and the Gaze

Gender has been a crucial aspect of concepts of the gaze. In the history of art, the fact that paintings were for the most part geared toward male viewers, as art historian Griselda Pollock has noted in her work on modernity and the spaces of femininity, had as much to do with the commerce of art as it did with the social roles and sexual stereotypes of men and women.[14] Until quite recently, most collectors of art were men, and the primary viewing audience of art was composed overwhelmingly of men. In a typical depiction of a female nude, a woman is posed so that her body is on display for the viewer's easy appreciation. There is a long tradition in art of understanding the female nude as the project and possession of the male artist. In these paintings, the women are posed as objects of an active or "male" gaze, and their

FIG. 3.17
Lorenzo Lotto, *Venus and Cupid*, early 1500s

FIG. 3.18
Titian, *Venus With a Mirror*, c. 1555

returning looks are more often downcast, indirect, or otherwise coded as passive. John Berger wrote that in this history of images, "men act, women appear."[15] Berger notes (like the Guerrilla Girls) that the tradition of the nude in painting was almost exclusively about images of nude women who were presented for male viewers.

There has been throughout the history of art a convention of depicting women gazing at themselves in mirrors, with their bodies turned toward the presumed spectator of the painting. The use of the mirror as a prop serves two functions. Mirrors were used by painters such as Titian to offer another view in the image, to create multiple planes within a painting that could be seen by the stationary spectator. The mirror is also a code for femininity. Venus looks at herself while the Cupid figures attend to her. Thus, while she is on display for the presumed male spectator, the convention of the mirror establishes her gaze as narcissistic. These codes of imaging the female nude have long traditions in art, and they are also liberally used by advertisers. This Ralph Lauren ad (fig. 3.19) sells romance to the spectator through the eyes of the woman. She gazes outward at the spectator and away from the man who is embracing her. Ironically, this can have the effect of making the man in the picture appear to be a mere prop, with no agency. The woman's connection is with the viewer who meets her look.

Theories of the gendering of spectator and the gaze in cinema find their origin in a groundbreaking essay about images of women in classical Hollywood cinema, published in 1975 by filmmaker and writer Laura Mulvey. This essay, "Visual Pleasure and Narrative Cinema," used psychoanalysis to propose that the conventions of popular narrative cinema are structured by a patriarchal unconscious, positioning women represented in films as objects of a "male gaze."[16] Mulvey argued that Hollywood cinema offered images geared toward male viewing pleasure, which she read within certain psychoanalytic paradigms, including scopophilia and voyeurism. The concept of the gaze is fundamentally about the relationship of pleasure and looking In psychoanalysis, the term scopophilia refers to pleasure in looking and exhibitionism—taking sexual pleasure in being looked at. Both of these terms acknowledge the ways in which reciprocal relationships of looking can be sources of pleasure. Voyeurism is the pleasure one takes in looking while not being seen looking. It carries the negative connotation of a powerful, if not sadistic, position within the gaze. The idea of the cinematic apparatus as a mechanism for voyeurism has been noted by film scholars,

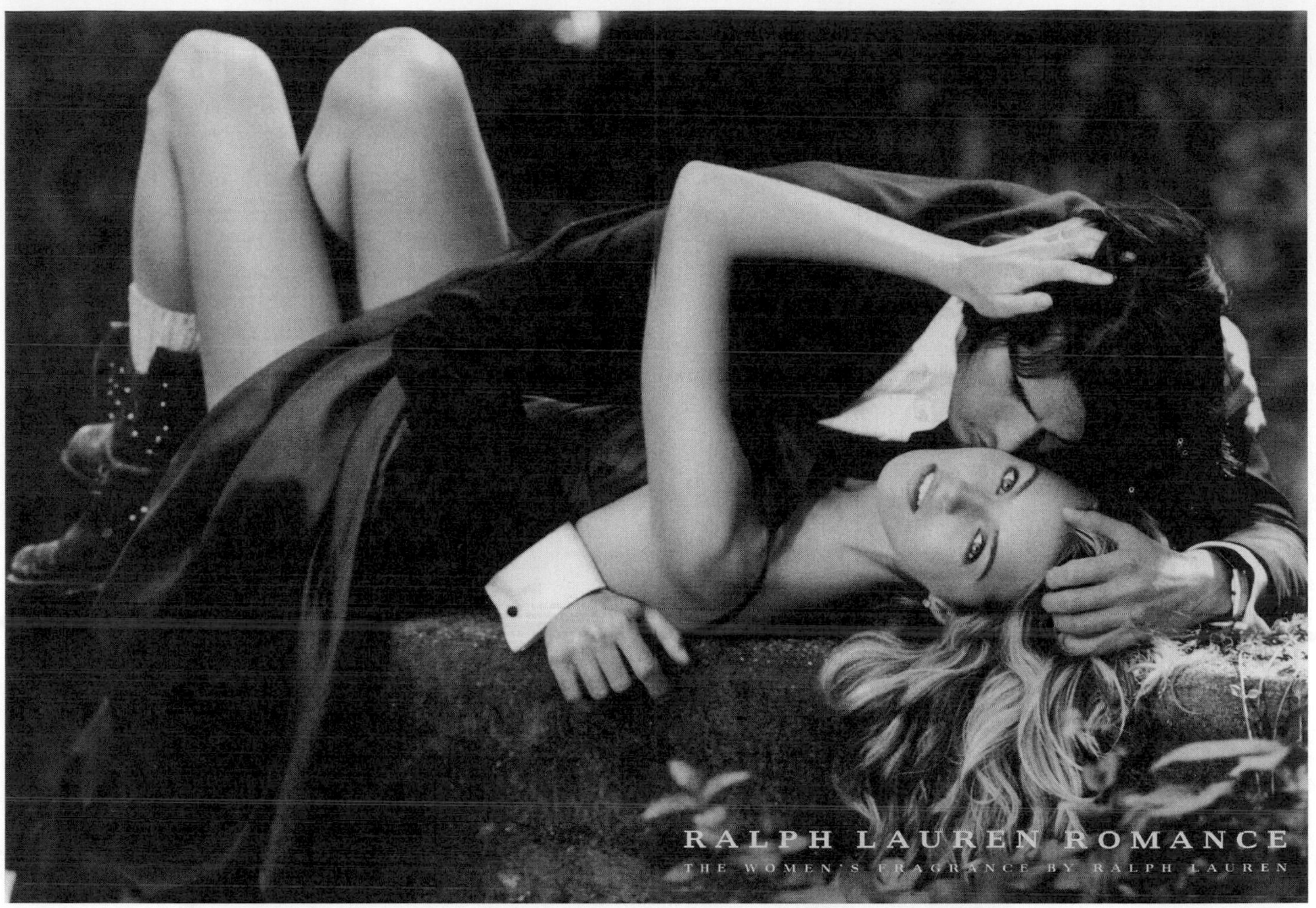

RALPH LAUREN ROMANCE
THE WOMEN'S FRAGRANCE BY RALPH LAUREN

FIG. 3.19
Ralph Lauren Romance ad, 2007

because, for instance, the position of viewers of cinema can be seen as voyeuristic. In watching films in a theater, spectators sit in a darkened room, where they cannot be seen looking. Characters on screen can never really return the spectator's gaze. In Mulvey's theory, the camera is used as a tool of voyeurism and sadism, disempowering those before its look. She and other theorists who pursued this line of thinking examined certain films of classic Hollywood cinema to demonstrate the power of the male gaze.

Alfred Hitchcock's *Rear Window* (1954) is a popular example of a film that is explicitly about gendered looking. The film's main protagonist is Jeffries (James Stewart), a photographer who has broken his leg and is temporarily confined to a wheelchair in his New York City apartment. Jeffries spends much of his time seated at a window that affords him a perfect view into the windows of the various people who live in the building across the way, where he believes he has witnessed evidence of a murder. *Rear Window* has been read by film theorists (including Mulvey) as a metaphor for the act of film viewing itself, with Jeffries standing in for the cinematic audience. Confined to a fixed position, like the film viewer, his gaze is similarly voyeuristic in that he freely looks at but is not seen by the objects of his gaze. Like characters in a movie, his neighbors are apparently unaware that this audience of one exists, much less that he has seen them up close in the intimate setting of their homes. The windows frame their actions just as the camera frames narrative

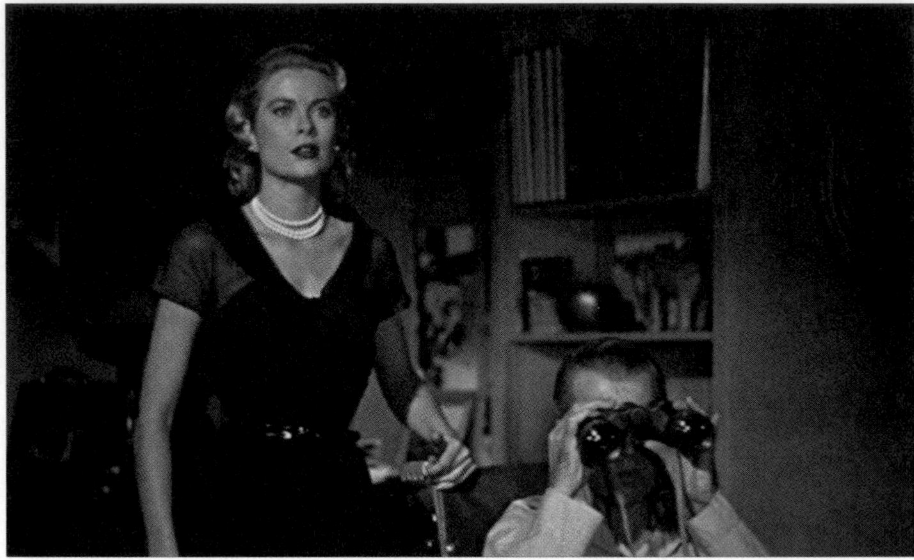

FIG. 3.20
James Stewart and Grace Kelly in Alfred Hitchcock, *Rear Window*, 1954

action in a film, both determining and restricting what Jeffries can know about their lives and generating in him a desire to see and know more. In the film, we see through his point of view as he observes his neighbors and tracks the movements of his girlfriend Lisa (Grace Kelly) as she becomes his mobile surrogate, his "private eye." Lisa steals up the fire escape across the way to search for murder clues in the off-screen space beyond the window frame that is off-limits to Jeffries and us, the film viewers.

Rear Window is a quintessential example of a film that depicts the male gaze as a practice in which men look at female bodies, containing them (through the device of the binoculars, for example) and rendering them objects of visual pleasure. Yet, as the example of Lisa's investigation suggests, the male gaze is not as controlling and powerful as this interpretation suggests. Film scholar Tania Modleski has pointed out that one can reread the interplay of gazes and power in *Rear Window* in quite a different way. She argues that Hitchcock's films are defined by an ambivalence about femininity, in which women who know too much threaten patriarchal structures.[17] In *Rear Window*, she argues, the character of Lisa has her own interpretation of what has taken place across the way, and the film ultimately validates her view.

Jeffries gains power by looking, but he is emasculated by his confined state and must rely on the eyes and legs of a woman to gain access to knowledge. The cinematic viewer, like Jeffries, is confined to a fixed seat and the field of vision offered by this position and the camera's restricted framing of the scene. The gendered relations of power of the cinematic gaze are clearly quite complex. Indeed, not only is Jeffries frustrated in his attempts to know more, but he is also punished for looking. Once Jeffries gets caught looking, he becomes vulnerable and trapped; the murderer comes looking for him. Clearly, male looking is not without its limitations and its consequences.

Mulvey's formulation was enormously influential, and it was published at a time when a number of artists in the 1970s were already engaging with issues of the gendered gaze. In this 1971 work, the American painter Sylvia Sleigh turned the tables on both Ingres and the gendered mirror trope by portraying her male model in the classical odalisque nude pose. We know this figure is male because of the title of the painting. Sleigh's young model lounges with his back to the spectator-painter in the vulnerable pose made famous by Ingres's *Odalisque*, his gracefully curved spine and buttocks exposed to the spectator's view. The absence of any telling body parts makes it ambiguous that this feminine figure is in fact a man, a confusion that is amplified by the face that gazes narcissistically at its own image in a mirror, in which we see reflected soft features and long, wavy hair. The face is in fact rudely cut off in the framing of the body on the canvas, appearing there only in the mirror image above the faceless torso. In that mirror, Sleigh has also painted the reflection of her own face. She appears in the painted reflection seated before the reclining nude, gazing on him

FIG. 3.21
Sylvia Sleigh, *Philip Golub Reclining*, 1971

FIG. 3.22
Robert Mapplethorpe, *Arnold Schwarzenegger*, 1976, © The Robert Mapplethorpe Foundation. Courtesy Art + Commerce

with her arm actively outstretched to the canvas where she has begun a painting, presumably the one we are seeing completed here, not unlike Velázquez in *Las Meninas*. This painting serves at once as a nude that riffs off of the classical style of rendering the female body and also as a self-portrait of the artist, who appears clothed, in makeup and with her hair done up in a professional-looking bun that contrasts starkly with the nude model's flowing mane.

The 1970s and 1980s were also a time when artists began to push at the boundaries of representation in relation to race, sexuality, and gender. Foremost among these artists was the American photographer Robert Mapplethorpe, who composed many works that convey physical beauty in a manner that emphasizes the fine line between standards of masculine and feminine anatomy and physiognomy, between erotica and art, and between beauty and its exaggeration and distortion. Mapplethorpe, who died of AIDS in 1989, is well known for his stark and edgy portraits of well-known figures of art and music countercultures and models and bodybuilders such as Arnold Schwarzenegger and Lisa Lyon, the first world champion of female bodybuilding. He was at the center of the culture wars during the 1990s, when political conservatives and religious fundamentalists demanded that the U.S. Congress stop funding the National Endowment for the Arts after it had funded a posthumous exhibition of Mapplethorpe's work that included graphic portrayals of gay sexuality. His photographs also incited controversy among visual theorists, who have both critiqued and celebrated his explicit representations of themes and issues such as racialized sadomasochism.[18] Is this sleek and crisp portrait of Arnold Schwarzenegger—former bodybuilder, action film star, and politician popularly known as the "Governator of California" during the 2000s—a kind of beefcake exploitation of Schwarzenegger's pumped-up body, or is it a cultural commentary on male sexuality, glamour, and body norms and ideals? The image treats Schwarzenegger's body as an object in itself, beautifully lit, sculpted, aesthetically pleasing, and photographed on stage next to a theatrical curtain. He flexes his muscles for the camera within the conventions of bodybuilding performance. Yet the exhibition mode of the image frames his performance within visual codes that fetishize his body. Mapplethorpe's work can signal an array of meanings about male sexuality, particularly in retrospect.

FIG. 3.23
Ana Mendieta, *Silueta Works in Mexico*, 1973

In works by women artists of the 1970s, we find a wide range of examples of strategies that counter dominant traditions of representing the female body as a site of display and of women as narcissistically engaged with their own display for male consumption. A crucial figure in feminist body art of the 1970s was the Cuban-American artist Ana Mendieta, a well-known performance and earthworks artist of the 1970s and 1980s who died in a fall from an upper-story window from her New York apartment building in 1985 (her husband, the modernist artist Carl Andre, was tried for and acquitted of her murder). Mendieta produced a number of earthworks in which the trace of her body, marked like a crime-scene outline, is impressed in the sand, then sprinkled and lined with blood-red pigment and photographed. The emulsions of some of the photographs documenting these earthworks are marked with scratches and treated with color using hand-applied techniques. Mendieta's work is internationally regarded as among the most important contributions to the feminist art of the twentieth century that critically rethought the representation of the female body—its overinscription in paintings by men, as well as the absence from history of works made by the hands of women artists.[19] In her body works, Mendieta's image is an imprint, an outline that reminds the looker of the historical absence of the hand of the woman artist. She refuses the spectator's gaze on her body by erasing her literal form while leaving its trace.

Changing Concepts of the Gaze

The theoretical concept of the male gaze has been debated, reworked, and rethought in the decades since Lacanian film theory first engaged with the idea. In addition, representations of gendered power relations and their relationship to the gaze have expanded to include a broad range of gendered image codes. Thus the theoretical paradigms through which the gaze and spectatorship are understood have been transformed, and the ways in which the gaze is enacted through images has produced new kinds of possibilities of identification. Mulvey's essay launched more than three decades of writing about modes of spectatorship, and Mulvey herself revised her thinking about visual pleasure in an essay of 1981.[20] One of the key factors in the original concept of the gaze that has been rethought is the way that it could not account for the pleasures of female viewers (except by seeing them as masochistic or as viewing "like men") or for the male figure as the object of the gaze. Meanwhile, feminist critics have continued to mine the theories of sexual difference put forth by Freud and Lacan. Even analyses of classical Hollywood film have broken free from the strict model of the dominating male gaze and female object of the gaze. For instance, Mary Ann Doane used psychoanalysis to theorize about female spectators of films made specifically for women viewers, such as the genre of the woman's film of the 1940s (also known as "weepies").[21] Some theorists have since argued that gendered viewing relations are not fixed, that viewers readily deploy fantasy to occupy the "wrong" gender position in their spectatorial relationships to films. Women can identify with the male position of mastery or exercise voyeuristic tendencies in looking at men or women. Men can be looked on with pleasure and desire by men or women. Although pleasure in looking may be strongly tied to one's sexuality, we may take pleasure in looking in ways that do not strictly conform to the codes of our respective sexual identifies. Pleasure and identification are not dictated by one's biological sex, or even by one's sexuality.

Some films defy the conventions of looking in film and present women's gazes with agency. For example, the 1991 film *Thelma & Louise* defies traditional formulas of the gaze and shows the complexity of the power relations of looking. The film begins with a scene in which the two women (played by Susan Sarandon and Geena Davis) take a photograph of themselves. Here, the women control the camera, belying the dominant view that women are objects, not subjects, of the gaze. One of the women, Thelma, gazes with lust at a hitchhiker whom the women pick up (Brad Pitt, in one of his first movie roles) and who is situated by the camera as an object before the gaze. The women are driving a convertible, which makes them visible to the gazes of men on the highway (when they are trying to flee), yet they resist those gazes by confronting those men, questioning that dynamic, and using guns (classically the possessions of men in film) to do so. *Thelma & Louise* is a film in which the viewer's identification through the narratives asks all viewers, men and women, to identify with the two female protagonists in a genre (the road movie, the buddy

FIG. 3.24
Susan Sarandon, Geena Davis, and Brad Pitt in Ridley Scott, *Thelma & Louise*, 1991

film) that has been traditionally male. As such, it defies the simple definition of the male gaze of Hollywood cinema.[22]

Scholarship on spectatorship and the gaze in the 1980s and 1990s began to radically modify many of the early concepts of power and the gaze in ways that are similar to these kinds of representations. Film scholars have rethought questions of spectatorship in relationship to history and mass culture, to reception studies and studies of the audience, to issues of race and spectatorship that question the emphasis on the gender binary of the original model and the resistance of black viewers, to new formulations about how different kinds of viewers can occupy the male gaze, and to the concepts of transgressive female looking and lesbian spectatorship.[23] Our pleasure in looking may be strongly tied to our cultural and sexual identifies and preferences, but we must always remember that looking practices are strongly bound up in fantasy. We may use images to conjure fantasies about who we are, what we do, and what others do in frame or on screen, and these fantasies may be quite different from what we would do with our bodies and with others in life. Visual fantasy is not a blueprint for reality. Perhaps the most comprehensive examination to date of spectatorship and the question of the constitution of the subject in terms of race and cultural identity in visual culture is Coco Fusco and Brian Wallis's exhibition and catalogue titled *Only Skin Deep: Changing Visions of the American Self.*[24] This exhibition and book are among the first comprehensive works to take on an overarching compilation and analysis of photography, video, and film traditions across the sciences and the arts through which racial identities were imaged, constructed, and challenged. They examine works from across news media, science images, art photography, and independent video to raise questions about the place of race and cultural identity in changing patterns and practices of spectatorship and representation.

Analyses of pornography, which ranged from feminist critiques about the repression of women to arguments against the censorship of sexualities, have also emerged out of spectatorship theory. In 1989, film scholar Linda Williams published a groundbreaking book, *Hard Core,* that analyzed pornography through psychoanalytic film theory, taking it seriously as a kind of cultural text that creates a variety of desires and subject positions.[25] This work opened the way for feminist film scholars to offer more nuanced theories of the function of pornography and, in the field of porn studies, to take up questions such as the agency of women workers and producers in the industry, as well as subgenres such as lesbian and gay pornography.[26] Spectatorship theory remains important in this field because it provides a method by which to consider the complex and sometimes contradictory ways in which viewers identify not only within their own identity category but also with different social and gender positions, crossing categories and identities often within the same viewing situation.

A rethinking of the processes of identification with the image has been crucial to new concepts of the gaze. Writers working in queer theory, a field that grew out of the gay and lesbian studies field of the 1980s, have been engaged in the project of moving away from identity-based readings of spectator relations and looking practices. One of the most powerful set of claims in spectatorship theory of the 1990s was the proposition that looking practices and pleasure in looking for any human subject are not tied to the spectator's biological sex or social gender position. To look "as a man," "as a woman," or "as a lesbian," for example, may be performed by a human subject of any sexual and social identity through processes of fantasy and identification. Associations and affiliations we make with and through processes of identification never preclude occupying the "wrong" subject position in our relationships with images. In her book *Uninvited,* film theorist Patricia White argues for a theory of lesbian spectatorship, mining works such as Hitchcock's *Rebecca* (1940) to make a case for lesbian representability in texts previously unrecognized as being open to readings of lesbian texts and subtexts.[27]

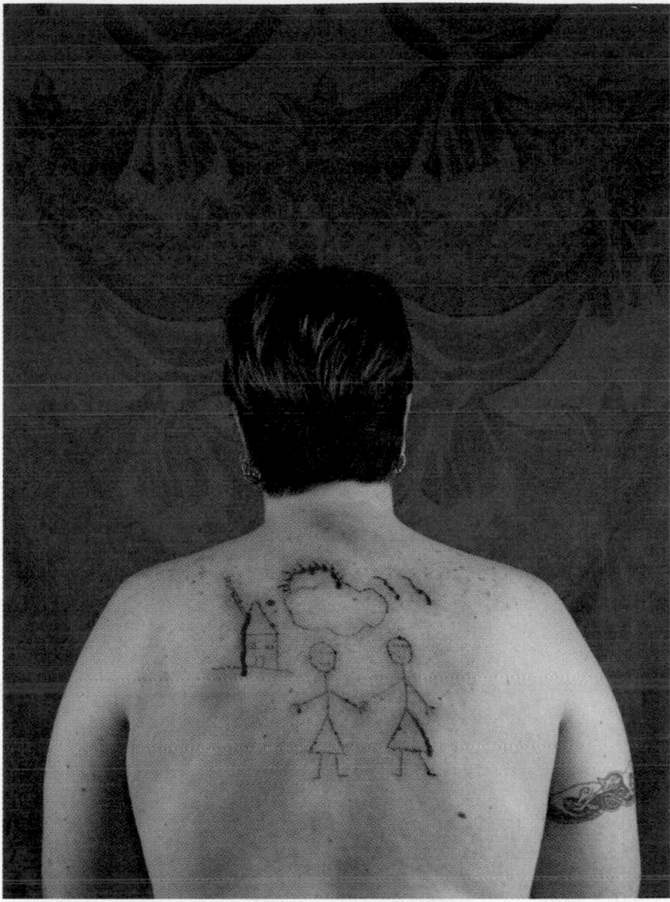

FIG. 3.25
Catherine Opie, *Self-Portrait / Cutting*, 1993

One tactic for mediating the dynamics of the gaze is to self-reflexively refuse to participate in its spatial domain. We can see the implications of the shift in the idea of what constitutes the gaze and the relationship of spectatorship and identification in the work of an artist such as Catherine Opie, whose photographic portraits examine lesbian subjectivity in everyday life. In this self-portrait, Opie turns away from the camera. Her back is a tableau on display for the spectator, but it is also a surface onto which the codes of heteronormativity have been painfully etched, with the childlike imagery of two stick figures in skirts holding hands before an image of a house with a peaceful sky above. The iconography is about the idyllic childhood dream of normative family life—the house, the couple holding hands, the puffy cloud—but the violence with which it has been etched on Opie's back and the image of the two women holding hands as the central element in the childhood dream of normativity demand that we reread the image as a reworking of the codes of normativity to allow lesbian partnership to be an element of the dream of family.

As we have noted, these changing views of scholarship and the idea of what kinds of images were important objects of intellectual inquiry have been paralleled by trends in image making across the fields of art, media, and advertising that reflect new concepts of gender and aesthetic conventions. Contemporary visual culture involves a highly complex array not only of images and spectators but also of gazes. Whereas many contemporary advertisements continue to sell products through traditional gender codes by portraying women in demure, seductive poses for a possessive male gaze, other ads play off these traditions by reversing them and showing both the pleasure of looking at men as objects and the power of women in action. In this Reebok ad (fig. 3.26), we see a woman in action, exercising in her apartment, oblivious to our gaze and determined in her body movements. This ad sells self-empowerment (exercise, control of one's body) and self-determination ("I believe that a man who wants something soft and cuddly to hold should buy a teddy bear."). Certainly, the male gaze still operates in this image in that we are invited to assess this woman's appearance in looking at her, no matter our gender or sexual orientation. Yet this woman's active stance and defiant words are resistant to the traditional power dynamic of the gaze. This ad is a good example of what Robert Goldman calls "commodity feminism," in which feminist concepts of empowerment and strength are

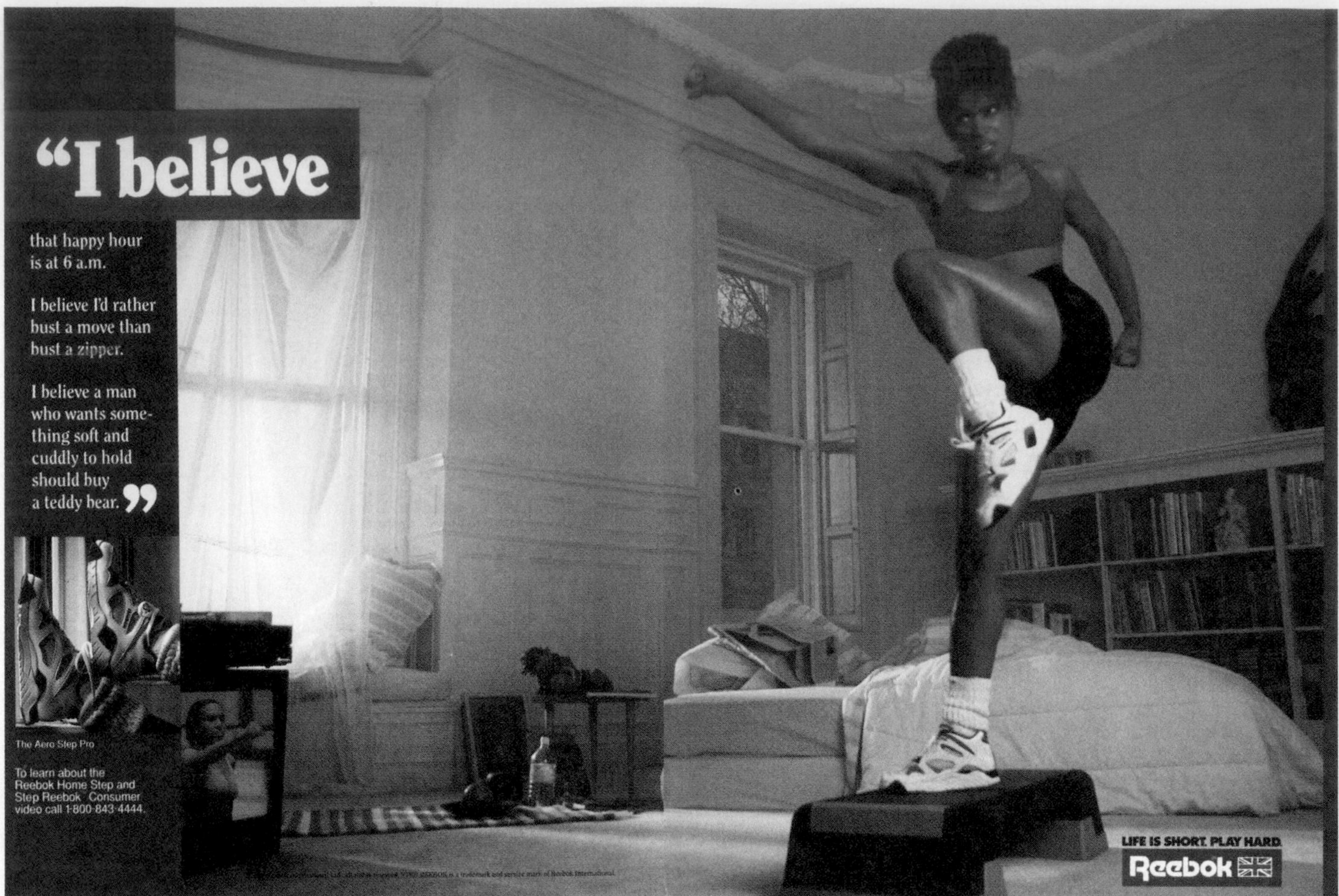

"I believe
that happy hour is at 6 a.m.
I believe I'd rather bust a move than bust a zipper.
I believe a man who wants something soft and cuddly to hold should buy a teddy bear."
The Aero Step Pro
To learn about the Reebok Home Step and Step Reebok Consumer video call 1-800-843-4444.
LIFE IS SHORT. PLAY HARD.
Reebok

FIG. 3.26
Reebok ad, 1990s

translated into the mandate that working out, producing a tight, lean, muscled female body, and consuming products such as running shoes is equivalent to having control over one's life.[28]

If the former tradition of imaging men was to show men in action (as we have noted, John Berger wrote that "men act, women appear"), since the early 1990s the influence of gay pornography (through the borrowing of image codes and in terms of the work of several high-profile fashion photographers) has dramatically changed the way masculinity is represented in consumer culture. This trend began with several famous campaigns, such as the Calvin Klein jeans campaigns during the 1990s, that used homoerotic codes in their images. What this means is that men are depicted as both masculine and as objects of the gaze, that they are increasingly posed in what would have been seen as demure, almost passive, poses before the camera. Yet, as codes of power and the gaze are changing, this is not read as disempowering them. Rather, these kinds of images, in which fashion designers and photographers are playing with gender and sexuality in order to establish themselves as cutting edge and trendy, represent a range of sexual roles and gendered power relations. In this Dolce & Gabanna ad, the male figure lies before the camera. He reclines before our gaze, he is there for us to look at, yet he has not lost his masculine power.

From feminist theories of female spectatorship forward, the idea of the subject as an ideal rather than as a historically or socially specific being has come under serious scrutiny. One of the central tensions between older modernist and current theories

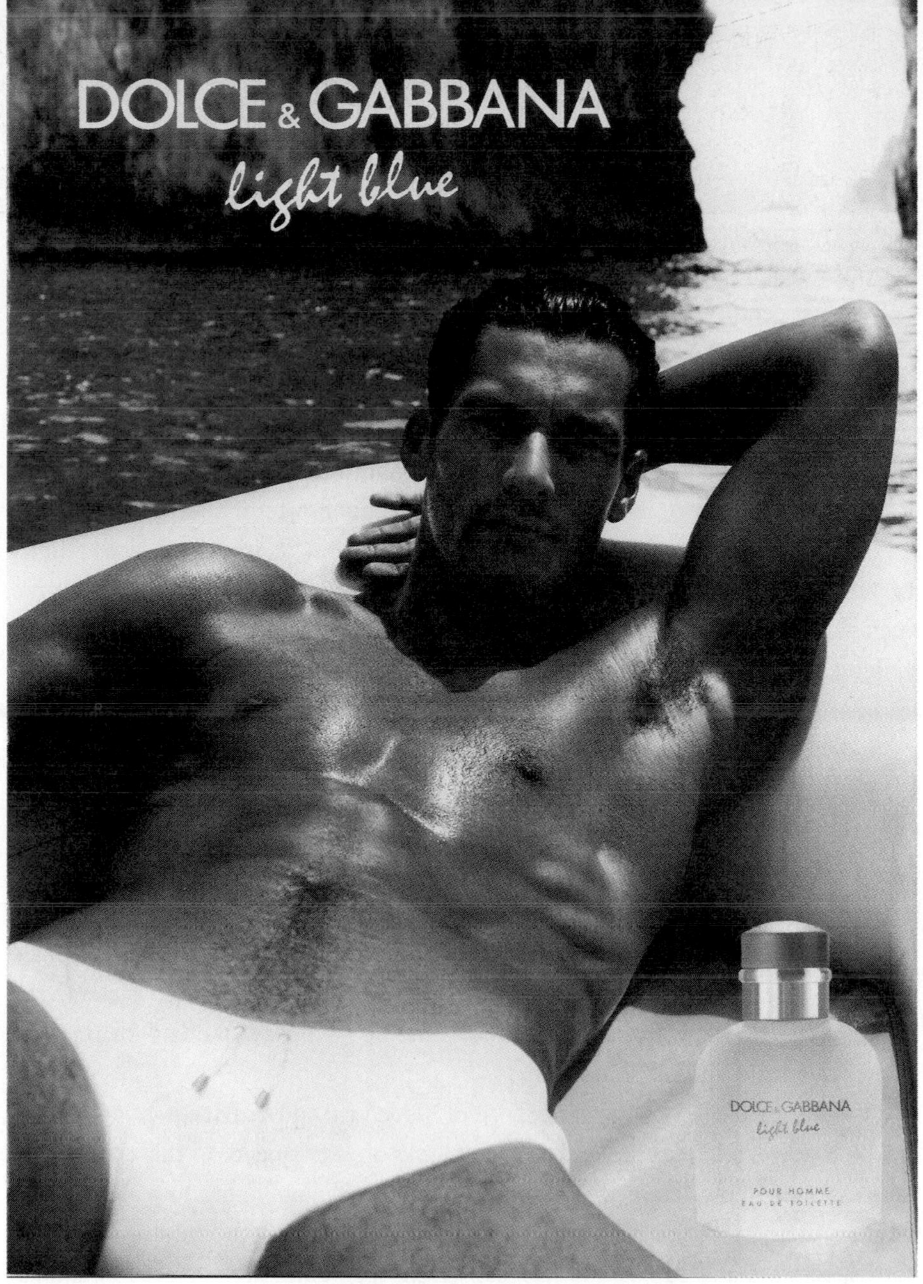

FIG. 3.27
Dolce & Gabbana ad, 2007

of film and media spectatorship is that between the construction of the ideal spectator and the recognition of the multiple subject positions and social contexts from which we view films. The concept of regressive cinematic viewers who are encouraged to repress their identities and to identify with the image has been replaced by a broader set of models about the multiplicity of gazes and looks that mediate power between viewers and objects of the gaze and that are much more allied with postmodern theory.

The concept of the spectator is one way of understanding practices of looking; it does not fully account for the engaged viewer practices we discussed in chapter 2. It has come into question with the kinds of viewing practices introduced by television and the digital screens of twentieth-century media forms. Television scholar Lynn Spigel has described the introduction of the home theater in postwar culture—the social space of the living room in which the family assembles as a group before the television set, which took the place of the hearth.[29] Televisual spectatorship and the field of the gaze it constructs are radically different from that of the movie theater or the museum gallery. With the multiplication of screens and image fields in everyday twenty-first century life, the look of any one subject can be divided not only among multiple screens within a given space (the computer displays and projections within a classroom, a home, and a library, which may include even the screen of one's cell phone or PDA) but also among multiple frames within any given screen as we keep open various files and programs and move among them, even looking away from these files to the screen of a television or a classroom projector and back again.[30]

Importantly, contemporary theories that engage with issues of race, ethnicity, and sexuality as factors in the construction of the gaze allow for much more nuanced understandings of the processes of identification with the image and the complex ways in which images interpellate spectators. This brings us back to where we began, with the human subject and the critique of the notion of the individual. It is precisely the intervention of such theories about looking and subjectivity that has helped us to rethink the relationship of looking to subjectivity. And the marketplace of images has become more self-conscious, playing with issues of power and looking, and in the process has produced new image codes in film, television, advertising, and on the Web. For instance, one might say that the exhibitionist tendencies of webcams might replicate the dynamics of the male gaze, yet one might also argue that the kind of image performance that we see through the use of webcams asks us to come up with new models for thinking about voyeurism and exhibitionism.

Images are central to the experience of modernity and provide a complex field in which power relations are exercised and looks are exchanged. In this chapter, we have examined how the media of photography and film are implicated in particular ways in the systems of power and knowledge of the modern state and how, as both spectators and subjects of images, we engage in and are subject to complex practices of looking and being looked at. In both chapters 2 and 3 we have focused on the role of the viewer in making meaning of the image and on theories about the viewer as subject. In the next chapter, we trace the history of how visual technologies have affected both concepts of realism and ideas about the political in the visual field.

Notes

1. Jürgen Habermas, "Modernity—An Unfinished Project," in *The Anti-Aesthetic*, ed. Hal Foster, trans. Seyla Ben-Habib, 3–15 (Port Townsend, Wash.: Bay Press, 1983).
2. Bruno Latour, *We Have Never Been Modern*, trans. Catherine Porter (Cambridge, Mass: Harvard University Press, 1993).
3. Michel Foucault, "The Repressive Hypothesis," in *The History of Sexuality: An Introduction*, vol. 1, trans. Robert Hurley, 15–49 (New York: Vintage, [1976] 1990).
4. Quoted in Jacqueline Rose, *Sexuality in the Field of Vision* (London: Verso, 1986), 190. See also Jacques Lacan, *Freud's Papers on Technique, 1953–54*, trans. John Forrester (New York: Norton, 1988).
5. Judith Mayne, "Paradoxes of Spectatorship," in *Viewing Positions: Ways of Seeing Film*, ed. Linda Williams, 157 (New Brunswick, N.J.: Rutgers University Press, 1995).

6. Michel Foucault, *The Order of Things: An Archaeology of the Human Sciences,* 3–16 (New York: Vintage, [1970] 1994).
7. Michel Foucault, "Panopticism," in *Discipline and Punish: The Birth of the Prison,* trans. Alan Sheridan, 195–228 (New York: Vintage, 1979).
8. Foucault, *Discipline and Punish,* 25.
9. Jacques Derrida, *Of Grammatology,* trans. Gayatri Chakravorty Spivak (Baltimore: Johns Hopkins Press, 1974). See also "Translator's Preface," liv-lxvii.
10. Edward Said, *Orientalism* (New York: Vintage, 1979), 1.
11. Malek Alloula, *The Colonial Harem* (Minneapolis: University of Minnesota Press, 1986).
12. Jill Beaulieu and Mary Roberts, eds., *Orientalism's Interlocutors: Painting, Architecture, Photography* (Durham, N.C.: Duke University Press, 2002).
13. Jane Gallop, *Reading Lacan,* 38 (Ithaca, N.Y.: Cornell University Press, 1985).
14. Griselda Pollock, "Modernity and the Spaces of Femininity," in *Vision and Difference: Femininity, Feminism and Histories of Art,* 70–81 (New York: Routledge, 1988).
15. John Berger, *Ways of Seeing,* 47 (New York: Penguin, 1972).
16. Laura Mulvey, "Visual Pleasure and Narrative Cinema," in *Visual and Other Pleasures,* 14–26 (Bloomington: Indiana University Press, 1989). Originally published in 1975 in *Screen.*
17. Tania Modleski, *The Women Who Knew Too Much: Hitchcock and Feminist Theory,* 73–85 (New York: Routledge, 1988).
18. See, for example, Kobena Mercer, "Looking for Trouble," in Henry Abelove, David Halperin, and Michele Aina Barale, eds., *The Lesbian and Gay Studies Reader,* 350–59 (New York: Routledge, 1993); and Kobena Mercer, "Reading Racial Fetishism: the Photographs of Robert Mapplethorpe," in *Fetishism as Cultural Discourse,* ed. Emily Apter and William Pietz (Ithaca, N.Y.: Cornell University Press, 1993).
19. See *Wack! Art and the Feminist Revolution,* ed. Cornelia Butler and Lisa Gabrielle Mark (Cambridge, Mass.: MIT Press, 2007). Catalogue for the exhibition of the same title originating at the Museum of Contemporary Art, Los Angeles, in March 2007.
20. Laura Mulvey, "Afterthoughts on 'Visual Pleasure and Narrative Cinema' Inspired by King Vidor's *Duel in the Sun* (1946)," in *Visual and Other Pleasures,* 29–38.
21. Mary Anne Doane, *The Desire to Desire: The Woman's Film of the 1940s* (Bloomington: Indiana University Press, 1987).
22. See Marita Sturken, *Thelma & Louise* (London: British Film Institute, 2000).
23. See Miriam Hansen, *Babel and Babylon: Spectatorship in American Silent Film* (Cambridge, Mass.: Harvard University Press, 1991) on spectatorship and the public sphere; Jackie Stacey, *Star Gazing: Hollywood Cinema and Female Spectatorship* (New York: Routledge, 1994) on reception studies of cinema and audience; Jacqueline Bobo, *Black Women as Cultural Readers* (New York: Columbia University Press, 1995), on black spectatorship; David Rodowick, *The Difficulty of Difference: Psychoanalysis, Sexual Difference, and Film Theory* (New York: Routledge, 1991), on theories of identification; Manthia Diawara, "Black Spectatorship: Problems of Identification and Resistance," *Screen,* 29.4 (Autumn 1988), 66–79, and bell hooks, "The Oppositional Gaze," in *Black Looks: Race and Representation,* 115–32 (Boston: South End Press, 1993), on the resistance of black spectators; and special issues of *Camera Obscura* 36 (September 1995) and *Wide Angle* (13.3 and 13.4, 1991) and Michele Wallace, *Dark Designs and Visual Culture* (Durham, N.C.: Duke University Press, 2004). In addition, Kaja Silverman, in her book *Male Subjectivities at the Margins,* shows how articulations of desire and gaze relationships situate men complexly in terms of the spectrum of sexual identifications and affinities available in the cinematic field of the gaze (New York: Routledge, 1992).
24. Coco Fusco and Brian Wallis, *Only Skin Deep: Changing Visions of the American Self* (New York: Abrams, 2003).
25. Linda Williams, *Hard Core: Power, Pleasure, and the Frenzy of the Visible* (Berkeley: University of California Press, 1989).
26. Linda Williams, ed., *Porn Studies* (Durham, N.C.: Duke University Press, 2004).
27. See Judith Mayne, *Framed: Lesbians, Feminists, and Media Culture* (Minneapolis: University of Minnesota Press, 2000); Chris Straayer, *Deviant Eyes, Deviant Bodies: Sexual Re-Orientation in Film and Video* (New York: Columbia University Press, 1996); and Patricia White, *Uninvited: Classical Hollywood Cinema and Lesbian Representability* (Bloomington: Indiana University Press, 1999).
28. Robert Goldman, *Reading Ads Socially* (New York: Routledge, 1992).
29. Lynn Spigel, *Make Room for TV: Television and the Family Ideal in Postwar America* (Chicago: University of Chicago Press, 1992).
30. See Anne Friedberg, *The Virtual Window: From Alberti to Microsoft* (Cambridge, Mass.: MIT Press, 2006).

Further Reading

Baudry, Jean-Louis. "The Apparatus: Metapsychological Approaches to the Impression of Reality in the Cinema." In *Narrative, Apparatus, Ideology: A Film Theory Reader.* Edited by Philip Rosen, 299–318. New York: Columbia University Press, [1975] 1986)..

———. "Ideological Effects of the Basic Cinematographic Apparatus." In *Narrative, Apparatus, Ideology: A Film Theory Reader.* Edited by Philip Rosen, 286–89. New York: Columbia University Press, [1970] 1986.

Beaulieu, Jill, and Mary Roberts, eds. *Orientalism's Interlocutors: Painting, Architecture, Photography.* Durham, N.C.: Duke University Press, 2002.

Bergstrom, Janet. "Enunciation and Sexual Difference (part 1)." *Camera Obscura.* 3–4 (Summer 1979): 33–69.

Bobo, Jacqueline. *Black Women as Cultural Readers.* New York: Columbia University Press, 1995.

Butler, Cornelia, and Lisa Gabrielle Mark, ed. *Wack! Art and the Feminist Revolution.* Cambridge, Mass.: MIT Press, 2007.

Cahoone, Lawrence. *From Modernism to Postmodernism: An Anthology.* Oxford, UK: Blackwell, 1996.

Cartwright, Lisa. *Moral Spectatorship: Technologies of Voice and Affect in Postwar Representations of the Child.* Durham, N.C.: Duke University Press, 2008.

Cowie, Elizabeth. *Representing the Woman: Cinema and Psychoanalysis.* Minneapolis: University of Minnesota Press, 1997.

Derrida, Jacques. *Of Grammatology.* Translated by Gayatri Chakravorty Spivak. Baltimore: Johns Hopkins Press, 1974.

Diawara, Manthia. "Black Spectatorship: Problems of Identification and Resistance." *Screen,* 29.4 (Autumn 1988), 66–79.

Doane, Mary Ann. *The Desire to Desire: The Woman's Film of the 1940s.* Bloomington: Indiana University Press, 1987.

———. *Femmes Fatales: Feminism, Film Theory, Psychoanalysis.* New York: Routledge, 1991.

Edwards, Elizabeth, ed. *Anthropology and Photography 1860–1920.* New Haven: Yale University Press, 1992.

Erens, Patricia, ed. *Issues in Feminist Film Criticism.* Bloomington: Indiana University Press, 1991.

Foucault, Michel. *Madness and Civilization: A History of Insanity in the Age of Reason.* Translated by Richard Howard. New York: Routledge, [1961] 2001.

———. *The Order of Things: An Archaeology of the Human Sciences.* New York: Vintage, [1970] 1994.

———. *Discipline and Punish: The Birth of the Prison.* Translated by Alan Sheridan. New York: Vintage, 1979.

———. *Power/Knowledge: Selected Interviews and Other Writings 1972–77.* Edited by Colin Gordon. Translated by Colin Gordon, Leo Marshall, John Mepham, and Kate Soper. New York: Pantheon, 1980.

———. *The History of Sexuality: An Introduction.* Vol. 1. Translated by Robert Hurley. New York: Vintage, [1976] 1990.

Gallop, Jane. *Reading Lacan.* Ithaca, N.Y.: Cornell University Press, 1985.

Giddens, Anthony. *The Consequences of Modernity.* Stanford, Calif.: Stanford University Press, 1990.

Gillespie, Michael Allen. *The Theological Origins of Modernity.* Chicago: University of Chicago Press, 2008.

Green, David. "Classified Subjects: Photography and Anthropology: The Technology of Power." *Ten 8,* 14 (1984): 30–37.

Habermas, Jürgen. "Modernity—An Unfinished Project." In *The Anti-Aesthetic.* Edited by Hal Foster. Translated by Seyla Ben-Habib. Port Townsend, Wash.: Bay Press, 1983, 3–15.

Hansen, Miriam. *Babel and Babylon: Spectatorship in American Silent Film.* Cambridge, Mass.: Harvard University Press, 1991.

Holmlund, Chris. "When Is a Lesbian Not a Lesbian? The Lesbian Continuum and the Mainstream Femme Film." *Camera Obscura*, 25–26 (May 1991), 145–78.

hooks, bell. "The Oppositional Gaze." In *Black Looks: Race and Representation*. Boston: South End Press, 1993, 115–32.

Kaplan, E. Ann, ed. *Feminism and Film*. New York: Oxford University Press, 2000.

Latour, Bruno. *We Have Never Been Modern*. Translated by Catherine Porter. Cambridge, Mass: Harvard University Press, 1993.

Lutz, Catherine A., and Jane L. Collins. *Reading National Geographic*. Chicago: University of Chicago Press, 1993.

Mayne, Judith. *Cinema and Spectatorship*. New York: Routledge, 1993.

———. *Framed: Lesbians, Feminists, and Media Culture*. Minneapolis: University of Minnesota Press, 2000.

Metz, Christian. *Film Language: A Semiotics of Cinema*. Translated by Michael Taylor. New York: Oxford University Press, 1974.

Modleski, Tania. *The Women Who Knew Too Much: Hitchcock and Feminist Theory*. New York: Routledge, 1988.

Mulvey, Laura. *Visual and Other Pleasures*. Bloomington: Indiana University Press, 1989.

Nichols, Bill, ed. *Movies and Methods*. Berkeley: University of California Press, 1976.

Penley, Constance, ed. *Feminism and Film Theory*. New York: Routledge, 1988.

Rodowick, David. *The Difficulty of Difference: Psychoanalysis, Sexual Difference, and Film Theory*. New York: Routledge, 1991.

Rose, Jacqueline. *Sexuality in the Field of Vision*. London: Verso, 1986.

Russo, Vito. *The Celluloid Closet: Homosexuality in the Movies*. New York: HarperCollins, 1987.

Said, Edward. *Orientalism*. New York: Vintage, 1979.

Silverman, Kaja. *Male Subjectivity at the Margins*. New York: Routledge, 1992.

———. *Threshold of the Visible World*. New York: Routledge, 1996.

Stacey, Jackie. *Star Gazing: Hollywood Cinema and Female Spectatorship*. New York: Routledge, 1994.

Straayer, Chris. *Deviant Eyes, Deviant Bodies: Sexual Re-Orientation in Film and Video*. New York: Columbia University Press, 1996.

Thompson, Krista A. *An Eye for the Tropics: Tourism, Photography, and Framing the Carribean Picturesque*. Durham, N.C.: Duke University Press, 2006.

Weiss, Andrea. "'A Queer Feeling When I Look at You': Female Stars and Lesbian Spectatorship." In *Stardom: Industry of Desire*. Edited by Christine Gledhill. New York: Routledge, 1991, 283–99.

White, Patricia. *Uninvited: Classical Hollywood Cinema and Lesbian Representability*. Bloomington: Indiana University Press, 1999.

Williams, Linda. *Hard Core: Power, Pleasure, and the Frenzy of the Visible*. Berkeley: University of California Press, 1989.

———, ed. *Viewing Positions: Ways of Seeing Film*. New Brunswick, N.J.: Rutgers University Press, 1995.

———, ed. *Porn Studies*. Durham, N.C.: Duke University Press, 2004.

Williams, Raymond. *The Politics of Modernism: Against the New Conformists*. London: Verso, 1989.

Williamson, Judith. "Woman Is an Island: Femininity and Colonialism." In *Studies in Entertainment*. Edited by Tania Modleski. Bloomington: Indiana University Press, 1986, 99–118.

chapter **four**

Realism and Perspective

From Renaissance Painting to Digital Media

What do we mean when we describe one image or media text as "realistic" and another as "abstract"? We tend to take for granted the idea that images that reproduce the way something "really" looks are realistic. Realism is an important aspect of our sense of ethics as citizens in a world in which images proliferate as forms of communication and expression. We expect photojournalists to observe the conventions of realism when they document events for news stories. When they don't, we object. Most of us probably assume that we know realistic work when we see it.

In this chapter, we show that realism has been linked to a surprisingly varied set of conventions and approaches. Moreover, the same conventions have been linked to a diverse range of political agendas, demonstrating Saussure's dictum that the link between the signifier and the signified (between the image/object/sound and its meaning) is arbitrary and contextually specific. It would not be accurate, we propose, to draw a clear line between conventions of realism and conventions of abstraction. In looking back through the history of visual culture, we find many realisms and many motives and meanings linked to the familiar conventions, such as linear perspective, that have become synonymous with realism. Abstract images and art movements have in many cases incorporated some elements of realism (emphasizing the materiality of paint, for example) while explicitly rejecting other elements strongly associated with realism (perspective, for example), describing them as trickery or illusionism. The division between realism and abstraction is not as clear as we might at first believe. In this chapter, we examine some of the foundational aspects of realism in painting, with attention to what these terms mean in any given historical and political context, focusing on the system of linear perspective that is a cornerstone of pictorial realism in two-dimensional media such as painting, photography, film, and video. By the end of this chapter, we hope that readers will be equipped with a toolbox of techniques through which to discern the many different kinds of visual realism and abstraction at play in the everyday world.

A tenet of realism in the visual arts is that the realist image depicts something as it would be seen by the eye. The function of visual art, however, has not always been to reproduce objects, people, and events in the real world as the eye of the observer would see them. In the few examples of very early Christian art that have survived (the painted ceilings of the underground burial catacombs of Rome dating back to the second century, for example), pictorial elements appear to have served as forms of symbolic communication and expression among members of a marginal and persecuted religious sect whose means of public religious expression were severely limited. Emphasis is placed, in these ceiling paintings, on symbolism. Fish and loaves, for example, probably signified the Eucharist. Variations in scale and mixing of graphic and decorative elements with representational ones in a single scene suggest that concern with symbolism overshadowed any possible concern about making things look as they would to the eye.

As the Church acquired legal recognition and gained in stature, the production and display of Christian iconographic art and artifacts, from manuscripts and paintings to hand-hewn icons, gained broader support and recognition. By the fourteenth century, Christian works of art took on a new scale of value that surpassed their specific role in religious communication and expression. Patronage of individual artists and ownership and display of their revered original works, by the Renaissance period, was securely organized around the Catholic Church and the wealthy ruling families in Europe. By this period, the individual styles of artists and the original works produced in the studios of well-known masters were highly valued beyond their function as expression of religious meaning. By the time of the Renaissance, painting came to be a practice in which many artists explicitly labored to reproduce the appearance of a scene as it would be seen by the eye of an observer. This does not mean that art became more scientific and less spiritual but that the formal science of organizing pictorial space as a replica of what the embodied eye would see took on greater symbolic, spiritual, and philosophical meaning.

Works of art have long been invested with special powers beyond their role in basic symbolic communication and relative to their status as reproductions of what the eye might see. For example, when the tomb of the emperor of China's Chin dynasty, dating back to 200 BCE, was excavated, it was found to hold a clay army of 7,500 life-size clay warriors and horses, apparently placed there to offer protection to the emperor. The clay figures were not identical copies made from the same mold. Rather, they constituted a set of similar but unique figures made of clay coiled and shaped into individualized features and poses. Archaeologists believe they were meant to substitute for real, live soldiers. They believe the figures were put in the tomb to stand in for the actual soldiers whom it had been the practice, during the earlier Shang dynasty, to bury with the dead emperor in order to guard him. We might say this is a kind of realism, insofar as the statues were substitutes for actual soldiers (who must have been grateful for this change in approach to realism!).

In this chapter, we emphasize that reproducibility in images is not just about the capacity of art works and images to be copied (which we discuss in the following chapter) but also about the aim to copy, or reproduce, the real. Art and images are, in one view, a practice dedicated to the visual and material reproduction of things and events in the world. In this view, we might say that there are things in the world and then there are their representations. We might even say that so-called nonrepresentational or abstract art reproduces ideas or that it represents objects and events by abstracting aspects of them (their appearance, structure, or conceptual meaning). Cubism, for example, is an "abstract" art style in which the form of objects is reduced to planar shapes and these planes are then shifted around in space. Finally, reproduction can occur in the relationship between seeing and the work of art, in which seeing is understood to reproduce the real in the form of images that we hold in our thoughts and memories.

It is possible to read the history of art as the history of the relationship between ways of seeing and the forms that representation of the real has taken in different periods. Throughout history, conventions and techniques of representation have both given shape to and been shaped by that culture's particular conventions of seeing—a culture's understanding of how embodied vision works or its understanding of how the mind pictures the world. Conventions of representation in art and image making, we might say, both shape and reproduce their contemporary ways of seeing, and in so doing also give rise to and reproduce worldviews. With this relationship of visual reproduction, embodied seeing, and worldview in mind, we examine how visual codes of representing the real, and the technique of perspective and challenges to it, have shaped ways of thinking about the world and the place of humans within it.

Visual Codes and Historical Meaning

In looking at images from history, it is important to note initially that image codes and conventions reproduce historical meanings. Because visual codes and conventions change over time, we look at images of the past differently today than they were viewed during the time in which they were created. A viewer may make assumptions about the date of an image based not only on its content but also on its style, medium, and formal qualities. For instance, we might assume that a painting composed in a classical style was made prior to the modernist period or that a sepia-toned or black-and-white photographic family portrait predates the 1960s, when color photography became more common in the home photography market. Particular visual styles can thus help us to generally date an image, evoking an earlier moment in history.

FIG. 4.1
Julia Margaret Cameron, *Pomona, Portrait of Alice Liddell*, 1872

There are formal aspects of this photograph, for instance, that help us to determine its time period. As viewers, we can make certain assumptions about when it was produced, even if we know nothing about its origins. Its tone is soft brown sepia. Sepia toning of photographic prints was a common technique in nineteenth-century photography. The chemical conversion that occurred through sepia toning, a process using a chemical secreted from cuttlefish, made the print more resistant to the process of decomposition over time. As a result, a larger percentage of photographs that were toned this way have withstood the effects of time than have the untreated black-and-white prints of the era. Even if you did not know these facts, you probably were able to guess that this photograph was old because this sepia color has become a familiar signifier of an aged image in photographs and films. Other, more literal elements of the photograph hint at its age. The woman in the portrait is dressed in a style of the Victorian era. The uneven focus, and especially the soft focus at the edges of the frame that may invoke a sense of memory fading, suggests an era when the photographic process was not refined. This image is, in fact, from the Victorian era. It is photographer Julia Margaret Cameron's 1872 photograph titled *Pomona*. This is a portrait of Alice Liddell, the inspiration for *Alice in Wonderland*, at age twenty. Discussions about the photograph often make note of this fact, which adds to the photograph's value (by serving as a document of a historically significant person).

Historians and experts on photography value Cameron's portraits as important works in part because they stand apart stylistically from the prints of commercial portrait artists of the late nineteenth century. In the more prevalent style, the sitter's stature was often conveyed through stiff, formal poses and crisply focused detail. Cameron, whose photographic subjects were frequently women, capitalized on the problem of keeping the image in focus during the length of time needed for each exposure by using soft focus as an aspect of making photographic meaning. She compounded the ethereal effect of soft focus by placing her subjects in stylized naturalistic settings. Liddell's hair flows free, weaving into the leaves and branches that surround her. This is not the restrained bun or concealing hat, or the formal interior, that one would typically expect to see in a Victorian high society portrait.

Though embodying a new aesthetic for its time, Cameron's work also references a prior tradition of artmaking. Cameron's many portraits of women are done in a neoclassical style, a style that revives and reproduces aspects of classical fine art (which we discussed in chapter 3 in relation to neoclassical Orientalist paintings). She participated in the aesthetic and formal strategies of a group of unconventional painters and sculptors of the Victorian era who called themselves the Pre-Raphaelite Brotherhood. The name signified the group members' admiration for the symbolism and naturalism of the late Medieval and early classical Renaissance artists who worked in the period before the painter Raphael, whose *Small Cowper Madonna* is discussed in chapter 1. The Pre-Raphaelite artists appropriated the naturalistic style of the early Renaissance in their own contemporary aesthetics to make a statement against the prevalent Victorian-era aesthetic, which they saw as a cheapening commercialization of purer ideals. Thus Cameron's style and conventions of photography were not uniquely hers but rather reproduced, along with the Pre-Raphaelite Brotherhood's, a style and set of conventions from early Renaissance painters. In reproducing this style, she offered more than the look of the classical Renaissance era. Cameron's work made a statement not only about the artist's subjective taste (favoring more naturalistic settings, themes, and styles) but also about the politics inherent in the formal choices of media, technique, and aesthetics.

It is possible for an image that looks like this photograph of Liddell to have been made today using older imaging techniques or effects that simulate early photographs and Victorian neoclassical styles and techniques and by posing one's subjects in vintage clothing and settings. Yet, just as Cameron's photographs create a different meaning from the classical work from which she drew some of her conventions and style, so the use of her techniques and style would convey a different set of meanings now. An identical reproduction would not convey the same values of realism and authenticity. A photograph done in Cameron's well-known style today would signify, among other things, a reference to her neoclassical, Pre-Raphaelite-influenced aesthetic of naturalism, and this would take on meaning with reference to the conventions and media forms of portraiture in style now. We would regard a reproduction of this work's style as a copy of a former realistic style, a nostalgic remake, and not realistic in contemporary terms.

Questions of Realism

Both the Pre-Raphaelites and the neoclassicists revived and reproduced an earlier set of approaches to the representation of human form, and in so doing drew on older forms and meanings to make new meanings in their contemporary context. But they each had different ideas about what techniques and conventions produced the qualities of naturalism, realism, or beauty. By noticing changes in the *aesthetics* and styles of naturalist or realist images over time, we do more than simply chart taste or progress in the history of art. We also follow the development of different ways of seeing, different ways of knowing the world, and different views about value and meaning.

The term *realism* typically refers to a set of conventions or a style of art or representation that is understood at a given historical moment to accurately represent nature or the real or to convey and interpret accurate or universal meanings about people, objects, and events in the world. The goal of realist art is to reproduce reality as it is. But knowing this does not tell us how "reality" is understood in any given culture at any given historical moment or which conventions are considered the right ones for representing reality in any of those contexts. Different forms and techniques of realism have taken precedent at different places and times in history. Different ideas about realism have coexisted throughout history, as well, both across and within cultures. What constitutes realism in a given historical, geographic, or national context can be a charged political issue. Realist approaches have often been put forward as a direct means of political expression, sometimes to challenge the status quo of realist representation. The question for us is not which approach to realism has resulted in the most accurate representations of the world at any given time, but what do the different approaches to realism that we find in art and visual culture tell us about the culture and politics of a given social context. There is no universal standard for realism, and ideas about what constitutes realism can vary dramatically.

FIG. 4.2
Vladimir and Georgii Stenberg, *Man with a Movie Camera* film poster, 1929 © Estate of Vladimir and Georgii Stenberg/RAO, Moscow/VAGA, N.Y.

For example, socialist realism is a classical pictorial representational style of painting that was embraced as state policy in the Soviet Union in 1932. It was advanced as a direct counter to the principles of the Soviet Constructivist Realist Manifesto. The Manifesto, in keeping with the Leninist avant-garde tenets that informed the Russian Revolution in 1917, had proposed that geometric abstraction and objective forms and icons, rather than representational and pictorial styles, best represented the reality of the new, modernizing Soviet state and its forward-looking citizenry. Constructivists emphasized the realistic aspects of showing the artwork's materials and structural elements of form. They suggested that revolutionary artists should expose the means of production to viewers rather than hide technique and equipment from view. This poster for the filmmaker Dziga Vertov's film *Man with a Movie Camera* (1929), by well-known Soviet artists Vladimir and Georgii Stenberg, reveals the camera as a featured element of both the poster and the film itself.

FIG. 4.3
Dziga Vertov, *The Man with a Movie Camera*, 1929

Vertov's film is a primary example of using the strategies of reflexivity to capture the experience of life in the new modern Soviet city. Born Denis Kaufman, he took on a *nom de plume* that in Russian means "spinning top" to reflect his own physical existence as an observer caught up in the giddy motion and excitement of the new Soviet city and the postrevolutionary move to industrialize the nation. His newsreels of the 1920s, titled *Kino Pravda* (or film truth), captured life on the streets of Russia as viewed through the eyes of this "spinning top" cinematographer. The cameraman of Vertov's films seems to float through the dizzying spectacle of the new urban vistas under construction, his camera eye moving from sight to sight in modernity's display of architecture and engineering. *Man with a Movie Camera* is in the vein of the "city symphony" (a phrase used to describe lyrical film celebrations of the spectacular sight of urbanization), in which Vertov reflexively exposes the presence of the cameraman as a roving eye capturing the city for the pleasure of its Soviet viewing subjects. Footage of the cameraman's encounters with his subject matter reflexively emphasizes the conventions of filmmaking and viewing. The filmmaker documents the city, turning the camera out to "look back" at the camera filming him (and thus at "us" seated collectively in the audience). The seats of an empty film theater shot from a position at the rear of the audience fold open mechanically as if to invite us to be aware of our own status as viewers and to participate in this mass spectacle of urban transformation.

Vertov's film embodies a kind of realism in its attention to the day-to-day life of the Soviet people, though it is edited together in an abstract and fragmented, non-narrative fashion. Vertov's film-truth approach offers his viewers a practice of looking that glances and abstracts through the movement of the camera eye's framing and through the editing of fragments, allowing the viewer to see Soviet life from multiple perspectives in rapid succession. But each fragment captures the reality of everyday life (a factory process, a child playing) and the conjoining of fragments could also be said to be realist in its capturing of the frenetic and diverse pace of the city.

Soviet leader Josef Stalin mandated a turn back to classical pictorial realism in the 1930s, advocating a style that became known as socialist realism. This shift is

FIG. 4.4
Serafima Ryangina, *Higher and Higher*, 1934

represented here by one of numerous realist paintings made during this period depicting happy, healthy workers introducing technology to the Soviet countryside during the postrevolution period of modernization. The Stalinist Soviet state aimed to enforce art styles that could be used to promote nationalism among people in the countryside unfamiliar with the newer, more abstract style of work that was seen as more realist by the Constructivist avant-garde in the 1920s. Under Stalin's mandate of pictorial realism, it became very dangerous to make abstract art. Some of those artists who continued to produce abstract work were exiled to Siberian work camps. In 1974, the abstract painters Oscar Rabine and Evgeny Rukhin organized a public display of the unofficial abstract art being made by artists who defied the state mandate. They hung the works in a Moscow urban forest because indoor spaces were deemed off-limits for this kind of show. Officials used water cannons and bulldozers to tear the exhibition down, damaging and destroying many of the works in the process. Rukhin died in a mysterious fire at his art studio in the following year.

The introduction of socialist realism in the Soviet Union coincided temporally with the introduction of Poetic Realism in France, but in this case realism served a different sort of political agenda. Poetic realism is an approach to filmmaking developed in France during the 1930s in opposition to the narrative film style that prevailed in the French mainstream industry films, which were thought to pander to a complacent bourgeoisie in the period before the German invasion of France. It is a dark and lyrical style influenced by surrealism and associated with filmmakers sympathetic to the French Popular Front (an alliance of left-wing political groups). The term *realism* refers to the fact that this film style dramatized the real social conditions of the French working class, mostly through fictional tragic antiheroes. This movement includes such films as Marcel Carné's *Children of Paradise* (1945) and Jean Renoir's *Grand Illusion* (1938) and *The Rules of the Game* (1939). These films influenced Italian neorealist filmmakers of the late 1940s and 1950s, who came to be regarded as realists as well. Italian film critics, including Michelangelo Antonioni and Luchino Visconti, who were blocked from writing about politics in the magazine *Cinema* by its editor (who was the son of the Italian Fascist Benito Mussolini), turned to filmmaking to comment on the bleak economy and politics of post-World War II Italy. They used untrained actors from the working class and poor of Italy and filmed on locations such as the urban ghettoes of Rome and the poverty-stricken countryside of the rural south. Italian neorealist films such as Visconti's *Obsession* (1943), Roberto Rossellini's *Rome, Open City* (1945), and Vittorio De Sica's *Bicycle Thieves* (1948) introduced a new style of narrative fiction filmmaking that combined ironic and farcical political allegory with stark depictions of postwar poverty and ideological despair. As we can see, poetic realism and Italian neorealism relied on different formal and aesthetic conventions to evoke the real. Each style of realism expresses a particular worldview that vies with other realisms and other worldviews in particular social contexts.

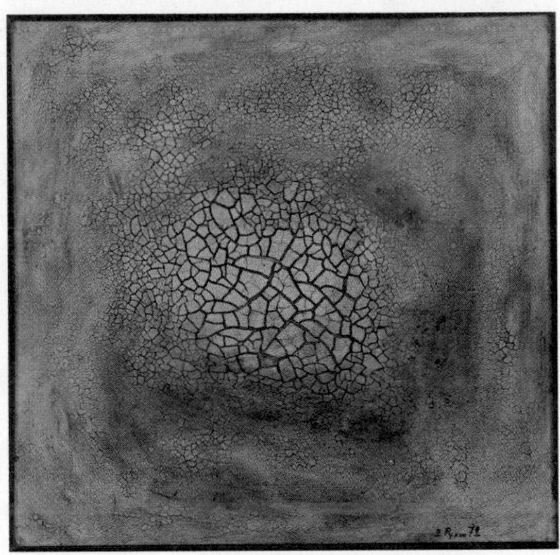

FIG. 4.5
Evgeny Rukhin, *Untitled*, 1972, Collection of Art4.RU Contemporary Art Museum, Moscow

For centuries, art's function was to reflect truths about society and nature back to subjects in the world. But, as the preceding examples show, ideas about what is truth and how the inquiry into truth and its representation is best conducted have varied. Michel Foucault, in his book *The Order of Things*, used the term *episteme* to describe the way that an inquiry into truth is organized in a given era. An episteme is an accepted, dominant mode of acquiring and organizing knowledge in a given period of history. Understanding the work of signs is an important means to identifying the episteme or dominant worldview of an era. Each period of history has a different episteme—that is, a different predominant way of ordering things or of organizing and representing knowledge about things. The episteme of the classical period is different from the epistemes of the modern and the postmodern periods. But we must keep in mind that later epistemes are not necessarily better or more advanced epistemes.

We illustrate this point with an example of spatial representation in an Egyptian funerary papyrus. The detail shown here is taken from the British Museum's second facsimile reproduction of the Papyrus of Ani (fig. 4.6), a copy of a funerary papyrus dated 240 BCE. The manuscript's illustrations (or illuminations) are organized in the form of vignettes, some with narrative or descriptive hieroglyphic text within the frame of each distinct drawing. In this detail, the Elysian fields are represented as if from above. But this seeming aerial view serves as a space in which text and image are organized sequentially, like a contemporary comic book. The composition does not suggest illusion of depth. Objects and figures are not consistently depicted as a viewing subject might see them if models were used to represent this scene in an actual physical space, even if it were seen from above. Space is organized instead according

FIG. 4.6
Papyrus from the Book of the Dead of Ani, Thebes, Egypt, Nineteenth Dynasty, c. 1250 BCE

to both spatial and pictorial codes of symbolism in which relative size and position in the frame signify the sequence of reading, the relative status of different figures, and other concepts. Spatial logic does not reflect the scene as it would be seen by eye. But this does not mean that the representation is primitive or that spatial logic is undeveloped. Rather, other epistemic systems of logic are at work here than those to which we are accustomed, and more than one way of using space is being invoked at once.

Out of these kinds of systems of symbolism and multiple spatial logics, both of which remained dominant in art in varying ways through the medieval period, perspective emerged as a set of techniques for bringing depth to two-dimensional pictorial space during the Renaissance. The organization of objects in space as seen from the position of a single fixed subject positioned before the frame as window on the world was not yet a dominant epistemic model in the representation of the world prior to the Renaissance, even if we can identify earlier discussions about perspective (Plato, for example, regarded techniques for rendering depth as a kind of deception, not realism) and earlier instances of drawings showing depth in the ancient period (in Roman Pompeiian wall paintings, for example, there are some examples of drawing that approximate depth). Our interest in perspective is not in its origins, however, but in its emergence as both a dominant representational method and a metaphor, in science as well as in art, of a dominant episteme.

Our discussion of realism that follows focuses on the role of perspective in painting and its relationship to an artistic episteme that dominated for many centuries. We then turn to the incorporation of aspects of perspectival space into the camera obscura and the photographic camera in the nineteenth century. Perspective has had a long life in different media forms. It has held strong as a signifier of realism across different periods and different epistemes, from the Renaissance to the present.

We focus on perspective as one of many possible visual systems because it allows us to consider the ways in which images can function as reproductions not only of the world and the objects and events in it but also of ways of seeing.

The History of Perspective

The word *perspective* comes from the Latin *perspicere*, meaning "to see clearly," "to inspect," or "to look through." Perspective refers to a set of systems or mechanisms used to produce representations of objects in space as if seen by an observer through a window or frame. In perspective, the size and detail of objects depicted corresponds to their relative distance from the imagined position of the observer. Artists, draftsmen, and designers have used the techniques and systems associated with perspective intensively since the Renaissance, incorporating and influencing research in mathematics, physics, and psychology about the mechanics of light, the eye, laws of optics, and mental aspects of perception.

We can trace the roots of perspective back to early sources, such the optical studies of Euclid, who demonstrated that light travels in straight lines, or the *Opticae Thesaurus Alhazani* (1572), a Latin translation of the tenth-century writings of Abu Ali Al-hasen Ibn Alhasen (Alhazen), a Muslim mathematician and astronomer. We begin our discussion about perspective, however, with the early Renaissance, because this is the period during which artists actively pursued the development of techniques for making paintings and drawings based on the model of a spectator situated before a scene as if looking through a window or screen. The Renaissance is the historical era that art historians have identified as the point from which perspective evolved as not simply another option in a battery of techniques of pictorial representation but as an important instrument in the era's episteme. It is important to stress that perspective was not simply a tool for representation. It has been an integral part of the epistemes of each era from the Renaissance forward, shaping practices of looking and serving as a metaphor for knowledge and being. Yet perspective has not been used in the same way or to the same ends in every era.

During the scientific revolution that took place from the mid-fifteenth through the seventeenth centuries, developments in science, in fields such as navigation, astronomy, and biology, prompted radical changes in the European worldview. These changes involved an erosion of the role of the Church in cultural and political authority. Many new scientific ideas, such as Galileo's theories about planetary movement, were seen as a threat to the Church and were the source of difficult struggle (Galileo was tried, for instance, for heresy for his scientific ideas). However, by the eighteenth century, science had emerged as a dominant social force. The Enlightenment, an eighteenth-century intellectual movement, saw an embrace of the importance of science and the concepts of rationalism and progress. The Enlightenment promised that the power of human reason would overcome superstition, end ignorance through the development of scientific knowledge, bring prosperity through the technical mastery of nature, and introduce justice and order to human affairs. Rationalism and the elevation of science and technology, trends associated with the philosopher and mathematician René Descartes, were thus firmly established in this time period and would lay the foundations for modernity beginning in the seventeenth century.

The linear perspective system demonstrated by the goldsmith and architect Filippo Brunelleschi in the early 1400s is widely regarded as the major turning point in perspective's emergence as a dominant way of organizing two-dimensional visual space. The system introduced by Brunelleschi, which was like the one later described in a book by Leone Battista Alberti, involved the concept of regarding the picture as a kind of mirror or window frame through which one sees the world. A famous story told about Brunelleschi by his biographer Antonio Manetti concerns perspectival drawing. Brunelleschi, the story goes, painted onto the surface of a mirror the outlines of the baptistery of the Florence cathedral for which he would later design a dome that would be regarded as his most important architectural accomplishment. The drawing followed the lines reflected in the mirror exactly. When he continued the outlines beyond the point where the buildings ended, he noted that they converged at the horizon. After completing the drawing, he had viewers face the baptistery and then peer through the back of the mirror-painting via a small peephole he had drilled into in its center. Another mirror was then positioned facing the viewer, allowing the viewer to see that the painting on the first mirror, reflected in the second mirror, looked nearly identical to the actual view from the peephole.[1] Brunelleschi's system differed from earlier, more intuitive and empirical forms of perspective in that the distances in the image could be measured with accuracy against the real structure. Not only did a drawing depict a building, but also the building's plan could be derived and even reproduced from that drawing. The architect studied classical Greek columns and architectural forms to try to derive the underlying system of measurement the Greeks used to arrive at what he regarded as such perfect designs.

The earliest publication on linear perspective as a geometric system was written by Alberti, a scholar who studied law, worked for the Church, and wrote about the lives of saints, painting, architecture, and sculpture before working as an architect. Alberti described linear perspective in Latin (in *De Pictura*, 1435) and then in an Italian version of the text (*Della Pittura*, 1436), making the principles of perspective available to artists who were literate but not scholars of Latin. "I first draw a rectangle of right angles," he wrote, "which I treat just like an open window through which I might look at what will be painted there."[2] Mathematical and optical rules that he argued were derived from nature itself are described as the source for this system, which is illustrated in this diagram. To demonstrate this system of drawing, he used the example of a

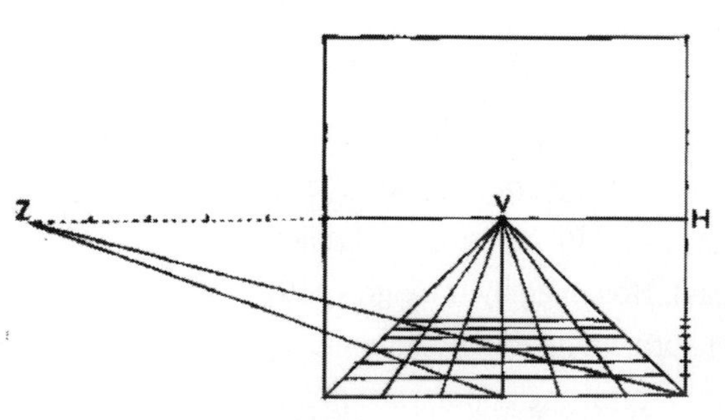

FIG. 4.7
Illustration from *Alberti, De Pictura*, 1435

floor composed of square tiles. The point marked "V" is the vanishing point toward which the parallel lines of the tiled floor converge, giving the effect that the floor recedes into space.

Variations on this system of perspective would be devised with two and three vanishing points, but in all models, a single, fixed spectator position remains the conceptual anchor. As Anne Friedberg writes in *The Virtual Window: From Alberti to Microsoft*, the trope of the window as the frame through which seeing is organized has a surprisingly long and relatively uncontested life in practices of mimetic representation, from the time of Brunelleschi to the digital era.[3] Friedberg emphasizes that Alberti's window was both a method and a metaphor for organizing space. The window has had a remarkably long life that, she suggests, may have found its culmination in the era of the computer as an optical screen that offers multiple frames and perspectives at once. We return to the visual and spatial logics of digital screens and the mobile and multiple standpoints they offer later in this chapter.

In art history, Alberti's writings on painting and architecture have come to be regarded as important articulations of a new art form. Brunelleschi drew the cathedral in part because he needed to know more about its structure in order to build its dome. Architectural drawing relies on the precision of a representational system that emphasizes the measurability of basic structure of forms in space. Brunelleschi's goals were at first quite different from those of the artists who were commissioned to paint scenes from the scriptures. Their aim was to represent religious views and stories, not to use drawings to plan buildings. When Renaissance artists incorporated perspective into their paintings of scenes from the scriptures, they often included buildings and distant landscapes as a means of referencing the new tool for indicating structures in deep space that Alberti had documented. Like Alberti's floor, landscapes and architectural interiors offered some of the best scenes for looking at and tracing the axes through an imaginary window, because they provided the most obvious and clear lines on which to base a drawing in linear perspective.

The individual body viewed close up was a less easy object to fit into this formula. In the *Cestello Annunciation* (1489) by Sandro Botticelli, a tempera painting on a wooden panel for the Church of the Convent of Cestello that now hangs in the Uffizi Gallery in Florence, the archangel Gabriel and the Virgin Mary are situated in the foreground of the painting. They are standing in an interior space on a tile floor, the lines of which serve to emphasize the painter's use of linear perspective and the single vanishing point, which can be found in the middle of the horizon line made visible in the open doorframe behind Gabriel. Distant buildings are strung along the horizon. The viewer is drawn to look in that direction by the receding path of a winding river. The frame within the frame gives the relatively shallow architectural interior in which the figures are painted an opening onto a second, much deeper space. This use of two spaces, one an architectural interior and one a landscape, allows the painting to contain two framed areas of space, one with high detail and precision but still relatively shallow (the room within the picture frame) and the second containing

FIG. 4.8
Sandro Botticelli, *The Cestello Annunciation*, 1489–90

a very deep space in a relatively small frame (the landscape framed in the doorway). The use of the precisely rendered, close, and relatively shallow architectural space of the room allows the characters to take precedence in the composition. The second space, the landscape, gives the painting a degree of depth that is unusual up to this point in painting's history. Yet the details of natural forms within the space of the landscape (water, trees, and sky) that cannot easily be captured in lines and edges are left relatively undetailed.

The emphasis on representing depth in linear perspective in this image can be seen when we compare it to prior depictions of the Annunciation, a popular subject among European artists. The second tempera panel of the annunciation we show here, the original of which also now hangs in the Uffizi, was painted by Simone Martini in 1333, more than a century and a half before Botticelli painted the *Cestello Annunciation*. This work is a triptych that served as the altarpiece in the Duomo in the city of Siena. In *The Angel and the Annunciation*, figures and objects are oriented in relationship to a relatively unified spatial logic. The space of the room depicted is even more shallow than that of the room in Botticelli's Annunciation, and there is no orientation toward a vanishing point, but some depth is nonetheless clearly indicated. The rendering of the vase and the chair, for example, suggest their positions relative not only to a floor but also to a wall at the deepest plane. Yet certain graphic elements continue to function through other representational codes. For example, a line of Latin text emanates from the archangel's mouth toward Mary, making clear the source and direction of speech. This is not, of course, meant to show what exists in space but rather to represent speech in a means similar to a graphic novel or comic frame. Like the early Egyptian papyrus frame, text (in this case representative of

FIG. 4.9
Simone Martini, *The Annunciation*, 1333

speech) introduces another logic into the frame, interrupting the unity of the visual logic that is based on what a viewer might physically see if positioned before models depicting this scene.

Our point is not simply to see implied depth in this work as a step toward the full-on geometric perspective of the classical period. The codes and conventions in Gothic and early Renaissance works contribute to a range of styles in use later. The symbolic, narrative, and textual strategies of this panel by Martini can be found in contemporary art forms such as the graphic arts and comics. Systems such as the perspectival grid may provide a sort of realism based on the idea of a spectator's fixed point of view, but we might also note that the use of perspective in the Botticelli does little to further the symbolic and the narrative elements so strongly present in Martini's version of the Annunciation and does not offer a means of representing the qualities of indistinct forms not well captured in line, such as the water of the river. Perspective is, rather, a formal exercise that frames an iconic scene. The iconic meaning of the figures, which is religious, stands apart from the iconic meaning of perspective, which is scientific. We might say that, apart from signifying actual space, the presence of perspective in the Botticelli annunciation iconically signifies scientific progress and newer, more advanced ways of seeing. The two meanings, religion and science, stand in tension to one another at this moment in history. As Friedberg observes, with the introduction of the device of the window frame as screen through which we see the world, *how* the world is framed becomes more significant than what is *in* the frame.

Throughout art history, the role of perspective in the formation of a modern scientific worldview has been interpreted in different ways. Recent accounts have stressed a paradox: paintings organized by the conventions of perspective take the fixed gaze of the individual spectator as the organizing locus. But at the same time, the system of perspective displaces the seeing individual with a mechanical device that approximates the human gaze. In 1927, the well-known German art historian Erwin Panofsky proposed that perspective, as it developed from the Renaissance period forward, became the paradigmatic, spatialized form of the modern world-view associated with the rationalist philosophy introduced by Descartes in the seventeenth century.[4] Rationalism is the view that true knowledge of the world derives from reason and not from embodied, subjective experience and empirical observation. Cartesian space, derived from Descartes's theories about rational ways of viewing the world, is contingent on the idea of an all-knowing, all-seeing human subject at the conceptual center of the world. But knowing requires recourse to tools beyond embodied vision. Space conceived on the rationalist model is knowable not just by seeing it but through mapping and measuring it with tools that aid and correct perception by the naked eye. The Cartesian grid, although not the same as Alberti's perspectival system, is an important tool in cartography and in systems for graphic and computer modeling, measuring, locating, and manipulating of forms in three dimensions on a two-dimensional plane. This system was developed in 1637 in two writings in which Descartes brought the geometry of Euclid together with the principles of algebra. In *Discourse on Method*, he introduced the idea of specifying the position of a point or object on a surface, bisecting them with two intersecting axes positioned across a grid. In *La Géométrie*, he developed the model further. By organizing space around three distinct axes, Descartes was able to provide a model for measuring, designing, and manipulating dimensional shapes with great precision. Descartes also mapped a theory of perception that attempted to define several vanishing points from which the dual vision of the eyes creates a scene simultaneously. This image, which was published posthumously in his *Treatise of Man*, attempts to map how perception works in rational, physiological terms.

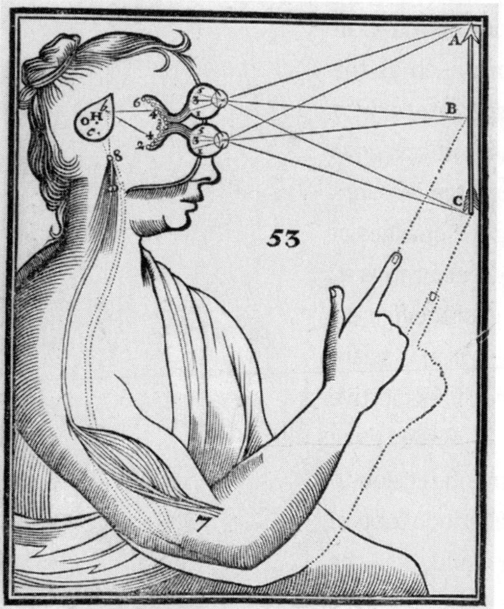

FIG. 4.10
René Descartes, *Theory of Perception*, 1686

Although Cartesian rationalism is often understood to be opposed to empiricism (knowledge based on experience and experiment), Descartes understood the importance of the senses to knowledge. He held, rather, that the body was subject to the laws of physics and operated like a machine but that the senses needed some help from mechanical instruments that embodied rational thought. He famously wrote: "All the management of our lives depends on the senses, and since that of sight is the most comprehensive and noblest of these, there is no doubt that the inventions which serve to augment its power are among the most useful that there can be."[5] His ideas about bodies both as machines and augmented by them are important precedents in the movement toward realms of science in which the senses and cognition are augmented, externalized, and even reproduced (computers, artificial intelligence, and intelligent machines, for example). Perspective embodies this dual interest of Descartes in the body as/and the machine and in the augmentation and displacement of embodied sensory performance through tools of reasoning. These tools, in his view, bring certainty to perception by putting embodied seeing to the test of a machine of instrumental reason.

In composing a picture using the geometric formula of perspective, the position of the observer is the central organizing principle. Yet at the same time the observer's position is *hypothetical*. This mathematical aspect of the system brought certainty to the image through measurements taken with mechanical instruments, augmenting vision's power. The instrument and the formula for seeing built into the system of perspective rendered the image objective, taking the authority of the individual embodied seeing eye and externalizing it. This was done by determining the view according to a set of rules and formulas that provided the safeguard of objectivity derived from the instrument and not from the fallible human observer.

In 1972, John Berger, like the art historian Panofsky before him, interpreted perspective as a system that anticipated Cartesian rationalism and the instrumental objectivity of modern science: "every drawing or painting that used perspective," he stated, "proposed to the spectator that he was the unique centre of the world."[6] If we accept this idea, then we are bound to see the history of Western painting from the Renaissance forward as a march toward the Cartesian worldview, in which instruments of scientific reason put the individual human subject at the center of the universe but at that same time displaced him with a machine. The art historian Norman Bryson later refined art historical accounts of perspective's trajectory toward a rationalist modern worldview, proposing that the perspectival system documented by Alberti in *De Pictura* offered a representation of a self-knowing viewpoint paradoxically removed from the spatial conditions of embodied subjectivity.[7] Alberti's system, Bryson proposed, situated the viewer as both the origin and the object of the look, while at the same time positing a divine, disembodied, and objective viewpoint. The development of scientific perspective in the mid-fifteenth century is thus widely seen as the result of a Renaissance interest in the fusion of art and science, with intensification of the movement toward science into the modern period for which Cartesian mathematics and rationalism would become dominant modes of knowledge. Although perspective placed the human observer at the locus of the image and, as Berger argued, at the center of the world, it also displaced the human subject with an instrument of mechanical objectivity and reason.

Perspective and the Body

Representation of the body in perspectival space, as we have noted, poses an interesting challenge for geometric perspective. As we can observe in the two Annunciation paintings, techniques for rendering space advanced at a different pace from techniques for rendering the body as a dimensional entity. In early perspectival paintings, the body is not given the same precise treatment as volumetric space in itself, even where multiple bodies are rendered accurately to recede in space relative to one

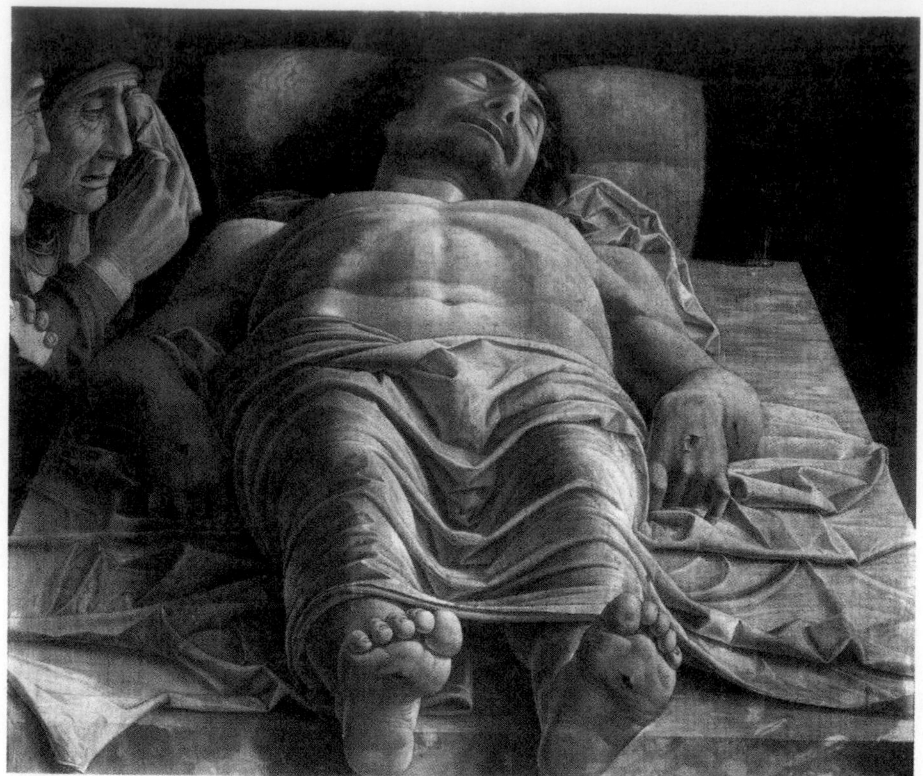

FIG. 4.11
Andrea Mantegna, *The Lamentation over the Dead Christ*, c. 1480

another. Recall that in ancient Egypt, representations of the size of an object or person represented a figure's social importance relative to others in the picture, rather than representing distance from other objects or from the imagined position of the painter or a human observer. A few years before Botticelli painted his *Cestello Annunciation*, Andrea Mantegna painted this work on canvas, titled *The Lamentation over the Dead Christ* (another popular theme among Renaissance painters). This painting of Christ laid out on a marble slab, his genitals draped but his chest and arms left bare, is widely shown to represent anatomical foreshortening, the set of techniques used to render the body as an entity with spatially oriented features within its own outline and not simply as a simple object afloat in the perspectival space around it. Mantegna, a court artist who lived in Padua, painted this dramatic work near the end of his own life with the intention of having it displayed in his own funerary chapel. However, his family sold it to cover his debts, and so it hangs instead in the Pinacoteca di Brera of Milan, where it is revered as an iconic example of the use of perspective to achieve a high level of anatomical realism.

Mantegna adjusted the drawing so its most important feature, the head, would not look too tiny. Precise accuracy in the use of perspective to render a human body up close receding in space with anatomical detail would result in the appearance of exaggeration or gross distortion, which is still a possible interpretation of this classic example of dramatic foreshortening of a figure receding into a relatively shallow space. The strict use of perspective on a body viewed up close like this can result in a compression of form in space that, when unmodified, gives the optical effect of distortion. We might ask, Is Mantegna's drawing a realist rendering of the body,

FIG 4.12
Albrecht Dürer, *Draftsman Drawing a Nude*, 1525

then, or is it an exaggerated view? In this image, the flesh is rendered so precisely as to give the appearance of stone, and severe compression makes Christ's feet and chest cage loom and his face appear oddly squashed.

The limits of perspective can be seen as well in a well-known engraving produced in the sixteenth century by the German printmaker and painter Albrecht Dürer. The engraving depicts an artist in the process of creating a work of linear perspective to render the human body, but with a twist that would seem to indicate the artist's self-consciousness about the role of perspective in creating a powerful "seeing through," as he described it.[8] In this image, the draftsman looks through a grid at a curvaceous model, attempting, apparently, to render her body within the laws of perspective. The photo historian Geoffrey Batchen writes that this image could appear to be a critique of perspective as a form of looking, for not only is the draftsman's page blank, but we as viewers are allowed see the technical trick used to produce an image of the "real."[9] It may be said that the scientific grid gets in the way of sexually pleasurable looking at the nude. The simpler point we wish to make is that the early stories of the perspectival grid emphasize the applicability of the process to the organization of built architectural space and not to the particularities of the scale and form of the human body. The precision of the perspectival grid, as we saw in Mantegna's *Lamentation*, does seem to turn the body to stone. Mantegna's subject was death, but insofar as the body depicted in art history is more typically alive, the precision of line and fixity of form in space afforded by the grid system can drain the qualities of mobility of fluidity from the image that are characteristic of the living body. Indeed, Dürer, who made copies of Mantegna's works to master his style, produced an engraving and painting titled *Adam and Eve* (in 1504 and 1507, respectively) that are noteworthy for the fact that the nude figures were rendered not from life but according to what Dürer believed to be perfect proportions. In his draft manuscript for a book on human proportions, he wrote, "One may often search through two or three hundred men without finding amongst them more than one or two points of beauty. You therefore... must take the head from some and the chest, arm, leg, hand and foot from others...."[10] Thus, for Dürer, realism is achieved by making a composite of views and parts from a variety of observed forms. Realism, in this case, is achieved not by seeing one scene from the fixed perspective of an

FIG 4.13
Albrecht Dürer, *Adam and Eve*, 1504

imagined spectator but by combining parts of views sketched at different times of different bodies in different places and merging them into a composite whole. Thus the history of anatomical rendering provides insights into another potential history of visuality in modernity (that of composites, collage, and remixes) than that of the dominant role of perspective.

This raises the question of how the potentially distorting or deceptive aspects of these systems of viewing have been understood over time. It has been widely held among historians, for instance, that cultures such as ancient Greece philosophically rejected the use of techniques designed to reproduce what the human eye sees, regarding them as forms of trickery and claiming that the mirror reproduction of human form was not the purpose of art. The Renaissance era embraced the idea that it was art's social function to reproduce human vision in an instrumental manner. Indeed, Leonardo da Vinci wrote in his diaries, "Have we not seen pictures which bear so close a resemblance to the actual thing that they have deceived both men and beasts?"[11] His point is that the most innocent, untrained spectator would recognize a drawing rendered in perspective to be objectively representative of the object or scene it is meant to depict.

Da Vinci's point about deception is interesting in light of his unique work in a technique called perspectival anamorphosis. This technique is demonstrated in a drawing he rendered in 1485. If one holds the drawing perpendicular to one's face, one sees an abstract relationship of marks and lines. But by holding the image at an acute angle leading away from one's face, one can see a drawing of an eye coming into view, its proper perspective made visible by the receding plane of the drawing surface. It is interesting that surrealist artist Salvador Dalí used anamorphic perspective in some of his paintings, not to invoke realism but as a technique for making surrealist plays on meaning. For Dalí, this perspective was used to invoke a kind of mental play in the spectator as he or she tries to reconcile perceptual oscillation between two referents that appear to be embedded in the same form. In this painting by Dalí, we can easily pick out the symbolism that is so often the focus of popular discussions about the famous painter's work, but there are also three examples of perceptual anamorphosis. Look closely at the bust of the French Enlightenment philosopher and social reformer Voltaire that sits on the pedestal on the piano. Voltaire's eyes, nose and chin are made up of two Dutch Renaissance merchants in stereotypical collars and hats. Looking carefully as well at the fruit in

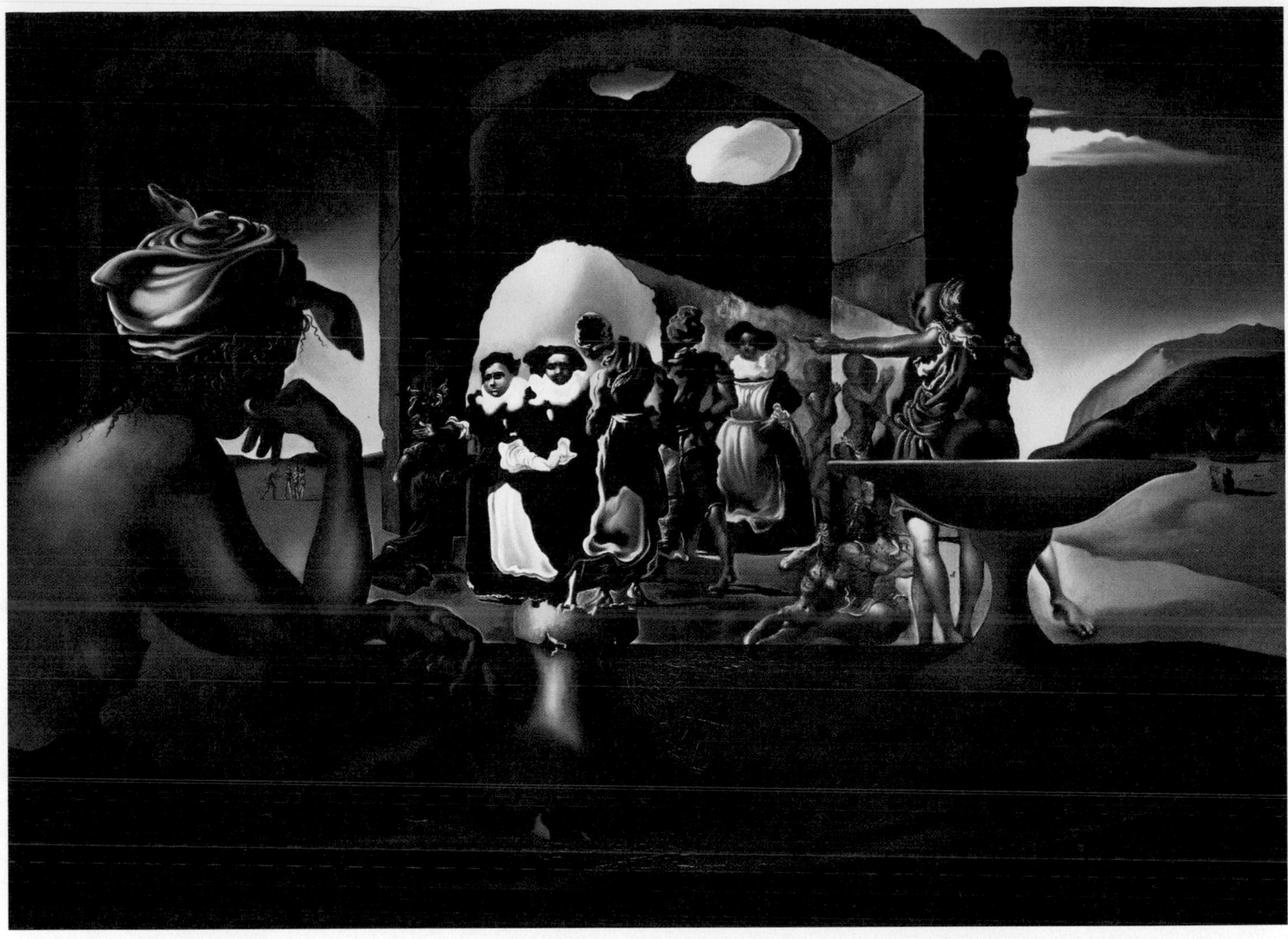

FIG 4.14
Salvador Dalí, *Slave Market with the Disappearing Bust of Voltaire*, 1940

the dish next to the bust, you may notice that the plum doubles as the buttocks of the man positioned in the distance behind the piano and the pear doubles as the base of the distant hill. In playing with our expectations that images offer perspectival ways of seeing, this image can evoke a surreal worldview in its representation of unexpected views and double meanings. As we have seen in this section, the confines of linear perspective have produced a range of strategies for play of the visual.

The Camera Obscura

Today, perspective is recognized as one among a number of possible means of representing space, as one possible technique of realism among others; it no longer characterizes our era's episteme in a totalizing way. However, the value of perspectival realism continues to derive from its status in a tradition that emphasizes the usefulness of scientific instrumentation in producing representations that are seen as more reliable and consistent than seeing with the unaided human eye. With the development and use of the camera obscura from the tenth to the nineteenth centuries, followed by its adaptation to the design of the photographic camera,

FIG. 4.15
Camera Obscura, 1646

single-point perspective continued to hold its own as the standard for documenting space in an objective manner. Yet, at the same time, the photographic camera brings us back to a notion of empiricism that is a counterpoint to the rationalism through which we have interpreted perspective's history.

The camera obscura is a simple device that is based on the phenomenon that light rays bouncing off a well-lit object or scene, when passed into a darkened chamber (a box or a room) through a tiny hole, create an inverted projection, which can be seen on a surface inside the chamber. This phenomenon is mentioned in the writings of Euclid, Aristotle, and the Mohist philosopher Mo Jing in fifth-century China. The Chinese scientist Ken Suo, during the Song dynasty, described the geometrical attributes of this phenomenon in his book of 1088 a.d., the *Dream Pool Essays*. A key figure in the camera obscura's development was the tenth-century Muslim mathematician Alhazen, whom we mentioned before. Whereas the ancient Greeks believed that light emanated from the eye, Alhazen demonstrated that in fact light enters the eye. His camera obscura was modeled on this phenomenon, and through it he shifted the study of the physics of light from philosophy (theorizing about the phenomenon) to empirical experimentation.

Camera obscuras ranged from freestanding rooms and tents to the small boxes that Louis Daguerre and William Fox Talbot would adapt into photographic cameras. In the nineteenth century, camera obscura structures were built in parks and places of natural beauty throughout the American and European landscape. Jonathan Crary has written that the camera obscura is a central factor in the reorganization and reconstitution of the subject from the sixteenth through the eighteenth centuries. It is important that the "viewer" of a camera obscura has a different relation to the images than the viewer of two-dimensional image, precisely because one stands within the space of a camera obscura in order to see its view, what Crary calls an "interiorized observer to an exterior world."[12] This gives the camera obscura, according to Crary, a distinct phenomenological difference from the system of perspective. The camera

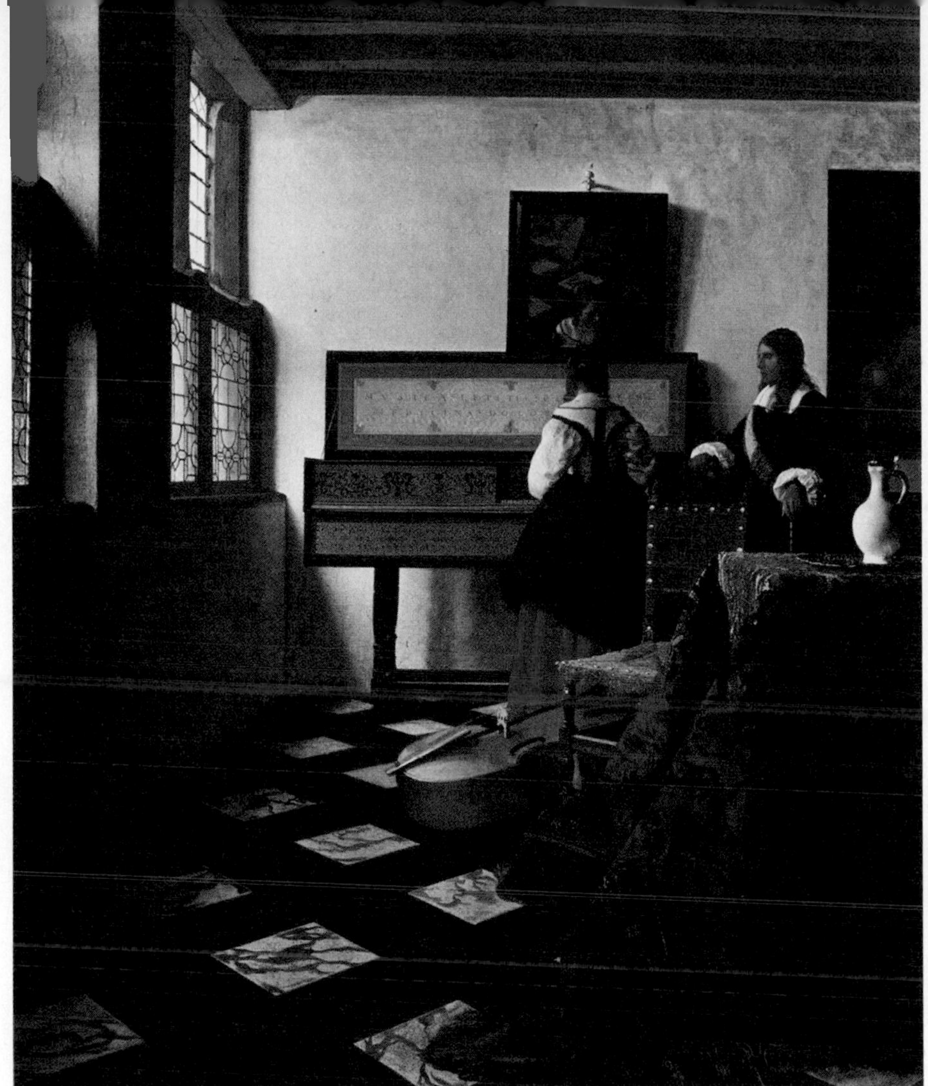

FIG. 4.16
Johannes Vermeer, *Lady at the Virginals with a Gentleman (The Music Lesson)*, 1662–65

obscura was a philosophical model for two centuries, Crary states, "in both rationalist and empiricist thought, of how observation leads to truthful inferences about the world."[13] Although the camera obscura's influence had a long history, in the nineteenth century it was transformed from being a metaphor for truth to being a metaphor for those aspects of society that conceal or invert (as the camera obscura structure does to light) the truth. For Karl Marx, for instance, the way that the light comes into the camera obscura and is then inverted was a metaphor for how bourgeois ideology inverts the actual relations of labor and capital and substitutes appearance for reality.

Camera obscuras were also found in artist's studios, where they were used, much like the perspectival grid, as a drawing instrument. In *Secret Knowledge: Rediscovering the Lost Techniques of the Old Masters*, the contemporary British painter David Hockney put forward a highly controversial thesis that certain painters, from the Dutch Masters (painters of the Baroque period) to French neoclassical painters such as Ingres, used devices including camera obscuras and concave mirrors.[14] For example, in this painting by Johannes Vermeer, the distorted perspective and highlights are suspected to be artifacts of the lens. Although Hockney's theory about lenticular vision is contested by some art historians, it is interesting to note that lenses and viewing devices were not uncommon or suspect objects during this earlier era. Vermeer's friend and executor of his bankrupt estate was Antony van Leeuwenhoek, the Delft fabric merchant who ground his own lenses for the simple homemade microscopes he fashioned to magnify living organisms and who is considered to be one of the first microbiologists.

Whether or not Hockney's thesis is correct, it is important to note that whether a historical work is produced "by eye" or with the aid of a perspectival grid, a camera obscura or a microscope affects the perceived and actual value of the work. This may seem surprising in an era when seeing through visual instruments and displacing authority from the body to the instrument are taken for granted in visual productions of which the aim is accurate rendering or modeling. These techniques were accepted among the conventions of fine art and scientific vision in Vermeer's time as well. Yet the objections to Hockney's thesis are based not only on his evidence but also on skepticism about the idea that a fine artist who painted by hand would resort to tricks of the trade—in particular, we might say, an artist such as Vermeer, whose work is revered for its verisimilitude. Perhaps also, there is concern about the value of these paintings in light of the possibility that their makers used visual technologies more extensively than had been believed. The idea that the value of the original fine-art painting resides in its nonmechanical nature—the fact that it is made by hand and by eye and not with the help of technology—hangs on in art history even as ever more complex instruments of reproduction are increasingly used to make art that is collected, regarded as museum worthy, and gains in value in the twenty-first-century fine-art market.

Challenges to Perspective

Perspective in its more traditional forms has, throughout its long history, remained tied to the idea of an objective, as opposed to a subjective, depiction of reality. However, human vision, as many art historians have noted, is infinitely more complex than perspective's model of a stationary viewer and a world organized around line and space suggest. When we look, our eyes are in constant motion, and any sight we have is the composite of many different views and glances. We can identify other systems of representation that emphasize elements of the visual field other than line and space, the elements abstracted in perspective.

Many styles of modern art that followed the invention of photography defied the tradition of perspective. Impressionism, for instance, was an art movement of the late nineteenth century that featured works that used visible brushstrokes and impressionistic depictions of light to capture a sense of human vision differently. Impressionists shifted their focus to light and color and aimed for a visual spontaneity that some critics have compared to a photographic snapshot. But the impressionist work is not a moment captured in time, like a photograph, but an image that evokes the ongoing play and movement of light and color in the experience of looking. Impressionist painters turned to landscape paintings rendered

FIG. 4.17
Claude Monet, *La Gare Saint-Lazare*, 1877

through the empirical experience of being in the midst of nature, observing and subjectively recording the changes in light and color experienced during the painting session. Claude Monet's painting *Impression, Sunrise* (1872), which now hangs at the Musée Marmotton Monet in Paris, inspired a French critic to coin the term *impressionism* in a view that mocked the new approach. Impressionism was greeted, as many changes in representational style are, as a disturbing way of looking, prompting some French cartoonists to predict that the images would cause pregnant women to miscarry.

Monet examined the process of looking by painting different works of the same scene in a series to show subtle changes due to shifting light and color over time. These series include paintings of a particular view of the Rouen Cathedral done at different times of day and renderings of the movement and variation of patterns of light and color among the water lilies floating in the pond in his garden. He made numerous paintings of the Gare St. Lazare train station in Paris, each a portrait of the scene as it appeared in the different lighting and colors resulting from changes in weather and time of day. Whereas most of the impressionist works depicted landscapes and pastoral scenes, these images of the Gare St. Lazare evoke the bustling new modern world, with smoking locomotive trains and industrial landscapes. In works such as these, Monet demonstrated the complexity of human vision and depicted it as a fluid process that interacts with nature. Whereas Renaissance figures such as Brunelleschi sought the objective laws of nature and trusted instruments over sensory information, impressionists such as Monet emphasized the sensory, embodied experience of seeing as a process through which nature could be known. The train station never looks the same; it is not simply one set view but many impressions. The act of seeing is thus established in these works as active, changing, never fixed; here, vision is a process. In later years, Monet would paint many versions of his now famous garden in Giverny, each a portrait of the garden's changing light and color, creating a view of nature as vibrant and dynamic.

FIG. 4.18
Claude Monet, French, 1840–1926, *Arrival of the Normandy Train, Gare Saint-Lazare*, 1877, oil on canvas, 59.6 × 80.2 cm, Mr. and Mrs. Martin A. Ryerson Collection, 1933.1158, The Art Institute of Chicago

Although impressionism was an avant-garde movement that challenged conventional

FIG. 4.19
Georges Braque, *Woman with a Guitar*, 1913

ways of seeing in its time, it has been for many decades a very popular style for art reproductions. Impressionist paintings are widely reproduced and marketed on posters, calendars, and coffee mugs. The reason may be that much of the subject matter of impressionism, with the exception of some of the work of Vincent van Gogh, is cheerful and pastoral. The images tend to be light and vibrant, pretty to look at and experienced as restful or joyful by many viewers who know little about the style's history. This is quite different from many other modern art styles, such as Cubism, in which both form and subject matter are more challenging.

New ways of looking were a primary focus of the avant-garde in the late nineteenth and early twentieth centuries. What it means to look was thus a central concern of modern art at a time of rapid social change that included the increased visibility of photography as a new way of documenting and representing the world. Beginning around 1907, the Spanish painter Pablo Picasso and the French painter Georges Braque became interested in depicting objects from several different points of view simultaneously. Cubism was a style that deliberately challenged the dominant model of perspective through an analytic system that broke up the perspectival space of the conventional painterly style. These paintings seemed to proclaim that the human eye is never at rest but is always in motion, perceiving the world from multiple vantage points at once. The cubists painted objects as if they were being viewed from several different angles simultaneously, with surfaces colliding and intersecting at unexpected angles. The coherence and unity of perspectival depth is thus shattered and pieced together in unexpected and ambiguous ways. Space in cubist paintings becomes shallow and fragmented. The spectator is led to focus on the disunity of the painterly space itself, appreciating the scene's difference from the representational and compositional unity of earlier styles of painting. In this painting by Georges Braque, a rendering of realistic space and light has been discarded for a kinetic view of ordinary objects and labels through different angles and fragments. The painting is intended

FIG. 4.20
Pablo Picasso, *Les Demoiselles d'Avignon*, 1907

to suggest a referent: a woman playing a guitar at a café table, with newspapers and bottles in view. But this scene is composed as a synthetic series of simultaneous glances of the scene. This was, according to the cubists, a means of depicting the restless and complicated process of human vision. We could compare this painting to another still life, the eighteenth-century still life by Roland de la Porte that we discussed in chapter 1. Each image is a still life, but Braque's vision defies the singular perspective of Roland de la Porte's realist image. Each painting presents itself as a representation of how we really see. But whereas the Roland de la Porte painting posits a singular spectator looking toward the image, the Braque offers the restless view of a spectator in constant motion. It is important to note that the cubists were interested in creating not fantasy worlds but new ways of looking at the real. John Berger has written, "Cubism changed the nature of the relationship between the painted image and reality, and by so doing it expressed a new relationship between man and reality."[15]

Pablo Picasso's well-known painting *Les Demoiselles d'Avignon* (1907) is one of the most famous examples of the Cubist style. Picasso, like many other modern artists, was influenced during this period by the styles of African sculpture and masks, and this painting, of prostitutes in a brothel in Avignon, demonstrates how the distinct abstraction of the body in African art was borrowed and recoded in cubism as a means of demonstrating the European idea of seeing from multiple angles simultaneously. In defiance of the codes of Western art and linear perspective, Picasso adapted to painting some of the compositional elements of the angular figurative style he observed in the African art and artifacts that were newly displayed in Paris museums during this period of intensive French colonial expansion into Africa. It is not incidental to the meaning of the painting, of course, that it, like the Braque painting, depicts the figures of women. In the case of the Picasso, the women present defiant, if not hostile, faces to the spectator.

The relationship of modern artists to the aesthetic styles of African art, defined at the time as "primitive" art, has been the source of much debate, in particular around issues of colonialist appropriation and authorship.[16] Picasso's painting was the signature work in the well-known 1984 exhibition at the Museum of Modern Art in New York titled "'Primitivism' in 20th Century Art: Affinity of the Tribal and the Modern." The show presented the work of European modernists alongside the work of African artists that may have inspired their forms, yet the African art was presented without artist names or dates. Critics of the exhibition argued that this presentation format was a form of colonialism that was both Eurocentric and one of cooptation. Thus this mask, made by an artist in Zaire and reproduced in exhibition, was seen in the exhibition context as an example of primitivism that inspired modern art, rather than as a form of abstraction with its own set of cultural connotations. Though these styles, such as cubism, were seen as particularly modern views that defied tradition, they were also borrowing without attribution abstract styles that were understood as traditional in many parts of Africa and Latin America. Importantly, those styles that seem in the context of European American art to be particularly modern and forward looking, hence avant-garde, were influenced by art traditions that had much longer histories of abstraction and that also had long histories of defying or simply not observing the conventional codes of perspective.

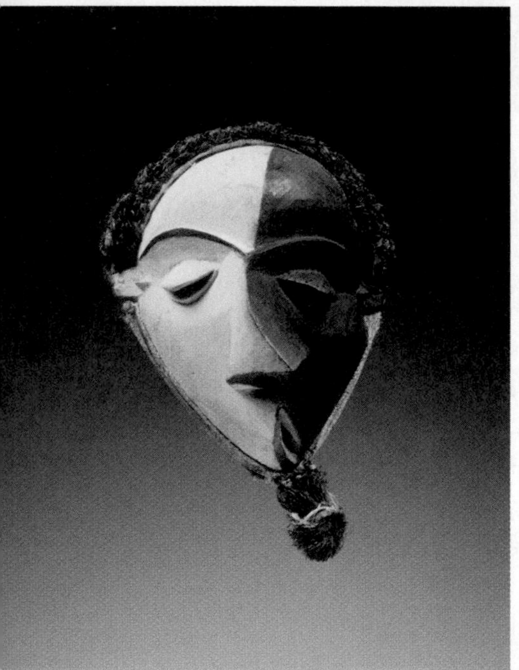

FIG. 4.21
Mbuya (sickness) mask, Zaire. EO.1959.15.18, collection RMCA Tervuren, Photo: © R. Asselberghs, RMCA Tervuren

Challenges to the prevalence of fixed perspective as a system for organizing the appearance of the real can be found at the levels of metaphor and symbolism. In this 1914 painting by Giorgio de Chirico, titled *Melancholy and Mystery of a Street* (fig. 4.22), the Italian artist exaggerates perspective to create a sense of unease in the spectator. Each building in this eerily vacant cityscape recedes at a dramatic angle to its own slightly different vanishing point. The painting is organized according to a perspectival system in which structures are not precisely aligned. The faceless figure in the foreground threatens to be overtaken by the looming shadow that advances from the background. This painting is an example of de Chirico's metaphysical works,

FIG. 4.22
Giorgio de Chirico, *Melancholy and Mystery of a Street*, 1914

FIG. 4.23
Ico game cover, remake of Giorgio de Chirico, *Melancholy and Mystery of a Street*

which are intended to show states of mind or consciousness rather than to depict objective reality accurately. De Chirico's painting inspired the image template for the Japanese video game designer Fumito Ueda's well-known video game, Ico, which was released in 2002 (fig. 4.23). Ico departed from the visual style of many video games and acquired a cult status in part for its rejection of certain aesthetic conventions of games. Here, the de Chirico image is transposed into an image that evokes a journey through a metaphysical and fantastic landscape.

The longevity of traditional linear perspective suggests a cultural desire for vision to be stable and unchanging and for the meaning of images to be fixed. In fact, the act of looking has been highly changeable and contextually meaningful, not in any ideal sense, throughout modernity. Rational objectivity may be an accurate general characterization of the modern episteme, but the mobilization of the seeing subject and the fascination with distortion (and depiction of perspective as a technique of illusionism) that the anamorphosis process suggests indicate that we should take seriously alternative paradigms of looking. Artistic movements such as cubism and surrealism have continually sparred with the dominant worldview for which perspective is the paradigm. The intent of the artists working in these styles is not to replace that episteme with a new worldview but to emphasize the status of perspective and its worldview as culturally situated and determined by social conditions of seeing and representation. The purpose of abstraction is to make obvious the historical and contextual making of perspective by that emphasizing it is not a universal principle. This occurs in works such as impressionist paintings that bring other aspects of seeing into play or through strategies such as those used in cubism that analyze and restructure the spatial logic of perspective.

Modern artists working in subsequent image styles also challenged perspective along with other techniques in the twentieth century. In painting, photography, and film spanning approximately the 1910s through the 1960s, modernist artists questioned traditions of representation organized around the model of the Cartesian subject as the locus of the pictorial world. In some abstract modern paintings, form became the content itself. In addition, some modernist artists shifted the emphasis from the painting as a representation to the painting as a document of the painter's physical and emotional experience in marking the canvas. The painting becomes a record of the actual performance of the painter as he or she actively made the work of art. The drip-and-splash "action painting" that was abstract expressionist Jackson Pollock's trademark style demonstrates this approach. To create paintings such as the one reproduced here, Pollock placed his canvas on the floor and walked around its perimeter, vigorously pouring and dripping his paint from a can right onto the surface in broad gestures. Instead of using brushes, he manipulated the paint with sticks, trowels, or knives. Sometimes he added sand, broken glass, or other materials to the paint. Action painting drew from the surrealist interest in automatism, a technique of writing, drawing, and painting in which the producer marks the surface with spontaneous gestures, giving little or no attention to the aesthetic form that results. The guiding concept was that this technique would result in more direct, uncensored release of the inner feelings of the artist and that the marks on the canvas would express these feelings without direct pictorial symbolism. The spectator, in turn, could feel the energy and emotion of the artist in contemplating the turbulent lines and shapes that serve as a record of the painter's spontaneous activity. These paintings were not named after anything (this one is called simply *Number 1*), because they did not represent or symbolize anything beyond the painting and its process of being made. Art criticism of the period emphasized the aesthetic qualities of the works as

FIG. 4.24
Jackson Pollock, *Number 1, 1948*

representations of the artist's process and materials rather than as representations of how he or she saw the world or a scene.

Concept, process, and performance were essential aspects of many modernist artists' practices and were the source of categories designating subcategories of modernist art (such as conceptual art, process art, and performance art). Conceptual art involved the production of works in which the idea or concept was more important than the visual product. Some artworks were in fact devoid of pictures, containing only words describing a concept. The French painter Yves Klein combined the conceptual approach with process-, performance-, and action-based painting. Rather than making the canvas a record of his own bodily action, he instructed nude female models to roll in a single color of paint (a hard, bright royal blue) and then had them roll and drag their bodies over canvases before live audiences to the accompaniment of a musical composition he called the "Monotone Symphony" (one sustained chord), producing paintings that were records of their action. The process was a work of art in itself—both action and performance art.

This kind of work, which was launched under the name of new realism, subverted the older realist tradition of "painting from life" in which studio artists painted posed nude models. Klein took the whole body of the model and used it as a direct source of imprinting the canvas, as if the body were one big live brush. Just as the photograph is seen as a direct imprint of light in the codes of photographic realism, here the painting shows the literal imprint of the bodies physically touching the canvas with every surface. Yet these imprints are highly abstract, because they are devoid of representational conventions such as foreshortening, shading, line, variation in color and tone, and perspective. This work from Klein's series of body images has a title, *Anthropometry of the Blue Period*, that directly evokes the nineteenth-century practice of measuring bodies to derive information about normalcy, health and intellect (we discuss these practices further in chapter 9). These images interpellate the spectator into their world in a way that does not invite identification or pleasure in looking in the typical sense. They invite us to think about the physical materiality of the body and the paint, the "having been there" of a nude body that rolled in the viscous paint, like a child plunging its hand into finger paint and then smearing the canvas. Here, the body of the model is the surrogate for the painter's hand in composing the image. We are expected to imagine the process and the scene of the painting being made, not a posed scene that was copied.

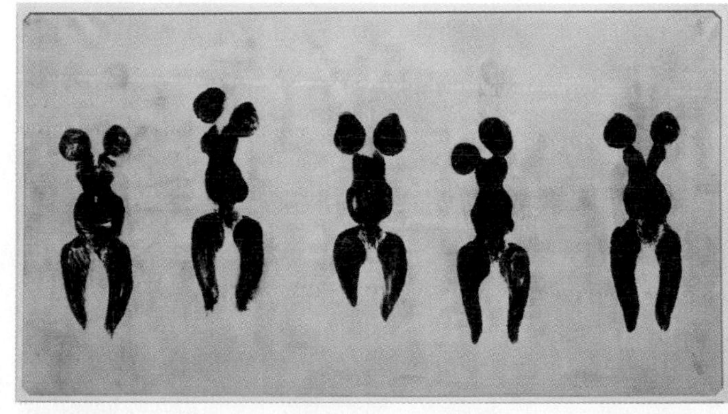

FIG. 4.25
Yves Klein, *Anthropometry of the Blue Period (ANT 82)*, 1960

For the 1950s, this was a radical approach to organizing pictorial space because it broke dramatically with the idea that paintings were meant to represent what we see. Even impressionist paintings offered a semblance of seeing a scene, emphasizing the importance of light and color in that process. Klein's paintings were so notorious that the particular color of paint he used in all of these pieces became widely recognized as "Yves Klein Blue." He in fact patented the color under the name International Klein Blue, although it was never commercially manufactured (he died young, at age thirty-four, before this and other ideas of his were realized).

Klein's process paintings were later riffed in the work of the Cuban-American artist Ana Mendieta (discussed in chapter 3), who left imprints of her own nude body in the sand in natural settings (earthworks) and then photographed the imprints, reworking the photograph to emphasize the surface of the image as a trace of the hand and body of the artist. Whereas Klein used the female nude as living surrogate for the hand and brush, Mendieta used her own body as marker, symbolizing women's physical absence as mark-makers from the history of art, even as nude female bodies are overrepresented as the object of the male painter's gaze.

The idea that a perspective-based view of the world is actually no more than one of the many different ways of representing human vision has been taken further by many contemporary artists, many of them playing with the codes of photographic truth in doing so. For instance, in this photo collage, David Hockney composes an image of a desert intersection through many snapshots taken from different positions. Hockney's composition suggests that this mundane roadside is experienced not in one view but in many fleeting views from many perspectives over time. It is not just one viewer who contemplates this scene from multiple perspectives, but perhaps hundreds or thousands of viewers who catch a fleeting, mobile glimpse of it as they drive by it once or as they pass it on their commute multiple times in a day, week, or month. His image is a portrait of the vibrancy of everyday vision and the fleeting and serial nature of seeing on the go in modern life.

FIG. 4.26
David Hockney, *Pearblossom Hwy., 11–18th April 1986 (Second Version)*, 1986

Other contemporary artists have continued to play with perspective. This painting by Mark Tansey, *Innocent Eye Test* (1981), makes a witty postmodern commentary about the history of perspective. It does so with drawings that employ the conventions of perspective and volumetric rendering to represent objects and scenes as they might be seen through a window on the world. Tansy renders, in seemingly exacting realist form, a hilariously preposterous scene in which men show a cow a painting

FIG. 4.27
Mark Tansey, *The Innocent Eye Test*, 1981

of cows, a large-scale work draped like a great masterpiece, also rendered in impeccable realist style. Men, presumably curators, art historians, and social scientists, observe the cow observing. One wears a scientist's lab coat and takes notes, another holds a pointer, as if ready to draw the cow's attention to some aspect of the painting.

Tansey is making a joke about realism and the idea that its codes might be apparent to the innocent, untrained eye of animals. His joke is highly relevant to the art-historical context of the new realism of the early 1980s that challenged modernist abstraction's resistance to representation, which had become dogmatic. During the decade at the start of which Tansey painted this work, many painters returned to the codes and conventions of classical realism as developed in the Renaissance in a reaction against the abstract and conceptual work of the 1960s and 1970s that emphasized the real of the canvas and paint, the real of the codes, and the artifice of pictorialism. *Innocent Eye Test*, Tansey explains, is not simply a return to old ideas about realism. He states, "In my work, I'm searching for pictorial functions that are based on the idea that the painted picture knows itself to be metaphorical, rhetorical, transformational, fictional. I'm not doing pictures of things that actually exist in the world. The narratives never actually occurred."[17]

By saying that the picture "knows itself," Tansey is saying that his painting was received in a social context in which the audience knows better than to believe that art's function is to mimic vision, to fool the eye of the spectator, or to present a view of the real as if seen from the eye, rendered mechanically or otherwise. By 1981, the year this painting was first exhibited, there is no museum spectator who is innocent of the artifice, the techniques, and the mechanical processes that underlie the effects of pictorial realism in painting. There would be no way to return to the "innocence" of an earlier era in which perspective awed or fooled the viewer into believing they were seeing the real thing. Viewers approaching Tansey's work were likely to get the joke, which is a reflexive one not only about (not) being innocent about techniques of realism and the politics of representation (people are not cattle) but also about the art historian's and critic's desire to see and to study scientifically how spectators see,

FIG. 4.28
The Sims 2: FreeTime, Hobby: Cuisine, 2004

making the spectator into a kind of test animal. Tansey's painting is, in part, a joke about the history of representation and a joke about the academic study of practices of looking that had come into style as well.

Perspective in Digital Media

The codes and conventions of realism have continued to change in the context of electronic visual technologies. Digital imaging in particular has presented new modes through which the viewer can experience a multiplicity of perspectives on a multiplicity of virtual worlds within the same screen. Video games, for example, brought new kinds of perspectives and interactions with other players and with the technology itself to the experience of viewing images. The emphasis on the phenomenological experience of the body of the producer, so evident in the modernist paintings of Klein and Pollock, continues in video game production. However, with games, the emphasis shifts to the embodied experience of the user. The video game is a form that was introduced after World War II in amusement devices that incorporated the kinds of display screens used in radar technology. In the earliest video games, analog devices were used to control the trajectory of mobile shapes on a screen. Some of these early games featured military themes in which, for example, the objective was to maneuver shapes with the goal of striking fixed targets literally drawn on the screen. In the early 1970s, coin-operated video games were installed in arcades as a form of popular amusement. One of the key aspects of video games is the level and degree of interaction with the technology and with other viewers that they invite. Unlike a movie or television program, which unfolds before our eyes without the requirement that we interact much with others or with the actual technology (beyond pushing buttons on the remote), video games typically require viewers to navigate elements of the game in particular ways or to interact with other users as a condition of their use. One's activity drives the game. For this reason, in writings about video games, the term *user* has become far more commonplace than *viewer* because it connotes physical, embodied experience with something beyond the delimited sensory experience of looking.

Digital media theorist Noah Wardrip-Fruin prefers to refer to games as *playable media* and to users as *players*. He does this in order to open up a descriptive category that would include on common ground both conventional video games and experimental media projects by artists and media producers that are game-like but without some of the qualities of commercial games (containing the goal of playing to win, for example). To choose the terms *user* or *player* is not to say that viewing is passive and involves only looking all the time but that the discourse of video games has adapted to a language that emphasizes the active nature of our engagement with media. As digital media theorist Alexander Galloway writes, "if photographs are images, and films are moving images, then *video games are actions*."[18] We are reminded of Pollock's action painting, in which the emphasis is on embodied movement and not what the canvas looks like. Galloway continues, "With video games, the work itself is material action. One *plays* a game. And the software *runs*. The operator and the machine play the video game together, step by step, move by move." The actual images of any video game are thus determined in part by the actions of the player in relation to the limitations of the game itself. This turning to "use" and "action" suggests that the new episteme features utility and embodied experience.

The look of video games is also crucial to the worlds that these games help us to imagine. Like the image from the ancient Papyrus of Ani discussed earlier, video games offer different kinds of perspectives all at once and do not always follow the conventions of geometric linear perspective. One way of seeing that is built into some video games is isometric, or axonometric, projection. Isometry means equal in measure. In isometric perspective, objects are not represented as becoming smaller as they recede in space, as they would be using linear perspective. Isometric perspective flattens the space within the frame without creating a sense of depth. The image has no vanishing point. Isometric spaces are often used when one frame is embedded in another, as is sometimes the case in video games. An isometric view places the viewer in a different relation to space than traditional perspective, inserting him or her into a kind of overhead view in which one is positioned as if at the top corner of a room, looking down toward the opposite, lower corner. This kind of perspective is used in some comic books and graphic novels, in which we find various kinds of flattened dimensional space invoked as settings in which action takes place.

In video games, the conventions of isometric perspective are common, though most game players probably do not pay much attention to this aspect of games. In *The Sims*, for instance, the space of the screen has a flattened effect so that viewer-players seem to be looking down on the screen from above, like omniscient viewers. Although traditional perspective was seen as granting the viewer a god-like, centralized view of a given scene, isometric perspective can be said to afford the players a potentially even more empowered position. This is so not only because it presents to the viewer an omniscient view of a virtual world but also because it also places the viewer in the position of interactively creating, engaging in, and moving through that world, maintaining a central position in it even as orientation within a scene changes.

Artist Jon Haddock juxtaposes traditional and isometric perspective by taking scenes from famous images and historical events and rendering them as if they were imaged in a video game. He calls these works "isometric screenshots." The photograph of a Chinese student stopping a tank that became an icon of the Tiananmen Square uprising (discussed in chapter 1) is rendered by Haddock into the flat perspective of a video game. In Haddock's image, the original photograph is reconceived through the conventions of isometric perspective, uncannily transforming the images into what looks like stills from a video game. The figures seem to be placed on the flat background of the street. Haddock has also appropriated a press image of Elián González, a Cuban boy who was taken by U.S. federal agents from his relatives' house in Miami in 2000 in the midst of an international battle over the child's custody and immigration status. The house in which the photograph was taken is reimagined through the perspective of a game structured like *The Sims*. The user can see into the building as if its roof could be removed for viewing. In transposing these images into isometric perspective, Haddock is pointing to the artificialities of both systems of looking, the original photographic view and its isometric remake.

Another crucial aspect of video games is their heavy use of point-of-view shots to situate the player in relation to the experience of moving through space. Lev Manovich, in his influential book *Language of New Media*, stresses that cinematic ways of composing screen space in depth and motion have consistently been invoked in such forms as video games and computer graphics in the late twentieth century. Many video games are designed to give the player the sense of a singular point of view with which one may identify one's own gaze, but this point of view is mobile. The convention of point-of-view shots has a long history in both cinema and comic books as a means through which the viewer is afforded the experience of seeing as if through the eyes of a character. Sometimes, this convention in cinema has been used to show the subjective (usually altered) vision of a character, such as the view of someone who could not see well or who is dreaming or drugged. More commonly, though, point-of-view shots in cinema depict approximately what a character sees and are preceded or followed by a shot of

FIG. 4.29
Jon Haddock, *Wang Weilen—Screenshot Series*, 2000

the character who is looking. Pursuit is a common theme for point-of-view shots. In one subgenre of video games, the image is designed in what is called a "first-person shooter" mode, in which the viewer is positioned behind a weapon and the screen offers scenes of prospective targets.

Video games are composed of *virtual* images. A common misconception about the term *virtual* is that it means "not real," or that it refers to something that exists in our imaginations only. There is also a misconception that whereas actual or representational images are produced through analog technologies, virtual images are produced through digital technologies and are specific to their era. In fact, virtual images are both analog and digital. Virtual images break with the convention of representing what is seen. They are simulations that represent ideal or constructed rather than actual conditions. A virtual image of a human body may represent no actual body in particular but may be based on a composite or simulation of human bodies drawn from various sources. For example, we can describe the composite bodies of Adam and Eve drawn by Dürer (discussed earlier in this chapter) as virtual insofar as there were no one look and no specific bodies as the source of this seemingly realist view. The realism of the virtual stems from the embodiment of ideal or composite elements, not correspondence with an actual referent.

Virtual, simulated images are central to the use of special effects in cinema. Most contemporary films use some form of digital special effects, even in scenes, such as crowd scenes, in which these effects are not readily obvious. They thus represent virtual worlds that are simulated on the screen. This is perhaps most obvious in those films in which real actors interact with animated characters, such as *Who Framed Roger Rabbit* (1988) or *Night at the Museum* (2006). Although we as viewers understand that these actors never experience physical proximity with these cartoon characters, the pleasure in watching such films is in seeing the blend of animation and live action. The world of the film, even as experienced by the actors themselves, is thus very much a virtual world insofar as no film set ever contained it.

Virtual technologies include the mundane and real-world augmentations of reality such as pacemakers and hearing aids. They also include simulations that aim to exist parallel to what we think of as the real world, such as flight simulation training systems and game systems that invite us to enter their imagined world on multiple sensory levels. Simulations and virtual reality systems incorporate computer imaging, sound, and sensory systems to put the player's body in a direct feedback loop with the technology itself and the world it simulates. The aim of such systems is to allow subjectivity to be experienced in and through the technology. Rather than offering a world to simply view and hear, as the cinema does, virtual reality systems create simulations that attempt to provide an experience in which players feel as if they are physically incorporated into the world on all sensory levels, with their bodies linked through prosthetic extensions. Increasingly, there are also examples of emerging "virtual institutions" and virtual worlds in which players interact in online environments, using avatars, in ways that replicate social structures of the real world through economic, psychological, legal, and other types of interactions.

One of the unique qualities of virtual reality systems is that they unleash the spectator from his or her bodily position in space, allowing a more free-floating experience of perception. In a virtual system, one might choose to occupy various positions within the virtual world, positions not possible within actual space. For example, in this virtual simulation inside a colon by biophysicist Richard Robb, created with the Virtual Reality Assisted Surgery Program (designed by Robb and Bruce Cameron), the human body (represented in the avatar figure) can assume any perspective he or she wishes to by selecting different views through the computer program. This system allows users such as medical students to take a virtual fly-through tour of the human colon. Increasingly, medical practitioners have devised the means to play with scale and generate virtual worlds in which the surgeon may enter the human body visually to see things never before seen (because they are too small or too remote) and operate at a scale never before possible (at the level of cells, for example). We discuss scientific images further in chapter 9.

It is important to note that the space of cyberspace and virtual technologies including virtual reality and video games is distinct from traditional, material Cartesian space. As we discussed before, Cartesian space, as defined by René Descartes, is a physical, three-dimensional space that can be mathematically measured. However, virtual space, or the space created by electronic and digital technologies, cannot be mathematically measured and mapped. The

FIG. 4.30
Richard A. Robb, virtual colonoscopy: 3D rendered image from CT scan

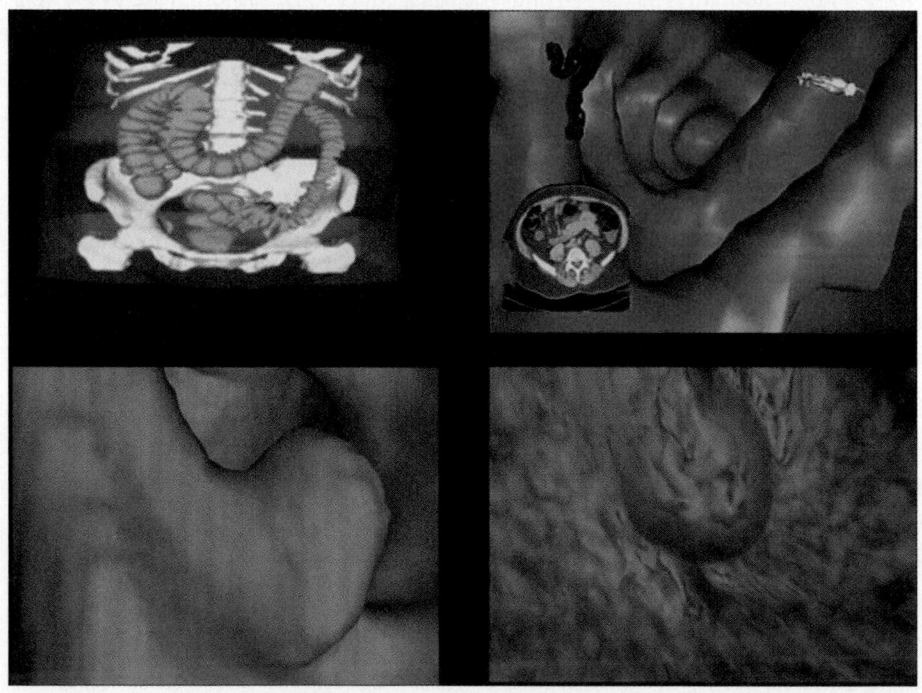

term "virtual space" thus refers to spaces that appear to be like physical space as we understand it but do not conform to the laws of physical, material, or Cartesian space. Many aspects of computer programs encourage us to think of these spaces as akin to the physical spaces that we encounter in the real world; however, virtual space exists in opposition to the rules of traditional physical space. Amusingly, when *The Simpsons* television show wanted to portray Homer Simpson as lost in virtual space in a well-known episode, it used a Cartesian grid to depict the space. Yet virtual space is a dramatic change in the forms of representation, space, and images as we have known them.

FIG. 4.31
Homer Simpson in cyberspace, from *The Simpsons, Treehouse of Horror VI: Homer^3*, 1996

We live in an image environment that is dramatically different from the world of Renaissance perspective, scientific rationalism, and modern worldviews through the end of the twentieth century that adapted perspective. Indeed, one of the shaping characteristics of contemporary visual culture is our reliance on a multiplicity of views, screens, and contemporaneous fields of action as we negotiate our lives. When we work on the computer, we are accustomed to looking at and moving between multiple screens and experiencing many different perspectives all at once. Since the development of the graphic user interface (GUI) of contemporary personal computers in the mid-1980s, in which computer information has been increasingly visualized through icons on the screen rather than text, the contemporary computer user is connected back through the history of systems of looking. Anne Friedberg writes, "In the mixed metaphor of the computer screen, the computer user is figuratively positioned with multiple spatial relations to the screen. 'Windows' stack *in front of* each other... or *on top of* each other.... on the fractured plane of the computer screen. The metaphor of the window has retained a key stake in the technological reframing of the visual field. The Windows interface is a postcinematic visual system, but the viewer-turned-user remains in front of... a perpendicular frame."[19] The window frame of the computer screen thus offers a new kind of seeing that, like cubism, engages with many screens and angles all at once.

We began this chapter by explaining that perspective is both a method and a metaphor for an episteme that would be captured in the worldview of Enlightenment rationalism. Rather than seeing in perspective the roots of a system of ever more perfect machines that reproduce seeing based on an ideal that locates agency and subjectivity in the unitary body, we might identify a hybridized network of relationships among perspective as a system, the body of the artist, drawing materials, drawing, the referent scene or body, and so on. This network of multiple human and nonhuman actors, objects, and technologies is generative of a worldview. The image, in this view, is neither a metaphor nor a reflection of the world, the human subject, or thought. It is an element with agency in its own right, engaging with us in our world. We might say that digital imaging's multiplicity of perspectives and its openings for multiple entry points and potential for new combinations of users and objects suggest many possible entry points into engagement in the ongoing making of worlds and worldviews. In the following chapter, we will discuss the role of visual technologies and reproduction as a key factor in this hybridized, multi-perspective worldview.

Notes

1. Antonio Manetti, *The Life of Brunelleschi*, trans. Catherine Enggass (University Park: Pennsylvania State University Press, 1970).
2. Leone Battista Alberti, from *On Painting*, excerpted in Janson and Janson, *History of Art*, 612.
3. Anne Friedberg, *The Virtual Window: From Alberti to Microsoft* (Cambridge, Mass.: MIT Press, 2006).
4. Erwin Panofsky, *Perspective as Symbolic Form*, trans. Christopher S. Wood (New York: Zone Books, [1927] 1997).
5. René Descartes, *Discourse on Method, Optics, Geometry and Meteorology*, trans. Paul J. Olscamp, 65 (New York: Bobbs-Merrill, 1965). See also Martin Jay, *Downcast Eyes: The Denigration of Vision in Twentieth-Century French Thought*, 69–72 (Berkeley: University of California Press, 1993).
6. John Berger, *Ways of Seeing*, 18 (New York: Penguin, 1972).
7. Norman Bryson, *Vision and Painting: The Logic of the Gaze* (New Haven: Yale University Press, 1986).
8. Geoffrey Batchen, *Burning with Desire: The Conception of Photography*, 110 (Cambridge, Mass.: MIT Press, 1997).
9. Geoffrey Batchen, *Burning with Desire*, 111.
10. Albrecht Dürer, from the book manuscript for *The Book on Human Proportions*, excerpted in Janson and Janson, *History of Art*, 620.
11. Leonardo da Vinci, *The Notebooks of Leonardo da Vinci*, ed. Edward McCurdy, 854 (New York: George Brazillier, 1958). *The Notebooks of Leonardo da Vinci* are online at www.gutenberg.org/etext/5000.
12. Jonathan Crary, *Techniques of the Observer: On Vision and Modernity in the Nineteenth Century*, 34 (Cambridge, Mass.: MIT Press, 1990).
13. Crary, *Techniques of the Observer*, 29.
14. David Hockney, *Secret Knowledge: Rediscovering the Lost Techniques of the Old Masters* (New York: Studio, 2001).
15. John Berger, "The Moment of Cubism," in *The Sense of Sight*, 171 (New York: Pantheon, 1985).
16. See the exhibition catalogue, William Rubin, ed., *"Primitivism" in 20th Century Art: Affinity of the Tribal and the Modern*, Volumes 1 and 2 (New York: Museum of Modern Art, 1984). Critiques of the exhibition include Thomas McEvilley, "Doctor Lawyer Indian Chief: 'Primitivism in 20th Century Art' at the Museum of Modern Art," *ArtForum*, 23.3 (November 1984), 54–61; and Hal Foster, "The 'Primitive' Unconscious of Modern Art," *October* 34 (Autumn 1985), 45–70.
17. Mark Tansey, quoted in Arthur C. Danto, *Mark Tansey: Visions and Revisions* (New York: HNA Books, 1992).
18. Alexander Galloway, *Gaming: Essays on Algorithmic Culture*, 2 (Minneapolis: University of Minnesota Press, 2006).
19. Anne Friedberg, *The Virtual Window*, 231–32.

Further Reading

Aristotle. *Poetics*. Translated by Ingram Bywater. New York: Modern Library, 1954.

Adorno, Theodor W. *The Jargon of Authenticity*. Translated by Knut Tarnowski and Frederic Will. Foreword by Trent Schroyer. Evanston, Ill.: Northwestern University Press, 1973.

———. "Understanding a Photograph." In *Classic Essays on Photography*. Edited by Trachtenberg, Alan. New Haven: Leetes's Island Books, 1980, 291–94.

Batchen, Geoffrey. *Burning with Desire: The Conception of Photography*. Cambridge, Mass.: MIT Press, 1997.

Berger, John. *Ways of Seeing*. New York: Penguin, 1972.

———. *The Sense of Sight*. New York: Pantheon, 1985.

Bernal, J. D. *Science in History, II. The Scientific and Industrial Revolutions*. Cambridge, Mass.: MIT Press, 1954.

Bryson, Norman. *Vision and Painting: The Logic of the Gaze*. New Haven: Yale University Press, 1986.

Bukatman, Scott. *Terminal Identity: The Virtual Subject in Postmodern Science Fiction*. Durham, N.C.: Duke University Press, 1993.

Crary, Jonathan. *Techniques of the Observer: On Vision and Modernity in the Nineteenth Century*. Cambridge, Mass.: MIT Press, 1990.

Danto, Arthur C. *Mark Tansey: Visions and Revisions*. New York: HNA Books, 1992.

Daston, Lorraine, and Peter Galison. *Objectivity*. New York: Zone Books, 2007.

Descartes, René. *Discourse on Method, Optics, Geometry, and Meteorology*. Translated by Paul J. Olscamp. New York: Bobbs-Merrill, 1965.

Elkins, James. *The Object Stares Back: On the Nature of Seeing*. New York: Harcourt, 1997.

Freidberg, Anne. *The Virtual Window: From Alberti to Microsoft*. Cambridge, Mass.: MIT Press, 2006.

Foster, Hal. "The 'Primitive' Unconscious of Modern Art." *October* 34 (Autumn 1985), 45–70.

Foucault, Michel. *The Order of Things: An Archaeology of the Human Sciences*. New York: Vintage, [1966] 1994.

Galloway, Alexander. *Gaming: Essays on Algorithmic Culture*. Minneapolis: University of Minnesota Press, 2006.

Gombrich, E. H. *Art and Illusion: A Study in the Psychology of Pictorial Representation*. Princeton, N.J.: Princeton University Press, 1960.

Goodman, Nelson. "Authenticity." *Grove Art Online*. New York: Oxford University Press, 2007.

———. *The Structure of Appearance*, 3rd ed. Boston: Reidel, 1977.

———. *Languages of Art: An Approach to a Theory of Symbols*, 2nd ed. Indianapolis, Ind.: Hackett, 1976.

Greenberg, Clement. *Art and Culture*. Boston: Beacon Press, 1961.

Harrigan, Pat, and Noah Wardrip-Fruin, eds. *Second Person: Role-Playing and Story in Games and Playable Media*. Cambridge, Mass.: MIT Press, 2007.

Hawkes, Terence. *Structuralism and Semiotics*. Berkeley: University of California Press, 1977.

Hockney, David. *Secret Knowledge: Rediscovering the Lost Techniques of the Old Masters*. New York: Viking Studio, 2001.

Holly, Michael Ann. *Panofsky and the Foundations of Art History*. Ithaca, N.Y.: Cornell University Press, 1985.

Janson, H. W., and Anthony F. Janson. *A Basic History of Art*. Englewood Cliffs, N.J.: Prentice-Hall, 1992.

——— *History of Art: The Western Tradition*, 6th ed.. New York: Abrams, 2001.

Jay, Martin. *Downcast Eyes: The Denigration of Vision in Twentieth-Century French Thought*. Berkeley: University of California Press, 1993.

Kember, Sarah. *Virtual Anxiety: Photography, New Technology, and Subjectivity*. Manchester, U.K.: Manchester University Press, 1998.

Kemp, Martin. *The Science of Art*. New Haven: Yale University Press, 1990.

Latour, Bruno. *We Have Never Been Modern*. Cambridge, Mass.: Harvard University Press, 1993.

Manetti, Antonio. *The Life of Brunelleschi*. Translated by Catherine Enggass. University Park: Pennsylvania State University Press, 1970.

Manovich, Lev. *The Language of New Media*. Cambridge, Mass: MIT Press, 2001.

McEvilley, Thomas. "Doctor Lawyer Indian Chief: 'Primitivism in 20th Century Art' at the Museum of Modern Art." *ArtForum* 23.3 (November 1984), 54–61.

Mitchell, W. J. T. *Iconology: Image, Text, Ideology*. Chicago: University of Chicago Press, 1987.

Nelson, Robert S., and Richard Shiff, eds. *Critical Terms for Art History*. Chicago: University of Chicago Press, 2003.

Panofsky, Erwin S. *Perspective as Symbolic Form*. Translated by Christopher S. Wood. New York: Zone Books, [1927] 1997.

Rubin, William, ed. *"Primitivism" in 20th Century Art: Affinity of the Tribal and the Modern*, Volumes 1 and 2. New York: Museum of Modern Art, 1984.

chapter five

Visual Technologies, Image Reproduction, and the Copy

Reproduction comes into play in different ways in visual culture. As we discussed in chapter 4, many works of visual culture reproduce the appearance of objects, people, or events in the real world. We may refer to instruments and technologies of visual production, such as the photographic camera, as reproducing the way the human eye sees. We may use the term *reproduction* to describe a copy of an original work. In theories of visual culture influenced by Marxist theory, the term *reproduction* is used to describe the ways that cultural practices and their forms of expression reproduce the ideologies and interests of the ruling class. In this view, the reproduction of ideology through media also reproduced the political order and its episteme.

In this chapter, we consider the reproduction of images through technological means and the social and cultural changes that accompany changes in technologies of reproduction. Our discussion spans from the early nineteenth century through the early twenty-first century, considering photography, cinema, television, and digital image techniques. We discuss visual technologies from the mechanical to the digital and the impact of reproducibility on the social meanings and value of images. The relationship of technology to the meaning of images is crucial. Just as the embrace of perspective was bound up with epistemic concerns about the subjective nature of embodied vision and the potential for greater objectivity through visual instruments, as we discussed in chapter 4, so changes in imaging technologies are part of broader epistemic shifts in the knowledge politics of their respective eras.

Visual Technologies

One way of understanding the history of imaging technologies has been to examine how the introduction of a particular invention, such as the photographic camera, changed things in the world (by changing the way we see, or changing how we use images, and so forth). We argue against this approach, because technology itself does not determine social change. Technologies are developed incrementally and in different directions over time, in response to changes in worldviews and through serendipity. People use the same technologies in different ways. Mistakes become common practices. Decisions to introduce a technology for particular reasons sometimes serve unanticipated ends. For example, when the U.S. Department of Defense first used the computer communication system called ARPANET for military email in 1971, they had no idea that within two decades this would become the basis for a network used by civilians, businesses, and governments around the world. Technology is not an autonomous force that brings about social effects after something has been invented. Likewise, inventions are not solely the product of human will or political and economic initiative. Rather, technologies interact with people and the forces of politics, economics, and other aspects of culture in various social and historical contexts, resulting in changes not only in the technologies themselves but also in social practices and uses. In other words, it can be argued that technologies have some agency—that is, that they have important and influential effects on society but that they are also themselves the product of their particular societies and times and the ideologies that exist within them and within which they are used.

The fact that visual technologies emerge out of particular social and epistemic contexts means that their possibility often precedes their development. The elements of the technique of linear perspective existed prior to its "invention" during the Renaissance. As we mentioned in chapter 4, the ancient Greeks understood the basics of perspective, yet they rejected it as a technique because it was in contrast to certain fundamental philosophical ideas that were prevalent in Greek culture then—for instance, a drawing using perspective might trick a viewer. The development of perspective as a dominant technique was the outcome of the social views of European culture in the early fifteenth century, of a particular episteme, that included the emergence over centuries of a paradigm of scientific reason culminating in the Enlightenment centuries later. Similarly, many of the chemical and mechanical elements necessary to produce photographic images existed prior to the time that several people working in different countries in the late 1830s "invented" photography simultaneously. The early uses of photography were both institutional (for medical, legal, and scientific uses) and personal (for portraits), and these uses influenced the ways that photographic technologies were developed. As photo historian Geoffrey Batchen writes, the origins of photography raise the question not of who invented photography but "at what moment did photography shift from an occasional, isolated, individual fantasy to a demonstrably widespread, social *imperative*?"[1] In other words, photography emerged as a popular medium not simply because it was invented, but because it fulfilled particular social demands of the early nineteenth century.

Photography emerged as a popular visual technology because it fit certain emerging social concepts and needs of the time—modern ideas about the individual in the context of growing urban centers, modern concepts of technological progress and mechanization, modern concepts of time and spontaneity, the desire to contain nature and landscape in mechanically reproducible form, and the rise of bureaucratic institutions in the modern state interested in documentation and classification. Photography is the visual technology that most helped to usher in the age of modernity to the extent that it epitomizes that era. Using Foucault's concept of *discourse*, we might say that photography emerged along with discourses of science, the penal system, medicine, the media, and other institutions of everyday life that made visual reproducibility one of the imperatives of modernity. The French novelist Emile Zola, a friend of the Impressionist painter Paul Cezanne, wrote: "We cannot claim to have really seen anything before having photographed it."[2] Many felt, like Zola, that photography epitomized the new and modern way of seeing that prevailed in the nineteenth century.

Motion and Sequence

We can apply these concepts to the emergence of visual technologies of motion. The introduction of sequential photography and motion picture film in the late 1800s corresponded with an increased desire to visualize movement in the increasingly mobile

FIG. 5.1
Jacques-Henri Lartigue, *Grand Prix of the Automobile Club of France*, 1912

and fast-paced society of late-nineteenth-century modernity. Indeed, the introduction of cinema projection devices was preceded by an interest in paintings and photographs representing movement that could not be grasped by the unaided eye. Jacques-Henri Lartigue's photographs of the antics of his wealthy family members engaged in their sports and hobbies captured the thrills offered by machines of mobility such as cars. In fig. 5.1, the wheels of the car appear elongated due to the speed with which they turn, an effect reproduced in comic drawings of cars in motion.

Notable among photographers exploring the depiction of motion was Eadweard Muybridge, who in the late nineteenth century produced a study of animal and human locomotion. Leland Stanford, the wealthy California governor after whom Stanford University is named, asked Muybridge to use his motion studies to settle a bet: Did the hooves of a horse ever leave the ground all at the same time in the midst of a gallop? The unaided eye could not discern this fact, because the movement was so rapid that this fact could not be discerned by eye with certainty. Working with railroad engineer John Isaacs, in 1878 Muybridge set up an elaborate system of twelve stereoscopic cameras, each set twelve feet apart on a stretch of track and rigged with an electrical trigger. As the horse covered the ground of the track, it tripped the triggers, setting off the shutter of each camera one immediately after another, resulting in a contiguous series of images of the horse in stages of motion. The sequence of images showed the exact position of the horse's hooves in a short cycle of the run, with one revealing that the horse did indeed become airborne for a fleeting instant with its legs tucked under its torso. Muybridge's project was one of many scientific and popular uses of the photographic motion study in

FIG. 5.2
Eadweard Muybridge, *Woman, Kicking*, 1887

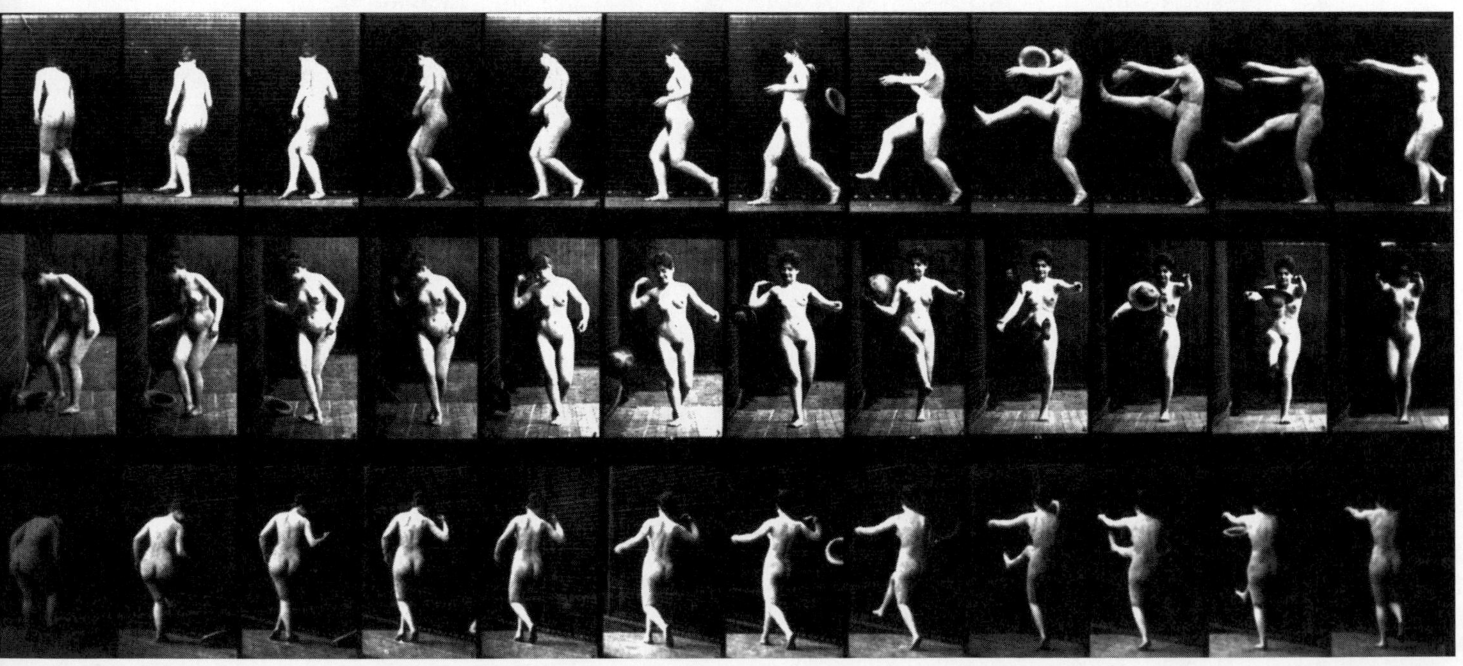

North America and Europe during this period. Muybridge also produced motion studies of humans: men performing athletic activities, such as wrestling, boxing, and throwing a ball; women performing mundane domestic tasks, such as pouring from a jug, carrying a bucket, and sweeping. Most of these studies depicted the human body unclothed, the idea being that one could better analyze human form if the body were not concealed. Although this nudity was clearly meant to be interpreted within the conventions of dispassionate scientific looking, we should not overlook the codes of gendered performance styles and the conventions of sexualized bodily display so obviously present in these images.

FIG. 5.3
Zoetrope

Photographic images of movement such as those by Muybridge set the stage for the development of cinema as did other forms of visual display that were proto-cinematic. In the decades prior to the cinema, entertainers on the vaudeville circuit, magicians, and traveling performers entertained spectators with a range of techniques that would later be regarded by historians as precursors to cinematic projection. A popular form of entertainment called the magic lantern show involved the projection of still photographic slides with narrative or descriptive accompaniment provided by a live performer. Although these were not moving images in a strict sense, the sequential arrangement of images, their projection for an assembled group, and the voice-over narration of the live performer lent a kind of flow and theatrical display element that would later be a strong feature of motion pictures. Projection machines variously called Zoetropes, Praxinoscopes, and Phenakistoscopes were designed on the model of the camera obscura, which we discussed in chapter 4, but included a kind of round drum that accommodated an interior light source. Inside the drum was placed a strip of photographs taken in a sequence, like Muybridge's *Horse in Motion* series. When a viewer spun the inner drum, the serial images each passed a peephole in a rapid sequence, giving the illusion of a flickering moving image.

Other viewing devices presented images that appeared to move into depth within the frame. The stereoscope was an instrument used in the nineteenth century that offered two separate views on the same scene arranged to replicate the positioning of the two eyes and then optically converged to simulate depth in the scene. The art historian Jonathan Crary states that the stereoscope dislocated the singular view of geometric perspective embedded in the instrument of the camera obscura, fracturing this unitary view into two slightly different views of a scene that, when

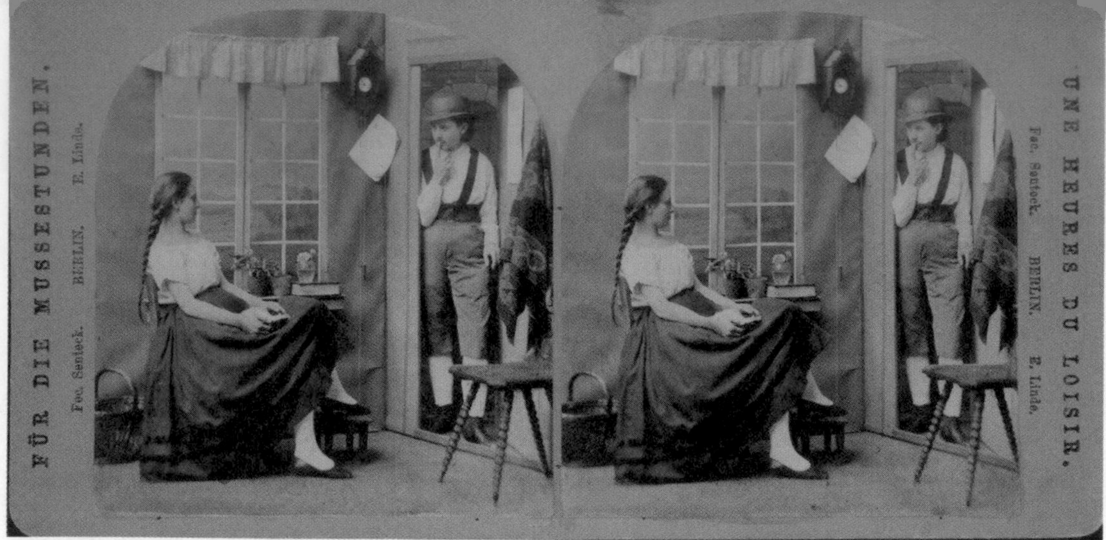

FIG. 5.4
E. Linde, *Leisure Time (Für Die Mussestunden)*, c. 1870s

seen together through a viewing device, appear to have a kind of animated, shifting depth. The scene seen through the device is actually somewhere between the two images, ironically not really reflecting anything as it would be seen by the unaided eye. Stereographic imaging was used in a variety of ways: as home amusement—with scenes of nature, shots of national monuments, and semipornographic views being the genres most popular among collectors—and for the illustration of astronomical and anatomical atlases. As this stereograph shows, a sense of the image (titled "Leisure Time") as creating a secret or titillating view was a common effect.

Whereas we associate motion pictures with the apparatus of the projector and the viewing context of the theater, the initial experiments of cinematic viewing in the United States were designed, much like the stereoscope, for viewing through an apparatus that allowed only one user at a time. In 1891, Thomas Edison publicly displayed a device called a kinescope, with which individual viewers could stand before a peephole through which they could watch a projection of a short motion picture film. These devices became popular in places of popular amusement such as Coney Island, where they were assembled in rows much like arcade games are now. Individual viewers could enjoy a short amusing vignette such as the *John and Mary Irwin Kiss* by peering through the peephole of the device. This viewing experience shared with the stereoscope the ability to make viewing the private, voyeuristic domain of the spectator, even if the spectator used the device in a public space.

The invention of cinema involved both the invention of a moving picture camera and projector and a flexible form of film (celluloid) that could be projected and reprojected without falling apart. Historians of cinema widely agree that the origins of the cinema lie not only in the invention of motion picture film and the ability to *make* films but also in the development of the projector, an instrument that could be used to *exhibit* films onto a surface in a projection that was large enough for an assembled group of people to watch the same film at the same time and in the same place, seated in different positions around the room. It was the ability of people to assemble in a group before a projected image, and not simply the ability to make and view moving images, that allowed the cinema to become a form of mass entertainment. With the introduction of the film projector, the experience of private viewing was replaced by the group experience of spectators in a theater, each looking from a slightly different proximity and angle to the screen. The theater setting of cinema entailed a break from the ideal of the singular, unitary spectator positioned at an ideal point before the frame.

Cinema added the elements of temporality, movement, and eventually sound to photography, allowing the photographic image to become a primary means of temporal narrative storytelling. Filmmakers at the turn of the century, such as D.W. Griffith and Edwin S. Porter, developed such narrative techniques as intercutting two scenes taking place at the same time in order to give the spectator a sense of being in both places at once. Filmmakers of the silent period (before the soundtrack was added to the film) also established the convention of cutting between two characters to indicate an exchange of dialogue between them. As viewers, we are familiar with these cinematic codes. For instance, when a shot of a character looking off screen is followed by another shot, we recognize that the second shot is intended to represent what the character in the first shot is looking at. In the 1930s and 1940s directors, camera operators and editors perfected techniques through which relatively short shots could be linked together with matches on action, continuity of direction, and other codes leading the spectator not to notice the cuts from shot to shot. This kind of "invisible" editing became a hallmark of the classical Hollywood "realist" fiction film style. Cinematic meaning is derived not from the individual film frame or take but through the linking together of images and takes into signifying chains. The juxtaposition or combination of two images to create a third meaning, a concept based on the dialectic (the idea that each meaning builds on the previous one to create a more comprehensive meaning) and theorized famously by the Soviet filmmaker Sergei Eisenstein, remains a central component of understanding how films make meaning. Montage became an important strategy for representing the passage of time both in mainstream films and in experimental films. In addition, experimental filmmakers of the mid-twentieth century contrasted mismatching frames and sequences to create rhythms or patterns of light and dark and fragmented movements to signify a break from the smooth, even flow of conventionally edited narrative cinema.

The nineteenth-century visual technologies of photography and cinema established complex new modes of representation that would then shift again with the development of electronic media such as television in the mid-twentieth century and the emergence of digital technology in the late twentieth century. It is important to remember that each new form of visual technology builds on the codes of previous technologies but that each constitutes as well a kind of epistemic shift. Cinema borrows codes of photographic realism and fantastical imagination from photography and adds motion and the layered meanings of sequential action. Television borrows many of the sequential, narrative, and genre conventions from cinema, yet its electronic technological nature changes its distribution and viewing contexts and presents the possibility of the live image. Digital technologies borrow from all these media, yet present a new set of meanings through their capacity for reshaping and malleability. We discuss some of these shifts in technologies of reproduction more throughout this chapter.

Image Reproduction: The Copy

When we think of technologies of reproduction, the idea of the copy easily comes to mind. The copy is not a new phenomenon. Shortly before the Egyptian historical period called the New Kingdom, the funerary scrolls previously rendered only for the coffins of dead pharaohs and court members began to be copied more widely and placed in the coffins of those who were not nobility. The afterlife, Janson and Janson propose in their canonical history of Western art, was thus democratized.[3] Whether or not this claim about copies and democratization holds up, it is true that the manufacture of scrolls for many people required a means of reproduction. The scrolls were rendered in ink on papyrus and formed into a continuous roll. These scrolls were adapted and revised over hundreds of years BCE. by Egyptian artisans who made copies by hand in special funerary workshops. Sections of each copy of the papyrus were written and drawn by different artists, and in some it appears that the scribes paid more attention to the quality of the image than to accurately copying and placing the text in the story. Segments by different artists were pasted together to make complete scrolls, much like a contemporary graphic novel to which different artists contribute parts. The work was done by these artists in advance with the name of the dead left blank in each copy, to be filled in later.

It is nevertheless the case that a valuing of the original, uncopied work has dominated the history of images. The work of art has been regarded throughout history as a unique and original object, with its meaning and value tied to the importance of the place in which it resided (a church, a palace, or a museum, for example). But even during the period before modernity, which has been described as the age of mechanical production, paintings and sculptures were potentially reproducible. In the Renaissance religious art was sometimes reproduced in the form of replicas (hand-hewn, hand-painted copies), and an "original" bronze sculpture required casting the true original, the work in clay, from a plaster mold. Thus in the case of bronze sculpture reproduction was, paradoxically, a means to making an original work.

Value is a key factor in the status of reproduction, originals, and copies. When works are produced in a series, reproducibility is often understood within a system of limited value. Even in the woodblock print, which was used, along with papermaking and silkscreening techniques, in Chinese antiquity, or in the sculpture cast from a mold (a practice that can be traced back to ancient Egypt), the value of each work in a print series is often determined by its status as one of a limited number. Typically, the lower the number in a series, the more rare, and hence potentially valuable, is each copy. The first in a series of silkscreens, for example, is more valuable than later prints. The easy reproducibility of the unique work of fine art in the photographic era has altered the way value is assigned in the art market, but not to the degree we might have anticipated. For example, there continues to be a strong market in contemporary fine-art original painting, despite the availability of reproduction options such as photography and high-resolution digital copying. The value of the original work still holds in the art market, even as reproductions have become more widely available and even as the copy becomes, in many cases, harder to distinguish from the original.

Some technologies of imaging are designed to produce multiple similar images. These include printmaking techniques such as engraving, etching, and woodcuts, which were popularized in the fifteenth and sixteenth centuries and lithography (popularized in the early nineteenth century). It has been argued, most notably by art historian William Ivins, that although great emphasis has always been placed on the social impact of the invention of the printing press in the mid-fifteenth century by Johann Gutenberg, the slightly earlier discovery of how to print pictures and diagrams was tremendously important to the emergence of modern life and thought. Without prints, Ivins states, "we should have very few of our modern sciences, technologies, archaeologies, or ethnologies—for all of these are dependent, first or last, upon information conveyed by exactly repeatable visual or pictorial statements."[4]

The "exactly repeatable visual or pictorial statement" has been central to the dissemination of knowledge since the early fifteenth century. However, the medium of photography changed the status of the image further by making it possible to reproduce preexisting works of art, such as paintings and frescoes, that were previously unique. This technological change had a profound influence on the meaning of images, and in particular two-dimensional visual art. The invention of photography coincided, paradoxically, with a cult of originality. Previously artists might produce several versions of the same painting, and there were traditions of making replicas of works, usually by the artist or under his or her supervision, in the same medium. However, with the rise of photographic reproduction, these practices faded. Instead, a reaffirmation of the unique image, one that had more value than the copy, took place precisely at the time when that original image could be easily reproduced in copies thanks to the photographic camera.

The photographic image presents a very particular set of issues to the relationship of reproduction, art value, and mechanical production. The camera obscura had been in use for centuries as a seeing and drawing device, but it was not until the 1820s that the French inventor Joseph Nicéphore Niépce would successfully expose permanent images in a process that took eight hours. With Louis Daguerre, Niépce later devised a means to create a silver compound that, when exposed to light in a camera obscura box, would leave behind an image impression. (1839 is usually given as the date for photograph's invention.) Daguerreotypes, as images from this technique are called, were eventually used a great deal in portrait photography and to capture scenes of the city (in fig. 5.5 as a panorama of Paris).

A crucial aspect of early photography is that the image produced by early photographic technique actually is an original. The daguerreotype is a single, negative

FIG. 5.5
Friedrich von Martens, *La Seine, la rive gauche et l'ile de la Cite (The Seine, The Left Bank and L'Île de la Cité)* (Panorama of Paris) c. 1845, panoramic daguerreotype

image that is seen in positive by the viewer. The term *negative* has come to mean an original from which we strike original prints, but this was not so for the daguerreotype and similar processes in use during the early 1800s. The negative served as the sole original. If a viewer takes the daguerreotype into his or her hand and turns it slightly, the metal plate's surface can be made to reflect light at an angle that allows the image to appear as a positive. William Fox Talbot developed a similar process, calling his images calotypes. The daguerreotype was widely produced in the United States, where Daguerre did not control the patent (as he did in England). Other processes, such as the ambrotype and the tintype, became more popular, as photographic techniques continued to change in the following decades. Roll film was introduced by George Eastman in 1884, another significant step that enhanced reproducibility.

The acceptance of the photograph in the fine art market, in which the concept of the original continues to reign, was neither easy nor fast in part because of the form's association with production by machine. As we have noted, photography was not the first technique to introduce reproducibility to the art market, Moreover, the quality of photographic reproducibility did not meet the art market's criteria of originality. If there is an original material form that we can point to in photography, it would be the negative, which holds great value as the source of prints. But only with the daguerreotype and similar processes has the negative been exhibited and sold as an original work of art. The problem of valuing the photograph as art is captured in the paradoxical concept of the "original print." With the photographic print on paper, the original resides, paradoxically, in copies struck from the artist's original negative.

The strong association of the photographic form with the mechanical instrument and the technical process, and not the hand of the artist, worked against the idea of photography as an art form. As we noted in chapter 4, claims that artists used the camera obscura to trace their works have the potential to devalue and even discredit those works. Classical works of art that carry too strong an association with the use of technical instruments run the risk of being devalued, because value continues to reside in the idea of the hand and eye of the individual artist as the source of creativity and genius. The individual work is valued in part because it is unique and in part because it was crafted through the direct touch and gaze of its individual creator. Even the action paintings of Pollock in the mid-1950s were valued because they were records of his bodily interaction with canvas and paint. Photography offers neither the direct touch nor the direct look of the artist on the work in its process of production. Both are mediated by the camera. Writings on photography throughout the nineteenth and early twentieth century emphasized the mechanical nature of the medium even as they also noted the ability of photography to capture evidence of spiritual life (it was believed by some that the device could reveal ghosts that did not appear to the unaided eye). It is this quality of instrumental objectivity that earned photography its strong place in science, medicine, and law as a means of documenting truths about events, objects, and people in the world. In this view of photography as an objective form, photography embodied the rationalism of the modern era, augmenting the eye.

The photograph has also been noted, by Roland Barthes and film theorist André Bazin, among others, for having a unique affinity with the real, which they describe as the "noeme" of photography. The term *noeme* comes from phenomenology, a branch of philosophy devoted to the study of embodied sensory experience, which is regarded as the root of being and knowledge. A conventional photograph of an object, person, or scene must by necessity have been taken in a space of copresence. The camera and film must have been there with the object in the photograph. Not so with the painting, which provides no guarantee of the artist's copresence with his or her subject, even if done in realist linear perspective. In a photograph, the light rays that hit the object are the same light rays that expose the film from which the image is made. In this view, the photograph is a realist form not simply because of its verisimilitude (likeness with its subject) but because of its guarantee of having been physically copresent with the person, object, or scene. Barthes, in his book *Camera Lucida*, reminds us that the photograph, unlike the drawing or painting, has the unique quality of conveying a guarantee that something "has been" because of the medium's requirement of being copresent, of sharing space and light with the object it represents. This emphasis on the empirical coexistence of the camera and the real scene (which is related to what semiotician Charles Pierce would call its indexical quality) has been a persuasive argument for the use of photographs, films, and videotapes in courtrooms as criminal evidence.

Like the touch of the hand of the artist, the photograph, in these accounts, is regarded as conveying the "touch" that guarantees the scene as an authentic record of the filmed object's or scene's having been there. In this sense, the photograph is empirical in both an epistemological sense (it provides knowledge of what has been) and an ontological sense (it guarantees that something has, in fact, been). Bazin gave this theory a spiritual spin when he compared this relationship of the real and the photographic image to that of the face of Christ and the shroud of Turin. This cloth, a piece of linen kept in the chapel of the Saint John the Baptist in Turin, is believed to have been worn by Christ at the time of his burial. It bears a direct imprint of the face of a person who appears to have been in agony. When an Italian lawyer and amateur photographer photographed the shroud in 1898 he was shocked to see on the photographic plate a clear and stark image of a man, who many believed to be Christ. The shroud was regarded as holding a special "something," a quality of realness that is uniquely Christ's because of its direct contact with his body. In this sense, the cloth is regarded as empirical evidence in a more strongly ontological sense, in that it is valued because it is believed to hold Christ's *being* (despite radiocarbon testing dating the cloth back to the medieval period, long after Christ's time).[5] With spirit photography, the photograph is regarded as empirical evidence of presence (being) and as a guarantee of knowledge (that ghosts exist despite their invisibility, because we can see their trace in the image). In this example, seeing is taken for knowing, with little attention to the artificial or artifactual aspects of the imaging process.

These are just a few examples of the use of photography in an episteme in which empiricism, not rationalism, dominates. The art historian Vered Maimon has argued that in its earliest decades the photograph was linked not to the rationalist enterprise and skepticism about embodied knowledge but to the inductive method and empiricism in philosophy and science. The photograph was not simply the outcome, after the camera obscura, of the desire for mechanical copies. It was also a tool of empirical investigation.[6] By considering the interests of early photographers and scientists who developed visual techniques for knowing the world empirically and through sensory experience, we can trace a different and equally important counterhistory to the dominant story told about photography's past.

Although the photograph is now regarded as a form of fine art, its status as art has been long debated and was hard won. Even though photography was invented in 1839, it was not until 1902 that photographs were formally shown in galleries of fine art. Photographers like Julia Margaret Cameron, whom we discussed in chapter 4, used photography to create images with a painterly look in reaction to the commercial aesthetic of the period. But at the turn of the century, artists such as Imogen Cunningham, Ansel Adams, and Edward Weston felt that this pictorialist approach, in which photographs were made to look like paintings, elided the true beauty of "straight photography," which emphasized the actual material qualities of the medium. In 1902, the photographers Alfred Stieglitz, Gertrude Käsebier, and Alvin Langdon Coburn broke away from their commercial peers (in a movement dubbed the Photo-Secession) and published a magazine, *Camera Work*, devoted to showing photography in lush reproductions. They held photo exhibitions in a space owned by Edward Steichen. By the end of World War I, these photographers had moved further from the pictorialist approach that characterized the documentary and commercial uses of photography that dominated the profession. The British art critic Clive Bell, in his classic 1914 essay *Art*, wrote that only "significant form" distinguishes art from not-art in arousing our aesthetic emotions. Art photographers established what was significantly photographic, emphasizing the unique qualities of the photographic surface, black-and-white imagery, and shadow and light that the technique afforded and that would arouse aesthetic appreciation within the terms of photography's own distinct codes. Art photographers thus gained acceptance for their medium as a form that has its own unique qualities, rather than capitalizing on the photograph as copy.

Walter Benjamin and Mechanical Reproduction

Many of the issues we have been discussing so far about image reproduction and the valuing of art were of particular interest to Walter Benjamin, a German critic of the twentieth century who was associated with the mid-century German political theorists collectively dubbed the Frankfurt School. Benjamin wrote a well-known and highly influential essay in 1936 about the cultural shift to reproducible forms in art, widely published in English under the title "The Work of Art in the Age of Mechanical Reproduction." Benjamin proposed that with the introduction of image forms such as photography and motion picture film, there is no original work to speak of but rather a series of copies (prints) that stand equally in the place of the singular original work. Reproducibility as a quality of the medium moved the artwork out from the centuries-long emphasis on uniqueness and authenticity as the qualities that confer value to it. Benjamin saw reproducibility as a potentially revolutionary element, because it freed art from its revered status as unique ritual artifact in traditions of iconic reverence and exchange. Art, newly understood as existing in forms designed for reproducibility and circulation, could be a democratizing force and could now become engaged in a more fluid socialist politics that included reception by the masses through the broader circulation of copies.

Benjamin argued that the long era of the closed ritual in which ownership and value of the artifact was based on the status of the work as unique and exclusive led to a reification of the work of art as commodity in a capitalist system. With reproducibility an integral feature of the medium, this system could be challenged. Reproduction was no longer simply a means of making less valuable replicas or faked copies of the unique work. The inherently reproducible form became much more pervasive by the end of the twentieth century, transforming art-making and art-marketing practices dramatically.

One of the paradoxes of the era of mechanical reproducibility is that advances in mechanical and digital reproduction techniques have been matched by advances in mechanical and digital techniques for verifying the authenticity of works of fine art claimed to be originals. Visual technologies such as X-ray imaging are now routinely used to discern fakes, forgeries, and changes made to original works.

Benjamin argued that the one-of-a-kind artwork has a particular *aura*. Its value is derived from its uniqueness and its role in ritual, meaning that it may carry a kind of sacred value, whether religious or not. Indeed, it is because it is one of a kind that it retains a sacred status. He wrote, "Even the most perfect reproduction of a work of art is lacking in one element: its presence in time and space, its unique existence at the place where it happens to be."[7] It is precisely this "presence in time and space" that Benjamin refers to as giving the image a particular kind of aura, making it feel authentic.

In Benjamin's terms, the authenticity of the aura cannot be reproduced. Traditionally, authenticity has meant genuine and reliable, not false or copied. The authentic is regarded as more "real" than the copy. Yet the concept of authenticity is used in many different ways today. Authenticity can refer to seeing or structuring an image as if without the help of the many technologies available to us today. The term is also used to refer to an enduring and timeless quality, such as "authentically" classical beauty, which can be found and reproduced. Authenticity is a quality that producers can attach to works through the use of a variety of codes that signify its various meanings. For example, in documentary film and video, the "authentic" realism of seeing as if without the help of visual technology is sometimes signified by a professional use of techniques associated with "amateur" filmmaking: random lighting, candid framing of shots, jerky camera movement, the use of long takes in editing, and inclusion of "natural" sound. These stylistic techniques are sometimes used to signify authentic life caught in action, not orchestrated and selectively edited.

Authenticity is also a quality that clings to the idea of a classic type within a category of people or icons. Indeed, the enduring power of the icon depends on its ability to retain the quality of authenticity under conditions of intensive reproduction. In

FIG. 5.6
Arrow ad, 2007

an era in which it has become second nature to alter and manipulate not only images but bodies to make them over into images of perfection, we retain a special respect for the "authentic" beauty of celebrities such as Cindy Crawford, America's famous supermodel of the 1980s who was noted for her "natural" beauty. Even after Crawford revealed to the British *Daily Telegraph* in 2006 that she had undergone numerous plastic surgeries, her beauty continued to be regarded as authentic and natural, even though it was revealed to be produced rather than given. Authenticity is also sought in the consumer market, as we can see in this advertisement for Arrow clothing as "Authentic American style." Authenticity is, in this case, not about originality and uniqueness. Rather, it is a free-floating signifier that is attached to this clothing in a way that is meant to indicate a style that is "classic" or "timeless." "Authenticity" thus can be easily reproduced, packaged, and sold as a quality attributed to particular looks or designs, but not to a single object or person.

Benjamin noted that the meaning of the original work of art changes when it is reproduced, because its value comes not from the uniqueness of the image as one of a kind but rather from its status as being the original of many copies. Reproduction plays an essential role in the dissemination of art. It is commonplace today for famous paintings to be reproduced in art books and on posters, postcards, coffee mugs, and T-shirts. It's important to note that ownership of original fine-art works of value remains beyond the reach of the middle-class consumer, who might come to know these works solely through book and art reproductions or through trips to museums. Exposure to original works of art remains a relatively rare experience, an option for those with the means and the incentive to travel to the museums and collections in which highly valued originals are displayed. The capacity for reproducibility thus produces a situation in which viewers may come to know, to love, and even to own a copy of a valued work of art but may never have seen that work in the original form in which its meaning and value are still understood to reside. The reproduction, paradoxically, becomes the form through which meaning and value are maintained and developed in original works.

For instance, Leonardo da Vinci's *Mona Lisa*, created in 1503, is one of the most famous paintings in the world. It is known to most people through its innumerable reproductions in art books and on postcards, calendars, refrigerator magnets, and other trinkets. As we noted in chapter 1, the original painting is on display at the Louvre, behind a shield of bulletproof security glass (it was doused with acid and marred by a rock by irate viewers in 1956, prompting stricter security measures for the work's exhibition). Over three million people flock to see it each year, standing before it fifteen seconds each on average. But they have seen its reproductions many times. The painting has been subject to innumerable parodies and remakes. For instance, in 1919 Marcel Duchamp took a cheap postcard version of the painting and drew a moustache and goatee on the famous portrait.

FIG. 5.7
Marcel Duchamp, *L.H.O.O.Q.*, 1930

This was one of numerous "readymades" that Duchamp produced, deploying a satirical irreverence that was characteristic of Dada art. He named the new work *L.H.O.O.Q.*, which when spoken quickly in French sounds like "elle a chaud au cul," vulgar slang for "she has a hot ass." As we noted in chapter 1, the smile can have many different meanings, and historically the smile of the Mona Lisa has been described as demurely feminine and coy. Here, Duchamp quite clearly recodes that smile as sexual, with the implication that Mona Lisa harbors sexual urges that are revealed in her smile. His intent was to take a painting that had achieved sacred status in the history of art and essentially write graffiti on it, an act of playful insolence toward the art world's reverence for masterpieces. Later the French surrealist painter Salvador Dalí paid homage to Duchamp's prank by remaking the *Mona Lisa*, giving her his own famous swirling moustache.

The *Mona Lisa*'s reproduction has extended to the digital age. The impact of computers and digital media on visual culture has often been compared to the impact of perspective during the Renaissance. Hence there are many references in digital culture to the Renaissance and in particular to Leonardo da Vinci as an icon of that era's merging of science and art. A reproduction of the *Mona Lisa* was one of the first images to be scanned and digitally reproduced on a computer in 1965, along with a portrait of computer scientist Norbert Wiener (who coined the term *cybernetics*). Copies of this "digital masterpiece" have been sold on the Web, where the image was described as "unique." In this case, *unique* means not one of a kind but unusual in concept. Computer programmer Eric Harshbarger became a sculptor and mosaic artist in 1999, working primarily with Lego blocks rather than pixels as his units of construction. His works include a reproduction of the *Mona Lisa*, a wall installation that required more than thirty thousand Lego pieces and measures six by eight feet.

FIG. 5.8
Eric Harshbarger, *Mona Lego*, 2000

Contemporary society is saturated with reproduced and mass-produced images. The idea that only a one-of-a-kind image can be authentic holds more limited currency in the twenty-first century. Many copies can exist of a photographic image, each of equal value, and cinematic, television, and digital images consist of many simultaneous images on many screens all at once. Their value lies not in their uniqueness but in their aesthetic, cultural, and social worth. A television news image can be considered valuable because it can be seen immediately and simultaneously on many screens at the same time. Digital images have no original—copies are of relatively equal quality and value. However, Benjamin's points remain valid today: (1) that the reproduction of a singular image (such as a painting) has an effect on the meaning and value of that original image and (2) that the mechanical reproducibility of images changes their relationship to rituals of meaning, use, and value in their respective markets. In the following sections, we discuss further his point that reproducibility is a political issue and the questions of copyright and ownership that reproducibility poses.

The Politics of Reproducibility

Benjamin argued that the result of mechanical reproduction was a profound change in the function of art. He stated, "Instead of being based on ritual, [art] begins to be based on another practice—politics."[8] Benjamin wrote this essay in Germany in the 1930s, as the rise of fascism and the Nazi Party was orchestrated in part by an elaborate propaganda machine of images. Germany's Third Reich anticipated much of the contemporary use of images in politics to groom the image of political leaders and the cult value that images can produce. Its images of grandeur, monumentality, and massive regimentation are now icons for both a fascist aesthetic and the practice of propaganda.

It is central to this concept that reproduction allows images to circulate with political meaning and that mechanically or electronically reproduced images can be in many places simultaneously and can be combined with text or other images or reworked. These capabilities have greatly increased the ability of images to captivate and persuade. In the 1930s, German artist John Heartfield produced photo collages against the Nazis (and their use of images of Adolf Hitler to further their political power) that had a biting political edge. The powerful effect of Heartfield's images is derived in part from his use of "found" photographic images to make political statements. In fig. 5.9, he portrays Hitler swallowing gold coins and taking the money of the German people. Heartfield borrowed from the style of German propaganda images at the time to make his political art, using the images of the Nazis against them. The photo-collage form allows Heartfield to make a political statement through reworking and combining familiar images in new ways—thus the photo-collage form gives the image a kind of visceral quality that a drawing might not accomplish.

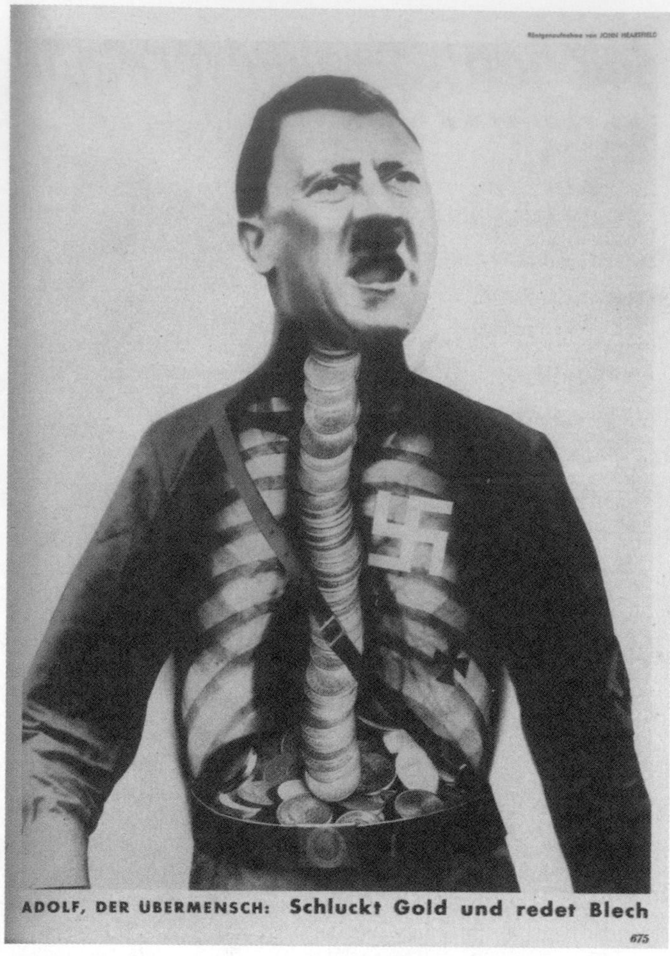

ADOLF, DER UBERMENSCH: Schluckt Gold und redet Blech

FIG. 5.9
John Heartfield, *Adolf as Superman: "He Swallows Gold and Spits Out Tin-Plate"*, 1932

The reproduction of a charged image can also heighten its political message. One image that has served as an icon for revolutionary politics is the famous photograph of Latin American revolutionary figure Che Guevara taken in 1961 by the Cuban photographer Korda (Alberto Díaz Gutíerrez). The photograph of Che looking outward and wearing a beret with a star on it has long been an important symbol in Cuba, where Guevara is a hero for his participation in the Revolution of 1959. As Ariana Hernández-Reguant explains in her discussion of the transformation of cultural politics of art and authorship under late socialism in Cuba, the image of Che can be tracked to read the broader changes in Cuba, from censorship to Cuba's version of *perestroika* and a market economy. The politics of image ownership and copyright brought new meaning and marketability to the photograph—and to its photographer—that had already taken on a vastly broad and diverse range of forms and meanings for an international public.

The reproduction of the photograph of Che has been a crucial aspect of the way in which Guevara became not only a hero of leftist Latin American politics (and more broadly an icon of revolutionary socialist politics throughout the world) but also a revolutionary martyr. The fact that Guevara is known as "Che" rather than "Guevara" points to the intimate sense of loyalty if not possession that people feel toward him and his image.

In the original photograph Che is wearing a beret, a hat that has become since that time a symbol of alternative and activist politics. Although the beret was traditional military gear in the French army and later during World War II in the British army as well, it has since the mid-twentieth century had an association with revolutionary politics. For instance, in the 1960s, the Black Panthers, who were very conscious of the role of images in revolutionary politics (as is clear in the extensive prints and posters produced by the artist Emery Douglas), wore black berets as a kind of uniform that connected back to Che's style. The single star on Che's beret, which designates his military rank of comandante as a guerrilla in the fight over revolutionary Cuba, is mythologized both as a designation of Che's unique valor and as a symbol of his celestial power in many reiterations of the Che image.[9] At this point in history, images employing even just the abstract

FIG. 5.10
Alfredo Rostgaard (OSPAAAL), *Portrait of Che*, 1969

silhouette of Che are widely recognized as symbols of this iconic figure.

The famous photograph of Che has been reproduced in many forms. In Cuba, where Che is a national hero of mythic proportions, the photograph has been used in many government posters to affirm the origins of the Cuban state in its revolution. In these images, Che is radiant, extending over the landscape. His larger-than-life presence looms over Latin America. Throughout the world, the Che image has circulated not only as an icon of both revolutionary politics and leftist uprisings but also as an icon of the charisma of revolutionary heroes. In this process, the image has often become increasingly abstracted, yet it remains recognizable even from a simply made beaded wall hanging that barely outlines its shape. Inevitably, the Che image has proliferated as a kind of quick shorthand to signify leftist or progressive politics and revolutionary movements. The image has spilled over into numerous commodity items. Che's image has been marketed on tote bags (with the slogan "Chénge the World") and mouse pads in part because it is so instantly recognizable. In Benjamin's terms the reproducibility of this image opens its potential to be deployed for political purposes. It also means that the original meaning of the image can be transformed through its constant iterations until it is just shorthand for a more general meaning, such as breaking with conventions. Is the meaning of Che diminished by the constant reiteration of his image on consumer fashions and trinkets—those very objects that Che himself might have critiqued for their role in commodity fetishism?

FIG. 5.11
Rafael López Castro and Gabriela Rodríguez, *Por la Ruta del Che (On the Path of Che), March for Latin American Student Solidarity 29 June–26 July 1998*

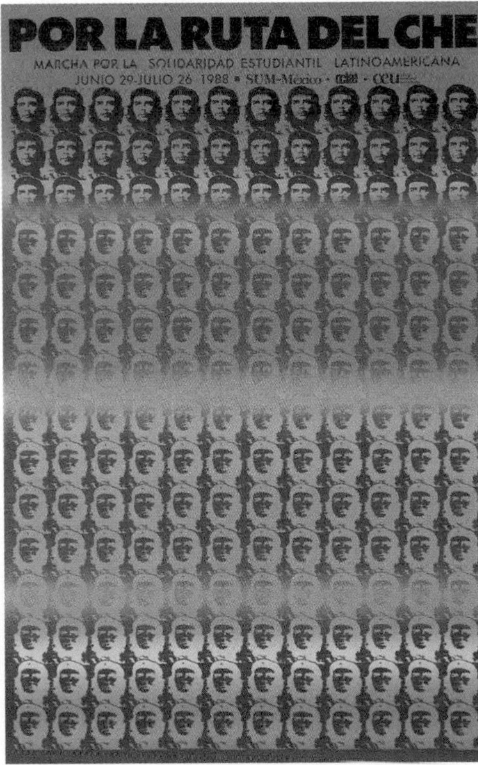

This reproduction of images also raises issues of copyright and ownership. In the socialist system of Cuba, the rights of photographer Korda to own the image of Che were limited. The image was used for many decades without copyright being invoked. In 2000, however, Korda successfully sued the British ad agency Lowe Lintas that had used the image in a Smirnoff vodka ad.[10] Hernández-Reguant writes that the lawsuit marks a change in Cuban politics that indicates both Cuba's entrance into the global economy and the emergence of a group of elite cultural producers who are able to exercise claims over the value of their work in foreign markets. Needless to say, there

FIG. 5.12
Che bead hanging, Havana, 1996

are multiple ironies in the competing values placed on the reproductions of Che's image (moral values of the revolution, national values of the Cuban state, and commercial values of the global marketplace) in a global economy.

The tradition of political art and images of protest, which expanded in significant ways in the era of mechanical reproduction, often stands in opposition to the concept that images should be unique, sacred, and have monetary value or should be copyrighted and owned by an individual. For instance, AIDS activists have produced images for the purpose of distributing as many symbols and messages as possible on the street through posters, buttons, stickers, and T-shirts. These images were disseminated in the 1980s and 1990s in cities around the United States as a means of using the street as a forum for protest art. The *Silence = Death* image (which has an inverted pink triangle in its center) was distributed in many forms and even spray-painted onto sidewalks in cities such as New York. The value of this image does not come from its reference to any original but is derived specifically from its proliferation. It is intended to make people recognize and reconsider their passivity precisely because it is an omnipresent symbol visible even in the moment of stepping onto the curb of a city street. The triangle refers to the pink triangle that homosexuals were forced to wear in Nazi Germany, just as Jews were forced to wear yellow stars. As such it is intended to refer to the tragic consequences of ignoring a crisis at hand. With the triangle placed upside down, this image recodes a homophobic symbol of the past by reversing its meaning from shame to pride. This act of appropriating and transcoding the original symbol has important political implications. The original symbol, here the pink triangle, is emptied of its former power and given new strength. The effectiveness of the *Silence = Death* image in conveying a message is directly related to its capacity to be reproduced many times and to exist in many different places at the same time. The more it proliferates, the more powerful

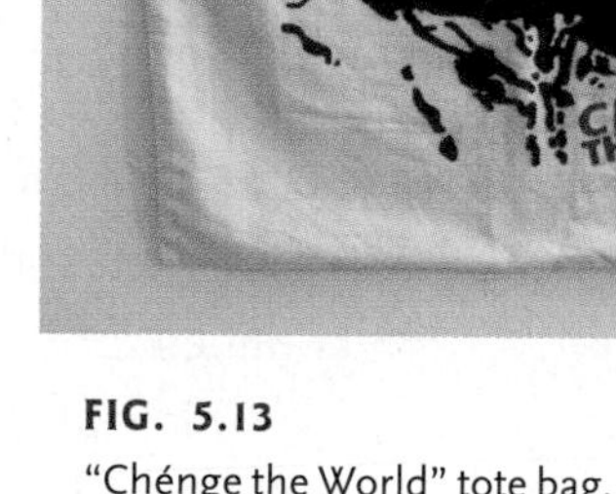

FIG. 5.13
"Chénge the World" tote bag.

FIG. 5.14
Che "Revolutionary Martyr" mousepad

FIG. 5.15
Alberto "Korda" Díaz Gutíerrez, photographer of Che photo, after winning lawsuit against agency Lowe Lintas and photo agency Rex Features, Sept. 8, 2000, Havana, Cuba.

its message. Importantly, it is not a copyrighted image but an image intended to be copied and passed around—an image that is free of charge and not owned by anyone.

FIG. 5.16
ACT UP, *Silence = Death*, 1986

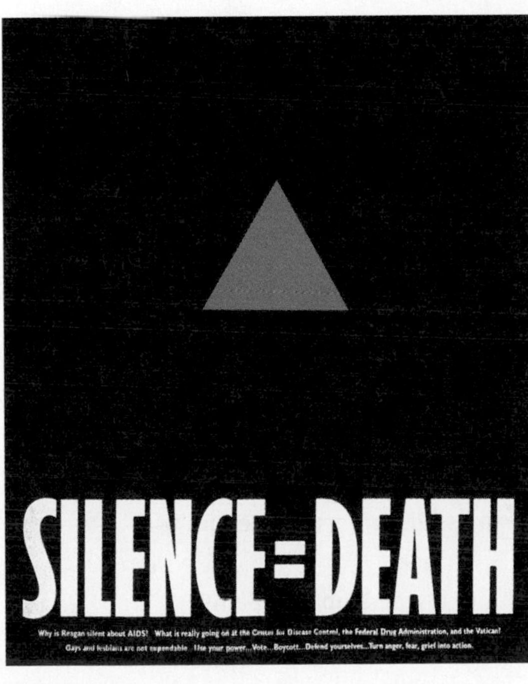

The proliferation of images through reproduction also means that images can be more easily accompanied by different kinds of text, which can dramatically change the signification of the image. Text can ask us to look at an image differently. Words can direct our eyes to particular aspects of the image; indeed, they can tell us what to see in a picture. We can see that the text that accompanies the Heartfield photo collage in fig. 5.9, "He swallows gold and spits out tin-plate," explains the image to us and makes clear its political meaning. It strongly condemns Hitler as a leader who is robbing the German people and selling them a lie. The words "Silence = Death" give a new meaning to the transformed pink triangle, encoding it with the message that silence about the oppression of gays is fatal.

Copies, Ownership, and Copyright

"The Work of Art in the Age of Mechanical Reproduction," like many of Benjamin's writings, is still highly influential (and widely reproduced) today. The essay anticipated changes in the art and visual culture of the twentieth and twenty-first centuries, which saw massive growth in technologies of visual reproduction. But Benjamin's essay could not anticipate the intensification of debates about image reproduction ownership rights that mushroomed alongside the new politics of reproducibility and the new techniques of reproduction in the digital era. One perspective on this era that is shared by many who enjoy the benefits of the new reproductive technologies is that computers and digital imaging have made the possibilities for reproduction and ownership of images virtually limitless. This situation raises issues about the status of rights to reproductions and changes in the legal structures through which the circulation of reproductions is regulated.

The possibilities for reproduction of any image are highly contingent on the legal management of images as forms of intellectual property. Moral codes and laws concerning copyright in particular not only regulate the flow of copies but also shape ideas about what constitutes a legitimate use of a copy and what constitutes an infraction of ownership rights. When is the right to an image protected by law? With the proliferation of means of reproduction in the twentieth century, ownership of the image emerged as a complex field of ethics and law in most national contexts. In this section, we briefly consider aspects of privacy, image rights, and intellectual property (copyright and trademark) with respect to images in the context of U.S. intellectual property law.

Copyright, taken literally, means "the right to copy." The term refers to not one but a bundle of rights. This bundle includes the rights to distribute, produce, copy, display, perform, create, and control derivative works based on the original. Although the concept would seem to facilitate copying by delineating rights to do so, it was in fact established to protect the rights of the owner or producer of an image from others wishing to make copies, if only for a limited period of time. This time limit has continually been expanded so that in 2008 it stands at the author's life plus seventy years, or ninety-five years if a corporation is the owner of the work. Copyright grants legal protection to the "expression of an idea," not the idea itself. The fixed expression is deemed to belong uniquely to someone—the photographer, writer, painter—who created it. Under the Berne Convention of 1886, copyright for a creative work does not have to be declared. One need not register or apply; rather, the work must be "fixed" (written, expressed, or documented in some medium).

Let us first consider the case of an original painting. Ownership of a painting belongs with its creator unless the painting is done as work for hire. When the painting is sold, ownership of the object itself is transferred, but the right to reproduce that object is not. The painter sells the object but not the "expression of the idea" that informs that object. The rights to the expression of the idea, as well as rights to reproduce, to distribute, and to make derivative works from the object, all remain with the artist. Within the terms of copyright law, reproductions of the painting are considered reproductions of the *expression of the idea* (which is protected as the painter's) and not simply reproductions of the *physical object*, the painting. The rights to reproduce the painting in the form of photographs for publicity and such can be negotiated, but they are not automatically transferred with the purchase of the painting. In other words, authenticity, in legal terms, resides in the painting as a unique expression of the painter's idea and not in the literal uniqueness of the object "the painting."

This is not to say that the value is not understood to inhere in the actual work itself. Continuing concerns about the presence of forgeries and fakes among works of famous painters in museums and private collections highlight the fact that although copyright law emphasizes the expression of the idea, we cannot dismiss the material value of the actual work. In the nineteenth and early twentieth centuries, techniques for authenticating works of art were the domain of connoisseurs who were trusted to know the real thing when they saw it. Some authenticators licked, smelled, and touched the painting for evidence of material likeness of the work to others by the same painter, and one expert describes a method for authenticating Cycladic sculptures in which the object is struck with a tuning fork. If the object emitted a dull thud, that would suggest authenticity. A ringing sound would indicate a possible fake. Sleuthing involved noting the inclusion of anachronistic elements in the scene (the wrong style of clothing, for example). By the middle of the twentieth century, forgery detection had become the domain of laboratory science, with chemical analysis of elements such as paint and paper introduced to determine anachronistic use of materials and X-ray imaging, CT scanning, and infrared examination used to determine underlying layers of paint and areas of structural change or repair. Spectrophotometry is a laboratory process used to date pigment by analyzing its chemical composition.

The work of Vincent van Gogh has been at the center of scandals concerning forgeries since the turn of the last century, culminating in the infamous Wacker affair, in which Otto Wacker, described as a charming trickster, was ultimately found guilty of fraud in the passing off of thirty-three forgeries as original van Goghs. Experts engaged in the debate over the forgeries noted the importance of technical means of discerning them, such as techniques for dating the canvas and paints or analyzing brush style, but many also noted that the most reliable test of authenticity was the viewer's intuition in picking up on the authentic style of the artist.

The case of copyright of the novel *Gone with the Wind* is a useful one through which to demonstrate how the notion of what aspect of the work embodies "unique expression" can change. Uniqueness is not always attached to the work as a whole. When the novel approached the end of its period of copyright protection, the estate of Margaret Mitchell, the novel's author, sought to prevent the work from falling into the public domain. They set out to find authors who would work on commission to write sequels to the story. Because this sequel writing was done for hire, ownership of the expression of the ideas in the sequels belonged to the estate and not to the writers. These sequels did not extend the life of the copyright of the book *Gone with the Wind*, but as the characters in the original book were portrayed in the sequels, the *characters* became the protected expressions of an idea. This all but ensured the estate the ability to stop others from incorporating those characters into their works. The original *Gone with the Wind* thus became protected by default, because any attempt to reproduce the novel would have to entail reproducing its characters, which were now newly protected from copy in the form of protected estate ownership rights to the sequels.

As we have noted before, reproduction also refers to the copy of one's image or likeness. To whom does one's image or appearance belong, and how is ownership of a likeness determined? John David Viera, writing on the question of privacy in documentary photography, raises this question first as an ethical (not legal) one. He discusses, among other cases, the portraits taken by photographers employed by the Farm Security Administration during the 1930s of poor migrant farmers caught in the economic and environmental devastation of the Great Depression and the Dust Bowl that wiped out farmland in the American midwest.[11] Consider Dorothea Lange's photograph *Migrant Mother* (fig. 1.24), which we discuss in chapter 1. The face of this woman has become a widely recognized icon of the Depression. Viera notes that individuals such as this woman gained no economic benefit from their loss of privacy. They have been subject to a seemingly eternal role as a symbol of human misery. The issue of obtaining consent from a photographic subject, he explains, buries the deeper problem of the subject's lack of ability to predict and control the meanings and uses of the image as it is reproduced and circulated in different contexts in the decades and centuries following the short moment during which it is taken. The instantaneity of the photographic moment in which the likeness of the subject is captured in an image that will be owned by the photographer belies the potential life of the image well beyond the scope of the photographic subject's control.

This question of consent and the individual right to privacy was especially complicated in the case of *Titicut Follies* (1967), the only American film banned for reasons other than obscenity and national security. The documentary, which exposed life in a Massachusetts correctional facility for the criminally insane, and its director, the lawyer turned filmmaker Frederick Wiseman, were at the center of a national controversy about what constitutes informed consent, the competency of subjects to consent (in this case, to being filmed), and the moral and ethical issues involved when personal humiliation is put on display to reveal violations of human rights and to effect social change on a larger scale. The film was subject to legal restrictions in force until 1992 concerning audiences (it was restricted to educational use only) and was finally opened to broad distribution markets in 2007, forty years after its production.

The likenesses of *public* personalities pose different issues with respect to privacy and exploitation. Only celebrities, Viera explains, have valuable public images and therefore seek to control the circulation of their likenesses. There are nonconcrete aspects of a star, such as persona, that create intangible forms of intellectual property that have confounded law. Viera considers the ownership of personality rights and the case of Bela Lugosi's performance on stage in *Dracula* (1931). The character Count Dracula dates from the sixteenth century and, by law, is not owned. Universal Film Studios contracted with Lugosi to photograph and reproduce, distribute, and exploit his *actions, poses,* and *appearances* in relation to this film. Lugosi's performance, however, transcended the copyrighted film. The public came to see Lugosi himself as synonymous with the character. Universal capitalized on this by marketing his likeness in the film in masks, costumes, and other tie-ins as the studio's property. Lugosi's son and widow, seeing this as a violation of their rights to ownership of Lugosi's image as a personal property right, sued the studio and lost, but by default. In *Lugosi v. Universal Pictures* (1979), the California Supreme Court ruled that Lugosi had had the right to *convert* his personal image into a property right, but because he had not done so during his lifetime, the right to do so had expired with his death and could not be revived by his heirs. Universal could continue to own the Lugosi Dracula image by default and could prevent others from using the image as well. Since the Lugosi decision, many states have passed laws, such as the California Celebrities Rights Act of 1984, protecting a person's "right

FIG. 5.17
Bela Lugosi, Jr. (right), with Dracula stamp art, 1997

of publicity," effectively reversing the initial decision against the rights of the Lugosi estate. However, it still remains unclear what aspects of likeness and personality are protected by these laws.

The word copyright suggests a policy that grants rights to copy. Copyright, however, is a policy that in actuality regulates and restricts copying, though it does not rule out reproduction entirely. In the United States, the Fair Use Doctrine (made law in the Copyright Act of 1976) permits copying without permission of the copyright holder in certain limited cases. A major factor in determining fair use is the question of whether the copy promotes or adds something new—whether it is transformative rather than simply derivative of the original. A major question concerns how the courts determine the difference between transformation and derivation of a work in an era when appropriation and parody are common forms in artistic production.

These areas of law sometimes converge in ways that demonstrate the complexity of the "bundle of rights" contained in the concept of the right to copy. For example, an unauthorized concert T-shirt bearing the name and image of the band The White Stripes would violate all three aspects of copyright law. Jack and Meg White, who constitute the band, own trademark rights to The White Stripes band name. Each individually owns publicity rights to his or her image and likeness. The photographer who took the picture would own the copyright to the photograph appearing on the T-shirt. He or she has the right to show or sell the image. However, that right does not include the ability to exploit the persona of the people or group depicted by using the image as a marketing tool or by selling the image to be used in this way. The manufacturer of the T-shirt may have purchased a copy of the photograph, but he or she would additionally need to purchase from the photographer the right to reproduce the photograph and, further, the right to reproduce it on a particular item (such as a T-shirt or poster). The manufacturer also would need to acquire permission from the trademarked band, as well as from Meg and Jack White as individuals whose likenesses are displayed in the photograph, to use their band name and likenesses on the T-shirt.

An example of a blatant engagement of the issue of copy and rights is Sherrie Levine's work *After Walker Evans*. In 1981, the New York gallery Metro Pictures displayed the work of the artist Sherrie Levine. Levine's exhibition consisted of a series of documentary photographs of the Burroughs family, tenant farmers in the destitute Depression-era South taken by the well-known photographer Walker Evans for the U.S. Farm Security Administration. Levine copied the photographs, which were no longer protected by copyright, from an exhibition catalogue of the work of Walker Evans, titled *First to Last*. She framed and displayed the copies with no additional alteration. (We discuss Levine's work in the context of postmodern art in chapter 8.) This case raises important questions about ethical and market issues concerning copies and originals, although it was not the source of a copyright dispute. Levine, in this act of explicit display of copies as the "original" works of the fine artist (herself), raised questions about the status of appropriation in art and the nature of creativity in the age of mechanical reproducibility. Here we find the issues of authenticity and image ownership and the question of what constitutes transformation versus derivation in the appropriation of another person's creative production. By moving the photographs into a gallery of contemporary fine art, Levine raised the question of the changing value of photography, and by reproducing these particular historical images of poverty in the era of Reaganomics, she raised questions about the meaning of historical records of national experience viewed through a different era's frame of reference.

The questions about art and reproducibility raised by Levine were further highlighted when the Levine show itself was copied by the artist Michael Mandiberg. Mandiberg's copy exists in digital form on two identical sites: AfterWalkerEvans.com and AfterSherrieLevine.com. Whereas the work in Levine's 1981 show was copyrighted, Mandiberg's digital sites invite browsers to download any image at whim, providing those who choose to do so with certificates of authenticity and ownership. The stated aim of Mandiberg's duplicate copycat sites is to create the possibility for ownership of a physical object with cultural but not economic value. Mandiberg thus quite shrewdly plays a game of one-upmanship with Levine on the issue of reproduction. He uses digital reproduction to restore to the Evans photographs their "original" status as existing in the public domain, as photographic icons of American collective memory and history. The

FIG. 5.18
Michael Mandiberg, image and certificate of authenticity from AfterWalkerEvans.com and AfterSherrieLevine.com, 2001

Certificate of Authenticity

Untitled (AfterSherrieLevine.com/2.jpg)

Michael Mandiberg

This certificate guarantees that the accompanying digital image printout, Untitled (AfterWalkerEvans.com/2.jpg), is an authentic work of art by Michael Mandiberg so long as the following conditions have been met:

1. The image has been printed 3.825" x 5" at the highest resolution setting of the printer, up to the full resolution of 850DPI. The image is centered on an 8.5" x 11" piece of paper which has been trimmed to 8" x 10" to fit in the frame — the image must remain centered on the 8" x 10" piece of paper.

2 The image has been framed in an 8" x 10" black pre-cut Nielsen & Bainbridge sectional frame kit, available inexpensively at most frame or art supply stores.

3 This certificate is signed by the printer of the image, trimmed to 8" x 10" and placed in the rear of the frame facing out so it can be read while looking at the back of the frame.

Print your name here: MARITA STURKEN

Sign your name here: [signature]

Date: 2-9-08

FIG. 5.19
Art Rogers, *Puppies*, 1980

digital form enhances rather than undercuts photography's role, in this case, as a medium of collective memory.

The 1992 court case of *Rogers v. Koons* takes us into yet another direction of inquiry concerning the bundle of rights and issues contained in copyright law. The professional photographer Art Rogers produced this image, titled "Puppies," which was reproduced on postcards and other goods. The well-known American artist Jeff Koons sent a copy of a postcard with this image, copyright label removed, to an Italian studio with instructions for its assembly in the form of a statue. The sculpture, which he titled *String of Puppies*, originally sold for a reported $367,000. When Rogers sued Koons and his gallery for infringement of copyright, Koons claimed his work was a parody and therefore was protected under the Fair Use Doctrine. The court's determination was that Koons could have constructed a parody on that general style but that in fact he had copied the specific Rogers image. It was not the Rogers artwork that was being parodied, specifically, but rather a broader style. *String of Puppies* therefore did not constitute fair use. It was derivative, not transformative. An interesting aspect of this determination is that the sculpture was considered derivative despite its obvious transformation of media (from photography to sculpture). Though the medium was changed, the concept remained derivative.

In 2006, the courts ruled in favor of Koons in another of his legal cases (*Blanch v. Koons*). For a work he titled *Niagara*, the artist appropriated a photograph by professional fashion and portrait photographer Andrea Blanch that had been published in *Allure* magazine. Koons argued that the work, a painting commissioned by

Deutsche Bank and the Guggenheim Museum, used popular images to comment on the social and aesthetic consequences of the mass media. The court ruled that use of the legs from Blanch's copyrighted image constituted fair use on the basis of multiple factors, including the fact that Koons's painting had an entirely different purpose and meaning from the original work and took a different form in a different social context (a gallery).

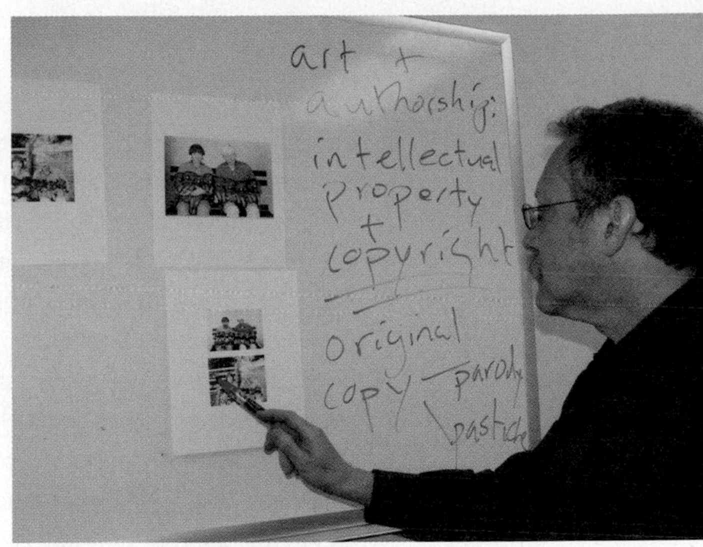

FIG. 5.20
Professor teaching issues of copyright raised by Jeff Koons's *String of Puppies*, 1998 and Art Rogers's *Puppies*, 1980

Trademarks that involve graphic or pictorial images constitute a slightly different set of legal concerns. A trademark is a symbol, word, or phrase used to identify a manufacturer's product and distinguish it from the goods of others. The "swoosh" logo that is synonymous with Nike lets us know that these sneakers are made by that company and that company only. It is not the sneaker in general that is trademarked (except in cases in which particular design features of the sneaker are trademarked). Rather, the unique mark that signifies a brand is the protected, trademarked entity. One acquires the right to a unique mark by being the first to use or register it. However, one may have the right to display a logo contested or limited if a similar mark is found to preexist in another national context, as was the case with the Nike logo in the 1992 Barcelona Olympics. A year before the Nike name was registered by the sports company in 1983, a Spanish lawyer had purchased the rights to the mark from a Catalonian sock company which had registered a mark incorporating the word Nike in 1932. The Nike company thus was threatened with restriction of its ability to display its sign in one of the major international brand marketing opportunities of the year.

Threat to ownership can also occur if a mark becomes "genericized"—that is, if its use becomes so widespread that the mark becomes synonymous with the generic type. Kellogg lost its challenge to a competitor's use of the name "shredded wheat," for example, because this form of cereal had become generic. In contrast, Xerox mounted a successful marketing campaign to "save" its mark from becoming generic. "Don't make a Xerox, make a Xerox copy" was the message they sent the public as a means of defending their unique mark. The ubiquitous yellow smiley face that has appeared on buttons, stamps, and computer emoticons since the 1960s, which we discuss in chapter 1, is an interesting example of the limits of genericide. The symbol is the subject of an ongoing lawsuit in which the London company SmileyWorld, who registered the mark, and the French designer Franklin Loufrani, who filed the trademark for SmileyWorld in France in 1971, opposed the use of the generic symbol by WalMart.[12] Credit for the design in the United States has informally gone to Harvey Ball of Massachusetts, who, in 1963, designed the yellow smiley button for State Mutual Life Assurance Company of America for a fee of forty-five dollars. Ball refused to register the icon, feeling that it belonged to the public and not to him alone, to the disappointment of his heirs.

These diverse cases of copyright, right of publicity, trademark practice, and Fair-Use Doctrine testing suggest that reproduction has become an important issue not only because copies and their technologies are more pervasive but also because the proliferation of copies and technologies for making them has made the stakes in owning the original that much higher. Fair use of copies is always dependent on interpretation of the Fair Use Doctrine, a set of guidelines that is unique to the United States and dependent on practical interpretation, not the word of law. But the question remains, What counts as "original" in an era of technological reproducibility and simulation? There is no easy or general answer to this question, as digital technologies have made the original hard to identify and the intangibles (persona, the expression of the idea) harder to document and trace.

Reproduction and the Digital Image

The digital image raises questions of reproduction and copyright to new levels of intensity. The digital camera has no negative, no "original" storage medium from which copies are made. Digital images differ from analog photographic images in ways that affect how they look, the ways in which they are generated, stored, and distributed, and the kinds of devices (digital cameras, cell phones, computers, iPods, websites, etc.) on which they can be created and displayed. Yet there are many similar ways in which digital images are used as analog photographic images were—as forms of personal expression, for family portraiture, and as documentary evidence.

Analog images by definition bear a physical correspondence with their material referents. An analog photograph gains its power in part through the sense that it is a trace of the real. Analog images, such as photographs and analog video images, are defined by properties that express value along a continuous scale, such as gradations of tone (or changes in intensity through increasing or decreasing voltage in video); thus analog signals can be regulated gradually, by "knob twisting," for instance. One way to see this is to consider the difference between an analog clock that measures time on a continuum in a circular fashion and a digital clock that counts forward in numeral increments. A traditional silver-based analog photograph is primarily composed of "grain," or numerous dots that together form the lights, darks, contrasts, and shapes of a recognizable image. In digital cameras, the roll of film on which is exposed a negative image is replaced with an electronic image sensor and storage microchip. The roll form, as we noted in our discussion of the funerary papyrus in chapter 4, has had a long history; its association with photography ends with this transition to a unit of reproduction that takes the form of a tiny chip on which hundreds of images can be stored in minute code, deleted, and replaced.

The significance of the negative as "original" stems not just from the fact that the negative was "there" at the take with the filmed object (we could argue that the chip was there as well) but that when a film negative is copied, there is degeneration of the "original" image. Multiple positive prints from the same negative will have about the same image quality, because all are one generation away from the negative. The information on the digital chip is not subject to degeneration because it is code that can be replicated without this kind of loss of detail. This code can be downloaded onto multiple storage devices and from device to device without any loss of image quality. With the digital camera, then, we have the quality of reproducibility built into the form in a way that eliminates dependence on a single original medium (the negative) from which the work derives. For this reason, we can say that the digital photograph breaks even further than did the analog photograph from the ideology of the original work. Not only is the digital photograph highly reproducible, but also reproducibility itself is a deeply inherent characteristic of digital technology.

Whereas analog cameras produce images that must be processed and developed, digital cameras allow the photographer to see the image on the camera immediately after the take, allowing even more instantaneous pleasure in the image than did the Polaroid snapshot of the 1960s, which developed right before the eyes of the consumer. One sees a positive image, not a negative, both with the Polaroid and the digital photograph. Here we see a relationship back to an earlier technology as this positive evokes the mirror effect of the camera obscura, in which the image consumed is the one projected on the surface of the chamber, and not in the form of a portable print.

A similar change in the status of timing and delay in seeing one's product, and seeing oneself, occurred in the film industry of the 1950s when magnetic tape was introduced to the sound recording process. The optical soundtrack, recorded in the form of a band of emulsion at the edge of the film that could be "excited" by a sound bulb, required developing before it could be played. Sound recorded on magnetic tape on the set could be played back immediately after the take. With advances in sound studios and sound recording on sets into the 1940s, some actors became obsessed with playback devices during shoots, listening to a sound take immediately afterward (much as football players watch a replay during halftime), redoing it to correct any perceived errors or problems. Whereas previously performers had to wait to hear the take, now they could hear their sound echoed back in a kind of mirror effect. The digital video and still digital camera have, since the 1980s, provided this same sort of near-instant feedback loop, by which a take can be followed almost immediately by looking at and changing the scene of the conditions of the take and redoing the scene. This capacity to use the photograph itself to redo a shoot in progress, however, was introduced relatively late, with digital photography in the 1990s.

The most widely discussed difference between conventional and digital photography concerns what happens after the take, before the print is struck. The pixel form of the digital photograph coincides with the technology available in digital image manipulation software programs such as PhotoShop. The convergence of the two systems happened not by chance but by design, in an industrial effort to strengthen markets for visual technologies by combining two or more forms that previously had been separate. Anyone with a digital camera, a home computer, and a cable can download images not only to print them out as they are but also to copy them into programs in which they can be edited, enhanced, corrected, and manipulated to alter composition, framing, color, and combinations of elements and scenes.

Digital photography has thus altered the noeme, the "that has been" effect, of conventional photography that we discussed in Chapter 5 by opening up the possibilities for "creative geography." This concept of creative geography was illustrated by the Soviet filmmaker Lev Kuleshov in 1922, who intercut images of pedestrians walking, one to the right and one to the left, in two sequences of film (in Moscow and Washington, D.C.) to give the spectator the sense that the two are in the same geographic space and will meet up. In digital programs such as PhotoShop, it is easy to be creative in placing oneself in locales that one has never visited or that do not exist in a kind of virtual tourism. As Lisa Nakamura notes, the potential for virtual tourism (visiting online museums and representations of distant places) increases with a global audience accustomed to living through the space of the screen.[13] With digital imaging, photography has lost some of its sense of "that which has been." But the reason is not that the camera does not need to be in the same place as the object it depicts (it does, unless we are speaking of a simulation). Rather, it is that we have become so used to the possibilities for creative manipulation of location, proximity, and historical period, all of which can be evoked with digital effects. This is enhanced by the status of the image itself, the materiality of which loses its importance. The rare and cherished old photograph of our grandmother at age five, fading and crumbling in the family album, becomes a bit less difficult to lose when we have preserved it in a digital file that can be stored, copied, sent via e-mail, or placed on a photo album website. The image becomes timeless in the sense that it can be preserved in a copy that will not erode over time and will not undergo degeneration of quality with copying, as a photographic original would. However, the history of technologies tell us that changes in format often render images and files in previous formats inaccessible and obsolete.

The capacity for manipulation and multiple contextualization is not new, of course, with the digital photograph. It has always been possible to "fake" realism in photographs. Many early photographers played with manipulation. In 1858, in photography's second decade as a popular medium, the British photographer Henry Peach Robinson exhibited *Fading Away*, a photograph of a young girl dying of consumption (tuberculosis). This 1858 portrayal of a young woman dying, surrounded by her grieving relatives, generated controversy for two reasons. Robinson was criticized at the time for exploiting such a painful scene. Representations of grief and death were common in painting, and the morbid and the tragic were no strangers

FIG. 5.21
H. P. Robinson, *Fading Away*, 1858, combination print from five negatives

to art of this period, but for some, this theme crossed a line in the medium of photography. The second objection concerned his technique. *Fading Away* is not one photograph; it is in fact a composite of five. This is a constructed image of what such a scene might look like. We are reminded of the 1504 engraving entitled *Adam and Eve*, discussed in chapter 4, for which Albrecht Dürer made a composite of the most beautiful parts of many different bodies from multiple sketches to assemble each figure. In each case, the scene is actually a virtual depiction.

Digital techniques have made it possible to build on this ability to artificially construct realism. Until the 1990s, tools for the manipulation and recontextualization of the analog photograph remained, for the most part, restricted to the commercial and fine art photographer. It was common practice for commercial photographers to use airbrushing and a range of other professional techniques to reframe, "clean up," combine, and modify their photographs. These techniques have now been transferred to a broader market. Today, it is a common practice to have personal photographs digitally reconfigured, to take now out-of-favor relatives out of wedding pictures, for instance, or to erase ex-boyfriends from treasured images. In many cases, this kind of toying with the historical record is relatively harmless. Yet we can also imagine a context in which all historical images are even more available for manipulation than they have been in the past. What changed with the digital photograph is not the *ability* to manipulate the image but the wide availability and accessibility of these techniques to the middle-class consumer, making not just image production but also image reproduction and alteration an everyday aspect of consumer experience.

Modes of display have also changed. Before, the print sent home from the drugstore lab might include a duplicate set to pass along to a family member that could be cherished along with the original in the family album. Now the "album" exists in the form of multiple duplicate compact discs that can be sent to family members far and wide or of image files to be sent via e-mail, all of them of equal quality. They can also be accessed on websites set up privately or through photo services established to facilitate personal databases such as these. The family photo album has thus moved online and is often much more publicly available than before. Digital archives are thus not just a new technical form. They are also a new way of experiencing history and memory.

The proliferation of the public display of personal images on homepages, blogs, and photo websites such as Flickr has also produced a new relationship between the personal image, commercial photography, and public space. Millions of personal snapshots proliferate on the Web, available for public consumption, and many users tell the stories on their personal blogs and Web diaries by regularly uploading images from their cell phones or laptops. As programs for easily searching images online, such as Google Image, and sites like Flickr have systems for tagging images and making connections between them, users are encouraged to create aggregates and groupings of images. Web users thus can easily assume the role of image collectors and curators as they download images and link to them online. Sites like Flickr allow users to see the links between images geographically, by subject, and by creator. Commercial stock photography businesses have suffered in the face of this burgeoning image database, most of which is guided by the ethos of creative commons. This sharing of images essentially transforms not only the means by which people use images to publicly tell their own personal stories but also the relationship of archives and image institutions to this vast online image collection. The Library of Congress uploaded part of its image collection to Flickr in 2008, so that its historical images could become part of that site's image environment and be the source of user comments and connections. All of these developments have implications for cultural memory and the role of the personal digital image within it.

FIG. 5.22
Deborah Bright, *Untitled*, from *Dream Girls* series, 1989–90

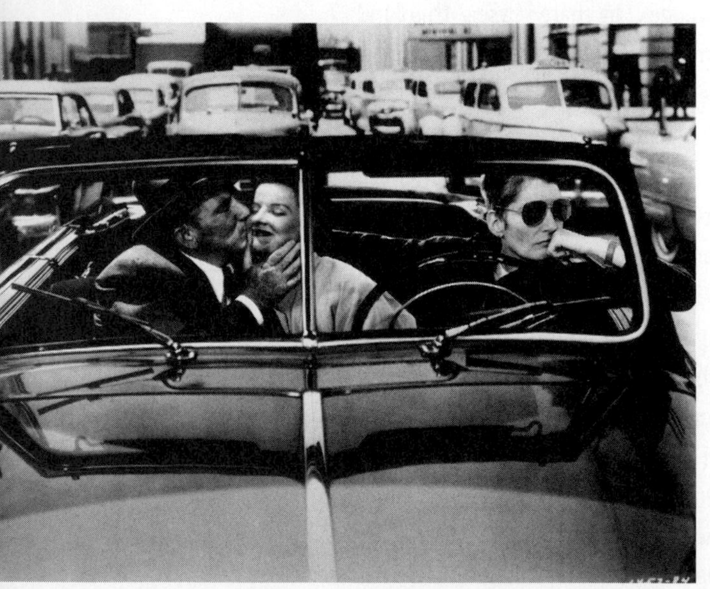

It is also the case that in the contemporary world of visual images, digital and analog forms of image manipulation are creating a broad array of images that defy traditional notions of time. The images of deceased celebrities have been digitally enhanced to have them say words they never spoke or to interact in scenes they never performed (such as a television advertisement in which the late Fred Astaire dances with a contemporary vacuum cleaner). There is ongoing discussion of the potential to create entire new films with virtual versions of now-dead film stars. How will popular culture recycle images of the past? Artist Deborah Bright uses this image context to comment ironically on the representation of compulsory heterosexuality in classic Hollywood films. Here, Bright sits in boredom as film stars Spencer Tracy and Katharine Hepburn embrace in "her" car. Image manipulation allows

Bright to recode the film image, to insert herself into its space of signification, changing its meaning. A nostalgic image of Hollywood romance becomes a critical commentary on the ideology that makes heterosexuality the accepted norm.

Peirce's concept of the indexical quality of signs (discussed in chapter 1) gives us another way to understand the changes taking place with digital technology. As we have noted, the power of the analog photograph is derived largely from its indexical qualities. The camera has coexisted in physical space with the "real" that it has photographed. Many digital images and all simulations lack this indexical relationship to what they represent. For instance, an image in which people are digitally inserted into a landscape where they have never been does not refer to something that has been. Like the Deborah Bright image of Tracy and Hepburn, all composites are fictions. Ironically, H. P. Robinson's famous photograph of a deathbed scene which we discussed earlier in this section was criticized in part on technical grounds, because the joins between the five composite parts used to make the one image were apparent in the print. Simulation is not unique to digital imaging, but the technology makes compositing easier to do and harder to notice. A "digital image" of a sound wave may represent an occurrence of a real sound event, but there is no "real" optical event to which the image bears an indexical relationship. This raises the question of what happens to the idea of photographic truth when an image that looks like a photograph is created on a computer with no camera at all. In Peirce's terms, this marks a fundamental shift in meaning from the photograph to the digital image. Here, index gives way to icon, as we take these computer-generated images to resemble real-life subjects in an iconographic way.

Questions of the verifiability and manipulation of images takes on particular importance in the context of photojournalism and documentary photography. There are very high stakes in the news industry in certain ethical codes of truth telling. These include, among other tenets, the idea that photographic news images are realistic and unmanipulated. In other words, as viewers we assume that the photographs we see in mainstream newspapers and news journals are unaltered (whereas we often assume that the images we see in certain tabloid newspapers are faked, compositing images of different celebrities to make it look like they are together). Discovery that a news organization has altered an image can spark scandal and debate, such as the debate over *Time* magazine's cover image of O. J. Simpson that we discussed in chapter 1. Yet, in the context of digital imaging, with its increased capacity to change images in seamless and realistic ways, can the idea of photographs as unmanipulated evidence survive? Some manufacturers of digital photographic software are developing "photo-authentication" tools that will be designed to track images to their camera source and to detect "improper" manipulation of images.[14]

There are numerous examples of controversies over the manipulation of images to produce more aesthetically pleasing "documentary" images. For instance, *National Geographic* moved the Egyptian pyramids closer together, *TV Guide* put Oprah Winfrey's head on the body of another woman, and in 2007 CBS doctored an image of news anchor Katie Couric for its public relations magazine *Watch!* to make her look slimmer. In the contemporary context of celebrity image making and public relations, these kinds of manipulations are quite common. But when these manipulations spill over into the domain of news organizations held to journalistic standards of objectivity, the codes are quite different.

Photojournalist organizations have produced increasingly explicit guidelines for any manipulation of photographs, guidelines that call into question practices that have had long uncontroversial histories in photojournalism. The debate has brought forward larger questions about the notions of objectivity that are attached to images published in journalistic contexts. Most news organization have instituted policies about digital manipulation, and discussions about whether to mandate labeling of images produced with digital manipulation have been underway since the early 1990s. The *Washington Post* stated in the early 2000s:

> Photography has come to be trusted as a virtual record of an event. We must never betray that trust. It is our policy never to alter the content of news photographs. Normal adjustment to contrast and gray scale for better reproduction is permitted. This means that nothing is added or subtracted from the image such as a hand or tree limb in an inopportune position.[15]

Policies such as this one raise questions such as what constitutes a virtual record, what counts as content and what counts as form, what is normal adjustment, and what constitutes trust in the history of the public's response to journalistic photography. Manipulation techniques

FIG. 5.23
2004 Bush campaign ad, "Whatever It Takes," in which a group of soldiers was electronically copied

have continued to proliferate and are now the norm in digital photography, chipping away at the photographic conventions that previously were associated with truth in photojournalism.

Thus, in contexts in which the stakes in the truth-value of the image are high, digital manipulation is seen within the framework of a discourse of image ethics. During the 2004 U.S. election campaign, the Bush campaign was forced to admit that it had used a doctored photograph of soldiers being addressed by the president in a video ad titled "Whatever It Takes." The original image had been edited to remove the president and his podium from the frame, and a group of soldiers was digitally repeated to fill in the space and make the crowd look bigger. If one examines the image closely, one can see the faces of soldiers repeated throughout the image. Given the implication in the ad that the image was an unretouched documentary image, the campaign was roundly criticized for this manipulation.

William J. Mitchell writes that digital images demand a new set of criteria from viewers as the "age of digital replication is superseding the age of mechanical reproduction." He writes:

> We might best regard digital images, then, neither as ritual objects (as religious paintings have served) nor as objects of mass consumption (as photographs and printed images are in Walter Benjamin's celebrated analysis), but as fragments of information that circulate in high-speed networks now ringing the globe and that can be received, transformed, and recombined like DNA to produce new intellectual structures having their own dynamics and value.[16]

Digital images assert a new kind of value, according to Mitchell—not the cult value of the single object or the exhibition value of the reproduced image but the "input value" of easy manipulation and distribution.

The vast array of photographic, electronic, and digital images that have emerged since the mid-twentieth century has also had the effect of changing certain painting styles. As we have noted, from its very beginning photography changed the social role of painting as a mode of representation. Although it is often stated that the emergence of photography helped free painting styles to move away from realism and into abstraction, in the late twentieth century the style of photorealism emerged among painters who self-consciously deployed a "photographic" style. Eric Fischl, a U.S. painter and sculptor strongly associated with the postmodern style of new realism of the late twentieth century, uses the photograph as a referent for paintings of the human body. His paintings looked "realist" according to photographic conventions, establishing the photograph as source and the painting as copy. This reverses the status of the photograph as copy and the elevation of the painting as original discussed earlier in this chapter.

Artist Chuck Close creates very large paintings that reflect the tonal precision of photographs in ways that take this one step further toward digital photography. Close photographs his subjects, draws a grid over both the photograph and a much

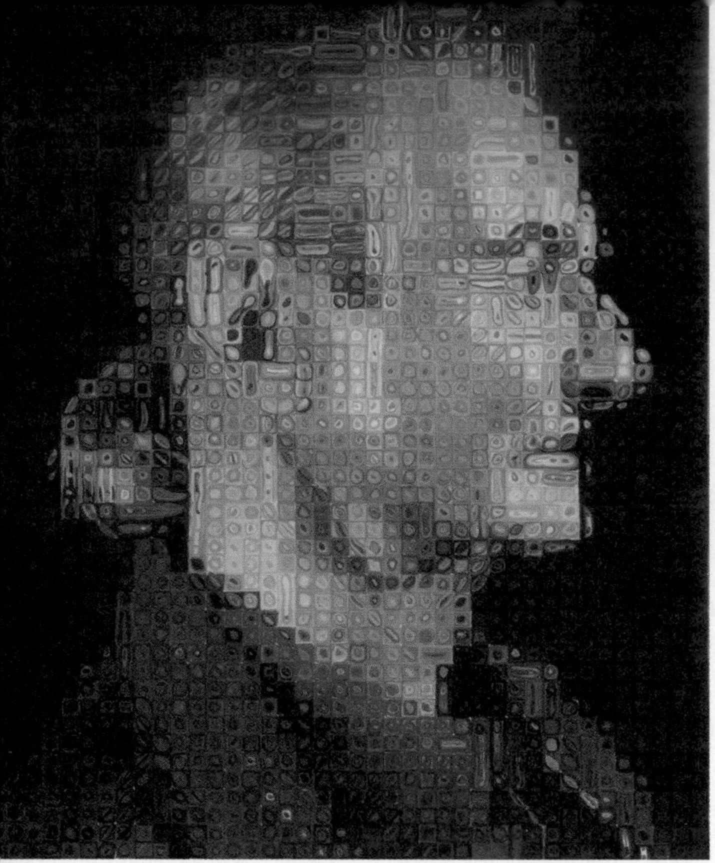

FIG. 5.24
Chuck Close, *Roy II*, 1994

larger canvas, and then paints the image one square at a time. The result, as seen in this portrait of artist Roy Lichtenstein (whose work we discuss in chapter 7), is an abstract rendering of the effect of the photographic and the digital. This image evokes both the grainy surface of a photograph and the grid structure of a digital image, with its multiple squares (pixels) that merge to form a likeness. Close thus deploys an early medium (painting) to create the effect of pixilation that we associate with digital media. If one moves too close to the image, it becomes an abstract grid of shapes and colors, but at a distance the face emerges. The image thus changes substantially according to the position of the viewer in relation to it. Close's image takes us back full circle, in a certain sense, by creating a painting that looks like a digital image.

In this chapter, we have considered aspects of reproduction as they have coincided, since the time of the Renaissance, with the development of visual technologies over the last two centuries. We began by noting the roots of reproduction in the Marxist notion of the term. According to this Marxist view, cultural practices and their forms of expression reproduce the ideologies and interests of the ruling class, which control the means of cultural production. Reproduction of ideology through media forms and texts is an important set of modalities through which a political order and its worldview are maintained. As we move further into the digital era, we can ask whether this notion of reproduction remains useful, given that images and media forms are no longer so tightly bound to the idea of representing a real, and visual technologies are no longer as pervasively regarded as replicating or objectively performing the work of the eye. As we come to regard the body as coextensive and interdependent with its technologies, we must also grasp changes in the meanings and contextual roles of reproduction. We will explore some of these issues in the later chapters of this book.

Notes

1. Geoffrey Batchen, *Burning with Desire: The Conception of Photography*, 36 (Cambridge, Mass.: MIT Press, 1997).
2. Georges Didi-Huberman, "Photography—Scientific and Pseudo-scientific," in *A History of Photography: Social and Cultural Perspectives*, ed. Jean-Claude Lemagny and André Rouille, trans. Janet Lloyd, 71 (Cambridge, UK: Cambridge University Press, 1987).
3. H. W. Janson and Anthony Janson, *History of Art: The Western Tradition*, 6th ed., 58 (New York: Harry N. Abrams, 2001).

4. William M. Ivins, Jr., *Prints and Visual Communication*, 3 (Cambridge, Mass.: MIT Press, 1969).
5. André Bazin, "The Myth of Total Cinema," in Hugh Gray, ed. and trans., *What Is Cinema? Volume 1*, 21–22 (Berkeley: University of California Press, 1967). Bazin also mentions the shroud in his "Ontology of the Photographic Image" in the same volume, 9–16.
6. Vered Maimon, "Talbot and Herschel: Photography as a Site of Knowledge in Early Nineteenth-Century England" (Ph.D. dissertation, Columbia University, 2006).
7. Walter Benjamin, "The Work of Art in the Age of Mechanical Reproduction," in *Illuminations*, trans. Harry Zohn, 220 (New York: Schocken Books, 1969); also in Walter Benjamin,*The Work of Art in the Age of Its Technological Reproducibility, and Other Writings on Media*, ed. Michael W. Jennings, Brigid Doherty, and Thomas Y. Levin (Cambridge, Mass.: Harvard University Press, 2008).
8. Benjamin, "The Work of Art in the Age of Mechanical Reproduction," 224.
9. David Kunzle, *Che Guevara: Icon, Myth, and Message*, 53 (Los Angeles: UCLA Fowler Museum of Cultural History, 1997).
10. Ariana Hernández-Reguant, "Copyrighting Che: Art and Authorship under Cuban Late Socialism," *Public Culture* 16.1 (2004), 4.
11. John David Viera, "Images as Property," in *Image Ethics: The Moral Rights of Subjects in Photographs, Film and Television*, ed. Larry Gross, John Stuart Katz, and Jay Ruby, 135–62 (New York: Oxford, 1988).
12. Thomas Crampton, "Smiley Face Is Serious to Company," *New York Times*, July 5, 2006.
13. Lisa Nakamura, "'Where Do You Want to Go Today?' Cybernetic Tourism, the Internet, and Transnationality," in *Cybertypes: Race, Ethnicity, and Identity on the Internet*, 87–100 (New York: Routledge, 2002).
14. Randy Dotinga, "Adobe Tackles Photo Forgeries," *Wired News*, March 8, 2007.
15. Quoted in Dona Schwartz, "Professional Oversight: Policing the Credibility of Photojournalism," in *Image Ethics in the Digital Age*, edited by Larry Gross, John Stuart Katz, and Jay Ruby, 36 (Minneapolis: University of Minnesota Press, 2003).
16. William J. Mitchell, *The Reconfigured Eye: Visual Truth in the Post-Photographic Era*, 52 (Cambridge, Mass.: MIT Press, 1992).

Further Reading

Barthes, Roland. *Camera Lucida: Reflections on Photography*. Translated by Richard Howard. New York: Hill and Wang, 1981.

Batchen, Geoffrey. *Burning with Desire: The Conception of Photography*. Cambridge, Mass.: MIT Press, 1997.

Bazin, André. "The Myth of Total Cinema." In *What Is Cinema? Volume 1*. Edited and translated by Hugh Gray. Berkeley: University of California Press, 1967.

Bell, Clive. *Art*. Charleston, S.C.: Dod Press/BilbioBazaar, [1914] 2007.

Berger, John. *Ways of Seeing*. New York: Penguin, 1972.

Benjamin, Walter. "The Work of Art in the Age of Mechanical Reproduction." In *Illuminations*. Translated by Harry Zohn. New York: Schocken Books, 1969, 217–51; and in *The Work of Art in the Age of Its Technological Reproducibility, and Other Writings on Media*. Edited by Michael W. Jennings, Brigid Doherty and Thomas Y. Levin. Cambridge, Mass.: Harvard University Press, 2008.

Druckrey, Timothy, ed. *Electronic Culture: Technology and Visual Representation*. New York: Aperture, 1996.

Gross, Larry, John Stuart Katz, and Jay Ruby, eds. *Image Ethics: The Moral Rights of Subjects in Photographs, Film and Television*. New York: Oxford, 1988.

———. *Image Ethics in the Digital Age*. Minneapolis: University of Minnesota Press, 2003.

Kunzle, David. *Che Guevara: Icon, Myth, and Message*. Los Angeles: UCLA Fowler Museum of Cultural History, 1997.

Hernández-Reguant, Ariana. "Copyrighting Che: Art and Authorship under Cuban Late Socialism." *Public Culture* 16.1 (2004), 1–29.

Hughes, Robert. *The Shock of the New*, rev. ed. New York: Knopf, 1995.

Ivins, William M., Jr. *Prints and Visual Communication*. Cambridge, Mass.: MIT Press, 1969.

Mitchell, William J. *The Reconfigured Eye: Visual Truth in the Post-Photographic Era*. Cambridge, Mass.: MIT Press, 1992.

Mulvey, Laura. *Death 24x a Second: Stillness and the Moving Image*. London: Reaktion Books, 2006.

Nichols, Bill. "The Work of Culture in the Age of Cybernetic Systems." In *Electronic Culture: Technology and Visual Representation*. Edited by Timothy Druckrey. New York: Aperture, 1996, 121–43.

Prince, Stephen, and Wayne E. Hensley. "The Kuleshov Effect: Recreating the Classic Experiment." *Cinema Journal* 31.2 (Winter 1992), 59–75.

van Dijck, José. *Mediated Memories in the Digital Age*. Stanford, Calif.: Stanford University Press, 2007.

chapter six

Media in Everyday Life

The media are pervasive in most of our lives, yet we tend to take them for granted. How do you start your day? Take this hypothetical account of a morning in 2008: having been awakened by the alarm on your cell phone or the strobe flasher on your Wake and Shake alarm clock, the first thing you look at is the digital time display. You might check your text messages, perhaps using screen reader or screen magnifier software. Over coffee, you check your e-mail and the news on your iPhone or laptop, maybe listening to the news on TV or radio, or listening as the screen reader's voice lists one page element after the next as you scroll through your e-mail. Maybe you glance at the traffic site that gives you live webcam footage of your commute. Driving to school or work, you might program your destination into the navigational system in the dashboard of your car and then follow a map that keeps you at the center with each move your car makes. Descartes would be pleased. Or maybe you have few of these technologies used by your peers in your college or in another country. Perhaps you can't afford them, or perhaps you choose not to participate in the mainstream consumer culture of technological devices into which we are interpellated by advertisements every day.

We are increasingly invited to experience the mundane routines of our everyday lives through screens or through information translated from those screens by voice output. Although we perform some of these activities alone, most involve participation with, or simply the presence of, other people (audience members in a movie theater, for instance, or other commuters, or computer users seated nearby in front of screens in a café, a classroom, or a library). For some of us, participation in these technologies requires being in a public space such as an

Internet café, a library, or a computer center. Many of these experiences incorporate multiple forms of visual or audiovisual media at once, and we may keep open many screens at once, clicking between them as we multitask. Importantly, many of them are so integrated into our lives that we don't think of these screens as separate from our everyday worlds. We may find ourselves anxious when these systems of communication and consumption fail us (when we misplace our cell phones or are unable to connect to the Web, for example), or when we read about the risks of radiation absorption in exposure to radiofrequency (RF) fields through the use of some of our devices, such as cell phones, for which manufacturers are required to post specific absorption rate (SAR) ratings in their product details. In most of these uses of technology, we are the recipients, as well as the authors, to varying degrees, of messages that are conveyed through a variety and mix of media forms. Increasingly, the media modalities that are integrated into our lives work in conjunction with one another, for example with digital cameras, iPods, and cell phones that connect to computers. Together these linked and converged technologies offer a kind of personalized media network that each of us negotiates to varying degrees on a daily basis. For instance, you go to a concert and take a picture of the band on your cell phone, then e-mail that image to a friend or send it to your blog, where it is instantly available for anyone to see. This one simple example makes clear that small transactions with visual media today can involve complex interconnecting systems, networks, and audiences.

In this chapter, we trace the concepts of the mass media, the public sphere, and media cultures through the twentieth century to the present, looking at how particular media forms have shaped our understanding of information, news events, national and global media events, and our sense of a public. As these examples show, very little of contemporary media falls under the rubric of *mass* media anymore. Rather, what we see is a shift away from the concept of audience as a mass to the idea of audiences or users as niche or narrowcast markets. In order to understand these contemporary media interactions, we begin by examining the early concept of mass media.

The Masses and Mass Media

The idea of "the masses" was introduced in the nineteenth century to describe changes in the structure of societies undergoing industrialization and the emergence of a massive working class. The masses were regarded as having influence on opinion and on social practice. According to the French sociologist Emile Durkheim, in industrial society, collective sentiments and a collective conscience of the masses came to *determine* what constituted a crime, rather than the collective simply standing in judgment of actions predetermined to be criminal. In other words, we do not condemn an action because it is objectively a crime; the action is deemed a crime because society collectively evaluates and judges the action, determining it to be a crime and condemning it.[1] It is the mass response in itself that shapes classification, laws, and judgment about actions, and it is this function of the collectivity—its determining social role—that characterizes the masses as such. The concept of the masses was used by political economists, including Karl Marx, to describe the working class during the rise of industrial capitalism. In media theory, the concept of the masses has generally been used with negative connotations. It has been used to characterize audiences as undifferentiated groups of people, individuals who are passively accepting and uncritical of media practices and messages authored by corporations with profit motives, whose messages support dominant ideologies and ruling class and/or government interests. The term *mass media* came into common use in the post-World War II era, a period marked by the dissemination of broadcast television throughout much of the world.

FIG. 6.1
Granada Cinema audience, Welling, England, c. 1938

Mass society describes social formations in Europe and the United States that began during the early period of industrialization and culminated after World War II. The rise of mass culture is usually characterized much like modernity: with the increased industrialization and mechanization of modern society, populations consolidated around urban centers. The large national (and later multinational) corporation, owned by a faceless board of investors, replaced the small-scale local company, whose owner might have been a neighbor. Mid-twentieth-century critics of mass society argued that urban populations lost their sense of community and political belonging and that interpersonal life and civic involvement slacked off under the pressures of crowding in the home, the workplace, and the streets. Corporate workplaces became sites of worker alienation not only because ownership was anonymous but also because assembly-line production had made the worker nothing more than a cog in the machine, replacing the satisfying work of completing assembly by hand from start to finish with the repetition of tasks that are boring or physically grueling to perform. Urban workers were disaffected from the harsh sounds and crowding in with strangers that came with life in the city. At the same time, workers who migrated from rural places were despondent about the distance separating them from loved ones left behind. Family and community life eroded as the large urban metropolis and then dispersed suburban enclaves replaced tight-knit rural communities.[2] Such characterizations emphasize the negative aspects of changes in modernity. They are linked to the concept that film, television, consumerism, and cheap amusements rose to provide some semblance of social connectedness among this exhausted and alienated populace.

To speak of people as members of a mass society is to suggest that they receive their messages through centralized broadcast forms of national and international media. The term implies that populations acquire the majority of their opinions and information through the one-way broadcast model and not through narrowcast media or through local channels of back-and-forth or networked exchange (members of the immediate community or family passing or sharing messages through conversation, for example).

The idea of a monolithic mass culture is linked to a particular historical period—the period of modernity and industrialization in which national newspapers and television broadcast media rose and dominated the industry through periods of monopoly and corporate growth. *Mass media* is a term that has been used since the 1920s to describe those media forms designed to reach large audiences perceived to have shared interests. It is used to refer to describe the conventions in which audiences receive regularly programmed entertainment shows or news about the events of the world, usually from a relatively centralized mass distribution source such as a newspaper corporation, a national television network, a major film studio, or a news and entertainment media conglomerate. The primary traditional mass media forms of the twentieth century were radio, network and cable television, the cinema, and the press (including newspapers and magazines); hence visual images were primary, though not the sole elements of that century's mass media.

Electronic and digital media, such as the Internet, the Web, cell phones, and wireless communication devices, as well as the rise of narrowcast television programming in conjunction with cable and satellite television systems, transformed the landscape of mass media in the 1980s, 1990s, and 2000s. Their increased prevalence and the varieties of uses to which these technologies were put by consumers demanded a rethinking of the term *mass* by the end of the twentieth century. Whereas previously mass media were produced and distributed under the auspices of corporations and the delivery of these messages to the masses was regarded as a major source of corporate and/or state power in any society with a strong mass media system, since the 1980s consumers have increasingly been recognized by media producers as occupying smaller, niche audiences that must be addressed according to their specific tastes, interests, and language groups. Today, consumers are also more likely to regard themselves as potential producers, as well as consumers who exercise choice, with regards to the media through which they interact in their everyday lives.

It is important to note the social impact of the expansion of the mass media from forms such as print and voice (such as black-and-white text-dominated newspapers and radio) into media that combine image, color, movement, text, and sound. Before radio, literacy was essential to the flow of information in society because books and handbills or newspapers were the primary forms of information and knowledge-sharing beyond the spoken word. Because only the educated minority could read and write, this portion of the society was largely in control of the exchange of information beyond word of mouth. Some critics of the media have argued that radio and television furthered this control by restricting authorship of information to those with access to the means of media production (media corporations), creating a society of producers (who represent the interests of the government or the ruling class) separate from consumers (who are duped by these mass media messages to accept the views of the government and the ruling class). The mass media of the late twentieth century have been both criticized and celebrated for inundating us with images. The French philosopher Jean Baudrillard used the term *cyberblitz* to describe the escalation of random and unpredictable media forms, images, and information that have bombarded us in postmodern society.[3]

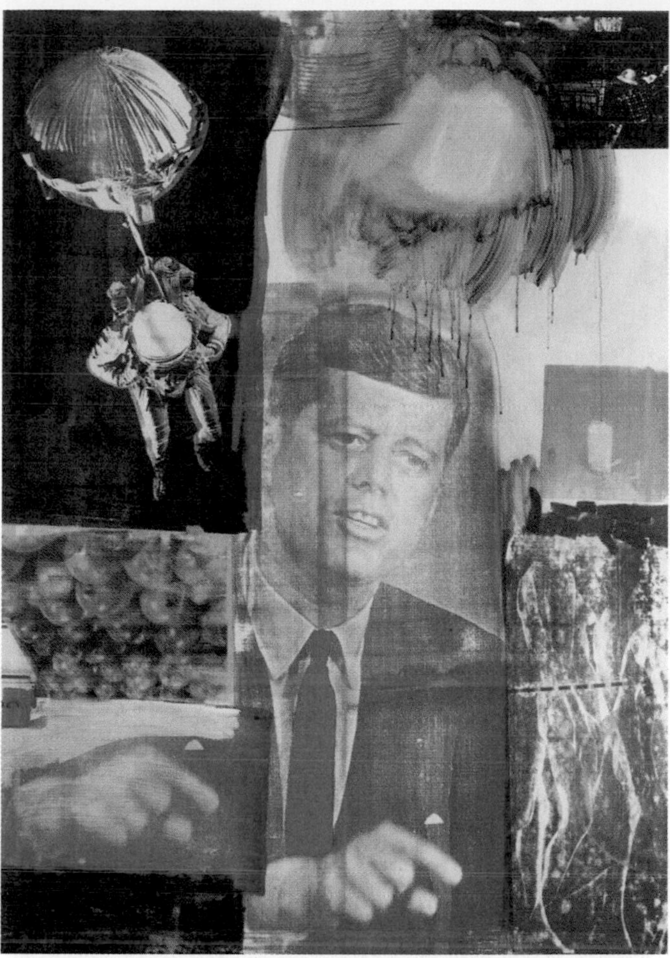

FIG. 6.2
Robert Rauschenberg, *Retroactive I*, 1964, © Robert Rauschenberg/ Licensed by VAGA, N.Y.

Artists have engaged with the experience of media overload by working with "found" images from news and entertainment media. In this 1963 silkscreen, Robert Rauschenberg creates a tension between news images and painting techniques. The work gives a sense of the ways that news images penetrated the lives of U.S. citizens in the 1960s. This collage, titled *Retroactive I*, is a part of a series of eight silkscreen prints in which Rauschenberg featured a photographic image of U.S. President John F. Kennedy. Kennedy is caught in a pose made familiar by news images, emphatically jabbing his finger to make his point. Rauschenberg completed the silkscreen series when Kennedy was assassinated in 1963. In *Retroactive I*, Kennedy's image is framed by screened reproductions of images from news stories about the space program. Kennedy's launching of the program was widely reproduced in the news media: "I believe that this nation should commit itself to achieving the goal, before this decade is out, of landing a man on the moon and returning him safely to earth." Rauschenberg reproduces and combines news images in montage, overlapping and painting over them, to comment on the juxtaposition of images and texts that make news and history in modern life and the complexity of media culture's layered meanings. He plays on the iconic status of Kennedy as a purveyor of visionary progress and democratic social change.

If Rauschenberg had simply drawn these pictures, they would not have had the same association with cultural memory that these recomposed found images carried then and that they carry now. We live in an era in which we have seen Kennedy's

FIG. 6.3
Shepard Fairey, Barack Obama "Hope" poster, 2008, obeygiant.com

image consistently deployed to represent an era of U.S. history for which there remains significant nostalgia. Most recently, Kennedy's appearance has been referenced in the poses, dress, and compositional framing of Barack Obama in the news media and popular iconography. Street artist Shepard Fairey created this limited silkscreen print during the presidential campaign of 2008 to fund a broad poster campaign for Obama. The image draws on the iconographic pose, attire, and framing we associate with portrayals of JFK in the popular media, as well as the style of graphic poster design used by the Bolshevist agitprop artists of the 1920s. These references associate the popular Democrat with the spirit of progress and hope experienced in two prior contexts. The graphic newsprint-like reproduction gives the work a sense of political urgency, playing with the idea of mass images and the random, eclectic manner in which they appear in our encounters with the billboards and digital displays of everyday life.

Kennedy was, in many ways, the first media president in the United States—that is, the first to be subject to the media coverage of television to a full extent. It is therefore ironic that his death was also emblematic of the role images play in shaping political events as history. The famous film footage of Kennedy being shot in Dallas in November 1963 while driving in a motorcade, was taken by a bystander, clothing manufacterer Abraham Zapruder, with his 8mm Bell and Howell home movie camera. Today video cameras are pervasive, but in 1963, relatively few people owned the portable home movie cameras available as luxury items for middle-class consumers. The original print of this short 26.6 seconds of film, known as The Zapruder Film, was sold by Zapruder to *Life* magazine with the stipulation that the frame showing the fatal shot would not be shown. The footage is considered to be an essential historical document, and has been relentlessly analyzed for what it reveals (and does not reveal) about the details of Kennedy's death. But it was shown publicly only as still images for many years until an illegal copy was aired on television in 1975. The U.S. government paid the Zapruder family $16 million in 1999 for ownership of the original film.[4] It is thus one of the earliest examples of an amateur film image having an important political impact and public circulation. Like many iconic images, the Zapruder film has been the focus of public fascination. It was reenacted in 1975 by the video

FIG. 6.4
Ant Farm/T.R.Uthco, *The Eternal Frame*, 1975

activist groups Ant Farm and T. R. Uthco, who restaged the event in Dallas in order to comment on the power of the image itself. Their video makes clear that the Zapruder film image of the assassination cannot be separated from the event itself, indeed that the image is, in essence, the event. Interestingly, the video captures the fact that most of the Dallas tourists who saw the Ant Farm reenactment mistook it for an official event and wept over the staged assassination. The Zapruder film has continued to fascinate. It was incorporated in a digitally enhanced form in the popular 1991 film *JFK* by Oliver Stone and was reenacted again in the late 1990s in a parodic music video by singer Marilyn Manson. This inter-referencing of media texts reminds us that mass media are not immune to interactions with other media cultures and popular culture.

Media Forms

The familiar definition of *medium* is a means of mediation or communication—a neutral or intermediary form through which messages pass. In this sense, *media*, the plural form of medium, refers to the group of communications industries and technologies that together produce and spread public news, entertainment, and information. When we refer to "the media" we usually mean a plurality of media forms (news, entertainment, radio, television, film, the Web, and so forth) and not one entirely unitary industry, though we may mean to imply that the members of the plurality produce a surprisingly homogenous set of messages. The term medium also refers to the specific technologies through which messages are transmitted. Radio is a medium, television is a medium, a megaphone is a medium, the Internet is a medium, your voice is a medium. Canadian media theorist Marshall McLuhan proposed in the 1960s that a medium is any extension of ourselves through a technological form. Media are not just those technologies that convey information. They include cars, trains, lightbulbs, and even vocal and gestured or signed speech. Media are forms through which we amplify, accelerate, and prosthetically extend our bodies in processes of communication.

It is widely agreed among those who study the media that a medium is not a neutral technology through which meanings, messages, and information are channeled unmodified. Even the medium of your voice, through conventions such as accent, loudness, pitch, tone, inflection, and modulation, encodes messages with meanings that are not inherent to the content of the message. The medium itself, whether that medium is a voice or a technology such as television, has a major impact on the meaning it conveys. There is no such thing as a message without a medium or a message that is not affected in its potential meanings by the form of its medium. This point has been driven home in media theory since 1964, when Marshall McLuhan published *Understanding Media: The Extensions of Man*.[5] It is impossible to separate messages, information, or meanings from the media technologies that convey them. First of all, there are phenomenological differences among media—that is, there are differences in the way we experience media that are particular to their material qualities. When we listen to television news, for example, our experience of information or content is shaped by the form and conventions of the medium (how images are framed, how stories are edited, what the newscasters wear, how they speak, who they are, and so on). When we watch a movie in a theater, our experience is affected by the cinematic apparatus—the dark room, the projection of film on the screen, the sound system, the excitement that the movie is a new release, the feeling we have, muted or otherwise, of fellow audience members watching along with us. Watching the same movie on a DVD at home changes the experience.

Television viewing has been described, since its origins in the mid-twentieth century, as a medium of distraction. Television is an ongoing electronic presence that is set to a timetable (an aspect that is changing with the emergence of On Demand, Pay Per View, and the issuing of television series on DVD) and continuously transmitted. Watching television is a social activity, even when done alone, in that we are likely to be aware of ourselves as part of a broader public tuned in to the same broadcast, in particular for popular shows. Watching is sometimes performed in a collective social space such as the living room, where people talk during programs, move in and out of the space, or simultaneously perform other activities such as eating or doing homework. We tune in and out of television. Cultural theorist Raymond Williams once wrote about television flow, the concept that viewers' experience of television involves an ongoing rhythm that incorporates interruptions (such as changes between programs and TV commercials).[6] Television, insofar as it is time based and establishes narrative flow over days, months, and even years (as in the case of ongoing soap operas), has a particular kind of continuity that weaves into patterns of daily experience in our lives. It provides a different phenomenological experience from that of other technology we use, such as the computer. When we engage in online social networks or online gaming, we sit alone before a computer screen, using a mouse and typing on a keyboard, but we nonetheless participate in a social space—the virtual space that can span a vast geographical area across which those who share in our online communication live.

There are also important political and cultural differences in how we understand and judge the media messages in our daily lives. We may, for instance, consciously or unconsciously rank modes of news media in terms of importance or credibility. We might, for instance, consider newspapers to be more reliable than television news, find twenty-four-hour cable news to be more reliable than network news, or see news on websites or news blogs as more or less truthful than other sources. We might consider news parodies to be more reliable sources because their biases are explicit, and there is no pretense of neutrality. The way we rank media is based on the position in which that medium stands in relation to older and newer media and on cultural assumptions about reliability and whether a network or show is primarily oriented toward entertainment, news, or information. We may think of Web news as being more "up to the minute" than televised news broadcasts, because the Web has come to be associated with speed of transmission, a global scope, and instantaneous border crossing.

The presentation of news in different media affects our perception of it. In the case of television news, for instance, aspects of the traditional television format can affect our sense of the veracity of the news. Our perception of television news is shaped by such elements as the cultural status of the newscaster (his or her gender, cultural identity, clothing and appearance, and accent and tone of voice), as well as by how he or she is situated on a set (with the image of a newsroom in the background or a screen into which images are inserted) and framed and edited and by the degree to which entertainment styles of television are used in broadcasts, with elaborate graphics, music, and stage sets meant to simulate everyday spaces such as living rooms. All of these aspects—casting, costume, makeup and hair style, composition, sets, and editing of image and sound—work within certain conventions of television news to confer meaning to what we tend to think of as the "content" of the story covered. In the United States, late-night comedy shows that parody the news (such as *The Daily Show* and *The Colbert Report*) are adept at making fun of the conventions of television news in order to show how the news media spin stories and miss stories. These shows act as forums through which the formulas, conventions, codes, and assumptions of television news are constantly being analyzed and parodied, interpellating an audience that reads those codes and uses them to re-interpret the news as it is presented in more conventional venues.

Most newspapers and television news channels translate their stories to websites through a set of conventions that include different text fonts to capture attention, the use of images to signal story lines, complex link structures, and a mix of advertising, video clips, still images, and different type sizes. Reading and viewing the news online requires a different set of skills from viewers than reading a newspaper, watching television news, or listening to the radio. Media, then, never operate wholly apart from other media forms. They implicitly refer to and comment on other media forms.

In the media landscape of the early twenty-first century, the boundaries between news and fiction and between entertainment and

FIG. 6.5
Jon Stewart on *The Daily Show*, January 25, 2007

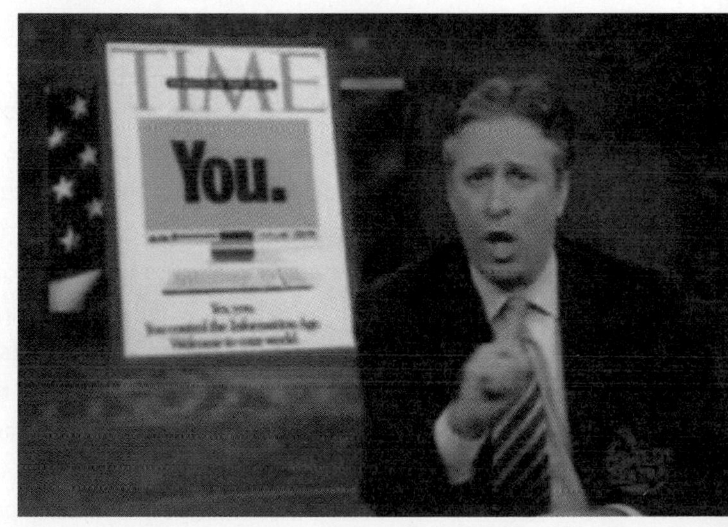

information are increasingly blurred. Entertainment television such as the *Idol* shows explicitly crafts the lives of featured contestants in narrative form. Evening television news programs feature stories linked to the story lines of drama shows that precede them in the television schedule, and reality television shows regularly funnel ousted contestants onto morning news shows the next day. Through these conventions of cross-referencing, entertainment is made to seem as important and relevant to our lives as are politics and real-life events.

The global media landscape of the late twentieth and early twenty-first centuries is highly complex. It is diverse both at the level of the media themselves and at the level of national and cultural boundaries. Traditional media forms such as newspapers are increasingly Web based; films are shown in theaters and internationally on television, are rented on videotapes and DVDs, are downloaded from the Web, and are distributed in highly developed underground economies throughout the world; television migrates to the Web through both official and user-generated productions. Since the 1980s, the film industry has been transitioning to digital production, with movie theaters slated to shift to digital projection by the next decade. Thus movies are becoming an electronic and digital form. *Convergence*, a term used in the 1990s to describe the coming together of media forms, has resulted in the merger of such previously discrete instruments and technologies as the still camera, the video camera, the telephone, the musical listening device, the Internet, and the video screen. With the convergences taking place among these forms, we see redistributions and mergers among previously discrete media sectors such as telecommunications, computer technology, television, and the motion picture industry. The "bundling" of a previously discrete range of services (cable, Internet, and telephone) into one provider is the result of convergence.

Not only does the contemporary media environment mean that the distinctions among media industries and sectors are less clear, but it also means that there are opportunities for media programming and consumption to be less monolithic and centralized. One striking example of the way that even the most centralized media context can be resisted is the Chinese student rebellion in Tiananmen Square in 1989, the famous image of which we discussed in chapter 1. This square is a well-known site of public political expression in China, with more than half a dozen significant protests taking place at this location since 1919. In 1989, when labor activists, students, and intellectuals joined together to protest government corruption and to call for democracy, the Chinese government blocked media coverage, banning foreign press from the country and tightly controlling coverage by the media of the People's Republic of China. Because the Internet was not yet widely in use in China, supporters of the protests used fax machines to circulate news information about the student protests and the brutal killing of students at Tiananmen Square internationally. This is one of many examples of the ways in which new media and telecommunications forms were deployed in acts of political resistance, even under circumstances of strict media repression.

Media access and information flow within and out of China continues to be controversial. Activists in China have used text messaging, instant messaging, and chat rooms to organize protests against issues such as pollution and corruption and to protest the police task force set up to monitor the Internet, but increased monitoring has resulted in the erasure of information sometimes minutes after a posting appears. The Golden Shield project, a network firewall set up by the PRC Ministry of Public Security in 1998, is widely regarded as far from impenetrable, and with software such as Freenet it becomes increasingly easy for Internet users in China to send and retrieve information without being detected. These details demonstrate that even under tight state regulation the Internet remains a space of negotiation and multidirectional flow.

Broadcast, Narrowcast, and Webcast Media

When we consider different kinds of media forms, the reach with which they create audiences is a key factor. An important distinction between media forms is that between broadcast (with one central source broadcasting a signal to many venues) and narrowcast (targeted, via cable and other means, to niche audiences) media. As television became more widespread in the post-World War II era, it was largely a national broadcast medium, with some amounts of local programming in some countries. Initially, long-distance national transmission was facilitated through cables or antenna (CATV stood for "community antenna television," which was used as early as 1938 in England and 1948 in the United States, where it was used to transmit in mountainous regions), and by the 1960s, satellite transmission was introduced to facilitate long-distance broadcasting. Throughout regions such as Africa, satellite has made more sense because of the drawbacks of laying cable in areas of low population, and satellite remains South Africa's dominant transmission form. The broadcasting model replaced early narrowcast or community-based television, with satellite transmission making global communications a real possibility. With this expansion of regions and increase in potential markets, networks produced programs that appealed to more universal or "mass" cultural interests, replacing the earlier community television model.

The emergence of cable in North America, East Asia, Australia, Europe, and parts of the Middle East and South America during the 1970s and 1980s introduced the narrowcast model, allowing the development of community-based programming after twenty years of its near absence in the earliest television markets. It also allowed the development of specialty cable channels, twenty-four-hour news channels, and increasingly multilanguage programming that has served diasporic audiences throughout the world. Chinese, Korean, Indian, and Spanish-language channels serve diasporic communities throughout the world, and such channels as CNN, the BBC, and TV5 from France, among others, are distributed globally via cable systems. In the United States, this has also meant the rise of "minority" networks such as Black Entertainment Television (BET). Important in global narrowcasting are the Spanish networks that serve audiences in Latin and North America, such as Telemundo and Univision. The proliferation of stations and programming options that has escalated into the 2000s may give the appearance of expanded choice. However, it should be noted that providing more networks and programs to choose from to consumers is not the same thing as providing more venues for different voices and opinions. Freedom to choose among a broader range of consumer products cannot be equated with freedom of expression. In fact, some critics of the cable phenomenon have emphasized the intensification of existing problems in the television industry with the advancement of cable networks, such as lack of diversity in management and hiring and the proliferation of conventional programming that deploys racial, ethnic, and gender stereotypes.

The development of the Internet in the 1960s and 1970s, with the subsequent expansion of the home computer market and the making public of the Web in the early 1990s, dramatically changed the media landscape of broadcast and narrowcast media. The primary shift that the Internet and the Web introduced was toward multidirectional communication networks that converge media forms, so that people engaging with their media are considered to be active "users" rather than passive viewers. This began, in the early days of the Internet, with simple forms of text-based exchange, such as e-mail and e-mail list discussion groups. The public introduction in 1991 of the Web, in combination with the development of consumer-oriented imaging capabilities and graphic interfaces, resulted in even more dramatic changes in computer-based spectatorship and authorship. On the Web, with today's technologies, viewer-users can make and modify their own images and videos with relative ease. Users may upload content and images to personal websites and to centralized Web forums, and, in some cases, have their images, videos, or blogs viewed by thousands of other viewers.

Stories of success on the Web get a lot of attention. For example, after the YouTube film clips of Joe Bereta and Luke Barats, Gonzaga University students who won a film competition in Spokane, Washington, generated more than a million hits, NBC gave them a six-figure contract to produce situation comedies and sketches. Stories such as this proliferate as major media conglomerates used consumer venues such as YouTube both to scout talent and to pursue and quash apparent cases of copyright infringement. By 2007, NBC and Viacom were both embroiled in copyright infringement cases against Google involving footage posted on YouTube (which was acquired by Google in 2006). One of the important questions that these cases address is to what extent the corporations that own websites are protected from liability for the actions of their users. The courts will be interpreting the potential scope of the Safe Harbor Provision of the Digital Millennium Copyright Act of 1997, which was set out to protect website owners from liability but that requires them to remove infringing material once notified by those who own the rights to it. When the 1997 Act was created, access to the high-speed Internet connection was rare, but by 2007, a much larger percentage of people have access to high-speed connections from among a vastly larger number of users globally (estimates range over a billion), making video sharing far more prevalent, as is indicated by YouTube's global popularity.

We might say that the ability of the small-scale, unknown producer to reach a mass audience with appropriated images is serendipitous—it is dependent on his or her ability to work within and around laws that protect freedom of speech and fair use and those that uphold the intellectual property rights of the legal owners of media texts and images. These patterns are, of course, driven by the corporate strategy of making public the numbers of hits to any given site and allowing end users to search by this metric of site popularity. Majority taste thus emerges in contexts such as YouTube as an indicator of potential industry success, even if that success is relatively short-lived (because much of the talent contracted through these venues gets a short window of opportunity in which to succeed—the life of the network contract). Yet such sites also radically transform the concepts of broadcast and narrowcast media.

During the 1990s and early 2000s media critics warned of the emergence of a global digital divide. The early developers of the Internet lauded the medium's capability of expanding connectivity and bypassing formal structures of communication oversight and management. "Information wants to be free" was one of the catch phrases of the medium's early years, and this ethos of accessibility has been maintained to a surprising degree despite the corporate takeover of vast sectors of the Web through domain ownership and the use of the medium to enhance promotion and advertising—through pop-ups and banner ads on your "free" account on Yahoo, for example. As computer ownership and access became an accepted aspect of everyday middle-class life in the democratic West, people in developing nations were the first to achieve the kind of "freedom" of access envisioned by the medium's developers, increasing the divide between themselves and the majority of people in developing nations for whom computer access was a technological and economic impossibility. Having access to the Internet requires enhancement of networks such as telephone or cable lines, making a prerequisite of access either government or corporate initiative to extend access routes beyond areas with a solid potentially paying consumer base.

Responding to these concerns, some of the innovators and promoters of global digital culture have been developing alternative programs such as One Laptop Per Child, a global initiative launched by MIT computer pioneer and *Wired Magazine*'s founding investor Nicholas Negroponte to make computers available to all schoolchildren in selected poor remote and urban locations in which Internet penetration and Web access is low for geographic and/or economic reasons.[7] This program is designed not only to benefit children, who can use these solar-powered computers for learning in the classroom, but also to promote computer and basic literacy among adults by making these computers available for students to take home to their parents each night. The idea behind this initiative is that if participation in a global network becomes recognized by the "haves" as a requisite for democratic participation in everyday life, it becomes the responsibility of those with access to transfer or disseminate the technology to those who do not have the means to buy into it for themselves.

The explosion of consumer-user productions, home entertainment, and Web media suggests that the model of broadcast communications has lost much of its dominance. Yet media industries have become increasingly consolidated, as networks, cable channels, newspapers, film studios, and other entertainment media are now part of huge media conglomerates (particularly in the United States). Thus, whereas traditional media industries are losing audiences, media conglomerates such as Viacom, Disney, Fox, General Electric, and News Corporation are actively staking out ownership over new media forms.[8] This consolidation of ownership has been enabled by the loosening of government regulation. Media scholar and activist Robert McChesney has chronicled the changes in Federal Communications Commission (FCC) policies throughout the 1990s and 2000s that have further limited government regulation of media ownership, facilitating private-sector mergers and new kinds of monopoly conglomerates that span telecommunications, television, print journalism, the film industry, the Web, entertainment and amusement venues, and a surprisingly diverse range of other sorts of industries (food, oil, clothing, toys).[9] McChesney argues that the new global media comprise a small world of big conglomerates.

The History of Mass Media Critiques

The capacity of the mass media to reach so many viewers both nationally and globally has historically given the media industry a significant amount of power. The coincidence of the rise of the mass media with industrialization and movements of populations away from rural communities to urban centers prompted some theorists to see the mass media as contributing to the erosion of interpersonal and group life and as fostering increasingly centralized models of communication and identity. The historical argument, put forward most famously by communication scholar Herbert Schiller in his numerous publications, from *Mind Managers* (1972) to *Information Inequality* (1996), warned of the takeover of public space by private media interests and the control of mass communications by the military-industrial complex. His criticism of U.S. media imperialism spanned the period from the introduction of video to the rise of the Internet. Schiller states that mass media function, in effect, as a tool of cultural imperialism and provide a centralized means of mobilizing the new global mass society around a unified political ethos handed down from dominant nations to less powerful nations and populaces. Schiller proposed that as nations modernize through the introduction of communication and media systems, along with industrial development, the external purveyors who introduce modernization (transnational media corporations, for example) entice, pressure, or bribe national government and corporate leaders to embrace and promote the values and structures of the (usually Western and capitalist) political system in which the media company is based. The idea is that mass broadcasting, with its ability to reach large numbers of people across national boundaries with the same messages, fosters conformity to dominant ideas about politics and culture.[10]

Schiller's basic critique of the media has been continued by some contemporary media critics. In 2006, television studies scholar Timothy Havens noted the surprising statistic that only a few thousand professionals are responsible for the acquisition and distribution decisions of television markets around the world and that these professionals base their decisions not on audience tastes but on institutional incentives. His argument is that the market drives decisions about the program choices available to viewers globally.[11] This fact makes it clear that diversification of programming does not necessarily indicate diversification of ownership and decision making about that programming. In contrast, other critics, such as television scholar John Fiske, who wrote about popular culture and mass media in the 1980s and 1990s, introduced the argument that mass media forms changed the dynamics of the flow of information by making more information directly available to nonliterate people, thus rendering possible a more democratic flow of information.[12] Media theorist Ien Ang expanded on this idea when she proposed that the very notion of audience is imagined or constructed within the commercial and public service sectors as a convenient way to conceptually group together potential consumers, which, though convenient for marketing purposes, cannot capture viewers' specific and diverse tastes, interpretive strategies, and practices.[13] Contemporary critics of the mass media such as Robert McChesney have also argued that new technologies continue to serve as powerful tools for propaganda or mass persuasion. This conventional view emphasizes the top-down unifying potential of various communications technologies together as "the media," singular. Theorists such as Fiske and Ang offer a more plural view, stressing that members of audiences engage with television in ways that are both specific to their cultural context and at times resistant to normative and/or dominant ways of looking and interpreting. However, unlike many of the theories of viewer strategies that we discussed in chapter 2, many approaches to media regard viewers as passive if not gullible recipients of media systems and messages.

One view of the mass media is to denounce them as a form of propaganda. One key example of this effect is the use of film to support the rise of Nazism in Germany prior to World War II. The German film director Leni Riefenstahl (1902–2003) is well known for her work with the Nazi Party to produce propaganda to enlist the German masses in the Nazi Party ethos. Her 1935 film, *Triumph of the Will*, documents a Nazi rally in Nuremberg in 1934. It is considered by many to be one of the most powerful examples of the use of visual images to instill and affirm political beliefs in its audience. The 1934 rally was planned and constructed as a mass visual spectacle with the film process well in mind. Adolf Hitler, who served

FIG. 6.6
Leni Riefenstahl, *Triumph of the Will*, 1935

as the film's executive producer, had the rally choreographed and filmed with an array of special techniques, including aerial photography, telephoto lenses, multiple cameras, and an elaborate tracking-shot system to give the impression that the whole nation was united behind him at a moment when his party and leadership had just weathered a major challenge from the National Socialist Party. Special equipment was constructed to provide optimal access to the events for more than thirty cameras and a vast crew, led by Riefenstahl. The film is composed of strikingly dramatic compositions in which Hitler is featured as both the master eye that takes in all of the populace assembled and the full scope of the city and the single object that rivets the gaze of the vast crowds assembled before him. The film opens with grand aerial tracking footage of Hitler's plane swooping in over the city, intercut with shots of the city from the plane's-eye view as Hitler presumably scopes out his domain. We later see many shots of Hitler in the crowds, taken from a low camera angle to emphasize his stature and placing him at the focal point of cheering crowds who search out the chance to see him and gaze raptly on him when he is finally in their view. *Triumph of the Will* is an example of the way that practices of looking can work in the service of overt nationalism and idolatry.

Of course, we cannot equate all propaganda with Nazism and its ways of generating ideological positions. Images can be used for many political purposes, and media serve different social purposes in different cultures. For instance, in "The Work of Art in the Age of Mechanical Reproduction," Walter Benjamin called for the use of the presses by revolutionary student and worker groups rather than by governments and corporate interests. Whereas in the United States and many other countries, televisions were introduced as home appliances that took center stage in the relative domestic privacy of the family home, in countries such as Germany and Japan television was at first more frequently viewed collectively in public spaces. Television emerged during the era of Nazism as a nationalized industry that was used to forge a strong collective ideology. As such, it was a tool of mass persuasion not unlike mass rallies, at which people physically gathered to express their support for the party. In this sense, the practice of looking collectively in a public space at the same spectacle was an important experience in the forging of a mass ideology. This is true whether we are talking about crowds of people looking at Hitler himself in a rally or rooms full of people gazing at a television program that supported Nazism. The concept of the media as propaganda is one approach to understanding the mass media's promotion of mass ideology, one that sees audiences as undifferentiated masses easily persuaded by media messages.

Other critics of the mass media, many of them working with empirical methodologies influenced by behavioral communications research, have used several different models to understand media effects. The "hypodermic needle" or "magic bullet" effect was a popular model for understanding media effects in the mid-twentieth century, and its influence can still be felt today in the writings of critics who blame the media for modeling violent behavior through computer games and action and crime genre movies. The hypodermic-needle model proposes that the media have a direct and immediate effect on audiences, fostering passive follower behavior among viewers "drugged" by media texts that "inject" ideas into their viewers. This model was influenced not only by observations of media effects under Nazism but also by observations of rising consumption in response to the growing advertising and persuasion industries. Yet this model did not account for the complex back-and-forth negotiation of meanings and practices among media texts, technologies, producers, and audiences.[14]

Studying the effects of the mass media on social behavior has been a common model for thinking about media since the Payne Fund supported studies in the 1930s on the effects of motion pictures on children that concluded that children were deeply influenced by the content of the movies and that children who watched movies regularly did poorly at school. These studies, now largely discredited, were the first of many that fanned public fears about the influence of media (television, the Internet, etc.) on children. Television has, because of its dominance as a social medium, been the subject of many studies concerned with the effects of the media on social cohesion and political engagement. In the 1950s, for instance, the U.S. Congress held hearings on the effects of television on juvenile delinquency, and today, concerns about children, video games, and the Internet are a common topic of effects research. With every publicized example of violence or threatened violence by a child at a school or in the home, questions about the role of the media resurface anew, with politicians sometimes resorting to outdated research to support their views that images of violence serve as direct models for behavior. The extent to which political leaders have failed to understand how media work and how ill served we are by simplistic effects models is made clear by media scholar Henry Jenkins, who was called before the U.S. Congress to testify on the topic of "selling violence to our children" through the media. In his account of this experience, Jenkins recalls the reductive assumptions and misunderstandings about how media representations work and how media panics are started and his own largely unheeded attempts to offer the means for thinking about the complex ways that viewers make meanings. Popular culture, Jenkins noted, is not the root of the problem.[15]

Models for thinking about the influence of media and popular culture on social behavior have also come from the context of philosophy and art. One well-known analysis of collective practices of looking and the media that was influential in the 1960s is Guy Debord's 1967 *Society of the Spectacle*. Debord was a founding member of Situationist International, a group of French social theorists with links to the

FIG. 6.7
Poster for exhibition "The Situationist International: 1957–1972," ICA Boston, October 1989-January 1990

modern art movements of futurism, Dadaism, and surrealism. They sought to blur the distinction between art and life and called for a constant transformation of lived experience. Debord describes how the social order of the global economy exerts its influence through representations. The spectacle is both an "instrument of unification" and a world vision that forges a social relationship among people in which images and practices of gazing are central. All that was once directly lived, he argued, has become mere representation.[16] The Situationists have since become a kind of symbol of strategies of resistance to media influence in the 1960s. Artists and writers refer to them in retrospect, as this exhibition poster shows, to show how radical was their critique of mass influence. They were interested in using guerrilla tactics and innovative publication styles to intervene into the homogenized experience of everyday life.

The term *spectacle* refers to an event or image that is particularly striking in its visual display to the point of inspiring awe in viewers. We commonly think of spectacle as involving enormous scale of some kind—fireworks displays, awe-inspiringly large images, IMAX movie screens. Yet Debord and the Situationists were primarily interested in spectacle as a metaphor for society, in how we live in an ongoing and constant spectacle. Although Debord and the Situationists were rooted in the social movements of the 1960s, it could be argued that the relevance of their ideas and the world of spectacle have reached new heights in the decades since, in particular in relation to media spectacle and the "empty" spectacle of political events. The virtual worlds of computer games, virtual environments, and simulated life are all examples of spectacles behind which there is no "there" there.

One of the most influential critiques of the media and the industrialization of culture came from the Frankfurt School theorists, who applied Marxist theory to the study of culture in the postwar years and whose work was equally influential in the 1960s, along with Debord's. This group, which included Max Horkheimer, Theodor Adorno, and Herbert Marcuse, among others, published a series of essays criticizing the capitalist and consumerist orientation of postwar entertainment and popular media forms, including popular movies, television, and advertising. Most of the members of the Frankfurt School had fled from Europe in the 1930s to the United States to escape the threat of impending fascism, but to a large degree they also found American society to be dangerous in what they saw as its degradation of culture into cliché, mass-produced sentimentality, empty schlock, formulas, and so on. According to the Frankfurt School theorists, the "culture industry" is an entity that both creates and caters to a mass public that, tragically, can no longer see the difference between the real world and the illusory world that these popular media forms collectively generate. In their classic essay on the culture industry, Max Horkheimer and Theodor Adorno set up a contrast between mass entertainment and fine art.[17] In this distinction of high and low culture, they criticize the culture industry for generating images that are nothing more than style and propaganda for industrial capitalism, reproducing the status quo and obeying the dominant social order. In their view, the culture industry generates false consciousness among its consumers, encouraging the masses to buy mindlessly into the belief systems or ideologies that allow industrial capitalism to thrive. As we have noted, Horkheimer and Adorno began their theories of media as Jewish intellectuals in Germany during the rise of Nazism in the 1930s. Their view of media was thus initially formulated in a time and culture in which the media were being used effectively to create a particularly destructive and murderous national Fascist ideology, and they wrote "The Culture Industry" in the United States in 1944, while World War II was still in full force.

The homogenization of culture was a central aspect of the Frankfurt School's critique, in particular the way in which the industries that produce culture shun innovation in favor of standardized products. If culture is a commodity, they argued, then its value has been reduced to the price of a ticket. Commodified culture produces a kind of pseudoindividuality, they argued, in which certain kinds of talentless celebrities evoke uniqueness even though they themselves are without individuality. Frankfurt School theorists, among other critics, emphasized that the mass media made palatable, and even seemingly inevitable, the domination and oppression inherent in a capitalist economy.

The question of what the "masses" or viewers in general might actively do with the mass media was not a central concern of the Frankfurt School or its followers. Though they were concerned with the effects of media on the masses, they did not generally consider just how people interpret and use the media forms they encounter. The ideas of resistant viewing, cultural appropriation, and subjective or psychical factors were introduced by other theorists to modify their model later, in response to the criticism that their view was too universalizing. The Frankfurt School theorists also set up a divide between art and mass culture, and in so doing established a high and low culture dichotomy (even as they claimed that much high art had sold out to the culture industry, too). Although the Frankfurt School model of media is flawed in its condescension toward the viewer (seen as a dupe of the system) and its inability to examine the complex negotiations that take place between viewer and cultural products, their criticism of the effects of the industry of culture—summarized in the phrase, "the whole world is passed through the filter of the culture industry"—still resonates today.[18] In part due to the Frankfurt School's contributions, it has become something of a commonplace idea that we experience life in and through our practices of looking at and experiencing media and art.

Since the late 1980s, critics have questioned the high art/mass culture divide, suggesting that our experiences with the media during the late twentieth century are too complex and varied to be adequately characterized in sweeping categories such as mass consciousness or mass culture. We have many cultures, many media industries, and many ways of representing meaning; hence the concepts of a unified mass culture and a singular media industry are not useful for talking about present conditions. There is no longer one mass audience. Rather, the populace is fragmented among a range of cultures and communities, some of which may respond to art and media in ways that challenge or even transform the dominant meanings generated by the mainstream culture industry. Moreover, the culture industry no longer makes a unified set of products. It increasingly produces a diverse range of art and media designed to appeal to niche audiences. Hence the media can include counterhegemonic forces that challenge dominant ideologies and the social orders they uphold. Yet one glance at television programming throughout the world can tell us that on the topic of the standardization of culture, the Frankfurt School had a point—the repetition of formats, genres, narratives, formulas, and conventions of most mainstream film and television today demonstrates a remarkable global standardization of culture. Although we may think that the medium of the Web media breaks with this standardization, much of what we encounter on the Web is also remarkably homogenous.

The paradoxes of contemporary media include this range: from standardized entertainment programming to ironic and resistant programming or interpretations of programming to the broad range of Web media produced by users themselves, some of which is innovative but much of which can look like the most conventional standardized programming. Yet many would argue that the fragmentation of media has also opened up new terrain in new media for many users (whereas, ironically, those media forms become less experimental and more conventional in other ways). It is clear that the term *media cultures*, in the plural, best describes the visual culture of the twenty-first century.

Media and Democratic Potential

Although the anxious and fearful view of how the mass media can change a society proliferated throughout the twentieth century, there was also a counterview that regarded the mass media as a promising set of venues for democratic ideals. This view sees communications technologies as empowering tools for use by citizens to promote an open flow of information and exchange of ideas, thereby strengthening democracy. It emphasizes the potential for various individual media forms to be used by individuals and groups to advance positions of resistance or countercultural perspectives.

An example of the media's potential to foster diversity of expression is community-based or public-access cable television. As the U.S. FCC set the ground for the introduction of cable in 1972, the regulatory agency mandated cable companies to set aside three channels for educational, local governmental, and public use in the top television markets. Any group or individual wanting to use this airtime would be guaranteed at least five minutes of program time per week. Cable companies were required to provide community access to production technology and facilities. Community-based television, in the form of local access programming in the United States and of subsidized programming in other national television systems, is produced at low cost by members of the community and is geared toward local audiences. It is a model of television as a means for citizens to feel connected to their communities and to gain more information about local issues. Public-access programming made possible programming by Paper Tiger Television, a New York news media nonprofit organization that since the 1980s has produced media critiques, beginning with a cable show featuring cultural critics and figures in the art world as hosts of an alternative investigative view of current news, such as *Noam Chomsky Reads the* New York Times: *Seeking Peace in the Middle East* in June 1985. (Paper Tiger expanded into Deep Dish Television, which distributes independent media via satellite.) Though public access is minimal in its audience scope and short-lived (it has been gradually scaled back with escalating deregulation of cable from the 1980s forward), this kind of programming nonetheless serves as a model for a democratic idea of a mass media that serve diverse or "minority" needs and interests. In one early episode of Paper Tiger television, many episodes of which were shot on a cheap set that was meant to look like a New York City subway car, media critic Herb Schiller reads the *New York Times*,

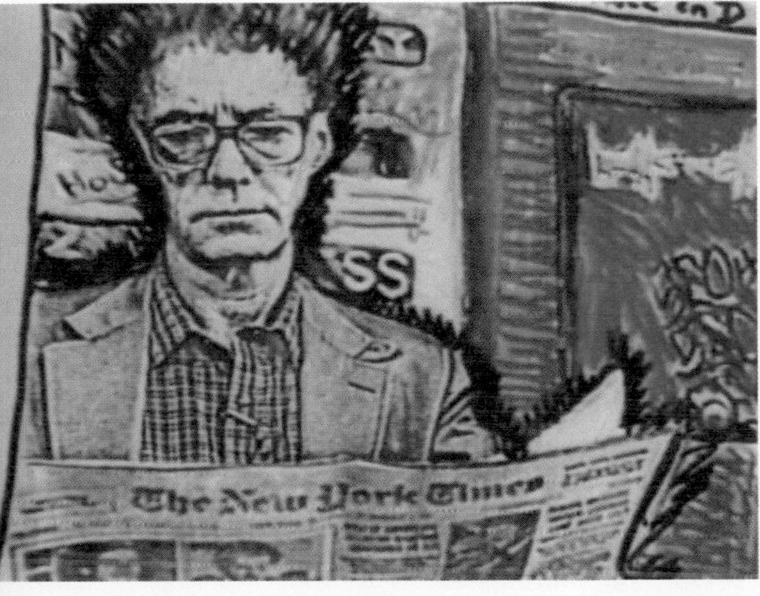

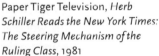

FIG. 6.8
Paper Tiger Television, *Herb Schiller Reads the New York Times: The Steering Mechanism of the Ruling Class*, 1981

pointing out the ideologies embedded in the language and editorial choices of one of the most respected of American newspapers.

The view of media as potentially democratic challenges the very idea of a mass media or a mass society. It stresses instead the potential of individual media forms for the development of community and identity on a much smaller scale. For example, the range and variety of television programming on cable, despite the fact that this medium contains many channels that emulate the mass appeal of network television, presents too varied a terrain to offer a unified idea of what public culture can and should be. Some cable network channels are geared toward specific language audiences, such as Spanish-, Chinese-, or Korean-speaking diasporas. Others are oriented toward audiences constituted according to taste, interests, age, or gender. However, when we look to ownership we see less diversification; for instance, Disney owns the ABC network. It also owns the Disney Channel for child audiences; Disney Asia (and Disney Malaysia, Disney UK, etc.); Lifetime Television network, which is geared toward women viewers; A&E (Arts and Entertainment); and many other channels.

Among those who have seen media as having great democratic and liberatory potential, Marshall McLuhan, who wrote most influentially in the 1950s through the 1970s, had the most widespread impact on media theory. McLuhan was known for coining catchy phrases, of which "the medium is the message" and "global village" have had the most longevity. McLuhan argued that television and radio were like natural resources, waiting to be used for the benefit of increasing mankind's collective and individual experiences of the world. He also stated that the media were simply extensions of our natural senses, helping us better to hear, see, and know the world and, moreover, helping us to connect ourselves to geographically distant communities and bodies. His analysis in the 1960s and 1970s of how the speed of information's flow through the media has affected local, national, and global cultures was tremendously influential.

McLuhan felt that media technologies give greater potential for power to our individual bodies by extending our senses and thereby extending our individual power in the world. Part of the "message" of the medium is the new, bigger scale that is introduced to individual experience through the very act of using a technology that increases the scope of connectivity. One of his examples is a hypothetical man in Africa who does not understand English but listens to BBC radio news every night. According to McLuhan, just hearing the sounds of the broadcaster's voice makes this man feel empowered. The content is not essential. The "message" consists in this man's relationship to the world, enriched and expanded through the experience of global media access. Interestingly, McLuhan chose an example in which we can imagine a recent colonial relationship between the man's country (presumably a former colony of England, as it receives the BBC) and the medium's national source (England). In contrast to McLuhan, we might want to ask, Can it be that the man might have a more contradictory relationship than one of "empowerment" through this association with the media broadcast of a past colonial power?

FIG. 6.9
Cover of *Guerrilla Television*, designed by Art Farm, 1971

Might the recipient of news broadcasts from the colonial center respond as a listener who is critical of and resistant to the broadcast and speak out on that basis?

Portable, consumer-grade video technology became available in the late 1960s, making it possible for artists, activists, and local community and political groups to make their own videotapes for the first time. Some saw this as a means of countering dominant television and news messages with militant, activist guerrilla television. Proponents of guerrilla television argued that to put the means of production in the hands of ordinary citizens would empower these citizens to express themselves more freely and defy the power of the mass media. This was regarded as a positive outcome of the new communications revolution that could foster a global media village. For instance, in 1972 a group of video activists calling themselves TVTV (for "Top Value Television") took their Portapak video equipment to the Republican National Convention that reelected President Richard Nixon to make their tape *Four More Years* (1972) ("four more years" was the slogan of Nixon's reelection campaign; the collective had already made a tape of the 1972 Democratic Convention, called *The World's Largest TV Studio*).[19] TVTV used their access to the convention to actually interview the press and get a view of the convention from many perspectives, such as that of anti-Nixon protestors, that were not included in network television coverage. Their resulting production gave a visceral sense not only of the maneuverings of the press on the floor of the convention but also of the protests that were taking place in the streets outside the convention hall. The gritty, kinetic style of TVTV, like other activist videos produced in the 1970s, demonstrated a resistance to mainstream television styles, and the group's tactics of looking "behind the scenes" at the media itself was radical at a time when the conventions of television news were highly staged. Their strategies resonate powerfully with the approach of students on college campuses in 2008 campaigning for Barack Obama under the sign of "change" by using personal networks and the Internet as a means for grassroots networking.

FIG. 6.10
Skip Blumberg interviewing news reporters in TVTV, *Four More Years*, 1972

Many of McLuhan's ideas are now being recycled as ways of looking at new media. In fact, he is considered to be the "patron saint" of *Wired Magazine*, which was established in 1993 as a key publication about Internet technologies and Web culture. *Wired*'s ethos is one of techno-utopianism, and McLuhan's catchy aphorisms, such as his concept of the media creating a "global village," have resonated powerfully with the idea that digital technologies and the Internet create new forms of community. In 1965, McLuhan stated, "There are no remote places. Under instant circuitry, nothing is remote in time or in space. It's now."[20] His words now seem prescient. Yet, although McLuhan's notion of the global village resonates in profound ways in contemporary cyberculture, it cannot help us to understand the ways in which globalization has created new kinds of inequalities between those who are plugged in and those who are not.

Yet Web culture continues to spawn democratically inspired initiatives. Founders of the Web and advocates of the free global flow of information have emphasized technology access as a means of promoting development. A leader in Web initiatives such as this is the W3C, a World Wide Web Consortium founded by Tim Berners-Lee, the inventor of the Web, the aims of which include the promotion of nonproprietary standards in Web languages and protocols. In 2008, the W3C hosted a workshop in Brazil on the potential role of mobile and Web devices in providing services for underprivileged populations. Initiatives such as this one and the One Laptop Per Child project described earlier in this chapter extend a humanitarian and utopian view of the media prevalent in the McLuhan tradition since the 1960s. Whereas for some who embrace this model democratic ideals drive the spread of technology, for others libertarian entrepreneurship is also a strong motivating factor. The view that the Internet and the Web should remain free of government regulation and commercial ownership is strong among the founders of these forms of media and communication.

The concept of media fostering democratic potential is seen by many people as having been realized most recently with a wide range of activities on the Web in a broad range of "second-generation" websites known as Web 2.0. These sites, such as blogs, wikis, social networking sites, sites of person-to-person economic exchange (such as eBay and Craigslist), and Web media sites such as YouTube move well beyond the model of the Web as users retrieving information from sites. The simple fact that new software developments facilitated easy access to uploading content to the Web enabled an explosion of activity in the early 2000s in which Web "users" become Web "producers." One of the primary aspects of this shift is a change in the notion of the "amateur" and the concept of the "expert"—thousands of political news blogs challenge the system, videos of recent events are instantly posted online, Wikipedia encyclopedia entries are coauthored by multiple users. Is this democratization in action?

These changes in how the Web is accessed and used have been greeted by a discourse about how these Web media sites are facilitating democratic potential. It is important, therefore, to consider that even though many aspects of Web 2.0 indicate important new forms of democratic engagement, opening up spaces for political and cultural debate, participants in such social networking and Web media sites, however large a number, still constitute a very small percentage of Web users. Inevitably, hierarchies evolve within open systems such as this, and the sheer amount of information posted on blogs on any given day creates a kind of saturation. As mainstream media become more consolidated and news entities are cut back, the explosion of the blogosphere offers an important countersphere of debate and discourse. There is simply no doubt that images produced by nonprofessionals can acquire audiences on the Web through such websites in a way that has never happened before. Whether this is a video of a teenager enacting light saber moves from *Star Wars*, a scripted serial show created by nonprofessionals that gets them a Hollywood contract, the image of a politician making a potentially unpopular comment, or photographs taken by Iraq War veterans, these images have the potential to be seen by a global audience.

Media and the Public Sphere

The many different forms of media that exist simultaneously today are also a means through which concepts of a *public* are created. Thus the idea of the media having democratic potential contributes to a broader sense of a viewing public, national publics, and a global public, interconnected at least in part through media forms. The concept of a public has been the subject of debate from the early twentieth century and has given rise to vigorous debate about the differences between public and private. Michael Warner has written that a "public" can be defined as a space of discourse, which involves a relation among strangers, in which public speech is both personal and impersonal, a social space constituted through the "reflexive circulation of discourse," that is, the circulation and exchange of ideas.[21] Warner notes that one effect of the Internet on this circulation of ideas is that it has been speeded up. That is, the circulation of ideas in more traditional media such as newspapers and television took place at daily and weekly intervals, whereas now it takes place within the instant temporality of the Web.[22]

The notion of a public has been deeply allied with the concept of a public sphere as a site in which the public debates and discusses the issues relevant to its time. This model is based on the idea that there are distinctly separate public and private spheres and that the state is separate from private market interests. Yet the political terrain of all modern societies involves, to varying degrees, elements of private interest. Furthermore, the notion of a separation of public and private spheres is based on traditional definitions of gender, race, and class that must be rethought. The division between public and private depends on the belief that women should be relegated to the domestic sphere of the home and men to the public arena of business, commerce, and politics.

The concept of a public sphere in which public discussion and debate can take place has itself been the subject of debate since the beginning of the twentieth century. A public sphere is ideally a space—a physical place, social setting, or media arena—in which citizens come together to debate and discuss the pressing issues of their society. Social commentator Walter Lippmann postulated, in the 1920s, that the public sphere was nothing more than a "phantom"—that it was not possible for average citizens to keep abreast of political issues and events and give them due consideration given the chaotic pace of industrial society. Definitions of the public sphere have since then been enormously influenced by the ideas of German theorist Jürgen Habermas. Habermas postulated that modern bourgeois society has had within it the potential for an ideal public sphere. Habermas saw the public sphere as a group of "private" persons who could assemble to discuss matters of common "public" interest in ways that mediated the power of the state. With the rise of newspapers, salons, coffeehouses, book clubs, and private social contexts in which debate over public issues could take place, the liberal European and American middle class of the eighteenth and nineteenth centuries might seem to have had the potential for a public sphere of genuine debate within civil society. Habermas postulates that this public sphere has always been compromised by other forces within modern society, including the rise of consumer culture, the rise of the mass media, and the intervention of the state in the private sphere of the family and home.[23] In ideal terms, he saw that public sphere as emblematic of participatory democracy, a public context in which citizens could debate public issues regardless of their social status and in which rational discussion could produce positive social change. In addition, Habermas believed that the public sphere was a public space in which private interests

FIG. 6.11
Café Capoulade, Paris, 1925. Café culture was emblematic of the concept of the nineteenth-century public sphere

(such as business interests) were inadmissible, hence a place in which true public opinion could be formulated.

Habermas's theory of the public sphere has been endlessly debated. The nineteenth-century public sphere described by Habermas was restricted to the participation of bourgeois white men, and criticisms of his work have seen the exclusion of others, such as women, blacks, citizens of other ethnicities, noncitizens, and working-class people, as not simply the problem of the restrictions of a previous society but as constitutive aspects of this way of conceiving the public. In other words, this criticism states that the idea of a unified public sphere is not only a fallacy but is also based on exclusion (hence not truly public). Oscar Negt and Alexander Kluge wrote a well-known critique of Habermas in 1972 (translated into English in 1993) in which they argue that the public sphere imagined by Habermas needs to be reconceived as a working-class ("proletarian") public sphere and that the model of the nineteenth-century European bourgeois public sphere had been too easily transformed into fascism, as it was in Germany in the 1930s. Negt and Kluge also updated the concept of the public sphere to include media, both media industries and alternative media, as a form of counterpublic.[24] In other words, they looked for some positive contribution by media to discussions within the public sphere rather than dismissing media, as Habermas had tended to do, as the enemy of rational public discourse.

Contemporary attempts to understand how the public converges and functions have proposed the idea of multiple public spheres and counterspheres rather than one single voice or constituency. For instance, political theorist Nancy Fraser has pointed out that historically women were relegated to the private domestic sphere of the home and elided from the public spaces and discourses of middle- and upper-class European and white men. She puts forth the useful alternative theory of a women's or a feminist countersphere, among other counterspheres of public discourse and agency.[25] A counterpublic understands itself to be subordinate in some way to the dominant public sphere but is still a site from which people attempt to speak up in society. Theorists such as Fraser suggest that we can envision many publics that can overlap and work in tension with each other: working-class publics, religious publics, feminist publics, and so forth. Along these line, feminist media critics such as Lynn Spigel have critiqued the assumptions about the distinction of public and private as a means of negating not only the space of the domestic sphere as a site of women's labor and activity but also the integration of media and domestic space.[26] Michael Warner notes that the sexual cultures of gay men and lesbians can be seen as a counterpublic in that it is a sphere of discussion, debate, and the circulation of ideas that is conscious of a distinction from a more dominant public and that is structured by alternative dispositions and protocols, "making different assumptions about what can be said or what goes without saying."[27]

There are many ways in which traditional broadcast media attempt to create a sense of public dialogue through formats such as "town meetings" on television, call-in talk shows, and formats that address controversial issues by having representatives of concerned populations and groups debate together. One example of the ways that the Internet and television are being used together to promote public access is TV Worldwide's AT508.com Internet TV channel, which was launched in 2002 at the World Congress on Disabilities. The channel offers free live webcasts of events such as forums on disability access issues and a review of the effectiveness of Section 508 of the Rehabilitation Act of the U.S. Congress (a law that preceded the Americans with Disabilities Act of 1990), which mandates federal agencies to provide information and information technology access to employees with disabilities on a par with the level of access experienced by nondisabled employees. Not only are these webcast forums *about* access, but they also enhance or make possible participation by individuals who otherwise might be unable to attend or to participate fully in such meetings in person due to mobility or sensory disabilities. For instance, in 2007, when wildfires were spreading throughout Southern California, communities potentially threatened by fire and smoke could closely chart the progress of fire and shifts in the wind through Web venues ranging from weather sites documenting the direction and quality of wind to maps indicating the fires' geographic spread to local news broadcasts showing footage and reporting on the direction of spread. They could also use their cell phones and the Internet to keep in touch with neighbors, friends in other neighborhoods, and local fire and police officials. People did not simply watch the news from afar. They participated in networks of communication as active producers and disseminators of crucial information in a rapidly changing situation in which they were directly involved.

Although Habermas's image of the nineteenth-century public café is appealing, the fact of the matter is that most publics communicate in mediated ways, through discussion groups, newsletters, journals, bookstores, conventions, conferences, festivals, zines, websites, chat groups, e-mail, text messaging, blog discussions, online worlds, and other forms of media. The ideal public sphere imagined in the context of modern societies is also more global in its constitution and more embedded in the production of culture. Arjun Appadurai deploys the term *public culture* to suggest the dimensions of a broader transnational public culture in which global cultural flows of not only media but also people are key factors in the formation of notions of a public in the twenty-first century. We discuss the circulation of images in a global public culture in chapter 10.

National and Global Media Events

One of the primary functions of media has been to promote feelings of connectedness in audience members. Media can affirm national sentiment and offer a sense of national connection. By airing an issue or event internationally, broadcasters signal global importance and offer a means of connecting affected communities across vast distances. In his highly influential 1983 analysis of nationalism, *Imagined Communities*, Benedict Anderson wrote that the modern nation-state is an imagined political community—imagined as both limited (with borders) and sovereign (self-governing). Anderson famously noted that the nation is "*imagined* because the members of even the smallest nation will never know most of their fellow-members, meet them, or even hear them, yet in the minds of each lives the image of their communion."[28] Anderson argued that many factors cohered in the modern nation-state to aid in the creation of these feelings of community, among them the rise of national newspapers. Although Anderson did not discuss television, one can certainly argue that television has been a central medium in the creation of national identity, in particular in times of crisis. Thus some critics have noted that Anderson's concept of "print capitalism" should be extended to include "electronic capitalism."[29] Because of its capacity for instant transmission, its public presence, and its situation within the domestic sphere of the home, television has played a primary role (as radio did before it) in fostering a sense of national identity and a collective public sphere, in particular in the latter half of the twentieth century. In its creation of the sense of participation in a national audience, television has also aided in the creation of a shared national identity through television series and miniseries. For instance, as Arvind Rajagopal has written, Hindu nationalism in India was fostered by the enormously popular television series *Ramayan*, a Hindu epic, shown on state-run television from 1987 to 1990. The Hindu epic, a nostalgic view of a Hindu past, was effectively deployed via television to signal a religious national mobilization.[30]

As we already noted, in many postwar cultures television was viewed in public places before it had fully saturated the home television markets. For instance, in Japan most television viewing took place in large outdoor plazas before the late 1950s, when more Japanese households acquired television sets. Shunya Yoshimi writes that professional wrestling was a popular genre of these outdoor broadcasts, which sometimes drew thousands of viewers.[31] Later, businesses such as restaurants began to capitalize on the popularity of public viewing by installing television sets for their customers' use. In Great Britain, as seen here, prior to the television era national sentiment was rallied through the use of mobile movie trailers that brought newsreels out of the theaters and into the public square, where citizens could bond over war news in a more public and interactive manner than the darkened private theater could allow. Collective public viewing can thus interpellate viewers as part of a national audience. When Anderson wrote of the imagined community of the nation, he stressed

FIG. 6.12
A British crowd watches a film of the Royal Air Force projected from a mobile movie truck, October 1940

the importance of the sense of experiencing events at the same time. The fact that television can be transmitted instantaneously across great distances helps to create this sense of national or global community connectedness through the simultaneous experience of watching broadcasts of live events together with viewers dispersed across different locations. The public space created by these media is virtual rather than physical.

Over the past few decades, media events have affirmed the key role of television in creating a sense of simultaneous audiences while also expanding into a broad range of simultaneous media at work. Thus media events can be simultaneously local, national, and global, and they can involve an extraordinary range of producers, sources, and media. Let us take, for example, one of the most global of media events in the past decade, the terrorist attacks of September 11, 2001, in which four planes were simultaneously hijacked, one crashing into rural Pennsylvania and one into the U.S. Pentagon in Virginia and two planes crashing into the twin towers of the World Trade Center in New York City, which collapsed within two hours of the crash. Although little is publicly known about what the hijackers anticipated about news coverage of 9/11, it is commonly speculated that they strategized the timing of the hijackings to produce the largest potential global audience for their acts. When the first plane hit the North Tower, only a few cameras caught an image of the crash, and these images were taken purely by chance. Jules Naudet, a French filmmaker shooting a documentary about New York City firefighters, happened to glance up with his camera as the plane flew over him and struck the tower. That image would be central to *9/11*, the documentary that he and his brother would then produce about their experiences that day.[32] When the South Tower was hit by a second plane more than fifteen minutes later, there was an extraordinary number of people watching, not only from the street and rooftops of Lower Manhattan but also on screens and monitors receiving broadcasts of the live footage being recorded by the numerous television cameras that had been brought in to cover the scene of the first crash. Film and television documentaries that incorporate street-level footage of the second plane approaching the tower typically include not only the image but also the sound recorded at the scene. Accompanying the footage of the plane striking the second tower, we hear the horrified exclamations of the hundreds of people watching, along with the cameras, from below. Though the camera lenses were trained on the plane above heading into the tower, the live sound allowed us to picture the hundreds of spectators watching from the ground below, staring up in shock and disbelief that the unthinkable "event" of fifteen minutes earlier was about to happen for a second time. Television viewers watching the live broadcasts at a safe distance could watch with these witnesses, feeling their shock and fear through the medium of voice.

9/11 was a global media event of unprecedented proportions in which millions of viewers throughout the world saw images of the twin towers hit and falling, if not live, then within the span of a very short period of time. It was also an event

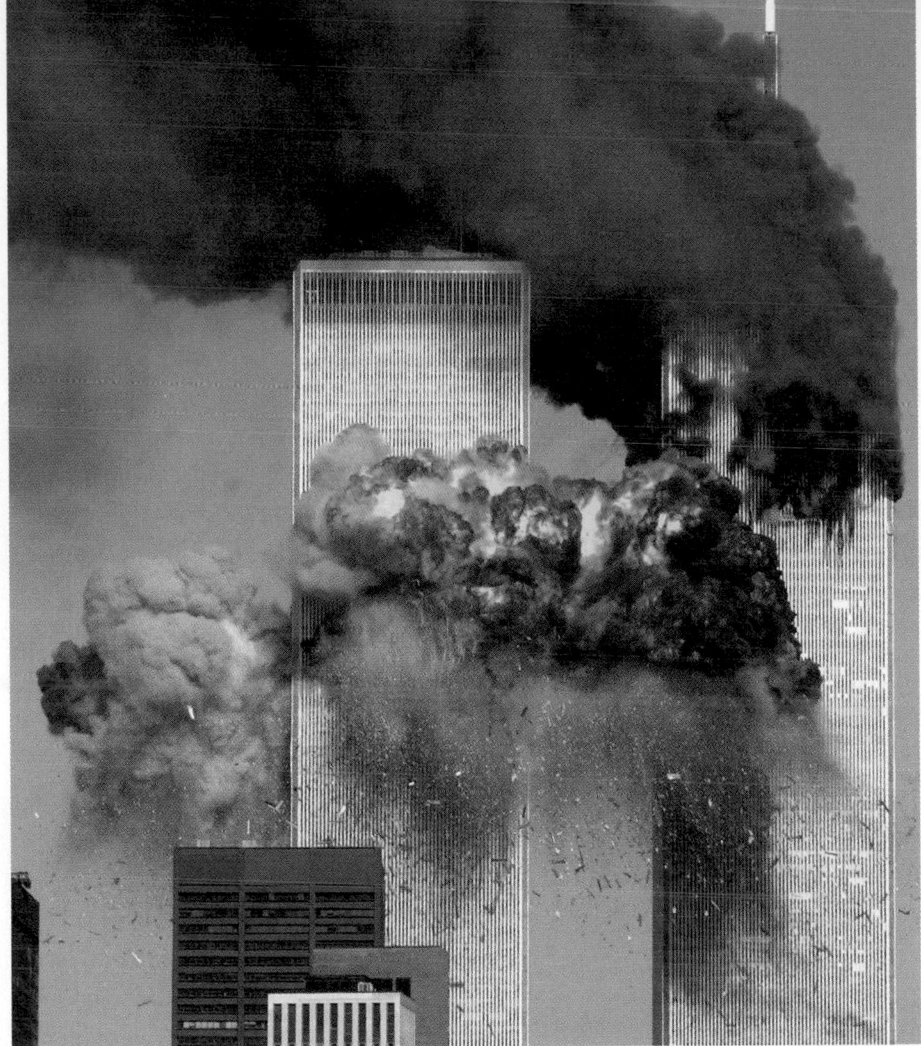

FIG. 6.13
Iconic image of World Trade Center towers being hit by second airplane, September 11, 2001

of immense spectacle—the image of the second tower exploding has been commonly referred to as the equivalent of a "movie," due to the unreality of the spectacle. This was an event that most thought simply could never really happen, except in the movies. It is now common to characterize the terrorist attacks of 9/11 as acts intended to produce above all an unforgettable image. As Slavoj Žižek has written, "we can perceive the collapse of the WTC towers as the climactic conclusion of twentieth-century art's 'passion for the Real'—the 'terrorists' themselves did not do it primarily to provoke real material damage but *for the spectacular effect of it*."[33] It is important to note that it is one of the primary aspects of spectacle that it overshadows and erases the actual violence behind it—in this case, the spectacle of the explosion erases the people who were incinerated within it. The point is not that spectacle is more important than real violence, but that spectacle is understood to have the potential to generate vast, global shock waves of violence that go beyond the actual destruction of life and property in the single event. These shock waves include invasions, sanctions, ethnic and religious conflict, and wars fanned by media spin.

The images of the twin towers exploding and then falling were instantly transmitted via satellite around the world. These images were recorded by photographic, digital, and video cameras, and disseminated via television transmission, websites, newspapers, magazines, and e-mail. Although the meaning of 9/11 has since been effectively nationalized, in particular in the political rhetoric that followed it, it was a media event that made clear the global reach of the media. In an event such as this, we can see an array of intersecting media vectors through which information and images are simultaneously transmitted. The passengers on the hijacked planes and the people trapped in the World Trade Center used cell phones and sent e-mail to contact the police, family, and friends. Those connections created other networks of information flow via additional phone calls, e-mails, and text messages among relatives, friends, rescue workers and the press. In the case of United flight 93, it was through these communication vectors—specifically through cell phones—that passengers on the plane learned that several other planes had been hijacked and had crashed. This news apparently motivated passengers to attempt to take over the plane, leading it to crash in a field in rural Pennsylvania rather than its potential intended target somewhere in Washington, D.C. Over the hours that followed the hijackings, radio call-in shows were a forum for other vectors of exchange, and air travelers notified loved ones that they were safe by using e-mail. The television images transmitted instantly around the world were rapidly disseminated into many different formats and viewing contexts. Ironically, as the towers fell, they took with them an enormous television antenna and various cell phone transmitters, temporarily eliminating television reception and cell phone connection to many New Yorkers. Media industries clearly have an infrastructure that remains quite material and physical, even when our communication occurs in the realm of the virtual. In the week that followed, television in the United States remained focused on the crisis, with regular programming and advertising suspended. Such a dramatic change in the media activity of everyday life signaled not only the depth of the national crisis but also the shock it had produced.[34]

FIG. 6.14
Missing persons posters, New York, September 19, 2001

In the weeks and months that followed, still photography emerged as a uniquely important medium. In New York City, distraught family members searching for their missing loved ones created flyers, using snapshots and family photographs to show relatives missing in the wake of the disaster, hoping they might be spotted, or might turn up in hospitals or among caregivers in the wake of the event. People in New York and surrounding areas created public shrines to mourn the dead, placing images of missing people and of the twin towers amid flowers and notes of grief and loss. Amateur photographs of the events of that day and its aftermath, taken by observers and by rescue workers, circulated though informal networks and were shown at several open exhibitions mounted in public venues throughout the city in the months afterward. Professional and amateur images have circulated in the media and in coffee-table books. In addition, websites have been central to discussions of 9/11, to the memorialization of those killed, and to the circulation of theories, including conspiracy theories, about what actually took place that day.

We can thus see how the meaning of a highly mediated event such as 9/11 is inextricably tied to the images that were produced and that continue to circulate about it through many venues and the media vectors that defined it. Its meaning as an event is inseparable from the iconic image of the towers falling and its spectacular qualities. The various ways in which this image has been used politically, whether as a tool of recruitment for Islamic fundamentalism or as the means by which the U.S. government justified subsequent wars, is enabled by its spectacular qualities. Yet, as the posters of missing people and the circulation of images in everyday networks show us, within the fabric of global media events such as 9/11, images can also be used in intimate and deeply moving ways; these show that media events are constructed by these broader systems of media vectors, but these are often accompanied by, interwoven with, and interlinked with images at the ground level.

Contemporary Media and Image Flows

It is important to note that there are many contexts of political change, violent conflict, and social injustice that are not covered by the media—through censorship, lack of access, and political indifference. The stories told through the media are always incomplete and always caught up in editorial decisions that cannot be separated from broader power structures. Newspapers, magazines, television channels, and Web media are owned by media conglomerates with political interests at stake. Sometimes this ownership results in direct and clear censorship as in the case where particular stories are stifled because they might reflect negatively on the parent company or one of its subsidiaries. More often, media institutions censor themselves, knowing that business survival depends on observing the boundaries of audience taste and opinion, as well as the interests of the dominant political system. Dependency on markets and government support makes it difficult if not impossible for media corporations to play the role of watchdog when it comes to reporting issues that involve potential infringements upon rights and freedoms by those who determine the financial stability of the corporation.

We can see how this affects media content in examining the image context of the war in Iraq, which began in 2003, and which has received restricted media coverage in particular in the United States, since its beginning. The U.S. military has systematically limited the activities of reporters and photojournalists in war zones since the Persian Gulf War of 1991. In the case of the Persian Gulf War, this was done by keeping reporters largely out of the areas in which combat fighting and bombing were taking place, so that the U.S. coverage of the war consisted mostly of images of weapons (and the images generated by cameras attached to those weapons)—a tactic that succeeded largely in erasing the Iraqi war dead from the television screens and news magazines of the American public. In the Iraq war, the U.S. military chose the tactic of embedding reporters within particular platoons and patrols, so that reporters saw the action of a particular group of soldiers and became identified with those soldiers. As the situation of the war worsened and security concerns heightened, news coverage of the war was heavily restricted by security concerns. Reporters Without Borders reports that between 2003 and March of 2006, 216 reporters and media assistants were killed in the Iraq war.

FIG. 6.15
Government images of U.S. Iraq war dead arriving at Dover Air Force Base, censored by the government, c. 2003

U.S. news organizations have historically refrained from showing images of American dead, though they have had no such restrictions on showing the enemy dead. Yet there are long traditions of showing the arrival of the American war dead at various military bases around the country. Since the Vietnam War, the U.S. military has treated the images of the flag-draped coffins as potentially political, if not incendiary. Since the Persian Gulf War in 1991, the Pentagon has banned the taking and publication of photographs of the flag-draped coffins of American soldiers returned to the United States. This has taken on extreme measures in the Iraq war. Even as the Pentagon has created its own archive of images taken by its own photographers, it has refused to release these images. This policy has been met with objections. A funeral protest at the 2004 Republican National Convention in New York included hundreds of empty coffins, conveying the message that we are allowing our war dead to go faceless, unrecognized. In April 2005, after two Freedom of Information Act suits, the U.S. government released a group of the images.[35] In releasing the second group of images, which were immediately placed on the website of the nonprofit organization the National Security Archive and published in many major newspapers, the military chose to black out (or "redact") the faces of the soldiers who were carrying the coffins.

The political consequences of this kind of image restriction are many. Here we focus on the meanings generated by the released images. The military stated that it redacted the faces and insignia of the soldiers who were carrying the coffins and participating in the honor ceremonies for reasons of privacy. This claim seemed disingenuous to concerned citizens who responded that by rendering the soldiers faceless, the military effectively made the photos unusable, without the emotional and subjective meanings they would bear if we were able to see the mens' faces. The use of black rectangles (or digital pixelization to create a blur) in order to block content of an image has a long history and carries with it a set of associations about secret information, obscene imagery, or potential guilt. The black rectangles in these images block out the faces of the soldiers, screening out, in effect, their identities as individuals and any expression they may have had. This visual act also has the potential to make the soldiers and the ceremony they are participating in appear shameful or secretive.

Yet at the same time that the mainstream U.S. military and the U.S. media operated to restrict the kinds of images that were disseminated from the war, much more than European media, for instance, the changes that had taken place in the global media environment made evident the fact that the image story of the war would take place through new forms of image flow and circulation. Two examples make this clear: first, the rise of the Arab cable network Al Jazeera and the use of this network by radical fundamentalist groups such as al-Qaeda as a channel through which to broadcast video proclamations; and second, the release to the press in 2006 of a large number of images of sadistic torture and abuse of prisoners by U.S. soldiers at the Abu Ghraib prison in Iraq; these images circulated casually among soldiers and friends prior to the media exposé that revealed not only the extensiveness of prisoner abuse, but also the pervasive acceptance among soldiers of the practice of public sexual humiliation of prisoners for the apparent pleasure of display through photo documentation. These image networks made clear that traditional news organizations, such as the BBC and CNN, which had perceived themselves to be the source of news for global audiences throughout the world, are increasingly challenged by the media that have emerged in particular regions (Al Jazeera and Al Arabiya in the Middle East, Univision and Telemundo in Latin America) with very different, and sometimes more local, ways of depicting news events. In addition, a network such as Al Jazeera, which was begun in 1996 and is based in Qatar, emerged in defiance of state-run television in the Middle East, which had been heavily censored in countries such as Saudi Arabia.

The emergence of networks such as Al Jazeera was also coincident with the use of video as a tool of violence by many fundamentalist groups. Al Jazeera has been the primary news outlet through which al-Qaeda has released videos of Osama bin Laden's speeches. In addition, some militant groups have produced videotapes of the on-camera beheadings of prisoners (most notably the killing of American journalist Daniel Pearl in Pakistan in 2004). These images were then posted on websites. In these contexts, the image itself has been a means to broadcast a political warning and message, and the new networks of image distribution, through which images moved quickly from websites into other distribution networks, have facilitated the ways in which these images have made the news, as they have then been reported on (though mostly not shown) in mainstream media networks.

That the dynamics of the global flow of images had changed with events surrounding the Iraq war was most obvious in spring of 2004 when photographs taken by U.S. soldiers at Abu Ghraib prison in Iraq were published in several news publications and shown on television in the United States. In this media event, we can see all of these elements of the role of the image in violent conflict converge: the Abu Ghraib images document torture and abuse, but their circulation also further humiliates the prisoners in the photographs by exposing their humiliated bodies to a vast global public.[36] The act of photographing was clearly a means of heightening the men's physical and sexual abuse. The photographs are essentially snapshots, many with U.S. soldiers posing in them like tourists. For instance, this well-known image shows Private Lynndie England, who in 2005 was sentenced to three years in prison on charges relating to the documented abuses, holding a prisoner on a leash like a dog. In other images, soldiers posed like tourists pointing out something humorous while gesturing at hooded, naked male prisoners or at the corpses of prisoners who had been killed. The sexual humiliation that the camera heightens is also a form of cultural and religious humiliation. These are Muslim men forced to expose their bodies to a white female captor, who might be said to be the bearer of a male imperial gaze. The images began as private titillation, and were passed around in a personal network that included England's former fiance, Specialist Charles Graner, who was sentenced to ten years for his involvement in the Abu Ghraib abuses. The photographs were released to reporters and circulated through international media networks, beginning with a *60 Minutes II* news report and an article by Seymour M. Hersh in the *New Yorker* magazine in spring 2004. As the images circulated, some news stations branded their broadcasts of the images with their network logo, as if to claim ownership of them, and blurred or blocked out sections, but the debasement they document was nonetheless obvious. These

FIG. 6.16
Private Lynndie England holding a prisoner on a leash at the Abu Ghraib prison, Baghdad, Iraq, 2003

images raise important questions about the role of the visual in the psychology of sadism that permeates both warfare and racism.

Perhaps the most famous of the Abu Ghraib images is that of a hooded man standing with his arms outstretched with wires attached to his body. It fits within an iconography of suffering that extends back to the Christ figure on the cross and before.[37] The image of the hooded man was broadcast on news websites and then was appropriated in cartoons and remakes, including the iRaq culture jam that we discuss on page 85. The Abu Ghraib photographs demonstrate the ways in which images still play an important role as evidence. These images document what has been, providing evidence of facts that would otherwise be beyond the belief of the general public. Moreover, these images tell us something about the social relationship between seeing and sadism. Although we have discussed many of the ways in which images are censored, not reproduced, and suppressed in some form, it is important to recognize that the enhanced circulation of images, even ones as troubling as these, plays a key role in exposing injustice around the world, even when the making and circulating of the images can be bound up in that injustice.

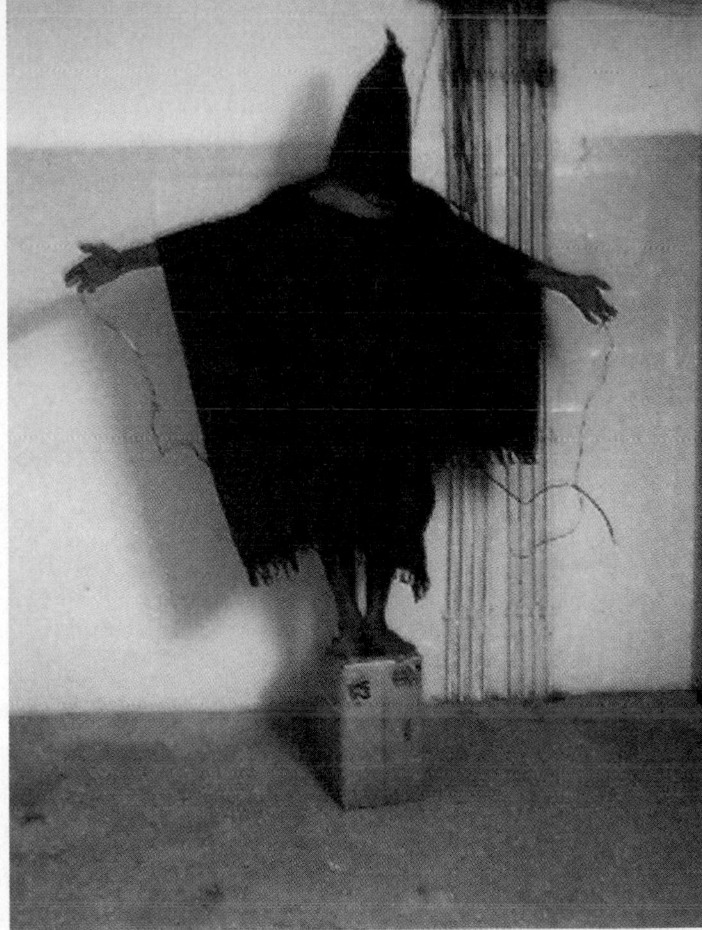

FIG. 6.17
Iconic image of hooded prisoner at Abu Ghraib prison, Baghdad, Iraq, 2003

It is thus important to see the constant negotiation of power that exists in the media. Power is not simply held by one group or individual entity over another. It is always enacted across people and groups in complex, shifting, and uneven dynamics. The media are indeed in the control of powerful business and government entities, and they do influence our thinking. but audiences in a wide range of cultural and national settings resist, appropriate, and transform media texts not only at the level of consumption but also as producers of new meanings and new texts. Moreover, media consumers transform the technologies they use, adapting them to new settings and new uses. The rise of independent media has challenged the hegemonic control of media, yet it is not simply a site of resistant culture, but rather the source of a broad range of ideological positions and productions. For instance, when media coverage of Hurricane Katrina in 2005 failed to fully address the racial and class dynamics of the government's response to the disaster, independent filmmaker Spike Lee went to New Orleans to make a densely detailed, revealing, and scathing video commentary that aired on the HBO cable channel one short year later. Lee's *When the Levees Broke: A*

FIG. 6.18
Josie Harris and Tania Butler of the Lower Ninth Ward of New Orleans in Spike Lee, *When the Levees Broke: A Requiem in Four Acts*, 2006

Requiem in Four Acts is not simply about the natural disaster but about the political and social dynamics that escalated its most damaging impact on the black and poor citizens of New Orleans. It shows the institutional failure of the local and national government to ensure safety in advance of the storm for the residents of poor areas, such as the low-lying Lower Ninth Ward, and the subsequent failure of the government to address the needs of the citizens during the flood, when more valuable properties were afforded greater attention, and after the flood, when citizens remained without homes seemingly indefinitely. Controversies continue about the government's ineptitude and indifference and the continuing environmental risks to remaining residents housed in trailers offgassing levels of formaldehyde that exceed government limits and living in areas without basic services such as adequate water and sewage lines. Enhanced image reproducibility, flow, and technologies made it possible for Lee to generate a critical text dense with audiovisual evidence that twenty years ago it would have been impossible to obtain, particularly in under one year. Moreover, Lee's position as an "independent" director is no longer a barrier that places filmmakers in this category on the margins of visibility and the fringes of social commentary. The Web and digital editing were crucial factors in these changes. The contradiction between media as the product of global powers and media as technologies for local meaning and use exists not because the theories we rely on to assess the media are faulty but because the status of media in contemporary cultures is contradictory and mixed in exactly this way. We discuss the global flow of images, cultural forms, and ideas and global surveillance and monitoring at more length in chapter 10.

Notes

1. See Anthony Giddens, *Emile Durkheim: Selected Writings*, 123–24 (Cambridge, U.K.: Cambridge University Press,1972); excerpt from Emile Durkheim, *The Division of Labor in Society*, 1933.
2. See, for example, David Reisman, *The Lonely Crowd: A Study of the Changing American Character* (New Haven: Yale University Press, 1950); and Herbert Marcuse, *One-Dimensional Man* (Boston: Beacon, 1964), which can be found online in full at http://www.marcuse.org/herbert/pubs/64onedim/odmcontents.html.
3. Jean Baudrillard, "Design and Environment, or How Political Economy Escalates into Cyberblitz," in *For a Critique of the Political Economy of the Sign*, trans. Charles Levin, 185–203 (St. Louis: Telos Press, 1981).
4. See Marita Sturken, *Tangled Memories: The AIDS Epidemic and the Politics of Remembering*, chapter 1 (Berkeley: University of California Press, 1997).
5. Marshall McLuhan, *Understanding Media: The Extensions of Man* (New York: Mentor, 1964). Republished in 1994 by MIT Press, Cambridge, Mass.

6. Raymond Williams, *Television: Technology and Cultural Form* (New York: Schocken Books, 1974).
7. http://www.laptopgiving.org.
8. See Eric Klinenberg, *Fighting for Air: The Battle to Control America's Media* (New York: Metropolitan, 2007).
9. Robert McChesney, *Rich Media, Poor Democracy: Communication Politics in Dubious Times* (New York: New Press, 2000).
10. Herbert I. Schiller, *Communication and Cultural Domination* (White Plains, N.Y.: International Arts and Sciences Press, 1976).
11. Timothy Havens, *Global Television Marketplace* (London: British Film Institute, 2008).
12. John Fiske, *Reading the Popular* (London: Unwin Hyman, 1989).
13. Ien Ang, *Desperately Seeking the Audience,* 35–36 (New York: Routledge, 1989). See also Ien Ang, *Watching* Dallas*: Soap Opera and the Melodramatic Imagination*, trans. Della Couling (New York: Routledge, 1990).
14. Paul Lazarsfeld, Hazel Gaudet, Bernard F. Berelson, *The People's Choice: How the Voter Makes Up His Mind in a Presidential Campaign* (New York: Columbia University Press, 1948).
15. See the account of this report to Congress by Jenkins at http://www.sirlin.net/Features/JenkinsGoesToWashington.htm (accessed March 2008).
16. Guy Debord, *The Society of the Spectacle* (Detroit: Black and Red Books, [1967] 1970), passages 3–5 in section 1, "Separation Perfected."
17. Max Horkheimer and Theodor W. Adorno, "The Culture Industry: Enlightenment as Mass Deception," in *Dialectic of Enlightenment, Philosophical Fragments*, trans. Edmund Jephcott, 94–136 (Stanford, Calif.: Stanford.: Stanford University Press, [1947] 2002).
18. Horkheimer and Adorno, "The Culture Industry," 99.
19. For a discussion of TVTV and guerrilla television, see Deirdre Boyle, *Subject to Change: Guerrilla Television Revisited* (New York: Oxford University Press, 1997).
20. Paul Benedict and Nancy DeHart, eds., *On McLuhan: Forward through the Rearview Mirror,* 39 (Toronto: Prentice Hall Canada, 1996).
21. Michael Warner, *Publics and Counterpublics,* ch. 2 (New York: Zone, 2002).
22. Warner, *Publics and Counterpublics*, 97–98.
23. Jürgen Habermas, *The Structural Transformation of the Public Sphere*, trans. Thomas Burger (Cambridge, Mass.: MIT Press, 1989).
24. Oskar Negt and Alexander Kluge, *Public Sphere and Experience: Toward an Analysis of the Bourgeois and Proletarian Public Sphere*, trans. Peter Labanyi, Owen Daniel, and Assenka Oksiloff (Minneapolis: University of Minnesota Press, [1972] 1993).
25. Nancy Fraser, "Rethinking the Public Sphere: A Contribution to the Critique of Actually Existing Democracy," in *The Phantom Public Sphere*, ed. Bruce Robbins, 1–32 (Minneapolis: University of Minnesota Press, 1993).
26. Lynn Spigel, *Welcome to the Dreamhouse: Popular Media and Postwar Suburbs* (Durham, N.C.: Duke University Press, 2001).
27. Warner, *Publics and Counterpublics*, 56.
28. Benedict Anderson, *Imagined Communities,* 15 (London: Verso, 1983).
29. Arvind Rajagopal, *Politics after Television: Religious Nationalism and the Reshaping of the Indian Public,* 24 (Cambridge, U.K.: Cambridge University Press, 2001).
30. Rajagopal, *Politics after Television*, 25.
31. Shunya Yoshimi, "Television and Nationalism: Historical Change in the National Domestic TV Formation of Postwar Japan." *European Journal of Cultural Studies* 6.4 (2003), 459–87.
32. *9/11*, directed by Jules Naudet, Gédéon Naudet, and James Hanlon (2002, Paramount Pictures).
33. Slavoj Žižek, *Welcome to the Desert of the Real!,* 11 (London: Verso, 2002).
34. See Lynn Spigel, "Entertainment Wars: Television Culture after 9/11," *American Quarterly* 56.2 (June 2004), 235–70.
35. Two Freedom of Information suits were filed, in April 2004 by Russ Kick, the webmaster of www.memoryhole.com and in April 2005 by Professor Ralph Begleiter of the University of Delaware. See the National Security Archive (at George Washington University) website: http://www.gwu.edu/~nsarchiv/ (accessed March 2008).
36. On the Abu Ghraib images, see Nicholas Mirzoeff, "Invisible Empire: Visual Culture, Embodied Spectacle, and Abu Ghraib," *Radical History Review* 95 (Spring 2006), 21–44; Allen Feldman, "On the Actuarial Gaze: From 9/11 to Abu Ghraib," *Cultural Studies* 19.2 (March 2005), 203–36; and W. J.

T. Mitchell, "The Unspeakable and the Unimaginable: Word and Image in the Time of Terror," *ELH* (Summer 2005), 291–310.

37. See Hassan M. Fattah, "Symbol of Abu Ghraib Seeks to Spare Others His Nightmare," *New York Times*, March 11, 2006, A1; Philip Gourevitch and Errol Morris, *Standard Operating Procedure* (New York: Penguin, 2008); and Errol Morris's film *Standard Operating Procedure*, 2008.

Further Reading

Ang, Ien. *Desperately Seeking the Audience*. New York: Routledge, 1989.

———. *Watching* Dallas*: Soap Opera and the Melodramatic Imagination*. Translated by Della Couling. New York: Routledge, 1990.

Allen, Robert, ed. *Channels of Discourse, Reassembled: Television and Contemporary Criticism*. Chapel Hill: University of North Carolina Press, 1992.

Anderson, Benedict. *Imagined Communities*. London: Verso, 1983.

Appadurai, Arjun. *Modernity at Large: Cultural Dimensions of Globalization*. Minneapolis: University of Minnesota Press, 1996.

Baudrillard, Jean. *Simulacra and Simulation*. Translated by Sheila Faria Glaser. Ann Arbor: University of Michigan Press, [1981] 1995.

———. *For a Critique of the Political Economy of the Sign*. Translated by Charles Levin. St. Louis, Mo.: Telos Press, 1981.

Baughman, James L. *The Republic of Mass Culture: Journalism, Filmmaking, and Broadcasting in America since 1941*. 2nd ed. Baltimore: Johns Hopkins University Press, 1997.

Benedict, Paul, and Nancy DeHart, eds. *On McLuhan: Forward through the Rearview Mirror*. Toronto: Prentice Hall Canada, 1996.

Boddy, William. "The Beginnings of American Television." In *Television: An International History*. 2nd ed. Edited by Anthony Smith. New York: Oxford University Press, 1998, 23–37.

——— *Fifties Television: The Industry and Its Critics*. Urbana: University of Illinois Press, 1992.

——— *New Media and Popular Imagination: Launching Radio, Television, and Digital Media in the United States*. New York: Oxford University Press, 2004.

Boy, A. H. S. "Biding Spectacular Time." *Postmodern Culture*, 6(2) (January 1996), http://www.monash.edu.au/journals/pmc/issue.196/review-2.196.html.

Boyle, Deirdre. *Subject to Change: Guerrilla Television Revisited*. New York: Oxford University Press, 1997.

Buckingham, David, ed. *Reading Audiences: Young People and the Media*. Manchester, U.K.: University of Manchester Press, 1993.

Chapman, Jane. *Comparative Media History: An Introduction: 1789 to the Present*. Cambridge, U.K.: Polity, 2005.

Couldry, Nick. *Media Rituals: A Critical Approach*. New York: Routledge, 2003.

Crary, Jonathan. "Spectacle, Attention, Counter-Memory." *October* 50 (Autumn 1989): 96–107.

Dayan, David, and Elihu Katz. *Media Events: The Live Broadcasting of History*. Cambridge, Mass.: Harvard University Press, 1992.

Debord, Guy. *The Society of the Spectacle*. Detroit: Black and Red Books, [1967] 1970. Reissue translated by Donald Nicholson-Smith. New York: Zone Books, 1994.

——— *Comments on the Society of the Spectacle*. Translated by Malcolm Imrie. London: Verso, 1990.

Ellis, John. *Visible Fictions*. London: Routledge and Kegan Paul, 1982.

Ewen, Stuart, and Elizabeth Ewen. *Channels of Desire: Mass Images and the Shaping of American Consciousness*. New York: McGraw Hill, 1982.

Fiske, John. *Understanding Popular Culture*. London: Unwin Hyman, 1989.

———. *Reading the Popular*. New York: Routledge, 1991.

Fraser, Nancy. "Rethinking the Public Sphere: A Contribution to the Critique of Actually Existing Democracy." In *The Phantom Public Sphere*. Edited by Bruce Robbins. Minneapolis: University of Minnesota Press, 1993, 1–32.

Habermas, Jürgen. *The Structural Transformation of the Public Sphere*. Translated by Thomas Burger. Cambridge, Mass.: MIT Press, 1989.

Hansen, Miriam. *Babel & Babylon: Spectatorship in American Silent Film*. Cambridge, Mass.: Harvard University Press, 1991.

Havens, Timothy. *Global Television Marketplace*. London: British Film Institute, 2008.

Horkheimer, Max and Theodor W. Adorno. "The Culture Industry: Enlightenment as Mass Deception." In *Dialectic of Enlightenment. Philosophical Fragments*. Edited by Gunzelin Schmid Noerr. Translated by Edmund Jephcott. Standford, Calif.: Stanford University Press, [1947] 2002.

Huyssen, Andreas. "Mass Culture as a Woman: Modernism's Other." In *After the Great Divide: Modernism, Mass Culture, Postmodernism*. Bloomington: Indiana University Press, 1986, 44–62.

Klinenberg, Eric. *Fighting for Air: The Battle to Control America's Media*. New York: Metropolitan, 2007.

Klinger, Barbara. *Beyond the Multiplex: Cinema, New Technologies, and the Home*. Berkeley: University of California Press, 2006.

Kintz, Linda, and Julia Lesage, eds. *Media, Culture, and the Religious Right*. Minneapolis: University of Minnesota Press, 1998.

Lazersfeld, Paul F., and Robert K. Merton. "Mass Communication, Popular Taste and Organized Social Action." In *Media Studies: A Reader*. Edited by Paul Marris and Sue Thornham. Edinburgh, U.K.: Edinburgh University Press [1948] 1996, 14–23.

Ledbetter, James. *Made Possible By: The Death of Public Broadcasting in the United States*. London: Verso, 1997.

Paul Marris and Sue Thornham, eds. *Media Studies: A Reader*. Edinburgh, U.K.: Edinburgh University Press, 1996.

McCarthy, Anna. *Ambient Television: Visual Culture and Public Space*. Durham, N.C.: Duke University Press, 2001.

McChesney, Robert. *Rich Media, Poor Democracy: Communication Politics in Dubious Times*. New York: New Press, 2000.

——— *The Political Economy of Media: Enduring Issues, Emerging Dilemmas*. New York: Monthly Review Press, 2008.

McLuhan, Marshall. *Understanding Media: The Extensions of Man*. Revised Edition. Cambridge, Mass.: MIT Press, [1964] 1994.

Meehan, Eileen R. "Why We Don't Count: The Commodity Audience." In *The Logics of Television*. Edited by Patricia Mellencamp. Bloomington: University of Indiana Press, 1990, 117–37.

Negt, Oskar, and Alexander Kluge. *Public Sphere and Experience: Toward an Analysis of the Bourgeois and Proletarian Public Sphere*. Translated by Peter Labanyi, Owen Daniel, and Assenka Oksiloff. Foreword by Miriam Hansen. Minneapolis: University of Minnesota Press, [1972] 1993.

Nightingale, Virginia. *Studying Audiences: The Shock of the Real*. New York: Routledge, 1996.

Rajagopal, Arvind. *Politics after Television: Religious Nationalism and the Reshaping of the Indian Public*. Cambridge, U.K.: Cambridge University Press, 2001.

Robbins, Bruce, ed. *The Phantom Public Sphere*. Minneapolis: University of Minnesota Press, 1993.

Ross, Andrew, and Constance Penley, eds. *Technoculture*. Minneapolis: University of Minnesota Press, 1992.

Schiller, Herbert I. *The Mind Managers*. Boston: Beacon, 1973.

———. *Culture, Inc: The Corporate Takeover of Public Expression*. New York: Oxford University Press, 1989.

———. *Communication and Cultural Domination*. White Plains, N.Y.: International Arts and Sciences Press, 1976.

———. *Information Inequality: The Deepening Social Crisis in America*. New York: Routledge, 1996.

Silverstone, Roger. *Television and Everyday Life*. New York: Routledge, 1994.

Smith, Anthony, ed. *Television: An International History*. New York: Oxford University Press, 1995.

Smulyan, Susan. *Selling Radio: The Commercialization of American Radio, 1920–1934*. Washington, D.C.: Smithsonian Institution Press, 1994.

Spigel, Lynn. *Make Room for TV: Television and the Family Ideal in Postwar America*. Chicago: University of Chicago Press, 1992.

———. *Welcome to the Dreamhouse: Popular Media and Postwar Suburbs*. Durham, N.C.: Duke University Press, 2001.

Staiger, Janet. *Media Reception Theories*. New York: New York University Press, 2005.

Thompson, John B. *The Media and Modernity: A Social Theory of the Media*. Stanford, Calif.: Stanford University Press, 1995.

Tracey, Michael. "Non-Fiction Television." In *Television: An International History*. 2nd ed.. Edited by Anthony Smith. New York: Oxford University Press, 1998, 69–84.

Warner, Michael. *Publics and Counterpublics*. New York: Zone, 2002.

Williams, Raymond. *Television: Technology and Cultural Form*. New York: Schocken Books, 1974.

Yoshimi, Shunya. "Television and Nationalism: Historical Change in the National Domestic TV Formation of Postwar Japan." *European Journal of Cultural Studies* 6.4 (2003), 459–87.

Žižek, Slavoj. *Welcome to the Desert of the Real!* London: Verso, 2002.

chapter **seven**

Advertising, Consumer Cultures, and Desire

We are confronted with advertising images constantly through the course of our daily lives, in newspapers and magazines, on television, in movie theaters, on billboards, on public transportation, on clothing, on websites, and in many other contexts in which we may not even notice them. Logos (signs, pictograms, or characters that represent a brand) are ubiquitous. They appear on clothing and shoes, on household objects, cars, knapsacks, computers, cell phones, and other electronic devices. Because consumers are so accustomed to the presence of brands and ads and see so many ads over the course of a typical week, they tune ad messages out. In today's media environment, advertisers and marketers are compelled to constantly reinvent the ways in which they address and hold the attention of increasingly jaded consumers, who are always on the verge of turning the page, hitting the television remote control, fast forwarding on their TiVos, or browsing to a new website.

Consumer products and brands and the advertising that sells them aim to present an image of things to be desired, people to be envied, and life "as it should be." Advertisements present an abstract world, often a fantastic one, that is situated not in the present but in an imagined future. Ads make promises—the promise of a better self-image, a better appearance, more prestige, and fulfillment. As we discussed in chapter 2, as viewers we have a range of tactics with which to interpret and respond to the images of advertising, to negotiate meaning through them, or to ignore them. Many contemporary advertisements interpellate consumers as savvy viewers who understand that ads promise more than they can deliver. Some ads present themselves as something other than ads—as art, as culture jams, and as forms of entertainment. Marketers sometimes use techniques of guerrilla marketing and viral marketing by which they attempt to tap into social networks in which consumers communicate with each other, and have made their messages integral to the online social networking that proliferates today. Consumerism is deeply integrated into the daily life and the visual culture of the societies in which we live, often in ways that we do not even recognize. As we discuss further in this chapter, the boundaries between ads and culture jams, between art and advertising, and between consumer culture and alternative cultures are increasingly blurred and hard to distinguish.

Consumer Societies

Consumer cultures have developed out of the rise of modernity and the historical emergence of capitalism as an economic force throughout the world. Capitalism as a system depends on the production and consumption of large amounts of goods, well beyond those that are necessary for daily living. The concept of consumer choice is central to capitalist consumer cultures. As this ad promotes, the idea of individual choice has a high value in the world of consumerism. Here, the relatively minor option of choosing between different diet sodas is promoted as a special experience—one that the graphic design of the ad equates to a palate of colors that can be used to make art. Individual choice is sometimes proposed in the language of advertising as an enormously important thing, crucial to a person's happiness and to the functioning of a society.

FIG. 7.1
Diet soda ad, 2006

Consumer societies emerged in the context of modernity in the late nineteenth and early twentieth centuries with the rise of mass production in the wake of the industrial revolution and with the consolidation of populations in major urban centers that took place in the eighteenth and nineteenth centuries throughout much of the industrialized world. In a consumer society, the individual is confronted with and surrounded by a vast assortment of goods. The characteristics of those goods change (or appear to change) constantly. Thus even products that are sold as exemplifying tradition and heritage, such as Quaker Oats cereal, are marketed through constantly changing advertising messages. In a consumer society there are great social and physical distances between the manufacture of goods and their purchase and use. This means that workers in an automobile factory may live far from where the cars they help build are bought and sold and may never be able to afford to buy one of the cars they make themselves. Increased industrialization and bureaucratization in the late nineteenth century meant a decrease in the number of small entrepreneurs and an increase in large manufacturers; this situation in turn resulted in people traveling longer distances to work. This is in contrast to feudal and rural societies of the past, in which there was proximity between producers and consumers, as in the case of a shoemaker whose shoes were sold to and worn by residents in the village where he worked.

Mobility and concentrations of populations in urban areas are aspects of modernity that have contributed to the rise of consumerism. As urban centers expanded in the nineteenth century and systems of mass transit were built in the late nineteenth and early twentieth centuries, people began to live increasingly mobile lives, traveling by trains to cities and through urban spaces on mass transit systems. As the automobile became a popular mode of transportation in the early twentieth century and highway systems were built throughout many countries after the Second World War, newer kinds of mobility continued to emerge. The world of consumerism is closely tied to the increased mobility of people in their daily lives. As places filled with mobile crowds and mass transit, city streets became forums for advertising.

In a consumer society, there is a constant demand for new products. Old products are sold with a new look, added features, a new design, or simply new slogans and ad campaigns. A capitalist economy is dependent on the overproduction of goods, which requires the production of desire for those goods among consumers who may not truly need them. In a consumer society a large segment of the population must have discretionary income and leisure time, which means that they must be able to afford goods that are not absolutely necessary to daily life but that they may want for an array of reasons, such as style or status.

Consumer societies are integral to modernity. The mass production and marketing of goods depended until the late twentieth century on large sectors of the population living in concentrated areas, so that the distribution, purchase, and advertising of goods had an available audience. The rise of online commerce since the late 1990s has dramatically reconfigured this relationship of consumerism to space. Initially, online consumerism promised to eliminate the necessity of bearing overhead costs of a physical retail space (a store, a mall) for the sale of goods to consumers (while at the same time adding significant amounts for shipping to consumers). Yet it has also emerged simultaneously with the expansion of global chain stores, such as the Gap, Victoria's Secret, Barnes and Noble, and many others, as well as the success of big-box retailers and massive discount stores such as Costco and Wal-Mart. This means that we find many of the same stores in central shopping districts of cities around the world, from Tokyo to London to New York. Global consumerism thus features this kind of homogenization at the same time that it offers a broad array of media venues to consumers, who can purchase goods online or through exchange networks such as eBay and Craigslist. Many aspects of these patterns of consumption are not wholly new, though; online consumerism recalls the nineteenth- and early-twentieth-century practice by which those people living in rural areas relied on mail-order catalogues to purchase many of their goods. For rural children growing up during the early to mid-twentieth century, before the broad expansion of mall culture, the delivery of each season's Montgomery Ward and Sears and Roebuck catalogues was a highly anticipated event. It was one of few sources through which rural consumers could engage in the kind of "window shopping" world of consumer fantasy that urban dwellers could experience in their walks by department stores and that suburban dwellers engaged in through trips to the local mall.

With the emergence of the consumer society of the late nineteenth century, the workplace, the home, and commerce became separated, which in turn had a significant effect on the structure of the family and gender relations. As people moved into urban centers and away from agrarian lifestyles in which all members of the family play crucial roles in production, the distance between the public sphere of work and commerce and the private sphere of the home increased. Women were relegated to the domestic sphere and men were assigned to the public sphere. As the manufacturing industry expanded, women and men were increasingly perceived as two distinct kinds of consumers who could be targeted through different kinds of marketing strategies linked to different sets of goods.

The new experience of urban life and modernity of the late nineteenth and early twentieth centuries has often been characterized as the sensation of standing in a crowd, being surrounded on a daily basis by strangers whom one will never know, and the both giddy and overwhelming feeling of the city as a kind of organism. In this modern context we can see another important aspect of consumer societies: the source of concepts of the self and identity are constituted in a larger realm than the family. It has been argued that in consumer societies people derive their sense of their place in the world and their self-image at least in part through their purchase and use of commodities, which seem to give meaning to their lives in the absence of the meaning derived from a closer-knit community.

The rise of consumerism thus took place within a context of shifting values. One of the fundamental changes in turn-of-the-century European-American societies that was integral to the rise of consumer culture was the emergence of what historian T. J. Jackson Lears calls the "therapeutic ethos."[1] These societies shifted over a period of time from valorizing a Protestant work ethic, civic responsibility, and self-denial to legitimating ideas of leisure, spending, and individual fulfillment. Whereas the religiously influenced ethos of the eighteenth and early nineteenth centuries affirmed the values of saving and thriftiness, in the late nineteenth century these societies gained a new emphasis on spending and on imagining that the path to betterment was through the increased acquisition of goods. In this constantly changing modern culture, the feeling that life was often troubling and overwhelming prevailed. This allowed the idea to take hold, one promoted by the emerging consumer market, that everyone was potentially inadequate and in need of improvement in some way. Commodities fit the bill as things imagined to aid in self-improvement and promising self-fulfillment.

This therapeutic discourse is an essential element of consumer culture. The idea that consumer products will offer self-fulfillment is crucial to marketing and consumption. Modern advertisements were able increasingly to speak to problems of anxiety and identity crisis and to offer harmony, vitality, and the prospect of self-realization, all values in the emerging modern culture; their products were offered as solutions. In the late nineteenth century, for instance, soda drinks were thought of as health tonics and sold at drugstore soda fountains. This ad participates in the therapeutic ethos by offering to late nineteenth-century consumers the promise of relief for physical and mental exhaustion, what we would call "stress" today. As anxieties about social appearance and personal improvement became more pervasive, many advertisers changed the messages of their products. Lifebuoy soap, which had been sold for its antiseptic properties with a sailor or a nurse as its symbol, was repackaged to be a preventative for "B.O." (body

FIG. 7.2
Coca-Cola ad, 1890

FIG. 7.3
Lifebuoy ad promising a solution to "BO," 1930s

Lever Brothers' ads for Lifebuoy soap introduced "B.O."—for body odor—into the vernacular.
Courtesy of Unilever HPC.

odor) by the 1920s. In the early twentieth century, many advertisements began to use the comic strip form to tell stories in order to sell products, a form that presages the narrative form of television advertisements.

As the therapeutic ethos that undergirds consumerism emerged in particular ways in North America and in parts of Europe in the late nineteenth and early twentieth centuries as those societies embraced industrial capitalism and consumerism, it would also emerge in the context of other societies that did not have the same traditions of Protestantism. For instance, the emergence of consumerism in postwar Japan was driven by the country's painful emergence from the devastation of World War II and the loss of its imperial monarchy. In China, consumerism, and along with it credit cards, emerged in the late twentieth century hand in hand with a socialist system that maintains values of communal good not unlike those of Protestant affirmations of community. Thus many aspects of contemporary Chinese society embrace values of self-improvement and self-fulfillment through consumerism, even though those values are in conflict with the values of communism that have structured Chinese society since the establishment of the People's Republic of China in 1949. Consumerism has taken hold quite differently in different societies precisely because of the social values and economic and political systems under which they operate.

FIG. 7.4
Arcade of the Galleria Umberto I in Naples, Italy, 1890s

The rise of consumerism in European-American societies in the late nineteenth century created new kinds of spatial and mobile relationships for citizens in relation to their environments. Shopping was transformed from a mundane task, in which the consumer purchased unbranded bulk goods by standing at a counter and asking a merchant for them, into an activity of leisure and entertainment. Much of this transformation was accomplished through the creation of visually pleasing spaces for shopping in the city. In the early nineteenth century, for instance, shopping arcades began to emerge in European cities such as Paris, Milan, and Berlin. These arcades were covered streets that contained multiple small shops along each side. The arcade anticipates the shopping center by creating a space walled off from nature, a space in which the strolling of the shopper among products is as much part of the experience of shopping as the actual purchase of goods. In fact, the arcades were known as much for the visual splendor of their spaces—beautiful mosaics, crystalline glass windows and ceilings—as for the individual goods on display and for sale within. Like a theme park of endless consumption, the arcades became a place to go to, to stroll through, as well as to buy things. It is no surprise, then, that when cultural critic Walter Benjamin set out to describe the glittering seductions of commodity capitalism, he concentrated on one city, Paris, and its arcades.[2] The arcades maximized the potential for looking. Benjamin wrote, "both sides of these passageways, which are lighted from above, are lined with the most elegant shops, so that such an arcade is a city, even a world, in miniature."[3] Benjamin, whose major life work was an unfinished, massive study based on the modern street life of the arcade, *The Arcades Project*, saw the shopping arcades as the essence of modernity, in which the street is turned into a kind of interior space and the unruliness of the city is made manageable.

Visual pleasure was an enormous part of the arcades' attraction—it was a place to look at the spectacle of glass and metal structures, the packaging of goods, and fellow strollers. In the late nineteenth century, this kind of visual pleasure in the experience of shopping as entertainment was manifested in the rise of the department store. These enormous "palaces" to consumerism were built in major cities as destinations for citizen-consumers, from residents of the city to visitors from the countryside. The department store announced itself as a site of both commerce and leisure and was constructed in order to display the largest possible number of goods to a consumer, who was imagined as strolling through its aisles. With enormous staircases, luxurious goods on sumptuous display, and elaborate décor, the department store intended to be awe inspiring. For instance, writer Emile Zola called Le Bon Marché, the first department store of Paris, a "cathedral of commerce."[4] The big windows of department stores were designed as forms of spectacle that extended the store onto the street and invited consumers into the store. The idea of displaying goods where roaming consumers would see them from all angles coincided with increased attention to the aesthetics of package and product design.

Window shopping and browsing thus gained a kind of currency with this new consumer environment as mobility emerged as a key aspect of modern life. Window shopping is, in many ways, a modern activity, one that is integral to the modern city that is designed for pedestrians, strolling, and crowds. With the emergence of a consumer culture in the nineteenth century that depended on visual codes for pleasure, philosophers and writers described the figure of the *flâneur,* a man who strolls the streets of cities such as Paris, observing the urban landscape in a detached way while moving through it. The *flâneur,* who was a subject of fascination for poet Charles Baudelaire and later for Walter Benjamin, was, according to Benjamin, at home in the streets of the city, in particular in the shopping arcades of Paris. The *flâneur* is a figure who moves through the city in an anonymous fashion and whose primary activity is looking. Sean Nixon writes that these new contexts—of shopping arcades

FIG. 7.5
A nineteenth-century flâneur, from *Physiologie du flâneur*, 1841

and *flâneurs* and visually appealing goods, in other words of new kinds of cityscapes and shop display—created a new kind of "technology of looking" organized around consumption and leisure.[5]

This visual culture of *flânerie* and window shopping in the nineteenth and early twentieth centuries was related to the more mobile vision of modernity. As Anne Friedberg writes, evidence of the increased mobility of vision can be seen in the nineteenth-century interest in panoramas (large 360-degree paintings that the spectator viewed while walking past them or turning in the center to see the full image), dioramas (theatrical compositions of objects and images that moved before immobile viewers), and the emergence of photography in the early nineteenth century and motion picture film at its end.[6] In the nineteenth century, *flâneurs* were men, because respectable women were not allowed to stroll alone in the modern streets. As window shopping became an important activity, in particular with the rise of the department store, it allowed what Friedberg calls the *flâneuse,* a female window shopper, to emerge in more contemporary contexts. Friedberg notes that theories of film spectatorship can also help us to understand the broader function of spatial, mobile practices of looking in the consumer culture of the city. There are many kinds of gazes at play in the visual culture of modernity, from the cinematic predecessors such as the panorama to the cinematic gaze to the gazes at work in the urban environment of pedestrians, commerce, and mall display. Thus the new ways of looking in modern society were not limited to shopping but extended into all areas of urban life. David Serlin has argued that in thinking about the figure of the *flâneur* we should consider not only gender but also sensory ability. He discusses a photograph of the famous American blind advocate Helen Keller window shopping in Paris to emphasize that shopping entails not only visual consumption but also tactile and aural pleasures.[7]

These cultures of visuality and mobility continued to change throughout the twentieth century. With the increased distances traveled by people in automobiles in the city and countryside in the early to mid-twentieth century, billboards became a central venue for advertising. Although advertisements had been painted in large scale on city buildings for decades and billboards were a part of the urban landscape, the development of the automobile in the 1910s changed not only the landscape of communities and industries but also the experience of consumerism.

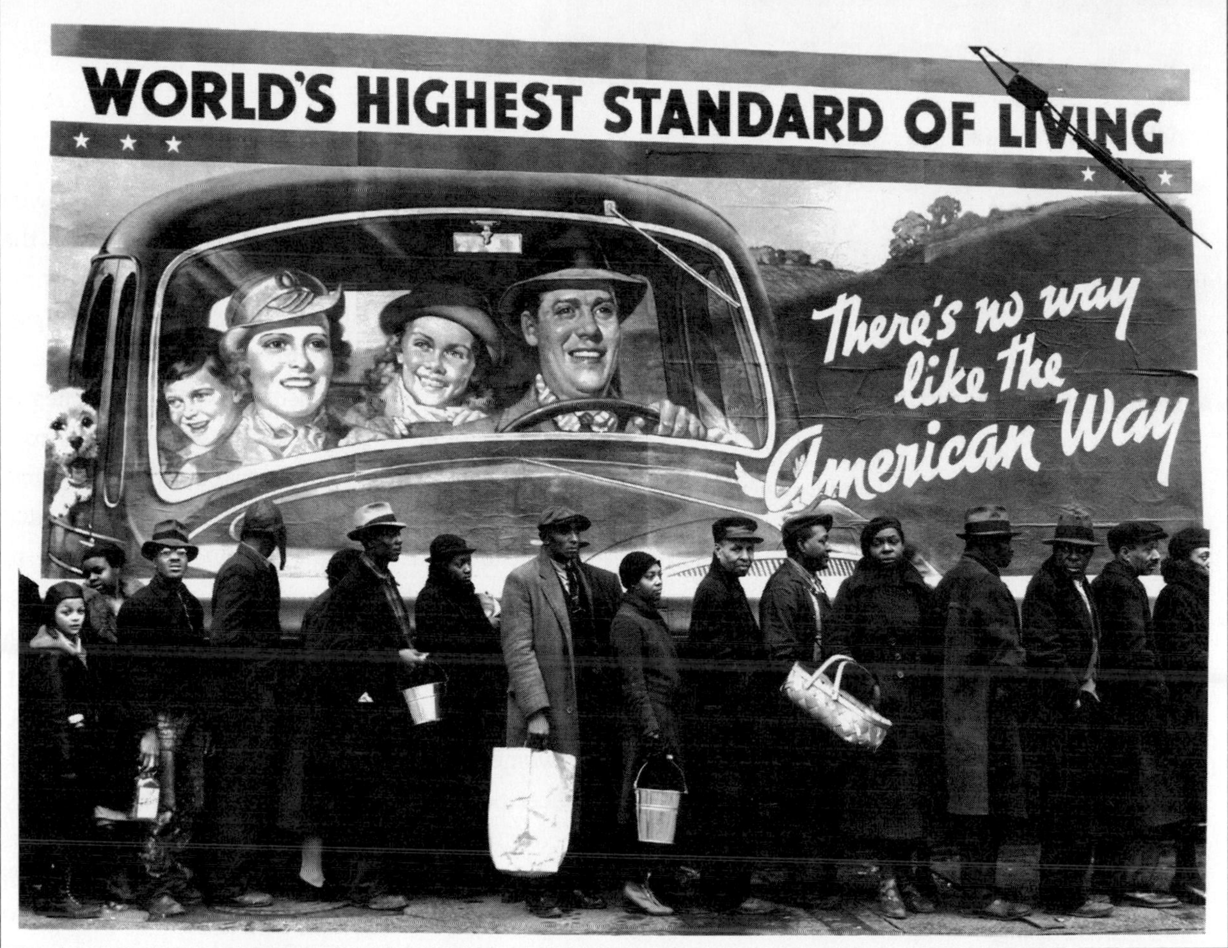

WORLD'S HIGHEST STANDARD OF LIVING
There's no way like the American Way

FIG. 7.6
Margaret Bourke-White, African-American flood victims lined up at Red Cross relief station, 1937

Billboards were designed to be seen on the go, and the automobile was increasingly seen as a consumer product connoting freedom and consumer mobility. During the Great Depression in the 1930s in the United States, billboards were sometimes incorporated into documentary photographs to make ironic commentary, contrasting the promise of American consumerism and the reality of joblessness, poverty, and soup kitchens. In this well-known image by the American documentary photographer Margaret Bourke-White, the destitution of victims of a flood, who are lined up by a Red Cross relief station in 1937, during the height of the depression, is juxtaposed with the advertising campaign of the National Association of Manufacturers, which shows a happy white family driving in their car as emblematic of the "American way." Bourke-White's image not only exposes the racial divisions in the United States during that time, with these black citizens waiting with their few possessions overshadowed by the image of untroubled consumer happiness presented in the billboard, but it also uses this juxtaposition to undercut the ideological simplicity of the image and its selling of the idea that the United States has the "highest standard of living."

Billboards were part of a broader trend in which advertisers reenvisioned the viewing practices of consumers. As Catherine Gudis notes in her book *Buyways*, the billboard became an iconic form for the idea of the consumer on the move, for whom advertisers needed to provide design within an "aesthetics of speed." She writes, "as part of this new aesthetics, advertisers refined their use of the trademark,

FIG. 7.7
Carnation canned milk billboard, Los Angeles, 1958

the slogan, and the massed image that allowed for quick impression."[8] Gudis notes that the outdoor advertising industry credited the movies with creating new kinds of viewing strategies and a familiarity with speed (and large-scale images) among consumers. Thus the integration of mobility into the consumer's visual consumption of advertising that began in the urban centers of the nineteenth century expanded exponentially by the mid-twentieth century to the wider landscapes of the interstate and cross-country highway and toll road. Graphic designers of billboard ads often played with point of view and with the frame of the billboard. In this 1958 Carnation billboard, the image is designed to give an overview from the consumer's perspective (the hand indicates that it was targeted at women), with the product magically pouring itself. The visual extension of the saucer beyond the billboard frame creates a visually arresting image for the motorist-consumer who is passing by.

In the postwar period, the consumer embrace of the automobile as a symbol of individualism, freedom, and conspicuous consumption was part of a broader social engagement with consumption as a kind of civic duty. In the United States, consumerism was increasingly associated with citizenship, with the idea that to be a good citizen was to be a good consumer. This gave rise to what historian Lizabeth Cohen calls "a consumers' republic." Cohen defines this "republic" as an economic and cultural context in which the highest social values are equated with the promises of consumerism, so that consumerism is understood by citizens to be the primary avenue to achieving freedom, democracy, and equality.[9] Thus individual consumerism, rather than social policy, was offered beginning in the 1950s in the United States as the means to achieve the promise of social change and prosperity. This resulted, Cohen notes, in more social inequality along racial lines, a decrease in voter participation, and increased social and political segmentation.[10]

We can see that over a very short period of history, consumerism came to be understood as essential to the economic stability of many societies and has ultimately come to be understood as a primary activity of citizenship and belonging. As we discuss further, our relationships to consumer products can be deep and highly personal, and we construct our identities in part in relationship to brands. All of these changes represent radical shifts from the way in which citizens thought about their identities prior to the late nineteenth century. Today, consumption continues to be thought of as a practice of leisure and pleasure and as a form of therapy. It is commonly understood that commodities fulfill emotional needs. The paradox is that those needs are never truly fulfilled, as the forces of the market lure us into wanting different and more commodities—the newest, the latest, and the best. This is a fundamental aspect of contemporary consumer culture—that it gives us pleasure and reassurance while tapping into our anxieties and insecurities and that it promises what it can never fulfill.

Envy, Desire, and Belonging

Advertisements speak the language of transformation. They promise consumers, whether explicitly or implicitly, that their lives will change for the better if they buy a particular product or brand. In speaking to viewers/consumers about changing themselves, most advertising is always constructing consumers as dissatisfied in some way with their lifestyles, appearances, jobs, relationships, and so forth. Many ads imply that their product can alleviate this state of dissatisfaction. They often do this by presenting figures of glamour that consumers can envy and wish to emulate, people who are presented as already transformed, and bodies that appear perfect and yet somehow attainable.

The attachment of the value of art to a product can give it a connotation of prestige, tradition, and authenticity. Some contemporary advertisements make reference to artworks of the past in order to give their products the connotation of wealth, upscale leisure, and cultural value attributed to works of art. General references to painting style, such as the still-life painterly style of this Grey Goose pear vodka ad, suggest that a product has cultural value through its association with fine art and, here, French culture as well. Ads such as these construct consumers as having cultural knowledge. They offer to consumers a kind of added cultural value—what we call *cultural capital*. The work of French sociologist Pierre Bourdieu, discussed in chapter 2, can be useful in understanding this process. Bourdieu identified different forms of capital in addition to economic capital (material wealth and access to material goods), including social capital (whom you know, your social networks and the opportunities they provide you), symbolic capital (prestige, celebrity, honors), and cultural capital, which refers to the forms of cultural knowledge that give you social advantages.

FIG. 7.8
Grey Goose La Poire ad, 2007

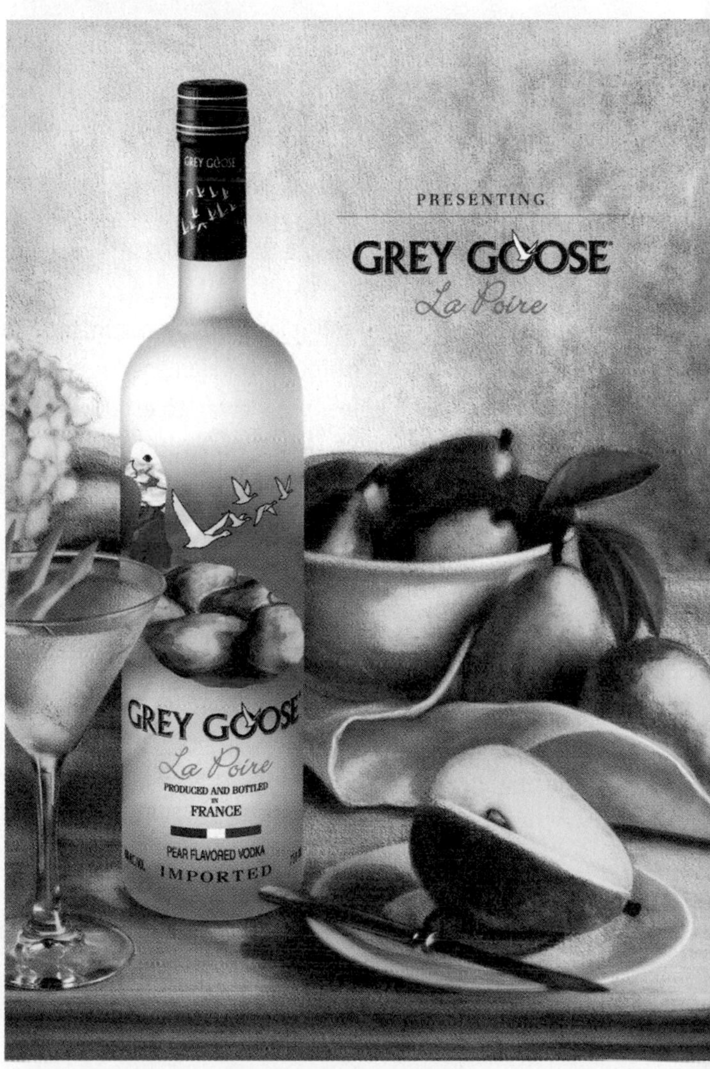

HYUNDAI
Drive your way™
It gives. You take. What a beautiful relationship.
Incredibly well equipped for $27,495. It's your turn to be pampered, and the all-new Azera is up to the task. With power rear sunshade, dual-zone climate control, all the personal space you could ever want, and America's Best Warranty,™* it's the car that just keeps on giving. And at the price, it keeps the taking to a minimum. thenewAZERA.com
A Hyundai like you've never seen before
AZERA

FIG. 7.9
Hyundai ad, 2007

Cultural capital can come in the form of rare taste, connoisseurship, and a competence in deciphering cultural relations and artifacts. It is accumulated, according to Bourdieu, through education, privileged family contexts, and long processes of inculcation.[11] Bourdieu's formulation allows us to see how value is awarded in most capitalist societies not simply through money but through forms of knowledge that are often part of an elite social context and how ads can construct consumers as having different kinds of cultural knowledge—in the case of the Grey Goose ad, of painting styles, French culture, and the still-life genre of painting.

Advertising functions largely to create consumer relationships to brands and to establish brands as familiar, essential, even lovable. Many ads address consumers, then, about their relationship to a brand rather than to a particular product. In this ad, the text promises that the consumer's relationship to the car will be one of affirmation ("It Gives, You Take"), and the image of the car in motion conveys the sense of dynamism. We cannot see through the darkened windows of the car, so it is as if it is driverless, beckoning to us, the viewer, to establish a relationship with it. Such a message is, of course, also designed to remind viewers of their actual, less-than-simple personal relationships, in which such an equation (they give, you take) would be considered inappropriate and certainly not "beautiful."

We can say, then, that advertising asks us not to consume products but to consume signs in the semiotic meaning of the term. Thus this ad is selling the sign: Hyundai as ideal relationship partner. Ads set up particular relationships between the signifier (the product) and the signified (its meaning) to create signs in order to sell not simply products but the connotations we attach to those products. When we consume commodities, we consume them as commodity signs—we aim to acquire, through purchasing a product, the meaning with which the product is encoded. It is also a convention in advertising that ads speak in important terms about products that may in the long run have very little importance. Ads thus operate with a presumption of relevance that allows them to make inflated statements about the necessity of their products. In the real world, the statements of most ads would appear absurd, but in the world of advertising, which integrates fantasy, they make perfect sense because we are aware that when we buy a product as generic as water, we are also in fact buying an image of taste—not in the sense of flavor, but in the sense of style.

Advertising sometimes sells belonging (to a family, community, generation, nation, or special group or class of people), attaching concepts of the nation, community, and democracy to products. Hence the ideological function of many advertisements takes the form of speaking a language of patriotism and nationalism in order to equate the act of purchasing a product with the practices of citizenship. In other words, ads that use an image of America or Britain or other nations to market products are selling the concept that in order to be a good citizen and to properly participate in the nation, one must be an active consumer. Many advertisements depict the family as a site of harmony, warmth, and security, an idealized unit with no problems that cannot be solved by commodities. Indeed, commodities are often presented as the means by which the family is held together, affirmed, and strengthened. Advertisements affirm this meaning that people relate to each other on the most intimate levels through consumerism, depicting commodities as facilitating familial emotion and communication (such as the giving of jewelry or flowers and other commodities to signal affection and value).

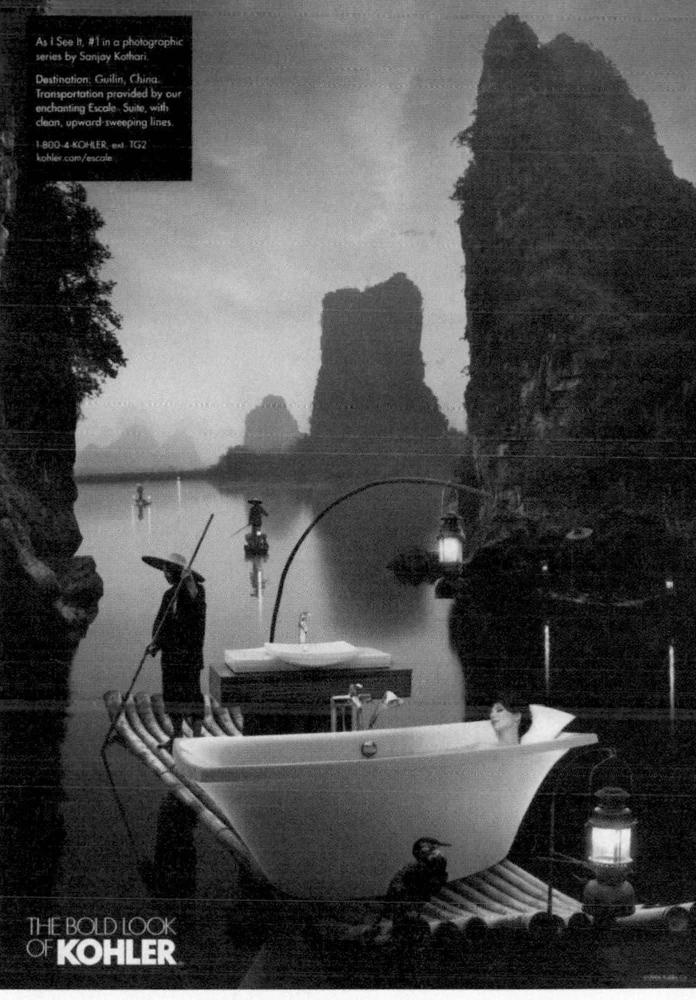

FIG. 7.10
Kohler ad, 2006

In the same way that advertising sells the idea of belonging, it also establishes codes of difference in order to distinguish products. Ads often establish norms by demonstrating things that are different from the norm; this happens through the process of marking and unmarking. As we discussed in chapter 3, the unmarked category is the unquestioned norm, and the marked category is the one seen as "different" or "other." For instance, in ads in the North American and European markets, an apparently white model is unmarked, the normative category, precisely because consumers are not meant to register the fact of his or her whiteness, whereas an apparently nonwhite model is sometimes marked by race, insofar as his or her appearance is intended to connote a racialized meaning. Traditionally, race has been used in advertising to confer to a product a kind of exoticism and foreignness. For example, there has been a long tradition of advertisements that use images of the "islands" and unidentified tropical locales to sell commodities such as cosmetic products and lingerie as exotic and "primitive." In this ad, Kohler sells the experience of its bathtub by suggesting an exotic Chinese locale, complete with natives to push the relaxing consumer on bamboo rafts. The dreamlike fantasy of the image

fresh american style
SUITS, DRESS SHIRTS & TIES
SHOP ONLINE AT TOMMY.COM

FIG. 7.11
Tommy Hilfiger ad, 2005

makes it clear that the Chinese location is one of mystery, with "boldness" then implied to be a quality of the consumer. Ironically, although these products promise to white consumers the qualities of otherness, commodity culture is in actuality about the denial of difference in that it encourages conformist behavior and sameness through the act of consumption.

Increasingly, markers of ethnicity and race are used in advertisements to demonstrate social or racial awareness and to give a product an element of cultural sophistication. There is an increasing number of ads that use models of many different ethnicities in an attempt both to unmark race and to attach to their products the meaning of social awareness. In this Tommy Hilfiger ad, for instance, the mix of races is intended to connote American multiculturalism, with the models posed almost like a family photograph to signify belonging to the nation. In ads such as these, race is specifically marked to connote multiculturalism and racial harmony. Thus, although these ads aim toward racial inclusiveness, part of their message is also that the product is hip enough to be sensitive to racial difference and diversity.

John Berger wrote that advertising is always situated in the future. He was referring to the way in which the present is depicted in advertising as lacking in some way. It is helpful for us to return to the psychoanalytic theory of Jacques Lacan. He suggests that desire and lack are central motivating forces in our lives. We all experience something missing from our lives that we seek, most often in the form of pursuing another person whom we desire. We try to fill this lack but it is never really satisfied, even when our basic needs are met. Our lives are structured by a sense of lack, Lacan suggests, from the moment that we recognize that we are separate entities from our mothers. This separation, experienced as a splitting, marks the point at which we recognize ourselves as subjects apart from others. In Lacan's terms, we are always searching to return to some state of wholeness that we believe we once had prior to this moment of recognition. We constantly strive, through relationships and activities such as consumerism, to fill that lack. It is this drive to fill our sense of lack that allows advertising to speak to our desires so compellingly. Advertisements often recreate for us fantasies of perfect ego-ideals, facilitating a regression to this childhood phase.

This fundamental lack is always unfulfilled. There is never a moment, in psychoanalytic terms, when lack is replaced by full satisfaction, precisely because of desire's origins in various stages of infantile and childhood development. This sense of lack is a crucial engine in our psyches, motivating us to keep searching for the things (relationships, material goods, activities, things) that will help us to feel whole, to acquire states of being that we experience as always just out of reach. According to Lacan, this feeling of lack structures our psyches in profound ways, so that dissatisfaction, not only with ourselves but also with the commodities that promise to fulfill but never succeed in fulfilling our lack, is a central aspect of the human subject. In terms of consumer culture, lack provides an explanation for the process by which we feel pleasure in consuming yet always feel that we need more or feel disappointment afterward in what we have purchased.

Commodity Culture and Commodity Fetishism

A consumer culture is a commodity culture—that is, a culture in which commodities are central to cultural meaning. Commodities are defined as things that are bought and sold in a social system of exchange. The concept of commodity culture is intricately allied with the idea that we construct our identities, at least in part, through the consumer products that inhabit our lives. This is what media theorist Stuart Ewen has called the "commodity self," the idea that our selves, indeed our subjectivities, are mediated and constructed in part through our consumption and use of commodities.[12] Clothing, music, cosmetic products, and cars, among other things, are commodities that people use to construct their identities and project them outward to those around them. Advertising encourages consumers to think of commodities as central means through which to convey their personalities. Sometimes advertising speaks to the commodity self by selling the idea that one becomes a particular kind of person through acquiring and using a brand—one might be a Pepsi or Coke person, for instance, or a Puma or Adidas person. Such a tactic sells a kind of pseudoindividuality, which the Frankfurt School theorists defined as a feature of the products of the culture industry, in which a false sense of individuality is sold simultaneously to many people.

The concept of the commodity, in particular the way that commodities are given meaning and value, is crucial to an understanding of consumer cultures. Analyses of commodities and how they function come to us primarily through Marxist theory, which is both a general analysis of the role of economics in human history and an analysis of the ways that capitalism functions. It is precisely because Marxist theory has a critique of capitalism that it can help us to understand how capitalism functions, given that capitalism is a system of values that most of our societies are so familiar with that we rarely examine its underlying assumptions. As we discuss further, Marxist theory is limited in how it can help us understand contemporary consumerism precisely because the complexity of the relationship of culture and consumerism today is something Marx could never have imagined in the nineteenth century. Nevertheless, some of the core concepts of Marxist theory remain useful in thinking about consumerism today. Commodities have both use value, which refers to their particular use in a particular society, and exchange value, which refers to what they cost in a particular system of exchange. Marxist theory critiques the emphasis in capitalism on exchange value over use value, in which things are valued not for what they really do but for what they are worth in abstract, monetary terms. As the Frankfurt School theorists would say, we value the price of the ticket over the experience itself; this would explain why sometimes goods sell more when their prices are raised.

A look at different kinds of products can help us to see how exchange value works. Certain kinds of products have important use value in our society—food and clothing, for instance, that we feel we cannot live without. Yet we can see that within those categories, there is a broad range of exchange values. A loaf of mass-produced bread has a significantly lower exchange value than a loaf of high-end specialty bakery bread, though they both have the same use value. Similarly, a Mossimo shirt made in China and purchased at the local Target will have a significantly lower price tag than a designer shirt (most likely also made in China) by Quicksilver or Roxy and bought at Macy's. Both have the same use value as clothing but different exchange values. But here, of course, we can see how this theory does not take into account other forms of value that are equally meaningful in our society—the designer shirt may seem important to one's sense of style and commodity self, perhaps even to the image one feels is necessary for one's school or workplace. The idea of use value is tricky, because the concepts of what is and is not useful are highly ideological—one could argue endlessly about whether or not certain so-called leisure goods are "useful," and it is difficult to assess the use value of such qualities as pleasure and status.

One of the most useful concepts in understanding how consumerism creates an abstract world of signs and symbols separate from the economic context of commerce and production is the idea of commodity fetishism. This refers to the process by which mass-produced goods are emptied of the meaning of their production (the context in which they were produced and the labor that created them) and then filled with new meanings in ways that both mystify the product and turn it into a fetish object. For instance, a designer shirt does not contain within it the meaning of the context in which it is produced. The consumer is given no information about who sewed it, the factory in which the material was produced, or the society in which it was made. Rather, the product is affixed with logos and linked to advertising images that imbue it with cultural meanings quite apart from those of its specific production conditions and context. This erasure of labor and the means of production has larger social consequences. Not only does it allow the development of a broader social context of devaluing labor, making it hard for workers to take pride in their work, but it also allows consumers (most of whom are also workers) to remain ignorant of working conditions, the consequences of the global outsourcing of labor and the global production of goods, and the relationship of brand image to corporate practices.

FIG. 7.12
Roz Chast cartoon, 1999

The tensions between consumerism and the role of labor have only become stronger in postindustrial global capitalism, in which the production of goods has been increasingly outsourced from western centers to developing nations around the world. Many products designated "made in the United States" (such as some automobile brands) are in fact assembled in the United States from parts that are made in other places around the world. With the rise of the shipping container in the late twentieth century, goods could be shipped in large metal boxes that are taken directly from ships to tractor-trailers and railway cars for distribution. The price of shipping goods around the world fell significantly, allowing an increased outsourcing of labor. This means that most of the goods produced for developed nations are made by low-paid laborers in developing nations. Thus the distance in global capitalism between the workers who produce commodities and the consumers who purchase them has only grown larger, in both geographic and social terms. For instance, most of the clothing that is sold in North America and Europe is manufactured by low-paid workers in China, Korea, Indonesia, the Philippines, and India. Indeed, only a very small fraction of clothing sold in the United States, one of the world's largest markets for clothes, is made by workers in the United States. Rising oil prices at the end of the decade of the 2000s may impact the cost of shipping goods and that cost may be incorporated into the pricetags of consumer goods, but this situation is unlikely to change the practice of outsourcing labor. The complexity of global outsourcing means that consumers may feel helpless when we do learn of the labor conditions of manufacture because we feel there is little we can do to address them. This cartoon by Roz Chast makes fun of the process that many of us experience when we think about the troubling relationship between labor exploitation and the goods we own and then decide just to wear our clothing anyway.

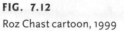

Commodity fetishism is the inevitable outcome of mass production, the practices of advertising and marketing, and the distribution of goods to many different consumers. It is essentially a process of mystification that not only empties commodities of the meaning of

FIG. 7.13
Miata ad, 2007

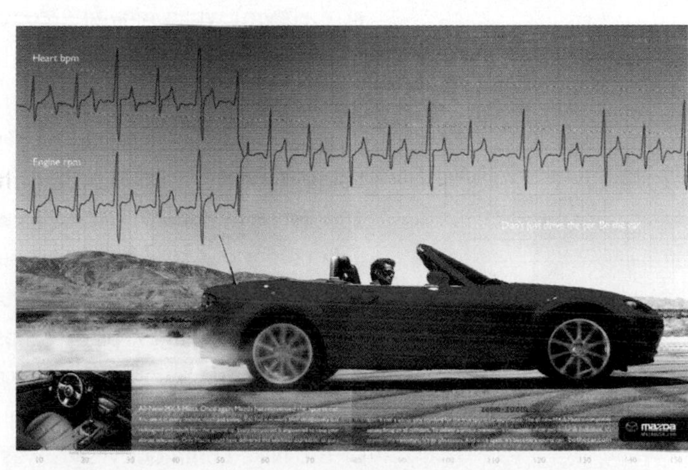

IN THE REAL WORLD
LADIES AREN'T SUPPOSED TO
LOOK LIKE HELL
AND WEAR SKIMPY CLOTHES
AND BLOT THEIR MAKEUP WITH THEIR SHIRT.
BUT HERE THINGS ARE DIFFERENT.
MY MASCARA IS RUNNING
MY KNUCKLES ARE COVERED WITH EYE SHADOW
AND NO ONE JUDGES ME.
OR THINKS MY PELVIC THRUSTS
ARE SOME KIND OF MATING CALL.
AND NO ONE TELLS ME WHAT TO DO
ALTHOUGH THE MIRROR POINTS OUT THAT
MY BRA STRAPS ARE SHOWING.
JUST DO IT.
NIKEWOMEN.COM

FIG. 7.14
Nike ad, 2007

their production but also fills them with new, appealing meanings, such as empowerment, beauty, and sexiness. This fetishization often affirms deeply personal kinds of relationships to commodities. This Miata ad (fig. 7.13) asks the consumer to imagine him- or herself as one with the car ("be the car") by using the graphic chart of heartbeat and rpm merging together, accompanied by the requisite image of the man in the sports car in action, driving through the desert. Such an ad promises masculine affirmation through the fantasy of the car that will extend one's body and commodity self through speed and the fantasy of mastery and control. This mystification of the meaning of the car erases the production context in which the car was made.

It is easiest to see commodity fetishism at work by looking at instances in which it fails. For instance, Nike shoes for women have been promoted as signifiers of female self-empowerment, healthy women's bodies (as opposed to the dangerously thin ones in many fashion ads), feminism, and hip social politics. As this ad shows, Nike is adept at selling empowerment (here, permission to "look like hell" at the gym) while retaining codes of the gaze and appearance management (none of these women even remotely "look like hell"). The text here sells empowerment, independence, and action.

However, in 1992, there was public outcry over the fact that Nike had outsourced the production of their shoes to factories in Indonesia, South Korea, China, and Vietnam, where women were underpaid and working under terrible conditions. The companies to which they outsourced production were not in compliance with Nike's own stated Code of Conduct, which, for example, condemned child labor and mandated fair wages, placed caps on shifts, and mandated implementation of programs benefiting workers' health and safety. When these conditions became known, the process of commodity fetishism was momentarily ruptured. The empowerment of the Nike commodity sign was undermined by revelations about the actual labor

FIG. 7.15
Doonesbury strip on Nike, by Garry Trudeau, 1997

conditions that produced Nike shoes and that were disempowering to the women making them. The shoes could no longer be stripped of the meaning of their conditions of production and "filled" with the signifiers of feminism and women's healthy living. The company had to respond to criticism and to change its practices in an attempt to redeem its image as a company that supports women's health and human rights. Nevertheless, the publicity around Nike and labor is seen by marketers as dramatically affecting its brand status.

In the context of today's blog culture, corporations have been forced to pay much greater attention to consumer critiques and complaints when such comments can create dramatic and immediate negative publicity if they take off on the Web. Brand managers regularly scan the Web for negative comments on a brand, and often respond directly to them. Many corporations have also created extensive policies around the relationship between corporate image and labor practices, sustainability, and civic responsibility. For instance, as the labor practices behind numerous brands and products were exposed, many corporations responded by directly discussing labor. Coca-Cola is one of the many global companies that responded to the potential of negative media attention by devoting a significant portion of its website to information about its labor practices and programs devoted to worker health and education. Maps with dots signifying not only the location of plants but also the worker advocacy and support programs in place at these plants make Coca-Cola appear to play the role of a humanitarian organization in some regions. Transparency coupled with promotion of a brand characterized in part by humanitarian principles has become a prudent marketing strategy among large corporations operating plants in developing nations.

FIG. 7.16
Chocolates as Valentine

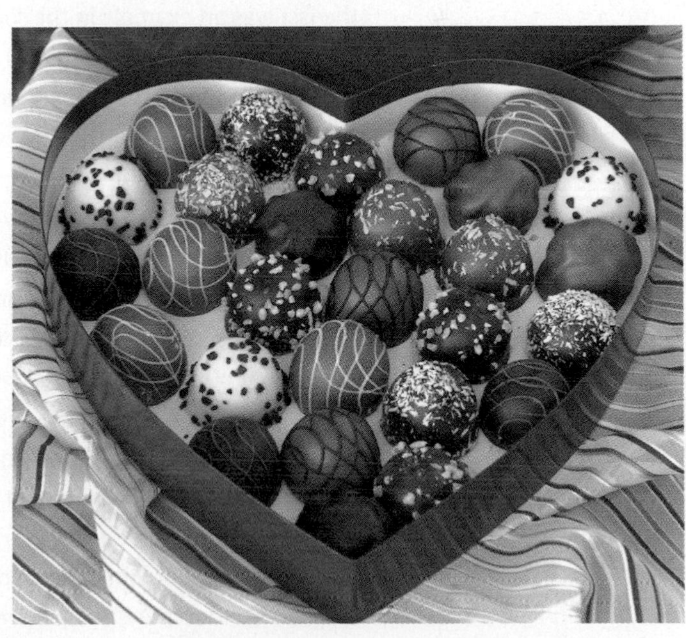

We can see many of the issues surrounding commodity fetishism and the erasure of labor in relation to chocolate. As a commodity, chocolate is associated with desire—both people's desire for and pleasure in consuming chocolate and in chocolate's popularity as a favored gift for Valentine's Day or romantic encounters, connoting taste, pleasure, and romance. However, in 2001, a series of reports by Knight Ridder that revealed the existence of inhumane working conditions for children, including slavery, on cocoa farms in West Africa effectively disrupted the commodity fetishism that surrounds chocolate products. Some sectors of the industry, hoping to avoid a global boycott of their products and more strict government oversight of industry trade, joined ongoing efforts with nonprofits and government agencies to assess the scope of the abuses and to work toward certifying that slavery would be eradicated, as well as to establish on-site monitoring of cocoa farms. A survey funded by the U.S. Labor Department and the chocolate industry placed the number of child laborers (paid workers, as well as those working under conditions of slavery) at 284,000. In some of these cases children as young as age eleven were enticed by the promise of pay to leave their homes for jobs that required twelve-hour workdays with little food, little or no pay, inhumane living conditions, and beatings. These revelations prompted calls to eradicate child slavery in the chocolate industry by 2005 (a goal that was not met). Media publicity about the labor that produces chocolate has escalated to try to chip away at the unreflective commodity fetishism of chocolate (and its association with romance) and to bring attention to the workers who harvest it.

A significant fact about this trend is that it was neither a subculture nor a movement on the margins of the mainstream that brought the issues to mass attention. The chocolate alliance includes mainstream nonprofit organizations such as Catholic Relief Services (through their Fair Trade Web venue), government organizations (U.S. AID and the U.S. Labor Department), and many of the major chocolate companies and professional organizations themselves. Some public schools have used the issue as an example in the social studies curriculum. The situation has, however, most broadly been presented as one that was caused by inhumane practices "over there" (in Africa), supposedly unbeknownst to the companies that benefited from the labor, and that must be "fixed" by more stringent oversight by "our" industry managers and nonprofit human rights observers. This idea of managerial oversight is based on a model of external oversight that looks much like the panopticon model of the gaze described by Foucault, in which guards watch over inmates of a prison (discussed in chapter 3). The prisoners know they are under watch, though they cannot actually see the guards. In effect, the prisoners internalize the gaze of the guards and obey the rules, making it immaterial whether the guards are really at their posts or not. The idea, in the case of the response to cocoa farms, is that the cocoa farm operators need paternalistic oversight to make them change their practices rather than considering the fact that farmers might be facing a much more high-stakes market in which they cannot easily compete. The alliance is, by and large, not addressing the broader economic conditions of global capitalism that are driving crop prices in a more competitive market. At the same time, advocates are making inroads with consumers through niche advertising and production, making *fair* trade a component of new humanitarian discourse about consumer choice in globalization alongside the more familiar neoliberal buzzword *free* trade. The problem remains that fairly traded goods cost more than conventional goods, making these niche products available only to those with enough income to choose to pay more for their chocolate products. We might ask, Why is "fair trade" a niche mark that we must choose to identify with through the purchase of select, specially marked, and more expensive products and brands, and not simply an unmarked requirement of all industry products?

We might also ask, Why does the obsession with products such as chocolate continue in light of the facts of its production? People love chocolate. Indeed, many characterize themselves jokingly as "chocolate addicts." Yet commodity fetishism is quite powerful as a process of masking the labor that produces goods or of making people feel powerless in the face of even the most stunning information about inhumane labor practices. Because these practices exist far from consumers, the reality may seem abstract and easy to be skeptical about. Yet it is also the case today that consumers are increasingly interested in being informed about where goods are produced in the global economy and under what conditions. Consumer activists have become increasingly skilled in informing consumers about the conditions under which certain consumer products are made and encouraging informed and responsible consumerism. As we see in the case of Coca-Cola, making the conditions of labor an explicit marketing strategy through philanthropic-like corporate worker programs makes good advertising sense.

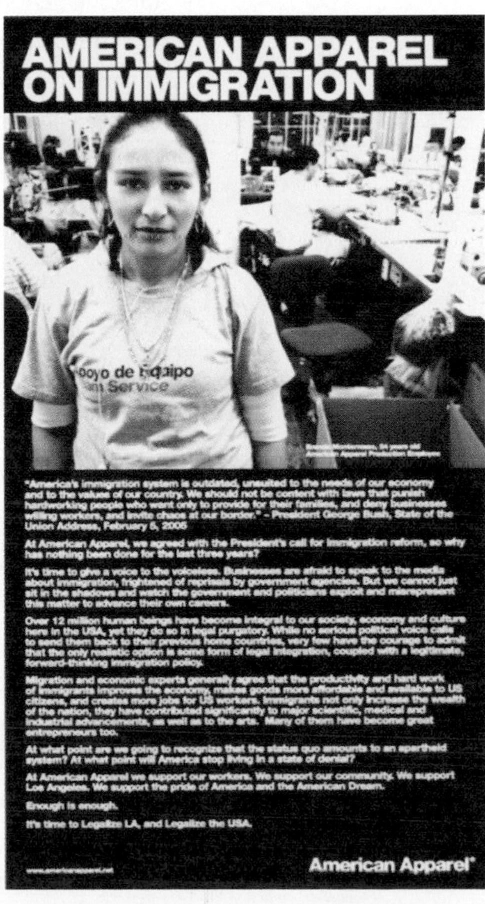

FIG. 7.17
American Apparel ad, 2007

American Apparel is an example of a clothing company that has refused the outsourcing model, keeping its production local and making its devotion to worker conditions and rights a blatant aspect of the company's brand image in marketing campaigns that have been both embraced for their advocacy of workers and condemned for their allusions to sex and porn. This company has described itself as pioneering standards of social responsibility through the labor practices instituted at its initial Los Angeles factory. The manufacturing of its clothing line is organized around a "sweatshop free" factory environment, inviting the public to pay attention to their practices and even offering the company as a model of successful marketing without outsourcing and exploitation. The labor practices of the clothing line, which has expanded from its original Los Angeles factory to Canada, Japan, and New York, are a key part of their products' brand-name identity. The system is based on a model the company called "vertically integrated manufacture," in which workers in a given factory, such as the original one in downtown Los Angeles, get company-subsidized affordable health insurance for their families, as well as a living wage (according to the company website, sewers got twice the federal minimum wage in 2008; the minimum was $5.85, and American Apparel sewers in the Los Angeles factory made $12 an hour). American Apparel sells its brand by selling the image of its worker policies, often putting its workers in its ads, and talking about their ethnic identities—situating them, in effect, within global capitalism and advocating for immigrant rights. This ad (fig. 7.17) specifically foregrounds the Mexican identity of the American Apparel workers in order to attach to the brand not only ethnic identity but also a politics of advocacy for immigrant workers. Yet the company is also notorious for using explicitly sexualized imagery to sell clothes, with many ads displaying their subjects in suggestive poses and states of undress, and the company has been the focus of sexual harassment suits. The selling of sexuality is not new, of course. But in the case of American Apparel, it is explicitly linked to social awareness.

There have been numerous public scandals over the use of sexual images in ad campaigns. For example, an Abercrombie and Fitch holiday catalogue prompted a call for boycott of the company's goods in Illinois and led to complaints that the catalogue was unfit for minors. In 2005, Abercrombie and Fitch paid $45 million in settlements to members of a class action suit (*Gonzalez v. Hollister*). More than ten thousand individuals who filed claims (because they were rejected for jobs or otherwise affected by discrimination in the workplace) charged that the company engaged in workplace discrimination by hiring largely white staff. The company changed some of its practices following this settlement, including curtailment of its practice of recruiting from white sororities and fraternities. Abercrombie and Fitch's advertising practices of the late 1990s through the mid-2000s were widely criticized not only for the excessive portrayal of whiteness but also for the company's stereotypical and racist portrayals of Asians in items such as T-shirts bearing the slogan "Wong Brothers T-Shirt Service, Two Wongs Make It White." Following boycotts and protests on college campuses, the T-shirt line was discontinued. Dwight A. McBride, author of *Why I Hate Abercrombie and Fitch*, discusses the implicit marketing of the gay male image as white through the A & F clothing line and its advertising and photographic campaigns prior to the settlement of the lawsuit, linking this nearly all-white image of laid-back male luxury culture to a history of homosocial woodsy sport culture that was a major part of the brand appeal in the early years of the company (it was founded in 1892).[13] Examples such as these make it clear that there is a complex dynamic between commodity fetishism, global outsourcing, and the marketing of cool, which we discuss further.

All of these examples demonstrate both the values and the limitations of Marxist theory for understanding advertising strategies and marketing practices. Throughout the twentieth century, cultural theory has largely been focused on critiques of consumerism. The Frankfurt School theorists, whom we discussed in chapter 6, saw the escalating role of commodities as a kind of death knell for meaningful social interaction. For these theorists, commodities were "hollowed out" objects that propagated a loss of identity and eroded our sense of history. For them, for instance, to think that a specific consumer item might make one's life meaningful was to engage in a corruption of the truly valuable aspects of existence. In this book, we aim to see the contemporary consumer within a framework that allows us to see the practices of consumers as more complicated than this. Not all consumption practices leave us disempowered.

FIG. 7.18
Stuart Davis, *Lucky Strike*, 1921, Art © Stuart Davis/licensed by VAGA, N.Y.

In contrast, critics who engage with the imagery of consumerism and popular culture have often treated consumption as symbolic of popular culture. Throughout the history of advertising, artists have worked as illustrators within the industry and advertising styles have sometimes paralleled painting and design styles. Conversely, artists have also mined the iconography of brands and logos to make comments on consumer culture, sometimes with a kind of affectionate reference to familiar brands. In this 1921 painting, *Lucky Strike*, American artist Stuart Davis used a cubist style to invoke Lucky Strike cigarettes and their meaning as an American brand. Davis deconstructs the then-familiar colors and shapes of Lucky Strike package and rearranges them in the cubist style that flattens shapes and creates tensions between colors and forms, equating the brand, and the practice of advertising itself, with the new, modern, cutting-edge aesthetic of cubism.

Davis's work prefigures the pop art movement of the 1960s, when a critique of the American obsession with consumption paralleled the rise in production and consumption of consumer goods. During the 1960s, the Frankfurt School writings and ideas of the 1930s were revived in a political and social context in which commercialism was condemned as one of the symptoms of capitalist society gone wrong. During this time, the newly emergent counterculture eschewed notions of material success and commodity culture. Yet, in the art world, pop art engaged with mass culture in a way that did not condemn it. Pop was an attack on distinctions between high and low culture. Pop artists took images from what was considered to be low culture, such as television, the mass media, and comic books, and declared these images to be as socially significant as high art. Pop also engaged playfully with advertisements and commercialism, appropriating design elements and techniques that

FIG. 7.19
Andy Warhol, *Two Hundred Campbell's Soup Cans*, 1962

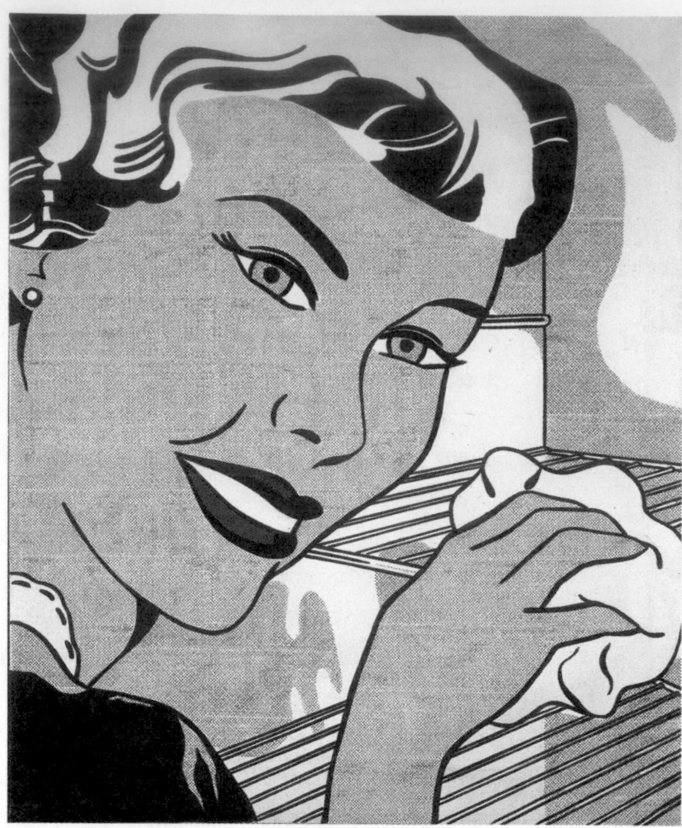

FIG. 7.20
Roy Lichtenstein, *The Refrigerator*, 1962

were a part of commodity culture and incorporating them into works of fine art to be shown in galleries and museums.

By incorporating television images, advertisements, and commercial products into their work, the artists who produced pop art were responding in a very different manner from the Frankfurt School to the pervasiveness of commodity culture. Rather than condemning mass culture they mined its imagery and techniques, demonstrating their love of and pleasure in popular culture even as they critiqued it. For instance, Andy Warhol painted and printed images of Campbell's soup cans to question the boundaries between art and product design and to celebrate the aesthetic repetition of mass culture. Warhol's painting has a flattening effect that comments simultaneously on the banality of popular culture and mass production and on the familiarity of the Campbell logo. The multiplicity of the soup cans refers to the inundation and overproduction of goods in a commodity culture, in which repetition prevails. Yet at the same time the painting is an affectionate homage to package and ad design, and to a consumer culture that values the familiarity and convenience that reproduction offers.

Other artists turned to "low culture" forms such as comic strips and advertisements. In search of a means to paint an "ugly" picture, Roy Lichtenstein made paintings and prints that drew on the form of the comic strip, referencing not only on the flat surface of the comic form but also the stories that comics tell. Lichtenstein's highly formal works are smooth and pristine, in contrast to the painterly brushstroke style of abstract expressionist painting. Their subject matter is the world of popular culture and consumerism. In their appropriation of the dotted surface of screen-printed comics, these works are a tribute to this commercial form and to consumer goods. *The Refrigerator*, a painting of 1962, is like a large, oversized comic frame. Lichtenstein blew up the grain of the image so that the viewer can see its dot texture. In this close-up of a woman cleaning a refrigerator, he makes reference to commercial images of housewives typical of 1960s ads, in which they appear smiling while performing boring housework. Here the comic-book form reference is meant both affectionately and as a means of making a social critique of consumer culture and its false promises and stereotypes.

Brands and Their Meanings

The role of the brand has been central to commodity culture. Brands are product names that have meaning attached to them through naming, packaging, advertising, and marketing. Branding originated in the late nineteenth century. Certain kinds of products, such as soap and oats, had previously been sold in bulk out of bins and purchased by consumers by weight. These products were given labeled packaging when companies began to see the advantage of naming products and marking their packaging with meanings that distinguished the qualities of a company and its products from other similar products offered by competitors. Along with packaging and advertising, companies began to promote themselves under brand names. Brands encompass all of the symbolic elements of a company's goods and services. The process of branding may include the look of the packaging, the typeface of package and ad print, and product, packaging and ad design concept and language, as well as the content and form of the product itself. Sometimes, it is a company that becomes a brand and not just the specific product, though certain products may come to embody the meaning and the message of the company brand. The practice of trademarking brands and the design, look, and language linked to particular brands and products as the intellectual property of companies began during this period as a means of protecting companies from infringements on their market by companies making knock-offs meant to be mistaken for the original. Thus bulk oats became Quaker Oats, with the Quaker Oats man signifying moral purity, health, and tradition as qualities of the company contained in their product. Bars of glycerine soap marketed by the Pears Company of England were labeled to clearly designate the product as a specific brand, distinguishing this soap from the similar products marketed alongside it. The company entreated consumers to use soap every day with the new ad slogan, "Have You Used Pears Soap Today?" One of Pears Soap's most famous ads used the painting *Bubbles*

FIG. 7.21
1888 Pears Soap ad using the 1886 painting *Bubbles* by John Everett Millais

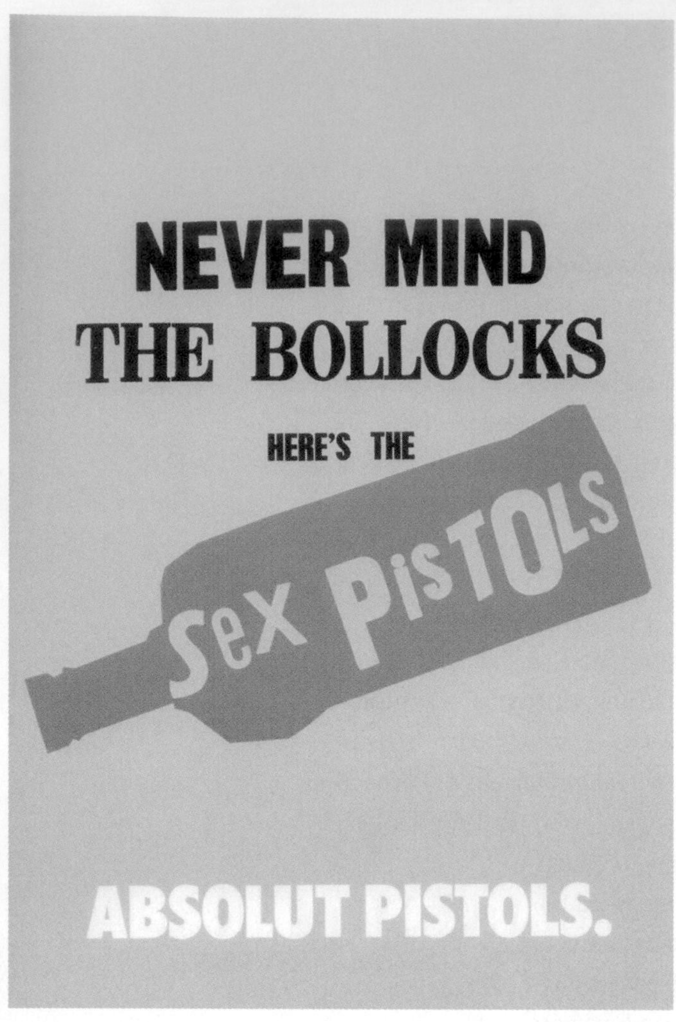
NEVER MIND
THE BOLLOCKS
HERE'S THE
Sex PisTOLS
ABSOLUT PISTOLS.

FIG. 7.22
Absolut ad remake of Sex Pistols album cover, 2001

(1886) by well-known British painter John Everett Millais to sell the image of childhood innocence as a sentiment or quality that could be acquired with the use of this soap, which was promoted as being pure and simple. This move toward branding signaled the interrelationship of art and advertising that would follow. Manufacturers and ad agencies today employ artists of all sorts (musicians, photographers, illustrators) to make ads and even present these ads as as works of fine art. In the use of the Millais painting, the Pears Soap company gained a kind of cultural authority, though Millais was criticized by the contemporary art world for allowing the painting to be used to sell soap.[14]

Although the origins of branding in the rise of consumer society can show us how products were turned into brands, the extent of branding culture and the complexity of consumers' relationships to brands today have changed dramatically since that time. As Marcel Danesi writes, "Brands are one of the most important modes of communication in the modern media environment."[15] A brand is a product name that we know about, whether or not we own or ever intend to purchase the product. The refinement of brand meanings can often take place over long periods of time and many advertising campaigns and is influenced by cultural factors beyond the reach of the company and its marketers. Branding is a complex process of naming, marketing, and cultural circulation.

Logos and visual style are crucial to the overall meanings of brands, and often brand meaning is established through the repetition of visual motifs. For instance, Absolut has advertised its vodka for years through a campaign that uses the shape of its bottle as an ongoing motif, often in playful ways. Absolut established its brand through this visual motif and the cleverness with which its ads have riffed on the clear bottle's shape, helping its brand to become instantly recognizable. Even people who have never purchased or tasted Absolut vodka know its brand name. In addition, Absolut has turned its ad campaign into art, not only commissioning ads from famous artists (Andy Warhol, Keith Haring, and Ed Ruscha, among others) but also publishing several coffee-table books specifically about the advertising campaign. The Absolut campaign thus awarded its vodka the value of cultural knowledge, interpellating viewer-consumers who recognize the work of certain artists or who get the joke. Among its many series, Absolut did a number of ads that made reference to famous record album covers, including the cover of the well-known 1980s punk band the Sex Pistols' album *Never Mind the Bollocks, Here's the Sex Pistols.* This campaign demonstrates the kind of incorporation and appropriation of alternative cultures and cultural resistance that such corporate advertising can accomplish. The Sex Pistols, famous for their anti-establishment stance, are now in an ad selling vodka to a younger generation and, perhaps, to a nostalgic baby boomer generation that wants to remember its former days of cultural resistance. Through this long-term campaign with its repeating visual motif, Absolut has established its brand as arty, original, and culturally informed.

The use of a visual motif can also be seen in the well-known iPod advertising campaign which sets silhouetted dancing figures against brightly colored backgrounds. This campaign, which appeared in the mid-2000s, uses the silhouette form to suggest that anyone could be the iPod listening figures, whose profiles subtly suggest just enough attributes to identify them as certain hip types. We can discern the cut of jeans and the style of hair and shoes—enough to suggest particular cultures and subcultures of coolness, youth, and sometime even racial or ethnic identity. The iPod brand gains specific meaning through these silhouettes of joyful dancing, with the delicate white lines suggesting the iPod headphones leading to the dancer's ears. Thus the iPod ad motif became quickly well known because of these key repeating visual elements—silhouette, bright color backgrounds, and white headphone wires.

It is key to the success of products such as the iPod that consumers create deep, sometimes emotional, connections to their brands. The equation of brand, image, and self thus takes hold. This means that identity is no longer the signifier of a product; rather, identity is the pure product that we consume, either as information or as image. This is demonstrated in the way that featured merchandise from films and television shows for children has become more than a secondary set of markets. The commodity sign of these toys now precedes and almost overtakes the "original" source of the movie in revenues and popularity. Thus in the mid-2000s little children might awaken between Frog Princess sheets wearing Bee Movie pajamas and rise to eat breakfast off Horton Hears a Who plates while watching the Rugrats in Pooh

FIG. 7.23
iPod billboard, 2008

chairs. Corporate conglomerate "authors," such as Disney/Capital Cities/ABC and Nickelodeon, have launched a rich intertextual world populated by myriad logos and trademarked characters. Branding has become not just a way of selling goods but an inescapable mode of everyday communication in the new commodity culture of the twenty-first century.

One of the key stakes in brands is that they are seen as unique and irreplaceable with other brands or products. One manifestation of this function gone awry (from the standpoint of corporations) is the generic use of trademarks. If you were to say that you might "Xerox" pages from this book, you would be using language that takes the brand name for the generic activity of photocopying. Lawyers refer to the way that trademarks become part of public culture as *genericide*. The owner of the mark loses rights to the name if it takes on a meaning for the generic type in the market, rather than for the particular branded product. Manufacturers of Coke and Kleenex are eager to get us to identify their products with quality—and to get us to think of their product each time we desire a facial tissue or a cola. They are not, however, eager to have us kill off their product's difference by using its name for the generic type each time we reach for the competitor's product. To remain profitable, even those brands that go global and seek ubiquity need to retain their distinguishing features and their identity. When the mark of a product gains true universality, its company must invest large sums in ad campaigns to dissuade the public from taking the brand for the type. The brand, into which companies have invested fortunes, must not lose its ability to function as a profit-generating commodity. Companies promoting products such as Kleenex and Xerox may at first spend millions to ensure that their product comes to mind when a consumer has a need for that category of product. But when this mission is successful, some companies such as Xerox have found themselves spending large sums on ad campaigns aimed to stop the use of their product name as a verb. Despite the fact that Xerox has already entered the Oxford English Dictionary as a verb, Xerox corporation has commissioned ads explaining that we photocopy documents, we do not *xerox* them. Ownership of a very valuable label is at stake in this campaign.

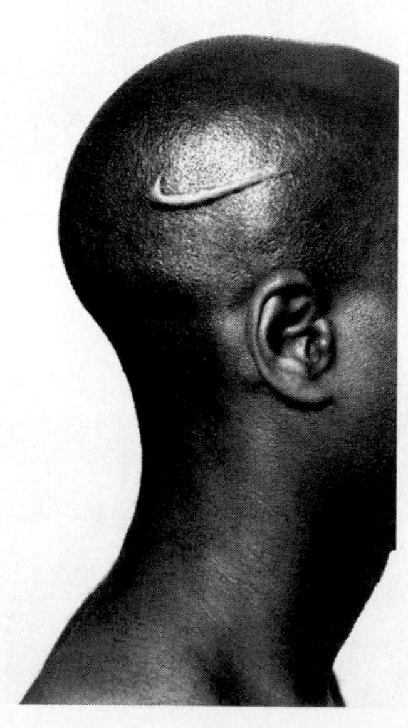

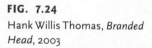

FIG. 7.24
Hank Willis Thomas, *Branded Head*, 2003

Artist Hank Willis Thomas comments on the depths of brand culture in his series *Branded*. He makes connections between the original meaning of branding, which was to mark the flesh of a person or animal, the history of slavery, and the relationship of branding to black culture. In this image, the branding of the Nike logo onto the shaved head of a black man refers not only to the intensity of consumer devotion to brands but also to the violence of such commodification. Willis Thomas refers to the particular

FIG. 7.25
Hank Willis Thomas, *Priceless*, 2004

role that young urban black consumers have played in the marketing of high-end athletic wear and products that want to convey "street cred." In some cases, young black men are cast in advertisements for products marketed to middle-class, white suburban consumers. Thomas also depicts the distance between the world of black urban youth and the language of privilege that dominates consumerism in this image, *Priceless*, which refers to the well-known MasterCard campaign. The original MasterCard campaign sells the idea that products and services (airplane tickets, jewelry, gifts) are quantifiable (and quantifiable on one's MasterCard bill) but that the emotional experiences that they bring are beyond monetary value, hence "priceless." In this work, Thomas shows the tragically quantifiable aspects of the funeral of a young black man. It is precisely Thomas's reference to the original ad campaign that allows this image to make a biting commentary on the relationship of racial identity and disenfranchised lives to commercial commodity culture and to violence associated with street crime linked to gang drug commodity culture.

The Marketing of Coolness

In many modern industrial societies, advertising as a profession underwent a dramatic change in the 1960s, as advertisers and marketers began to see themselves as creative professionals rather than as craftsmen who worked according to scientific rules about how persuasion operates. This occurrence is commonly referred to as a "creative revolution" in advertising. In response to the general social upheaval of the times, with an emerging emphasis on youth culture, and to the fact that consumers were increasingly mobile and (by the 1980s) in possession of television remote control devices, advertisers began to place more emphasis on being entertaining and intriguing. They used humor, parody, and new innovative styles as the rigid hard-sell and rule-bound conventions of selling were rejected and the idea that creativity would sell products began to dominate. Importantly, this change was part of a larger cultural dynamic through which marketers and advertisers began to see youth culture and alternative cultures as sites that could be appropriated to mark commodities as hip and cool. The marketing of coolness, which began in the 1960s, thus defines a much larger social shift in which advertisers and marketers attempted to attach the ever-elusive quality of coolness to an array of consumer products. The attribute of "cool" is usually seen as unique, distinct, and uninfluenced by the marketplace. A young person who is cool, for instance, would commonly be seen as having an innovative style and not caring what others think, someone that others aspire to be like. As cultural critic Thomas Frank has argued, in the 1960s advertising began to appropriate the language of the counterculture and to aim to make certain brands seem hip and cool. Although the counterculture at that time actually saw itself as rejecting the values of consumerism and going back to nature, Frank argues that not only was the counterculture not as anticonsumerist as it presented itself to be but also those ideals were easily appropriated to sell products. He writes:

> The counterculture seemed to have it all: the unconnectedness that would allow consumers to indulge transitory whims; the irreverence that would allow them to defy moral puritanism, and the contempt for established social rules that would free them from the slow-moving, buttoned-down conformity of their abstemious ancestors. In the counterculture, admen believed that they had found both a perfect model for consumer subjectivity, intelligent and at work with the conformist past, and a cultural machine for turning disgust with consumerism into the very fuel by which consumerism might be accelerated.[16]

This trend has only increased since that time, with many brands being sold through associations with youth culture and with marketers striving to attach coolness to brand names. This embrace of youth culture is really about selling the idea of youth as a "posture" rather than selling youthfulness, with youth signifying innovation and hipness. "Cool" brands, such as iPod and Nike, succeed in retaining coolness through complex strategies of marketing and reinvention. The appropriation of cool markers by marketers requires a constant re-evaluation of what is in style, and a constant turnover of styles and goods. What was cutting-edge cool one month becomes uncool the next when a particular look or item goes mainstream. In the 2000s, the cycle of appropriation and innovation has sped up to the degree that cultures seeing themselves as alternative must constantly reinvent themselves to remain a step ahead of the curve. In some contexts, the marketing of coolness has simply been about using signifiers of coolness, such as hip-hop or alternative music groups, on the soundtrack of advertisements. There are many paradoxes in this shift: the selling of products through values that appear to reject consumer culture; the attachment of youth culture to a range of brands that are marketed to a range of consumers, not just young consumers; the selling of brands through ads that pretend not to be ads; the social embrace of consumerism as a means to project the idea that we are all above consumerist values; and the selling of coolness, an attribute that is supposed to be genuine and difficult to reproduce.

The marketing of coolness is a symptom of a larger cultural phenomenon of the speeding up of trends and a blurring between mainstream and marginal cultures. Mainstream producers, such as fashion designers and athletic shoe manufacturers, pay marketing consultants (known as "cool hunters") to go out into the streets and find out what trendsetting cool kids are wearing and doing.[17] They then use those ideas to make products for mainstream consumers. Once those products become mainstream, they are no longer cool, and the trendsetters who want to remain at the margins of or in defiance of mainstream culture have to come up with new innovations. This process is only speeded up by technologies such as cell phones, social networking websites, text messaging, and other forms of rapid communication technologies. Marketers interested in charting trends in youth culture have turned more recently to borrowing the modes of social networking behavior to gather data, paying youth consumers to do video diaries or to take a camera out and interview their friends and consumer activities. Such strategies take into account that traditional market research, which relies on surveys and focus groups, is limited in what it can decipher about consumers' desires and essentially ineffectual with savvy young consumers.

Thus cultural trends emerge and fade at rapid speed, and consumer culture, which is racing to catch up to those trends, is also rapidly in flux. Ironically, this speeding up of trends and cultural innovation as mainstream manufacturers appropriate the styles of subcultures on the margins has the same effect as the long history of planned obsolescence in manufacturing, in which products are made not to last too long or consumers are sold the idea (as automobile owners have been since the 1960s) that they have to trade in their models after two years in order to stay current. The makers of computers and electronic technologies, such as the iPod and the iPhone, have capitalized on this trend in selling the idea that these devices become dated within short periods of time, requiring consumers to invest in the latest and newest version. On the day that the new iPhone was released in 2008, consumers lined up the night before outside many Apple stores, with lines extending for blocks by morning, in order to be among the first to own this device. Being among the first to use such a device carries a lot of prestige.

These trends in consumerism also necessitate new forms of address to contemporary consumers. Ads cannot interpellate consumers in traditional ways if consumers are too distracted, knowing, and savvy about ad styles and tactics. Thus some contemporary advertisements speak to consumers in voices that depart from the overbearing narrations of ads in the past that explicitly told consumers what to do. Some ads presume a significant amount of knowledge on the part of consumers about cultural trends and codes. Much of the marketing of coolness can be seen in relation to postmodern styles of advertising and popular culture, with their emphasis on parody and pastiche and their interpellation of a knowing consumer. These advertisements deploy a postmodern style to talk to consumers about their status as ads. This Ketel One ad is from a larger campaign in which each ad consists of a headline and a blank page that says nothing about the product itself. Here the line, "Can you find the subliminal message in this advertisement?" assumes, of course, that the viewer-consumer is familiar with the idea of subliminal advertising, or the

Dear Ketel One Drinker
Can you find the subliminal message in this advertisement?

FIG. 7.26
Ketel One ad, 2006

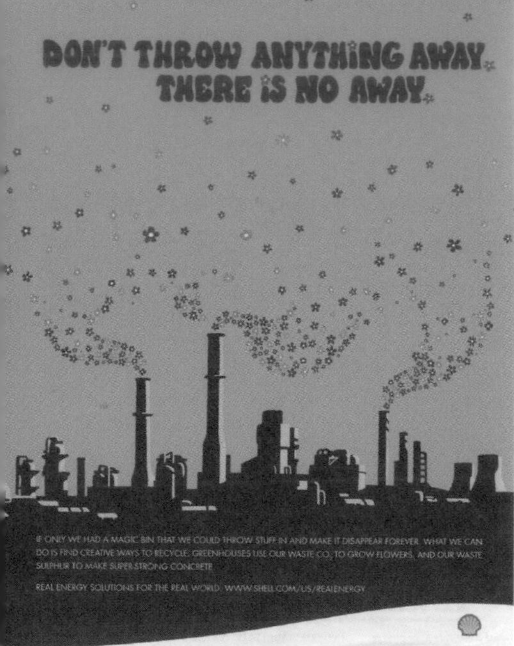

DON'T THROW ANYTHING AWAY.
THERE IS NO AWAY.
IF ONLY WE HAD A MAGIC BIN THAT WE COULD THROW STUFF IN AND MAKE IT DISAPPEAR FOREVER. WHAT WE CAN DO IS FIND CREATIVE WAYS TO RECYCLE. GREENHOUSES USE OUR WASTE CO₂ TO GROW FLOWERS. AND OUR WASTE SULPHUR TO MAKE SUPER-STRONG CONCRETE.
REAL ENERGY SOLUTIONS FOR THE REAL WORLD. WWW.SHELL.COM/US/REALENERGY

FIG. 7.27
Shell ad, 2007

idea that ads can contain hidden messages within that will appeal to consumer's subconscious. The joke of the ad is multileveled. First, the ad is making a joke about the fact that the "subliminal message" of the ad is in its blank page, thus making fun of the entire concept of subliminal advertising. In so doing, it is interpellating a knowing consumer, who rejects the model of an easily duped consumer. Second, the ad is also pointing to the fact that it is both an ad and an anti-ad simultaneously. Such ads can address the consumer in an obsequious voice, a voice that says, "we know that you know how ads work and that you are not easily fooled. We are not going to condescend to you. We respect your intelligence. We are going to bring you into the process of meaning-making." This is a form of metacommunication, in which the ad speaks to the viewer about the process of viewing the ad. This technique allows advertisers to address jaded consumers in a new way and to potentially get their attention. Such ads acknowledge the banality of simply displaying the product seductively in an era of image and ad saturation. (We discuss postmodern style at length in chapter 8.)

Selling social awareness is another strategy of cool marketing. There has been a trend over the past twenty-five years toward green marketing, through which advertisements equate products with awareness about the environment and a "green" lifestyle. Although much of this marketing is in relation to products that are designed to be less harmful to the environment, commodity fetishism makes it easy for advertisers to equate products that have no environmental benefits with greenness. Chevron oil company, for instance, ran a campaign, People Do, that for many years equated its logo with environmental projects even though its message was about how individuals (rather than corporations) can make a difference. Such ads allowed Chevron, one of the world's worst environmental offenders, to sell itself as a "green" company. A more recent Shell Oil Company ad appropriates 1960s pop style to imagine the emissions from a Shell refinery as flowers and sells the message of individual recycling to help the environment as a kind of neo-hippie Flower Power movement championed this time by the big corporate polluter.

FIG. 7.28
Kenneth Cole ad, 2002

The trend of fashion designers selling social awareness took hold in the 1990s when Benetton, then a very popular youth-oriented line of clothing, did a series of campaigns that equated the Benetton logo with awareness of social problems throughout the world. Other fashion designers, such as Kenneth Cole, have used their ad slogans to sell both their merchandise and the idea that fashion can relate to social awareness. For instance, in the months after 9/11, when advertisers were attempting to find the proper tone for their ads and to link patriotism to their ads, Kenneth Cole released a campaign that reminded Americans that there were other ongoing crises in the world, with the tag line "On September 12, 14,000 people still contracted HIV." Kenneth Cole ads, often featured on billboards in urban areas such as New York, often play with social messages in clever ways that allow the ad to signal social awareness while appearing not to take it too seriously.

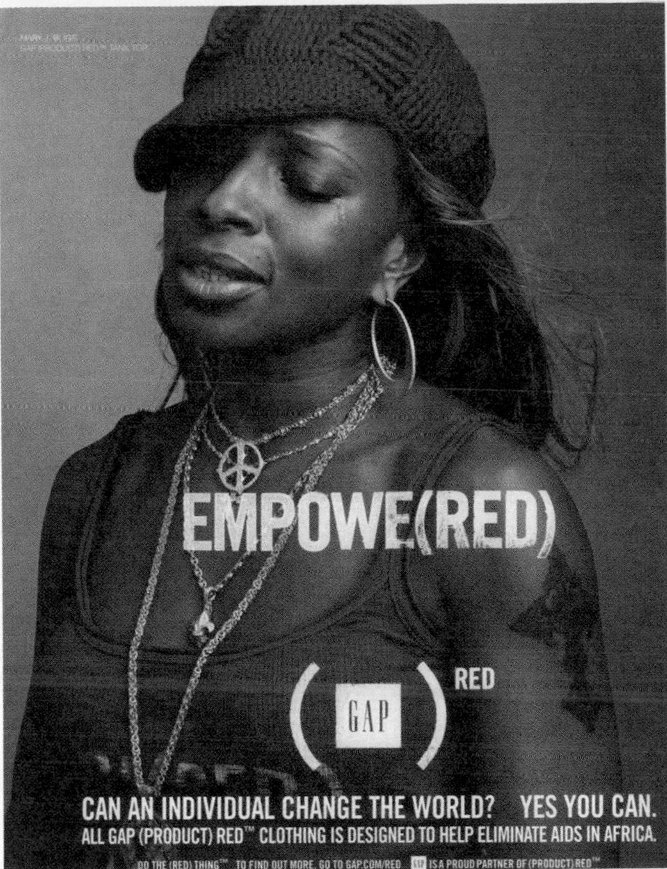

FIG. 7.29
Gap (Product) Red™ ad with Mary J. Blige, 2006

The marketing of social awareness involves creation of signs that equate social awareness with coolness and the attachment of social ideals to particular products. As this trend has increased, philanthropic organizations have created mechanisms to incorporate consumerism into charity contributions, thus selling the idea that certain kinds of purchases can be both philanthropic and pleasurable. (Product) Red, a branded initiative begun by U2 singer Bono to raise funds for the Global Fund to Fight AIDS, tuberculosis, and malaria, works on this premise. Project (Red), which is licensed to companies including American Express, Gap, Apple, and Hallmark, uses celebrities such as singer Mary J. Blige to sell designated goods, with a percentage of sales going to charities. It is important to note that these campaigns, which can effectively raise money for social campaigns, promise not only that the purchase of a product will help social causes but also that the acquiring and wearing of such commodities will advertise one's own social awareness to friends, and will serve as a kind of advertisement about the importance of the social issues linked to the campaign. Some argue, however, that the campaign is not cost-effective, given the significant funds spend by these companies to advertising the brand.

These new trends of social awareness and coolness marketing have emerged along with a broad set of changes in terms of how consumers see ads and the kinds of entertainment media that people are watching. The most fundamental change to the landscape of advertising and marketing has been the role of the Web as a form of entertainment media and a central medium for social networking. As traditional media such as newspaper, magazines, and television and cinema continue to lose audiences (and advertising revenue) and Web media gain a more central role in people's lives, the advertising industry has had to retool its strategies for getting viewer-consumer attention. The increased consumer use of DVRs such as TiVo that allow viewers to easily bypass ads, the changes in multiplatform media, and the rise of iPod culture have all changed the terrain through which advertisers can achieve the "eyeballs" they need to warrant their cost. Over the last decade, advertisers have used strategies of guerrilla and viral marketing to try to tap into existing social networks and have their ad messages travel through word of mouth. The concept of "guerrilla" marketing borrows its language from the history of political movements that use unconventional warfare and surprise attack to achieve their goals. Guerrilla marketing is "stealth" marketing, in that it tries to present itself as something other than marketing. Guerrilla marketers pay people to recommend drinks while at a bar or to extol the virtues of their cameras while pretending to be tourists. Viral marketing more specifically deploys the viral, meme networks through which people pass on ideas to their friends, most of them involving e-mail and cell phone communication networks.

As marketers become more sophisticated in tapping into social networks such as Facebook and MySpace, they are creating new models for thinking about their relationship to consumers, models that increasingly use information from consumers to influence product design and marketing, and that are designed to create useful activities for consumers. "Utility," rather than coolness, is thus the new buzzword in marketing in the age of Google with its high usage of the Web for information-seeking. Advertisers are thus tapping into pre-existing online communities to create profiles for their brands, and creating products, such as Nike+, that are designed to create communities rather than to just sell material goods. Nike+ is a device that records data about a runner's physique and their route while running, which they can then upload to a website and share with other runners, creating a new communities of runners. The product sold by such branding is actually a community rather than a simple device.

The computer technologies that have created these new forms of entertainment media and dramatic changes in consumer attention have also created the potential for much more consumer monitoring in the form of database gathering on consumer behavior. Consumerism and advertising on the Web create direct data about purchases and ad viewership because the Web itself can be easily designed to create data about user traffic. Retailers and marketers use an array of strategies, including discount cards, membership cards, registration requirements, and so forth, to gather information on consumer purchases and increasingly are targeting consumer messages to niche groups of consumers. In addition, digital technologies allow advertisers to insert different ads into television shows according to different markets. Such strategies move away from the big national advertising campaigns toward fashioning messages for increasingly targeted groups of consumers. At the same time, new technologies have also created increasingly important consumer exchange networks that replicate barter systems, such as eBay and Craigslist, that allow people to sell goods to each other directly, eliminating retailers altogether. Although many stores can use these networks, most of the exchange that takes place on them is

FIG. 7.30
Coca-Cola product placement on *American Idol,* with judges Simon Cowell, Paula Abdul, and Randy Jackson, 2005

through small businesses and individuals who negotiate with each other directly.

Ironically, one of the primary strategies used by advertisers to counter the rapidly disappearing audience of consumers recalls the beginnings of radio and television in their early years of corporate sponsorship. Product placement is used increasingly in film and television as a means to integrate advertising messages into the programming itself. In the television genres of reality TV and home and personal improvement shows, such product placement is integral to the shows' very premises—the products constitute the "improvement" of the show. So, for instance, a program such as *Queer Eye for the Straight Guy,* popular in the mid-2000s, integrates product placement by having the five gay male consultants specifically recommend certain brands to the straight guy whose home décor, clothing, and personal maintenance they are aiming to improve. Such a show also sells the idea that people can connect and transcend their differences (including differences in sexual orientation) through the cultures of taste and consumption. Other television programs simply hawk products by putting them noticeably on the screen. Many competition reality shows feature specific and blatant marketing of products as part of the competition contests. Yet, these kinds of product placement can easily incorporate ironic humor. On *American Idol* Coca-Cola's logo is obviously featured on the cups placed before judges, who have jokingly turned the labels to the cameras with deliberate emphasis to suggest their reluctant compliance with product placement mandates, and host Ryan Seacrest has plugged new Apple products such as the iPhone with noticeable irony. In more subtle ways, networks and film companies make elaborate deals to incorporate products into their scripts and put them on display within the narrative. Although such strategies are increasingly commonplace, they risk angering viewers, who may perceive such direct selling as crass commercialism and detrimental to the viewing experience.

FIG. 7.31
Hans Haacke, *The Right to Life*, 1979

Anti-Ads and Culture Jamming

Artists have long used the form of advertisements not only to affirm popular culture and advertising, as the pop artists did, but also to critique it. Artist Hans Haacke, whose work has often focused on the conflicts of interest of the corporate sponsorship of museums, created a whole series of works that use the codes of advertising as forums for political critique. Haacke has consistently produced works that address the workers who are rendered invisible by the process of commodity fetishism and the costs to these workers of their labor. In a 1979 image, Haacke used the famous Breck shampoo campaign of the 1970s that featured the motif of a well-coiffed "Breck girl" to make a political critique of Breck's labor practices. The Breck girl was an icon of 1970s advertising in a campaign that used painted images of models (here, Cybill Shepherd) to create their look. In Haacke's remake, the text refers specifically to the fact that American Cyanamid, Breck's parent company, gave women workers of childbearing age whose jobs posed reproductive health risks the "choice" of losing their jobs, transferring, or being sterilized. Haacke's "ad" is thus not only a play on Breck's campaign, but it is also a political statement about the treatment of workers and the kinds of oppressive practices that corporations are allowed to use against workers. The image marks the absence of the female Breck worker in the original Breck ad and her differences from the idealized Breck girl.

FIG. 7.32
1969 Breck ad of Cybill Shepherd

Haacke's work was ahead of its time. Ad remakes proliferate today. This practice of culture jamming borrows from the legacy of the Situationist group of artists and writers in France in the 1960s, the most famous of whom was Guy Debord, who advocated political interventions at the level of daily life to counter the passivity and alienation of modern life and spectacle. In his manifesto on culture jamming, Kalle Lasn borrows from the Situationist philosophy (discussed in chapter 6) to advocate a kind of jamming of the messages of consumer culture. The term culture jam was coined by the band Negativland in a reference to the citizens' band radio term for jamming someone's broadcast. Lasn writes,

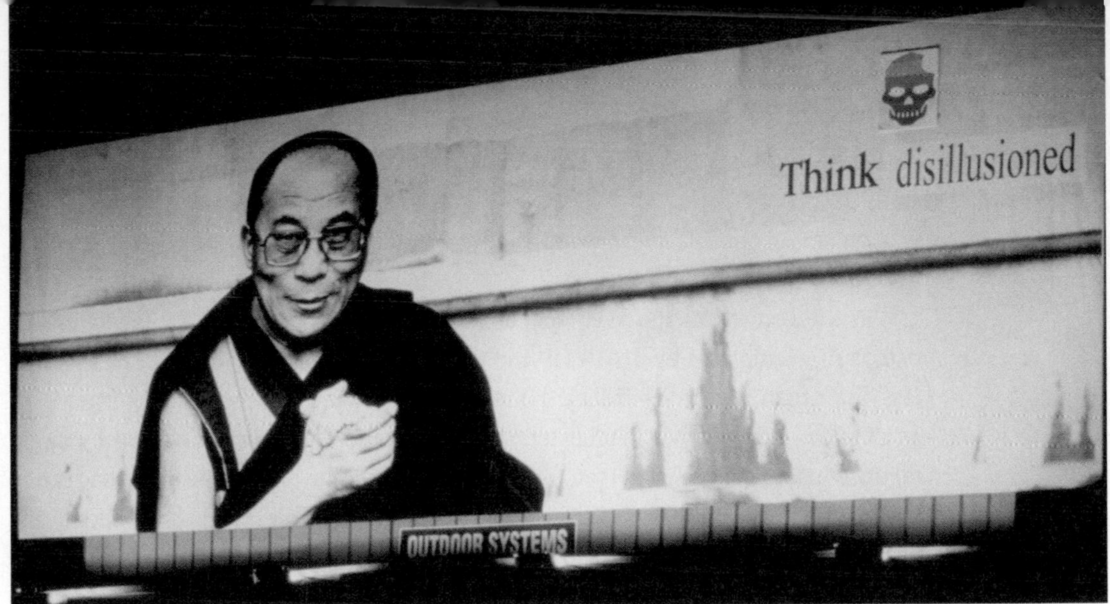

FIG. 7.33
Billboard Liberation Front billboard remake of Apple Think Different ad, 1990s

"culture jamming is, at root, just a metaphor for stopping the flow of spectacle long enough to adjust your set."[18] One of the primary strategies of the Situationists, whose work inspires these culture jammers, was called "détournement," or the rerouting of messages to create new meanings.

Some of the first culture jams began with the use by activists of spray cans to rewrite the messages of billboard advertisements, changing the slogans in the hopes of startling viewers into thinking about those messages differently. For instance, in Australia in the late 1970s and 1980s, a movement took place in which a series of billboards were "rewritten" or vandalized by activists wielding spray paint. Members of the group (and others who were inspired and just used the name) signed their work "BUGA UP," an acronym for Billboard Utilizing Graffitists Against Unhealthy Promotions, referring to Australian slang that means to screw something up or ruin it.[19] For a period of time, they achieved popularity for their work in changing the messages of ads, in particular ads for cigarettes and alcohol. BUGA UP would change brand names from "Southern Comfort" to "Sump Oil," "Marlboro" to "its a bore" and "Eyewitness News. Always First" to "We are witless nits: always are."

Since the late 1970s, a group in San Francisco called the Billboard Liberation Front (BLF) has also been reworking billboards against their intended messages. The group redesigns billboards so that it is not readily obvious that they have been tampered with. The BLF states that the group is not antibillboard (in fact, several of its members work in the advertising industry). They state, "To Advertise is to Exist. To Exist is to Advertise. Our ultimate goal is nothing short of a personal and singular Billboard for each citizen."[20] The group reworked the well-known Apple Computer "Think Different" slogan, from a campaign equating Apple with many unique figures of history (here the Dalai Lama), by rewriting it as "Think Disillusioned." The BLF continues their work, often deploying humor and a trickster stance, at a time when advertisers are increasingly attempting to coopt styles of anticorporate messages. After a 2008 campaign about the role of AT&T in the war on terror, the BLF announced that it was leaving the United States for "safe houses" in Europe.

In the context of the Web and digital imaging technologies, the reworking of billboards exemplified by BUGA UP and the BLF has been replaced by the easier (and less risky than repainting billboards) strategy of reworking advertising images and posting them on the Web. Adbusters, the organization (and magazine) run by Lasn, regularly posts culture jams that "détourne" the message of ads to expose bad labor practices and the negative effects of certain products. This culture jam effectively uses the aesthetic of a Nike ad about empowering women to visualize the underpaid Nike worker and her struggles to survive. Such reworkings of images demonstrate the capacity of artists and consumer-viewers to rework commercial images to create new kinds of messages. Today, reworkings of ads, parodies, and remakes abound on websites such as YouTube, many of them without explicit political messages, at the same time that advertisers themselves are deploying new tactics and creating ambiguous brand meanings through postmodern style that often seem quite similar to culture jam tactics. Thus the distinction between ads and anti-ads is increasingly difficult to make.

FIG. 7.34
Culture jam of Nike ad

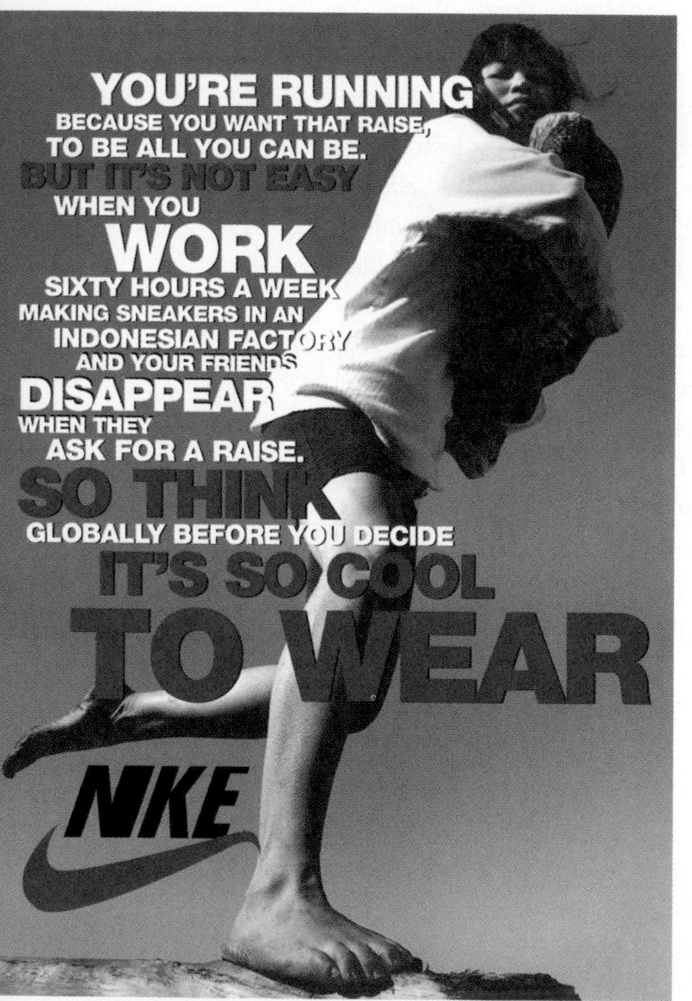

As we noted in chapter 2, brand cultures have been subject to critique for decades. The use of brands in alternative cultures and new forms of retailing, however, has shifted the relationship among brand culture's consumers and producers. There are many levels at which logos and product signifiers are used by both producers and consumers to create meaning on the streets, on our bodies, and in our chance visual and verbal exchanges in the public spaces of modernity. Branding on the Internet has involved new kinds of consumer relationships with brands that involve visual appeal in the absence of the feel and smell of goods that one experiences in stores. Kelly Mooney and Nita Rollins bring the philosophy of the open source movement to branding in *The Open Brand*, proposing that shopping online is no longer enough. Consumers' desire to have relationships with brands like the relationships we, consumers, have with each other as people. For Mooney and Rollins, the *open* in open source means On demand, Participatory, Emotional, and Networked. They suggest that old school branding practices should be extended to the Web, where brands can make emotional connections with consumers more powerfully than ever before. This suggests a kind of interactive fetishism in which consumers can engage in the character of the brand rather than simply being subjected to static, mass-circulated campaigns that tell us what to buy and what our products mean.[21] Figures such as Shepard Fairey, whose screened and stenciled street art in the 1980s inspired the offshoot Obey clothing label (a company dedicated to "manufacturing quality dissent since 1989," discussed on pages 61–62), produces T-shirts and personal fashion items, are emblematic of complex relationships of branding and politics that defy simple definitions of branding culture and alternative, counter-hegemonic culture.

The publication of Naomi Klein's popular diatribe against branding, *No Logo*, came on the heels of the 2000 Ministerial Conference of the World Trade Organization, an event that was subject to vehement protests by activists from around the world on site in Seattle and internationally, making the antiglobalization movement highly visible.[22] Klein's book shows how branding is connected to globalization in multiple ways. Offshore, outsourced industry relies on underpaid labor in sweatshops far from the corporate center. Copyright laws silence critical dissent. Big-name global brands drive out small local businesses unable to compete. Klein's book is an important critique of branding, the rise of multinationals, and the relationship of these to a global economy that is in crisis in the 2000s. The book chronicles the important British legal case in which McDonald's restaurant sued David Morris and Helen Steel, the authors of a pamphlet critiquing the nutrition claims and business practice of the popular global chain. The case, which came to be known as the McLibel suit, was won by Morris and Steel on the grounds of right to freedom of expression and a breach of their right to a fair trial. Klein's book was joined by other critiques of consumerism such as Eric Schlosser's *Fast Food Nation: The Dark Side of an American Meal* and *SUPER SIZE ME*, the 2004 Academy Award-nominated film by Morgan Spurlock who, interested in the wave of obesity in the United States, ate only McDonald's food for thirty days, demonstrating how a fast-food diet puts consumers' health in serious jeopardy. The critique of branding had spawned a movement dedicated to finding

FIG. 7.35
Copyleft symbol

routes that would move beyond the binary of consumerism and the rejection of brands espoused in works such as *No Logo.* Viral licensing is one such approach. In this tactic, the owner of a work marks each copy with a symbol signaling the user's right to make copies. The copyleft symbol is a logo that protects the right of the user to copy with acknowledgement to the author, without the threat of legal action on the basis of intellectual property rights.

Cultures are always in flux and are being constantly reinvented; they are always the site of struggles for meaning. In the culture of late capitalism, when the meanings of coolness and hipness are understood to be central to the exchange of commodities, there is a continuous appropriation of the styles of marginal cultures, which are in turn in a constant state of reinvention. And in the cultural realms of art, politics, and everyday consumer life, mainstream values are constantly questioned and political struggles are waged. As subversions and resistances at the cultural margins are appropriated into the mainstream, new forms of cultural innovation and refusal are found. As new technologies create new environments for social networking and the construction of personal identity, branding cultures have adapted their strategies to create an integral relationship to these online cultures, which in turn have both accommodated and resisted this process. Thus, in late capitalism, the boundary between the mainstream and the margins is always in the process of being renegotiated.

Notes

1. T. J. Jackson Lears, "From Salvation to Self-Realization," in *The Culture of Consumption: Critical Essays of American History 1880–1980*, ed. Richard Wrightman Fox and T. J. Jackson Lears, 3–38 (New York: Pantheon, 1983).
2. Walter Benjamin, *The Arcades Project*, trans. Howard Eiland and Kevin McLaughlin (Cambridge, Mass.: Belknap, 1999).
3. Walter Benjamin, *Charles Baudelaire: A Lyric Poet in the Era of High Capitalism*, 36–37 (London: New Left Books, 1973).
4. Emile Zola, quoted on the Le Bon Marche website: www.lebonmarche.fr (accessed March 2008).
5. Sean Nixon, *Hard Looks: Masculinities, Spectatorship and Contemporary Consumption*, 63–69 (London: UCL Press, 1996).
6. Anne Friedberg, *Window Shopping: Cinema and the Postmodern* (Berkeley: University of California Press, 1993).
7. David Serlin, "Disabling the *Flâneur*," *Journal of Visual Culture* 5.2 (August 2006), 193–208.
8. Catherine Gudis, *Buyways: Billboards, Automobiles, and the American Landscape*, 68 (New York: Routledge, 2004).
9. Lizabeth Cohen, *A Consumers' Republic: The Politics of Mass Consumption in Postwar America*, 7 (New York: Vintage, 2003).
10. Ibid., 401–10.
11. Pierre Bourdieu, *Distinction: A Social Critique of the Judgement of Taste*, 80–83 (Cambridge, Mass.: Harvard University Press, 1984).
12. Stuart Ewen, *All Consuming Images: The Politics of Style in Contemporary Culture* (New York: Basic Books, 1988).
13. Dwight A. McBride, *Why I Hate Abercrombie & Fitch: Essays on Race and Sexuality* (New York: New York University Press, 2005).
14. http://bubbles.org/html/history/bubbhistory.htm (accessed March 2008).
15. Marcel Danesi, *Brands*, 3 (New York: Routledge, 2006).

16. Thomas Frank, *The Conquest of Cool: Business Culture, Counterculture, and the Rise of Hip Consumerism*, 119 (Chicago: University of Chicago Press, 1997).
17. See Malcolm Gladwell, "The Cool Hunt," and Douglas Rushkoff, *Merchants of Cool*, PBS Frontline documentary.
18. Kalle Lasn, *Culture Jam*, 107 (New York: Quill, 1999).
19. See Simon Chapman, "Civil Disobedience and Tobacco Control: The Case of BUGA UP," *Tobacco Control* 5 (1996), 179–85.
20. Jack Napier and John Thomas, "The BLF Manifesto," http://www.billboardliberation.com/manifesto.html (accessed March 2008).
21. Kelly Mooney and Nita Rollins, *The Open Brand: When Push Comes to Pull in a Web-Made World* (Berkeley, Calif.: New Riders Press, 2008).
22. Naomi Klein, *No Logo: Taking Aim at the Brand Bullies* (New York: Picador, 1999).

Further Reading

Baudrillard, Jean. *Simulations*. Translated by Paul Foss, Paul Patton, and Philip Beitchman. New York: Semiotext(e), 1983.

Benjamin, Walter. *Charles Baudelaire: A Lyric Poet in the Era of High Capitalism*. London: New Left Books, 1973.

———. *The Arcades Project*. Translated by Howard Eiland and Kevin McLaughlin. Cambridge, Mass.: Belknap, 1999.

Berger, John. *Ways of Seeing*. London: Penguin Books, 1972.

Bollier, David. *Brand Name Bullies: The Quest to Own and Control Culture*. Hoboken, N.J.: Wiley, 2005.

Bordo, Susan. *Unbearable Weight: Feminism, Western Culture, and the Body*. Berkeley: University of California Press, 1993.

Bourdieu, Pierre. *Distinction: A Social Critique of the Judgment of Taste*. Cambridge, Mass.: Harvard University Press, 1984.

Cohen, Lizabeth. *A Consumers' Republic: The Politics of Mass Consumption in Postwar America*. New York: Vintage, 2003.

Coombe, Rosemary. *The Cultural Life of Intellectual Property: Authorship, Appropriation, and the Law*. Durham, N.C.: Duke University Press, 1998.

Danesi, Marcel. *Brands*. New York: Routledge, 2006.

Ewen, Stuart. *All Consuming Images: The Politics of Style in Contemporary Culture*. New York: Basic Books, 1988.

Frank, Thomas. *The Conquest of Cool: Business Culture, Counterculture, and the Rise of Hip Consumerism*. Chicago: University of Chicago Press, 1997.

Friedberg, Anne. *Window Shopping: Cinema and the Postmodern*. Berkeley: University of California Press, 1993.

Gladwell, Malcolm. "The Coolhunt." *New Yorker*, March 17, 1997: 78–88. Reprinted in *The Consumer Society Reader*. Edited by Juliet Schor and Douglas Holt. New York: New Press, 2000, 360–74.

Gladwell, Malcolm. *The Tipping Point: How Little Things Can Make a Big Difference*. New York: Little, Brown, 2000.

Goldman, Robert, and Stephen Papson. *Sign Wars: The Cluttered Landscape of Advertising*. New York: Guilford, 1996.

Gudis, Catherine. *Buyways: Billboards, Automobiles, and the American Landscape*. New York: Routledge, 2004.

Haacke, Hans. "Where the Consciousness Industry Is Concentrated: An Interview with the Artist by Catherine Lord." In *Cultures in Contention*. Edited by Douglas Kahn and Diane Neumaier. Seattle: Real Comet Press, 1985, 204–35.

Hebdige. Dick. *Subculture: The Meaning of Style*. New York: Routledge, 1979.

Hillis, Ken, Michael Petit, Nathan Scott Epley, eds. *Everyday eBay: Culture, Collecting, and Desire*. New York: Routledge, 2006.

Horkheimer, Max and Theodor W. Adorno. "The Culture Industry: Enlightenment as Mass Deception." In *Dialectic of Enlightenment: Philosophical Fragments*. Edited by Gunzelin Schmid Noerr. Translated by Edmund Jephcott. Stanford, Calif.: Stanford University Press, [1947] 2002.

Jhally, Sut. *The Codes of Advertising: Fetishism and the Political Economy of Meaning in the Consumer Society*. 2nd ed. New York: Routledge, 1990.

King, Peter. "The Art of Billboard Utilizing." In *Cultures in Contention*. Edited by Douglas Kahn and Diane Neumaier. Seattle: Real Comet Press, 1985, 198–203.

Klein, Naomi. *No Logo: Taking Aim at the Brand Bullies*. New York: Picador, 1999.

Lasn, Kalle. *Culture Jam: How to Reverse America's Suicidal Consumer Binge—and Why We Must*. New York: Quill, 1999.

Lears, T. J. Jackson. "From Salvation to Self-Realization." In *The Culture of Consumption: Critical Essays of American History 1880–1980*. Edited by Richard Wrightman Fox and T. J. Jackson Lears. New York: Pantheon, 1983, 3–38.

Lears, T. J. Jackson. *Fables of Abundance: A Cultural History of Advertising in America*. New York: Basic Books, 1994.

Leiss, William, Stephen Kline, and Sut Jhally. *Social Communication in Advertising: Persons, Products and Images of Well-Being*. 2nd ed. New York: Routledge, 1990.

McBride, Dwight A. *Why I Hate Abercrombie & Fitch: Essays on Race and Sexuality*. New York: New York University Press, 2005.

Mooney, Kelly, and Nita Rollins. *The Open Brand: When Push Comes to Pull in a Web-Made World*. San Francisco: New Riders Press, 2008.

O'Barr, William M. *Culture and the Ad: Exploring Otherness in the World of Advertising*. Boulder, Colo.: Westview Press, 1994.

Paterson, Mark. *Consumption and Everyday Life*. New York: Routledge, 2006.

PBS Frontline. *Merchants of Cool*. (2001) http://www.pbs.org/wgbh/pages/frontline/shows/cool/.

PBS Frontline. *The Persuaders*. (2003) http://www.pbs.org/wgbh/pages/frontline/shows/persuaders/.

Schor, Juliet B., and Douglas Holt. *The Consumer Society Reader*. New York: New Press, 2000.

Schudson, Michael. *Advertising, the Uneasy Persuasion: Its Dubious Impact on American Society*. New York: Basic Books, 1984.

Sivulka, Juliet. *Sex, Soap, and Cigarettes: A Cultural History of American Advertising*. Boston: Wadsworth, 1997.

Turow, Joseph. *Niche Envy: Marketing Discrimination in the Digital Age*. Cambridge, Mass.: MIT Press, 2006.

Walker, Rob. *Buying In: The Secret Dialogue Between What We Buy and Who We Are*. New York: Random House, 2008.

Williamson, Judith. *Decoding Advertisements: Ideology and Meaning in Advertising*. London: Marion Boyars, 1978.

chapter eight

Postmodernism, Indie Media, and Popular Culture

Jia Zhang-ke's 2004 film *The World (Shijie)* takes place in a vast amusement park, called World Park, outside of Beijing. Since 1993 about one and a half million people have visited this park each year to experience "the world" through small-scale replicas of iconic buildings and structures that are major tourist destinations throughout the world: a replica of lower Manhattan (with the Twin Towers still standing), the leaning Tower of Pisa (where, as in Italy, people pose for pictures as if they are holding up the tower), the Eiffel Tower, the Taj Mahal, the Egyptian Pyramids, the Tower of London, and a replica of China's own Red Square. These sites can be visited on a "global voyage" taken by foot, speedboat, or battery-operated car. There are several World Parks in China, each a site where Chinese citizens, whose ability to travel outside China is still restricted by the government, are invited to "visit" the world through these replicas. "See the world without ever leaving Beijing!" the park slogan announces. The film focuses on the employees at the park, young Chinese and immigrant workers from Russia, who dress in costumes to perform spectacles of different world cultures—Bollywood-type dances in Indian costumes, flight attendant costumes for the simulated airplane trip that never leaves the ground, and so on. When these young workers communicate with each other via text messaging on their cell phones, the film reverts to animated sequences in which the characters imagine themselves flying through various park landscapes and out of the park.

In *Simulacra and Simulation*, the French philosopher Jean Baudrillard suggests that, with the rise of media technologies for making models of the real, the relationship between the model (the map) and the real social territory it charts

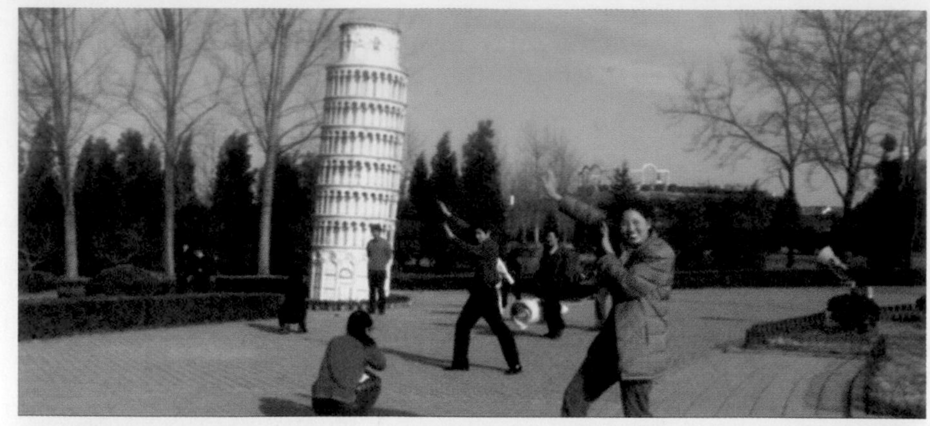

FIG. 8.1
Stills from *The World* (*Shijie*), 2004

changed in the postwar years of the twentieth century. As we entered into a *postmodern* era characterized by media and technologies of simulation, we lost sight of "the real." Our confidence in referents declined as we came to see the simulation as taking the place of the real. He wrote: "In the hyperreality of pure simulacra, then, there is no more imitation, duplication, or parody. The simulator's model offers us 'all the signs of the real' without its 'vicissitudes.'"[1]

Beijing's World Park is a postmodern simulation in Baudrillard's terms. It is a place where the experience of visiting "real" places is presented as a substitute for actually visiting them. With its small-scale pyramids and miniature Eiffel Tower, World Park is not unlike the Venetian Hotel in Las Vegas, where visitors can "experience" Venice by riding in gondolas on artificial canals, or the Paris Las Vegas Hotel which has, like World Park, a replica of the Eiffel Tower. It is also not unlike Main Street U.S.A. at Disneyland in California, where visitors can experience small-town America and which was one of the examples used by early theorists of postmodernism, most notably Baudrillard, to talk about simulation as a key factor in the postmodern condition. Another similar site is the planned theme park in Dubai, Dubailand, which will include in its Falcon City of Wonders *life-size* replicas of famous world monuments. Yet the World Park, both in actuality and as portrayed in Zhang-ke's film, introduces several important new elements into the question of the postmodern. As the site in the world in which global capitalism's territorial expansion is perhaps at its most explosive, China has embodied the contradictions of being a postindustrial, globalizing postmodern culture that is also undergoing expanded modernization and industrialization. As Jia Zhang-ke, the director of the film, states, "those artificial landscapes are very significant. The landscape in the World Park includes famous sights from all over the world. They're not real, but they can satisfy people's longing for the world. They reflect the very strong curiosity of people in this country, and the interest they have in becoming a part of international culture. At the same time, this is a very strange way to fulfill those demands. To me, it makes for a very sorrowful place."[2] Indeed, the film ends with a scene in which workers in a gritty, industrialized neighborhood close to and in contrast to the glittery World Park, dark, anonymous figures, are asphyxiated by the fumes from trying to heat their meager quarters, a reminder of the degree to which most of the world's populations live not in the world of simulations, virtual communication technologies (like the animated sequences of text-messaged fantasies in the film), or postindustrial work but in rural and urban poverty.

We begin with this example to make clear a fundamental aspect of postmodern society, identity, and style: we do not live in a postmodern world. Rather, we live in a world in which aspects of postmodernity are in constant tension with aspects of modernity and premodern existence, a world that is both preindustrial and postindustrial, in which many of the qualities that characterized modernity (the speeding up of time and compression of space that resulted in part from urbanization, industrialization, and automation) have become conditions in postmodernity alongside and in relation to virtual technologies and the flows of capital, information, and media in the era of globalization. Many of the paradigmatic aspects of modernity, including the period's emphasis on science, technology, and progress, remain quite dominant in postmodern societies. At the same time, structures of feeling, to use Raymond Williams's term, took shape in the late twentieth century that can be characterized as late modern or postmodern. These include the ease with which we interact in simulated environments; the jaded sense that everything has been done before; a preoccupation with remakes, remixes, appropriations, and pastiche; and regard of the body as a form that is physically malleable, adaptable to models we have in mind through bodybuilding, surgeries, and drug therapies.

Baudrillard described the late twentieth century as a period during which images became more real than the real, creating a kind of hyperreality in which simulation replaced reproduction and representation. Images fascinate us, he explained, "not because they are sites of the production of meaning and representation," but "because they are sites of the *disappearance* of meaning and representation, sites in which we are caught quite apart from any judgment of reality."[3] According to Baudrillard, Western culture was epitomized, in the late twentieth century, by the dull flickering of computer and television screens. America has become paradigmatic of global looking practices ruled by the simulacra of virtual media images. Unlike representations, which make reference to a real, simulacra stand on their own without requiring recourse to real objects or worlds elsewhere. Baudrillard introduced the concept of simulation to describe the collapse between counterfeit and real, and the original and the copy, that exists in a culture that had become strongly organized around digital technologies. Baudrillard's ideas were extremely influential, in particular in the 1980s, in presenting new paradigms for thinking about what might distinguish the experience of postmodernity from modernity. His concepts give us an immediate and dramatic sense of the role of the image both as it has been transformed through digital technologies and as the dominant paradigm for contemporary identity, though not through the concept of representation per se. It is the image as simulation that epitomizes postmodernity.

In this chapter, we address the concepts of postmodernity, postmodern society, and postmodern style and how they intersect with and work in tension with modernity and modernism. The philosophical engagement with the concept of postmodernism, which began in the 1980s, was both an attempt to understand changing concepts of the human subject and an analysis of the effects of globalization, postindustrialization, computerization, and communication technologies on concepts of the self and on worldviews in late modernity. As postmodern theory has matured, the concept of simulation, a paradigm of the postmodern which epitomized its origins, is seen in the more current context of digital technologies, genetics, network theory, rhizomes, pastiche and remake culture, independent media, and new kinds of economic and spatial relationships that have resulted from globalization and trade liberalization. This does not mean that forms of simulation are not still important symptoms of the postmodern worldview—the enormous popularity of such online worlds as Second Life testify to the ease with which people move between interactions in simulated worlds and identity construction in real life. Yet, although early invocations of Baudrillard and simulation were used to proclaim the end of the real and the dominance of the image, such pronouncements seemed glib and privileged in a world that is still dominated by real poverty, manual labor, and violent conflict. The phenomenological experience of living in a fleshly body that can be injured, can feel pain, and can become ill and die is something that simulation cannot supersede or replace with virtual experience. The film theorist Vivian Sobchack makes a scathing critique of Baudrillard's theory of simulation on the grounds that in celebrating the technologically augmented and simulated body he fails to acknowledge the vulnerability of the lived body.[4] Contemporary engagements with postmodernism, we argue, are most useful when they engage with the contradictions of these coexisting tensions.

To return to the film *The World*, the world as created through simulation is, of course, always the product of someone's labor. In the film, the low-paid workers who come from poor rural areas or who are brought in from other countries, such as indentured laborers from Russia, keep the simulation afloat. The World coexists with a world of industrial pollution, poverty, and human relationships that makes up the lives of these workers and the people who visit. In reflecting on the postmodern aspects of contemporary societies and our ease with interacting in and experiencing things within simulated environments, we are also tapping into issues of space, global culture, fantasy, and communication technologies, many of which are about concrete material effects. In this chapter, we consider how the underlying meanings of postmodernism translate into postmodern styles in art, popular media, and advertising. These styles offer new forms of address to postmodern subjects and viewers who remain situated within a world of late modernity—a world in which the needs and conditions of everyday embodied experience remain basic to life, even as we come to view life itself on the level of the molecular and the genetic and even as we come to experience the pharmaceutical and surgical enhancement of the body as a natural aspect of everyday life.

Postmodernism and its Visual Cultures

It is difficult to identify a precise origin of postmodernism, though many critics associate it with the time after 1968. Opinions differ as to whether postmodernism is a period, a set of styles, or a broader set of politics and ideologies. Some theorists have used the term *postmodern* to describe the postwar "cultural logic of late capitalism," a phrase famously used by cultural critic Fredric Jameson as the subtitle of his enormously influential 1991 book on postmodernism.[5] This definition of postmodernism emphasizes the formative role of economic and political conditions, including postwar globalization, the emergence of new information technologies, new flexible forms of production, and the breakdown of the traditional nation-state, in the emergence of postmodern modes of cultural production. Others begin with the cultural objects themselves, identifying postmodernism as a set of styles—indeed, as a creative explosion of style and surface image in reaction to the rigid attention to form and underlying structure in modernism. The latter approach has been criticized for implying that postmodernism is simply a style that an artist or producer might choose to embrace or reject rather than a cultural trend that is integral to changes in culture, the economy, and politics.

Postmodernism has been characterized as a response to the conditions of late modernity linked to the late stages of capitalism. Thus postmodernity refers not just to a style and a form of subjectivity that emerged in late modernity. It also refers to changes in the social and economic conditions that help to produce these styles and ways of being a subject. We have noted that modernity refers to a period of history characterized by industrialization, an emphasis on the value of science as a means of achieving progress, and an ethos of progress and freedom associated with Enlightenment philosophy and political theory. Postmodernity is tied to shifts that include the demise of the nation-state and the dissolution of national sovereignty; the skeptical embrace of science and technology in the wake of the Holocaust and the nuclear bombing of Japan, which showed how scientific ideas could be turned against humankind and toward acts of unthinkable violence and destruction; and the promotion of trade liberalization in a world increasingly characterized by uneven global flows of money, goods, and people. Not only the rise of a world economy but also advances in technologies of travel, information, and health care contribute to a postmodern world characterized by mobility, changeability, and flow rather than by universals of truth and unity. Thinkers such as David Harvey have characterized postmodernism as an economic, post-Fordist culture of flexible accumulation and argued that we are experiencing a "phase of time-space compression that has a disorienting and disruptive impact upon political-economic practices, the balance of class power, as well as upon cultural and social life."[6] Harvey's work has been influential in framing the "postmodern condition" within material and economic conditions, such as the deployment of new organizational forms and new technologies of production, the speeding up of production and distribution, outsourcing of labor, new technologies of control and management for production and labor, and accelerated turnover of production and consumption. All of this has had the effect of speeding up culture and the circulation of goods, and changing the meanings attached to goods to reflect the accelerated, digital life we lead in late capitalism.

It is widely agreed that there is no precise moment of rupture between the modern and the postmodern. Rather, as we have noted, postmodernism intersects with and permeates late modernity, a period during which Enlightenment notions of liberalism, modernization, and progress continue to compel development in many of the poorer and less developed nations and economies and during which modernist approaches based on scientific truth and technological advancement continue to be invoked. The 2000s have been characterized as a decade of neoliberalism, meaning that classical liberalism was revived to rationalize the use of economic and trade liberalization as a means of promoting economic growth and democratic freedom. Neoliberalism finds its precedent in the Enlightenment model of liberalism, a doctrine of individual freedom that included such measures as limited government and the protection of personal property rights and civil liberties. The proliferation of images and image-producing apparatuses such as the cinema and video and the digital imaging devices that can be characterized as postmodern have been met by criticism steeped in modernist ways of thinking about the real and the true. Although we can say that postmodernism describes a set of conditions and practices occurring in late modernity, modernism and postmodernism are not concepts that are strictly period-specific or successive. Aspects of postmodernism can be seen in the early twentieth century and in the early twenty-first century; aspects of modernity and postmodernism, as well as modern and postmodern styles, coexist both in unison and in tension.

There are, however, social aspects of postmodernity that can be distinguished from those of modernity. Modern thought was characterized by a sense of knowing that was forward looking and positive and the belief that one could know what was objectively true and real by discerning the structural relations that underpin social formations and natural phenomena. The postmodern is characterized by the questioning of the supposed universality of structural knowledge, as well as a skepticism about the modern belief in the universality of progress: Do we really know that progress is always a good thing? Can we really know the human subject? How can any experience be pure or unmediated? How do we know what truth is? Whereas modernity was based on the idea that the truth can be discovered by accessing the right channels of knowledge to arrive at structural and material bases, the postmodern is distinguished by the idea that there is not one but many truths and that the notions of truth are culturally and historically relative constructions. In their emphasis on the cultural and historical relativity of truth and meaning, mid-twentieth-century thinkers as diverse as the cultural anthropologist Margaret Mead and French philosopher Michel Foucault can both be characterized as presciently postmodernist in this sense. The postmodern entails a crisis of universality and cultural authority, that is, a profound questioning of the very foundations of truth that shore up our knowledge of social structures and our means of producing knowledge about social relations and culture.

For these reasons, postmodernism is described as a questioning of master narratives (or metanarratives). A master narrative is a framework that purports to explain society, if not the world, in comprehensive terms. Religion, science, Marxism, psychoanalysis, Enlightenment myths of progress, and other theories that each set out to explain all facets of life are master theories or master narratives. Metanarratives involve a sense of an inevitable linear progress toward a particular goal—enlightenment, emancipation, self-knowledge, and so forth. French theorist Jean-François Lyotard characterized postmodern theory as profoundly skeptical of these metanarratives, their universalism, and the premise that they could explain the human condition.[7] Hence postmodern theory has undertaken to examine philosophical concepts that were previously perceived as beyond reproach or question, such as the ideas of value, order, control, identity, centralized power, or meaning itself. It has involved a scrutinizing of social institutions, such as the media, the university, the museum, the practices of science and medicine, and the law, in order to analyze the assumptions under which they operate and the ways that power works within them in a manner more distributed and complex than previously recognized. One could say that postmodernism's central goal is to put all assumptions under scrutiny in order to reveal the values that underlie all systems of thought and thus to question the ideologies within them that are seen as natural. This means that the idea of authenticity is always in question in postmodernism.

We have noted that style is an important defining characteristic of postmodernism. The term postmodernism has been used to describe some of the styles and approaches to making images that have circulated more prominently since the late 1970s. We could argue that postmodernism defines an ethos, a set of sensibilities, or a politics of cultural experience and production in which style and image predominate. Thus, although postmodernism may not be about style alone, style is one of the chief characteristics of a postmodern ethos. The term postmodern has been used to describe fashions and even politicians who produce themselves through myriad media images and texts, generating identities as simulacra—hyperreal identities with no recourse back to a real person, their composite media image being more real than real.

The distinctions between modern art styles and postmodern styles reveal overlapping strategies and interests. For instance, modern literature, film, and art were often engaged in a critique of the assumptions of modern thought and with the alienation of modern life. One could argue that Marcel Duchamp and his fellow Dada artists were some of the first postmodernists in the early twentieth century from the moment that Duchamp placed a urinal on a pedestal, signed it with a fake name (R. Mutt), and called it art, in the process critiquing the very foundations of the art system. We can say, however, that modernist art and theory were distinguished by elitism toward media and popular culture, whereas postmodernism has been at one with the popular from its origins. Although postmodernism is not just style and image, it relies heavily on style and image to produce its worlds. In the period associated with late (post-World War II) modernist thinking and movements, critics spoke from positions they imagined to be outside—specifically, politically or aesthetically above—popular culture in order to criticize that culture or to reveal the ideological investments hidden beneath the glitzy surface of representations and images. Postmodernism dispels the idea that surface does not contain meaning in itself or that structures lie beneath the mask of surface appearances. The modernist way of thinking about structure did not stop with the emergence of postmodernism; this approach to art, criticism, and theory continued throughout the 1980s and 1990s, overlapping with tendencies associated with the postmodern.

Postmodernism thus has a very different mode of analysis from modernism of popular culture, mass culture, and the surface world of images. Whereas opposition to mass culture and its saturation of the world with images is one of the hallmarks of modernism, postmodernism emphasizes irony and a sense of one's own involvement in low or popular culture. The forms of low, mass, or commercial culture so disdained by modernists are understood, in the context of postmodernism, as the inescapable conditions in and through which we generate our critical texts. One signpost of the difference between a modern and a postmodern critical sensibility is the acknowledgement within the latter that we cannot occupy a position outside of that which we analyze; we cannot get beneath the surface to find something more real or more true. As postmodern theorist Santiago Colás puts it, "We may attempt to forget or ignore mass culture, but it will neither forget nor ignore us."[8] Postmodernism complicates the divisions between high and low culture, elite and mass consciousness, and in doing so makes it impossible to occupy a critical viewpoint on culture from outside or above it. This also means that the postmodern condition and postmodern style define a context in which consumerism is integrated into life and identity in complex ways. Thus one of the primary aspects of postmodernism is that it entails a reflexive recognition of our lived relation within the world at the level of consumption, branding, images, media, and the popular. Appropriation, parody, pastiche, and self-conscious nostalgic play are just some of the approaches associated with postmodernism. Thus we could say that the rise of remix culture is the result of shifting postmodern sensibilities coupled with the emergence of a set of technological practices enabled by the Web and digital technology. This means that remix and remake culture are not only evidence of new kinds of cultural and consumer practices but are also integrated into new concepts of identity and agency.

One of the criticisms of much postmodern theory has been that it can be apolitical in its jaded irony. Irony is certainly a strong characteristic of theories that spin out on style, simulation and surface or those that characterize the postmodern condition, as both Jameson and Gilles Deleuze and Félix Guattari did in the 1980s, as a form of cultural schizophrenia in a way that ignores the degree to which schizophrenia is a mental disorder rather than a mere metaphor of the fragmentation of everyday life.[9] The question of how postmodernism can be related to politics and whether or not postmodernism is politically regressive (while being culturally progressive) has been debated over the past few decades as a response in part to the centrality of theorists such as Baudrillard and his pronouncements of the end of the real and its representations. It is worth noting that modernism was tied to a range of political viewpoints, from apolitical avant-garde movements such as cubism to an embrace of the Soviet project to futurism's ties to fascism in Italy.

Yet many thinkers have tried to make postmodern concepts offer an opening into politics rather than bystepping it. Postmodern thought has been keenly engaged in the questioning of modern concepts of the self and identity, emphasizing fragmentation and plurality. These concerns open our thinking to include new ways of being human subjects and new ways of thinking about how identities (racial, ethnic, gendered, etc.) are in fact varied and plural sites from which to speak. David Harvey writes that one response to the space-time compression of postmodernism has been a kind of blasé been-there-done-that attitude. However, the enhanced flows of information and people in postmodernism has also led to a response in which people are imagining new ways of making community, new ways of having local and global involvement in humanitarian issues and social movements, and new ways to show respect for otherness.[10] For example, with the Internet, advocacy organizations like Greenpeace have been able to build a stronger international communications base than was possible with telephones, mail, print brochures, and local meetings. Postmodern ways of organizing that build on networking, viral marketing, and recognition of consumer savviness have been successful not only for corporate advertisers, but also for activist and advocacy groups, allowing for outreach to a wider base of potential participants internationally while also fostering a stronger sense of community among members. Thus the critique of modernism and the emphasis on what modernism leaves out, which is an essential part of postmodern theory, can be seen as a means through which those voices and representations foreclosed on by modernism can be heard and visualized differently. At the same time, postmodernism signals the rise of a generalized self-consciousness and a reflexive questioning of traditional metanarratives in all facets of everyday life as a means of rethinking the limits of previous paradigms. In doing away with master theories and master narratives, postmodernism leaves open possibilities and the means for recognizing the relative openness of the way things happen as they unfold in time. For Gilles Deleuze, *becoming* is an important term that captures the importance of moving beyond negative historical precedents in order to create something new. As theorists of the late twentieth century became boxed in by the explanatory logics of theories that could never be verified and that reproduced the same logics they critiqued, the writings of Deleuze offered a useful tool box of concepts with which to produce readings of cultural circumstances that could help us to move beyond the modernist goal of knowledge as an end in itself. Deleuze emphasized the usefulness of a rhizome's structure, in which new ideas and practices sprout up in heterogeneous, de-centered ways, much as tubers or bulbs propagate, as compared to the more centralized and orderly progression of the roots of a tree.

Addressing the Postmodern Subject

Just as the historical and cultural context of modernity created new kinds of human subjects, we can say that postmodernism and postmodern style speak to new kinds of human subjects. In interpellating these subject positions, postmodern texts participate in an exchange of signification that helps to shape how viewers engage with cultural texts, negotiate their meaning, and construct their identities in relationship to them. In looking at how postmodern style informs popular culture, art, literature, architecture, and advertising, we can see how these forms of address speak to and help to constitute (or make) new kinds of postmodern subjects.

Postmodern media texts generally speak to viewers as subjects who are in the know about codes and conventions of representation and simulation. The dominant mode of address in these texts takes the viewer to be someone who will not be fooled by techniques of propaganda and illusionism, someone who will get the reference, who is media and image savvy, as we discussed in the previous chapter about advertising. During the postmodern period, references to the real world outside the film may be as much to the world of other films or the world of a genre. Intertextuality is one means through which the referent is tied not to a reality but to another representation or simulation, as well as to a realm of consumer products tied in to the film and its cast of characters.

Let's take the case of the stylistic, cultural, economic, and global aspects of animation. Beginning in the mid-1990s, studio animated films shifted dramatically in their style. This did not happen in isolation from other genres and markets. The market for sophisticated children's programming had been growing, with Disney aiming for an adult market from the time of *Snow White* (1934) onward and with television programs such as *Sesame Street* (starting in 1969) using parody and adult-level humor geared to engage parents and children alike. Japanese animated television shows and feature films generated huge fan bases in the United States beginning with *Astro*

Boy, the animated television series of the 1960s based on a comic of the 1950s by the legendary manga artist and animator Osamu Tezuka, which was remade with success for the U.S. market in the 1980s and again in 2003. The Mighty Atom boy was for a time as popular in Japan as Mickey Mouse was in the United States. The Giant Robot (Mecha) science fiction subgenre (originating in Japan and South Korea) generated international cult attention after the release of *Mobile Suit Gundam* in 1979 and was the foundation for popular children's animation series such as *The Transformers*. The series was adapted for U.S. Saturday morning television (though still animated in Japan), along with the introduction of a Transformer toy line in 1984, the year that the Federal Communication Commission began to allow toy companies to use cartoons to promote products such as toys and lunch boxes. Transformers started out as a Japanese toy line by Takara (with the characters called Microman and Diaclone). *Transformers* (the television show and the movies) thus was part of broader intertextual market synergy that took effect through child-consumers engaging with available toy product lines off the radar of sleeping parents. It also coincided with the broad popularity of animated characters who were neither animal nor human. These cartoon worlds were composed of technologically advanced robots, "mecha" (mechanical beings), bearing little resemblance to biological life (yet who are, as the still shows, specifically gendered).

FIG. 8.2
Still from *Transformers: The Movie*, 1986

Although most of these animations were analog, not digital, productions made in the early 1980s, they featured digitized robotic beings with artificial intelligence and mechanical- and computer-augmented superhuman powers. Children identified with these collectives of fully robotic figures in a futuristic world, characters fully invested with computerized artificial life. To be robotic was, in these shows, the norm. The referent of the real biological living being in a natural world as the source of the animated figure in its world was no longer in place. Moreover, the text itself blatantly took as its referent not only the futuristic world of artificial life but also the real-life world of toys that could be bought and brought home. Children actively participated in a cycle of consumption that involved watching one's desired toys appear in animated shows and shopping "online," as it were, by using the TV screen as a site to select characters, sets, and accoutrements appearing in the world of the shows to later buy and play with at home. Baudrillard's account of the simulation engendering the real is relevant to this example of 1980s Saturday morning cartoons in which the simulation of intelligent life prefigures a world of "real" products in which the child may come to live (if the parent buys the toys). This postmodern approach to the screen was amplified in the experience of the Japanese-produced arcade video games that began to appear in the United States with the release of Space Invaders (designed by Tomohiro Nishikado and developed by Taito Corporation) in 1978 and Pac-Man (designed by Toru Iwatani and developed by Namco) in 1980. Video games would provide yet another textual field in which animated characters could be cross-marketed.

At the same time that child viewing practices were transformed by the aesthetics and logics of these animated computer-era action figures and toys, Japan was undergoing a transformation of its culture industry. After the devastation of World War II and the bombings of Hiroshima and Nagasaki, comic books (manga) and animated films (anime) became media venues not only for children but also for adults, addressing issues such as politics, history, and culture and including genres ranging from drama, comedy, and romance to satire, pornography, and explicit violence. One of the earliest anime for adults was the 1970s *Lupin Sansei*. Based on a manga series by Monkey Punch (the pen name of mangaka Kuzuhiko Kato), this anime TV and feature film series combined adult humor and slapstick violence. Not only were there narrowcast genres of anime for groups (girls, or Shojo, and boys, or Shojen, anime, for example); sectors of the industry produced entertainment geared to adult subgroups such as young men and older women and to taste-specific groups within adult audiences.

The release of Katsuhiro Otomo's animated feature *Akira* in 1988 marked anime's incorporation of a cyberpunk technological aesthetic. Animated film became a venue for the figuring of dark, dystopian postmodern views of the future demise and collapse of the industrial landscape of modernity in which we continue to live out our postmodern existences. Based on Otomo's original manga, the film *Akira* begins with a nuclear explosion that destroys Tokyo in 1988 and launches a third World War. The film then jumps forward to Neo-Tokyo in the year 2019, a city decimated by the blast, the war, and ongoing political violence but also displaying the advances of science and biotechnology as they segue in warped ways with the landscape of devastation (the character Tetsuo, who ultimately dies, develops paranormal abilities after serving as a government test subject, and his body acquires bizarre superhuman qualities). *Akira*'s international cult success was due in part to its explicit reach to the adult audience that had embraced science fiction texts such as Ridley Scott's *Blade Runner*, a film that media scholar Scott Bukatman has recognized as one of the most significant examples of a film that embodies a postmodern ethos in its film style, set design, and narrative (while retaining aspects of modern style).[11] *Akira* stood apart from most other anime of the period in its use of lip-synched dialogue and fluid motion across numerous action scenes. The film spoke to a new kind of postmodern viewing subject—one who could readily identify with the jaded, apocalyptic view of a postmodern life lived in the ruins of modernity, and who could identify with the sense of resignation about the bleak future people faced as a result of the technological "progress" modernity had demonstrated with the bomb.

FIG. 8.3
Still from *Akira*, 1988

Both *Blade Runner* and *Akira*, though quintessentially postmodern films, seem to suggest, as we did earlier in this chapter, that we do not live in a fully postmodern world but in a world in which postmodernity is lived in the crumbling ruins of modernity. This is the postindustrial world of the late stages of industrialism in which the collapsing of time and compression of space have resulted in a kind of imploded destruction of the built environment and nature. Through these films, viewers engage with simulated environments with the jaded sense that we know what is to come and that our bodies may be physically malleable and changeable through technology and medicine. Those changes to our bodies may not be in our own hands. For example, in *Akira* the character Tetsuo's paranormal mental abilities were the result of experimentation on him by the government. These films are part of a dystopian postmodern worldview that was predominant in the 1980s and that continues in some fiction and media of the 2000s. This worldview emerged in many geographic settings simultaneously and in the aftermath of World War II, which was experienced in vastly different ways by different national subjects. Whereas in the United States *Akira* is a *Blade Runner*-like cyberpunk fiction about the demise of industrial capitalism, for Japanese audiences *Akira* makes obvious reference to the aftermath of Hiroshima and Nagasaki and the attempt to rebuild a culture from unthinkable devastation and in the face of international defeat and an ethically unconscionable act of violence against the history and citizenry of a nation. Animation and cartoons, in this postwar context, served a particular role in allowing a populace to be represented and to speak, even indirectly through media consumption and exchange, about an unthinkably violent trauma. The unnatural hair color and physical abilities of simulated and fantastic anime figures are expressive means of moving away from the codes of realism in which disaster and tragedy are so typically encoded.

The new popular animated films that began in the mid-1990s with such Pixar productions as *Toy Story* (1995), one of the first fully CGI (computer graphics imagery) feature films, and *A Bug's Life* (1998) used techniques and styles of computer animation that, like their precedents in the globally distributed Japanese animated film, were aimed at adult audiences, as well as children. These Hollywood animations proved enormously successful financially, beginning a trend in U.S.-produced digital animated features that crossed the child-adult market. These films succeed financially in appealing to a broad range of viewers and producing a thriving DVD market, while as cultural texts they also deploy styles that speak to a new kind of viewing subject that is also quintessentially postmodern. They do this through a complex mix of conventional storytelling and layered ironic quotation referencing other cultural products.

Let's take as our example the film *Shrek* (2001), which was based on a children's book by the cartoonist William Steig and which has since become the first of a *Shrek* franchise. *Shrek* draws on the conventions of the traditional fairy tale, with the story of a princess who has been cursed and is waiting for her prince to rescue her, a fairy godmother, an annoying sidekick, fantastic fairyland kingdoms, and a feat that the hero must accomplish in order to win the princess. As a cultural text of postmodern style, *Shrek* is layered with references to earlier fairy tales, characters from other animated films, and Hollywood labor and industry practices. It is filled with reflexive jokes about representation. The film does this while also pursuing a conventional love story with a moral about loving oneself as one is instead of aspiring to look and be like everyone else. The text operates on many levels simultaneously and addresses viewers who will understand the references (or at least will understand that multiple references to other texts are being made) and who are capable of reading the film's parodies of fairy tales while also engaging with the pleasure of seeing a conventional love story. Thus some viewers might read this scene, in which the princess fights off a band of robbers by using martial arts moves, as a reference to the technologically enhanced fight scenes in *The Matrix* (1999), which were themselves references to the style of Hong Kong martial arts films.

FIG. 8.4
Still from *Shrek*, 2001

This is an example of intertextual meaning, in which the reference to *The Matrix* brings into *Shrek* meanings associated with another film. It is a joke in the film, of course, that the princess is trained in kung-fu fighting, and having her fight like Keanu Reeves in *The Matrix* pokes fun at the *Matrix* style and how it takes itself so seriously. Intertextuality, a term derived from literature, literally means the insertion of part of one text, with its meanings, into another. One of the fundamental aspects of intertextuality is its presumption that the viewer knows the text that is being referenced. Intertextuality is neither a new aspect of popular culture nor specific to postmodernism. After all, the use of celebrities in ads throughout the twentieth century to sell products can be seen as an intertextual tactic. The stars bring to the ad the meaning of their fame and the roles they have played. Well-known actors carry meanings from texts in which they have appeared with them into new texts. For example, we never see Adam Sandler solely as the characters he plays in a particular film; rather, we see him simultaneously as those characters he has played and as Adam Sandler, movie star and comedian, playing those characters. However, contemporary intertextuality operates on a level that is much more ironic and complex, addressing a media and visually savvy viewer who is familiar with image conventions and genres. A popular culture text such as *Shrek*, which derives its meaning in part from constant referencing to other popular culture products, is deploying many layers of intertextual meaning to tell its story and speak to and entertain viewers. Such a text addresses its viewers as savvy individuals jaded by contemporary popular culture, as audience members who have seen it all and who are used to being immersed in image culture.

These aspects of postmodern style point to the way in which postmodernism is, in some of its manifestations, about citation or quotation both in terms of referencing other texts and in terms of putting things in quotes to indicate a kind of distancing irony. Texts, rather than referring to real life, refer to other texts. The Italian semiotician Umberto Eco once wrote that in the age of postmodernism, a person can no longer say to someone, "I love you"; what they can say is, "as Barbara Cartland says in one of her romance novels, I love you."[12] As we noted before, postmodernism involves using mass and popular culture as a point of reference for our real-life activity. Such citation also points to another central aspect of postmodernism, which is the sense that older models of how to address audiences don't work anymore, and the sense among consumers that everything has been said and done before. We discuss parody and remake culture, which are results of this trend, later in this chapter. Here we focus on how this notion of there being nothing "new" anymore results in a kind of endless layering of citation. Postmodernism is distinguished from modernism in relation to the concept of the new. Modern thought, as well as modern art and literature, was very much about a sense of the new, the avant-garde, the radical new idea. In postmodernism, the sense that everything has been done before gives way to relentless quoting and remakes, a context in which the only way to get noticed is to be ironic, to quote—not only words but also clothing and appearance styles, whether we cite the past through wearing 1970s clothing or the latest fashions (which also cite the past).

Reflexivity and Postmodern Identity

The practice of making viewers aware of the means of production by incorporating them into the content of the cultural product was often a feature of modernism. In most modern work, this was a strategy used by artists as a form of political critique that asked viewers to notice the structure of the show in order to distance them from the surface pleasures of the text. This idea of distancing is an important one, because it means that viewers can be engaged at a critically conscious level. Bertolt Brecht, a well-known German Marxist playwright and critic of the 1920s and 1930s, proposed the concept of distanciation as a technique for getting viewers to extract themselves from the narrative in order to see the means through which the narrative of a cultural work (such as a play or movie) gets us to buy into a particular ideological viewpoint. Reflexivity, in which the text refers to its own means of production, undermines the illusion or fantasy aspects of the narrative, encouraging the viewer to be a critical thinker about the ideology conveyed by the narrative.

Postmodern popular culture and art take this modern concept of reflexivity further but with different effect. In many postmodern reflexive texts, much of the political critique of reflexivity has been tempered with humor or is simply not present in the text. Media producers offer us reflexive techniques of disillusionment not as tools for critical and distanced reflection on the real economic and cultural conditions behind the text but as forms of intellectual play. It is thus an irony of media history that the techniques and conventions of discontinuity, reflexivity, and narrative fragmentation that were tied to a political project of critique by socially conscious media producers have become the codes of advertisers and media producers who use these codes for intellectual play without offering viewers any significant critical or political message beneath the reflexive joke.

Self-awareness of one's inevitable immersion in everyday and popular culture has led some postmodern artists to produce works which reflexively examine their own position in relation to the artwork or the artwork's institutional context. The work of photographer Cindy Sherman is a good example of this approach. In the 1970s, Sherman began to make photographs in which she was her own model. She struck poses evoking actresses in film stills and photographed herself in sets designed to evoke popular cinema genres such as melodrama. These images do not reproduce particular film stills or stars. Rather, they evoke the style of a particular moment or genre, such as the Hollywood female star and studio publicity stills of the 1940s and 1950s.

FIG. 8.5
Cindy Sherman, *Untitled*, 1978

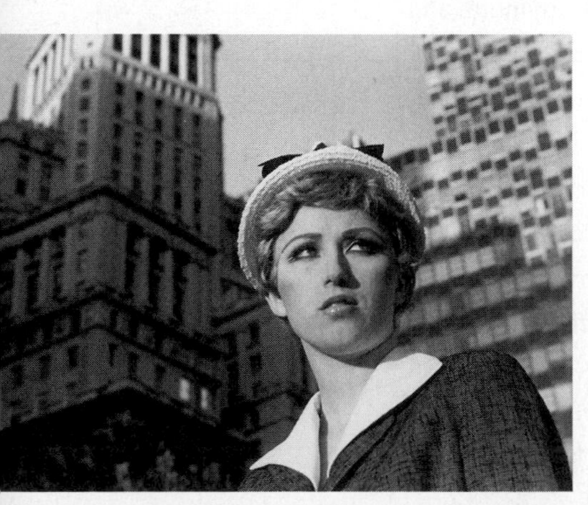

Sherman's photographs can be seen as portraits that are neither about herself, as she is always disguised and playing a role, nor about some other real subject, film star, or character. Rather, they are ironic and deliberate imitations or simulations of a type.

Sherman self-consciously appropriates the general styles, gestures, and stereotypes, performing them in conceptual interpretations. This series is a response to an era of feminist film criticism that challenged representations of women, the male gaze, and structures of identification that we discuss at length in chapter 3. Feminist film critics asked, How might women, as objects within the male gaze, identify within a position of active looking? Sherman's photography indirectly but powerfully engages these theories of looking and sexual difference by giving us visual texts that comment reflexively on women's place on both sides of the camera, as bearer of the look and as image. Indeed, many of Sherman's earliest photographs show her dressed in the garb of the height of the Hollywood studio era. The women she invokes are not the icons of her own generation but those of the studio-era films that appeared in syndication on television in the after-school hours during the decades in which Sherman grew up, the late 1960s and 1970s. Sherman's compositions reflexively pose questions for viewers about spectatorship, identification, the female body image, and the appropriation of the gaze by the woman photographer as her own subject. Sherman actively inserts herself into the media that she reflexively critiques, shifting the context from mainstream cinema to fine art. Rather than taking a critical stance from outside the image and its mode of production, Sherman inserts herself not only into the image but also into the process of its production, making the viewer aware that the woman in the image is also the woman behind the camera, both the bearer of the look and the object of the gaze. She enmeshes herself in the world being critically interrogated in her work. This is one of the key things that distinguishes Sherman's commentary as postmodern against the modernist critical-readings-from-above offered by feminist film criticism of roughly the same period: Sherman offers her critique reflexively through visual practice rather than deploying words to critique visual culture. In this, she participated in an important postmodern trend that still holds strong: Using visual cultural practice to engage in cultural critique about visual culture, rather than turning to words as if words were a more intelligent or more trustworthy form.

References to nostalgia for other historical periods is another hallmark of postmodern art captured in Sherman's photographs. Like much postmodern culture, Sherman's photographs feed our nostalgia for bygone eras at the same time that they offer reflexive critique of that engagement with nostalgia. Her double position as both producer of the scene and object of the gaze, however, introduces an edge of irony and reflexivity. Irony refers to a deliberate contradiction between the literal or dominant meaning of something and its intended meaning (which can be the opposite of the dominant meaning). Irony can be derived from contexts in which appearance and reality are in conflict. Sherman's photographs comment not only on the conditions of that past but also, ironically, on the artist-producer's awareness of her own pleasurable engagement in the visual culture of nostalgic fantasy that she evokes. By situating herself as both artist and subject, Sherman invites us to think reflexively about our own subjectivity and gendered processes of identification, cultural memory, nostalgia, and fantasy in our engagement in postmodern visual culture. This makes her photographs ironic images that also instruct us in seeing practices of looking. Her work helps us to see looking as an activity that is historically determined, and as a practice in which we are actively situated rather than as an activity that we may stand outside of to critique from above.

Sherman's work points to the ways in which identity is perceived in postmodernism to be a much more flexible category than it was in modernism. As we have noted, concepts of identity in postmodernism understand the subject to be fragmented, pluralistic, and multifaceted. The constant questioning of postmodernism is integral to its rejection of modern concepts of the subject. The idea that we perform our identities, rather than the idea that they are fixed within us, is a key aspect of postmodernism.

We can see this by looking at the work of another artist who, like Sherman, uses photography to play off ideas of identity and performance. In her work called *Projects* (1997–2001), Nikki S. Lee combines performance art and ethnography (the study of cultures through empirical means). She not only observes but also adopts the styles of particular subcultures and identity groups (such as skateboarders, punks, drag queens, hip-hop musicians, Latinos, Korean school girls, seniors, tourists, exotic dancers, and yuppies). To infiltrate these groups, she changes her hair, style of dress, weight, and mannerisms. Her aim is not to fool people into believing she is an authentic member of these groups, but to experiment with the idea of forging new identities through cultural performance. Introducing herself to members of each group she infiltrates, she explains her artistic project and then gradually gains acceptance over the course of a few months. Once Lee is a part of the group, she has someone take snapshots of her in her new social environment, and these photographs then are put on display as part of her artwork. She also produced a film about this project (*A.K.A. Nikki S. Lee*, 2006).

Lee's engagement with the production of an identity she does not authentically own or occupy points to the postmodern idea that identity is produced through performance. On one hand, Lee is engaging in a process of imitation through disguise and performance, one that could be said to reduce identity into simple categories of signification that can be copied and reproduced without a lived relationship to their meanings. On the other hand, Lee's integration into these groups attests to her strong capacity to transform her being beyond appearances. Lee, who is Korean-American, states that her performative images are an extension of her own identity, which she defines as a constantly changing set of relationships. As art critic Russell Ferguson writes, "despite the seriousness of her preparation and the apparent success of her 'disguises,' Lee is on one level never playing a role at all."[13]

In Lee's work, as in Sherman's, the role of photography as a form of portraiture of a simulation is crucial. We can recall how portraiture was an essential early practice in photography to establish identity and individuality. Yet, in modern art movements, the image's function as a register of truth and meaning came under

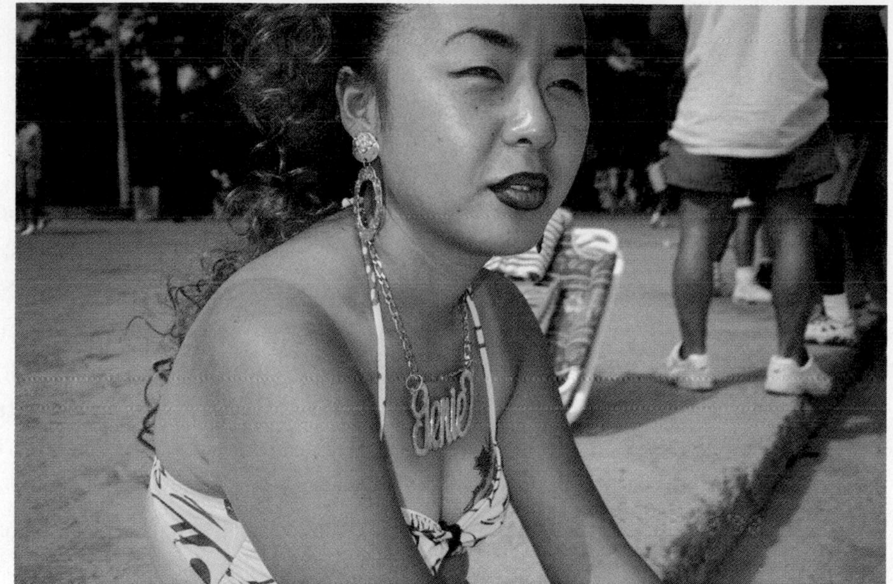

FIG. 8.6
Nikki S. Lee, *The Hispanic Project* (25), 1998

scathing scrutiny. Postmodernism responds to modernism not by going beyond the material form of the image to some newer, more accurate register of truth but by embracing the surface and appearances as important aspects of meaning, not simply as something put on top of the real thing, the structure. The status of Sherman's images as self-portraits that perform identity make clear that the self is not an authentic subject to be accessed through introspection, and the image does not give the viewer access to the artist's deeper self. In Sherman's work, the portrait is all surface and artifice; in Lee's work it gives us access only to the performance of identity. This does not, however, mean that the artists are shallow or that they have no substance. Rather, in postmodernism, the surface is understood to be a crucially meaningful element of social life and not simply the illusion put over the real, like makeup hiding a blemish. We can no longer look below the surface for depth and true meaning, because we will find no hidden truth there but rather just a different way of seeing.

In this context, Lee's work questions notions of identity as innate, calling into question not only the stability and authenticity of identity and social groups but also the question of social integration. One of the things that is striking about her images is that they are quite convincing. In these casual snapshots, no one appears to be posing. They appear "authentic," signaling, perhaps, Lee's "success" at the performance of integration. Yet Lee also clearly stands apart in these images despite her ease within them. This is most obvious in the images that address issues of ethnic and racial identity—although she looks entirely comfortable in the "Hispanic Project" images, her Asian ethnic identity is also evident within them. Yet her performance also points to the performance of others in her images, the codes by which we can easily detect a particular subculture or social group.

The taking on and off of identity and identity's performative nature have been a feature of pop artists since the 1980s with the integration of musical performance with video. Thus, with the emergence of music videos when MTV was established in 1982, visual performance became more explicitly a part of the pop music industry. Madonna was an early icon of the music video form, and, as we discussed in chapter 1, she popularized the strategies of appropriation and parody by adopting the look of the Madonna, and then adopting a Marilyn Monroe look, followed by numerous transformations of style and image over the course of her career. Madonna can be described as the quintessential postmodern pop figure of the 1980s and early 1990s in that she made the transformation of style a stylistic signature in itself. Also in the 1980s, pop singer Michael Jackson exhibited a similar penchant for bodily transformation as a means of nostalgic reference to past icons, undergoing a series of surgeries and treatments to change the look of his face and skin. These two vocal artists' construction of themselves as images, transforming their looks according to a familiar cultural referent, is emblematic of postmodern culture. Jackson's appearance eventually became completely different from his original look, as he used plastic surgery to erase any physical markers of black identity and whitened his skin to an extreme pallor.

These examples of changing and performing identity in pop icons points to broader issues of identity and the postmodern body. In postmodernism, the body is imagined to be easily transformed: One can change one's gender through cross-dressing or surgery, one can change one's race through changing skin tone and using colored lenses, and one can change one's appearance and shape through gym workouts, liposuction, plastic surgery, prosthetics, or changing one's hormonal makeup. In many ways, these concepts of the body are in sharp contrast to the image of the body in modernity, in which the body was perceived to be boundaried, stable, and fixed (one lived one's life with the body and its attendant identities—gender, race, sexuality—with which one was born). Concepts of the body in postmodernism are thus fully integrated with contemporary concepts about the integration of technologies into bodies, creating cyborg bodies that are part machine and part human, the metaphors of the interchange and malleability that are a part of digital culture, and the concepts of the body as a genetic map of DNA that have emerged over the past twenty years with the rise of genetic science. The postmodern body is also a body perceived through information science, and this has consequences for how the relationship of the body and identity is conceived. Fragmentation, malleability, fluidity, and the possibility of "reprogramming" the body (an obvious computer metaphor) become the dominant metaphors for conceiving the body in this context.

The fluid postmodern body is potentially one of shape-shifting, a body that can be resculpted into new shapes and forms. This concept has been explored by the French performance artist Orlan in relation to the iconic images of art. Orlan underwent a series of cosmetic surgeries performed with plastic surgeons in art galleries with an audience present. In these works, aspects of her face were combined with facial features taken from paintings, such as those of the fifth-century painting *Zeuxis*, to create not simply a new model but a kind of hybrid antimodel that short-circuits ideals and norms such as beauty and the natural. Body and identity become infinitely malleable in a culture in which the image is the ultimate register of experience. Orlan's work suggests that there is no "real," original body to which we might return in our quest to model ourselves after some fantasy of what we hope to become: the image of an image. Her performances cast the physical body not just as the screen on which meaning is simply inscribed to be erased and redrawn (as we might do with makeup) but as the structurally malleable and changeable material through which models are brought to life in the real. Once again we see the precession of the simulacra enacted in a postmodern practice of appropriation and pastiche, but in this instance we see the degree to which material transformation entails risk, violence, and loss. Although plastic cosmetic surgery has become an everyday consideration for many members of middle- and upper-class Western cultures, the loss of identity and the pointed embrace of the bizarre and the ugly in the service of aesthetics that Orlan performs takes this to the extreme. In doing so, she highlights the degree to which we have taken choice and self-fashioning to a limit that has surpassed notions of self-unity and the rootedness of the human subject in the natural and the biological body that grounded the Enlightenment subject.

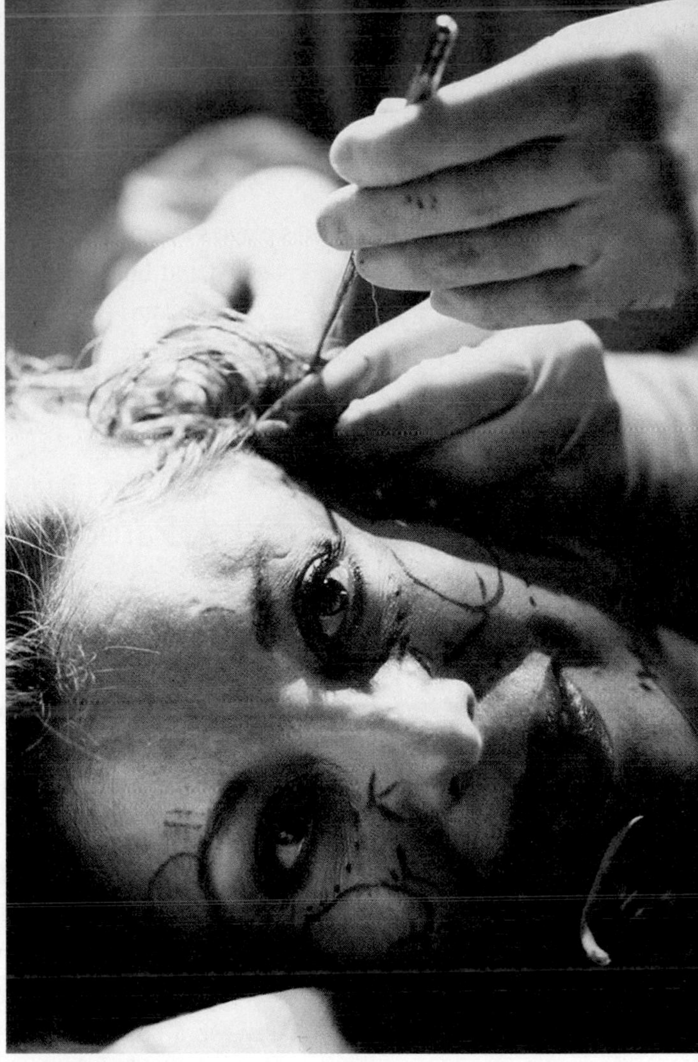

FIG. 8.7
Orlan, 7th *Operation*, 1993

The idea of the authenticity of the appearance of the face is pursued by media theorist Lisa Nakamura in her examination of alllooksame.com, a website designed by Dyske Suematsu that is devoted to the interrogation of the idea that one can "read" racial identity from the face. The person accessing the site is offered eighteen pictures of faces that are identified as either Japanese, Korean, or Chinese. The player is asked to guess the correct national identity of the face based on his or her knowledge about the typical appearance of members of these groups. The site then calculates the score of the player, which is on average a seven, whether or not the player is an "insider" or "outsider" in one of the cultural groups represented, showing that racial classification is more easily gotten wrong than right. Suematsu began the site as a joke, but with the rise of racial profiling in the 2000s it takes on a cultural role as an instructive lesson in the conceptual and political limits and problems of racial classification. As Nakamura points out, the "truth" about race is not a visual truth. Identity is always complex and diverse, and visual signifiers, as we saw earlier in this book, are always open to different meanings. Eye shape, hair color, and other physical qualities of appearance are no different in this respect. The site makes players interrogate the cultural and political bases on which racial taxonomies are imagined and built. Nakamura, through her examination of player responses to this site, interrogates the racial visual essentialism and reductionism built into racial profiling and extended in what Nakamura describes as the "ethnic absolutist identity politics" of those who uphold authentic and purist or essentialized notions about racial identity.[14]

Pastiche, Parody, and the Remake

As we have noted, postmodernism has been characterized by a kind of fatigue with the new and the sense that everything has been done before. Postmodernism asks: Can there ever be new ideas and images, things that have not been thought of or done before? Does it matter? The world of images today consists of a huge variety of remakes, copies, parodies, replicas, reproductions, and remixes. In the arenas of art and architecture, as well as popular culture, the idea of an original image or form seems to have been thoroughly subverted.

One of the key terms used to describe this culture of imitation, remake, and parody is *pastiche*. Film theorist Richard Dyer has written that the primary way to understand pastiche is as an imitation that announces itself as such and that involves combining elements from other sources.[15] The term *pastiche* is derived from the Italian word *pasticcio,* which refers to a combination of elements that evokes, according to Dyer, assemblage, collage, montage, *capriccio* (a style of composing that combines elements from different places), medley forms, and hip-hop forms of sampling, scratching, and riffing. Dyer thus points to the fact that pastiche has a long history in image making. Within the realm of imitation and quoting that constitutes pastiche, we can find different kinds of combinations and relationships to the original texts—from ironic quoting to parody to remakes to mashups. Pastiche has a very particular relationship to history. As a strategy it can often involve pilfering from history and combining historical elements in ways that have little historical meaning but are rather a kind of play.

One of the key strategies of pastiche is a questioning of the status of the original. As we discussed in chapter 5, use of this technique can raise legal questions because determining the legal ownership of the fragments of work appropriated as elements in a pastiche can be a complex matter. Artist Sherrie Levine made a series of works in the 1980s that are emblematic of this kind of postmodernism pilfering and borrowing that questions ownership and the original. Levine simply rephotographed famous images—in blatant violation of their copyright, the signifier of authorship and authenticity—and displayed them as her own. In *After Edward Weston (#2),* Levine rephotographed Weston's famous image of his son, Neil, entitled *Torso of Neil* (1925). Weston's image is situated in a long history of male nudes, which Levine's "theft" disrupts precisely because it is explicitly presented as copied, rather than concealing its status as a copy. However, her choice of this male nude is provocative, given that Weston was known for his depictions of the female nude. Levine's work is a defiant critique of the idea of an original and a feminist critique of the idea of the male artist as master. It presents the viewer with a questioning of the differing value of images and the entire question of reproduction. In addition, like new technologies that allow images to be easily "reauthored," Levine's aesthetic style questions the very foundations of authorship. One of the principles put in question in Levine's work is the idea of the original. Levine's photographic appropriations, like the photographs of Cindy Sherman, raise questions about the role of the artist as the sole creator of a unique work. Who is the "real" artist here, Levine or Weston, and which is the "real" work of art, the copy or the original? Do we care about the "real" or the "true" in the era of reproducibility? This work questions the idea of originality in art and the value of the aura that is placed on it in museums, galleries, and the art market. In works such as these, the question of the referent (the real object to which a work refers) becomes quite complicated. These images are reworkings of representations, which are part of a potentially endless reworking of images for which the original referent is no longer identifiable.

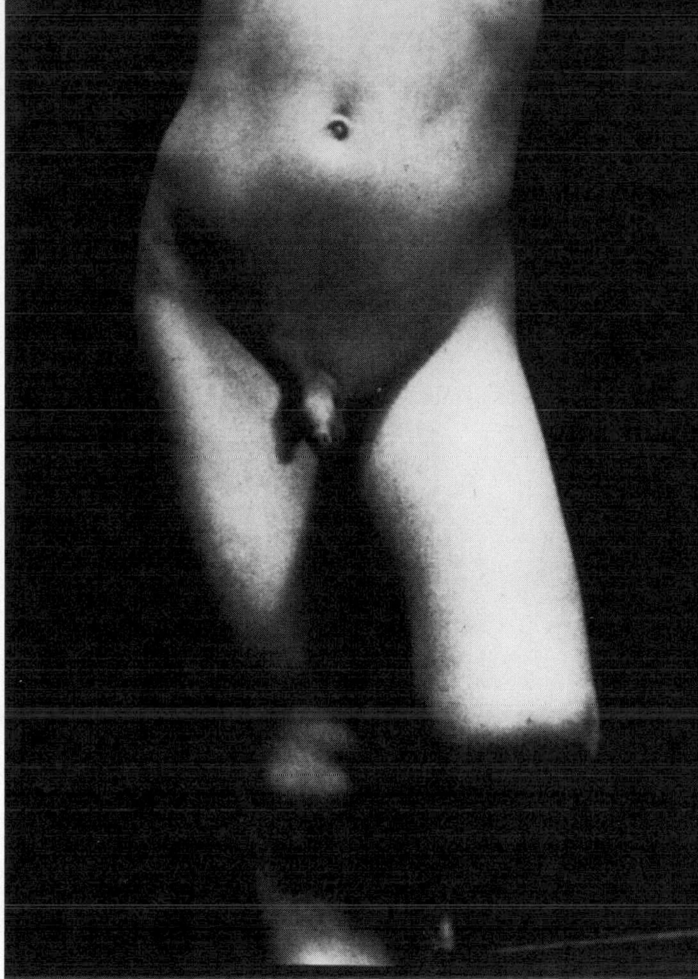

FIG. 8.8
Sherrie Levine, *After Edward Weston (#2)*, 1980, © S. Levine. Courtesy of the artist and the Paula Cooper Gallery

When pastiche is engaged in reworking elements of the past, it can also fall into the category of parody. For instance, throughout most of the period of classical Hollywood film, many films were created to fit specifically into genres, such as the Western, the gangster film, the romantic comedy, or the action picture. One of the essential aspects of genre theory is that specific genres (in film, television, literature, etc.) establish certain conventions and formulas that are recognizable to viewers, whose pleasure derives in part from a combination of seeing familiar elements and seeing the variation in them from one film to the next. Although genres still thrive in the context of popular culture, with new genres being created in television all the time, we are now in an era in which the vast majority of genre works are genre parodies. Importantly, these texts work at two levels at once, participating in the codes of a genre at the same time that they are self-consciously parodying those codes. So, for instance, a horror film such as *Scream* (1996) is a parody of the genre of horror films that knowingly taps into viewer's knowledge of the genre's conventions and formulas. Directed by well-known horror film director Wes Craven, the film repeatedly refers to the conventions of horror films in

FIG. 8.9
Psycho, 1960, with *The Simpsons* remake

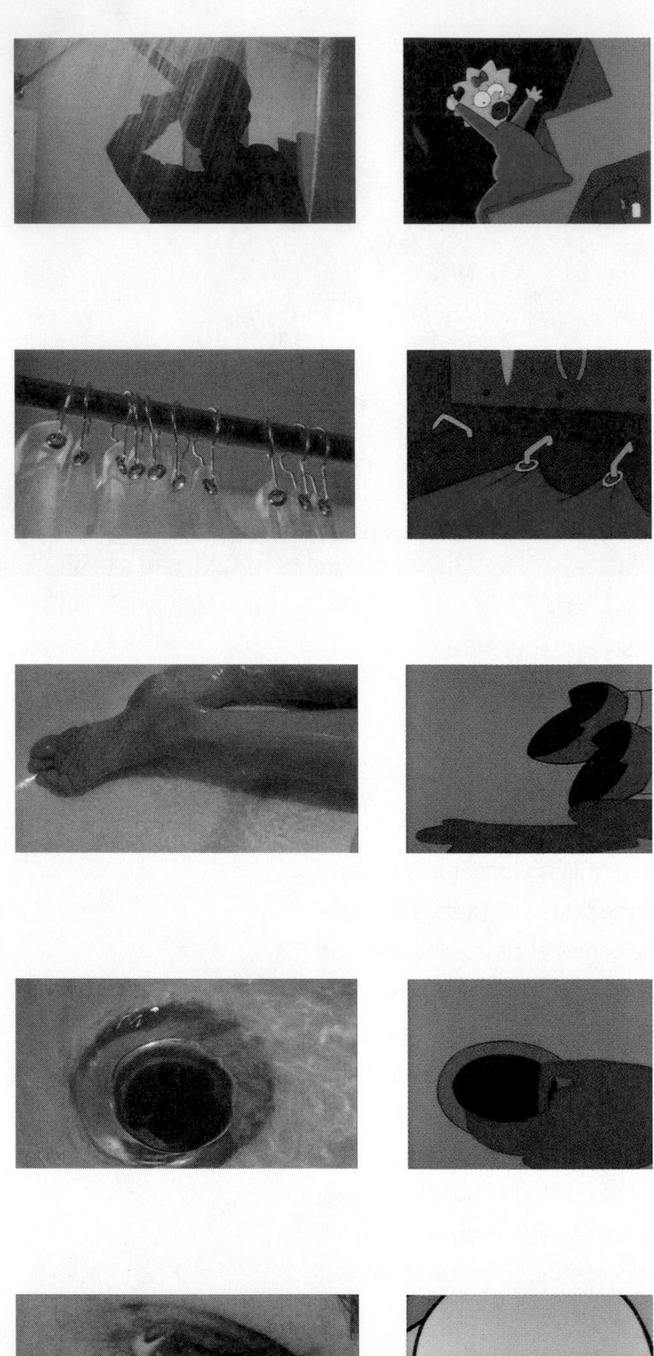

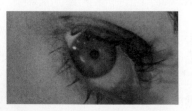

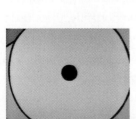

which characters are always killed after they have sex or are attacked after they say "who's there?" In addition the film is peppered with dialogue about the movies ("You've seen one too many movies"; "Life is like a movie, only you can't pick your genre"). Yet it is also a film that is as scary to watch as any horror film. After the making of *Scream*, most films within the genre of horror film continued this tactic of addressing viewers who were genre-savvy, with such films as *Scary Movie* (2000) taking the genre parody to camp levels.

A television show such as *The Simpsons*, which often remakes old films in its story lines, uses parody to play off the codes of film and cultural history. The series has over the years produced a huge number of parodies of well-known films.[16] When the show remade the famous shower scene from the 1960 Alfred Hitchcock film *Psycho*, it did so by incorporating particular plot elements of the film into its existing locale and characters. With many humorous and absurd plot lines, the episode did not ask viewers to take its reworking of *Psycho* seriously, merely to share in its homage to aspects of the film, such as the close-up of Janet Leigh's eye as she lies dead in the bathroom (remade as Homer's eye as he lies on the floor). The meaning of the show, and its humor, are dependent on viewers engaging with the differences between the show's parody and the texts it is pilfering. As we stated earlier, this does not constitute the kind of strategy deployed by modernists, who used reflexivity to make viewers stand back in critical distance, but rather suggests a deliberately playful engagement that allows us to enjoy our involvement in both the old text and its parodic remake. We used the word *play* to characterize the kind of parody that we see in *The Simpsons* because pastiche of the past rarely intends to make a statement about the status of the historical text it references. Rather, the remake uses the old text to create a layered intertext between the two works, summoning in viewers the depth of feelings that extend across both texts and the time periods between them.

The remake has also been a subject for artists. The artist Jeff Wall layers his works with references to philosophical ideas of writers such as Walter Benjamin and to canonical works of art, such as Rodin's *The Thinker* or Manet's Le *Déjeuner sur L'Herbe*. Many of his works are direct pastiche remakes of famous works of art, displayed as large backlit transparencies. In *A Sudden Gust of Wind (after Hokusai)* (1993), Wall remakes a famous 1831–33 print by the Japanese artist Katsushika Hokusai, which depicts peasants responding to a gust of wind with Mount Fuji in the background. The original Hokusai print is a woodcut, with an abstract printmaking texture, made by an artist who also produced a famous image of a cresting wave in woodcut style. The Hokusai image here is part of a series of works of different views of Mount Fuji and an early representation of movement. In this Hokusai image, the gestures of the figures indicate movement captured in an instant as a figure whose sight is obstructed by a blowing scarf lets go of papers that fly through the air. In its representation of an instant, the Hokusai print anticipates the instantaneity of photographic imaging (it was made just a few years before photography emerged in Europe). In contrast, the Wall photograph derives its meaning from its status as a photographic remake of an older form, a woodcut. Wall stages his images to make them look spontaneous. A similarly posed group of

FIG. 8.10
Jeff Wall, *A Sudden Gust of Wind (after Hokusai)*, 1993

FIG. 8.11
Katsushika Hokusai, *A High Wind on Yeijiri*, from *Thirty-six views of the Fuji*, c. 1831–33

figures respond to the papers flying up in the gust of wind, against the backdrop not of Mount Fuji but of a drab industrial landscape. When exhibited, the image creates the effect, as many of Wall's works do, of an elaborate canvas, at once photographic, cinematic (with its evocation of movement and its backlit effect), and painterly. It is not incidental that Wall's image was created using digital imaging tools that allowed the artist to seamlessly combine elements from more than a hundred shots.[17]

Postmodernism is often accused of ignoring history, of pilfering past image and appearance for clever play. Yet, as Linda Hutcheon writes, history is a key point of inquiry for postmodernism. Postmodern questioning raises important epistemological questions about the project of history and the degree to which we have access to the past. Hutcheon writes that postmodernism "suggests no search for transcendent, timeless meaning but rather a re-evaluation of, and a dialogue with the past in light of the present."[18] In postmodernism, there is an acknowledgement that we can only know the past through the fragments of its remnants. The French artist Christian Boltanski engages deeply with questions of memory, history, and the image, in particular of the event that shadowed twentieth-century world history: the Holocaust. In many of his works, Boltanski takes the signifiers of the Holocaust (photographs of Holocaust victims, archival boxes, discarded clothing and shoes) and replicates them as a means of reflecting on how the Holocaust hovers over European-American culture. Boltanski has created works called inventories that evoke archives, with piles of boxes that may or may not contain records or objects, and has created installations of piles of clothing in which visitors are obligated to walk across the clothing that evokes the emptying out of bodies. He thus references the effect of the Holocaust while refusing its codes of representation. He has stated, in trickster fashion, "My work is not about XXXXXXX it is after XXXXXXX."[19]

The role of the photograph as an icon of memory and history is a key feature of Boltanski's work, in which he signals "the complex suspicion that surrounds photography's documentary claims in a postmodern and post-Holocaust world," according to Marianne Hirsch, who also states that Boltanski's work is "devoted to uncoupling any uncomplicated connection between photograph and 'truth.' "[20] Boltanski has produced many works that rework images from the past, though never solely to excavate history. Rather, he engages in a form of postmodern pastiche with photographs as unknowable artifacts that are easily dislodged from their historical referents. In some of his works, such as this version of *Reserves* (1989), he took images of Jewish schoolchildren from the 1930s, rephotographed them, and then placed them behind lights. The faces of the students have become a blur, each a haunting image with dark eye sockets, lit by the harsh light of a desk lamp that evokes both interrogation and the glare of historical analysis. Nothing is known about the fate of these children whose faces are scrutinized up close by the camera. This work is thus not, like most art about the past, about retrieving the identities of these children; rather, it invokes the imminence of their death at the time of the photograph's taking. The clothes stacked beneath evoke the possessions left behind by Holocaust victims, the empty clothing that signals absence.

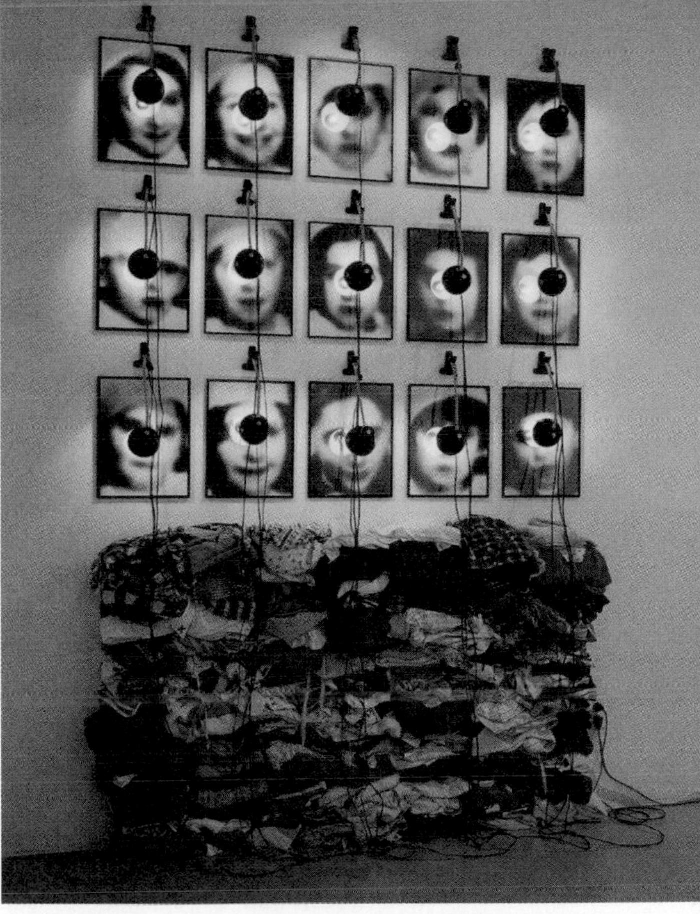

FIG. 8.12
Christian Boltanski, *Reserves: The Purim Holiday*, 1989

Ultimately, Boltanski's work engages with the question of the individual and memory in ways that make us think about how we know the past. Richard Dyer writes that pastiche, like the concept of the death of the author that we discuss in chapter 2, critiques the concept of the modern subject as the center and author of discourse. "Accepting that [we] are in the realm of the already said may be a source of anguish," Dyer states, if we are invested in ideas of the originating position of knowledge and authority. Pastiche articulates affective content, he states, through imitation:

> It imitates formal means that are themselves ways of evoking, moulding and eliciting feeling, and thus in the process is able to mobilize feelings even while signalling that it is doing so. Thereby it can, at its best, allow us to feel our connection to the affective frameworks, the structures of feeling, past and present, that we inherit and pass on. That is to say, it can enable us to know ourselves affectively as historical beings.[21]

Through pastiche and these kinds of postmodern engagements with history, we can see how seeing the past remains within the present.

Indie Media and Postmodern Approaches to the Market

Postmodern style and forms of address are derived not simply from changes that have taken place in popular culture and the art world. Postmodern culture is also produced through changes that have taken place in the production, dissemination, and marketing of media forms. The emergences of independent media forms and productions have capitalized in particular on the Web as an alternative venue for marketing media apart from the confines of the industry. Postmodern styles have emerged not only out of a set of economic and cultural shifts but also through a redefinition of authorship and the relationship of production, distribution, and consumption that has been enabled by changing technologies and new cultural practices.

Indie films give us an example of a new postmodern kind of market for media. Indie films are those movies produced outside the Hollywood studio system, a national studio system with a solid economic base, or an economically stable and thriving sector of a nation's privatized industry (such as Bollywood). Whereas at the beginning of the independent film movement producers saw themselves as standing apart from and against the mainstream film industry, by the mid-1980s indie filmmakers began to use stylistic strategies associated with postmodernism, such as reflexive narrative form, the remake, and parody, and business and marketing strategies that both drew on and reworked industry standards and practices to make and promote their films. It is actually the case that the Hollywood industry itself grew out of oppositionality. Hollywood was the place to which filmmakers fled to escape the control of the Motion Picture Patents Company that dominated and controlled film production on the east coast of the United States in the early decades of the cinema. Those producers who moved to California to set up studios had escaped the control of the existing studio monopoly. When the Hollywood studios gained control of the industry in the 1930s and 1940s, monopolies made it difficult for producers not associated with the major studios to get their films shown in the popular chain movie theaters whose bookings were controlled by studio interests.

The independents were the smaller film companies such as that of the African American director Oscar Micheaux, whose company produced films that were shown in cinema houses in urban centers such as Chicago that catered to black clientele in the era of segregation. With the loosening of control over distribution and exhibition that came after the Hollywood Antitrust Case of 1948 and the subsequent demise of the Hollywood Production Code that required industry board approval of content and imagery in all distributed releases, U.S. film culture became more diversified in the range of films shown, with independent art houses exhibiting foreign, art, and independent films that continued to fail to get bookings at the major chains. The postwar availability of lightweight 16mm cameras made possible a kind of independence in film production through lower-cost supplies and equipment that was less unwieldy and expensive. Independent film came to be associated both with the art house film (associated with highbrow tastes and European or Scandinavian film cultures) and with a modernist avant-garde approach to film in aesthetic and political movements around the world. In national contexts including England, the United States, France, Germany, and Japan, filmmakers opposed the dominant national styles, themes, and structure of mainstream cinema by producing films that offered new styles, themes, and structures. Critique of the corporate means of production took many forms in the 1960s and 1970s, ranging from this kind of extreme formalism to the fragmented narratives, allegorical stories, and reflexively political films of the French New Wave.

In the 1980s, independence took on a new and more postmodern meaning as filmmakers began to critique Hollywood style through strategies such as reflexive narratives and appropriations of genres and styles from earlier periods of cinema. When a few independent filmmakers, including Jim Jarmusch (*Stranger than Paradise*, 1984) and Spike Lee (*She's Gotta Have It*, 1986), broke precedent by achieving box office success with low-budget independent features, industry investors linked to or operating outside the big six studios made possible a degree of financial stability and even success that allowed these directors to rise to a degree of national name recognition. While experimental filmmakers remained on the margins, financing their films themselves, these postmodern directors worked the margins between the counterculture and the mainstream, playing the fine line between countercultural figure and cultural critic while deploying the postmodern strategy of working from within the popular even as one appropriates, parodies, and critiques it. Indie filmmakers of the 1980s and 1990s embraced the contradiction of working through popular form and mainstream business strategies, even while remaining outside the centers of power (the big studios).

In the decades of the 1980s and 1990s the economic structures of popular culture were changing, as we saw in the case of the television industry's expansion to cable, to embrace a broader array of tastes and to offer a wider range of consumer choices. The rise of directors such as the Coen brothers, Quentin Tarentino, and Michel Gondry in the 1990s is part of a trend toward the market's strategic support of a diverse range of products and styles, rather than opting to subsidize only the products and performers that achieve wide mass-audience success. A cynical view of this trend would note that marginal subcultures no longer have the ability to survive unless an investor snaps them up to make money. This case is well illustrated in the example of popular music. One can find a CD of an indie band signed to a middle-sized label in Target stores; that band might achieve a high ranking on iTunes charts for sales; yet that same band might not have name recognition among even a fraction of a typical college class. We can be cynical about the wiliness of investors who have learned to capitalize on the niche audiences of countercultures, marketing music, films, and even clothing for smallish market segments with the idea that small market incomes will add up in a diverse world of consumers hoping to define themselves as unique through their styles.

The fragmentation of the market, however, has supported the growth of a significant independent sector in the 2000s. With iTunes and other means of Web marketing, bands can bypass the restrictive terms of record labels and contracts as they accrue a fan base. In 2007, the British alternative rock band Radiohead broke protocol by making its seventh album, *In Rainbows*, available on its initial release as a digital download for whatever price one chose to pay on the band's website. When the album was released for retail sales, it rose quickly to number one on the United World Chart, Billboard, and the UK Album Chart, ranking, according to many reviews, as one of the best releases of the year. Radiohead was making a statement in their strategy of releasing their music for optional cost to fans about the restrictions on the Web as media and music corporations struggle to maintain ownership rights to—and profits from—media and music that is infinitely copyable. Their strategy was not the modernist one of working against the industry by acting wholly apart from its systems and practices. Rather, their tactic was to work within an accepted system of advertisement and distribution, going with the Web dictum that "information (or, in this case, music) wants to be free" while also challenging the increasing privatization of the Web and its flagrant use as an instrument of the global market. The payment that constitutes ownership of the copy became the object of a very public statement about the restrictions on ownership maintained by record companies that keep independent artists from exercising artistic freedom. As companies dictate not only the marketing practices of bands but also the look and sound of bands as elements of style that contribute to mass audience appeal, styles are reduced to the tastes suggested to be the most marketable by audience surveys and industry market analysts. The postmodern musical artist, in the case of Radiohead, acts as independent producer, making decisions not only about style but also about publicity and release strategies that are typically controlled by record companies and producers. Creativity is thus exercised not only in the music per se but also in the means of making that music public. Radiohead's strategy in marketing was postmodern in the sense that they did not simply resist the mainstream and work outside the industry. They worked within the framework of the industry to find a new route through which to achieve publicity and to reach a broad fan base.

As we see in the case of bands such as The White Stripes, who build their careers steadily on the basis of personal choices about forms of expression, style, and ways of performing and marketing, economic success in the context of postmodernism can be built through the cultivation of niche audiences and narrowcast marketing. The revivals of the careers of punk performers such as Patti Smith and the Smiths (whose member Morrissey is a popular indie solo artist in the 2000s), who in the 1970s and 1980s embraced left politics and insistence on a right to a personal style, is indicative of a trend toward the independent as someone who is not exactly an outlier or opponent of mass culture. These independents may coexist with performers who collectively represent a multiplicity of politics and styles, no one of which can be pointed to as representing a dominant worldview or mass style. For some of those who continue to believe in the role of media as a tool of social change, this incorporation of those independents at the margins into a differentiated and wide-ranging middle ground dulls the political edge of the independent, reducing marginality and oppositionality to just another style. Postmodernism, then, as a politics that relies on style for its expression, runs the risk not only of reducing real social conditions to mere media effects but also of reducing political expression to image. Whether the independents of the 2000s can effect social change in meaningful ways remains for readers to see... in real life.

Postmodern Space, Geography, and the Built Environment

Just as we can say that the experience of modernity changes concepts of space and time, with the rise of urbanization and communication technologies creating a separation of time and space and a distinction between space and place, postmodern space also creates new kinds of experiences.[22] Modern space began a separation of time and space (through the railroad and other modern technologies) that would continue to increase in the context of postmodernism and the rise of digital technologies, virtual experiences, and the rise of wireless technologies. Concepts of postmodern space have tended to focus on simulation and the emergence of non-places. Simulations, on the one hand, as we noted at the beginning of this chapter, have been a dominant theme in postmodernism, and the rise of such online worlds as Second Life is an indicator of the ease with which contemporary interactions that take place entirely online and in simulated spaces have become normalized in particular social contexts. An online world such as Second Life has 3D animation through which users create virtual people and identities (visualized through avatars), virtual societies, economies, cities, buildings, and legal systems. The enormous popularity of Second Life, which has more than one and a half million users all around the world, testifies to the pleasures involved in participating in online communities. Second Life has been a site at which architects and artists produce work for online viewers and audiences, at which universities hold classes, and at which much real-world activity finds an online 3D counterpart. Many activities take place in Second Life, including, as fig. 8.13 shows, political activities such as antiwar protests. Much can be said about how such online games and worlds encourage particular kinds of fantasy lives and imaginary activities. Here we note that, however crudely rendered despite their 3D aspect, the visual elements of these online worlds are crucial to their popularity and their fantasy elements. Thus architects can design buildings in Second Life that avatars can "teleport" to as a means to experiment with design. Importantly, the interrelationship of online activities and "offline" or real-world activities in a "world" such as Second Life is highly continuous in these contexts; this defies in many ways the early formations of Baudrillard and others about how simulations cancel out and take the place of the real.

FIG. 8.13
Antiwar protest on Second Life, December 1, 2007

The concept of the "nonplace" is, on the other hand, a kind of physical space that demands less presence of people within it. Space has often been defined in the context of postmodernism as sites of distraction and waiting—the freeway, the airport, the Internet café—spaces that are defined by being en route to somewhere else, or spaces in which people are connected virtually to other spaces rather than being "present" in actual space. Marc Augé refers to these as nonplaces, sites in which we are solitary, disconnected, and distracted, sites that are defined in a certain sense by the lack of presence they demand from those within them. As we noted in chapter 4, virtual space defies the laws of Cartesian space in that it is not mappable or graspable; it thus demands new models for thinking about how we are situated in space.

Questions of how the built environment has changed in relationship to the shifts of space, time, and concepts of identity of postmodernism can be seen as crucial to the practices of postmodern architecture. On the one hand, postmodern architecture raises questions about how to think about space, history, and context; on the other hand, it reveals many aspects of the postmodern engagement with mass culture, popular culture, and kitsch. With the publication of the book *Learning from Las Vegas* in 1972, the architects Robert Venturi, Denise Scott Brown, and Steven Izenour insisted that architects must be more attentive to the tastes and styles characterizing the spaces that are truly enjoyed by the masses in their everyday lives. They turned their attention to the built environment of the kitschy hotels and fast-food joints of the Las Vegas strip. They broke with the style of architects including Le Corbusier, whose book *The Decorative Arts of Today* was a critique of ornamentation and craft in the interiors of everyday spaces. Architects at mid-century embraced an aesthetic that emphasized clean, stripped-down design, modularity, clarity, repetition, and flowing lines. Buildings in urban spaces were designed without ornamentation and their rooms outfitted with identical window coverings to give a uniform look to their exteriors, all to reduce the design to the

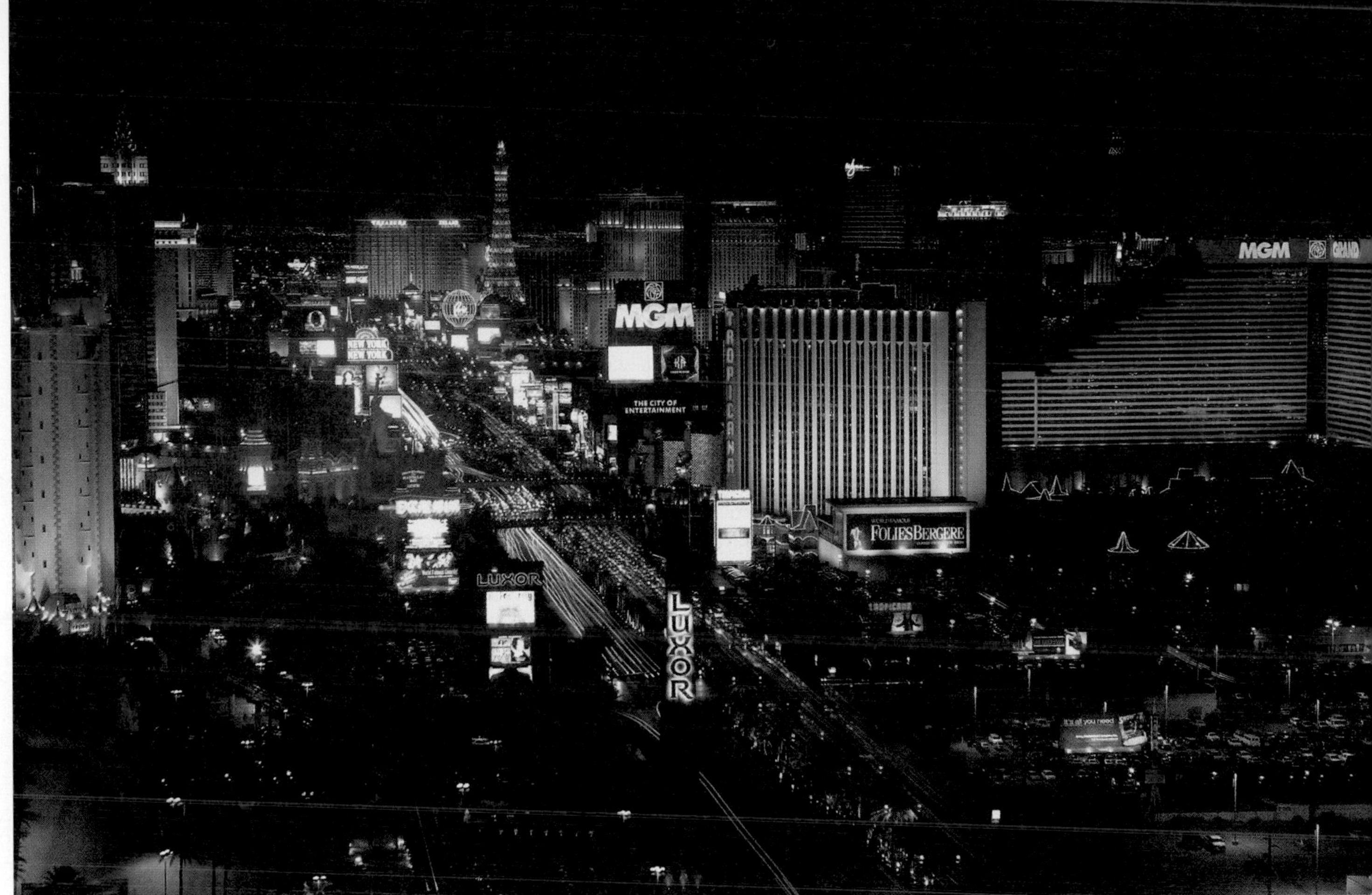

FIG. 8.14
The Las Vegas strip

beauty of form. This style was the epitome of modernism in its embrace of a philosophy that saw truth in material form and universal beauty in the basic elements of design and that saw crass and cheap consumerism reflected in purely decorative detailing and symbolism for the sake of symbolism, apart from functionality.

Venturi's firm reacted against the functionalism and minimalism of these mid-century architecture firms whose built environments, they felt, were wrongly ignoring the pleasures and tastes of the everyday person and the importance of design for design's sake to the ability of human subjects to feel comfortable and at home in their spaces of work, home, and leisure. They turned the tables on what they saw as a modernist contempt for the everyday person and his or her pedestrian tastes. The everyday, in the form of sculptures of chickens, larger-than-life donuts and other visual jokes adorning fast-food joints and the tacky flourish and flashing lights of cheap motels, was represented in *Learning from Las Vegas*, which helped architects and a broader readership notice the importance of the visual culture of mass consumption that had grown up in the years since World War II. Appropriation, pastiche, and bricolage were everywhere apparent in the design of the Vegas Strip, not as intentional expressions of a culture of critique but as means through which the postmodern subject communicated and interacted with and through its built environment. The tacky, the trashy, and the crass were embraced as an iconography and design form of the masses, who did not ignorantly embrace these approaches but who saw humor and took pleasure in the tongue-in-cheek display of "bad" taste and cheesy glitz. *Learning from Las Vegas* became a postmodern primer for theorists of modernism who, through this book, came to understand that the ideal of universal design, with its insistence on functionality and its rejection of decoration, metaphor, and symbolism, ignored the important ways that these elements functioned as cultural signifiers of the masses spontaneously forging a world of expression from the ground up, out of the consumer spaces of postwar culture.

This critique of the failures of modern architecture is a key aspect of postmodern architecture. Architecture critic Charles Jencks writes that postmodern architecture emerged when modern architecture died, with the demolition of the Pruitt-Igoe housing project in St. Louis, Missouri, in 1972. The Pruitt-Igoe complex had been constructed according to the progressive ideals of modern architecture when it was built in 1951, with a style influenced by Le Corbusier's concepts of urbanism; yet it had failed as a structure for public housing, becoming a site of crime, vandalism, and decay.[23] Jencks and others see the double coding of postmodernism as a means for it to communicate to residents and workers in ways that these modern buildings failed to do. Thus postmodern architecture can stress contextualization (buildings that speak to the architectural environments in which they are situated) and the capacity to speak on several levels at once, signaling simultaneously references to high architecture and mass culture.

As a key strategy of postmodern architecture, pastiche relates to this strategy of contextualization. Many architectural designs of postmodern style deploy a kind of plagiarizing, quoting, and borrowing of previous and current styles, through which the very notions of architectural lineage and authenticity are radically called into question. For example, Philip Johnson's well-known design for the AT&T building (now the Sony building) in New York is a modern tower topped with a sculpted pediment, often referred to as a Chippendale motif. The building creates an unusual profile in the New York skyline and, in a certain sense, the reference to Chippendale style, or to furniture, makes the building, which has a similar high archway entrance, seem like a kind of wardrobe piece, as if it is simultaneously being ornate and making fun of ornamentation. The building's playful engagement with ornamentation is also a reaction against the functionalism of modern architecture. Importantly, this kind of architectural pastiche of mixing different historical styles makes no statement about history and has no sense of rules about what is "right" for design but rather is a playful quoting, borrowing, pilfering, and combining of different design styles, genres, and forms. Pastiche works in defiance of the concept of progress—the idea, for instance, that styles get better as they evolve. The notion of progress so fundamental to modernist design and architecture is thus implicitly critiqued by postmodernism's studied disregard for the new. In modernism, style follows a linear course, each new style building on and progressing forward from the last by introducing more functionality or a better design. In postmodernism, styles can be mixed with no sense that we are moving toward something better.

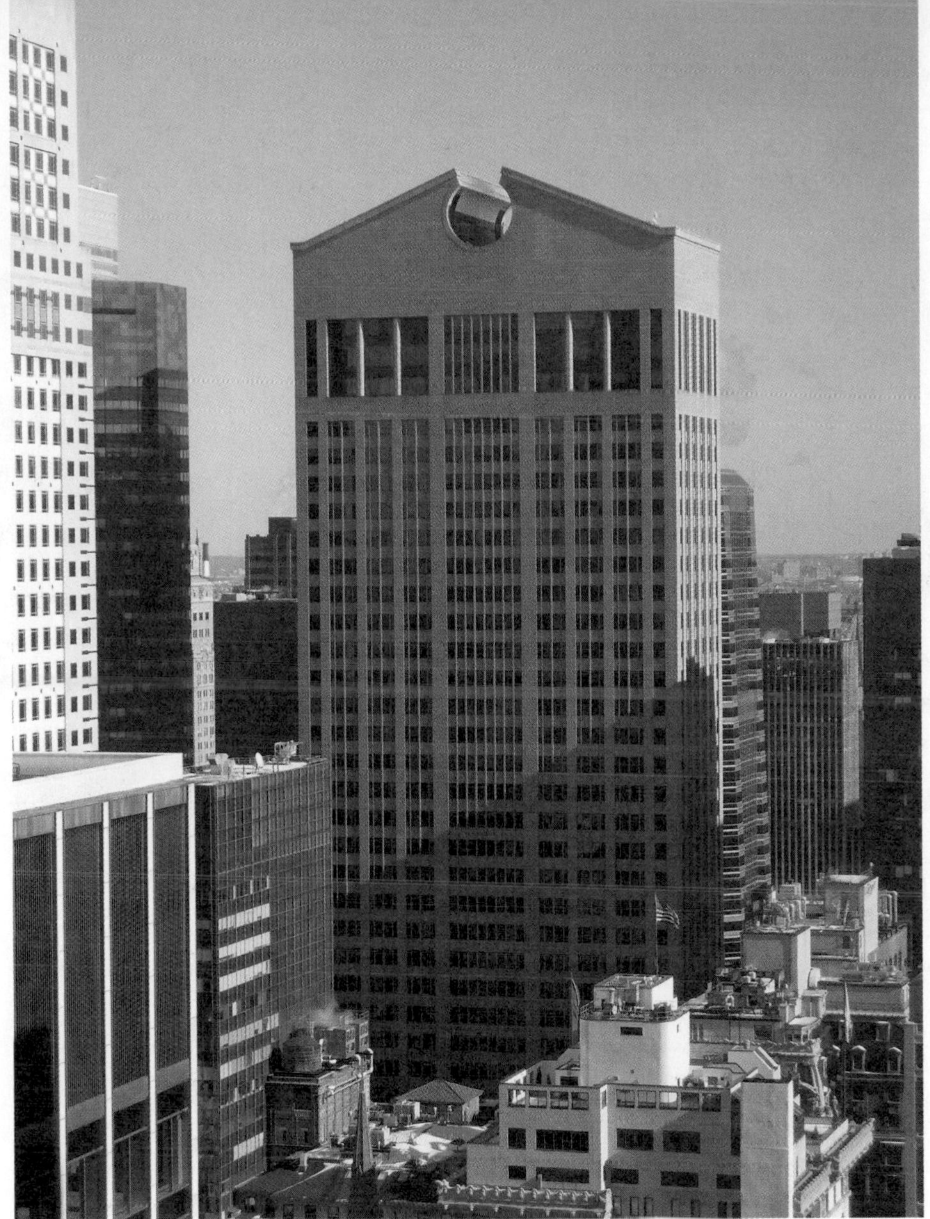

FIG. 8.15
Philip Johnson, AT&T building, now the Sony building, New York

In addition, many elements of postmodern buildings explicitly defy the notion of architecture as functional. An arch may have no structural function, and its use may reside in the humor of existing without a function, as mere decoration. A passage may lead nowhere, a facade may conceal nothing, and a Greek column might stand next to a Gothic arch. This is all done toward a playful undermining of some basic architectural principles and a celebration of surface that works simultaneously as a joke about architecture's functional role. Pastiche allows elements of architectural form to act as free-floating signifiers, detached from their original historical or functional context, which can constantly change meaning from different angles and in different contexts. In keeping with the respect for low and consumer culture epitomized in *Learning from Las Vegas*, many of the most famous architectural designs of the postmodern period have been spaces of public consumption, such as shopping malls.

Playing with the functionality of buildings is also a key aspect of postmodernism design. Thus a building such as the Centre Georges Pompidou in the Beaubourg

FIG. 8.16
Renzo Piano and Richard Rogers, Centre Georges Pompidou building

section of Paris (for this reason, the building is commonly known as Beaubourg), which was designed by Renzo Piano and Richard Rogers and which houses the Museé d'Art Moderne Nationale and other cultural institutions, has a design that turns the building inside out, with the functions of the building, such as air ducts and air conditioning, plumbing, and elevators color coded and placed on the exterior in the "exoskeleton" of the building. Rather than masking the functions of the building on its interior, the building displays these functional systems as its ornamentation, on its skin. Here we could say that the building is playing with the elements of building function, making them look like colorful elements at play in the surrounding environment.

Postmodern architecture has also redirected attention toward a more pluralistic set of structures for habitation, rejecting the preoccupation with corporate structures and high-art cultural institutions that were embraced in modern architecture. The architecture of sheds and shantytowns are forms engaged with by the contemporary architect Teddy Cruz, whose designs and writings are situated across transnational contexts such as the border cities of San Diego and Tijuana. In contrast to the modernists and many of the postmodern architects who worked primarily in the design of large-scale structures built for those corporations or individuals at the wealthiest end of the economic spectrum, Cruz emphasizes the importance of the built spaces of those at the lowest end of the economic spectrum—the border settlements and shantytowns of migrant workers, for example, or the cardboard structures of people who are homeless and living in the margins of urban spaces, under roadway bridges and in the urban canyons of public parks. Cruz considers the logics of postmodernity—its production of global subjects in the form of migrant

FIG. 8.17
Teddy Cruz design for housing in Tijuana

workers, undocumented immigrants, and homeless families who craft a new kind of nomadic living out of the everyday materials at hand, such as the castoffs of urban construction sites and the packaging left over from purchases in the consumer and business sectors.

One of the primary issues that hovers over the concepts of postmodernism is the degree to which they are a response to the fading and shifting aspects of modernism and the degree to which they signal a new era of some kind, a new episteme, a new way of thinking and being, a new way of making art, popular culture, and buildings, a new way of writing fiction, and so on. The self-consciousness of postmodernism is potentially itself a phenomenon that will fold in on itself until its viability seems limited. As we noted in the beginning of this chapter, we do not live in a world of postmodernism but rather in a world in which the tensions of modernity and postmodernity are active and present, a world that has many populations living in what can only be called premodern life situations of poverty and subsistence. How those worlds are entering into modern and postmodern domains can be dramatically different from the traditional trajectory of European-American societies. For instance, when locations of subsistence living acquire cell phone technology before they have a basic industrial economy, how does that change these contexts? These examples from postmodern architecture allow us to see postmodernism within a global frame that opens it up to political possibilities. Whereas Venturi's firm, in *Learning from Las Vegas*, emphasized the importance of seeing and respecting the visual culture of the commercial architecture of mass consumption, Cruz emphasizes the importance of seeing and noticing the visual and material culture of the bricoleurs, the appropriators, and the pastiche workers who use these postmodern approaches not simply to forge a new style but to live in the margins of a world economy. Global capitalism produces subjects who exist farther from the centers of economic wealth and technological advancement than ever before due to globalization's production of an ever wider economic divide yet who are nevertheless global, and it is their appropriative fashioning of the materials at hand to make do and find a place that shows us the tensions of the modern, the postmodern, the postindustrial, and the global at once.

Notes

1. Jean Baudrillard, *Simulacra and Simulation*, trans. Sheila Faria Glaser, 2 (Ann Arbor: University of Michigan Press, 1981).
2. Valerie Jaffee, "An Interview with Jia Zhange-ke," *Senses of Cinema* (June 2004), www.sensesofcinema.com (accessed March 2008).
3. Jean Baudrillard, *The Evil Demon of Images*, trans. Paul Patton and Paul Foss, 29 (Sydney: University of Sydney, 1988).
4. Vivian Sobchack, "Beating the Meat/Surviving the Text: or, How to Get Out of This Century Alive," in *Cyberspace/Cyberbodies/Cyberpunk: Cultures of Technological Embodiment*, ed. Mike Featherstone and Roger Burrows, 205–14 (Thousand Oaks, Calif.: Sage, 1995).
5. Fredric Jameson, *Postmodernism, or, the Cultural Logic of Late Capitalism* (Durham, N.C.: Duke University Press, 1991).
6. David Harvey, *The Condition of Postmodernity: An Inquiry into the Origins of Cultural Change*, 284 (Oxford, U.K.: Blackwell, 1990).
7. Jean-François Lyotard, *Postmodernism: A Report on Knowledge*, trans. Geoff Bennington and Brian Massumi (Minneapolis: University of Minnesota Press, 1984).
8. Santiago Colás, *Postmodernity in Latin America: The Argentine Paradigm*, ix (Durham, N.C.: Duke University Press, 1994).
9. See, for example, Gilles Deleuze and Félix Guatarri, *A Thousand Plateaus: Schizophrenia and Capitalism*, trans. Brian Massumi (Minneapolis: University of Minnesota Press, 1987).
10. Harvey, *The Condition of Postmodernity*, 350–51.
11. Scott Bukatman, *Blade Runner* (London: British Film Institute, 1997).
12. Umberto Eco, *Postscript to the Name of the Rose*, 67–68 (New York: Harcourt Brace Jovanovich, 1984).
13. Russell Ferguson, "Let's Be Nikki," in *Nikki S. Lee: Projects*, 17 (Ostfildern-Ruit, Germany: Hatje Cantz, 2001).
14. Lisa Nakamura, *Digitizing Race: Visual Cultures of the Internet*, 70–94 (Minneapolis: University of Minnesota Press, 2007).
15. Richard Dyer, *Pastiche*, 1–6 (New York: Routledge, 2007).
16. Numerous fan web sites chart these parodies, including http://www.joeydevilla.com/2007/09/22/simpsons-scenes-and-their-reference-movies/ (accessed March 2008).
17. Peter Galassi, *Jeff Wall*, 43 (New York: Museum of Modern Art, 2007).
18. Linda Hutcheon, "Beginning to Theorize Postmodernism," *Textual Practice* 1.1 (1987), 25.
19. Christian Boltanski, quoted in Ernst van Alphen, *Caught by History: Holocaust Effects in Contemporary Art, Literature, and Theory*, 93 (Stanford, Calif.: Stanford University Press, 1997).
20. Marianne Hirsch, *Family Frames: Photography, Narrative, and Postmemory*, 257 (Cambridge, Mass.: Harvard University Press, 1997).
21. Dyer, *Pastiche*, 180.
22. See Anthony Giddens, *The Consequences of Modernity* (Stanford, Calif.: Stanford University Press, 1990).
23. Charles Jencks, *The Language of Post-Modern Architecture* (New York: Rizzoli, 1984).

Further Reading

Anderson, Perry. *The Origins of Postmodernity*. London: Verso, 1998.

Augé, Marc. *Non-places: Introduction to an Anthropology of Supermodernity*. Translated by John Howe. London: Verso, 1995.

Baudrillard, Jean. *The Evil Demon of Images*. Translated by Paul Patton and Paul Foss. Sydney: University of Sydney, 1988.

———. *Simulacra and Simulation*. Translated by Sheila Faria Glaser. Ann Arbor: University of Michigan Press, 1994.

Cahoone, Lawrence. *From Modernism to Postmodernism: An Anthology*. Oxford, U.K.: Blackwell, 1996.

Colás, Santiago. *Postmodernity in Latin America: The Argentine Paradigm*. Durham, NC: Duke University Press, 1994.

Deleuze, Gilles, and Félix Guattari. *A Thousand Plateaus: Schizophrenia and Capitalism*. Translated by Brian Massumi. Minneapolis: University of Minnesota Press, 1987.

———. *Anti-Oedipus: Capitalism and Schizophrenia*. Translated by Robert Hurley, Mark Seem, and Helen R. Lane. Minneapolis: University of Minnesota Press, [1977] 1983.

Docherty, Thomas, ed. *Postmodernism: A Reader*. New York: Columbia University Press, 1993.

Dyer, Richard. *Pastiche*. New York: Routledge, 2007.

Friedberg, Anne. *Window Shopping: Cinema and the Postmodern*. Berkeley: University of California Press, 1993.

Galassi, Peter. *Jeff Wall*. New York: Museum of Modern Art, 2007.

Goldman, Robert. *Reading Ads Socially*. New York: Routledge, 1992.

——— and Stephen Papson. *Sign Wars: The Cluttered Landscape of Advertising*. New York: Guilford, 1996.

Hall, Stuart. "On Postmodernism and Articulation: An Interview with Stuart Hall." In *Stuart Hall: Critical Dialogues in Cultural Studies*. Edited by David Morley and Kuan-Hsing Chen. New York: Routledge, 1996.

Harvey, David. *The Condition of Postmodernity: An Inquiry into the Origins of Cultural Change*. Oxford, U.K.: Blackwell, 1990.

Hirsch, Marianne. *Family Frames: Photography, Narrative, and Postmemory*. Cambridge, Mass.: Harvard University Press, 1997.

Hutcheon, Linda. *The Politics of Postmodernism*. 2nd ed. New York: Routledge [1989] 2002.

Huyssen, Andreas. *After the Great Divide: Modernism, Mass Culture, Postmodernism*. Bloomington: Indiana University Press, 1986.

Jameson, Fredric. *Postmodernism, or, The Cultural Logic of Late Capitalism*. Durham, N.C.: Duke University Press, 1991.

Jencks, Charles. *The Language of Post-Modern Architecture*. New York: Rizzoli, 1984.

Lyotard, Jean-François. *Postmodernism: A Report on Knowledge*. Translated by Geoff Bennington and Brian Massumi. Minneapolis: University of Minnesota Press, 1984.

Martin, Lesley A., ed. *Nikki S. Lee: Projects*. Essay by Russell Ferguson. Ostfildern-Ruit, Germany: Hatje Cantz, 2001 (distributed in U.S. by Distributed Art Publishers, New York).

McRobbie, Angela. *Postmodernism and Popular Culture*. New York: Routledge, 1994.

Venturi, Robert, Denise Scott Brown, and Steven Izenour. *Learning from Las Vegas: The Forgotten Symbolism of Architectural Form*. Cambridge, Mass.: MIT Press, 1972; rev. ed., 1977.

Wallis, Brian, ed. *Art after Modernism: Rethinking Representation*. New York: New Museum, 1984.

chapter nine

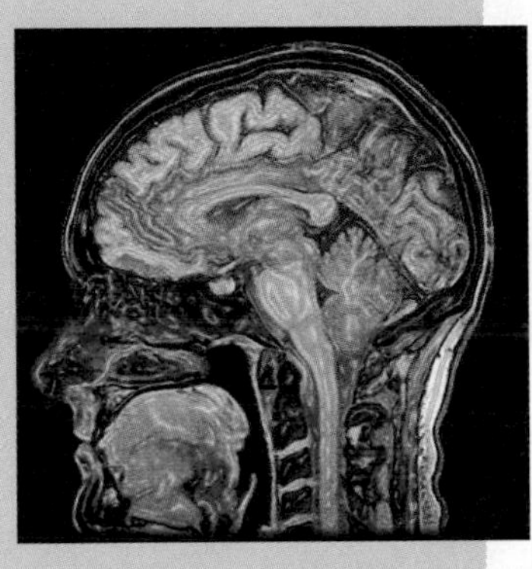

Scientific Looking, Looking at Science

Throughout this book, we have emphasized the ways that images and ways of looking in certain contexts affect how we look across a range of social arenas. We have stressed that our experiences and interpretations of images are never singular, discrete events but are informed by a broader set of conditions and factors. The term *visual culture* encompasses a wide range of forms, from fine art to popular film and television to advertising to visual data in fields that we tend to think of as distinct from culture—the sciences, law, and medicine, for example. Because scientific imagery often comes to us with confident authority behind it, in the form of images made by experts, we may assume these images are objective representations of knowledge, whether we view them through the popular media or through professional publications. But as we show in this chapter, scientific images and looking practices are as dependent on cultural context and culturally informed interpretation as images from popular culture, art, and the news.

Scientific looking does not occur in isolation from other cultural contexts, although society may have some stake in seeing science as a separate social realm, less encumbered by ideology or cultural meaning. The idea that science is a separate social realm, dedicated to discovering laws of nature unaffected by ideologies or politics, has been a myth surrounding the hard sciences. Scholarship in science studies of the past few decades has shown, however, that scientific knowledge depends on social, political, and cultural meanings and that what kind of science is practiced and rewarded is a highly political issue. Using Michel Foucault's term, we can analyze how the discourses of science, like all discourses, change over time, allowing for new subject positions to emerge and new ways of speaking about science to come into being.

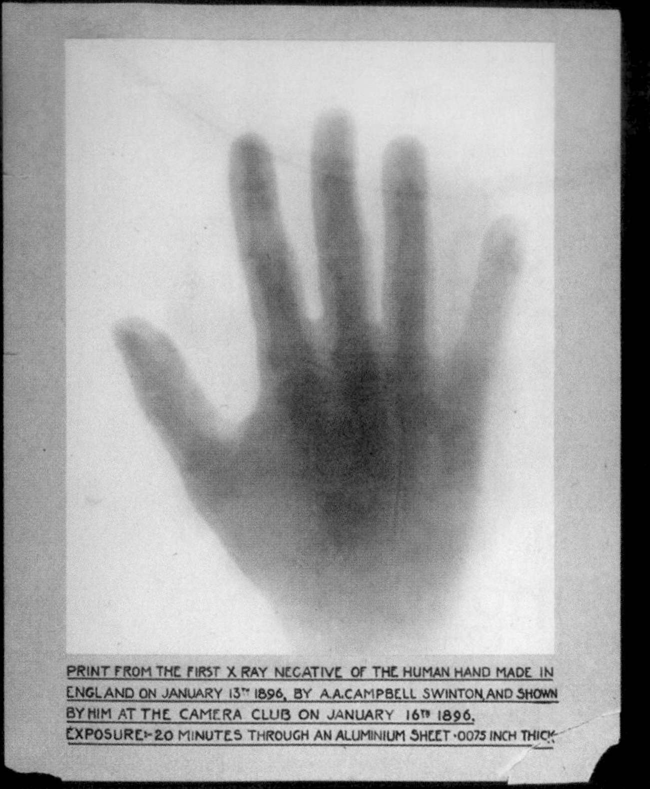

PRINT FROM THE FIRST X RAY NEGATIVE OF THE HUMAN HAND MADE IN ENGLAND ON JANUARY 13TH 1896, BY A.A.CAMPBELL SWINTON, AND SHOWN BY HIM AT THE CAMERA CLUB ON JANUARY 16TH 1896.
EXPOSURE:-20 MINUTES THROUGH AN ALUMINIUM SHEET ·0075 INCH THICK

FIG. 9.1
X-ray negative of the human hand, 1896

It is crucial to our inquiry that we see scientific images as integral to the production and meanings of images in popular culture, art, advertising, and the law. Although scientific images carry with them particularly strong meanings (as evidence of the real or truth, for example), they are also aesthetic objects. Take, for instance, this image from 1896 of the first X ray taken of a hand in England. The image was a technological achievement yet is nonetheless aesthetically pleasing. The hand seems to be a shadow here, evoking not only its form and the bones within it but also a sense of presence of the body and the meaning of hands as a symbol of individuality. The soft tones of the image give it an ethereal quality, evoking a hand from the past.

Since the origins of photography in the early nineteenth century, scientific and medical images and imaging methods have been important aspects of the history and development of photography, motion picture film, and digital media. It is an interesting paradox that although photographs have played an important role in experimental practice, as well as in the production of scientific, medical, and legal evidence, cameras are still banned as means of documentation in U.S. courts of law. With the rise of computers and digital imaging in the late twentieth century, images and visual inscriptions of data became more important aspects of conducting experiments, rendering information, and communicating ideas in science and medicine. The rise of technologies such as X ray, CT (computed tomography) or CAT (computerized axial tomography) and PET (positron emission tomography) scanning, ultrasound, and MRI (magnetic resonance imaging) throughout the twentieth century leads us to suggest that there was a worldwide shift toward the visual means of representing knowledge and evidence in science and a growth in the area of expert images—images we understand to make sense within specialized terms legible to trained professionals who can read their codes. Continuing the previous century's scientific interest in developing instruments such as the microscope and methods such as anatomical dissection, twentieth-century scientists developed technologies for seeing even in cases in which the object or process under study is not easily visualizable or not understood to have optical properties.

"Seeing the unseen" is a motif that has recurred throughout the long history of science and medicine. This motif was newly energized with the introduction of digital imaging and rendering techniques at the end of the twentieth century. Think of ultrasound imaging in medicine, in which sound waves are used to measure the boundaries of interior soft-tissue structures and the resulting measurements are translated into moving images, or the practice of using computer animation to visually represent the speed and trajectory of sound waves in physics. In these examples, acoustic events and data are represented in visual images. Here we encounter another paradox concerning imaging technologies in science and medicine: some of what we look at in scientific and medical imaging is not what we would typically consider to be within the domain of the visual. Visualization has escalated to encompass the acoustic and tactile world with the increased availability of digital rendering and display mechanisms. The increased use of visualization processes and visual images to represent all sorts of sensory information has changed not only how scientists pursue knowledge but also what scientists seek to know. In other words, knowledge—its objects and its processes—has changed with this shift toward the visual in ways of knowing the world.

British theorist of science and medicine Nikolas Rose proposes that in the twenty-first century, we have come to know life through a biomedical paradigm, and we have begun to experience our bodies at the scale of the molecular, a scale we cannot exactly see but which we conceptualize through systems of scientific representation such as genetic code. It is at the molecular level that we understand and engineer life itself in the twenty-first century.[1] We see this reflected in scientific representations of molecules and genes depicting forms or aspects of life. We also experience life on an everyday level as something that can be managed and lived at the molecular level. For example, we understand our diseases in terms of their molecular structures and genetic bases. We understand that drug therapies work in our systems on a molecular level. Research into areas such as stem cells and nanotechnology (working with matter at an ultrasmall scale) suggests a shift in the scale through which we understand life to be organized and managed on an everyday basis. Visualization and imaging technologies provide a crucial set of tools for structuring knowledge about life at this molecular level. It is not easy for us to perceive life at this minute level without technologies designed to bring to light that which cannot be seen by the unaided eye. These new means of visualizing and understanding the body are organized through a network of metaphors. Thus concepts of the body as genetic code are related to concepts of the body as molecular, which are in turn related to concepts of the body within the framework of the digital, as something that can be modified, reworked, and transformed at the cellular level. These systems are both literal, describing ways of knowing the body, and metaphorical, helping to shape new ways of imagining the self as a lived, material entity. Whereas before, anatomy and physiology may have organized our way of seeing the body in terms of essential structure or as a system fundamentally in motion, now we see the body as a multiplicity of tiny oscillating units that play off one another in a network, units that we cannot see or control but which can recombine through covalent bonds, driven by charges and impulses, or driven by forces such as environment, pharmaceuticals, or imaging systems such as MRI

FIG. 9.2
Lesson in anatomy, c. 1493

(which is based on the idea of capturing a register of the decay time of proton spin). Not only is the body understood to be organized through these units in motion, but it is also understood to be changeable at this level of detail and specificity, with drug and genetic therapies, for example.

Thus it is important to keep in mind that science and culture are always mutually engaged. Indeed, science is a set of cultures, and its practices are culturally specific. Science intersects with other areas of knowledge and culture and draws on those systems in its day-to-day practices. In this chapter, we consider the various ways that images come into play both in scientific practices and in media appropriations of scientific methods and approaches. We put forward the view that ways of scientific looking are culturally specific and are always caught up in other cultural practices of looking. We begin with a discussion of how human bodies have been imagined in the history of science and medicine and then discuss more contemporary examples.

The Theater of Science

The anatomy of the body has been a topic of representation and source of interest for artists throughout many centuries. As we noted in chapter 4, the Renaissance was a period during which art and science were seen as parallel points of inquiry. Art historian Erwin Panofsky wrote that the rise of anatomy was integral to Renaissance art. Nowhere was this more evident than in the work of Leonardo da Vinci, who performed more than thirty dissections in his lifetime. Panofsky notes that as the science of anatomy became established, "painter-anatomists" depicted the bodies being dissected.[2] It is important to note that Leonardo's prominence throughout history as an artist who used scientific methods and whose work and identity became icons of science is due in part to the overlap of science and art in his work. Da Vinci's famous image of the human figure, *Vitruvian Man*, which was created around 1487, is a representation of the proportions of man based on the treatise *De Architectura* by

FIG. 9.3
Leonardo da Vinci, *Vitruvian Man*, c. 1487

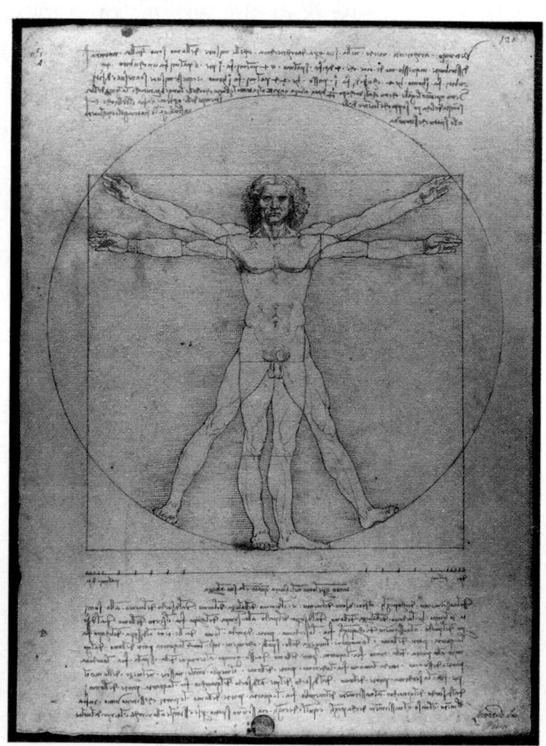

the Roman architect Vitruvius, which made reference to the relationship of geometry to ideal human proportions. The artist saw the human body as a microcosm of the universe. In depicting the figure within a circle and a square, the image is largely thought to convey da Vinci's concept that the body exists within both the material realm (symbolized by the square) and the spiritual realm (represented by the circle). *Vitruvian Man* is a world-renowned image from the history of art that has since come to symbolize practices of medicine and health. It is widely reproduced as a symbol of the interrelationship of the human body to laws of mathematics and structure in nature.

Representations of the practices of science and medicine throughout history have retained much of this fascination with anatomy. The sense that one can understand the body by cutting into it, physically or virtually, and exposing its organs to visual inspection has remained strong in medicine and science. As we discuss later in this chapter, the development of modern techniques for imaging the body's interior, such as X ray, CT scan, and MRI, replace the paradigm of anatomical knowledge through physical dissection with the belief that the body can be known through representational systems that allow us to see through the body's skin into its interior. But prior to these scientific developments, the practice of actually seeing the body's interior was limited to dissection and anatomical science. José van Dijck proposes that these imaging practices, from anatomy to X ray to endoscopy to digital scans, construct a transparent body, a body that the image appears to render more visible yet which in the process only becomes more complex.[3] In early modern society, many dissections (of animals and humans) were performed publicly. Anatomy theaters were, from the sixteenth century onward, a form of spectacle through which anatomists attempted not only to educate but also to entertain their audiences of colleagues, students, and lay spectators. In these theaters, the practice of science was presented as a wonder and a view into the mysterious borderland between life and death.

The anatomy theater of Leiden in the Netherlands, which was built in 1596, was an important site for this kind of theatrical practice of anatomy. In this print, the theater is represented with a dissection underway at the central table, surrounded by animal skeletons and onlookers. This image is both a representation of the anatomy theater and a symbolic rendering of its interactions of animal and human forms and between the living spectators and the skeletal forms that inhabit the space. The Leiden theater was widely known and a popular site for visitors, so much so that guidebooks to the collection of anatomical

FIG. 9.4
Leiden Anatomy Theater, 1610

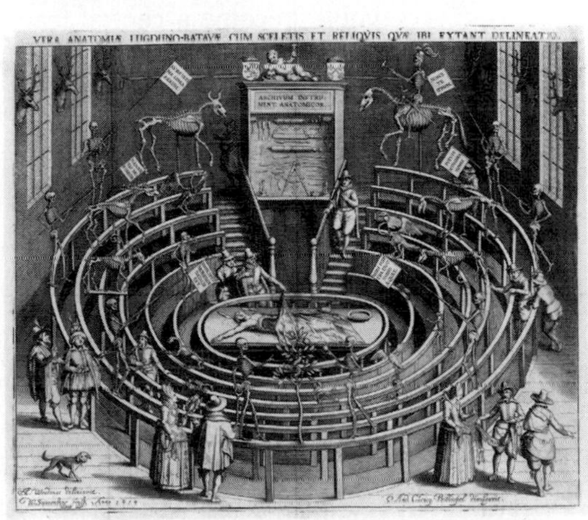

specimens held there were created in the late 1600s. The theater and Anatomy Hall included arrangements of skeletons that were intended to convey moral messages about the deceased, most of whom were criminals whose bodies the physicians had dissected in the theater. Such moralizing displays were justified by the status of these corpses as former criminals.[4] Van Dijck notes that it was the anatomist, rather than the cadaver, who was the actor and focal point of the anatomical theater.[5]

One of the most famous historical images of anatomy is Rembrandt's *The Anatomy Lesson of Dr. Nicolaes Tulp*, painted in 1632. In this painting, the observers attending the annual public dissection at the Amsterdam Guild of Surgeons gaze on both the corpse and a medical textbook which lies to the right. The main focal point of the painting is not simply the corpse (that of Aris the Kid, a criminal hanged earlier that day) and the exposed arm on which Dr. Tulp, the Amsterdam city anatomist, begins his dissection, but also on the gazes of the onlookers. This image opens up depictions of the theater of science to our observation of the pleasures and fascinations of the observers of such displays. The image is, in fact, a composite that Rembrandt created from his own observations. Rembrandt cast the face of the dead man in shadow (*umbra mortis*) to suggest death. Such a painting is thus not simply a document of the practice of science in its time, it is also a portrait of the social relations around that practice, with the inclusion of important figures of Amsterdam society in the painting as a means to affirm their social standing against the body of a social outcast.

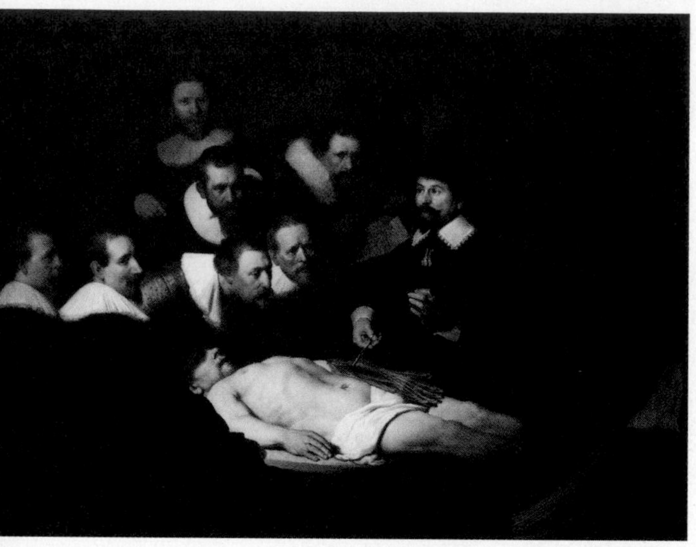

FIG. 9.5
Rembrandt van Rijn, *The Anatomy Lesson of Dr. Nicolaes Tulp*, 1632

A fascination with the dead body and an association of morbidity and crime would become a central feature of the visual spectacle of modernity. As Vanessa Schwartz writes, the Paris morgue became the site of spectacular displays in the late nineteenth century when certain types of dead bodies, in particular those of children who drowned in the Seine River or the body of a dismembered woman, were put on display. Hundreds of thousands of Parisians came to see these corpses as if the morgue were a kind of free theater. The morgue photographed the unidentified dead whose bodies had decomposed, but they also put unidentified bodies on display for public view in the exhibition room, creating a spectacle that commentators compared to the pleasures of viewing goods in department store windows. As Schwartz notes, "To many observers, the morgue simply satisfied and reinforced the desire to look. . . . One newspaper put it simply: 'people go to the morgue to see.' "[6] We are reminded of the Weegee photograph, *The First Murder*, discussed in chapter 1. As the spectacle of the morgue became too infamous, the Paris police closed it down for public consumption, but not before the morgue officials had begun to create wax replicas of the corpses, a practice that would give rise to the city's wax museums.

The desire to look into and upon the body is also a part of the fascination with the emerging practice of surgery in the late nineteenth century. One of the most famous American realist paintings of the nineteenth century is Thomas Eakins's *The Gross Clinic* (1875). It depicts Dr. Samuel Gross at age seventy in a fancy black coat, presiding in a theater-like setting at the Jefferson Medical College. Dr. Gross is at the center of the composition and he is brightly lit, surrounded by assistants and by figures in the shadowy background. But the body under surgical intervention draws our attention. Surgery was not practiced at this time in a sterile environment, but rather in an open setting with onlookers (Eakins would create another painting, *The Agnew Clinic*, in 1889, that shows a surgical theater that is more brightly lit and clean). Eakins was a key figure of nineteenth-century realism, and the painting is often admired for its realistic depiction of the surgical theater, with the bloodied hands of the doctors as the focal point of the work. At the time, the painting was considered to be shocking (Gross's bloodied right hand holds a scalpel), and the painting was rejected for the 1876 Centennial Exhibition. It has since been analyzed from many perspectives, including a psychoanalytic one that considers the painting's dynamic of gazes and the ambiguous gender status of the patient on the table.[7] At the center of these discussions about the painting is the question of how to interpret the woman on the left of the painting, who may be a relative or perhaps the mother of the patient. She responds to what she sees differently from the professional men, who exhibit clinical distance. She expresses emotional distress, recoiling from the scene and hiding her face (like the woman in fig. 1.1) in order to obliterate the view that the others in the painting so eagerly take in. She is, as Michael Fried argues, the surrogate for the viewer who both wants to look and is overcome by the spectacle.[8] We can also see behind her Eakins sitting and calmly drawing the spectacle around him. The painting is thus a portrait of our simultaneous revulsion and fascination with the body and

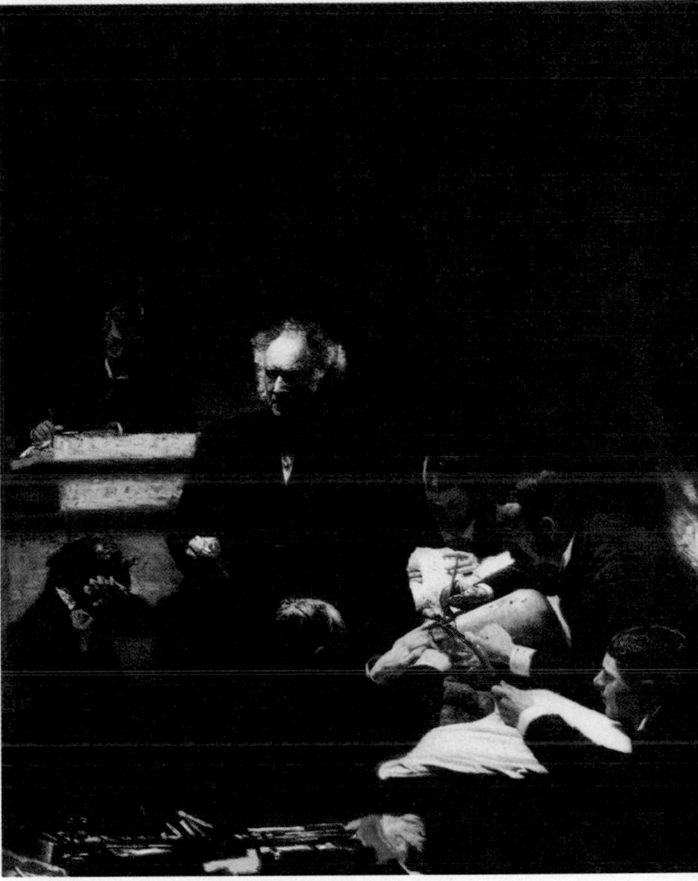

FIG. 9.6
Thomas Eakins, *Portrait of Dr. Samuel D. Gross (The Gross Clinic)*, 1875

its interior at the same time that it is emblematic of the tradition of likening bold acts of looking to heroic acts of healing.

With the development of photography in the early nineteenth century and the development of technologies to see into the body, beginning with the X ray in 1895, the relationship of images to science becomes one of providing evidence of the body's interior and cataloguing the body into types. Yet the relationship of anatomy to imaging has not faded into the past. In fact, two recent manifestations of the imaging of anatomy have demonstrated that the early practices of anatomy theaters retain a visual power: the Visible Human Project and the Body Worlds exhibition. Each raises the same kinds of questions that traditional anatomy has raised, and each makes evident the powerful desire for the transparent body.

The Visible Human Project (VHP) is a venture funded by the U.S. government and created at the Center for Human Simulation at the University of Colorado, Boulder. It involves taking two bodies, the Visible Male and the Visible Female, and creating digital images of them essentially slice by slice. The bodies were frozen and then literally sliced, and those slices were then digitally photographed to create a virtual body of each. The final images were then placed on public view on the website of the project in the mid-1990s and are available on CD. Proponents of the project saw it as a valuable educational tool that can supplement if not take the place of standard anatomical dissection. Inevitably, of course, this project of scientific images has complex cultural meanings, and questions have arisen about the ethics involving the bodies used for the project. The corpse used to make the Visible Male turned out to be that of a death row inmate who donated his body to the project in exchange for execution by lethal injection instead of the electric chair.[9]

The widely seen Body Worlds exhibition is another contemporary example of medical display, this time of actual dead bodies that have undergone a preservative process called plastination and that are put on display in various poses in an exhibition that has traveled the world. Gunther von Hagens, the notorious director of the Body Worlds project (and its Institute of Plastination in Germany) assumes the role of both a scientist and an artist, fashioning himself in the image of the late German artist Joseph Beuys to the point that he has been referred to as "die Leichen Beuys" ("the cadaver Beuys").[10] Von Hagens actually performed a public anatomical dissection in London in 2002, thus situating himself quite specifically in the history of the public anatomical theater. Von Hagens's project has been highly controversial. He has been accused of using the cadavers of Chinese prisoners, which his organization denies, although they are unable to verify the origin of the earlier Chinese corpses that they used. This resulted in the demand by the New York State Attorney General's Office in 2008 that the exhibition state that it could not verify whether some specimens were from victims who were tortured or executed in Chinese prisons. Hagens's process of bodily plastination has also been debated on moral grounds. The displays of the exhibit not surprisingly tend to affirm traditional gender stereotypes, with male figures in active scenarios, such as a soccer game, and the female figures shown in traditional states, such as pregnancy. The figures are posed with their layers of flesh pulled back to reveal organs, nerves, blood vessels, and muscle tissue. Some are posed to reference well-known art historical images. The Body Worlds project is disturbing not only because it involves the transformation and display of actual bodies but also because it transgresses particular categories of art and science display. As van Dijck notes in *The Transparent Body*, the project transgresses the boundaries between body and model, organic and synthetic, object and representation, fake and real, authentic and copy, and human and posthuman. In addition, the exhibition, like many of the other sets of images we have discussed here, bridges art and science and science and entertainment. It is this interrelationship between art, science, and popular consumption that underlies our discussion in this chapter. The desire to see art and science, or popular culture and science, as separate has a long history in Western philosophy, yet scientific images almost always beg the question of whether these domains can ever really be kept absolutely separate.

Images as Evidence: Cataloguing the Body

The images we have been discussing follow a trajectory from symbolic and allegorical representations of science to realist modes of representing science in action. Scientific images have also played an important role as evidence in science and medicine. The photograph has played a particularly important role as evidence in this regard. Mechanical and electronic image-producing systems, such as photography and motion picture film, television, computer graphics, and digital photography, bear the legacy of positivism, a philosophical belief that true and valid knowledge about the world is knowledge derived from objective scientific method. Positivism was advanced by the philosopher Auguste Comte in the mid-nineteenth century at about the same time that photography gained popularity. Forms of positivism gained ground in the twentieth century, informing a broader ideology in which thinkers questioned the validity of subjective reasoning and the soundness of philosophical and spiritual metaphysics as means of understanding and explaining the world. Positivism has informed such fields as law, medicine, journalism, and the social sciences in cases in which practitioners favor objective study and measurement as means of more clearly perceiving reality without the subjective bias of empirical looking and thereby advancing progress, knowledge, and justice in the world. The photographic camera was regarded, in a positivist view, as a useful tool for mechanically observing, measuring, and studying the real world in a manner that could check, balance, or correct the errors introduced by subjective human perception.

The notion of photographic truth, as we noted in chapter 1, hinges on the ideas that the camera is an objective device for capturing reality and that it can render this objectivity despite the subjective vision of the person using the camera. The photographic image is thus, in its more positivist uses and contexts, regarded as an entity that is less burdened with the intentions of its maker than hand-rendered representations and is believed to offer the potential for revealing facts and truths. Yet, as we have seen, photographic images are nonetheless subjective cultural and social artifacts. Despite the black-boxing (hiding away inside the device) of their mechanisms, photographs require their producers to make subjective and culturally informed decisions, such as framing, composition, lighting, contextual display, and captioning. The easy manipulation and combination of digital images only takes these qualities of analog images further. Much of the meaning of camera-generated images is derived from the combination of the camera's persistent reputation for capturing reality with a high degree of objectivity and the photograph's capacity to evoke a sense of wonder through its capacity to make visible that which is difficult to see. This was done, in some cases, by freezing in time events that are so fleeting that they would be missed by the unaided eye, by magnifying small objects or by telescopically drawing closer objects outside the range of unaided vision, or by rendering nonoptical events into visual artifacts (images of sound waves, for example). Such photographs can be experienced as both magical and truthful at once.

With its emergence in the nineteenth century, photography was immediately seen as a powerful medium for science and medicine. It was taken up by scientists in laboratories and in the field and by physicians in medical hospitals and clinics and was integrated into existing medical optical devices. Photographs in these contexts provided visual records of phenomena and experiments. They were used to document diseases, to perform diagnoses, and to record and graphically represent scientific data. In modernity, the idea of seeing farther and better, beyond the capacity of the unaided human eye, had tremendous currency; in modern thought, to see is to know. The camera was imagined by some to be an objective aid to vision, if not an instrument with which to see the unseen, invisible aspects of the world. Every aspect of the physical world was subject to this expanded optical model of the gaze. Photographers took cameras up in hot-air balloons to photograph aerial views that few had seen before, much as astronauts would later do in their explorations of space and the moon. Scientists attached photographic cameras to microscopes to magnify views of structures too small for the unaided human eye to see. X rays, introduced to medicine as a diagnostic medium in the 1890s, offered a new vision of the interior of the living human body. At the time of their introduction, X rays were widely regarded as wondrous because they provided views of a previously unseen dimension of the body in its living state. At the same time, they were received with awe and fear because of the skeleton's iconographic association with death.[11] The microscopic and interior aspects of the body were just some of the frontiers that photography helped to traverse in the positivist era. The idea of the image or the imaging instrument as that which helps us see more, better, or further than the human eye continues to be a theme in scientific discourse in the twenty-first century. As we have noted, the development of photography launched a new era of scientific image-making focusing on bodily exteriors, interiors, and specimens (microscopic studies of tissue or blood, for example). In this section we discuss the use of photographs of the bodily exterior as a means of classifying people. In the following sections, we discuss the cultural and social implications of imaging inside the body.

Photography's use in systems set up to classify people is an important aspect of the history of photography. Modern systems of scientific taxonomy introduced in the eighteenth century by the Swedish botanist Carl Linnaeus grouped animals in a manner that did away with the subjectivity and arbitrariness of descriptive names alone. Linnaeus introduced a dual system that divided animals according to generic (genus) and specific (species) names. The Linnaean system grouped species according to an ideal morphology (shape). Taxonomists, or classifiers, who built on the Linnaean system of nomenclature in the natural sciences placed animals into more specific categories, such as class, family, and subspecies. They did not simply name and group animals on an even playing field. Rather, they ranked them according to a larger worldview that emphasized evolution and development. A taxonomic scheme reflects an evolutionary history (a phylogeny) from simpler to more complex, advanced forms. These schemas could be used to show or to predict how interbreeding within a species resulted, or may result, in changes due to the selective or random breeding in or breeding out of traits within the type.

The classification of humans was also of great interest during the nineteenth century, not only within the emergent field of human biology but also among public institutions charged with the function of providing services and managing humans. In the nineteenth century, as Foucault has explained, institutions charged with the management of populations divided their charges according to nomenclatures, such as the poor and the infirm, the feeble-minded, and criminals. These institutions—charity homes, hospitals, prisons—documented and classified the many human subjects who passed through their doors as a means of managing people in institutions rather than in private homes or the public spaces of communities. To feed and clothe an institutionalized population, the prevailing ideology stated, one must know how many and what age, size, and kinds of individuals are present. The desire to keep track of these burgeoning institutionalized populations stemmed in part from an emerging understanding among managers of these institutions that classificatory systems could be used as a means of social organization and control. These practices are key features of what Foucault called *biopower*.

The regard of the camera as an objective recording device made it a logical tool for managers to turn to in documenting and classifying the many residents of their institutions. In asylums for what was known as the feeble-minded, for example, photographic documentation was used to study individual cases and then classify residents into groups on the basis of empirically visible features thought to signify distinct mental disease states. Prisons managers used photographs not only to identify and classify the physical features of general criminal types but also to create identification records for each individual subject. The photographs were also useful in identifying repeat offenders. They supplemented forensic techniques such as fingerprinting (introduced in the nineteenth century) and preceded biometric scanning and DNA identification profiles (introduced in the late twentieth century). In the criminal justice system, the photograph (or today the DNA "biological photocopy") is a tool for getting at the truth of individual identity, used in the hope of eliminating the problems of failing to identify or misidentifying repeat offenders. The visual categorization of people according to types, and according to specific identity-linked characteristics, became common practice in hospitals, mental institutions, and government agencies by the end of the nineteenth century, and many of these institutions continue to employ photography as a tool for cataloguing subjects, diseases, and citizens into the twenty-first century.

FIG. 9.7
Skulls of women criminals, collected by Lombroso, in his *Atlas of the Criminal Man* (1896–97)

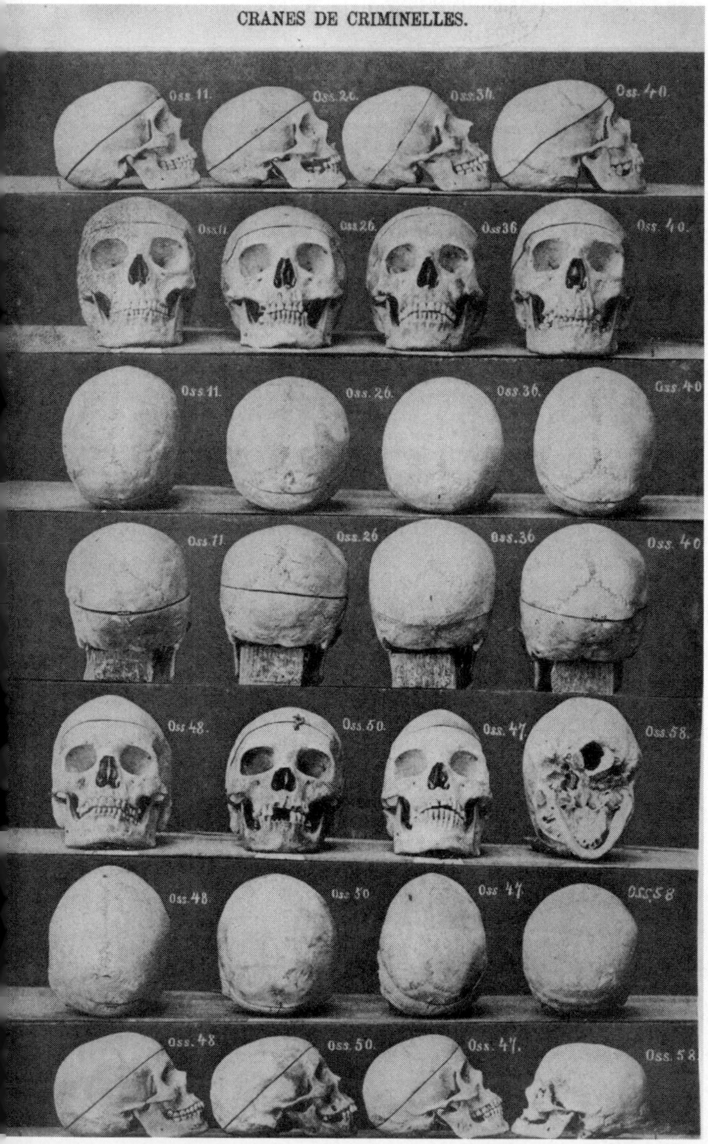

CRANES DE CRIMINELLES.

The practice of using drawings and photography to catalogue types according to the body's morphology, or shape, and appearance initially drew on the now-discredited technique of phrenology, popular between 1820 and 1850, and craniology, a slightly later phenomenon of the nineteenth century. Practitioners of phrenology, craniology (or craniometry), and physiognomy believed that the outward physical human body, and most particularly the cranium and the facial features, could be read for signs of temperament, moral capacity, health, or intelligence. Craniology is the nineteenth century science of skull measurement and tactile and visual analysis deployed to establish racial taxonomies for comparing the skulls of different races. Natural scientists used craniology to make claims about the supposed superiority of people of European or Anglo descent, and to try to show that people of African or Asian descent have more recent evolutionary ties to primates.[12] The use of these sciences of physical measurement and assessment by touch and sight was largely motivated by the racist agendas of colonial societies, which deployed science to justify their subjugation of nonwhite peoples, whom they claimed to be incapable of self-determination because of their supposed developmentally lower levels of intelligence, well-being, and so on. Physiognomy—interpreting the outward appearance and configuration of the body, and the face in particular—was popular prior to the 1900s, as represented in the work of Barthélemy Coclès who, in his *Physiognomonia* of 1533, went so far as to claim that the eyelashes of men signify inward sentiments such as pride and audacity. Understanding humankind to be categorizable into different racial groups and physical types was a central drive of nineteenth-century science. As we can see in this 1850 chart of the "Principal Varieties of Mankind," these systems typically placed the white European male in the center, with other racial types at the periphery.

FIG. 9.8
Depiction of human races with Europeans at the center. Color engraving by British artist John Emslie, *Principal Varieties of Mankind*, 1850

Physiognomists used photography as a tool to refine this sort of physical representation, measurement, and classification in ways that were also familiar in everyday life. Contemporary readers of Sherlock Holmes may puzzle over the line uttered by Moriarity, who, on meeting Sherlock Holmes, observes: "You have less frontal development than I should have expected." This comment reflects the sentiment, popular at the time, that the outward appearance of the face and the formation of the skull could be read for signs of inner intelligence, breeding, and moral standing. These qualities were also thought to be linked to racial type. In *The Races of Man*, a popular nonfiction book written in 1862 by John Beddoe, who would become a president of the Anthropological Institute, it is stated that there is a difference, both physical and intellectual, between those in Britain with protruding jaws and those with less prominent jaws. The Irish, Welsh, and the lower classes were among those with protruding jaws and a corresponding lower state of intelligence, Beddoe argued, whereas men of genius had less prominent jaws. Beddoe developed what he called an Index of Nigressence, a system of morphological classification on the basis of which he proposed that the Irish were closer than the English to the so-called Cro-Magnon man and thus had links with what he called the "Africinoid" races, which he regarded as lower in the evolutionary scale. In Beddoe's writing, we can see how a visual "science" of the body can be used to support a deeply racist cultural ideology. A modernist interpretation of craniology, phrenology, and physiognomy would tell us that these were pseudosciences, mere cultural ideology, and not true science. These practices produced myths, not facts about human life. A postmodern interpretation would take this analysis a step further to say that all science, including the most advanced contemporary practices, offer knowledge that is no less cultural, no less informed by ideology. This is not to say that the findings and claims of contemporary

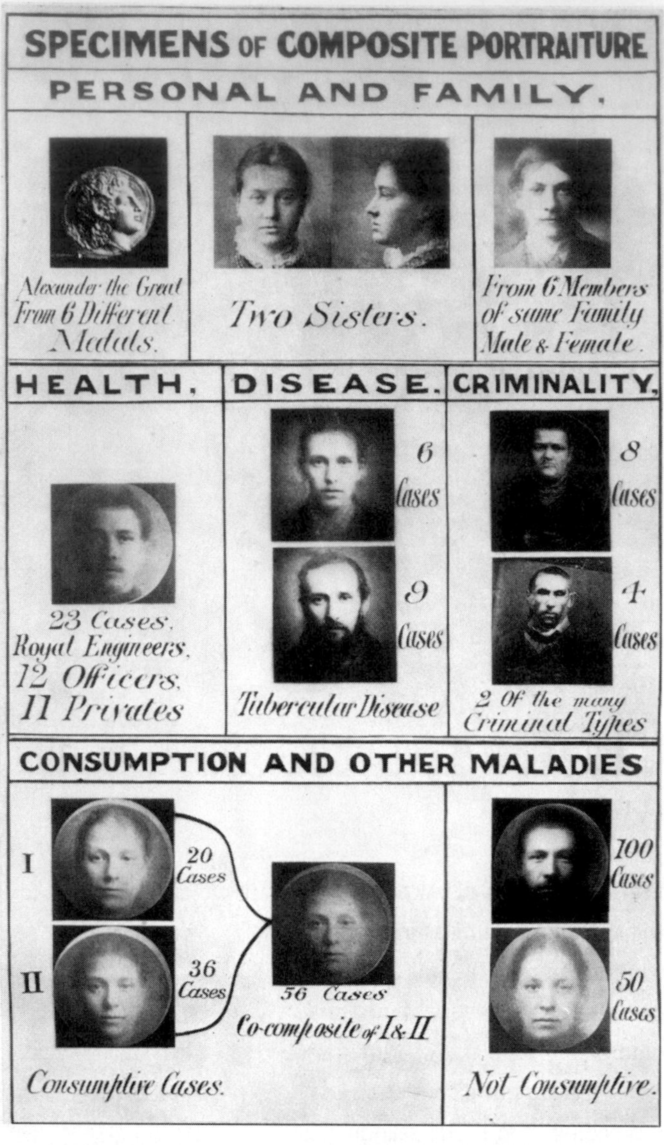

FIG. 9.9
Composite photography from Sir Francis Galton, *Inquiries into Human Faculty and Its Development*, 1883

are false, but that they are determined by current social thinking, and by the national, political, and economic contexts of the scientific practice. This *relativist* view of science was the subject of intense debate and critique in the 1990s, when authors, including Paul Gross and Norman Levitt in their 1994 book *Higher Superstition*, famously defended older ideals of truth and certainty, attacking the postmodern view that knowledge is socially constructed and contextual.

Craniology, phrenology, and other sciences of categorization were related to the science of eugenics, which was devoted to the practice of both studying and controlling human reproduction as a means of improving the human race. Eugenics was founded by Sir Francis Galton, author of a number of books, including the influential title *Hereditary Genius* (1869). In the eugenic view, not all races were deemed worthy of reproducing; that is, eugenics was guided by the belief that certain types and races should not breed in order to eliminate their traits from humankind. Galton, who was British, used measurement and the new method of statistics to "read" medical and social pathology off the surface of the body, and to analyze and compare traits. The frontispiece that appears in his 1883 *Inquiries into Human Faculties* shows us photographs of criminals, prostitutes, and people with tuberculosis. He was interested in producing a visual archive of types he regarded as deviant—types that deviated from norms of social behavior and mental and physical health. Galton even went so far as to make composite portraits of various people thought to have a given condition (see the superimposition of portraits of different people with consumption in the frontispiece reproduced here). He thought that these composites would better represent the general type of a category of people. His typologies, divided according to race, social deviance, and physical and mental pathology, were interlinked in troubling ways, suggesting that certain biological populations were more or less prone to illness and/or social deviance than other types. This idea would feed into racist eugenic political programs such as Nazism in Germany that used scientific discourse to justify genocide (the killing off of an ethnically or culturally linked group of people who are believed to constitute a genetically distinct group).

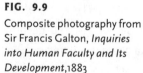

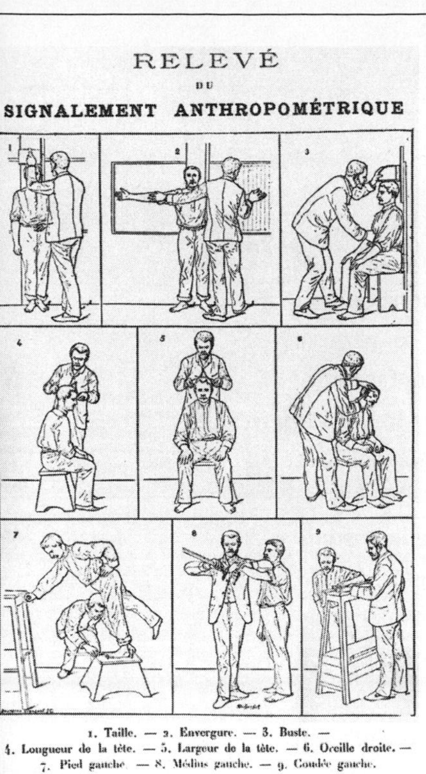

FIG. 9.10
Bertillon's system for anthropometric measurement, 1893

Simultaneously, photographic categorization was used as a practice to establish criminality as a trait linked to particular bodily characteristics such as a low forehead or narrow ("beady") eyes. In nineteenth-century Paris, police official Alphonse Bertillon created a system of measurement (or anthropometry) to identify the body types of criminals. Bertillon used photographs of subjects from the side and front as a means to identify what he saw as criminal characteristics, thus creating the first modern-day mug shots.[13] He created a vast archive of cards containing photographs of individuals measured against a system of types and anthropometric descriptions. Allan Sekula writes that "the projects of Bertillon and Galton constitute two methodological poles of the positivist attempts to define and regulate social deviance. . . . Both men were committed to technologies of demographic regulation."[14] Bertillon's system of anthropometry was used widely as a form of identification of faces and features such as ears before fingerprints became a more common source of identification at the turn of the century.

This kind of image cataloguing was used not only in the regulation of people caught up in the criminal justice system; it also quickly became a common practice in the nineteenth century to photograph hospital patients and people with particular medical conditions. As Foucault noted, the practices of organizing people in social institutions such as prisons and hospitals tend to be similar. In both prisons and hospitals, images were used to establish visual markers of what was considered to be normal and abnormal, and those markers were thus also in turn used to identify supposed criminal or sickly types. For instance, Cesare Lombroso, an Italian psychology and medical law professor, was convinced, like Bertillon, that criminality was biologically rooted, and he used photographs to classify physical traits of the criminal. In the mid-nineteenth century, Guillaume Duchenne de Boulogne, a French physician, used photographs to document experiments in which he applied electronic shock to subjects' faces in order to create a system for understanding facial expression. Duchenne's aim was to establish the universality of human expression, and photography was an essential tool in his project. In fig. 9.12, the subject is placed before the camera for a mug shot. In such a project we can see the power of the desire to catalogue and to create a map of human expressions alongside that of physical types.

FIG. 9.11
Alphonse Bertillon, *Identification anthropométrique: Instructions Signaletiques*, 1893

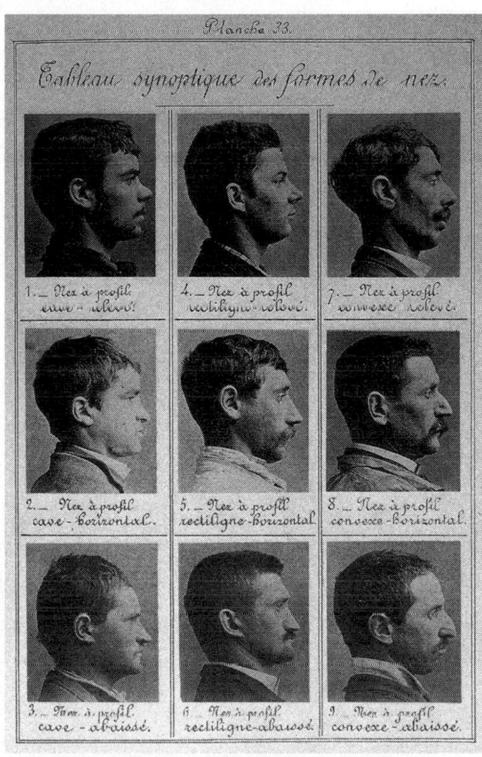

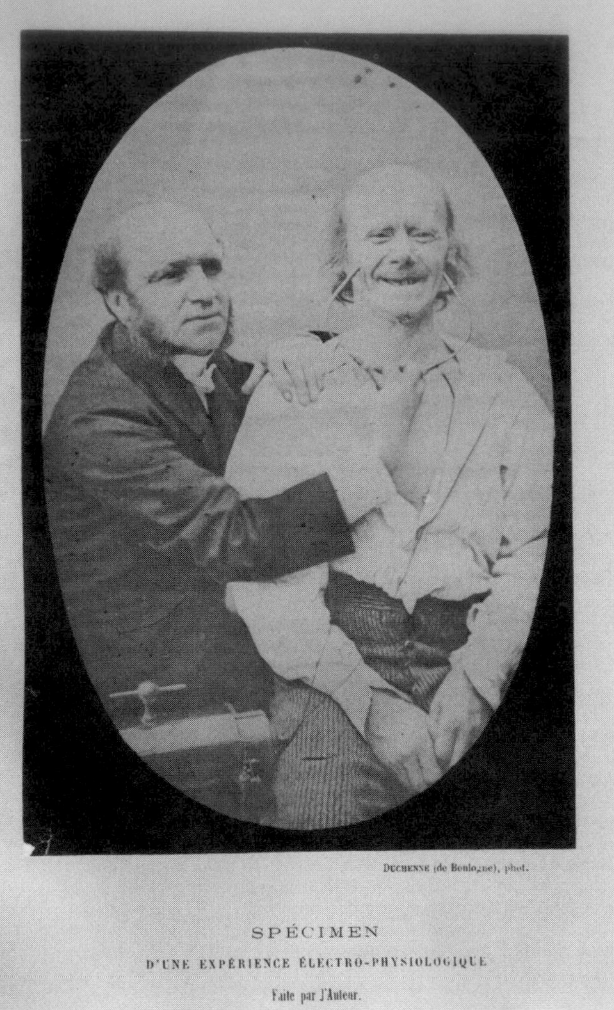

ÉLECTRO-PHYSIOLOGIE PHOTOGRAPHIQUE.
DUCHENNE (de Boulogne), phot.
SPÉCIMEN
D'UNE EXPÉRIENCE ÉLECTRO-PHYSIOLOGIQUE
Faite par l'Auteur.

FIG. 9.12

G.-B. Duchenne du Boulogne, experiments with facial expressions using electrical shock, from *Mécanisme de la physionomie humaine ou analyse électro-physiologique de l'expression des passions*, 1862

Ironically, Duchenne's subjects were not really feeling the emotions they seem to model. Rather, Duchenne was administering electric shocks to their facial muscles, forcing them to perform expressions we tend to assume spontaneously when feeling certain emotions. (One can surmise that the emotion these people probably felt was fear about being subject to electrical shock.)

The role of performance in medical study of this period is clearly evident in the now famous photographs and drawings of hysterical patients made in the late nineteenth century under the French neurologist Jean-Martin Charcot. This neurologist and his students and colleagues devoted themselves to the analysis of hysteria, a diagnostic category no longer in use but popular among neurologists of that period to describe a mysterious sequence of bodily symptoms they observed among their patients. Hysteria was a diagnosis given most often to women who were considered overly emotional and who performed episodes of dramatic behaviors and complained of unusual, sometimes fleeting physical symptoms (minor pains and pressures, loss of sensation) that neurologists believed to be psychogenic (to have a psychological rather than physical cause). At the Salpêtrière, the mental institution Charcot directed, neurologists kept those diagnosed with hysteria apart from others and conducted a battery of visual studies of these women in various stages of their hysterical episodes. These studies included observation of live performances by women who were provoked to fall into hysterical outbursts on cue before audiences of doctors and trainees and the photographing of women under hypnosis, as well as drawing from life and sequential photographs documenting the appearance of the body as these women passed through different phases of dance-like outbursts followed by collapse into exhaustion. Charcot and his colleagues believed that empirical observation was the key to knowledge, and saw the photograph as an ideal means of extending one's ability to observe and analyze. It was a common practice for them to hypnotize patients and then to photograph the gestures that they performed under suggestion. This woman (in fig. 9.13), for instance, acts surprised while in a hypnotic state.

FIG. 9.13
Charcot, woman under hypnosis asked to act surprised

In all of these images, the sense that the photograph creates an empirical trace of abnormalities and disorders is key to its use. The camera was, in these settings, a scientific tool for constituting groups of people as other (meaning different from the socially accepted norm). This use of the camera was prevalent not only in the medical and biological sciences but also in the social sciences, such as anthropology. In fig. 9.14, taken in the late nineteenth century, the photograph is embedded in the discourses of medicine and race, as well as in the discourse of colonialism. This image of an Asian man, posed against a grid while holding his braid, is an example of the use of anthropometry to support claims about qualitative and developmental differences among races. This man's nudity is coded within a discourse of science that establishes him as an object for cool and dispassionate study by scientists, not to be explicitly appreciated in a sexual or aesthetic manner. The grid imposed over the figure suggests that the image is meant to be used to determine how this body compares to physical norms and standards of size and proportion. The photograph does not invite the viewer to regard the man it depicts as an individual but rather to "measure him up," to see the physical differences that set him apart as a type from those whose measurements fit within accepted cultural standards and norms.

Looking back at photographic studies that use systems of observation and measurement, now discredited as both racist and unscientific helps us to consider the ways in which contemporary ideas about "truth" in scientific practices are the product of particular discourses at a given moment in history. The meanings we assign to that which is visible and measurable change, but we nonetheless rely on these meanings to make claims about universal facts and truths concerning bodies and the qualities and abilities we perceive them to possess. The critique of empirical observation has led us to recognize the ideological limits of such claims about seeing and its relationship to facts and to knowledge. Yet, even with this critique of empirical realism, aspects of these early scientific practices underlie current practices such as the application of facial recognition technologies for security purposes. Systems developed for use in airports, border crossings, and other sites of heightened security use electronic technologies to map the face as a series of interconnecting points. As communication scholar Kelly Gates points out, contemporary biometric technology finds its precedent in the problematic sciences like physiognomy and craniology which suggest that one's moral character might be inherent in one's genes and might also be visible in one's physical

FIG. 9.14
Anthropometric study of a Chinese man according to John Lamprey's system of measurement, 1868

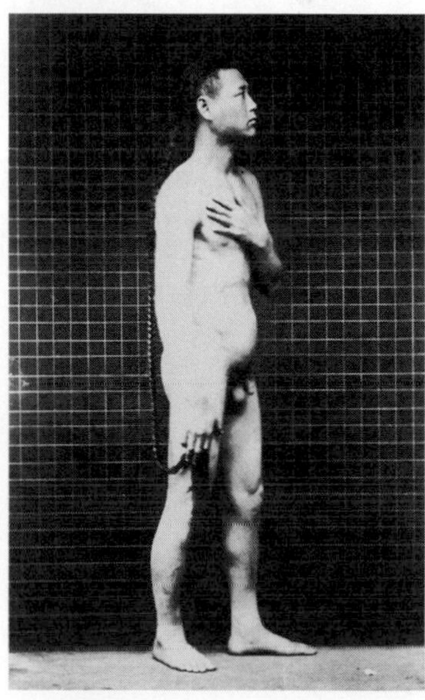

form and appearance. These technologies are used to support the practice of racial profiling, which has been subject to strong criticism for its assumptions about the link between racial or ethnic identity and moral tendencies.[15]

Imaging the Body's Interior: Biomedical Personhood

As we have noted, the integration of photography into the practices of science and medicine and the dominance of the narrative of science as seeing into new realms would be realized in powerful ways with nineteenth-century image techniques, such as X ray, that allowed the body's interior to be visually rendered, and in the development of twentieth-century technologies of digital and magnetic imaging. Here science promotes the concept of images seeing truths beyond the human eye and giving humankind insight into the mysteries of the body. Like the anatomy theaters, the images of the body's interior have clinical meaning, allowing for new knowledge about the body's organs and functions that is inseparable from the cultural meanings they generate. Thus these images help to shape the meaning of the body in ways that tell us a great deal about ideology, gender identity, and concepts of disease.

The process through which images change meaning according to variations in context, presentation, textual narrative, and visual reframing is well illustrated in the history of the X-ray image. When X rays, a form of ionizing radiation, were introduced as a tool in medical diagnosis in the late 1890s, the public responded with curiosity and fear. An X-ray image is produced by exposing the body to ionizing radiation and allowing the waves that pass through the body to register on a photographic plate or screen. Because the rays do not penetrate bone as readily as soft tissue, the X-ray image provides a relatively clear depiction of the skeleton and variations in bone density. These images suggested to those who saw them for the first time in the X ray's early years that the technique gave its practitioners superhuman visual powers, allowing them optically to invade the private space of the body. This fantasy took on an erotic cast, as seen in the work of some illustrators who made humorous cartoons, such as this one from 1934 which dramatizes the fantasy of a male cameraman using the rays to peer through women's clothing and flesh.

FIG. 9.15
Fantasies of X-ray views, 1934

Ultrasound images provide another example of a kind of medical looking that has been invested with public meaning and in which cultural desires are made explicit. Sonography, the process of imaging the internal structures of an object by measuring and recording the reflection of high-frequency sound waves that are passed through it, was introduced to medicine experimentally in the early 1960s and became a cornerstone of diagnostic medical imaging by the 1980s. Whereas X rays create images of dense structures (such as bones) and involve the use of potentially harmful ionizing radiation, ultrasound allows doctors to discern softer structures and (debatably) does not damage tissue.

Ultrasound provides an instructive example of how visual knowledge is highly dependent on factors other than sight. We tend to think of the ultrasound image as a kind of window into the body through which we see structures previously unseen and unknown. But in fact ultrasound involves the visual only in the last instance, almost as an afterthought to a process that is markedly lacking in any aspect of visuality. Ultrasound had its foundation in military sonar devices designed to penetrate the ocean with sound waves and measure the waves reflected back as indicators of distance and location of objects. In this technique, sound is utilized not for hearing or communication per se but as an abstract means of deriving measurements. The data measurements of sound waves acquired through sonar are computed to assemble a record of object location and density in space, but this record need not be visual. It could take the form of a chart, a graph, a picture, or a series of numbers. The data derived from sonography is analyzed with computers and translated into graphic images or three-dimensional objects. Paradoxically, sonography is a "sound" system that involves neither hearing nor the production of noise per se. It is because there exists a cultural preference for the visual that ultrasound's display capabilities have been adapted to conform to the conventions of photography and video and not to the standards of, say, the graph or the numerical record.

Ultrasound has been used widely in obstetrics, in which practitioners had long sought means to image the fetal body, tracking its development and identifying abnormalities, without placing the fetus or the pregnant woman at risk. However, less than a decade into the sonogram's use in obstetrics, studies began to show that pregnancy outcomes were only minimally affected by the use of the technique in routine prenatal care; that is, there was little evidence that the technique offered any clear benefits with regard to outcomes. Rates for prenatal ultrasound use doubled in Britain in the 1980s despite this lack of evidence and of official mandates supporting its use. Why was this imaging technique so popular among obstetricians and their patients, and why does its use continue in the routine monitoring of normal pregnancies?

One answer is that the fetal sonogram serves a purpose beyond medicine; in other words, the fetal sonogram is not simply a scientific or medical image. It is also an image with deep cultural, emotional, and even, for some, religious meaning. It is worth noting that the history of prenatal images includes a long history of imagining the fetus or embryo to be a person in the womb. Indeed, even Leonardo da Vinci created realistic images of fetuses, possibly based on his studres of newborn babies. As we have noted before, images can change social roles and be used in new contexts, as with art in advertisements and police photos on news magazine covers. The medical image of the fetal sonogram became a cultural rite of

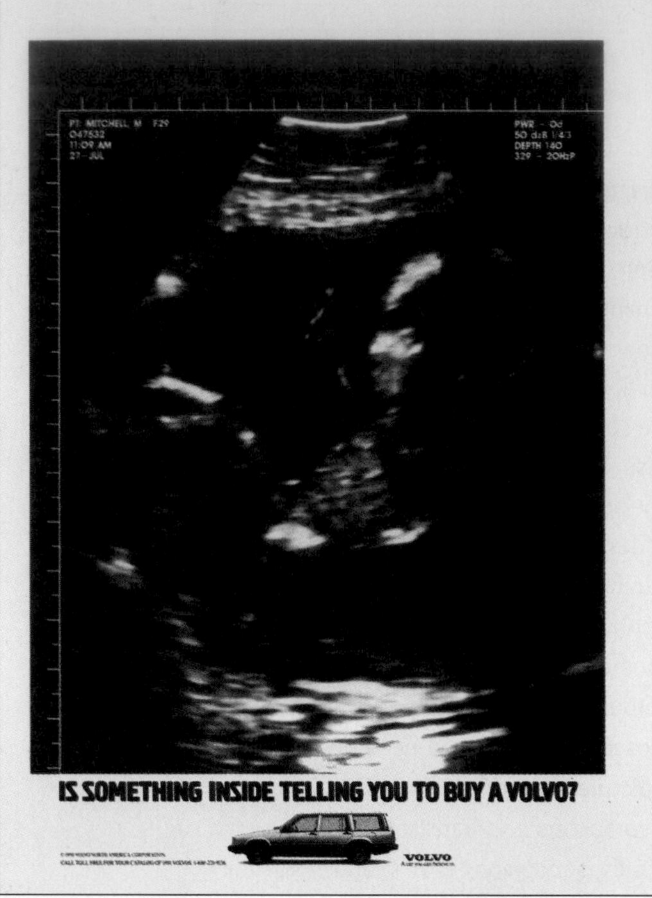

FIG. 9.16
Volvo ad featuring a fetus, 1990

passage in which women and their families get their first "portrait" of the child-to-be in sonogram form. Future parents relate to the sonographic image, pinning it up on the refrigerator and showing it to coworkers at the office as one would display a first baby picture. Sonograms now routinely turn up as the first image in a baby book. Similarly, clinical medical images are increasingly viewed by patients as they are created. Beginning in the 1990s, patients undergoing ultrasound and endoscopic procedures (in which a tiny fiber-optics camera is passed into narrow orifices and channels to record a moving image of the interior) were able to view their procedures in real time, and it is sometimes the case that patients are given copies of the tape or an image to take home. Medical images such as ultrasounds and MRIs have also been integrated into nonmedical advertisements to signify special care of the body or to evoke the authority of scientific knowledge in a given practice. The role of the fetal sonogram as an icon of one's imagined future family is evident in this 1990 advertisement that plays on Volvo's reputation as the safe family car. This advertisement features a fetal sonogram with the message "something inside you is telling you to buy a Volvo."[16] It appeals to an imagined maternal desire to protect the fetus, while also playing on cultural anxieties about women's bodies not being safe enough spaces for the fetus without the help of a technological safeguard. It is the image of this partly formed "child," through its persuasive address as icon of family, that "tells" the viewer she must conform to cultural messages about the woman's obligation to minimize fetal risks. Here the fetus not only resembles a large child, but is also positioned as if in the driver's seat, thus drawing a parallel between intrauterine and car safety.

The idea that women visually bond with their future children through the image of the sonogram has circulated in obstetrical discourse since the early 1980s and prompted the claim, reported in one study, that the sonogram may encourage women who are ambivalent about their pregnancies to choose not to terminate them. In other words, the image is understood to have the power to encourage future mothers to experience emotional bonding with their future children more powerfully than textual descriptions or graphic abstractions of the fetus ever could. This has sparked a debate among cultural analysts and medical practitioners, and it remains a vexed issue in part because the boundaries between the medical and the personal image are blurred.[17] However, one point of agreement is that in the case of the fetal sonogram the biomedical image takes on the aura of a portrait. The sonogram is a document of the fetus's status as a social being (a real person) and not just a biological entity waiting to become a person. We do not often hear accounts of people bonding with, say, an X ray or a bone scan, seeing it as a personal portrait. The fetal image has evoked a kind of response more typically associated with a family photograph or home video, giving it a status that goes beyond that of a medical record.

This view of the sonogram as a social document helps to award to the fetus the status of personhood (and a place in family and community) more typically attributed to the infant after birth. In this sense, sonograms serve a nonmedical cultural function that justifies the technique's use. The concept of a fetus as a person has been a central factor in legal cases that have allowed the fetus to be represented in legal terms by adults who feel they may speak on its behalf and who are pitted against the wishes or rights of the pregnant woman who may, for example, seek abortion, or who may require medical treatment that can place the fetus at risk.[18] In these cases, the concept of fetal personhood has been introduced in legal, religious, and social settings in arguments that in some cases have pitted the rights claimed for the fetus as an autonomous person against the legal rights of the mother to determine the fate of her own body and health. The image of the fetus thus acquires meanings beyond its most literal medical meanings in obstetrical screening and diagnosis.

This complex set of factors has fueled political debates about fetal images since 1965, when *Life* magazine published on its cover a photograph widely mistaken to be a depiction of a living fetus. The photograph was one of a series by the Swedish science photographer Lennart Nilsson, whose popular book *A Child is Born* depicted fetuses at various stages of gestational development until birth. Nilsson's earliest fetal photographs were enhanced and modified shots of specimens; yet they were often mistaken for photographs of living fetuses taken in utero. This image is accompanied by the caption, "Living 18-Week-Old Fetus," yet inside the magazine readers are informed that "the embryos shown on the following pages have been surgically

FIG. 9.17
April 30, 1965, *Life Magazine* cover with Lennart Nilsson photograph of a fetus

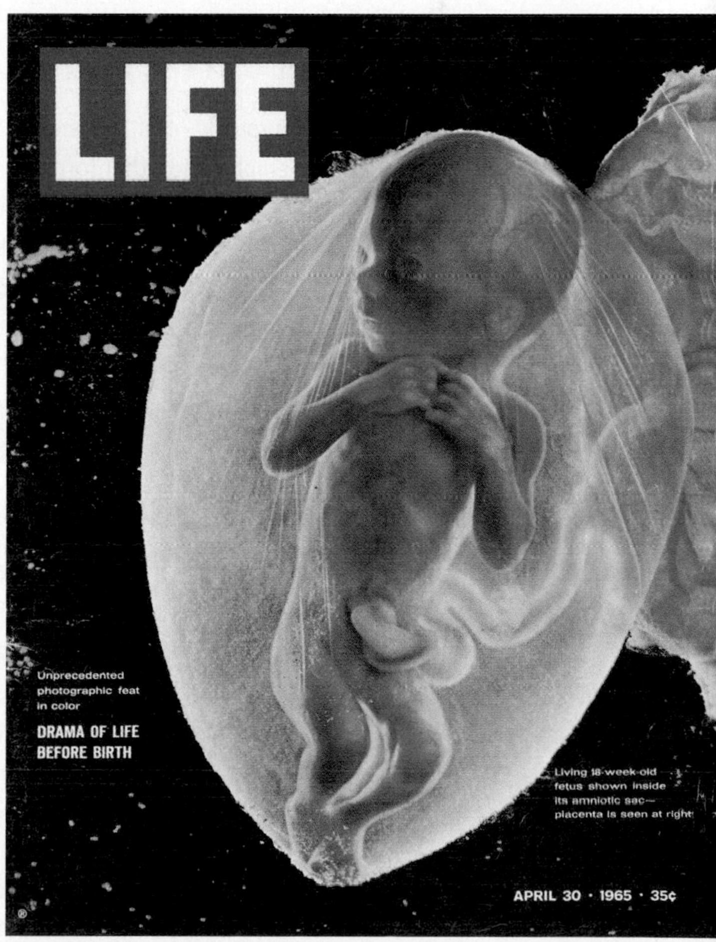

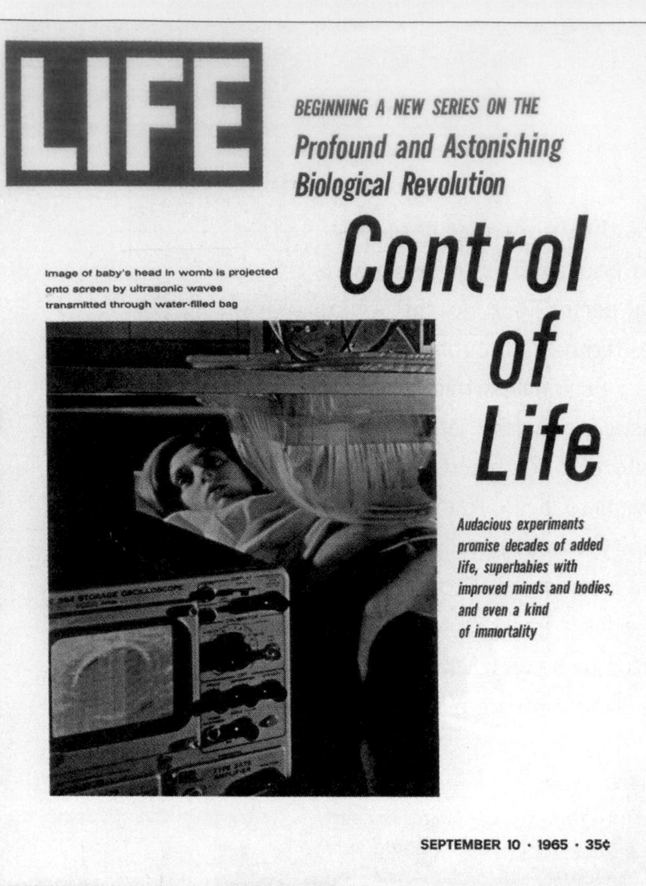

LIFE
BEGINNING A NEW SERIES ON THE
Profound and Astonishing
Biological Revolution
Control
of
Life
Image of baby's head in womb is projected
onto screen by ultrasonic waves
transmitted through water-filled bag
Audacious experiments
promise decades of added
life, superbabies with
improved minds and bodies,
and even a kind
of immortality
SEPTEMBER 10 · 1965 · 35¢

FIG. 9.18
September 10, 1965, *Life Magazine* cover

removed for a variety of reasons." Thus this is an image of a fetus that has been removed for medical reasons from the body of its mother, not a living fetus. Nilsson's technical strategies included rendering the color photographs in golden and orange tones, suggesting warm flesh and flowing blood, and staging the specimens in poses suggesting infant gesture and behavior. The misperception of these earliest images as depictions of life was also fed by *Life* magazine's featuring, in the same year, a cover story about the "control of life," announcing a "profound and astonishing revolution" in biology after which medical science would produce "superbabies" with improved minds and bodies. This cover featured a woman undergoing a fetal ultrasound, with the fetal head visible in a small, grainy black-and-white image on the monitor depicted at the corner of the photograph. These images, along with Nilsson's book, present scientific imaging as evidence of the control over and improvement of human life. The central narrative of these images is that medical photography and other forms of interior biomedical imaging are evidence of nothing short of a miracle in modern culture. The "miracle" refers both to control over human reproduction and development but also, by implication, to scientific imaging—the fact that the photographic camera can actually capture evidence of this mastery over life. Nilsson would continue to develop his techniques, and in the 1990s he would use endoscopic technologies to create images of fetuses that were actually living in the womb, producing images of live fetuses at seven weeks of development.

Some feminist critics of science have noted that Nilsson's images do more than provide compelling images of fetuses. They also have the effect of erasing the mother. Taken when many of the actual fetuses photographed were actually nonliving specimens outside the womb, these images depict fetuses as if alive and floating in space, as if they are not actually within the body of a woman.[19] The fetus in fig. 9.17 is set against a background that evokes the stars in the broader universe. Just a few years later, filmmaker Stanley Kubrick would evoke this image in his 1968 cult film, *2001: A Space Odyssey*, which featured a fetus floating in space as a metaphor for the cyclical nature of human existence. The fetus seems mystical in these images. Moreover, it is awarded personhood through the image process itself. Hence it has been argued that these images, along with ultrasound images, provided the emotional and political means for the rights and interests of the fetus to be seen in opposition, in medical and legal terms, to the rights and interests of its mother. It is thus not accidental that images of the fetus have become central icons in the debate over abortion in the United States. The compelling idea of fetal personhood that is projected onto the sonogram has provided powerful fodder for the anti-abortion movement. This was made clear in 1984 with the release of the videotape *The Silent Scream*, in which Bernard Nathanson, a physician and former abortion provider, mounts a case against the practice of abortion through visual tactics, showing what he describes as real-time ultrasound images of a twelve-week-old "unborn child," an abortion, and aborted fetuses. Nathanson explicitly states that the sonogram's moving image convinced him to change his political stance because it led him to believe he was seeing a "living unborn child" and not a mere fetus.

The Silent Scream provides many examples of the manipulation of images to demonstrate certain "truths." A rebuttal tape made by Planned Parenthood of King County, Seattle, in 1985 reveals that in *The Silent Scream* Nathanson consistently used images and models of fetuses older than the stage under discussion to give the impression, for example, that a first-trimester fetus is physically fully developed. In attempting to show that the fetus "sensed danger" with the insertion of instruments used in abortion, Nathanson sped up the real-time ultrasound image to make the fetus appear agitated and seem to throw back its head in a "silent scream," something Planned Parenthood assures us the fetus does not have the developmental capacity to do. In their rebuttal tape, Planned Parenthood experts show viewers the "real-time" footage again to demonstrate how the empirical truth is in fact staged. Techniques used by Nathanson, the Planned Parenthood experts suggest, are deceptive and manipulative because they influence our interpretation through language and manipulations of size and time scales. Whereas *The Silent Scream* banks on viewers' faith in the power of images to reveal the truth, the rebuttal makes the argument that images can seduce people into believing things that are not true. Yet history demonstrates that the simple process of debunking an image is not enough to defuse its power to make viewers believe it holds a particular truth. Images generate strong emotional responses, whether or not we are aware that they are manipulated. The prevalence of ultrasound suggests that people are moved by its images whether or not these images are always medically useful. Doctors and clients construct narratives about fetal personhood despite what is known to be true about fetal life and development.

Vision and Truth

Underlying images of the body's interior is a tension between the idea that truth is self-evident in the surface appearance of things and the contrasting idea that truth lies hidden in internal structures or systems of the body that scientific representational techniques can uncover. The belief that the truth lies beneath the surface and needs to be seen to be fully understood has prevailed in Western culture since the time of the Greeks. It is common in contemporary culture to regard looking inside someone as a means of seeing their "true" identity.

The idea that bodily truth can be made visible was a topic of particular interest to French philosopher Michel Foucault in his book *Birth of the Clinic*. This account of the creation of hospital-based teaching and research in 1790s France is pertinent to discussions of science and visuality, though its particular focus is the clinic. Foucault describes the replacement of traditional methods of diagnosis of reading the surface symptoms of an illness by the practice of anatomical dissection and looking for empirical evidence beyond the physical surfaces of the body. In chapter 3, we discussed the institutional gaze identified by Foucault in terms of surveillance and inspection. He was also interested in the identification of signs and symptoms, specifically how the "medical gaze" elicited truths hidden within bodies rather than through direct self-evidence of pathology. Dissection rejected older ideas about where to look for the truth, but it still adhered to an ideology of visual truth in which it was assumed that all a doctor had to do was gaze into the depths of the body for its truth to be revealed.

In the rise of the natural sciences in the nineteenth century and in biomedicine today, vision is understood as a primary avenue to knowledge, and sight takes precedence over the other senses as a primary tool in the analysis and ordering of living things. Hence an ultrasound image taken by a doctor will be perceived as more reliable than a woman's description of her bodily sensations of pregnancy—or what has been termed "felt evidence." Foucault identifies the introduction of a new (clinical) regime of knowledge in which vision plays a distinctive role in our regard of bodies and subjects. At the same time, vision can play different roles in contemporaneous regimes of truth; there is not one but multiple medical and scientific ways of looking.

The looking Foucault describes is crucially linked to other activities that give meaning to what vision uncovers: experimenting, measuring, analyzing, and ordering, for example. These are the activities that separate the idea of appearances as self-evident from the analytical clinical gaze Foucault describes. The paradox of the clinical gaze and its legacy is that vision may predominate, but it is nonetheless dependent on other sensory and cognitive processes. This paradox becomes all the more pronounced as we move into the twenty-first century and the age of the digital image.

During the last decades of the twentieth century, biomedicine introduced a broad range of imaging technologies such as MRIs, CAT scans, ultrasound, and fiber optics, in addition to the historical technology of X rays, to produce images of the body's interior. Increasingly, digital rather than analog technology is being used to map the body, and this means in turn that cultural concepts of the body have begun to reflect concepts of the digital. The history of imaging the body's interior has been, as we have noted, not simply a history of medical and scientific investigation but also a history in which the body is constructed through aesthetic choices and image-enhancing techniques. Scale is enormously important in our reading of many of these images, in particular those images that use microscopic lenses to envision the body's cells that are invisible to the human eye. Here, again, Lennart Nilsson has been a key figure. Nilsson's images, published in books with titles such as *The Body Victorious, The Incredible Machine, Behold Man,* and *Life,* use the technology of electron microscopy to depict the body as a series of landscapes. Indeed, it can be said that the history of microscopic photography has been about representing the body as a kind of landscape that can be discovered and claimed like a foreign land. This effect is heightened by the use of color to highlight and distinguish different parts of the body, yet such colorization has the effect of making the body appear unnatural. Here, images of the body's interior evoke the tradition of the sublime, in which landscape painting and photography have evoked transcendence of the real. There is no doubt that such images evoke awe and wonder and offer all kinds of visual pleasure. At the same time, the decontextualization inherent in the images and the changes in scale due to the enlargement of microscopic elements both have the effect of making these images of bodies seem otherworldly. The anthropologist Emily Martin, in her book *Flexible Bodies,* which is a study of the metaphors of conquest and power through which we describe the human immune system, interviewed people about their responses to these kinds of images of the body's interior and found that, although people marveled at the techniques of the images, most were ambivalent about seeing them as representative of their own bodies.[20]

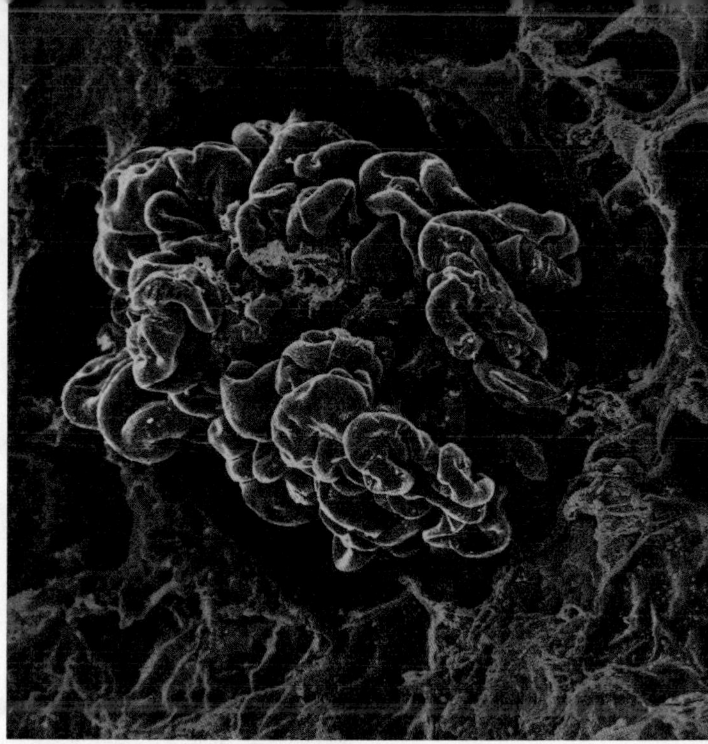

FIG. 9.19
Microphotograph of glomerulus—a ball of capillaries by Lennart Nilsson

The kinds of advances in imaging technologies that allow photographers such as Nilsson to photograph the minute elements of the body are paralleled by the development of tools for scanning the body's interior, such as MRIs and computed tomography. Until the late twentieth century, routine medical imaging was limited to X rays. It is now commonplace for medical practitioners to use MRIs, sonograms, CT scans, and PET scans to read soft tissue and organs within the body. These images are central to how the physical body is understood and interpreted by medical professionals and how people experience their own bodies when they see these images. Of these images, brain scans appear to hold the most cultural

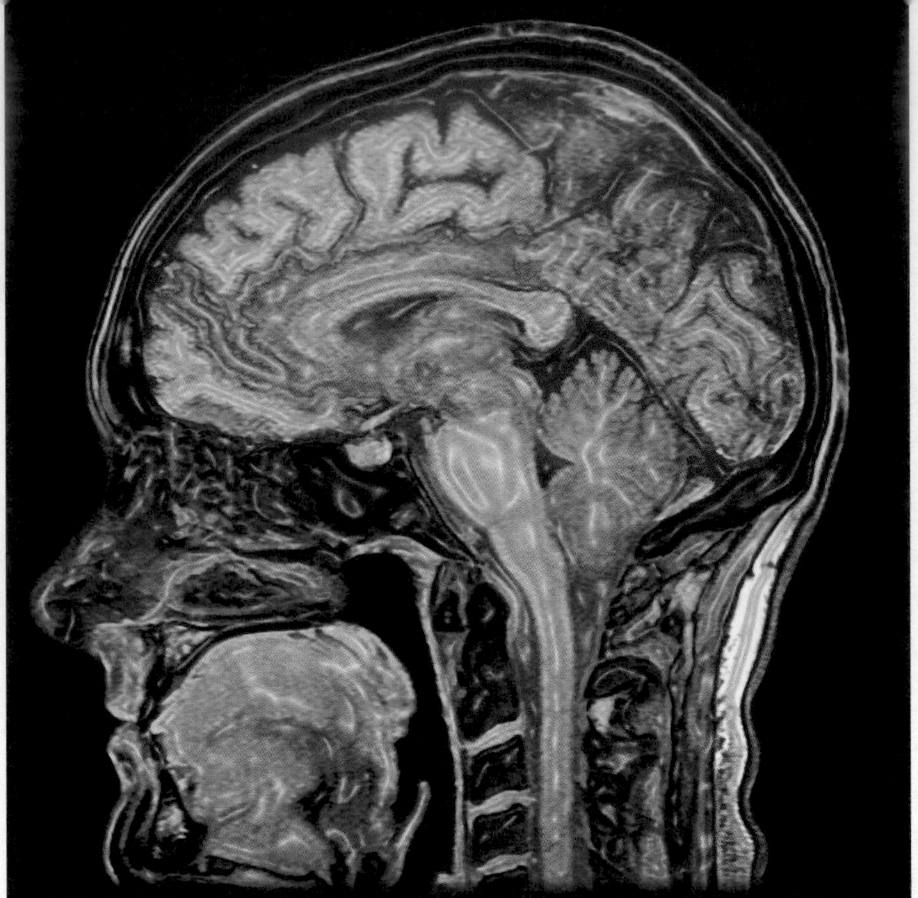

FIG. 9.20
Digitally enhanced MRI scan of the head, 2004

power, given that the brain appears to be the most elusive and complex of the human organs. Science studies scholar Joseph Dumit notes, in his book *Picturing Personhood*, that PET scans of the brain have quite regularly circulated in popular media as visual evidence of particular kinds of mental states and disorders. Dumit is careful to note that what such images mean to experts is quite complex, but in their colored renditions of brain activity, they appear to tell the public something visually about normalcy and abnormality. Dumit notes that as early as 1983, *Vogue* magazine ran an image of three PET scans of brains that were labeled Normal, Schizo, and Depressed, thus demonstrating the ease with which such images are deployed to designate "brain-types."[21] As Dumit notes, such images are much more effective in demonstrating abnormalities than they are in establishing norms, yet in the case of mental illnesses, it is much easier to diagnose patients using traditional psychiatric evaluative techniques than to read an image of the brain. However, precisely because of the positivist legacy of machine imaging, brain scans carry enormous power to suggest the "facts" of brain disorders. They have thus been introduced in legal contexts to affirm, for instance, the mental disorder of a defendant, and judges have taken a variety of tactics to mediate their powerful effect as evidence of brain function. Just as with the electron microscopic images of the body as a kind of landscape, these images are often colorized (both as part of the imaging process and to enhance the view of the brain) in ways that render the brain an aesthetic object. The effect of these images can be seen as a contemporary outgrowth of the nineteenth-century imaging technologies that were deployed specifically to visually demarcate abnormalities. Thus this antidrug ad from the National Institute on Drug Abuse uses PET scans to visually demonstrate the difference between a "normal" brain and a brain on the drug Ecstasy. Given the complexity of PET scans and how what they measure changes over time, there are many arguments one could make about how this image sets up too easy a contrast here to make its point. However, it is precisely because the image is coded as evidence that the ad carries the power potentially to persuade someone to consider not using Ecstasy.

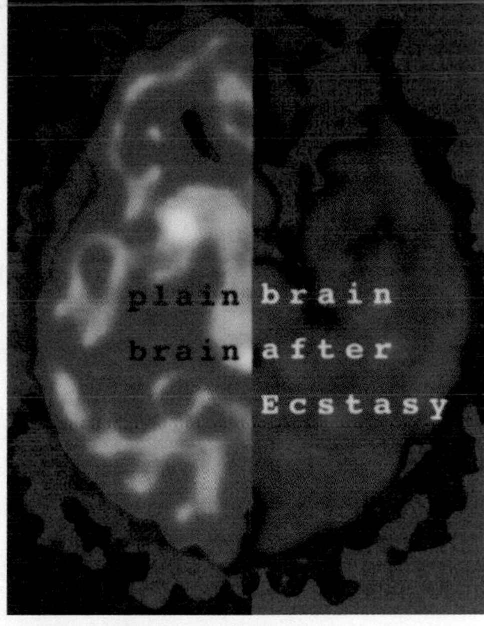
plain brain
brain after
Ecstasy

FIG. 9.21
Plain Brain/Brain after Ecstacy, National Institute on Drug Abuse 25th Anniversary poster, using PET scans as a scare tactic

Imaging Genetics

As we have noted throughout this chapter, the modes of image making that define the body and its interior are central not only to medical practices of diagnosis but also to how the body is perceived to function and to have meaning. Thus the image of the body as a set of digital slices (as in the Visible Human Project), as readable through brain scans, or as biometrically unique, as in biometrics, all contribute to a sense of the body not only as readable but also as malleable and transformable. This Dow Human Element ad, from an extensive 2007 campaign, sells the idea that in the chart of chemical elements there is also a human element. The campaign imagines each person as an element in the Periodic Chart of Elements, with a corresponding number. The ad copy reads, "a world that includes the Human Element along with hydrogen, oxygen, and the elements, is a very different world indeed." The body is seen

FIG. 9.22
Dow Human Element ad, 2006

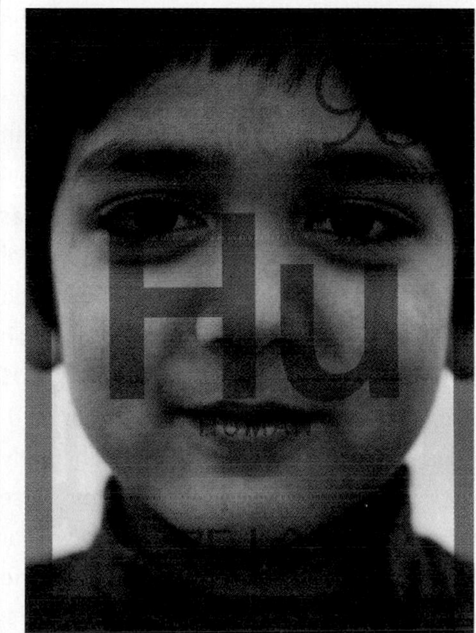
Hu
AND JUST LIKE THAT, THE LAWS OF CHEMISTRY CHANGE. A world that includes the Human Element, along with hydrogen, oxygen and the other elements, is a very different world indeed. Suddenly, chemistry is put to work solving human problems. Bonds are formed between aspirations and commitments. And the energy released from reactions fuels a boundless spirit that will make the planet a safer, cleaner, more comfortable place for generations to come. A world that welcomes change is about to meet the element of change: the Human Element.
DOW

body is seen as coded by science, as elemental, and as something that can be easily segmented and atomized.

One of the key influences in these scientific and postmodern concepts of the body has been the Human Genome Project (HGP), a global scientific endeavour which aims to create a complete genetic "map" of the human genome. Genetics captured the scientific and popular imagination at the end of the twentieth century. Beginning in the 1990s, genetics has become the scientific field that scientists and the public turned to for clues about the origins of everything from smoking to schizophrenia, from cancer to criminal behavior. With the rise of specialties such as gene therapy, genetic counseling, and genetic testing and the focus on the HGP and its mapping of the human genome, genetics has become the primary paradigm through which the human body is imagined. Genetic science is not simply about identifying the genes that constitute the human chromosome, it is also about identifying genes linked to disease, behavior, physical appearance, and a host of other conditions and factors. Genetic therapy understands genes as they relate to medical aberrations and pathologies. Just as nineteenth-century scientific practices of measurement were used to shore up ideologies of racial difference, gene therapy is used to map differences among human subjects and has the potential to be used to designate those who are outside the "norm" in troubling ways. Echoing Foucault, science studies scholars Dorothy Nelkin and Susan Lindee explain that with the shift to a genetic model, "Images of pathology have moved from gross to hidden body systems. Once blacks were portrayed with large genitalia and women with small brains. Now the differences are in their genes."[22] Genetics has thus emerged as a new and potentially problematic marker of biological and cultural difference, taking the place of nineteenth-century physiognomy and craniology. We now "see" at the molecular and genetic levels.

The appeal of the genetic model of the body lies in part in its rendering of the body as a kind of accessible digital map, something easily decipherable, understandable, and containable—a body that is seemingly less mysterious than the body that is popularly conceived and individually experienced. The Human Genome Project is presented as the means through which the body's potential for disease can be remapped and restructured and as the beginning of what has been called a new era of medical science, the "age of the genome." The map of the genome, which was fully sketched out in an initial stage by 2003, has resulted in the identification of 1,800 disease genes and provided the basis for more than 1,000 genetic tests for human conditions. The HapMap project was begun in 2005 to map the full spectrum of genetic diseases. (In a procedure that is typical of medical protocols, the volunteers whose DNA was used for the project are deliberately anonymous, in ways that are reminiscent of the bodies used for anatomy.) José van Dijck notes that the metaphor of the "mapping" of the genome carried with it the implication of a frontier terrain, with scientists cast as explorers like Lewis and Clark. Popular discussion of the HGP employs not only the language of blueprints, instructions, and codes but also the metaphors of "treasure hunts," "pioneer adventures," and images that invoke colonial expeditions, with analogies made between Columbus and the HGP scientists.[23] It is important to note that metaphors about science are not simply ways of talking; they are constitutive of what science sees, and they affect how scientific practices are conducted and understood inside and outside the lab. These metaphors are not the constructions of a misguided media that fails to "see" science accurately. Rather, they are the chosen metaphors of geneticists themselves, who adopt these models to describe their own work. The HGP has been characterized by scientists and the media as the culmination of modern science in its potential for control over the human body; it is thus not incidental that the project regularly uses Leonardo da Vinci's *Vitruvian Man*, which we discussed earlier, on its publications and brochures, as if that image signaled the beginning of science with the HGP its ultimate outcome.

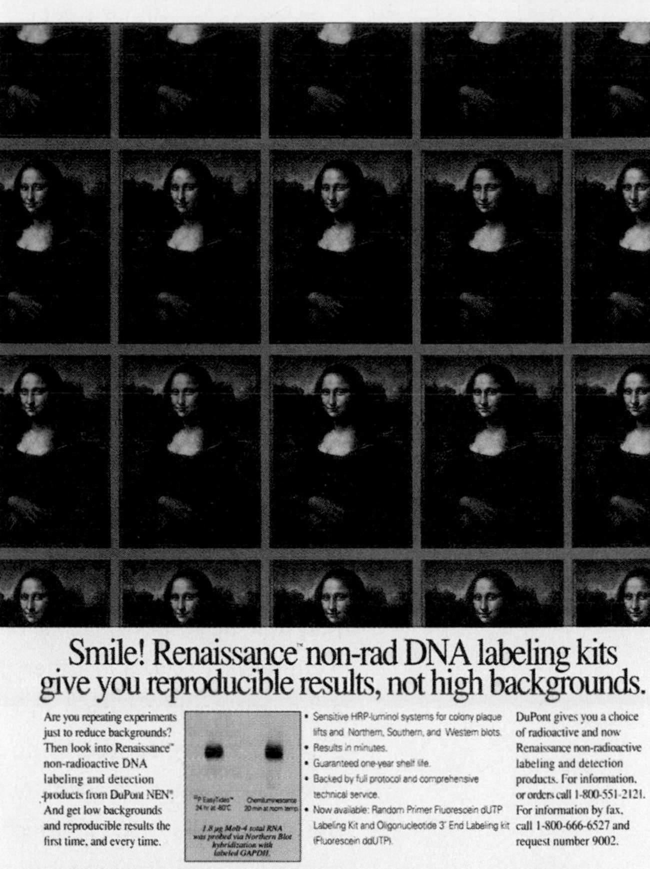

FIG. 9.23
Du Pont Renaissance™ ad, 1995

References to the Renaissance abound in genetics in ways that reveal underlying narratives about reproduction, replication, and the alliance of art and science. In these analogies, the Renaissance is perceived to be an era of immense movement forward in human creativity and fine art, and the current era of biotechnology is seen, by analogy, to be equally historically important. These connections are encapsulated in this 1995 ad for a Du Pont DNA labeling kit that is called Renaissance. Here, the ad appropriates Andy Warhol's work, *Thirty Are Better Than One* (1963), which is composed of numerous copies of the *Mona Lisa*, to refer to the replication qualities of the product. The image is effective, yet it carries many unintended ironies. Science studies scholar Donna Haraway has written of this ad, "without attribution, Du Pont replicates Warhol replicates da Vinci replicates the lady herself. And Renaissance™ gets top billing as the real artist because it facilitates replicability."[24] It is, of course, a further irony that Du Pont trademarked the Renaissance product name, thus claiming intellectual property rights for the name of an historical epoch to sell the idea of reproduction.

In earlier epochs of science, we have shown, practices of looking were central to discriminatory systems claiming to be objective knowledge systems. The identification of visible and measurable differences in skin tone and color and body shape and size were (and still are) means through which stereotypes are constructed and discriminatory practices are carried out and justified. Today, these appearance-related markers of natural difference are supplemented or replaced by the supposedly more accurate sign of the invisible gene as a marker of difference. We now live in a "reality" we understand to exist at the molecular, invisible level. But when the marker of difference is invisible to us, are the marker and difference itself taken out of the realm of our influence and debate? As an invisible marker, genetic code seems more fixed and more factual, far from the field of discourse, outside of historical context and the social field of power and knowledge. If differences are genetically determined and therefore immutable (except perhaps through gene therapies or drug treatments), it becomes easy to imagine that socialization may not be responsible for or effective in changing differences of mental capacity, physical skill, and other attributes of human beings. For instance, a genetic argument could be used to claim that criminals commit crime because they are genetically predisposed to do so, hence we need not waste money on programs designed to improve their social environments. The mapping of genes has raised the specter of a world in which people could be discriminated against by insurance companies and other institutions simply because of their genetic makeup, and laws are now being enacted to protect against this eventuality. The existence of the genetic map in and of itself presents a kind of empirical knowledge, however limited, that has through its very existence the capacity to trump other kinds of ways of framing disease and difference (leaving out environmental factors, for instance). Importantly, the concept of the body that we gain through the genetic model is one of mutability, as genetic science not only to identify genes but also to change them has become a primary engine of scientific research. This research is not only about potentially changing disease-causing genes but also about changing appearance and cognitive abilities—the genes for skin color have been identified, for instance. The specter of pharmaceutical companies applying for patents on such genetic information has not quelled concerns that the age of the genome will replicate many of the discriminatory sciences of eugenics and create new models for the norm.

FIG. 9.24
Human chromosomes, colored for animation, 2005

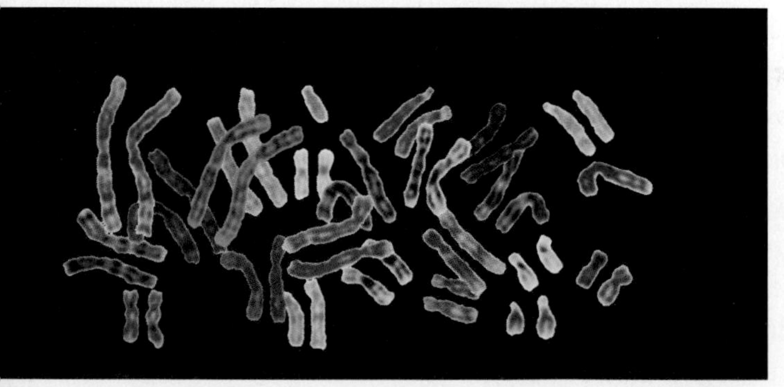

The production of images in genetic science carries with it the wonder of microscopic images that have, as we have noted, the effect of rendering the body as a kind of landscape. In this image, color coding to denote different chromosomes has the effect of turning microscopic chromosomes into playful creatures that look like pieces of candy. It is also the case that images of DNA sequences, rendered here to look like colorful ladders, sometimes include the icon of the mouse, invoking projects such as the HGP which have focused on the relationship of mouse genomes (sequenced in 2002) to human genomes. Because mice have almost the same set of genes as humans, they have been used extensively in gene research. Haraway writes that this resulted, in 1990, in the development of OncoMouse™, the first patented animal, developed by Harvard Medical School and licensed to Du Pont.[25] OncoMouse is a "transgenic" mouse whose genetic makeup is useful for studying cancer. As Haraway notes, the patenting of an animal, whose "natural habitat" is the laboratory, is emblematic of the complex border crossings found in biotechnology, between biology and technology, and between species.

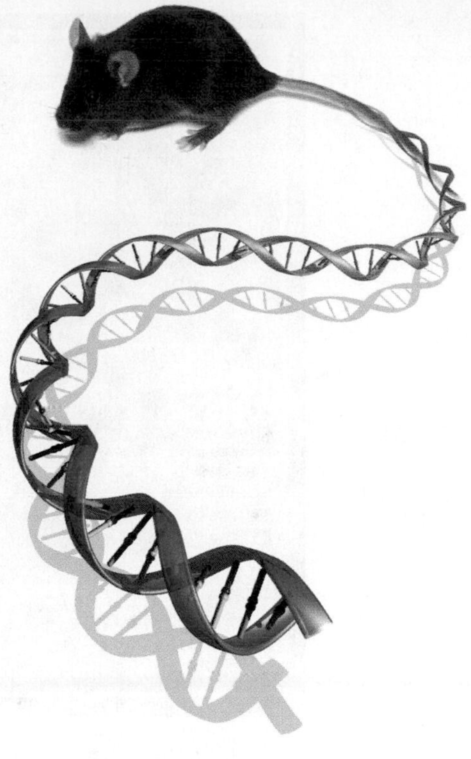

FIG. 9.25
The mouse as a symbol of DNA, 2002

The Digital Body

The image of the genetic body is also an image of the digital body, at once a body of microscopic entities, a set of bits that is mutable and plastic, easily combined and reassembled. These concepts of the body are aligned with concepts of the postmodern body that we discussed in chapter 8. The visual technique of morphing, for instance, makes it difficult to distinguish between one person and another, thus collapsing the boundaries between bodies that were once considered inviolable. Morphing techniques are sometimes used to make statements about universal humanity and the blending together of races; they also contribute to sense of the body as mutable and changeable. These morphed images recall the nineteenth-century composite photographs of Sir Francis Galton, which we described earlier. Fig. 9.26 shows one of the first widely circulated images using morphing digital technologies. This is the cover of a special issue of *Time* magazine devoted to "The New Face of America: How Immigrants Are Shaping the World's First Multicultural Society." *Time* presented a computer-generated composite of racial types, represented in a portrait of a young woman with dark hair and eyes and a medium skin tone. "Take a good look at this woman," the cover sidebar reads. "She was created by a computer from a mix of several races." The image was produced with Morph 2.0, the same software package used in the production of *Terminator 2: Judgment Day* (1991) and the legendary 1991 Michael Jackson video, *Black or White*. It is a computer composite that is 15 percent Anglo-Saxon, 17.5 percent Middle Eastern, 17.5 percent African, 7.5 percent Asian, 35 percent Southern European, and 7.5 percent Hispanic. Whereas Galton's composites presented types in hopes of breeding out those racial types deemed inherently pathological as part of eugenic science, *Time*'s composite suggests an amalgamation of races that appears to embrace a more multicultural future society, but one that is idealized in a genericized version of youthful female beauty.

The problems inherent in this tacit view of the new face of America as a stereotypically beautiful face become evident when we recall, as American literature

FIG. 9.26
"The New Face of America," *Time Magazine*, 1993

scholar Sue Schweik has written, the "Ugly Laws" that remained on the books in some cities of the United States, such as Chicago, as late as the mid-1970s, with the last arrest under these laws made in 1974.[26] The Ugly Laws forbade the public appearance of people with "unsightly" or "disgusting" appearances—people "diseased, maimed or mutilated," relegating these individuals to the hidden interiors of homes and institutions or to freak shows where they could be ogled as scientific and medical oddities, poorly paid for submitting their bodies to this sort of objectification. Whereas in some cases individuals with differences deemed ugly were ostracized and devalued, in others they were regarded as harboring special inner intellectual, moral, or spiritual powers. The latter was true for Joseph Merrick, the British man of the Victorian era who was the subject of a film by the director David Lynch. He was known as "the Elephant Man" due to his extreme facial and bodily malformations (he had a condition called Proteus syndrome). After years during which he was maltreated and exploited in workhouses for the poor and circus sideshows, he was befriended by a prominent doctor and the princess of Wales, who ushered him into Victorian London's high society, where he became a kind of cult figure admired and revered among the upper classes for the fine mind and soul his malformed body was believed to harbor.

The beauty in the "New Face of America" image is specifically coded within the science of genetics, the codes of the digital, and the cultural meanings of multiculturalism—here, beauty is precisely the mix of ethnicities and genes, the blending of difference. The visual culture of computer graphics aids fantasies of the forging of new peoples and new worlds in imagined and emergent genetic specialties such as cloning and selective breeding. As the *Time* article reveals, "Little did we know what we wrought. As onlookers watched the image of our new Eve begin to appear on the computer screen, several staff members promptly fell in love. This is a love that must forever remain unrequited."[27] But, as Evelynn M. Hammonds argues, the "Face of America" cover story enacts both a fear of racial mixing and a fantastic construction of a generic woman of color.[28] Stereotypic racial typologies remain in place as this attractive, idealized woman of color becomes an icon reflecting the unattainable desires of those who brought her to life on the screen. Although one might think of this woman as a person, she is a virtual person, with no referent in the real world. Composite photography had long been in use in forensics and criminal identification, and the digital software of morphing and composites was partly an outcome of this sort of practice. Visual constructions such as the "New Face of America," then, are not simply benign imaginings. They can serve as material "blueprints" for the scientific and social practices that they invoke, including selective breeding. They make these practices seem natural, easy, and inevitable.

Artist Nancy Burson has been a major force in the development of morphing not only in the art world but also in the crossover between art, science, and the broader culture. In the late 1980s, Burson was instrumental in developing computer software that contributed to the ability to make portrait images "age"—that is, to create a virtual rendering of the person as he or she could be predicted to look many years after the photograph was taken. This technique was an important breakthrough in locating missing persons and criminals, and images with "age progression" are now commonly circulated on flyers of those who are missing (in particular missing children). Burson's composite photographs and virtual renderings suggest some of the ways that the visual cultures of art and science are not as distinct as one might think. In the late 1990s, Burson created a series that commented on the legacy of physiognomy. Her series *Craniofacial* is composed of portraits of people with facial anomalies. Rather than taking these portraits in clinical, context-stripped settings and poses so common in the institutional imaging of aberrant facial structures, Burson shows us these faces in intimate, everyday settings emphasizing the routine normalcy of those deemed physically anomalous. Burson's *Human Race Machine* (2000) is a project that allows participants to visualize themselves as being of different races. She writes, "the concept of race is not genetic, but social. The *Human Race Machine* allows us to move beyond difference and arrive at sameness." If we compare the "New Face of America" and Burson's *Human Race Machine* to the early categorization charts of Bertillon and Galton, we can see the ways in which these overriding concepts of difference and sameness have guided not only the sciences of human classification but also humanitarian concepts governing the connections between humans.

FIG. 9.27
Nancy Burson, *Human Race Machine*, 2000

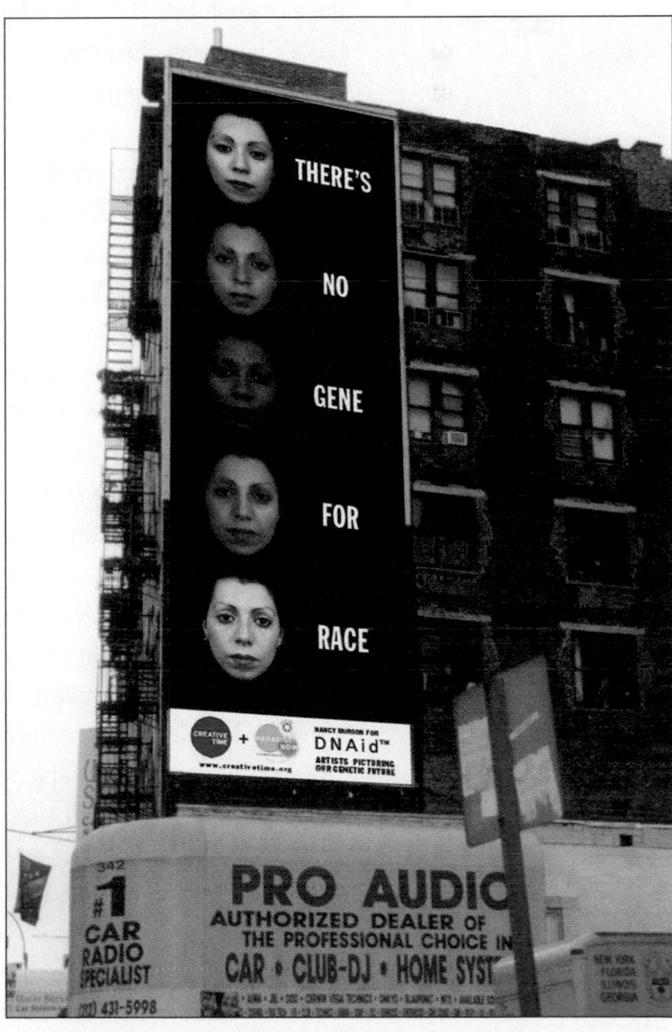

Contemporary imaging techniques such as morphing are indicators not only of the changing concepts of the postmodern, digital body but also of the relationship between the body and technology. One of the primary concepts for thinking about the relationship of the body and technology is the idea of the cyborg. A cyborg, or cybernetic organism, defines an entity that is part technology and part organism. The cyborg has its roots in early computer science and with the science of cybernetics, founded by Norbert Wiener in the postwar period, as a science that integrated communications theory and control theory. Cybernetics sees the human mind, the human body, and the world of automated machines and systems as having the common denominator of control and communication and proposes that the fundamental nature of the human organism can be reduced to an organizational pattern. The term *cyborg* was first proposed by Manfred Clynes and Nathan Kline in 1960 to describe "self-regulating man-machine systems," which they were exploring in relation to the rigors of space travel, with fundamental aspects of feedback and homeostatis.[29] Early computer scientists were thus working with the idea that man-made devices could be incorporated into the human body's regulatory feedback chains as a "participatory" stage of evolution with the desire for a "new and better being." Since the 1980s, the cyborg has been theorized as an identity that has emerged in the context of technoculture, a posthuman identity that represents the breaking down of traditional boundaries between body and technology and organism and machine. It was prominently theorized by Donna Haraway in her famous 1985 essay "The Cyborg Manifesto" as a means to think about the transformation of subjectivity in a late capitalist world of science, technology, and biomedicine.[30] Rather than suggesting that subjects experience technology solely as an external and oppressive force, Haraway wrote of the body-technology relationship as one filled with potential for imagining and building new worlds, potentially both liberatory and potentially threatening. There are, of course, people whom we might think of as literal cyborgs, people who have prosthetics and electronic devices embedded within their bodies, seemingly at one with technological devices. Much contemporary work in cyborg theory postulates that we are all, to a certain extent, cyborgs, given our complex bodily relationships with technology; for example, that our interaction with our computers, iPods, and cell phones means that we experience technologies as inseparable from our bodies. As this Hewlett-Packard ad shows, technologies are often sold to us with the promise that they will function as extensions of our bodies (as Marshall McLuhan once predicted), and these technologies are imagined to be integrated within our very eyes and vision. More recent work in the concept of the body-machine relationship develops on Haraway's point that we both fear and revere science and technology, enjoying

FIG. 9.28
HP ad: You and Your Camera See Eye to Eye, 2004

its benefits while remaining cautious about the economic, political, environmental, social, and emotional impacts of new technologies on the social worlds in which they are introduced and on which they draw for their raw material.

Visualizing Pharmaceuticals

Since the mid-1990s many countries, including the United States, have allowed direct-to-consumer advertising for prescription drugs. Advertising has become one of the ways in which consumer-patients receive information about medication choices. Direct-to-consumer (DTC) advertising, as this area of marketing is called, speaks directly to consumers, even though they can only purchase such a drug with a doctor's prescription. This kind of marketing has generated debates about advertising ethics and the logic of promoting drugs outside a medical context. Proponents point to surveys showing that most medical professionals feel that these ads have a positive effect in motivating patients to be active in their health care decisions. A similar argument can be made about the vast amount of medical information now available to people via the Web. Yet there is also significant concern that DTC ads make drugs seem better than they actually are.

If we consider DTC in relation to the history of images of science and medicine, and if we use the tools of cultural analysis to read their ideological messages, we can see the ways in which they construct particular kinds of subjects. The aim of these ads is, quite simply, to sell drugs and their continued use, and they do so by speaking to consumers as potentially abnormal and diseased subjects. Thus we could say that these ads interpellate consumers as subjects in need of chemical modification, as outside the norm, as subjects whose modification through the consumption of pharmaceuticals will aid them in becoming happier, more normal, and more fulfilled. It is thus a common convention in these ads, such as this Effexor ad, to have checklists that consumers might easily feel interpellated by (here, a checklist for the symptoms of depression). It is important to note that the aim of such an ad is to motivate a consumer to seek out such a drug remedy by asking (if not demanding) that their doctor provide access to it. In this ad, vague symptoms that might be considered normal responses to the strains of everyday life (stress, sadness, and trouble sleeping) are followed rhetorically and visually within the ad by the suggestion to "ask your doctor" to prescribe this product.

It is the convention of DTC ads that they offer abstract kinds of promises through the use of images of people in posttreatment states of being. By law, those ads that are indicated (meaning that they discuss the conditions that the drug is designated to treat)

FIG. 9.29
Effexor ad, 2008

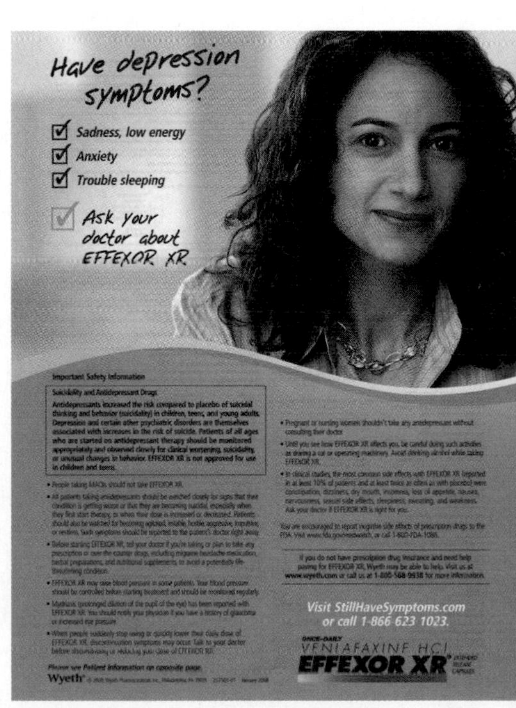

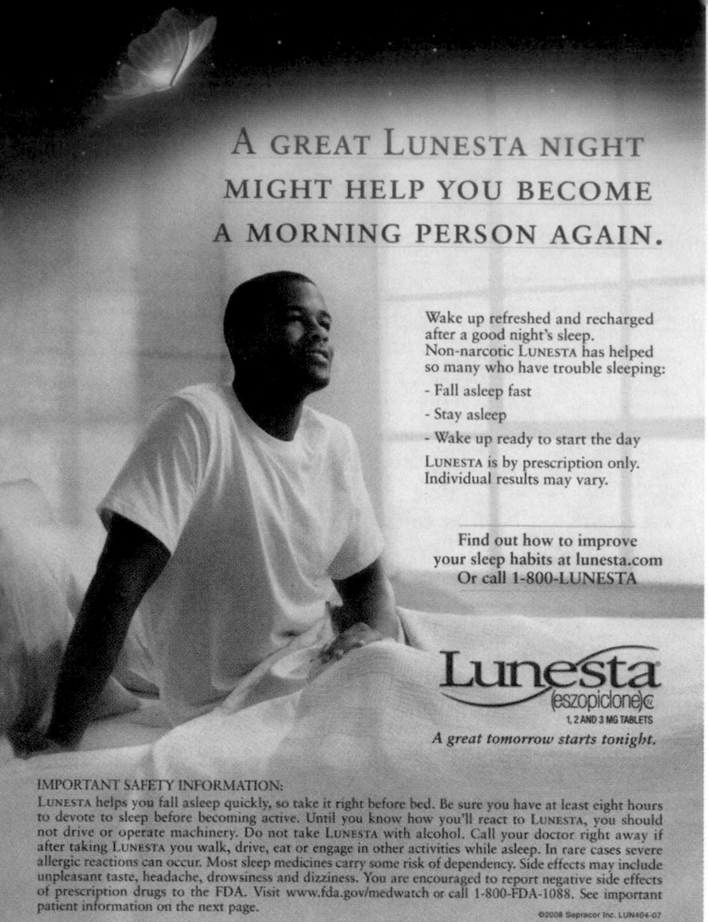

A GREAT LUNESTA NIGHT
MIGHT HELP YOU BECOME
A MORNING PERSON AGAIN.
Wake up refreshed and recharged after a good night's sleep.
Non-narcotic LUNESTA has helped so many who have trouble sleeping:
- Fall asleep fast
- Stay asleep
- Wake up ready to start the day
LUNESTA is by prescription only.
Individual results may vary.
Find out how to improve your sleep habits at lunesta.com
Or call 1-800-LUNESTA
Lunesta
(eszopiclone)
1, 2 AND 3 MG TABLETS
A great tomorrow starts tonight.
IMPORTANT SAFETY INFORMATION:
LUNESTA helps you fall asleep quickly, so take it right before bed. Be sure you have at least eight hours to devote to sleep before becoming active. Until you know how you'll react to LUNESTA, you should not drive or operate machinery. Do not take LUNESTA with alcohol. Call your doctor right away if after taking LUNESTA you walk, drive, eat or engage in other activities while asleep. In rare cases severe allergic reactions can occur. Most sleep medicines carry some risk of dependency. Side effects may include unpleasant taste, headache, drowsiness and dizziness. You are encouraged to report negative side effects of prescription drugs to the FDA. Visit www.fda.gov/medwatch or call 1-800-FDA-1088. See important patient information on the next page.
©2008 Sepracor Inc. LUN404-07

FIG. 9.30
Lunesta ad, 2008

are required to provide information about the potential negative side effects of those drugs. This often results in advertising texts that are comedically at cross-purposes, with soft-focus images of smiling people accompanied by small text that discusses horrifying potential effects. Nonindicated ads are not required to do this, but they are also not allowed to mention the conditions they are indicated for, thus creating ads that are abstract and mysterious, featuring feel-good situations with little concrete information. In general, DTC ads do not feature images of people taking drugs or receiving medical treatments, and they display a dominance of images of people looking happy and content in casual, leisure situations or making short, vague testimonials about how good they feel. In this Lunesta ad, the image of a contented person rising from his bed with a magical butterfly flying over him is used to sell a sleeping pill. Such an ad promises not only the capacity to sleep but also the transformative quality of such a drug to turn someone into a new kind of person, in this case, a "morning person." It is useful to remember Raymond Williams's well-known analysis of advertising as a "magic system" that transforms ordinary, material products into objects that promise a magical transformation.[31] DTC ads explicitly speak to consumers about the magical transformation that these drugs will provide for them. That there are risks in selling drugs this way is a key point in criticisms of DTC ads. For instance, the very popular drug Vioxx, which was used to treat arthritis and other muscular pain, had a very successful DTC campaign using former skating champion Dorothy Hamill to extol its transformative potential. When the Food and Drug Administration reported, in 2004, that Vioxx max have contributed to the deaths of almost twenty-eight thousand users, it was rapidly withdrawn from the market by its manufacturer Merck. Creating consumers for pharmaceuticals, which is what DTC ads do, thus involves a level of risk beyond that of most advertising.

In chapter 7, we noted that ads sell not only a product. They also sell something larger: a lifestyle, a national ideology, capitalism, or consumerism itself. Like other types of ads, DTC ads are not just about selling drugs as a normal, everyday part of our lives. They are also about selling science, medicine, and their institutions as essential aspects of our everyday existence and not just as places we might turn to for help during periods of illness. As Joseph Dumit puts it, the medicated citizen has become the norm. We are offered "drugs for life," that is, drugs that we may use every day for prolonged periods (such as Effexor or Prozac) to maintain a sense of normalcy, and not simply drugs to help us recover from sickness.[32] It is a key aim of DTC ads, for instance, to both encourage consumers to continue to use certain medications and to remind consumers to take their medication. The benefit to pharmaceutical companies in keeping consumers on drugs "for life" is clear. Going on a drug for life, or for an indefinite period of years, means participation in a consumer market for life, and not for the relatively brief period from illness to recovery.

FIG. 9.31
Oreck "Clean for the Cure" Vacuum, 2007

In the 2000s nonprofit health advocacy groups found canny ways to use corporate marketing and advertising not only to generate consumer health awareness but also to promote charity revenues. These strategies involve linking particular brands and products to a cause. In the Clean for the Cure campaign, Oreck Corporation, a manufacturer of cleaning appliances, donates fifty dollars to Susan G. Komen for the Cure® (a division of the nonprofit Komen Breast Cancer Foundation) for each purchase of its pink logo-emblazoned Special Edition Oreck XL Ultra vacuum. The charity benefits from donations and exposure through ads; the corporation benefits from the image of benevolence conferred by association with the charitable cause; and the consumer benefits from the good feeling of supporting an important cause while consuming. The vacuum, traditionally a tool of women's unpaid domestic labor, can be seen as an ironic vehicle for this message about empowering women.

The visual culture of the business of medicine and pharmaceutical companies extends beyond the advertising of products to consumers. Public debate over the role of pharmaceutical companies in relation to the business of health and the ongoing health care crisis in the United States has produced competing kinds of images. During the postmodern period, artists have been quite active in the production of images and media texts questioning the ties between private corporate interests and national health care. Artist-activists, most notably in the era of AIDS, have produced images and media texts that address concerns about patients' rights, the role and structure of corporate science in health care, and the role of the media in reporting on scientific advances in health care. In chapter 2, we discussed the innovative use of posters to raise public awareness of facts about HIV/AIDS during a period when public officials in areas most hard-hit by the epidemic gave the issue little funding and attention. The work of ACT UP (AIDS Coalition to Unleash Power) in the

FIG. 9.32
ACT UP, *It's Big Business*, 1989

1980s and 1990s introduced a whole new era of political visual culture about scientific practice. ACT UP explicitly challenged not only cultural perceptions about AIDS but also political policies concerning science and medical funding and research. ACT UP's visual campaigns, which included performances, sit-ins, videos, and posters, were an important venue for the distribution of accurate information about AIDS transmission at a time in history when science and medicine were not working to get out the message. ACT UP used images as an integral aspect of their provocative public interventions that aimed to get mainstream media to pay attention to the AIDS crisis. ACT UP used images such as this one, distributed as posters and stickers, to shock the public in the urban cityscape into thinking about the presence of people with AIDS, the inaction of the government in addressing the growing health crisis, and the role of pharmaceutical companies in the crisis. The visual culture of AIDS activism was one of the most transformative and effective interventions by nonscientists in the culture of science in the twentieth century, setting the model for activism in science in the twenty-first century.

As the images discussed in this chapter demonstrate, science is not created in a vacuum or in a world that is separate from social and cultural meaning. A cross-fertilization of ideas and representations exists between science and culture, and representations of science in popular media have a reciprocal influence on how scientists do science. Similarly, as we have shown, scientific images have cultural meanings that govern not only how they are produced and for what purpose but also how they are interpreted and gain cultural value. From the image of the anatomist at work to the photograph that makes a fetus appear to be alive to the MRIs and microscopic images that render the body into an aestheticized landscape to ads that sell science, the visual culture of science makes clear that the realms of science, culture, and politics are all intertwined.

Notes

1. Nikolas Rose, *The Politics of Life Itself: Biomedicine, Power and Subjectivity in the Twenty-First Century*, 4 (Princeton, N.J.: Princeton University Press, 2006).
2. Erwin Panofsky, "Artist, Scientist, Genius: Notes on the 'Renaissance Dammerung,'" in *The Renaissance: Six Essays*, by Wallace K. Ferguson et al. and the Metropolitan Museum of Art, 142 (New York: Harper Torchbooks, 1953).
3. José Van Dijck, *The Transparent Body: A Cultural Analysis of Medical Imaging*, 4 (Seattle: University of Washington Press, 2005).
4. Julie V. Hansen, "Resurrecting Death: Anatomical Art in the Cabinet of Dr. Frederik Ruysch," *Art Bulletin* (December 1996).
5. Van Dijck, *The Transparent Body*, 122.
6. Vanessa R. Schwartz, "Public Visits to the Morgue: *Flânerie* in the Service of the State," in *Spectacular Realities: Early Mass Culture in Fin-de-Siècle Paris*, 60 (Berkeley: University of California Press, 1998).

7. Michael Fried, *Realism, Writing, Disfiguration: On Thomas Eakins and Stephen Crane* (Chicago: University of Chicago Press, 1987); and Jennifer Doyle, "Sex, Scandal, and Thomas Eakins's The Gross Clinic," *Representations* 68 (Fall 1999), 1–33.
8. Fried, *Realism, Writing, Disfiguration*, 62.
9. See van Dijck, *The Transparent Body*, chapter 7; and Lisa Cartwright, "A Cultural Anatomy of the Visible Human Project," in *The Visible Woman: Imaging Technologies, Gender, and Science*, ed. Paula A. Treichler, Lisa Cartwright, and Constance Penley, 21–43 (New York: New York University Press, 1998).
10. Van Dijck, *The Transparent Body*, 59.
11. Lisa Cartwright, *Screening the Body: Tracing Medicine's Visual Culture* (Minneapolis: University of Minnesota Press, 1995).
12. See Stephen J. Gould, *The Mismeasure of Man* (New York: Norton, [1981] 1996).
13. Sandra S. Phillips, "Identifying the Criminal," in *Police Pictures: The Photograph as Evidence*, ed. Sandra S. Phillips, 20 (San Francisco: San Francisco Museum of Modern Art/Chronicle Books, 1997).
14. Allan Sekula, "The Body and the Archive," *October* 39 (Winter 1986), 6–7.
15. Kelly Gates, "Identifying the 9/11 Faces of Terror: The Promise and Problem of Face Recognition," *Cultural Studies* 20.4–5 (July/September 2006), 417–40.
16. See Janelle Sue Taylor, "The Public Fetus and the Family Car: From Abortion Politics to a Volvo Advertisment," *Public Culture* 4.2 (1992), 67–80; and Carol Stabile, "Shooting the Mother: Fetal Photography and the Politics of Disappearance," *Camera Obscura* 28 (January 1992), 179–205.
17. See, for instance, Rosalind Petchesky, "Fetal Images: The Power of Visual Culture in the Politics of Reproduction," in *Reproductive Technologies*, ed. Michelle Stanforth, 57–80 (Minneapolis: University of Minnesota Press, 1987).
18. See Valerie Hartouni, "Containing Women: Reproductive Discourse(s) in the 1980s," in *Cultural Conceptions: On Reproductive Technologies and the Remaking of Life*, 26–50 (Minneapolis: University of Minneapolis Press, 1997).
19. See Petchesky, "Fetal Images," and Stabile, "Shooting the Mother."
20. Emily Martin, *Flexible Bodies: Tracking Immunity in American Culture from the Days of Polio to the Age of AIDS*, 173 (Boston: Beacon Press, 1994).
21. Joseph Dumit, *Picturing Personhood: Brain Scans and Biomedical Identity*, 6 (Princeton, N.J.: Princeton University Press, 2004).
22. Dorothy Nelkin and M. Susan Lindee, *The DNA Mystique: The Gene as a Cultural Icon*, 102–03 (New York: W. H. Freeman, 1995).
23. José van Dijck, *Imagenation: Popular Images of Genetics*, 126–27 (New York: New York University Press, 1998).
24. Donna J. Haraway, *Modest_Witness@Second_Millennium. FemaleMan©_Meets_OncoMouse™*, 158 (New York: Routledge, 1997).
25. Haraway, *Modest_Witness@Second_Millennium.*, 79.
26. Sue Schweik, "The Ugly Laws of Disability Studies," lecture, 2003.
27. *Time*, "The New Face of America", 2 (Fall 1993).
28. Evelynn M. Hammonds, "New Technologies of Race," in *Processed Lives: Gender and Technology in Everyday Life*, ed. Jennifer Terry and Melodie Calvert, 113–20 (New York: Routledge, 1997). See also Lauren Berlant, *The Queen of America Goes to Washington City, 83–144* (Durham, N.C.: Duke University Press, 1997).
29. Manfred E. Clynes and Nathan S. Kline, "Cyborgs and Space," *Astronautics* (September 1960), reprinted in *The Cyborg Handbook*, ed. Chris Hables Gray, 29–33 (New York: Routledge, 1995).
30. Donna J. Haraway, "The Cyborg Manifesto," in *Simians, Cyborgs, and Women: The Reinvention of Nature*, 149–81 (New York: Routledge, 1991).
31. Raymond Williams, "Advertising: The Magic System," in *Problems in Materialism and Culture*, 170–95 (London: Verso, 1980).
32. Joseph Dumit, "Drugs for Life" *Molecular Interventions* 2 (2002), 124–27

Further Reading

Balsamo, Anne. *Technologies of the Gendered Body*. Durham, N.C.: Duke University Press, 1996.

Berlant, Lauren. *The Queen of America Goes to Washington City: Essays on Sex and Citizenship*. Durham, N.C.: Duke University Press, 1997.

Cartwright, Lisa. *Screening the Body: Tracing Medicine's Visual Culture.* Minneapolis: University of Minnesota Press, 1995.

Cartwright, Lisa. *Moral Spectatorship: Technologies of Voice and Affect in Postwar Representations of the Child.* Durham, N.C.: Duke University Press, 2008.

Daston, Lorraine, and Peter Galison. "The Image of Objectivity." *Representations* 40 (1992), 81–128.

Davis-Floyd, Robbie, and Joseph Dumit, eds. *Cyborg Babies: From Techno-Sex to Techno-Tots.* New York: Routledge, 1998.

Duden, Barbara. *Disembodying Women: Perspectives on Pregnancy and the Unborn.* Translated by Lee Hoinacki. Cambridge, Mass.: Harvard University Press, 1993.

Dumit, Joseph. *Picturing Personhood: Brain Scans and Biomedical Identity.* Princeton, N.J.: Princeton University Press, 2004.

———. "Drugs for Life." *Molecular Interventions* 2 (2002), 124–27.

Foucault, Michel. *The Birth of the Clinic: An Archaeology of Medical Perception.* Translated by A. M. Sheridan Smith. New York: Vintage, [1963] 1994.

———. *Madness and Civilization: A History of Insanity in the Age of Reason.* Translated by Richard Howard. New York: Routledge, [1961] 2001.

———. *The History of Sexuality: An Introduction, Volume 1.* Translated by Robert Hurley. New York: Vintage, [1976] 1990.

Hables Gray, Chris, ed. *The Cyborg Handbook.* New York: Routledge, 1995.

Hammonds, Evelynn M. "New Technologies of Race." In *Processed Lives: Gender and Technology in Everyday Life.* Edited by Jennifer Terry and Melodie Calvert. New York: Routledge, 1997, 108–21.

Gross, Paul R., and Norman Levitt. *Higher Superstition: The Academic left and Its Quarrels with Science.* Baltimore: Johns Hopkins Press, 1994.

Haraway, Donna J. *Simians, Cyborgs, and Women: The Reinvention of Nature.* New York: Routledge, 1991.

———. *Modest_Witness@Second_Millennium. FemaleMan©_Meets_OncoMouse™.* New York: Routledge, 1997.

Hartouni, Valerie. *Cultural Conceptions: On Reproductive Technologies and the Remaking of Life.* Minneapolis: University of Minneapolis Press, 1997.

Hayles, N. Katherine. *Chaos and Order: Complex Dynamics in Literature and Science.* Chicago: University of Chicago Press, 1991.

———. *How We Became Posthuman: Virtual Bodies in Cybernetics, Literature, and Informatics.* Chicago: University of Chicago Press, 1999.

———. *My Mother Was a Computer: Digital Subjects and Literary Texts.* Chicago: University of Chicago Press, 2005.

Hubbard, Ruth, and Elijah Wald. *Exploding the Gene Myth.* Boston: Beacon, 1993.

Jones, Caroline A., and Peter Galison, eds. *Picturing Science, Producing Art.* New York: Routledge, 1998.

Jordanova, Ludmilla. *Sexual Visions: Images of Gender in Science and Medicine between the Eighteenth and Twentieth Centuries.* Madison: University of Wisconsin Press, 1989.

Lombroso, Cesare. *Criminal Man.* Translated by Mary Gibson and Nicole Hahn Rafter. Durham, N.C.: Duke University Press, 2006.

Martin, Emily. *Flexible Bodies: Tracking Immunity in American Culture from the Days of Polio to the Age of AIDS.* Boston: Beacon Press, 1994.

McGrath, Roberta. "Medical Police." *Ten.8,* 14 (1984), 13–18.

Nelkin, Dorothy, and M. Susan Lindee. *The DNA Mystique: The Gene as a Cultural Icon.* New York: Freeman, 1995.

Nilsson, Lennart, with Mirjam Furuhjelm, Axel Ingelman-Sundberg, and Claes Wirsen. *A Child is Born.* New York: Dell, 1966.

Pauwels, Luc, ed. *Visual Cultures of Science: Rethinking Representational Practices in Knowledge Building and Science Communication.* Lebanon, N.H.: Dartmouth College Press/University Press of New England, 2006.

Penley, Constance, and Andrew Ross, eds. *Technoculture.* Minneapolis: University of Minnesota Press, 1991.

Petchesky, Rosalind. "Fetal Images: The Power of Visual Culture in the Politics of Reproduction." In *Reproductive Technologies*. Edited by Michelle Stanforth. Minneapolis: University of Minnesota Press, 1987, 57–80.

Phillips, Sandra S., ed. *Police Pictures: The Photograph as Evidence*. San Francisco: San Francisco Museum of Modern Art/Chronicle Books, 1997.

Rose, Nikolas. *The Politics of Life Itself: Biomedicine, Power and Subjectivity in the Twenty-First Century*. Princeton, N.J.: Princeton University Press, 2006.

Schwartz, Vanessa R. *Spectacular Realities: Early Mass Culture in Fin-de-Siècle Paris*. Berkeley: University of California Press, 1998.

Smith, Shawn Michelle. *American Archives: Gender, Race, and Class in Visual Culture*. Princeton, N.J.: Princeton University Press, 1999.

Stabile, Carol. "Shooting the Mother: Fetal Photography and the Politics of Disappearance." *Camera Obscura*, 28 (January 1992), 179–205.

Stafford, Barbara Maria, and Frances Terpak. *Devices of Wonder: From the World in a Box to Images on the Screen*. Los Angeles: Getty Research Institute, 2001.

Sturken, Marita. *Tangled Memories: The Vietnam War, the AIDS Epidemic, and the Politics of Remembering*. Berkeley: University of California Press, 1997, ch. 7.

Taylor, Janelle Sue. "The Public Fetus and the Family Car: From Abortion Politics to a Volvo Advertisement." *Public Culture*, 4 (2) (1992), 67–80.

Time. Special Issue. "The New Face of America." Fall 1993.

Treichler, Paula, Lisa Cartwright, and Constance Penley, eds. *The Visible Woman: Imaging Technologies, Gender, and Science*. New York: New York University Press, 1998.

van Dijck, José. *Imagenation: Popular Images of Genetics*. New York: New York University Press, 1998.

———. *The Transparent Body: A Cultural Analysis of Medical Imaging*. Seattle: University of Washington Press, 2005.

chapter **ten**

The Global Flow of Visual Culture

The circulation of images has changed dramatically over the past few decades. Whereas in the mid-twentieth century, images circulated through print media, national broadcast television networks, and the exhibition of film in theaters, today the two primary venues for the circulation, distribution, and consumption of images are satellite and the Web. This means that in the 2000s images move around the globe with ease and an instantaneous speed of transmission that was unheard of before the 1980s. Communication technologies that facilitate long-distance connection, from the telegraph to the telephone, have been proposed as potential avenues to world peace. Yet the globalization of communication technologies over the past few decades has shown that global image flows may allow an increased circulation of concepts, ideas, politics, and images, but this also helps to foster the growth of multinational corporations and the expansion of political influence by powerful nations over distant domains with fewer resources. Some paradoxes hover over analyses of global culture: transnational cultural flows create a homogenization of culture yet they also foster diversification, hybridity, and new global audiences. These flows are never truly equal. Globalization has increased the rich-poor divide. The poorest economies and the poor within the richest economies are paying the biggest price for globalization.

The media and visual images have been important forces in the changing status of the nation-state and the globalization of capital. Transnational and diasporic cultures, in which peoples are dispersed across national boundaries, are linked in part by consumption patterns and media cultures. Religious communities are linked across broad geographic areas through programming that includes webcast services, Internet radio, websites, and blogs.[1] The use of satellites by television networks and the proliferation of cable television have enabled diasporic communities to have access to television programming from their countries of origin in most locations around the world, and the rise of panethnic programming, such as Latino telenovelas that are aimed at multinational audiences, has dramatically changed the global landscape of television. Television news has been globalized with CNN International, the English-language television network that in 2008 claimed to reach 200 million households and hotels in 200 countries through cable and satellite feed; with Al Jazeera (produced in Qatar and watched globally, with English-channel hubs in Washington, D.C., London, and Kuala Lumpur); and with BBC World, generally one of the most watched channels in the world. The Web provides a globally linked network through which images, media forms, cultural products, and texts circulate throughout the world. Art also circulates on the Web, with art museums establishing global profiles through Web galleries, as well as opening branch museums around the world. Many films are produced in multinational studios and are distributed through global markets, as well as through global black markets of DVDs and downloaded computer files. People also move increasingly around the globe, as immigrants, workers, refugees, tourists, and consumers.

But the ideal of a global world without borders does not match the social reality of trying to forge such a world in the twenty-first century. Mobility (travel, communication exchange) may be easier than it was in the twentieth century, technologically speaking, but the reality is that national borders have tightened since 2001. Seyla Benhabib, a political theorist who is Turkish and Jewish, has consistently emphasized the importance of voluntary self-ascription to a religious or cultural identity, along with recognition that those who hold minority views or minority identities must be granted the same rights as those who constitute the majority.[2] Voluntary passage out of a national context in which one was born and into a national context in which one anticipates certain rights and freedoms is a desire held by many in the world today who hope for or who attempt such a transition (with or without success). However, since 2001 democracies have increasingly responded with distrust, hostility, and extradition to immigrants and exilic subjects who cross national borders seeking opportunity or asylum from political repression.

With some key notable exceptions, media, information, and images travel constantly throughout the world even if people cannot travel with the same ease, crossing boundaries of nation, culture, and language. Visual culture is key in this climate of escalated globalization. There is, though, a marked distinction between those nations among which images seem to flow with unrestricted ease and those where circulation is tightly monitored and restricted. Understanding how images circulate and what role they play in a global information economy is crucial to understanding practices of looking in the twenty-first century.

The Global Subject and the Global Gaze

Movements of peoples, ideas, information, and images have taken place throughout the history of the world. However, the concept of globalization has a much more recent, post-Cold War history. We discuss the history of theories of globalization later in this chapter. Here, we examine the ways in which the concepts of the global and of globalization has intersected with imaging practices to constitute the global subject, or "global citizens." How is it that we situate ourselves visually in relationship to the concept of the global?

One of the key historical demarcations of the concept of the globe came in the 1960s, when the space travels of the U.S. and the Soviet Union produced the first photographic images of earth as seen from space. Drawn images of the globe had of course been popular for centuries and were a key visual icon of empire; however, with the first photographic images of the whole earth, carrying with them the connotations of photographic evidence, a new embrace of the globe took place. During the 1960s, the National Aeronautics and Space Administration (NASA) Apollo space missions, which resulted in the landing of several astronauts on the moon in 1968, began producing images of the earth. One of the first images, Earthrise, taken by the Apollo 8 mission in 1968 and transmitted back to earth via television signals, shows the earth partially illuminated as it rises (just as a moonrise can be seen from earth). The spiritual meaning of this image was underscored by the fact that the astronauts read aloud from the Book of Genesis as they transmitted the image to earth.[3]

The declaration of Earth Day in 1970 marked a moment in history when the idea of a unified planet carried a strong humanitarian appeal to the mostly North American and European advocates of this celebration. However, a detailed photographic image of the earth in its entirety was not yet available to the public. Stewart Brand, who would later become famous as the founder of the *Whole Earth Catalog* (a compendium of tools and potential goods for going "back to the land" that was a kind of precursor to cyberculture and the Web and was an icon of the 1960s counterculture), began to lobby in 1970 for NASA to release an image of the whole earth seen from space. He distributed buttons that asked, "Why Haven't We Seen a Photograph of the Whole Earth Yet?" to such luminaries as Marshall McLuhan and Buckminster Fuller, and to members of Congress.[4] This image, called Whole Earth or "the blue marble," was released by NASA in 1972. It became an icon of the peace movement, symbolizing global unity and harmony. Brand, like others, thought that "no one would ever perceive things in the same way" after seeing

FIG. 10.1
View of Earth as photographed by Apollo 17 crew, 1972

FIG. 10.2
The Last Whole Earth Catalog, front and back covers

this image. Denis Cosgrove writes that the Whole Earth image was the product of the U.S. imperial mission in space, fueled by the Cold War in its space race with the Soviet Union, yet it prompted a broad popular discourse about world unity and the idea of "one world."[5] The well-known writer Archibald MacLeish wrote a poem about the Whole Earth image and proclaimed it an icon of global consciousness. Brand and others involved in the 1960s counterculture quickly deployed the Whole Earth image as an icon of alternative politics and the peace movement, and it was subsequently featured on the back cover of every edition of the *Whole Earth Catalog*. The Whole Earth image continues to have currency in the context of digital technologies and computer cultures. This IBM ad from the early 1990s (fig. 10.3), for instance, uses the image of the globe, placed within the reach of a baby, to signify "New challenges. New thinking." In an image such as this, the globe connotes science and knowledge as within the reach of the next generation, thanks to the new communications technologies offered by companies like IBM.

Satellites are a key factor in changing perspectives on visualizing the earth and in changing our ways of circulating the images through which we understand our lives. The development of satellite technology began, as did the earth images, in the postwar Cold War context of the space race. The 1957 launching of the first satellite by the Soviet Union, called Sputnik, began a period in which satellites would become a primary visualizing force, as the means to survey and spy on other nations, as a means of transmission for television and news images, and as the means through which most telecommunications, in particular cell phones, takes place. By the beginning of the twenty-first century, there were more than eight thousand satellites orbiting the earth. Lisa Parks writes, in her book, *Cultures in Orbit*, that "the globe is crisscrossed by satellite footprints, and the meanings of the televisual are increasingly contingent on them."[6]

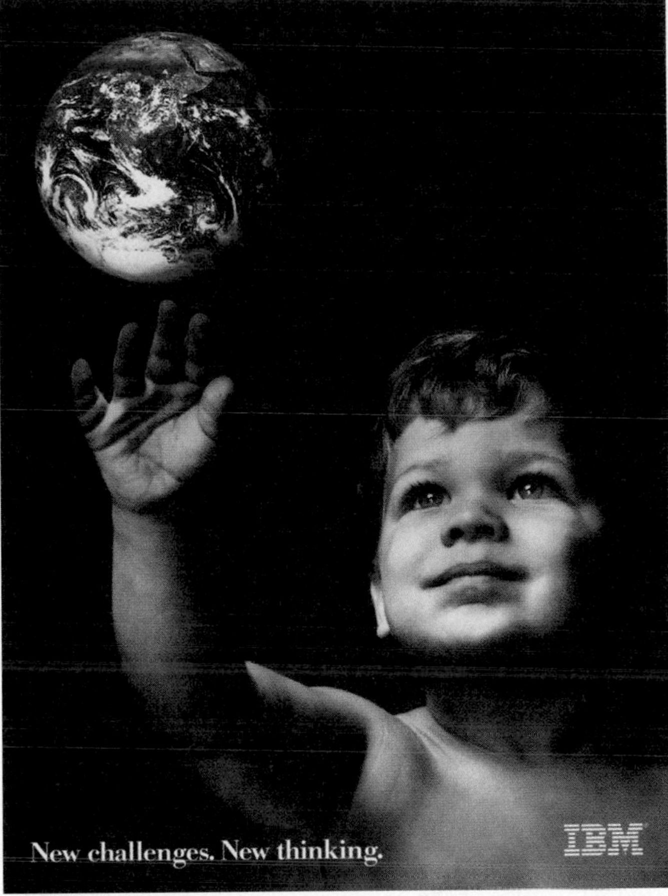

FIG. 10.3
IBM ad, 1992

During the 1960s and 1970s, people were fascinated with the idea of satellite transmission. Images transmitted across great distances could create an experience of simultaneous time in disparate places. Some artists' projects during this period involved performers situated in distant locales performing together by using satellite broadcast feeds. In the 1970s, live satellite feeds became a standard means of broadcasting important news events. Interconnectivity was a primary theme in the promotion of early uses of satellite in television markets. For instance, the 1967 BBC program *One World* used satellite technology to feature four "live" births throughout the world. Focused on the problem of the world's overpopulation, the program emphasized unity among all peoples, harkening back to the Family of Man, a famous photographic exhibition of the 1950s that showed links among various peoples around the world through photographs of different cultures. Parks proposes that satellites helped to create a "global presence" in which liveness and presence were "indistinguishable from Western discourses of modernization. Emanating from Western nation-states, the satellite spectaculars were as the cutting edge of the modern, the most current or present form of cultural expression.... Developing nations could only claim themselves as 'modern' if they were in the range of American, Western European, or Japanese satellite television signals, earth stations, or networks."[7]

People who have access to television and the Web have a broad array of satellite images available to them. These images situate them on the globe from the perspective of satellites orbiting the earth. For instance, it is a convention of weather reporting to show satellite images of the weather, and this in turn locates viewers, regionally and nationally, outside looking in on the spaces they and others occupy in the here and now. We can see storms coming our way through satellite tracking, and we can watch them as if from above even as we experience them from below. Viewers thus become accustomed, as Jody Berland writes, to viewing the weather and the skies from the perspective of looking down from them, rather than looking up at them.[8] This change in perspective afforded by satellites changes our relationship to objectivity and subjectivity in regard to knowledge about ourselves and the world. Whereas looking from outside and down upon the world suggests an enhancement of objective knowledge, the aerial satellite perspective also affords us a stronger sense of the subjective experience of living down inside the conditions we observe from above. Objectivity and subjectivity become more intertwined in our everyday experience of such things as weather and traffic conditions as we drive through the traffic jams reported to us on the radio in our cars, or as we collectively sit huddled in our respective houses under a violent downpour, viewing it from above through radar and live video footage broadcast on our TV screens.

Satellite imagery offers the awesome pleasure of seeing vast landscapes as if looking down from the clouds above, as well as the satisfaction of pin-pointing one's own location within that landscape even as one looks from a distance. These images provide both the wonder of viewing the earth with omniscience and the satisfaction of locating your own small place in that world—say, by using Google Earth to identify your neighborhood, your house, and even your car in the driveway, if you live in a region where Google Earth allows you to search by address. These images are a part of the history of modernity and visuality, in which an early fascination with photography was organized around a fascination with technologies for seeing things too small, too far away, or to hidden for the unaided human eye to see. Satellite images show us our world from a view in outer space that very few human beings in our lifetimes will ever see from that actual vantage point—what some would call a "god's eye view." Berland writes that satellite views of the earth produce a narrative of "this is one planet, one life, one world, one dream. This is the view of the globe from the eye of god.... This is the gorgeous, metaphysical triumph of the technological sublime, displaying itself in perfect harmony with the arcane laws of nature."[9]

A key feature of the everyday consumption of satellite images is the development of remote sensing as an aspect of the commercial satellite industry in the 1990s. Remote sensing involves the convergence of satellite, television, and computer imaging in the production of images of the earth from above. Until the 1990s, these images had for the most part been available only to government agencies and the military, which used them to spy on enemy states, among other things. With the opening up of this technology to private industry, an array of businesses emerged to sell satellite imaging programs to commercial and home users for work and leisure activities. Such images can be deployed for a broad range of political purposes. For instance, in the campaign to raise awareness about global warming, the use of satellite images has been highly effective in showing melting Arctic ice and glaciers and the expansion of desert terrains. In this sense, the image serves a role as empirical evidence of the facts of global warming that some industry-funded scientists have worked hard to contest. Some government scientists have used data about city lights to map the effects of urbanization on biological productivity. In this NASA image of city lights throughout the world, for instance, there is no correlation between population and the brightness

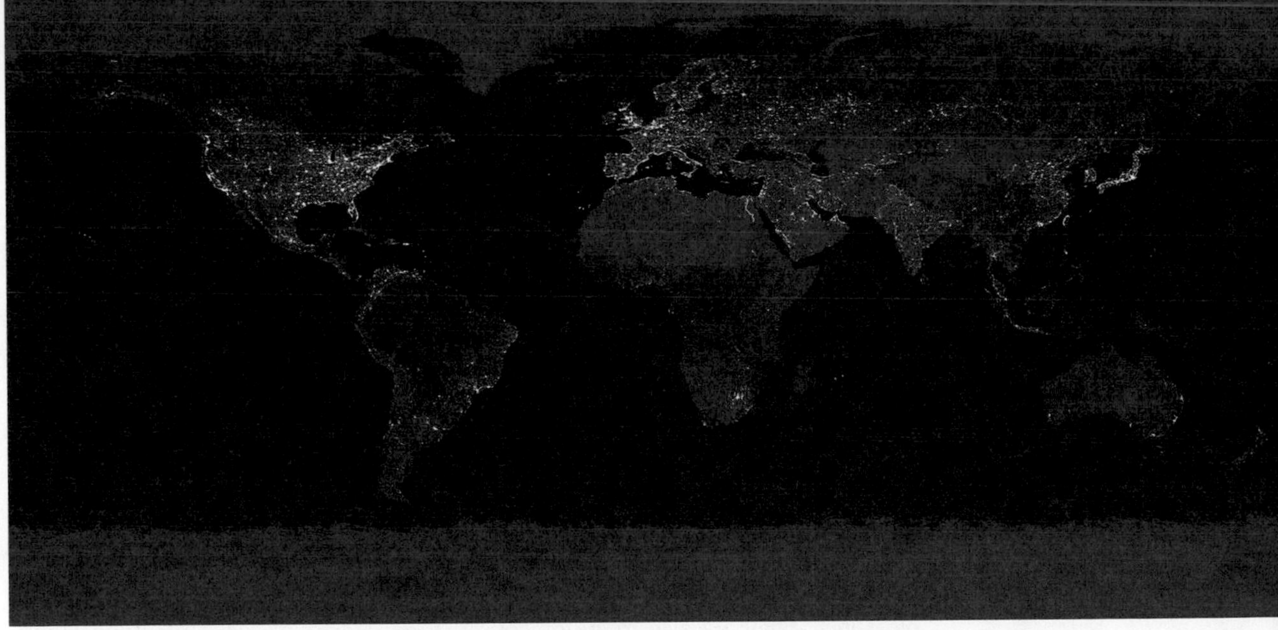

FIG. 10.4
NASA image of the Earth's city lights, November 2007

of the light; the correlation is, rather, between energy usage and light. It thus allows us to see those urban areas that consume the most energy. Such images not only provide the visual pleasure of mapping, but they also serve as dramatic visualizations of changes taking place in the natural and built environment, making them important historical and political documents of changes in consumption (of energy) wrought by industrialization and modernization. The concepts of appropriation and retooling are important ones in this context. Images generated from military satellites for national defense purposes can be used to map environmental destruction in the interests of protecting the earth from the devastating effects of technological progress and industrial development.

Geospatial technologies that produce digital images of the earth from satellites became enormously popular starting in 2005 with the release of Google Earth, a virtual globe program originally called Earth Viewer that combines imagery from satellite photographs, aerial photography, and 3D geographic information systems (GIS) images. Google Earth has popularized the viewing practice of seeing the earth from a satellite view, making this kind of viewing of the world emblematic of the information available to us in the digital era—images that were once the province of NASA and the military (the picture here was made with an early version of NASA's program). At the same time, it is clear that not all information is handled the same way on this system. Google Earth has been the object of some concern, in fact, among those who see the program as offering information about

FIG. 10.5
Huntington Beach, California, in NASA's World Wind 1.2, US Geological Survey

landscape and the built environment that may jeopardize national security, with locations such as the White House blurred to deter the use of the site to plot terrorist attacks on it. Not all countries, towns, and structures are represented in equivalent degrees of detail. In 2008, Las Vegas appeared with greater resolution than many other cities in the United States, simply because it is of great interest to tourists. Hamburg was the first city to appear in three dimensions, with even the textures of building surfaces appearing in relief. Like globalization itself, choices about where and how to represent parts of the globe in Google Earth show that all locales in the world are not equal.

We have been discussing the ways in which satellite images provide viewing pleasures. They are also, quite obviously, a key aspect of the contemporary surveillance society—what Berland calls our "satellite panopticon." The launching of satellites began during the Cold War, and military use was the primary motivation for their development. During the Cold War, spy planes had been a dominant form of gathering visual information, which took the form of aerial photographs. For instance, during the Cuban missile crisis in 1962, proof that the Soviet Union was building missile bases in Cuba was publicly announced in the U.S. with the presentation of aerial photographs that reportedly showed the missile silos. The use of satellites has helped to avoid the problems associated with planes entering into foreign airspace, a situation that has triggered several embarrassing, tense, and even tragic political misunderstandings and conflicts.

Global positioning systems (GPS) technology was developed in the aftermath of such a circumstance. The system was initially developed for use by the U.S. Department of Defense. But in 1983, Korean Flight 007 was shot down by Soviet military interceptors after the pilots of the commercial jetliner carrying 269 civilian passengers mistakenly crossed into Soviet airspace. Following this disaster, President Ronald Reagan issued a directive to make GPS available to the world for free, for the common good. He acted on the belief that if the pilots of Flight 007 had had access to a better navigational system they might have avoided their disastrous navigational mistake. Reagan's logic was that if satellite images could help us track enemy movement, they could also help us track our everyday paths, allowing us to plot our movements more carefully in a world whose borders are more permeable but not necessarily more free of restrictions and defenses.

The proliferation of satellite imagery inevitably provides the visual data for a society deeply invested in the practice of surveillance at every level. Navigational systems such as GPS, used in cars, boats, and planes, as well as in cell phones and computers, have spawned leisure activities such as geocaching, a sport that became internationally popular after 2000, with over 540,000 geocaches registered by the end of a decade in over 100 countries on seven continents. Geocachers hide small trinket-filled waterproof capsules, or caches, along with a log, in remote or odd locations, then post GPS coordinates, as well as descriptive clues about the location of the hidden capsule, to geocaching logs online.

GPS crosses military, science, service, and leisure uses because the system provides such comprehensive yet specific mapping data. GPS works an a model like the Cartesian grid. It allows the subject to put himself or herself, or the focal point of his or her own attention, at the center of the world contained in any given map. Not only do GPS systems help geologists measure volcanic expansion and fault line shifts with high precision and biologists to track the exact movements of animal life, but they also help emergency vehicle drivers to position themselves on the best route to people suffering accidents and emergencies. These systems help the everyday driver find his or her way on the road without using conventional paper maps. Unlike the paper map, on which we must imagine our current and anticipated position and the route between with a hesitant tip of the finger as our guide as we guess our best route and trace it out, the GPS screen tells us exactly where we are situated at each moment and where we must go at each subsequent moment to get to our anticipated destination (although we may disagree with its designation of the best route). It puts the user at the center of the world mapped by the image in a way that is mobile and fluid, allowing us to remain quite literally at a center that is always changing, from the present moment and place to the future anticipated time and place of arrival.

Cultural Imperialism and Beyond

We have been discussing the ways in which images and technologies allow us to situate ourselves in relation to the global. Now, we shift focus to examine the theories that help us make sense of the global flow of culture. One of the primary paradigms that has been used historically to understand the global movement of culture is imperialism. *Cultural imperialism* refers to how an ideology, a politics, or a way of life is exported into other territories through the export of cultural products. Twentieth-century communications theorists Armand Mattelart and Herbert Schiller argued that television is a means through which world powers such as the United States and the Soviet Union invaded the cultural and ideological space of a country with images and messages in place of an all-out military invasion. Television images and messages were seen to permeate the minds of the country's people with ideas about the value of U.S. or Soviet products, ideologies, and politics. In this view, television is able to cross boundaries and literally invade cultures in ways that bodies cannot. Through this programming, in the case of the United States, for instance, television would create global markets for U.S. products and promote global acceptance of U.S. political values.

An extreme example that illustrates this point is the U.S. government's Cold War-era practice of transmitting a radio broadcast, called the Voice of America, around the world, including into the frequency range of communist Cuba and in Soviet bloc countries. In 1985, the Reagan administration instituted Radio Martí and later TV Martí. These media venues were designed to broadcast the message of democracy to Cuba. After coming to power in 1959, Fidel Castro made Cuban television a national (as opposed to private commercial) industry and used the medium as a tool for the establishment of a new social order. Castro spoke for hours on television every evening, announcing new policies and even staging trials of captured infiltrators from the United States and opponents of the new regime.[10] Some saw the radio and television propaganda broadcasts of Radio and TV Martí as necessary interventions, countering Castro's own media propaganda. Others saw this form of media intervention as an act of cultural imperialism rather than an attempt to make democratic choices available to a population held captive by Castro's media rule. We might see this as an international political battle carried out at the level of looking practices. TV Martí, according to some critics, violated the spirit, if not the word, of the 1982 International Telecommunications Convention that determined that a country's airspace, like its land, was a part of its domestic property and hence these boundaries must not be violated. TV Martí raised important questions about the right of a nation to protect the airspace of media transmissions and to control the circulation of images in their seemingly immaterial state as they are transmitted over the airwaves. The debates over TV Martí have much to tell us about the limits of media globalization in a world in which information has become the most fluid and transmissible of global commodities and in which many speak of unchecked information flow as a democratic ideal.

Other analyses have shown that innocuous products of popular culture can have complex political meanings when they travel across national boundaries. In 1975 communication scholar Armand Mattelart and cultural critic Ariel Dorfman wrote a scathing analysis of the role played by the seemingly inconsequential figure of Donald Duck in promulgating U.S. imperialism in Latin America. In their manifesto *How to Read Donald Duck*, they argue that Donald and various other "innocent" Disney characters and stories presumably aimed at child audiences in fact were targeted also at adult viewers and that the narratives of these cartoons modeled for their Latin American viewers a relationship of dutiful respect for and submission to U.S. paternal authority.[11] Donald Duck and Mickey Mouse covertly sell to South Americans the sugar-coated belief that the United States is a place whose values and cultural practices should be emulated and whose economic presence should be welcomed. Mattelart and Dorfman point out that Disney, along with the U.S. government, worked to promote "good neighborliness" in South America in the 1940s, just as U.S. corporations were beginning to seek new markets for products and exploit the natural products and cheap labor available in South America. Donald Duck, for Mattelart and Dorfman, is an insidious icon of U.S. imperialist paternalism and self-serving benevolence during that period of history.

By the end of the twentieth century, media convergence and post-Cold War trade liberalization involved the establishment by the major U.S. networks of new sorts of channels and services outside the United States. These attempts to capture international markets occurred during an era fraught with competition from newer entities such as CNN that were savvy about capturing niche regional or language-based

FIG. 10.6
Columbian telenovela *Betty La Fea* and its American remake, *Ugly Betty* (Ana Maria Orozco as Betty La Fea and America Ferrara as Ugly Betty)

markets (CNN en Español, CNN Asia) while retaining a globally unified brand. Throughout the 1990s, NBC beamed a twenty-four-hour news service to Latin America from the network's offices in North Carolina, but the market is now dominated by CNN en Español. In 1999, NBC Europe stopped broadcasting to most of Europe and launched a computer channel in German, targeted to youth viewers, now a digital channel available through satellite and cable. In the realm of television news, CNN International became the major world player, with branded networks and services to 1.5 billion people in more than 212 countries by 2008.

Establishing niche markets globally while retaining network brand identity is harder across genres. An interesting case of a kind of reverse global flow is that of the show *Ugly Betty*, a popular ABC dramedy that premiered in 2006 and which was an adaptation of the popular Colombian telenovela *Yo soy Betty, la fea*. Whereas between 1978 and 1991 the epitome of global television was *Dallas*, the CBS prime-time soap about a Texas family that had aired in over 130 countries by the end of its run, by 2006 ABC had success with a show, *Ugly Betty*, that was an explicit remake from Latin American television. Although it would not be accurate to say that the tides of cultural imperialism had turned, it is feasible to suggest that the dynamics of global transmission, televisual and cultural, are far more complex than the simple one-way model of cultural imperialism suggested by Mattelart, Dorfman, and Schiller in previous eras.

It is a paradox of globalization in the early twenty-first century that the new liberalization and policies of open media flow have not created a more democratic flow of information for the people. Rather, "global" news venues such as CNN have become, in some contexts, a battleground for control over the shaping of world opinion. When national conflicts can be played out before the eyes of the world on news broadcasts internationally, coverage becomes crucial in generating foreign support. "Facts" may be more fluidly generated; however, they become harder, not easier, to verify independently in a media climate in which the flow of information is fast and thick but nonetheless highly monitored, restricted, and generated by countries maintaining strict control over media messages despite opening their doors to foreign journalists and providing more news to citizens. The case of CNN Asia in China during March 2008 allows us to demonstrate this paradox. When Tibetan protesters in China's Tibet Autonomous Region were reported to have been killed by Chinese police, reporters seeking verification and more information were blocked from the region. Tibetan supporters sent e-mails with video clips to CNN headquarters, but the footage of dead bodies was countered by stories generated at the mandate of Chinese authorities, who contested the reported facts and gave a new slant to the story by providing their own account of events in the region through, for example, state television footage of Tibetan rioters looting and burning Han Chinese stores. A CNN online news account by journalist Hugh Riminton captured this situation as one of "rival images" being used in the attempt to shape global news. The CNN Asia broadcast about the protests was blacked out, further limiting the already heavily restricted broadcasting of news, even by CNN, in China. In March 2008, CNN also reported on the first-ever interruption of the ritual lighting of the Olympic flame in Greece by French protesters who were also members of Reporters Without Borders, who wished to draw attention to the human rights violations by China against Tibetans. These reporters seized world attention by getting media coverage of their performance and calling for a boycott of the 2008 games in Beijing. Their interception of the torch ceremony shocked the public because of its transgression of a widely respected ritual of global connectivity, the lighting of a flame that would be carried by hand from Greece to China without expiring. The interruption of the ceremony suggested that the international spirit of fair competition and sportsmanship among nations represented by the flame was already jeopardized by China. The internationally broadcast ceremony became a prime place from which to launch a highly visual symbolic protest guaranteed to be seen by millions of people around the world.

It can be thus said that the national and the global are in constant, fluid tension, with national interests using global media to shape international opinion and with global forces struggling to work within the continued laws and rituals of the nation-state. Although the increased globalization of media venues may erode the centrality of national programming, it is also the case that media such as television still function to affirm national ideologies and to give people a sense of participation in an audience that is decidedly national. Concepts of the nation, of what it means to be an American or Chinese or French citizen, for instance, are often an integral part of programming that traverses national boundaries.

As we look at the contemporary terrain of global image flow and the dynamics of image generation, restriction, and appropriation, we can see that the United States is still a central source of entertainment programming around the world. The authors of *Global Hollywood 2* note that proportion of the world market that is commanded by the Hollywood film industry has continued to rise, doubling from 1990 to 2005, with the European film industries now one-ninth the size they were in 1945.[12] The climb to dominance of the U.S. entertainment industry worldwide, they propose, has had the effect of shrinking national production in other parts of the world.

Hollywood films make significant revenue outside the United States, so much so that Hollywood producers talk about "making it up in Europe," meaning that foreign revenues will recoup losses. Foreign revenues can exceed revenues earned within the United States. For instance, *The Lord of the Rings: The Two Towers* (2002) earned $921 million worldwide, of which $341 million came from within the United States. As we note later this in the chapter, there are vast industries in television and film throughout the world that are not Hollywood or U.S.-based. Nevertheless, entertainment media from the United States continues to have a strong market presence overseas. Productions are becoming more global both in their content and in their means of production, with the increasing reliance among studios on outsourcing aspects of their production work. Many "Hollywood" productions are also now multinational coproductions, as are many European productions. In fact, many Hollywood studios are owned by foreign multinational corporations (Columbia is owned by Sony, Universal is partially owned by the French company Vivendi). Some nations, such as Canada and France, attempt to mediate the dominance of U.S. entertainment media by promoting national production. The extraordinary amount of piracy whittles away the dominance of Hollywood in the world as well, at least at the level of revenue. Most mainstream Hollywood films can be found in bootleg DVD form on the streets of Shanghai and New York and online in the weeks before they open worldwide. Thus, although the worldwide dominance of Hollywood might seem to be an aspect of cultural imperialism and U.S. dominance, specific market conditions suggest that the picture is more varied and complex than it appears.

"Runaway" production, in which the labor that produces films and television programs is outsourced around the world, has had a major economic impact on the traditional sites of production such as Los Angeles. Yet the movements of industry professionals across national boundaries has always been a key aspect of Hollywood. Some of the most famous American classic Hollywood studio directors, such as Fritz Lang, Alfred Hitchcock, and William Wilder, were immigrants (many of them German refugees from World War II). The outsourcing of production and labor around the globe has many consequences on changing economies and on the kinds of cultural products that are generated in the studio system. It is worth noting, for instance, that the televisual and cinematic depiction of place has become increasingly generic, as certain locales (such as Toronto) have been used to simulate other places around the United States and elsewhere.

Global Brands

With the increased global marketing of key American brands in the postwar years, the idea of other places being "colonized" by American capitalism gained a great deal of currency. Major global corporations, such as Coca-Cola, with its trademarked logo and red colors, and McDonald's, with its iconic golden arches, expanded into foreign markets rapidly in the late twentieth century and became symbols of the global dominance of U.S. capitalism. Images representing these brands (graphic logos and advertisements) carry widely shared meanings that are easily read across different cultures, classes, and geographic spaces. As the American cultural anthropologist Robert Foster explains, Coca-Cola, as a global brand, has been marketed differently in different places. The company uses local strategies that make identification with the brand an aspect of an emergent national identity in different contexts such as, for example, Papua New Guinea.[13] Not only are there many ways to market this one brand, there are also multiple brands marketed under the banner of the one company. The company's marketing strategies, discussed in chapter 7, include generating not one but hundreds of brands across more than 200 countries, promoting the idea that the Coca-Cola business is essentially a local one, employing local people, paying local taxes, and serving local consumers products designed to suit their specific tastes.

In more recent years, global brands such as Nike and Starbucks have dominated in the circulation of commodity logos. On the one hand, these global brands can be seen as homogenizing forces, selling the same tastes and styles throughout diverse cultures. On the other hand, consumption habits and even specific products vary from region to region. One consequence of the status of global U.S. brands as symbols of U.S. capitalism has been that these brands and their corporate owners have been the targets of protests. For instance, when in 1999 French farmer activist José Bové organized protests against U.S. trade restrictions on Roquefort cheese, protesters chose to ransack a local McDonald's because in their view it symbolized the United States, even though the fast-food chain was not involved in the trade restrictions. Starbucks, with over 5,000 stores worldwide by 2007, became symbolic of global brand dominance in the 2000s. It was therefore chosen as the target of various protests in Lebanon, Israel, and New Zealand. Local resistance to Starbucks, including consumer boycotts of their products, has been prompted by the company's practice, until its economic falloff in 2008, of occupying sites left vacant by locally owned coffee shops whose proprietors could no longer pay the inflated rents that a large popular chain could easily manage.

FIG. 10.7
Mecca-Cola, Buvez Engagé

Resistance to global brands can also be seen in the creation of counterbrands that play off the logo of the original brand and offer themselves as politically viable substitutes. For instance, Mecca-Cola, which was launched in France in 2002, borrows the traditional red logo of Coca-Cola, with script that evokes Arabic lettering, selling itself as the anti-U.S. cola brand. The label of a Mecca-Cola bottle asks consumers to "buvez engagé," or drink with commitment. It is an irony of global marketing that many global brands sell themselves not as global products but as locally sensitive choices. Starbucks at one point suggested that its organizational philosophy reflects a kind of "tribal knowledge."[14] The company used the slogan "geography is a flavor" to sell the idea that the entire world is consumable through coffee, thereby marketing local "flavor" on a global scale, putting faraway places within the reach of the middle-class latte drinker.

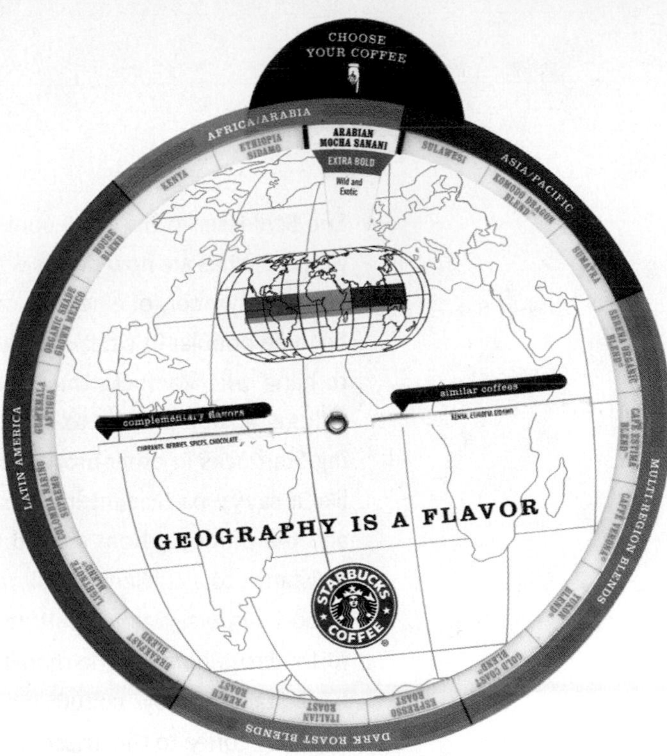

FIG. 10.8
Starbucks: Geography Is a Flavor Wheel, 2005

The Body Shop, a successful multinational chain retailer of body-care goods and beauty products (acquired by L'Oréal in 2006), refers to itself as a "multilocal" corporation and promotes itself in the language of the global village. The idea of the global village, which we discussed in chapter 6, emerged in the 1960s through the work of Marshall McLuhan. A global village refers to the concept that the media extend our reach across political and geographic boundaries, bringing the world together—shrinking it, as it were. The Body Shop specializes in selling products produced in specific developing locales to consumers throughout the world. The company emphasizes education and awareness of other cultures through the consumption of products that were made by "others." It does not directly advertise but instead produces brochures and educational materials that let the consumer know that the Body Shop supports women and underprivileged workers in the Third World in the manufacture of their products. In this case, educational brochures about the environment and animal rights, a "community trade" policy, and even an international human rights award given by the company stand in for product advertisements in promoting the company. As Caren Kaplan explains, the Body Shop paradoxically was able to emerge as a successful multinational corporation by trading on its image of sensitivity to local politics and environmental concerns.[15]

Global brands can also result in the emergence of specific cultural and national identities under the sign of the brand, rather than under the sign of an empire. In some contexts, such as mainland China prior to the 1980s, the symbol of Coke carried the meaning of cultural imperialism, symbolizing the spread of U.S. capitalism around the world. But in twenty-first century China, cultural imports such as McDonald's have become status symbols of modernity and China's new capitalism and the benefits of trade liberalization rather than symbols of cultural imperialism. Rather than signifying the unhealthy, cheap fast food famously critiqued by

Eric Schlosser in his 2001 book *Fast Food Nation*, McDonald's restaurants in major Chinese cities are now places where young people who want to associate themselves with the symbols of emerging capitalism like to congregate.[16] Similarly, Starbucks has become popular in cities such as Tokyo, where it offers young people a public place to hang out. Starbucks thus creates urban, modern spaces that signify global youth culture, linking patrons to their peers sipping lattes or specialty teas in similar looking Starbucks in other urban centers like New York and Paris. The draw is to appear like a savvy participant in global youth culture who appreciates the best of coffee and tea products from around the world. As these examples of appropriation and resistance to a challenged cultural and political status quo make clear, in the context of contemporary global culture, with the movement of cultural products back and forth across borders, the model of cultural imperialism is no longer a viable one for understanding how culture travels. Starbucks may signify the promotion of "good taste" in coffee to the masses in the United States, but in Tokyo it may signify a new freedom to participate in capitalist signifiers of consumption and Western tastes in a society whose popular drink is not coffee but tea.

Concepts of Globalization

Although the movements of people, products, ideas, and culture across national boundaries have taken place for centuries, the concept of globalization is largely understood as a set of conditions that have been escalating since the postwar period. These conditions include increased rates of migration, the rise of multinational corporations and the globalization of capital and financial networks, the development of global communications and transportation systems, a consequent sense of the decline of the sovereign nation-state in response to the "shrinking" of the world through commerce and communication, and the formation of new sorts of local communities not geographically bound (such as Web-based communities). Terms that are often used in association with globalization are *diaspora* (ethnic communities that are separate from their country of origin, such as the diasporic Chinese population in Toronto); *hybridity* (the mixing of peoples and cultures); *deterritorialization* (a separation of people from their traditional territories, often referring to a forced taking away of territory, also used by Giles Deleuze and Félix Guattari to indicate an opening up of meanings in new directions); *cosmopolitanism* (subjectivities that are situated beyond the nation, identified with the global or with traveling the world); *outsourcing* (of labor), and *transnationalism*. People increasingly move around the world, as travelers, tourists, guest workers, refugees, exiles, legal and illegal immigrants, and global citizens. As the distance between service workers and customers grows with, for example, the outsourcing of call centers, relationships of place and identity undergo change. We understand ourselves to exist within a global context, even as we identify ourselves as belonging to particular nations, regions, and cultures. These two aspects of identity—the global and the local—are not contradictory. They are interdependent.

Definitions of globalization vary, and each has particular political implications. U.S. Republican and former House speaker Newt Gingrich has compared media globalization to the rise of the telephone. Every American must recognize that we are now inevitably part of a world information system. That's why, he explains, when Iran gets a weapon we pay attention. For Gingrich, the global-village effect of globalization can bring our neighbors close—and too close for comfort. *New York Times* columnist Thomas L. Friedman outlines what some call the "TINA" (there is no alternative) outlook on globalization. In *The Lexus and the Olive Tree*, he puts forward his "Golden Arches theory": no two countries that both have McDonald's have waged a war against one another.[17] Friedman's point is that national gains (figured dubiously in the example of McDonald's) motivate mutual cooperation. Charles Norchi, the former executive director of the International League for Human Rights, has emphasized that globalization is not just about global communications and markets. It also includes a global discourse of rights.[18] Globalization, for Norchi, describes the progression of forces that have accelerated the interdependence of peoples to the point at which we can speak of a true world community. He dates this process from the period just after World War II, when the Universal Declaration of Human Rights was drafted, to the period after the Cold War, when ideological boundaries crumbled and technology and capital flowed more freely across some borders. At the same time, critics of globalization, such as Peruvian President Alejandro Toledo, have warned that globalization will make no sense if it does not address and help to reduce the extreme poverty that is increasing among most of the world's population into the twenty-first century. At a 2003 World Economic Forum, Tanzanian president Benjamin William Mkapa warned that the poor in all economies are paying the highest price in the process of globalization, as we see in the sharp escalation of the rich-poor divide throughout the decade of the 2000s. A large number of developing countries lost, not gained, economic ground in that decade. Arjun Appadurai has noted, likewise, that globalization's most striking feature is the runaway quality of global finance, with, for example, per capita incomes declining in Africa relative to changes in incomes in the industrial countries. A crucial issue during the 2008 collapse of the U.S. mortgage and investment markets was the devastating impact of these events on foreign markets. This is "a world of flows," Appadurai famously noted, "that are not coeval." These circumstances suggest to him "a new role for the imagination in society," in which we picture globalization not from the perspective of corporations but from below, from the perspective of the problems of "the global everyday."[19]

Appadurai offers a model for understanding the dynamics of globalization across a number of social and cultural realms.[20] He uses the suffix *scapes,* derived from the geographical metaphor of landscapes, as a framework for thinking about particular sorts of global flows. *Ethnoscapes* are groups of people of similar ethnicities who move across borders in roles such as refugees, tourists, exiles, and guest workers. The term *mediascapes* captures the movement of media texts and cultural products throughout the world. *Technoscapes* frames the complex technological industries that circulate information and services. *Financescapes* describes the flow of global capital. *Ideoscapes* represents the ideologies that circulate. Analyzing global flow according to "scapes" allows a critique of the different power relations within these cultural and economic movements and exchanges of products, people, and capital. It also provides an alternative to the traditional model of one-way cultural flow, allowing us to see the complex directions and scope of an image's or text's global circulation beyond the implied one-way reach of, say, broadcasting or imperial rule.

One of the key theoretical interventions into these issues is postcolonial theory. This approach considers the culture and social contexts of formerly colonized countries such as India, most African nations, and nations in the Middle East, most of which were decolonized in the mid-twentieth century, as entities that must be analyzed not simply in terms of their precolonial ways of thinking, but in light of changes to national forms of cultural expression that have incorporated and appropriated the languages, discourses, and techniques of their former colonizers. Postcolonial theorists also study the cultural and political expression of diasporic subjects, former subjects of colonialism who are immigrants or who live in exile. Thus Indians living in Great Britain are as much a concern of a postcolonial analysis of Indian culture as those who continue to live in India, Great Britain's former colony. Conditions of postcoloniality have resulted in hybrid cultures and large diasporic communities that are often connected to their country of origin through media networks and television and Web community networks. To make claims about authentic cultural expression unencumbered by influences from former colonial forces is to ignore the reality of mixing, appropriation, and cultural exchange through which both cultures, the former colony's and the former colonizer's, have changed. Edward Said's book *Orientalism*, which we discussed in chapter 3, is a foundational text of postcolonial theory. The complex of postcolonial societies and their cultural production and consumption makes clear how inadequate a model of cultural imperialism, with its concept of cultural products in one direction out from central powerful nations, is to understanding global cultural flows today. Cultural imperialists cannot control the complex movements of an image or media text's flow. The specific practices used by viewers to mediate and appropriate imported cultural products and images cannot be determined in advance by media producers. As we have discussed in previous chapters, viewers do not necessarily receive media texts as producers intend them to be seen, and they do not take them at face value. Rather, viewers make meanings based in part on the context in which they experience images. Meanings are also shaped by experiences and knowledges brought to the circumstances of viewing. Viewers may appropriate what they see to make new meanings, meanings that may be not just different from but even oppositional to the ideologies intended or received in these texts' original contexts. Although producers intentions in creating and disseminating messages to various markets is evident in most texts, it is also the case that cultural difference results in a broad range of responses to images, responses that cannot be accurately or easily predicted or controlled by producers.

Visual media is not the most central or the most important aspect of globalization. For the purposes of this book, however, we are most interested in looking at how visual culture contributes to the processes and concepts of globalization and at how images, in the form of cinema, television, animation, photographs, news media, digital imaging, and Web media, travel globally and are themselves global texts. Thus the global flow of images is central to how we understand visual culture today, as are the global aspects of image production and the increased cosmopolitanism and globalization of cultural narratives and texts.

Visuality and Global Media Flow

There are a number of different frameworks through which we can map out the complex ways in which popular culture is produced and in which it travels globally. As we noted before, even cultural products that appear to be "national," such as Hollywood films, are made and circulated through global networks. Enormously popular diasporic popular culture, from Hong Kong cinema to Telemundo telenovelas to Bollywood cinema, are produced for global audiences and distributed through global networks. Along with programs, which air in different markets, the genres of popular culture travel across national boundaries. For example, reality television programs that originate in the Netherlands and Great Britain, such as *Survivor* and *Idol*, have franchises across the globe and become nationalized in their particular iterations in other national networks. Finally, the narrative content of many popular culture productions reflect a global, if not cosmopolitan, worldview due to the fact that these shows cross so many cultures.

Hong Kong cinema is a classic example of how cultural forms are created in multinational and transnational contexts, and how these films and their production personnel and talent travel globally. The action films made in Hong Kong in the 1980s and 1990s were produced by a range of filmmakers from Japan, Taiwan, mainland China, the Philippines, and Australia and were enormously influential in the action film genre globally. Many Hong Kong kung-fu films, which began for theatrical distribution and then were distributed as direct-to-video productions and later as DVDs and for download, achieved enormous popularity globally.[21] By the late 1990s, as we discuss later, the influence of the Hong Kong film industry on Hollywood became increasingly evident, as Hong Kong's stars and directors moved to Hollywood in 1997 and mainstream Hollywood films such as *The Matrix*, made by a younger generation of filmmakers influenced by Hong Kong cinema, were produced in the United States.

What the Hong Kong cinema example makes clear is that Hollywood no longer has the global monopoly on popular film culture that it had in the middle of the twentieth century. It may be the case that some of the dominant film industries around the world are named after Hollywood, such as Bollywood cinema, the Hindi-language sector of the Indian film industries, and Nollywood, the Nigerian film industry of the digital era. But the film cultures of these industries are not derivative of the Hollywood style and model of production. The global climate of appropriation takes the form of transnational genre- and talent-swapping in which the trades are never equivalent in kind or value.

The term *Bollywood* refers not to a place precisely nor to Indian national cinema generally but to one of the country's seven regional cinemas: the Mumbai- (Bombay) based industry that produces films in Hindi or Hindustani, and increasingly in English as well, for a broad Indian diaspora and for non-Indian audiences. Cinema has a history of being enormously popular throughout India. But whereas in the 1920s more than three quarters of the films watched in India were made in the United States, Indian cinema audiences by the 1980s were consuming their own regional productions, as well as a mix of productions from Hollywood, Hong Kong, and other industries. The flow of cinema culture goes in multiple directions, however, and is not coeval (not happening at the same time and in the same ways or with the same kind or degree of benefit for all involved). Export is strong from Bollywood even as films are locally popular, with over eight hundred films a year produced and consumed by viewers not only in India but also throughout the Middle East, Afghanistan, Russia (where Bollywood films were popular even during the Soviet period, when U.S. films were banned from the region), and to diasporic South Asian populations in Europe, Australia, and the United States. Bollywood films are highly genre-based, with many similar elements repeated and borrowed from film to film, including lavish musical and dance scenes, melodramatic love stories, and the themes of conflicts between fathers and sons, redemption and the assertion of moral values, revenge, and happy endings.

Until the 1990s Bollywood productions were regarded as low in production values compared with those of Hollywood despite these films' huge budgets and lavish sets. The situation has changed in part due to changes in state and private support and funding structures (banks, formerly prohibited from investing in films, are now allowed to do so), with the introduction of new technologies and talent from other industries that comes with the globalization of the industry intensifying at the level of production. Hong Kong's film industry experienced an exodus of talent after 1997, when it shifted from a British Crown Colony to one of China's Special Administrative Regions. Bollywood and Hollywood were able to buy off many of the top figures of the booming Hong Kong industry in the wake of that transition. The globalization of the film industry has led to further cross-appropriation among national industries, with genres, styles, and talent going not only from Hollywood to India but also from Bollywood to the west. The important point is neither that Bollywood is struggling to catch up to Hollywood in quality nor that Bollywood has its own unique genres and styles that are culturally specific, though these statements may be partly true. Rather, we emphasize that Bollywood's changes are indicative of larger circumstances under globalization and trade liberalization in which cinemas formerly understood

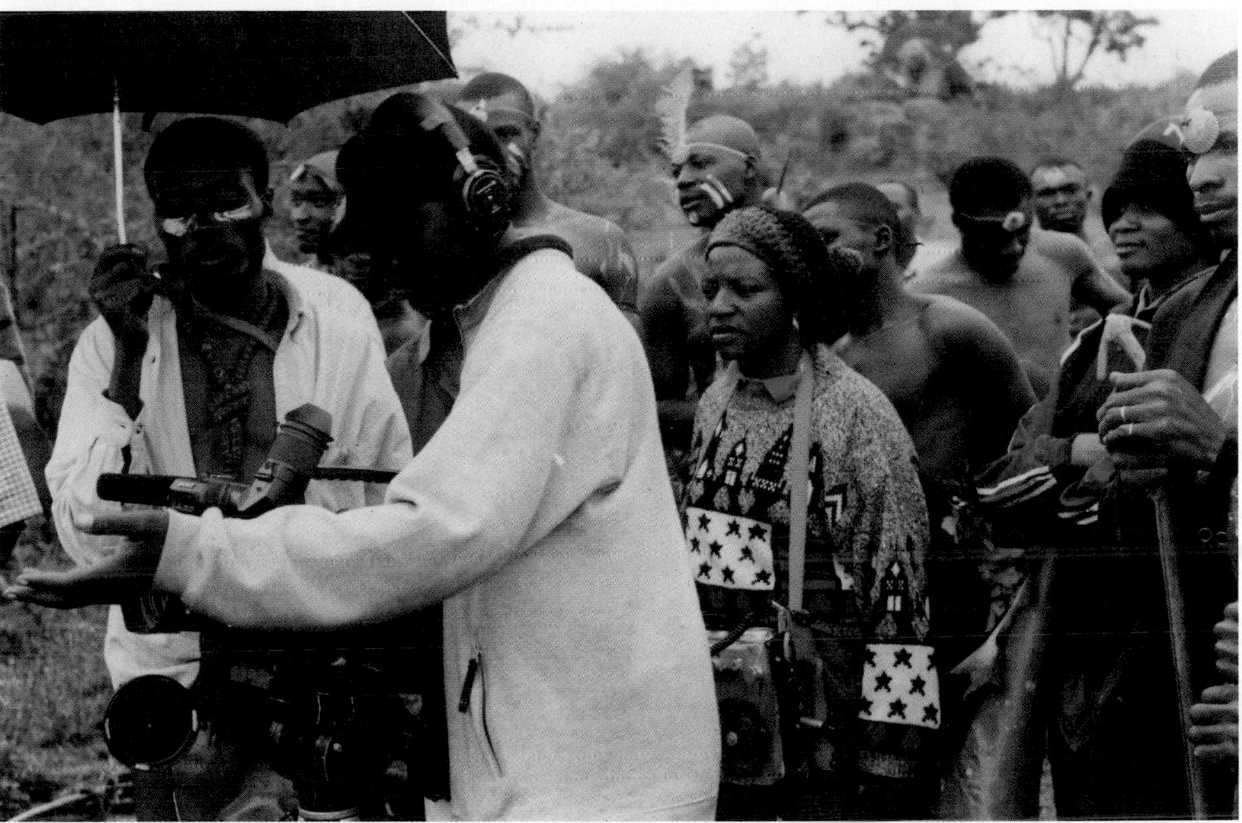

FIG. 10.9
Nollywood director Izu Ojukwu on set, courtesy filmmaker Jamie Meltzer, *Welcome to Nollywood* (2007)

to be representative of a nation-state or a nation-state's region can best be characterized as global and diasporic, representing a range of national and cultural influences, as well as a populace that travels and lives across many continents. Bollywood films are shown globally, even as the industry maintains an identity we think of as "national" or "regional." As media scholar Nitin Govil notes, the idea that Bollywood was ever supposed to represent the nation is a foundational fiction, as is the idea of the "nation" itself.[22] These sorts of identities are mobilized in ways that inevitably result in new kinds of serendipitous appropriations and mixing of elements that would have been unthinkable decades before. For example, action in *Krrish* (2006) was choreographed by Hong Kong's Tony Ching, making a Hong Kong kung-fu genre touch a characteristic of some of Bollywood in the 2000s.

The Nigerian film industry, or Nollywood, presents a very different picture from that of Hollywood or Bollywood. In the digital 2000s, Nollywood (a minimal celluloid-medium film industry) emerged out of relatively nowhere as a multibillion dollar industry that produces over a thousand films a year that go straight to DVD, a figure that places it behind only Bollywood and Hollywood in terms of quantity of production. Nollywood's huge production output is attributable to the small, hand-held video camera, especially the HD camera, straightforward computer-based digital editing, and DVD formatting. Nollywood features have supplanted U.S. films at the top of the DVD distribution market not only in Nigeria but also in many other African nations. Jamie Meltzer's 2007 documentary *Welcome to Nollywood* provides an interesting introduction to the Nollywood industry, which is an important new model of entrepreneurship and popular visual culture production. Whereas Bollywood gained success on features that took millions in investments and long production processes for each film, which then typically saw income in the years of video release, Nollywood productions remain relatively low-budget and films achieve market success quickly through the direct-to-DVD approach. The production and consumption cycle is lightning fast by comparison to other cinema industries.

One can look at the strength of these different industries and their cultivation of global audiences as testimony to the diversity of popular culture programming around the world. Yet, as the Bollywood example demonstrates, global culture can also be about genre conventions and repeating formulas. It is a relatively new phenomenon in television programming that "franchise culture" has emerged as a dominant global influence. Media scholars Michael Keane and Albert Moran write that format programming has become the new engine driving successful transnational television.[23] Program formats such as *Who Wants to be a Millionaire*, *Idol*, *Survivor*, *Big Brother*, and *The Weakest Link*, many of which originate in the Netherlands and Great Britain, are franchised out throughout the world, with localized version of the shows in the United States, Japan, Australia, the Philippines, Thailand, Hong Kong, and Singapore, among other locations. Franchising producers pay a licensing fee and then modify the format to their needs. This allows easy and relatively inexpensive programming decisions, in particular because most of these are reality TV or game shows, relatively easy formats that have been proven successful in other markets. Thus these formats travel around the globe and are modified for local markets, staying within the codes of the genre while changing to fit into local tastes. For example, *Big Brother* was run on the continent of Africa with participants from twelve different countries, prompting viewers to debate whether a reality TV show can bring a sense of unity to a fragmented and impoverished continent fraught with strife.

FIG. 10.10
Housemates from twelve different countries prepare for the African Fantasy Feast task in *Big Brother Africa*, Johannesburg, South Africa, 2003

Although the repetition of formats would indicate a commonality of programming, it is also the case that the movements of programs, styles, formats, and creative professionals around the world and into different popular culture markets has changed the kinds of films and television shows that are produced. The globalization of media platforms and film production has reconfigured the style and content of film series that we associate with classic Hollywood production. Take, for example, the ways in which the James Bond franchise has changed since its introduction in 1962. The well-known international icon James Bond first appeared in 1952 in a novel by the British author Ian Fleming. Bond was subsequently featured in a dozen novels and the longest running and second highest grossing film series of the twentieth century (behind *Star Wars*). The series began with *Dr. No* (directed by Terence Young in 1962), a film adaptation of the 1958 novel of the same title by Fleming, and included, by 2008, twenty-one feature films, with the twenty-second in production. The Bond franchise, which includes video games, comics, and other products, presents a variety of ways from which to study media globalization during the Cold War period and beyond. As British cultural studies scholars Tony Bennett and Jane Wollacott have noted, Bond is a character with many lives.[24] Not only was he penned by a series of authors in the making of the novels, but he was also performed by a series of film stars (six by 2009). The movies were filmed in a range of national contexts with plots almost as transnational in scope as the films' vast exhibition market range. The series was internationally marketed from the first episode and remains solidly transnational from production to exhibition. The films are all typically set in three or more countries. Their plots involve international business conflicts, international crime syndicates, and national security, and until the 1990s the series was structured thematically around Cold War binaries of the "free world" (largely represented by Great Britain) versus the Soviet Union—all displaying a nostalgia for the British Empire. For example, in *Dr. No* Bond does battle with a fictional terrorist organization called SPECTRE (Special Executive for Counter-intelligence, Terrorism, Revenge and Extortion). The goal of SPECTRE is to achieve world domination by instigating conflict between the world's superpowers, allowing them to bring one another down. *Quantum of Solace*, the twenty-second feature, scheduled for release in 2009, promises a Ukrainian "Bond woman" and sinister villain, suggesting a continuation of the Cold War-themed transnational intrigue. The Bond series exemplifies the conventions of genre and was the source of Umberto Eco's well-known structuralist analysis of plot conventions and binary oppositions (Bond/Villain, Bond/Woman, Duty/Sacrifice, Chance/Planning, and so on).[25]

To interpret the Bond series in light of globalization, we follow the trail of female performers who have occupied the roles of the many "Bond women" featured in the series. With few exceptions, Bond women have been white and European. The exceptions include three black Bond women (played by Gloria Hendry, Grace Jones, and Halle Berry) and two Asian women: Kissy Suzuki, played by Hama Mie (who is Japanese) in *You Only Live Twice* (1967), and Wai Lin, played by Michelle Yeoh, a highly respected martial artist. Yeoh's career path illustrates the dynamic of globalization as it affects an individual media star. By 1997, when Yeoh was cast opposite Pierce Brosnan in the Bond film *Tomorrow Never Dies*, she had been acting for ten years, had appeared in eighteen movies, and was one of China's top female stars in terms of income and reputation. The Malaysian-born star studied drama and dance in London at the Royal Academy of Dance. On returning to her home country in 1983 Yeoh became Miss Malaysia (and also Miss Mooba in Melbourne the same year), which resulted in a request for her to do a commercial in Hong Kong with the martial artist Jackie Chan (Sing Lung). While in Hong Kong she quickly became a sought-after performer in the Hong Kong film industry during its height. Her debut film was *Owls vs. Dumbo* (1984), made a year after she won the title of Miss Stomp Tokyo 1983. Her second feature, *Yes, Madam*, established her as a star in the Hong Kong industry. In 1996, Yeoh experienced a mainstream breakthrough with the American release of *Supercop*, a rerelease of the 1992 Stanley Tong action film *Police Story 3: Supercop*, in which she starred with Jackie Chan. Hollywood hyped Chan in the trailers and ads while barely mentioning Yeoh (billed then as Michelle Khan, her English marquee name). Yeoh performed her own stunts, including a scissor kick that took out two men at once and a motorcycle ride onto a speeding train. In 1997, the Hong Kong film industry saw an economic slump with the transition from British colony to Chinese autonomous region. Hollywood snapped up talent, including Chan and directors John Woo and Ang Lee. The Hong Kong action movie *Heroic Trio* (1993) was Yeoh's ninth film and had been a subculture hit among martial arts action movie fans internationally. *Heroic Trio* was brought back into distribution following the emergence of Yeoh as an international star opposite Brosnan in 1997, at age thirty-four. In that year *People* magazine named her one of the fifty most beautiful people of the year. In 2000, she starred in *Crouching Tiger, Hidden Dragon*, a blockbuster success directed by Ang Lee. If the Bond role had clinched her status as a mainstream star, *Crouching Tiger* secured Yeoh's position as the top female martial arts star internationally, with fan websites cropping up in French, Cantonese, Mandarin, English, and other languages to honor her.

Thus Yeoh made the leap from national to international stardom (her languages are English and Cantonese, though *Tiger* was in Mandarin), emerging not only as a movie star and beauty queen but also as an international sports star and as a martial arts cult figure. Thanks to global video marketing, *Heroic Trio*

FIG. 10.11
Michelle Yeoh in *Crouching Tiger, Hidden Dragon*, 2003

could be revived for market purposes in the form of multiple-language subtitled videos directed at a broad sector of the international market. Yeoh's featured role in the Bond series thus draws on the intertextual meanings she brings to her films, remapping the Bond geography from Cold War conflict to global culture.

Indigenous and Diasporic Media

The movement of people and images around the world has become more complicated in the early twenty-first century. Immigration and asylum for refugees have become heated subjects of political debate, diasporic communities have continued to grow, and homelessness looms large in countries like the United States with economic decline at the end of the 2000s. Media images are infused with dynamics that express the geographic dispersal of peoples, the breakdown of nation-states, the hybridization of cultures, and intensified concerns about national security and autonomy in a post-Cold War world in which borders have both eroded and become more desperately protected. An important aspect of this media environment is the emergence of indigenous and diasporic media.

One example of programming in the global media environment demonstrates the power of cultural products to reaffirm ethnic and local values over the homogenizing forces of a vast national communication system. In 1975, the Canadian Broadcasting Corporation introduced an accelerated coverage plan designed to provide Canadian programming throughout the country. This meant, in effect, that programs produced in southern Canada would be shown in the northern territories, where there was little production and representation of lifestyles. In 1982, the Inuit people of the Northern Canadian Arctic founded a satellite television broadcasting network. The Inuit Broadcasting Corporation (IBC) was established as an alternative to the southern Canadian media which had spread north. IBC linked Inuit communities dispersed across the continent by satellite, offering indigenous programming produced and broadcast in the Inuit language, Inuktitut, and representing Inuit cultural values, which had been dying out due in part to the influx of Canadian culture. The IBC, with its Inuit superhero, Super Shamou, the hero of a show in the late 1980s, and its own popular and educational programming and images, presents a powerful alternative to mainstream Canadian television and the popular media images already consumed by Inuit people. The example of the IBC suggests that indigenous and autonomous practices of looking can not only survive in an era of globalization but can also thrive by using global technologies in a manner that rethinks what local means. As the IBC website explains, the use of media technology

FIG. 10.12
IBC producer Barney Pattanguyak and Peter Tapatai as Super Shamou

has not only linked peoples who are geographically dispersed but also has helped to both preserve and reinstate cultural traditions and language practices that had been dying out. The IBC has been a model for using global media technologies to support cultural and political autonomy in the face of globalization. IBC produces programming that is internationally recognized as one of the most successful communication models for developing nations. Inuit communities are separated by huge distances in Nunavut, a region that makes up one-third of Canada's land mass. The only way in or out of many Inuit communities is by plane or skimobile. IBC programming travels by satellite via Television Northern Canada. The vast distances between communities make electronic communication of vital importance to the development of Inuit management of the North. Nunavut now has its own government, and Inuktitut is the official language of the Territory.

The IBC model is an important exception to the rule of global media imperialism in the age of cable and satellite television. Even cable holds the possibility of supporting alternative and local cultural interests. Whereas in the earlier narrowcast model distance and geography defined the limits of programming, in the cable television era (which began in the 1980s), "community" television at first meant programming for a "local" population that is dispersed around the globe. This means that diasporic communities throughout the world, that is, ethnic communities living in concentrations set apart from their homelands, may constitute the audiences of narrowcast programming. For diasporic and exiled peoples, television programming aired across national boundaries and narrowcast to their own communities can be a vital lifeline. "Local" programming across the geographic expanses of a diaspora provides what for some viewers may be a virtual home. Programming targeted to a particular cultural group may link viewers to a community whose geographic origin is no longer accessible—say, because viewers live in exile, because they cannot afford to go home, or because the homeland no longer exists (if it has been destroyed or overtaken through political upheaval). For example, beginning in the 1980s Iranian exiles living in Southern California and other parts of the U.S. have formed the audience for Persian-language television produced by fellow exiled Iranians. This cable programming focuses on Iranian media genres, culture, history, and values. Media scholar Hamid Naficy has written that U.S.-based Iranian television challenges the broadcast model.[26] This kind of programming works in opposition to the model of cultural imperialism by supporting local culture in a virtual community that is globally dispersed, without a unified geographic base. We are familiar with the role of the Internet in supporting virtual communities, but satellite and cable networks and programming like the IBC and Iranian television in Southern California prefigured such online communities and constituted them through the format of television.

The Web and the Internet can facilitate political connections among people who are separated from their homelands by providing an illusion of a "place" in which that group resides. The term "website" encourages users to think of a physical place, although such a place exists only within virtual space. For people who have been exiled from their homelands for political reasons, this idea of a website as a place is very meaningful. Pradeep Jeganathan has written about the sites that have emerged in the struggles of the Tamil movement in Sri Lanka.[27] The Tamil nation, called Tamileelam, which is held by its proponents to exist in certain provinces of Sri Lanka, is not recognized by the government of Sri Lanka. Under political duress, many Tamils migrated out from Sri Lanka in the 1980s to places throughout India, Europe, Canada, and Australia. The websites that sprang up to unite these Tamil populations form a virtual place in which this "nation" can exist. The location of the Tamil nation at eelam.com is somewhere in cyberspace, not in the desired location in Sri Lanka. This cyberspace address is a symbolic site at which this diasporic community maintains and generates unity in the absence of a real geographic home. In its existence on the Web, according to Jeganathan, where it is equidistant from all places in the world, eelam.com allows for the possibility that that geographic place will be reclaimed.

Globalized networks of electronic media and the Web have also provided the means for political movements to disseminate their ideas and build support throughout the world, thus constituting global communities of support. The Zapatista National Liberation Army/Ejército Zapatista de Liberación Nacional (EZLN), a political movement in Mexico that is centered in the region of Chiapas, has become an icon of a local movement with global support that has effectively used media and the Internet to disseminate political ideas. The Zapatistas, many of whom are of Mayan descent, began an insurgency in 1994 and created alternative forms of government within the Chiapas area. Supporters of the Zapatistas have effectively disseminated information from the rebels to a worldwide group of supporters. This has involved both high-tech and low-tech networks in which, for instance, messages are hand carried to those with access to computers. The Zapatistas are fighting for indigenous rights and control of the land and against the neoliberal policies and authoritarian rule of the Mexican government. They are proposing a broader global vision of civil society as well, which has resonated with other political movements around the globe, including antiglobalization activists working against the policies of the World Trade Organization.

Like the Black Panthers of the 1960s, the Zapatistas used style as a key factor in their global image. In order to mask their identities in the face of Mexican government oppression, they wear black ski masks that have become iconic of their political struggles. Thus images of figures with black masks have come to signify indigenous political movements. The Zapatistas use this symbolism to create an image for their movement, although it has traveled far

FIG. 10.13
Zapatista dolls

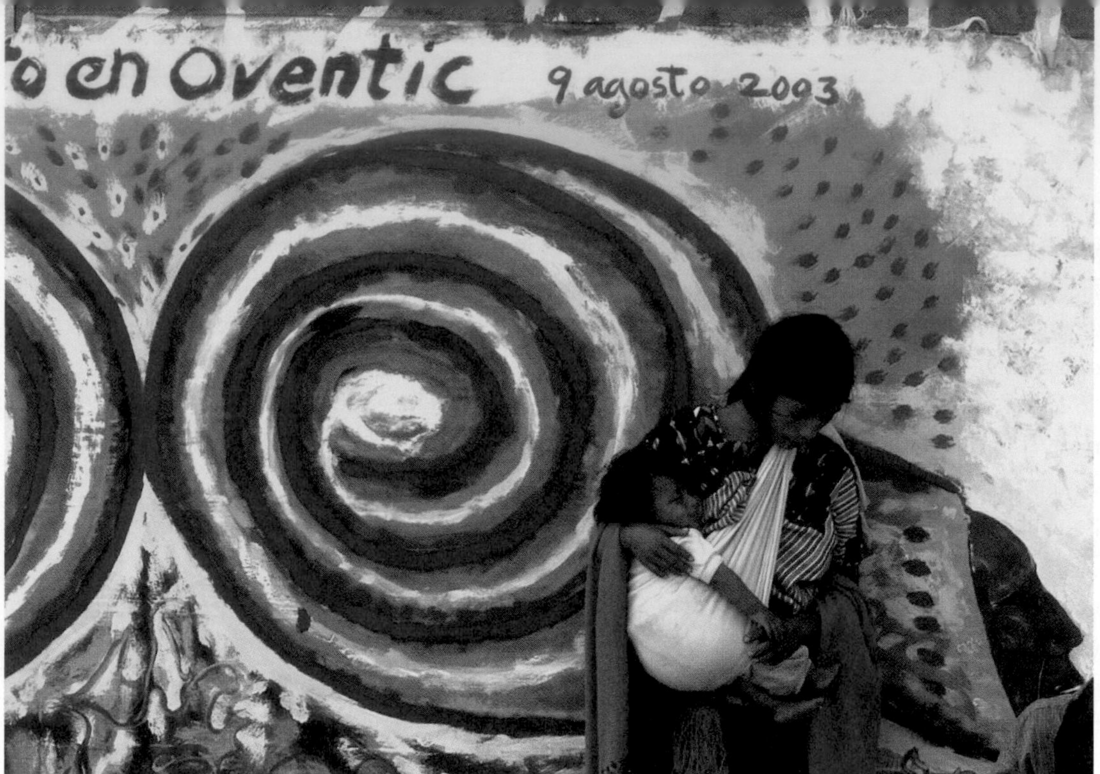

FIG. 10.14
A mural in the Mexican town of Oventic in Chiapas shows the symbol of the caracol, 2003

beyond the symbols. One can purchase tourist souvenirs of small Zapatista dolls throughout Latin America, which are sold along with other indigenous crafts. The symbol of the masked guerrilla has also cropped up in trendy stores, such as the Boxfresh in London, which used it in an attempt to sell hipness.

The Zapatistas have, through their leader Subcomandante Marcos, also participated in a sophisticated discourse about image making and the politics of indigenous peoples' relationship to tourist images. For instance, Marcos has sometimes taken photographic cameras from visitors and turned them back on them. Though Marcos is not himself indigenous, he is the spokesperson for the movement, which largely is composed of indigenous Mayans. In turning the cameras around, Marcos refers to the history of images of indigenous people as "images in museums, tourist guides, crafts advertising" in which they are seen "as an anthropological curiosity or colorful detail of a remote past."[28] As George Yúdice writes, "Marcos proposes to establish a different kind of relation by turning the gaze onto the spectators and photographers."[29] In addition, the Zapatistas have deployed symbols as icons of their movement that have important local meanings and that travel through global networks. For instance, they have adopted the caracol, or snail, as a key symbol for alternative forms of organization. The snail has significance within the Mayan tradition as a symbol of taking knowledge from the heart and taking it from the heart into the world. The caracol is also being used as a guiding geography for the five Zapatista communities, all called caracoles, and it has proliferated on T-shirts, in embroidery, and on murals in the area, sometimes with the snail sporting the signature black ski mask.[30] The Zapatistas make their movement global as well as local through the Web and other forms of media with this kind of sophisticated deployment of symbols and representations. Their global image presence demonstrates the degree to which earlier models of cultural imperialism are no longer viable in understanding global media flows. As Yúdice writes, "the Zapatistas' expert handing of the electronic media shows that there is no necessary contradiction between technological modernization and grassroots mobilization."[31]

Ethnicity and politics are, of course, not the only bases for community formation. The Web has supported the growth of communities organized around cultural interests, fandom, health and disability issues, and a multitude of other identities, themes, and concerns. The experience of illness and healthcare has changed dramatically with the rise of websites geared toward self-diagnosis and self-care, and most medical conditions and disabilities have an online organization with information and a chatroom or blog devoted to facilitating a sense of community among members, who may include friends, family, and healthcare professionals in addition to people with the condition around which the group is organized. For example, in 2004, people with Tourette syndrome and their friends and family could tap into the resources at globaltourette.net, accessing the means to communication, self-produced media production, and information about Tourette around the globe, in Spanish and English. How Tourette is understood around the world changes with this kind of cross-cultural communication among people who live with Tourette. The understanding of the syndrome no longer relies primarily on expert knowledge offered in medical and educational settings. This is just one of the examples of the Web's role in the democratization and globalization of information.

Borders and Franchises: Art and the Global

Globalization has also had enormous impact on the distribution, exhibition, and production of art. It is increasingly the case that cities are using art as a form of cultural tourism. Thus art as cultural capital has become a key factor in the transformation of urban centers into postindustrial cities. A great example of this trend is the Guggenheim Bilbao. The Guggenheim Museum, originally based in New York, has created a kind of franchise by constructing Guggenheim Museum branches in the northern Spanish city of Bilbao, in Venice, and in Berlin. The architect Frank Gehry was commissioned to design the Bilbao museum, which became a symbol of museum tourism in the 2000s. The art such a museum might have on its gallery walls is of less concern to tourists than the museum itself in occupying a place within a city that has a

FIG. 10.15
Guggenheim Bilbao, 2001, with Louise Bourgeois sculpture, *Maman,* in foreground

new, postmodern economy centered on luxury, new technology, new design, new ways of doing global business, and new ways of living the good life. Tourists are drawn not just to see art, but to see the new lifestyle of commerce, design, and consumption of which the museum has become symbolic. Postindustrialization, which is intricately linked to globalization, creates economic contexts such as this, in which gentrification and creative capitalism are seen as the answers to failing formerly industrial cities and economies. Gehry is well known for his postmodern architectural designs. His former home in Santa Monica, California, composed of layers of industrial materials such as corrugated sheet metal wrapped around a more conventional home, is an icon of postmodern architecture in its incorporation of construction materials and design shapes drawn from different periods and practices of building design and construction in Southern California and the United States. His designs for museums such as Bilbao (and several other projected Guggenheim branches), as well as Disney Hall in downtown Los Angeles, can be seen as modern rather than postmodern in that they deploy codes of universal design. These designs are not referencing the local historical context, as most postmodern architecture has aimed to do. The shiny roof and curving shapes of the Guggenheim Bilbao are not specific to Bilbao's history and architecture. Rather, they reference a distinct international Gehry style—a design that can easily be recognized and replicated anywhere in the world. It is as if Gehry has moved toward a kind of brand-like design approach that references both his own style and the Guggenheim franchise as global in character.

The use of museums to create the image of urban centers as the locus of creative global economies has proliferated over the past two decades throughout Europe, Asia, and the United States. In more recent years, this trend has also emerged in the Middle East, in the relatively liberal political states of the United Arab Emirates (UAE), one of the world's largest producers of oil and home to a population three-quarters of which is expatriated from other Arab nations. The UAE, a popular location for investors and developers in the 2000s, is the recent and planned site of new museum franchises and satellite campuses of American private universities. These institutions are accompanied by new, state of the art luxury hotels, restaurants, bars and condos to which global entrepreneurs are flocking in hopes of cashing in on the new opportunities for investment and the luxury lifestyle available in this booming location. In 2006, the Paris Louvre announced that it would create a satellite museum, its first, in the UAE city of Abu Dhabi. It was reported that the Louvre would be compensated $800 million for its project. The Louvre Abu Dhabi will be built by 2012 on Saadiyat Island, next to the Guggenheim Abu Dhabi and a new campus of New York University.

These examples of museum and university franchises and the purchasing of museum brands by wealthy Arab states are indicative of a new global creative economy. The power relationships that support this economy differs from previous colonial relationships of power in which the Western institution was the repository of knowledge and value. Previously the lion's share of world-class art and artifact from

FIG. 10.16
Pyramid at the Louvre, designed by I.M. Pei

around the world was acquired by and held in the collections of European and North American institutions. One had to travel to cities such as Paris or New York to see international treasures. With the practice of franchising, this centralization of culture is approaching its end. Global "sharing" suggests a kind of diasporic distribution of "world-class" culture and an expansion of the twentieth-century American Dream of consumer convenience and choice into a global, twentieth-first-century dream of technology and design supporting luxurious living. But who benefits from this distribution of culture, knowledge, and wealth? In 2008 new reports circulated globally relating the experiences of expatriate European and North American families unable to afford the glamorous lifestyle surrounding them in the UAE centers to which they had relocated in hopes of a better job and a better life than that offered in the declining economies at home. The trend toward franchising among museums may also be seen as a tactic of economic and ideological survival among museums in the declining economies of North American and European cities. These museums joined a globalizing economy in which new governments and new businesses saw benefit in acquisition of the cultural capital that would come with a vast government-funded institution with strong historical and site-specific iconic importance to the world. The Musée du Louvre, the Paris art museum, had opened to the public in 1793 as a site dedicated to the display of important and valuable works of art owned by the government to citizens of all classes, in keeping with the democratic principles of the French Revolution. The Louvre is by no means in economic decline. By 2007 the Louvre was drawing as many as 8.3 million visitors a year from around the world to see original works, including Leonardo's *Mona Lisa* and Delacroix's *Liberty Leading the People*, an 1830 painting that holds great significance as an icon of democratic freedom and that Delacroix painted, he said, because he felt that if he had not fought for his country, at least he should paint for it. ("Liberty" is represented as a barefoot, bare-breasted woman in a cap symbolizing the French Revolution brandishing the French Tricolore and a bayonet.) The Paris site of the Louvre is vast, having been constructed over eight centuries through a conglomerate of additions, including a fortress, a dungeon, a series of palaces, and finally a glass and steel pyramid designed by the postmodern architect I. M. Pei.

By building a version of itself in the oil-rich UAE, the Louvre might be said to be continuing the tradition of growth through architectural pastiche, the adding on of structures and works begun by royalty and turned to the goals of benevolence in which the spaces and artifacts of the world's high culture, from France and beyond, are made available to a vast public of everyday citizens in a series of special collections. The UAE acquires the status of high culture by bringing into its region and putting on display there a piece of the Louvre, not only through acquiring works that have blue-chip value in the global art market but also through erecting a building that bears the brand name of the original building itself, a physical icon of world class art. This is an instance of what some advocates of globalization call a "win-win" situation in which globalization allows the "have nots" to benefit (to see and own world-class art without leaving home) along with the "haves." The Louvre maintains and even expands its markets in a globalizing economy while Abu Dhabi, formerly without world-class art, gets its own collections and architectural sites for its expatriate community and tourist economy, as a way of lending culture and history to its new institutions of entertainment, leisure, and lifestyle. To see this situation as reflecting or even modeling the potential for an eroding of borders and a sharing of cultures between the West and the Middle East would be to accept a kind of Disney-like fairy-tale version of the reality of the political situation that exists between these regions as a whole. Recall that the UAE is being built on the culture not of indigenous locals but of expatriates and successful North American, European and Asian entrepreneurs, and low-paid immigrant labor. We might see these institutions as a kind of Disneyfication of the idea of global fine art. This view is supported by the construction in the UAE of a kind of island-map theme park of the world. In this project, the continental land masses are represented in miniature, like a sculptural frieze spread across the water. The UAE thus has its own Whole Earth image for the 2000s—one that can be photographed from above and experienced in its material form by visiting there in person.

But we must recognize that there is far more to this situation than the stunning buildings, collections, and consumer items that meet the eye. The art, buildings, hotels and restaurants are signifiers of new wealth and knowledge, but the links that make this visual and material globalization of beauty and culture possible are a market in oil and global financial industries as well as an expatriate citizenry eager to live the good life disconnected from the past. These circumstances make the UAE a crucial link between regions fraught by tensions that escalated profoundly and tragically in the 2000s. France and the United States have made explicit their profound distrust of many Middle Eastern nations and have in fact curtailed and more strictly regulated cultural and political transmission between the regions since the early 1990s. The cultural expansion of the Louvre and the Guggenheim, a New York museum, into

Abu Dhabi, as well as numerous American universities into Abu Dhabi, Qatar, and Dubai, present an exception to the dominant trend in politics between the Middle Eastern nations, which have in the vast majority of cases expressed a profound distrust of Western political and economic intentions and motivations in the region, and the West, which sees the majority of Middle Eastern nations and peoples as harboring explicit threats to national security in the wake of September 11. The Guggenheim and the Louvre in Abu Dhabi are certainly major icons of the "borderlessness" of global trade liberalization and cultural exchange in a world moving toward a global free market, but these icons hold deeply limited and ironic meanings given this mutual distrust between regions.

We would not suggest that these museums constitute a later form of cultural imperialism. Rather, the dynamics of this kind of cultural exchange are markedly different. We live in an era marked on the one hand by the opening of borders to trade, travel, and cultural exchange and on the other hand by the increased surveillance and monitoring of those borders even as flow across them increases. Battles over a natural resource are played out in the name of democratic freedom "for all" and not simply imperial right of ownership, making these new cultural icons of globalization function differently from simply top-down purveyors of Western values to ignoble "others." The nature of this kind of cultural movement remains to be characterized by students of art and visual culture who study and engage in the flow of art, artifacts, and goods in a century that has already been characterized with certainty as slated for harsh conditions, including the depletion of natural resources and the explosion of consumption of goods that were the outcome of modernity's industrial expansion.

The franchise model, as in television, is indicative of broader global trends in which the ideal is to forge a global network of display. But this ideal has met with challenges. It is no accident that the new museum global franchises are coincident with the demands by countries, including Peru, South Africa, and Greece, for the return of artifacts that were looted from their countries for the collections of Western museums. For example, for a century the Paris Musée de l'Homme held, and until 1974 kept on display, the remains of Saartje (or Sarah) Baartman, a Khoisan woman. Baartman was taken to London in 1810 from the area known as the Eastern cape of South Africa, where she had been a slave to a Dutch family. A brother of her owner had enticed Baartman to make the journey by promising her wealth. He put her body on display in French sideshows and society events, hawking her as an anatomical curiosity on the basis of her buttocks and labia (described as unusually large). Following a public and legal scandal in which it was charged that her display constituted a form of human bondage (the Slave Trade Act had been passed three years earlier), Baartman was taken to Paris, where she was displayed by an animal trainer, and then came to the attention of society women and men who eventually had her brought to the attention of French naturalists, including Georges Cuvier, who studied her living human form. After her death from smallpox in 1815, her remains were analyzed and put on display in the Musée de l'Homme until 1974, when they were put in storage in part as a response to objections about the ethics of showing the body of someone so wrongfully displayed in life as a mere scientific artifact. Efforts to have Baartman's body returned and buried according to Khoisan tradition were resisted until 2002, when Nelson Mandela, then president of South Africa, made a successful plea to France for her body's repatriation. Her body parts were returned, with the exception of her brain, which had disappeared from the collection, its location a mystery.

The Louvre's collection is, of course, works of art, not bodies. Yet the question of ownership and national rights remains crucial in an era in which we have seen numerous cases of restitution, many fraught with guilt, reluctance, righteousness, and conflicts centering on legal versus moral rights and in which claims of sovereign ownership on both sides are inevitably subject to the world's view and hence judgment. The Louvre's collecting practices were shaped in part by acquisitions made under colonialism, a relationship of domination that helped to rationalize French proprietary rights to a colony's cultural production. Proprietary rights to art and artifacts taken for display during the colonial era continue to be negotiated. The Metropolitan Museum in New York has holdings that are similarly shaped by acquisitions obtained during American industrial expansion into foreign regions, and the British Museum in London has a collection that clearly reflects the former practice of acquiring the cultural productions of colonies for display as means of demonstrating the power of the British Empire. It is well known that war and imperial expansion have created opportunities for the illicit acquisition of foreign works of art, and this practice has been hard to document and correct due to the chaos of warfare, in which repositories of art are not only targeted for destruction (as a means of wiping out a culture) but are also physically appropriated by enemy forces. Ownership battles have raged concerning artifacts going as far back as the Elgin Marbles, half of an original 500-foot sculptural frieze (or wall relief) taken from the Parthenon in Greece. The British ambassador to the Ottoman Empire removed this segment of the Parthenon wall in the early 1800s and took it to England to be put on display. The act was condemned as vandalism in 1816, and the British government then offered to pay, subsequently placing the frieze on display in the British Museum, where it can be seen today in its own special gallery, though Greece is still demanding its return. The Geneva Convention codified ownership of some of the tens of thousands of works of art stolen from Jews, who were among those from whom the Nazis had systematically stolen hundreds of thousands of works between 1933 and 1945. When Louvre employee Vincenzo Peruggia was apprehended in his attempt to sell the *Mona Lisa*, which he had stolen, to the Uffizi Gallery in Florence, he was regarded by many as a patriot for trying to return the painting to Italy. In recent years, the Getty Museum in Los Angeles and other institutions have returned some artifacts to their places of origin in an attempt to recognize, belatedly, that Western institutions can no longer assume this role as the rightful repository of the world's cultural gems, particularly when those gems were acquired through relations of domination. American anthropological and history museums have, under protest from Native Americans, returned Indian artifacts and bones to tribes, recognizing the importance of these items to the maintenance of local traditions and the crucial importance of allowing the proper burial of bodily remains. As in the case of Baartman, to strip a body of its cultural meaning in the service of scientific knowledge is now regarded as inhumane. Recognition of this fact came about after the Holocaust, when it became clear that not only were humans killed because of contempt for their cultural identity, sexual preference, or mental capacity, but they were also subjected to experimentation and the use of their body parts in industry, a practice rationalized by the claim of scientific and industrial gain. It is now widely accepted that to appropriate and put on display artifacts, human or object, is to strip them and their owners of the human right to self-determination. The discourse of sovereignty and local rights is a strong, sometimes antagonistic and sometimes consolidating, force within the discourse of free global transmission.[32]

The desire to situate oneself within the local and the national is always in tension with an embrace of the global; the movement of cultural products and visual images throughout the world is always about the way that cultural meanings and values change and power is negotiated. In this book, we have examined many of the changes that have taken place in the world of visual images throughout history. We have focused in particular on the ways that image technologies that emerged in the nineteenth and twentieth centuries have affected the kinds of images that are produced, how they are consumed and understood, and how they circulate in and across cultures. This complex history shows us how difficult it is to predict the future of images in the twenty-first century. Although convergence of industries and technologies is the focus of industry, it is also the case that people have important ritualistic relationships and distinct phenomenological experiences with different media that make them resistant to media and institutional convergence and conglomeration, and the sense of the visual varies from culture to culture. Clearly, the shift toward the digital will continue to affect notions of the real and the true.

Yet, at the same time, the image can never in itself encompass all that is entailed in living in the world. The material environment is crucial to an understanding and grounding of a global worldview. Building and engineering become more than just tropes of change. If we can say that visual culture was the paradigmatic form of the twentieth century, we may find that engineering and the built environment, the field in which we live in all of our sensory and motor capacities, is the focus of twenty-first century art. Natalie Jeremijenko, the Australian U.S.-based engineer-artist-activist, is perhaps the quintessential expression of this approach to art. As an engineering student in 1996, Jeremijenko, working under the sign of the Bureau of Inverse Technology, created a work she called the *Suicide Box*, a vertical-motion-triggered surveillance camera that was installed under the Golden Gate Bridge for 100 days, where it captured frame-accurate data of seventeen activities, some of which

FIG. 10.17
Natalie Jeremijenko, *Feral Robotic Dogs*, 2002

were suicides that otherwise would have gone undocumented unless and until the bodies were discovered. Jeremijenko's piece drew attention to the status of this gateway to Silicon Valley, the information capital, as the unrecognized suicide capital in an era characterized by fervor over information but also by alienation and despondency over life in late capitalism's urban centers. It also drew attention to the gaps in the kind of panoptic field of attention created by the use of surveillance systems, which by 2000 had become so prevalent in everyday life that one would be hard put to find a spot in a city outside a private home where one was *not* documented while moving through public space. Work like Jeremijenko's moves beyond institutional critique by using new technologies in experimental ways to intervene in practices of living, serving as examples of how we might retool digital culture toward a world that does not reduce itself to life on the screen as an escape from the real and the everyday. In *Feral Robotic Dogs* (2002), Jeremijenko upgraded commercially available robotic toy dogs, transforming them into an army of activist instruments programmed to identify and display data on the location and composition of urban pollutants. By making visible evidence that would otherwise be apparent only to expert observers with special equipment, Jeremijenko aims to widen access not only to material evidence but also to opportunities for political engagement in environmental issues. Whereas in the Enlightenment period art and science were put in one another's service, in the postmodern period science and popular culture are similarly made interdependent in the art of social change in an effort to motivate us toward making visible and addressing the environmental problems that have produced the conditions for the state of modernity in ruins imagined in films such as *Akira* and *Bladerunner.*

The circumstances of national borders, which were fervently fortified in the 2000s after 9/11, bring the issues of technologies, visuality, and the stakes and effects of environmental changes through globalizing industry to the fore. If we look, for example, to the border towns that flank the United States and Mexico, to the south we can identify increasingly intensified presence of fences and guards, including the presence of the civilian vigilante patrols that became prevalent in the late 2000s. Looking inland from the I-5 freeway that connects the California border town of San Diego to Mexico, we may notice something that looks from a distance like fields of cardboard boxes, condo villages assembled in landscaped rows by the hundreds, their numbers expanding day by day into former canyon land before the real estate collapse of the late 2000s slowed the frantic pace of their construction, which attempted to keep up with the need for affordable housing in a market that had outstripped even the solidly middle-class person's ability to own a free-standing house. If we look south of the California border further down that freeway, we may see rugged dry landscape, and a few miles beyond that we might spy yet another field of box-like assemblages. These are not condos but shantytowns, the mostly illegal settlements of impoverished factory workers and unemployed Mexicans.

These shantytowns are found close to the border, where we also find *maquiladoras,* foreign-owned plants that import materials and equipment on a duty- and tariff-free basis and assemble goods that are then reexported. The word *maquila* refers to the portion of grain given to the miller for processing one's raw wheat. Three hundred such factories were built in Mexico, most at the border where goods can conveniently cross back into the United States for consumption and where managers can live. They employ over a million Mexican workers at much lower wages than could be paid a few miles away, in the United States. The shantytowns were constructed in a process that epitomizes the practices of appropriation, pastiche, and bricolage described in relationship to works of art and cultural expression throughout this book. They are constructed by the hands of those who cannot afford to rent or own a home. These people are factory workers, day laborers who cross into the United States to work illegally in jobs such as housecleaning, construction, and landscaping. Dwellings are fashioned spontaneously from materials at hand: the cardboard, wood, corrugated steel, and PVC piping appropriated from the garbage left over from urban consumption and construction and from industrial deliveries and production. These towns built on squatted land spread out from the least habitable regions at the outskirts of cities where authorities are least likely to intervene.

In some cases, these towns have populations that approach and even surpass those of the cities they border. *Everyone Their Grain of Sand*, a 2005 documentary by the Los Angeles filmmaker Beth Bird, gives a detailed account of the land-rights struggle of the people of Maclovio Rojas, a Tijuana squatter village whose citizens had worked to establish a sustainable community, even building and staffing a school for the children of the town and petitioning for water and electrical power, only to have the government attempt eviction in order to make way for the site of a new multinational factory. The Mexico City- and San Diego-based architect Teddy Cruz, whose work is discussed in chapter 8, engages directly in this visual and material politics of housing in his practice as an architect, artist, international activist and local community organizer. Cruz draws from the aesthetic and formal strategies of those who fashion their houses from the castoffs of industrial production, using this style and this kind of material to fashion dwellings in places near the border of high visibility and in the museums and public spaces of urban centers far from these towns. In doing so, he brings the reality of life in the shadows of late capitalist industrialism and consumerism to the attention of the museumgoing public and the everyday person inhabiting the urban and suburban centers of modernity. The subjects who engage in this form of bricolage are no less modern, no less paradigmatic of the digital era than the typical student we tried to capture in our discussion of media in this book, the person who wakes to a cell phone's alarm clock and spends the day negotiating digital screens.

We encourage our readers to see the subjects who populate the periphery and build from waste not simply as the "have-nots" who should be helped through philanthropic means to be brought into the wealth of the digital age. Rather, as Cruz suggests, we should learn from the tactics and politics of those forced to live at the margins of late modernity's development. We might, like Cruz, embrace their assemblage-and-bricolage strategies as models of how to make fine art that comments on the conditions of everyday living at the border of two vying yet interdependent geographies and economies. The early postmodern decades saw cultural expression as a source for styles from which politics had been emptied out. Cruz encourages us to think about the politics that are inherent in the styles of bricolage and appropriation, and to become active in the politics that give shape to the styles we appropriate and to which we give new life and meaning. We should be astute cultural readers, discerning the meanings of these structures within a broader politics of everyday survival and work as cultural producers, not simply within the walls of museums and universities but in the institutions of environmental management, housing, health care, and food production that make the mundane and everyday landscape we see a place where we can live.

Working to change visual culture can shape life anew in all sorts of professions in ways that can change everyday life. Visual culture is not limited to the domains of art, photography, and media production. This is a new way to understand convergence. We saw this approach in the work of Duchamp, with his readymades that incorporated everyday objects and not just new technologies, and we see it enacted every day in the street art and institutional interventions of contemporary artists, ranging from Fred Wilson, who mined the historical museum, using its mundane artifacts to retell the history of racism, to Shepard Fairey, who mines the styles of poster art of the Soviet revolutionaries and the 1960s to find news ways of expressing political change through street art and cheap T-shirts, to the Guerrilla Girls, who became fed up with the continued exclusion of female artists from museums and took their practices into public performance and institutional critique. Whereas in the 1990s institutional critique took place inside institutions, Cruz's work suggests that in the 2000s the site of action is at the margins and in the spaces that cannot be contained within the walls and discourses of institutions. Everyday life and the public spheres of the borders, the streets, the Web, and the malls become sites not just where we can post signs but where we can also use visual culture to speak, act, build, and work to engineer social change.

Notes

1. See Linda Kintz and Julia Lesage, eds., *Media, Culture, and the Religious Right* (Minneapolis: University of Minnesota Press, 1998).
2. Seyla Benhabib, *Another Cosmopolitanism* (New York: Oxford University Press, 2006).
3. See Denis Cosgrove, "Contested Global Visions: One-World, Whole-Earth, and the Apollo Space Photographs," *Annals of the Association of American Geographers* 84.2 (June 1994), 270–94; and Neil Maher, "Gallery: Neil Maher on Shooting the Moon," *Environmental History* 9.3, http://www.historycooperative.org (accessed March 2008).
4. Vicki Goldberg, *The Power of Photography: How Photographs Changed Our Lives*, 52–57 (New York: Abbeville, 1991); and Fred Turner, *From Counterculture to Cyberculture: Stewart Brand, the Whole Earth Network, and the Rise of Digital Utopianism*, 69 (Chicago: University of Chicago Press, 2006).
5. Cosgrove, "Contested Global Visions," 286.
6. Lisa Parks, *Cultures in Orbit: Satellites and the Televisual*, 3 (Durham, N.C.: Duke University Press, 2005).
7. Parks, *Cultures in Orbit*, 23–24.
8. Jody Berland, "Mapping Space: Imaging Technologies and the Planetary Body," in *Technoscience and Cyberculture*, ed. Stanley Aronowitz, Barbara Martinsons, and Michael Menser, 124 (New York: Routledge, 1996).
9. Berland, "Mapping Space," 129.
10. See Michael Tracey, "Non-Fiction Television," in *Television: An International History*, ed. Anthony Smith, 78 (New York: Oxford University Press, 1998).
11. Ariel Dorfman and Armand Mattelart, *How to Read Donald Duck: Imperialist Ideology in the Disney Comic*, trans. David Kunzle (New York: International General, [1975] 1984).
12. Toby Miller, Nitin Govil, John McMurria, Richard Maxwell, and Ting Wang, *Global Hollywood 2*, 10–11 (London: British Film Institute, 2005).
13. Robert Foster, "The Commercial Construction of 'New Nations,'" *Journal of Material Culture* 4.3 (1998), 262–82.
14. See John Moore, *Tribal Knowledge: Business Wisdom Brewed from the Grounds of Starbucks Corporate Culture* (Chicago: Kaplan Publishing, 2006).
15. Caren Kaplan, "A World Without Boundaries: The Body Shop's Trans/National Geographics," *Social Text*, 13.2 (Summer 1995), 45–66.
16. Yunxiang Yan, "McDonald's in Beijing: The Localization of Americana," in *Golden Arches East: McDonald's in East Asia*, ed. James L. Watson, 39–76 (Stanford, Calif.: Stanford University Press, 1997).
17. Thomas Friedman, *The Lexus and the Olive Tree* (New York: Anchor Books, 1999).
18. Charles Norchi, "The Global Divide: From Davos..." *Boston Globe*, February 1, 2000, excerpted at http://www.globalpolicy.org/globaliz/define/davos.htm (accessed March 2008).
19. Arjun Appadurai, "Grassroots Globalization and the Research Imagination" *Public Culture* 12.1 (Winter 2000), 1–19.
20. Arjun Appadurai, "Disjuncture and Difference in the Global Cultural Economy," in *Modernity at Large: Cultural Dimensions of Globalization*, 27–47 (Minneapolis: University of Minnesota Press, 1996).
21. Meaghan Morris, "Transnational Imagination in Action Cinema: Hong Kong and the Making of a Global Popular Culture," in *The Inter-Asia Cultural Studies Reader*, ed. Kuan-Hsing Chen and Chua Beng Huat, 432–35 (New York: Routledge, 2007).
22. Nitin Govil, "Bollywood and the Frictions of Global Mobility," in *Media on the Move: Global Flow and Contra-Flow*, ed. Daya Thussu, 84–98 (New York: Routledge, 2006).
23. Michael Keane and Albert Moran, "Television's New Engines," *Television and New Media* 9.2 (March 2008), 155–69.
24. Tony Bennett and Jane Woollacott, *Bond and Beyond* (London: Palgrave/Macmillan 1987).
25. Umberto Eco, "Narrative Structures in Fleming," in *The Role of the Reader: Explorations in the Semiotics of Texts*, 144–72 (Bloomington: Indiana University Press, 1979).
26. Hamid Naficy, *The Making of Exile Cultures: Iranian Television in Los Angeles* (Minneapolis: University of Minnesota Press, 1993).
27. Pradeep Jeganathan, "Eelam.com: Place, Nation, and Imagi-Nation in Cyberspace," *Public Culture* 10.3 (1998), 515–28.

28. Subcomandante Marcos, "For the Photograph Event in Internet," EZLN communiqué posted February 8, 1996, and quoted in George Yúdice, *The Expediency of Culture: Uses of Culture in the Global Era*, 106 (Durham, N.C.: Duke University Press, 2003).

29. Yúdice, *The Expediency of Culture*, 105.

30. Rebecca Solnit, "Revolution of the Snails: Encounters with the Zapatistas," *Tomdispatch.com*, January 15, 2008, http://www.tomdispatch.com/post/174881 (accessed July 2008).

31. Yúdice, *The Expediency of Culture*, 106. On the Zapatistas, see also Lynn Stephen and Rosalva Aída Hernández Castillo, "Indigenous Women's Participation in Formulating the San Andres Accords," *Cultural Survival Quarterly* 23.1, April 30, 1999. http://www.culturalsurvival.org/publications/csq/csq-article.cfm?id=1117. Accessed July 2008.

32. On the subject of Sarah Baartman, see *The Life and Times of Sarah Baartman, "The Hottentot Venus,"* a video by Zola Meseko, South Africa/France, 1998, 52 minutes. Distributed by First Run/Icarus Films.

Further Reading

Allen, Robert C., ed. *To be Continued…: Soap Operas Around the World*. New York: Routledge, 1995.

Appadurai, Arjun. "Disjuncture and Difference in the Global Cultural Economy." In *Modernity at Large: Cultural Dimensions of Globalization*. Minneapolis: University of Minnesota Press, 1996, 27–47.

———. *Fear of Small Numbers: An Essay on the Geography of Numbers*. Durham, N.C.: Duke University Press, 2006.

Aufderheide, Pat. "Grassroots Video in Latin America" and "Making Video with Brazilian Indians." In *The Daily Planet: A Critic on the Capitalist Culture Beat*. Minneapolis: University of Minnesota Press, 2000, 257–88.

Bird, Beth, director. *Everyone Their Grain of Sand*. Women Make Movies, 2005.

Benhabib, Seyla. *Another Cosmopolitanism*. New York: Oxford University Press, 2006.

Berland, Jody. "Mapping Space: Imaging Technologies and the Planetary Body." In *Technoscience and Cyberculture*. Edited by Stanley Aronowitz, Barbara Martinsons, and Michael Menser. New York: Routledge, 1996.

Berwanger, Dietrich. "The Third World." In *Television: An International History*. 2nd ed. Edited by Anthony Smith. New York: Oxford University Press, 1998, 188–200.

Boddy, William. "The Beginnings of American Television." In *Television: An International History*. 2nd ed. Edited by Anthony Smith. New York: Oxford University Press, 1998, 23–37.

———. *Fifties Television: The Industry and Its Critics*. Urbana: University of Illinois Press, 1992.

Cairncross, Frances. *The Death of Distance: How the Communication Revolution Will Change Our Lives*. Boston: Harvard Business School Press, 1997.

Canclini, Néstor García. *Consumers and Citizens: Globalization and Multicultural Conflicts*. Translated by George Yúdice. Minneapolis: University of Minnesota Press, 2001.

Cheah, Pheng, and Bruce Robbins, eds. *Cosmopolitics: Thinking and Feeling Beyond the Nation*. Minneapolis: University of Minnesota Press, 1998.

Chen, Kuan-Hsing, and Chua Beng Huat, eds. *The Inter-Asia Cultural Studies Reader*. New York: Routledge, 2007.

Clifford, James. *The Predicament of Culture: Twentieth-Century Ethnography, Literature, and Art*. Cambridge, Mass.: Harvard University Press, 1988.

———. *Routes: Travel and Translation in the Late Twentieth Century*. Cambridge, Mass.: Harvard University Press, 1997.

Devereaux, Leslie, and Roger Hillman, eds. *Fields of Vision: Essays in Film Studies, Visual Anthropology, and Photography*. Berkeley: University of California Press, 1995.

Dorfman, Ariel, and Armand Mattelart. *How to Read Donald Duck: Imperialist Ideology in the Disney Comic*. Translated by David Kunzle. New York: International General, [1975] 1984.

Druckrey, Timothy, ed. *Electronic Culture: Technology and Visual Representation*. New York: Aperture, 1996.

Dudrah, Rajinder, and Jigna Desai, eds. *The Bollywood Reader.* New York: Open University Press/ McGraw Hill, 2008.

Edwards, Elizabeth, ed. *Anthropology & Photography 1860–1920.* New Haven: Yale University Press, 1992.

Foster, Robert. "The Commercial Construction of 'New Nations.'" *Journal of Material Culture,* 4.3 (1998), 262–82.

Fox. Elizabeth. *Latin American Broadcasting: From Tango to Telenovela.* Luton, U.K.: University of Luton, 1997.

Ginsburg, Faye. "Indigenous Media: Faustian Contract or Global Village?" *Cultural Anthropology* 6.1 (1991), 94–114.

Innis, Harold A. *Empire and Communications.* New York: Oxford University Press, 1950.

Inuit Broadcasting Corporation, Ottawa, Ontario. e-mail: ibcicsl@sonetis.com, http://siksik.learnnet.nt.ca/tvnc/Members/ibc.html (accessed March 2008).

Iwabuchi, Koichi. *Recentering Globalization: Popular Culture and Japanese Transnationalism.* Durham, N.C.: Duke University Press, 2002.

Jeganathan, Pradeep. "Eelam.com: Place, Nation, and Imagi-Nation in Cyberspace." *Public Culture,* 10.3 (1998), 515–28.

Karp, Ivan, Corinne A. Kratz, Lynn Szwaja, and Tomás Ybarra-Frausto, eds. *Museum Frictions: Public Culture/Global Transformations.* Durham, N.C.: Duke University Press, 2006.

Kaplan, Caren. "A World without Boundaries: The Body Shop's Trans/National Geographics." *Social Text,* 13.2 (Summer 1995), 45–66.

———. "Precision Targets: GPS and the Miltarization of Consumer Identity." In *Rewiring the "Nation": The Place of Technology in American Studies.* Edited by Carolyn de la Peña and Siva Vaidhyanathan. Baltimore: Johns Hopkins Press, 2007, 139–59.

Kintz, Linda, and Julia Lesage, eds. *Media, Culture, and the Religious Right.* Minneapolis: University of Minnesota Press, 1998.

Mattelart, Michèle, and Armand Mattelart. *The Carnival of Images: Brazilian Television Fiction.* Translated by David Buxton. New York: Bergin & Garvey, 1990. Republished by Westport, Conn.: Greenwood.

Meltzer, Jamie, director. *Welcome to Nollywood.* Cinema Guild, 2007.

Michaels, Eric. *Bad Aboriginal Art: Traditional, Media, and Technological Horizons.* Minneapolis: University of Minnesota Press, 1994.

Miller, Toby, Nitin Govil, John McMurria, Richard Maxwell, and Ting Wang. *Global Culture 2.* London: British Film Institute, 2005.

Morley, David, and Kevin Robins. *Spaces of Identity: Global Media, Electronic Landscapes, and Cultural Boundaries.* New York: Routledge, 1995.

Naficy, Hamid. *The Making of Exile Cultures: Iranian Television in Los Angeles.* Minneapolis: University of Minnesota Press, 1993.

Parks, Lisa. *Cultures in Orbit: Satellites and the Televisual.* Durham, N.C.: Duke University Press, 2005.

Schiller, Herbert I. "The Global Information Highway: Project for an Ungovernable World." In *Resisting the Virtual Life: The Culture and Politics of Information.* Edited by James Brook and Iain A. Boal. San Francisco: City Lights, 1995, 17–33.

Schon, Donald A., Bish Sanyal, and William J. Mitchell, eds. *High Technology and Low-Income Communities: Prospects for the Positive Use of Advanced Information Technology.* Cambridge, Mass.: MIT Press, 1999.

Shohat, Ella, and Robert Stam. *Unthinking Eurocentrism: Multiculturalism and the Media.* New York: Routledge, 1994.

Sinclair, John. *Latin American Television: A Global View.* New York: Oxford University Press, 1999.

Smith, Anthony, ed. *Television: An International History.* 2nd ed. New York: Oxford University Press, 1998.

Soong, Roland. "Telenovelas in Latin America," 1999, http://www.zonalatina.com/Zldata70.htm. Accessed March 2008.

Tomlinson, John. *Cultural Imperialism: A Critical Introduction.* Baltimore: Johns Hopkins Press, 1991.

Vink, Nico. *The Telenovela and Emancipation: A Study of Television and Social Change in Brazil.* Amsterdam: Royal Tropical Institute, 1988.

Yúdice, George. *The Expediency of Culture: Uses of Culture in the Global Era.* Durham, N.C.: Duke University Press, 2003.

Yan, Yunxiang. "McDonald's in Beijing: The Localization of Americana." In *Golden Arches East: McDonald's in East Asia.* Edited by James L. Watson. Stanford, Calif.: Stanford University Press, 1997, 39–76.

glossary

Abstract/abstraction In art, a nonrepresentational set of styles that respectively focus on material and formal qualities such as composition, shape, color, line, or texture rather than the overall pictorial representation of a reality external to the work of art. In advertising, the term is used to describe the fantasy world separated out from reality that is created by ads.

Abstract expressionism First used to describe expressionist art in Germany in the period after World War I, the term later became associated with artists including Willem de Kooning and Jackson Pollock after World War II through the 1950s. The works of art were viewed as a record of the artist's emotional intensity and physical spontaneity and gesture during the painting process. The compositions that resulted are highly abstract, but compared to the geometric abstraction of cubist paintings, they appear less formally organized and more spontaneous.

Aesthetics A branch of philosophy that is concerned with judgments of sentiment and taste. The term can also be used to mean the philosophy of art, which considers art's meaning and value in light of standards such as beauty and truth. Postmodern theorists questioned the universalizing claims of aesthetic judgment.

Affect Feeling or emotion, and the expression of feeling or emotion in the face and body. In visual studies, affect has been of great interest since 1995 with regard to the relationship between affect understood as internal feelings, as the outward, physical expression of inner feelings through facial expressions and gestures, and as the interpretation of our expressions and gestures by others. See *Psychoanalytic theory*.

Agency The capacity or power to act or to make meaning on one's own behalf relatively free of influence from social forces and the will of others. Foucault's model of power suggests that human subjects are never wholly free agents but are always shaped by and through the social institutions and historical contexts in which they live.

Alienation A term that has several meanings historically: in general, the sense of distance from others in one's social world, a loss of self, and a sense of helplessness that is an effect of life in modernity. In Marxism, alienation is a condition of capitalism in which humans experience a sense of separation from the products of their labor, hence from other aspects of life, including human relations. In psychoanalysis, alienation refers to split subjectivity and is a result of the fact that one is not in full conscious control of one's thoughts, actions, and desires because of the mediating forces of the unconscious. See *Marxist theory, Psychoanalytic theory, Modernism, Modernity.*

Analog The representation of data by means of physical properties that express value along a continuous scale. Analog technologies include photography, magnetic tape, vinyl recording, a clock with hands, or a mercury thermometer, in which highs and lows, darks and lights, and so forth, are measured along a scale that shows incremental change, such as that of electrical voltage. It could be said that we experience the world as analog, that is, as based on a sense of continuity. An analog image such as a photograph is distinguished from its digital counterpart in its basis on continuity in gradation of tone and color. A digital image is divided into bits that are mathematically encoded. See *Digital.*

Appropriation The act of borrowing, stealing, or taking over others' works, images, words, meanings to one's own ends. Cultural appropriation is the process of borrowing and changing the meaning of commodities, cultural products, slogans, images, or elements of fashion by putting them into a new context or in juxtaposition with new elements. Appropriation is one of the primary forms of oppositional production and reading, when, for instance, viewers take cultural products and reedit, rewrite, or change them, or change their meaning or use. See *Bricolage, Transcoding, Oppositional reading.*

Aura A term used by German theorist Walter Benjamin to describe a special quality that seems to emanate from unique works of art. According to Benjamin, the aura of unique works gives them the quality of authenticity, which cannot be reproduced. Aura is not a quality the work materially holds but one that is imputed to the work by a culture that holds it in high regard. See *Reproduction.*

Authenticity The quality of being genuine or unique. Traditionally, authenticity referred to a quality attributed to things that are one of a kind and original, rather than copied. In Walter Benjamin's theories of the reproduction of images, authenticity is precisely that special something that cannot be reproduced when an original is copied.

Avant-garde A term imported from military strategy (in which it indicated an expeditionary or scouting force that takes risks) into art history to describe movements at the forefront of artistic experimentation, leading the way toward major changes. Avant-garde is often associated with modernism and formal innovation and is frequently contrasted with mainstream or traditional art that is conventional rather than challenging.

Base/superstructure Terms used by Marx to describe the relations of labor and economics (considered the social base) to the social system and consciousness (regarded as superstructure) in capitalism. In classic Marxist theory, the economic base determines the legal, political, religious, and ideological aspects of the superstructure. See *Marxist theory.*

Binary oppositions The oppositions such as nature/culture, male/female, mind/body, and so forth, through which reality has traditionally been represented. Although binary oppositions can seem immutable and mutually exclusive, contemporary theories of difference have demonstrated the ways in which these oppositional categories are interrelated and are ideologically and historically constructed. This leads to the exclusion of other positions in the spectrum between these binaries. For example, sexuality exists along a continuum and not solely in the form of two poles of identity, male and female. The historical reliance on binary oppositions points to the way that difference is essential to meaning and how we understand things. See *Cartesian dualism, Marked/unmarked, Structuralism.*

Biopower A term used by French philosopher Michel Foucault to describe the technologies of power through which modern states rely on institutional practices to regulate, subjugate, and control their human subjects. Biopower refers to the ways that power is enacted on a collective social body through the regulation and discipline of individual bodies in realms such as social hygiene, public health, education, demography, census taking, and reproductive practices, among others. These processes and practices produce particular kinds of knowledge about bodies and produce bodies with particular kinds of meaning and capacities. In Foucault's terms, all bodies are constructed through the many techniques of biopower. See *Docile bodies, Power/knowledge.*

Black-boxed The inability of the user to see inside (metaphorically and sometimes literally) a machine and discern how it functions. What gets "boxed" are the structure and mechanisms of a particular technology that are not visible to its user.

Brand The naming and investment of meaning into companies or products in order to sell them as commodities. Branding began in the nineteenth century when products sold in bulk were given names, packaging, trademark symbols, and meanings (such as Quaker Oats). Contemporary brands have highly complex meanings created through advertising, logos, and packaging, and it is now common to speak of brand identity, brand identification, and "love of the brand," all of which demonstrate the depth of consumer relationships with brands.

Bricolage The practice of working with whatever materials are at hand, "making do" with what one has. As a cultural practice, bricolage was used by Dick Hebdige to refer to the activity of taking commodities and making them one's own by giving them new meaning. This has the potential to create resistant meanings out of commodities. The punk practice of wearing safety pins as body ornamentation is an example of bricolage. One origin of the term in cultural studies is derived from anthropologist Claude Lévi-Strauss in reference to how so-called primitive cultures differ in their processes of meaning making from dominant colonial cultures. See *Appropriation, Counter-bricolage.*

Broadcast media Media that are transmitted from one central point to many different receiving points. Television and radio, for instance, are transmitted across broad spectrums, from a central transmission point to a vast number of receivers (TV sets and radios). Low-power and local transmission are not broadcast but narrowcast media. See *Narrowcast media.*

Capitalism An economic system in which investment in and ownership of the means of production, distribution, and exchange of wealth are held primarily by individuals and corporations, as opposed to cooperative or state-owned means of wealth. Capitalism is based on an ideology of free trade, open markets, and individuality. In capitalism, the use value of goods (how they are used) matters less than their exchange value (what they are worth on the market). Industrial capitalism refers to capitalist systems that are based on industry, such as those of many European-American nation-states in the nineteenth and twentieth centuries. Late capitalism (which is also called postindustrialism) refers to late twentieth-century forms of capitalism that are more global in terms of economic ownership and structure and in which the primary commodities that are traded include services and information, in addition to manufactured, physically tangible goods. Marxist theory is a critique of the ways that the system of capitalism is based on inequality and exploitation of workers, allowing a few to prosper while many have only limited means. See *Exchange value, Marxist theory, Postindustrialism, Use value.*

Cartesian dualism The binary division, theorized by seventeenth-century philosopher René Descartes, that the mind and body are split, with the mind containing consciousness and reasoning while the body is only matter. The concept of mind-body split has its origins in Greek philosophy but was explicated at length by Descartes in relation to his concepts of consciousness and reason.

Cartesian space A term that refers to the mathematical mapping of space developed by the seventeenth-century philosopher René Descartes. Descartes's theories concerned a rationalist, mechanistic interpretation of nature. A Cartesian grid is the definition of space through three axes, each intersecting each other at ninety degrees to define three-dimensional space. Cartesian space is contingent on the idea of a rational human subject whose sensory experience is put to the test of judgment. See the discussion of virtual space under *Virtual.*

Cinéma vérité A movement of documentary cinema in the 1960s, in some contexts referred to as direct cinema, that promoted a naturalistic, supposedly unmediated recording of reality through the use of long takes with minimal editing, handheld cameras, and the rejection of voice-over narration and scripts. Although advocates of cinéma vérité felt that these techniques provided a more authentic way of representing reality, it can still be said that the choices they made through framing and their presence as filmmakers in these situations all had an effect on the "authenticity" of what they shot. Vérité directors include Jean Rouch and Frederick Wiseman, who is also associated with the direct cinema style. See *Direct cinema.*

Classical art Art that adheres to the styles and aesthetics of tradition. Typically the term is associated with ancient Greek and Roman art, referring to norms of balance, symmetry, and proportion.

Code The implicit rules by which meanings get put into social practice and can therefore be read by their users. Codes involve a systematic organization of signs. For example, there are codes of social conduct, such as forms of greeting or styles of social interaction, that are understood within a given society. Semiotics shows that language and representational media, such as cinema and television, are structured according to specific codes. Cinematic codes are the accepted ways of using lighting, camera movement, and editing within a given genre, period, or style. Codes may cross media, and various sets of codes may inform a single medium. For example, the painterly codes of chiaroscuro lighting or Renaissance perspective may be used in photographs and films. The term *code* has also been used by Stuart Hall to describe how cultural texts, such as television, can be encoded with meaning by producers and are then decoded by viewers. See *Decoding, Encoding, Semiotics, Sign.*

Colonialism The process of a nation extending its power over another nation, people, or territory. The term is used primarily to describe the colonization by European countries of Africa, India, Latin and North America, and the Pacific region from the sixteenth through the twentieth century (when struggles for independence produced the conditions of postcolonialism). Colonization was motivated by the potential exploitation of one nation's resources and labor by another and involved both the conquest of countries politically and economically but also the restructuring of the culture of the colonized, with enforced changes in language, among other things. See *Imperialism, Postcolonialism.*

Commodity/commodification Originally a term in Marxism, commodification is the process by which material objects are turned into marketable goods with monetary (exchange) value. Commodities are goods marketed to consumers in a commodity culture. See *Marxist theory.*

Commodity fetishism The process through which commodities are emptied of the meaning of their production (the labor that produced them and the context in which they were produced) and filled instead with abstract meaning (usually through advertising). In Marxism, commodity fetishism is the process of mystification that exists in capitalism between what things are and how they appear. Commodity fetishism also describes the process by which special life powers are attributed to commodities rather than to other elements in social life. For example, to suppose that a brand of car confers self-worth is to engage in commodity fetishism. In commodity fetishism, exchange value has so superseded use value that things are valued not for what they do but for what they cost, how they look, and what connotations can be attached to them. For instance, a commodity (such as bottled purified water) is emptied of the meaning of its production (where it was bottled, who worked to bottle it, how it was shipped) and filled with new meaning (mountain springs, purity) through advertising campaigns. See *Exchange value, Fetish, Marxist theory, Use value.*

Commodity self A term, coined by Stuart Ewen, that refers to how we construct our identities, at least in part, through the consumer products that inhabit our lives. The concept of a commodity self implies that our selves, if not our subjectivities, are mediated and constructed in part through our identification with commodity signs—the meanings that are attached to consumer products that we intentionally acquire through their purchase and use.

Commodity sign A term that refers to the semiotic meaning of a commodity that is constructed in an advertisement, brand, or logo. The representation of a commodity, or the product itself, and its meaning together form the commodity sign. Contemporary cultural theorists state that we do not consume commodities but commodity signs. That is, what we are really purchasing is the meaning of the commodity. See *Commodity/commodification, Sign.*

Conceptual art A style of art that emerged in the 1960s that focused on the idea of concept over aesthetic qualities or the material object itself. An attempt to counter the increased commercialism of the art world, conceptual art presented ideas rather than artworks that could be bought and sold and thus worked to shift the focus to the creative process and away from the art market and its commodities. Artists who worked in conceptual art include Joseph Kosuth, Hans Haacke, and Yoko Ono.

Connoisseur A person who is particularly skilled at discerning quality in a particular art. The term *connoisseur* is a class-based concept that has been traditionally used to refer to those with "discriminating" taste, that is, those of an upper-class status. The concept of connoisseurship has been criticized for representing upper-class taste as something that is natural, more authentic, more educated, and more discerning than popular taste.

Connotative meaning In semiotics, all the social, cultural, and historical meanings that are added to a sign's literal meaning. Connotative meanings rely on the cultural and historical context of the image and its viewers' lived, felt knowledge of those circumstances. Connotation thus brings to an object or image the wider realm of ideology, cultural meaning, and value systems of a society. According to Roland Barthes, myth occurs when we read connotative meanings as denotative (i.e., literal) meanings and thus naturalize what are in fact meanings derived from complex social ideologies. Freedom is a connotative meaning of the American flag, a meaning that is socially and culturally specific not natural. See *Denotative meaning, Myth, Semiotics, Sign.*

Constructivism An art movement in the Soviet Union following the 1917 Russian Revolution that deployed a modernist avant-garde aesthetic. Constructivism emphasized dynamic form and line as the embodiment of the politics and ideology of a machine-driven culture. The pro-Soviet artists of constructivism embraced the theories of Vladimir Lenin, ideas of technological progress, and a machine aesthetic. Its primary proponents were Vladimir Tatlin, El Lissitsky, and filmmaker Dziga Vertov. Soviet leader Joseph Stalin outlawed constructivism and embraced pictorial realism as the art form of the masses after 1932.

Convergence, media A term that refers to the combination of media together into one point of access or one conglomerate form. The combination of a telephone, wireless e-mail system, camera, and musical listening system in one device is an example of media convergence.

Cosmopolitanism Being a citizen of the world and having an identity that is more broadly defined than in a provincial or national context. Cosmopolitanism has a long history as a term and is used today most often in relation to theories of globalization. See *Globalization.*

Counter-bricolage A term coined by Robert Goldman and Stephen Papson for the practice used by marketers and advertisers to "borrow" and sell as commodities aspects of bricolage style. For instance, counter-bricolage occurs when styles of street youth are appropriated by manufacturers and then packaged and sold to consumers. See *Appropriation, Bricolage.*

Counter-hegemony The forces in a given society that work against dominant meaning and power systems and keep in constant tension and flux those dominant meanings. See *Hegemony.*

Cubism An early twentieth-century art movement beginning in 1907 that was part of the modern French avant-garde. Cubism began with collaboration between Pablo Picasso and Georges Braque, who were both developing new ways of depicting space and objects. Cubism was a deliberate critique of the dominance of perspective in styles of art and an attempt to represent the dynamism and complexity of human vision by representing objects simultaneously from multiple perspectives. See *Dada, Futurism, Modernism, Modernity.*

Cultural imperialism See *Imperialism.*

Culture industry A term used by the members of the Frankfurt School, in particular Theodor Adorno and Max Horkheimer, to indicate how capitalism organizes and homogenizes culture, giving cultural consumers less freedom to construct their own meanings. Horkheimer and Adorno saw the culture industry as generating mass culture as a form of commodity fetishism that functions as propaganda for industrial capitalism. They saw all mass culture as dictated by formula and repetition, encouraging conformity, promoting passivity, cheating its consumers of what it promises, and promoting pseudoindividuality. See *Frankfurt School, Pseudoindividuality.*

Cyberspace A term that refers to the virtual spaces of the computer screen, the Internet, the Web, and other telecommunications and digital technologies and systems. Sites of electronic exchange, such as the Web, are understood as constituting a kind of virtual geography in cyberspace. See *Cartesian space, Virtual, Web.*

Cyborg A term originally proposed by Manfred Clynes and Nathan Kline in 1960 to describe "self-regulating man-machine systems" or cybernetic organisms. Since that time, the cyborg has been theorized, most famously by Donna Haraway, as a means to consider the relationship of human subjects to technology and the subjectivity of late capitalism, biomedicine, and computer technology. It is argued that those who have prosthetics or pacemakers, for instance, are cyborgs, and cyborgs have populated contemporary science fiction literature and film. Contemporary thinking about cyborgs emphasizes how all subjects of contemporary postmodern and technological societies can be understood as cyborgs because we all depend on and have an integral relationship with technologies in everyday ways.

Dada An intellectual movement that began in Zurich in 1916 and later flourished in France with such figures as Marcel Duchamp and Francis Picabia. Dada was defined by the poet Tristan Tzara as a state of mind and was primarily anti-art in its sensibilities, with, for instance, Duchamp making "ready-mades" by putting ordinary objects such as a bicycle wheel and a urinal on display in a museum. Dada was irreverent concerning taste and tradition. It was influenced by futurism, though it did not fully share futurism's association with fascism and love of the machine. Other important Dada figures are the German writer Richard Hulsenbeck, the German artist Kurt Schwitters, and the French artist Jean Arp. See *Futurism.*

Decoding In cultural consumption, the process of interpreting and giving meaning to cultural products in conformity with shared cultural codes. Used by Stuart Hall to describe the work done by cultural consumers when they view and interpret cultural products (such as television shows, films, ads, etc.) that have been encoded by producers. According to Hall, factors such as "frameworks of knowledge" (class status, cultural knowledge), "relations of production" (which include the viewing context in which meaning is produced), and "technical infrastructure" (the technological medium in which one is viewing) influence the process of decoding. See *Code, Encoding.*

Denotative meaning In semiotics, the literal, face-value meaning of a sign. The denotative meaning of a rose is a flower. However, in any given context, a rose is likely to have connotative meanings (such as romanticism, love, or loyalty) that add social, historical, and cultural (connotative) meaning to its denotative meaning. See *Connotative meaning, Semiotics, Sign.*

Developing countries Those countries with a low standard of living, low HDI (Human Development Index), and a minimally developed or undeveloped industrial base. According to some theorists this is a more appropriate term to use than Third World. See *Third World, Globalization.*

Dialectic A term from philosophy whose use is varied and often ambiguous. In Greek philosophy, it referred to the dialogic process of question and answer as the means to higher knowledge. The term has generally been used to refer to a conflict or tension between two positions, for example the dialectics of good and evil. However, its use in philosophy (the Hegelian dialectic) refers to this conflict as a dynamic that produces social relations and meaning as they are enacted and resolved. In Marxist theory, history moves forward not in a continuous progression but through a chain of conflicts that are resolved only to bring new conflicts. Marxism speaks in this respect of theses and antitheses, for example an owner (thesis) and a worker (antithesis), whose antagonism leads to a synthesis through dialectical process. See *Marxist theory.*

Diaspora The existence of various communities, usually of a particular ethnicity, culture, or nation, scattered across different places outside of their land of origin or homeland. There are, for instance, large diasporic communities of South Asians living throughout England and the United States. Work in diasporic studies has stressed the complexity of such communities, who not only negotiate memory and nostalgia for original homelands but have the shared histories of migration, displacement, and hybrid identity of other local diaspora communities. See *Hybridity.*

Digital Representing data by means of discrete digits and encoding that data mathematically. Digital technologies, which technologically contrast with analog technologies, involve a process of encoding information in bits and assigning each a mathematical value. A clock with hands that move around a dial to show the time is analog, and a clock with a numbered readout is digital. A photographic image is analogic and continuous in tone, whereas a digital image is mathematically encoded so that each bit has a particular value and tone is represented in pixels. This allows the digital image to be more easily manipulated and copied without degeneration. See *Analog, Pixel.*

Direct cinema Closely related to cinéma vérité, direct cinema involved recording synchronized sound and footage of real-life action spontaneously, as it unfolded before the camera and crew. This technique broke with the use of voice-over narrative that had continued in some of the work of vérité directors such as Jean Rouch and involved minimal or no scripting, staging of action, editing, and general manipulation of materials filmed and recorded. Ricky Leacock, Robert Drew, D. A. Pennebaker, Frederick Wiseman, and Albert and David Maysles are some of the U.S. directors associated with this style. Their focus was primarily people in everyday institutions, from famous political figures to students and teachers, prison inmates and guards. See *Cinéma vérité*.

Discontinuity In avant-garde and postmodern styles, the strategy of breaking up a continuous narrative, interrupting stylistic flow with unexpected or contrasting elements, and circumventing audience identification in order to defy viewer expectations of smoothness and flow. Discontinuity might include jump cuts, a shuffling of chronological events, and reflexivity. See *Reflexivity*.

Discourse In general, the socially organized process of talking about a particular subject matter. More specifically, according to Michel Foucault, discourse is a body of knowledge that both defines and limits what can be said about something. Although there is no set list of discourses, the term tends to be used for broad bodies of social knowledge, such as the discourses of economics, the law, medicine, politics, sexuality, technology, and so forth. Discourses are specific to particular social and historical contexts, and they change over time. It is fundamental to Foucault's theory that discourses produce certain kinds of subjects and knowledge and that we occupy to varying degrees the subject positions defined within a broad array of discourses. See *Subject position*.

Docile bodies A term used by Michel Foucault to describe the process by which social subjects submit bodily to social norms. See *Biopower*.

Dominant-hegemonic reading In Stuart Hall's formulation of three potential positions for the viewer/consumer of mass culture, the dominant-hegemonic reading is one in which consumers unquestioningly accept the message that the producers are transmitting to them. According to Hall, few viewers actually occupy this position at any time because mass culture cannot satisfy all viewers' culturally specific experiences, memories, and desires and because viewers are not passive recipients of the messages of mass media and popular culture. See *Negotiated reading*, *Oppositional reading*.

Empiricism A method of scientific practice emphasizing the importance of sensory experience, observation, and measurement in the production of knowledge about something. An empirical methodology relies on experimentation and data collection to establish particular truths about things in the world.

Encoding In cultural consumption, the production of meaning in cultural products. Used by Stuart Hall to describe the work done by cultural producers in encoding cultural products (such as television shows, films, ads, etc.) with preferred meaning that will then be decoded by viewers. According to Hall, factors such as "frameworks of knowledge" (class status, cultural knowledge, and taste of the producers), "relations of production" (labor contexts of the production), and "technical infrastructure" (the technological context of the production) influence this process of encoding. See *Decoding*.

Enlightenment An eighteenth-century cultural movement associated with a rejection of religious and prescientific tradition through an embrace of the concept of reason. Enlightenment thinkers emphasized rationality and the idea of moral and social betterment through scientific progress. Kant defined the Enlightenment as "man's emergence from his self-imposed immaturity" and awarded it the motto of *sapere aude*—Dare to Know. The Enlightenment is associated with broader social changes, such as the decline of feudalism and the power of the Church, the increased impact of printing in European culture, and the rise of the middle class in Europe. It is considered to be an important aspect of the rise of modernity. See *Modernism, Modernity.*

Episteme The ideas and ways of ordering knowledge that are taken as true and accurate in a given era. The term was used by Michel Foucault, in his book *The Order of Things*, to describe the dominant mode of organizing knowledge in a given period of history, the ground on which particular discourses can emerge in that time. Each period of history has a different episteme. See *Discourse, Epistemology.*

Epistemology The branch of philosophy concerned with knowledge and what can be known. To ask an epistemological question about something is to investigate what we can know about it and how we know it.

Exchange value The monetary value that gets assigned to a commodity in a consumer culture. When an object is seen in terms of its exchange value, its economic worth (or monetary equivalent) is more important than what it can be used for (its use value). Marxist theory critiques the emphasis in capitalism on exchange over use value. For example, gold has significant exchange value though very little use value, as there are few practical functions for it. It serves to buy status. See *Capitalism, Commodity/commodification, Commodity fetishism, Marxist theory, Use value.*

Exhibitionism In psychoanalytic terms, taking pleasure in exposing one's body (or, its sexualized parts) to attract the attention of others. Some theorists have described certain films and Web projects to be fundamentally exhibitionist, as they are visually constructed to attract voyeuristic attention from spectators. See *Psychoanalytic theory, Scopophilia, Voyeurism.*

False consciousness In Marxist theory, the process by which the real economic imbalances of the dominant social system get hidden and ordinary citizens come to believe in the perfection of the system that in fact oppresses them. The biblical phrase "the meek shall inherit the earth" would be considered by Marxism to be an example of false consciousness, as it tells the downtrodden not to rebel against the system but to instead await later reward. Twentieth-century developments in Marxism see the concept of false consciousness as itself potentially oppressive because it characterizes the masses as unaware dupes of the system. In contrast, concepts such as hegemony emphasize the active struggle people engage in over meanings rather than their passive acceptance of ideological systems. See *Marxist theory, Hegemony, Ideology.*

Fetish In anthropology, an object that is endowed with magical powers and ritualistic meaning, for example, a totem pole. In Marxist theory, an object that is awarded "magical" economic power that is not in the object itself. For example, a dollar bill is a piece of paper that physically has no worth, yet it is given economic power by the State. In psychoanalytic theory, a fetish is an object that is endowed with magical powers to enable a person to compensate for a psychological lack. For example, a poster of a movie star may offer viewers a fantasy of possession or closeness with the absent star. Shoes, or even feet, may be psychically invested with the power to incite sexual desire for the sorts of bodies that have such feet, or that wear such shoes. The sexual response is displaced onto a part, an object, or a category of object, which takes on charged meaning in the absence of the body desired. See *Commodity fetishism*.

First World A term used in the post-World War II period of the twentieth century to refer to the countries of the West, as opposed to the Second World (the East) and the Third World. In this theory, the world is divided into West (First World) and East (Second World), with two major superpowers, the United States and the Soviet Union. As the Cold War has faded and the global dynamics of these countries have changed, the term has been considered to be less useful. See *Third World, Developing countries*.

Flâneur A French term popularized by nineteenth-century poet Charles Baudelaire, and subsequently theorized explicitly by cultural critics such as Walter Benjamin, that refers to a person who wanders city streets, taking in the sights, especially those of consumer society, in the era of industrialization and modernity, when consumer goods were first put on display in store windows and architecture was beginning to adapt to the need for spaces of consumption and display (such as arcades and department store windows). The *flâneur* is a kind of window shopper, with the implication that the act of looking at the gleaming offerings of commodity culture is itself a source of pleasure whether or not one actually ever purchases anything. The *flâneur* is simultaneously in the world of consumerism and detached from the cityscape around him. Originally, the *flâneur* was understood to be male, as women did not have the same freedom to wander the city streets alone, but recent cultural criticism, such as the work of Anne Friedberg, has sought to theorize the concept of the *flâneuse* as a female shopper consuming the seductive sights of the city. See *Modernism, Modernity*.

Frankfurt School A group of scholars and social theorists, working first in Germany in the 1930s and then primarily in the United States, who were interested in applying Marxist theory to the new forms of cultural production and social life in twentieth-century capitalist societies. The Frankfurt School scholars rejected Enlightenment philosophy, stating that reason did not free people but rather became a force in the rise of technical expertise, the expression of instrumental thinking divorced from wider goals of human emancipation, and the exploitation of people, making systems of social domination more efficient and effective. The key figures associated with the Frankfurt School are Theodor Adorno, Max Horkheimer, Herbert Marcuse, and later Jürgen Habermas. The early members fled Germany in the 1930s with the rise to power of the Nazis, and many of them came to the United States. See *Culture industry*, Pseudoindividuality.

Futurism An Italian avant-garde movement that was inspired by Filippo Tommaso Marinetti's *Futurist Manifesto*, which was published in 1909. The futurists were interesting in breaking free of tradition and embraced the idea of speed and the future. They wrote many manifestos and maintained a provocative and challenging style. Some of the futurist painters, such as Giacomo Balla, focused on painting objects and people in motion, and others worked in cubist styles. Marinetti famously forged links between futurism and Italian fascism, but futurists could be found all along the political spectrum. See *Cubism*, *Dada*.

Gaze In theories of the visual arts, such as film theory and art history, the *gaze* is a term used to describe the relationship of looking in which the subject is caught up in dynamics of desire through trajectories of looking and being looked at among objects and other people. For example, the gaze can be motivated by a the subject's desire for control over the object it sees, and an object can likewise capture and hold the look. A gaze is not exactly something one performs (as in the phrase, I gaze on your face); rather, it is a relation in which one is caught up (I am caught in the field of the gaze in which I look on your face and I see you look back at me, or not). In traditional psychoanalytic theory, the gaze is intimately linked to fantasy. Gaze theory was updated by French psychoanalyst Jacques Lacan, who put the gaze at the center of his approach to how individuals enact desire. Applying Freud's and Lacan's theories to film, 1970s psychoanalytic film theorists posited that in cinema, the gaze of the spectator on the image was an implicitly male one that objectified the women on screen. Since the 1990s, theories of the gaze have complicated this original model and have introduced discussion of a variety of different kinds of gazes, for example, gazes distinguished by sex, gender, race, and class.

Michel Foucault uses the term *gaze* to describe the relationship of subjects within a network of power—and the mechanism of vision as a means of negotiating and conveying power within that network—in a given institutional context. For Foucault, social institutions produce an inspecting, normalizing, or clinical gaze in which their subjects are caught and through which institutions keep track of their activities and thereby control and discipline them. In this formulation, the gaze is not something one has or uses; rather, it is a spatial and institutionally bound relationship into which one enters. There need not be a real subject who looks in order for the subject who is watched over to feel caught in the controlling gaze of an institution (such as a surveillance system). See *Mirror Phase*, *Panopticism*, *Psychoanalytic theory*.

Gender-bending Practices that call into question the traditional gender categories of male and female and heterosexual norms of representation and interpretation. For example, a gender-bending reading of a text might point out previously unacknowledged gay or lesbian meanings that may not have been intended by producers, but which nonetheless are plausible in an alternative reading of the codes.

Genre The classification of cultural products according to familiar, highly legible formulas. Genres follow recognizable formulas, codes and conventions. In cinema, genres include the Western, the romantic comedy, science fiction, and the action-adventure. In television, for example, genres include situation comedies, soap operas, news magazines, talk shows, reality TV, and home improvement shows, among others. Contemporary genre products are often parodies of the genre category itself.

Globalization A term used increasingly toward the end of the twentieth century to describe a set of conditions that have escalated since the postwar period. These conditions include increased rates of migration, the rise of multinational corporations, international trade liberalization initiatives, the development of global communications and transportation systems, increased postindustrialization, the decline of the sovereign nation-state, and the "shrinking" of the world through commerce and communication. Whereas some theorists take the conditions of globalization as a given, others see these conditions to be ideological, in the sense that their direction and force are not inevitable but are shaped by vying economic, cultural, and political interests. The term *globalization* also extends the concept of the local in that globalization's advancement depends on the formation of new sorts of local communities (such as those on the Internet) that are not bound by geography. See *Cosmopolitanism*.

Global village A term coined by Marshall McLuhan in the 1960s to refer to the ways that media can connect people from all over the world into geographically dispersed communities, giving the collective sense of a village to people that are separated geographically. McLuhan stated that the global village was created by instant electronic communication. He wrote, "The global village is at once as wide as the planet and as small as the little town where everybody is maliciously engaged in poking his nose into everybody else's business. The global village is a world in which you don't necessarily have harmony; you have extreme concern with everybody's else's business and much involvement with everybody else's life." It is a term that describes both the contemporary frenzy of media events and the connections created by people over distances through communication technologies. The concept of a global village puts a cheery spin on globalization.

Graphical user interface (GUI) The design in computer software, first developed in the 1980s for personal computers, and on the Web that allows users to make choices, enact commands, and move around screen space through the use of graphics and images rather than text. See *Web*.

Guerrilla television A term used by video artists and activists to describe alternative video practices begun in the late 1960s that used television technology to produce and show videotapes that were oppositional to the styles and politics of mainstream television. Guerrilla television was shot by participants in political movements, rather than by industry reporters, and was considered a vital part of direct political action.

Habitus A term popularized by French sociologist Pierre Bourdieu to describe the unconscious dispositions, strategies of classification, and tendencies that are part of an individual's sense of taste and preferences for cultural consumption. In this model, one's taste in music, décor, art, fashion, and so forth, are all connected and all derived from one's class position, educational background, and family context. According to Bourdieu, these value systems are not idiosyncratic to each individual but are derived instead from one's social position, educational background, and class status. Hence different social classes have different habituses with distinct tastes and lifestyles.

Hegemony A concept most associated with Italian Marxist theorist Antonio Gramsci, who rethought how power works in traditional Marxist theories of ideology. He shifted his thinking away from ideas about false consciousness and passive social subjects and toward human subjects as active agents. There are two central aspects of Gramsci's definition of hegemony: that dominant ideologies are often offered as common sense and that dominant ideologies are in tension with other forces and hence constantly in flux. The term *hegemony* thus indicates how ideological meaning is an object of struggle rather than an oppressive force that fully dominates subjects from above. See *Counter-hegemony, Ideology, Marxist theory.*

High/low culture Terms that have traditionally been used to make distinctions about different kinds of culture. High culture distinguishes culture that only an elite can appreciate, such as classical art, music, and literature, as opposed to commercially produced mass culture presumed to be accessible to lower classes. The distinction of high and low culture has been heavily criticized by theorists since the 1980s for its elitism and its condescending view of the popular consumer as a passive viewer with no taste.

Hybridity A term referring to anything of mixed origins that has been used in contemporary theory to describe those people whose identities are derived simultaneously from many cultural origins, ethnicities, or sexualities. Hybridity has been used to describe diasporic cultures that are neither in one place nor the other but of many places. See *Diaspora.*

Hyperreal A term coined by French theorist Jean Baudrillard that refers to a world in which codes of reality are used to simulate reality in cases in which no referent exists in the real world. Hyperreality is thus a simulation of reality in which various elements function to emphasize their "realness." In postmodern style, hyperrealism can also refer to the use of naturalistic effects to give an advertisement, for instance, the look of a realist documentary—"natural" sound, jerky "amateur" camerawork, or unrehearsed nonactors, yet which is understood to be a construction of the real. See *Postmodernism/postmodernity, Simulation/simulacrum.*

Hypertext A format for presenting text and images, which forms the basis of the Web, that allows viewers to move from one text, page, or website to another through hyperlinks. This means that any website, for instance, can have a number of links to other sites, to audio, video, and other graphics. The importance of this format is that it allows Web users to move laterally through a significant amount of material that is linked. See *Web.*

Hypodermic effect A theory of mass media that sees viewers as passive recipients of media messages who are not only "drugged" by the media but injected with its ideology. The idea of a hypodermic or narcotic effect specifically refers to the way in which viewers of mass media are allowed the impression that they are participating in a public culture while watching mass media forms such as television, when in fact passive viewing has replaced social and political action.

Icon Originally, the term icon referred to a religious image that had sacred value. In its contemporary meaning, an icon is an image (or person) that refers to something beyond its individual components, something (or someone) that acquires symbolic significance. Icons are often perceived to represent universal concepts, emotions, and meanings.

Iconic sign A term in semiotics used by Charles Peirce to indicate those signs in which there is a resemblance between the signifier (word/image) and the thing signified. For example, a drawing of a person is an iconic sign because it resembles him or her. Peirce distinguished iconic, indexical, and symbolic signs. See *Indexical sign*, *Semiotics*, *Symbolic sign*.

Identification The psychological process whereby one forms a bond with or emulates an aspect or attribute of another person and is transformed through that process. The term identification is used extensively to describe the experiences of viewers in looking at film. According to cinema theorist Christian Metz, cinematic identification can involve feeling oneself to be in the position of characters or the cinematic apparatus itself. One example would be to feel as if one were seeing in the place of the camera that appears to go everywhere in a scene. Viewers identify in complex ways that do not always map onto their actual social identities. For example, women may identify with male characters, straight men may identify with gay male characters, and so on.

Ideology The shared set of values and beliefs that exist within a given society and through which individuals live out their relations to social institutions and structures. Ideology refers to the way that certain concepts and values are made to seem like natural, inevitable aspects of everyday life. In Marxist theory, the term ideology has undergone several changes in definition: first, by Marx, to imply a social system in which the masses are instilled with the dominant ideology of the ruling class and that constitutes a kind of false consciousness; second, by French Marxist Louis Althusser, who combined psychoanalysis and Marxist theory to postulate that we are unconsciously constituted as subjects by ideology, which gives us a sense of our place in the world; third, by Antonio Gramsci, who used the term *hegemony* to describe how dominant ideologies are always in flux and under contestation from other ideas and values. See *False consciousness*, *Hegemony*, *Interpellation*, *Marxist theory*, *Psychoanalytic theory*.

Imperialism Derived from the word empire, imperialism refers to the practices of nations that aim to extend their boundaries into new territories, dominating them through processes such as colonization. In Marxist theory, imperialism is one of the means through which capitalism extends its power by creating both new markets to which it can sell its commodities and new labor forces that it can exploit to make those commodities at low cost. Cultural imperialism refers to how ways of life are exported into other territories through cultural products and popular culture. The United States is understood to routinely engage in cultural imperialism. See *Colonialism*.

Impressionism An artistic style that emerged in the late nineteenth century, primarily in France, that was characterized by an emphasis on light and color. Impressionist work emphasized a view of nature as unstable and changeable. Painters foregrounded the brushstroke and often painted the same scene many times to evoke how it changed with the light. Prominent impressionist artists included Claude Monet, Pierre-Auguste Renoir, Alfred Sisley, Camille Pissarro, and Berthe Morisot. Paul Gauguin, Vincent van Gogh, and Paul Cezanne are often referred to as post-Impressionists.

Indexical sign A term in semiotics used by Charles Peirce to indicate those signs in which there is a physical causal connection between the signifier (word/image) and the thing signified, because both existed at some point within the same physical space. For example, smoke coming from a building is an index of a fire. Similarly, a photograph is an index of its subject because it was taken in its presence. Peirce distinguished iconic, indexical, and symbolic signs. See *Iconic sign*, *Semiotics*, *Symbolic sign*.

Interpellation A term coined by Marxist theorist Louis Althusser to describe the process by which ideological systems call out to or "hail" social subjects and tell them their place in the system. In popular culture, interpellation refers to the ways that cultural products address their consumers and recruit them into a particular ideological position. Images can be said to designate the kind of viewer they intend us to be, and in speaking to us as that kind of viewer, they help to shape us as particular ideological subjects. See *Ideology*, *Marxist theory*.

Interpretant A term used by semiotician Charles Peirce in his three-part system of signification. The interpretant is the thought or mental effect produced by the relationship between the object and its representation (Peirce's definition of a sign). The interpretant is the equivalent of the signified in Saussure. Peirce stated that the interpretant could be endlessly commuted, that is, each interpretant can create a new sign, which in turn creates a new interpretant, and so on. See *Referent*, *Semiotics*, *Signified*.

Intertextuality The referencing of one text within another. In popular culture, intertextuality refers to the incorporation of meanings of one text within another in a reflexive fashion. For example, the television show *The Simpsons* includes references to films, other television shows, and celebrities. These intertextual references assume that the viewer knows the people and cultural products being referenced.

Irony The deliberate contradiction between the literal meaning of something and its intended meaning (which can be the opposite of the literal meaning). Irony can be seen as a context in which appearance and reality are in conflict, for instance when someone says "beautiful weather!" to emphasize that the weather is terrible. Irony is a key feature of contemporary postmodern style, in which meanings are signaled in quotes to signify knowingness.

Kitsch Art or literature judged to have little or no aesthetic value, yet that has value precisely because of its status in evoking the class standards of bad taste. Afficionados of kitsch thus recode kitsch objects, such as lava lamps and tacky 1950s suburban furniture, as good rather than bad taste. Kitsch can also refer to cultural objects and images that interpellate viewers in easy codes of sentimentalism.

Lack A term used in psychoanalysis by Jacques Lacan to describe an essential aspect of the human psyche. According to Lacan, the human subject is defined by lack from the moment of birth and his or her separation from the mother. The subject is lacking because it believes itself to be a fragment of something larger and more primordial. The second stage of lack is the acquisition of language. In Lacan's theory, desire, the human sense of always wanting something that is out of reach or unattainable, is the result of lack. Though we always seek pleasure through others, there is no person or thing that can truly satisfy that feeling of lack. In Freudian psychoanalysis, the term lack refers to the woman's lack of a penis/phallus, her lack being precisely what awards power to the phallus. See *Phallus/phallic, Psychoanalytic theory.*

Low culture See *High/low culture.*

Marked/unmarked In binary oppositions, the first category is understood to be unmarked (hence the "norm") and the second category as marked, hence "other." In the opposition male/female, for instance, the category male is unmarked, thus dominant (think of the universal use of the pronoun *he*), and the category of female is marked, or not the norm. Whiteness typically goes unmarked (we rarely see an author described as white because whiteness is regarded as the default category), but blackness is typically marked (stated as such, understood to mean different from ...). These categories of marked and unmarked are most noticeable when texts break with the norm. For instance, until quite recently, in the majority of advertising images, which have traditionally been directed at a white middle-class audience, white models were unmarked (the norm, hence their race was unremarkable), whereas models of other races and ethnicities were marked (that is, marked by signifiers that played up their race, such as "ethnic" jewelry or "exotic" settings). See *Binary oppositions, Other.*

Marxist theory Originating with the nineteenth-century theories of Karl Marx and Friedrich Engels, Marxist theory combines political economy and social critique. Marxism is, on the one hand, a general theory of human history, in which the role of the economic and modes of production are the primary determining factors of history, and, on the other hand, a particular theory of the development, reproduction, and transformation of capitalism that identifies workers as the potential agents of history. Emphasizing the profound inequities that are necessary for capitalism to function, Marxist theory is used to understand the mechanisms of capitalism and the class relations within it. Concepts of Marxism have evolved throughout the nineteenth and twentieth centuries with such theorists as Vladimir Lenin, Jean-Paul Sartre, Louis Althusser, Antonio Gramsci, Chantal Mouffe, and Ernesto Laclau. See *Alienation, Base/superstructure, Commodity fetishism, Exchange value, False consciousness, Fetish, Hegemony, Ideology, Interpellation, Means of production, Pseudoindividuality, Use value.*

Mass culture/mass society Terms used historically to refer to the culture and society of the general population, often with negative connotation. Mass society was used to characterize the changes that took place in Europe and the United States throughout the industrialization of the nineteenth century and culminated after World War II, when large numbers of people were concentrated in urban centers. The term *mass society* implies that these populations were subject to centralized forms of national and international media and that they received the majority of their opinions and information not locally or within their families but from a larger broadcast medium through which mass views were promulgated and reproduced. The culture of this society has been characterized as a mass culture, and this term is often synonymous with popular culture. It implies that this culture is for ordinary people who are subjected to and buy the same messages; hence this culture is conformist and homogeneous. Both these terms have been criticized for reducing specific cultures to an undifferentiated group.

Mass media Those media that are designed to reach mass audiences and that work in unison to generate specific dominant or popular representations of events, peoples, and places. The primary mass media are radio, television, the cinema, and the press, including newspapers and magazines. The term has been seen as less applicable to contemporary forms of computer-mediated communication, such as the Internet, the Web, and multimedia, as they do not involve mass audiences in the same way. See *Medium/media*.

Master narrative A framework (also referred to as a metanarrative) that aims to comprehensively explain all aspects of a society or world. Examples of master narratives include religion, science, Marxism, psychoanalysis, and other theories that intend to explain all facets of life. French theorist Jean-François Lyotard famously characterized postmodern theory as profoundly skeptical of these metanarratives, their universalism, and the premise that they could explain the human condition.

Means of production In Marxist theory, the means of production are the machines, tools, plants, equipment, infrastructure, and bodies through which humans transform natural materials into goods, services, and information for the market. In a small-scale agricultural society, the agricultural means of production include individual farmers growing their own produce and constructing their own tools. In industrial capitalism, the means of production include large-scale mass production of goods in factories. In late capitalism, the means of production include the production of information and media products and services. In Marxist theory, those who own the means of production are also in control of the ideas that circulate in a society's media industries. See *Capitalism, Marxist theory*.

Medium/media A form in which artistic or cultural products are made or a form through which messages pass. In art, a medium refers to the art materials used to create a work, such as paint or stone. In communication, medium refers to a means of mediation or communication—an intermediary form through which messages are transmitted. The term *medium* also refers to the specific technologies through which messages are transmitted: radio, television, film, and so forth. The term *media* is the plural of medium but is often used in the singular, as in "the media" to describe the constellation of media industries that together influence public opinion.

Medium is the message A phase popularized by Marshall McLuhan to refer to the ways that media forms hold meanings apart from their messages. McLuhan stated that a medium affects content because it is an extension of our individual bodies One cannot understand and evaluate a message unless one first takes account of the medium through which one receives it. Hence McLuhan felt that a medium such as television has the power to impose "its structural character and assumptions upon all levels of our private and social lives."

Metacommunication A discussion or exchange in which the topic is the exchange taking place itself. A "meta" level is a reflexive level of communicating. In popular culture, this refers to texts in which the topic is the viewer's act of viewing the text. An ad that addresses a viewer about the ways that the viewer is looking at the ad is engaging in metacommunication.

Mimesis A concept that originates with the Greeks that defines representation as a process of mirroring or imitating the real. Contemporary theories such as social construction criticize mimesis for not taking into account the way in which systems of representation, such as language and images, shape how we interpret and understand what we see, rather than merely reflecting it back to us.

Mirror phase A stage of development, according to psychoanalytic theorist Jacques Lacan, in which the infant first experiences a sense of alienation in its realization of its separateness from other human beings. According to Lacan, infants build their egos between six and eighteen months through the process of looking at a mirror body image, which may be their own mirror images, their mothers, or other figures and not necessarily a literal mirror image of their own bodies. They recognize the mirror image to be both themselves and different, yet as more whole and powerful. This split recognition forms the basis of their alienation at the same time that it pushes them to grow. The mirror phase is a useful framework through which to understand the emotion and power invested by viewers in images as a kind of ideal form and has been used to theorize about film images in particular. See *Alienation, Psychoanalytic theory.*

Modernism In literature, architecture, art, and film, modernism refers to a set of styles that emerged in the late nineteenth and early twentieth centuries that question traditions and conventions of representation (such as pictorialism, decoration and the concealment of form, narrative structure, and illusionism) in writing, architecture, and the plastic arts. Modernists emphasized and exposed the materiality of form, the conditions of production (equipment, structural elements) so often covered over in works of culture, and the role of the author or painter as producer embedded in the material conditions of the economic and physical world. Most modernist movements shared the general principles of breaking with past conventions of narrative and pictorial realism, foregrounding form over content, and drawing attention to structure and function. Modernism is akin with structuralism in its emphasis on seeing the world as composed of underlying formal systems that can be known and explained. Postmodernists and poststructuralists questioned this assumption that we can know the world by ascertaining its systems and structures. See *Postmodernism/postmodernity, Structuralism.*

Modernity Modernity refers to the time period and worldview beginning approximately in the eighteenth century with the Enlightenment, reaching its height in the late nineteenth and early twentieth centuries, when broad populations in Europe and North America were increasingly concentrated in urban centers and in industrial societies of increased mechanization and automation. Modernity is a time of dramatic technological change that embraces a linear view of progress as crucial to humankind's prosperity and an optimistic view of the future at the same time that it embodies an anxiety about change and social upheaval. It is characterized by an embrace of technology and progress, a sense of revolutionary change, and anxieties about this upheaval.

Montage Editing techniques, usually in film, that combine images in a sequence in order to indicate the passage of time. In classic Hollywood film, montage sequences were often done by special editors and indicated a rapid passage of time. In Soviet montage, the combination of images usually indicated clash or tension through the juxtaposition of different elements or scenes.

Morphing A computer imaging process by which one image is superimposed onto another, creating a third image that is a combination or blend of the two.

Myth A term used by French theorist Roland Barthes to refer to the ideological meaning of a sign that is expressed through connotation. According to Barthes, myth is the hidden set of rules, codes, and conventions through which meanings, which are in reality specific to certain groups, are rendered universal and given for a whole society. Myth allows the connotative meaning of a particular thing or image to appear to be denotative, hence literal or natural. In Barthes's famous example, an image in a popular magazine of a black soldier saluting the French flag produces the message that France is a great empire in which all young men regardless of their color faithfully serve under its flag. For Barthes, this image affirms the allegiance of French colonial subjects at the level of myth, erasing evidence of resistance. Myths are a subset of *ideology*. See *Connotation, Ideology, Semiotics, Sign.*

Narrowcast media Media that have a limited range through which to reach audiences and hence are capable of carrying programming tailored to audiences that are more specific than broadcast audiences. Cable television is a primary example of narrowcast programming, with many channels narrowcasting to specific communities (on local city or municipal channels) or to audiences with specific interests (such as independent film). See *Broadcast media.*

Negotiated reading Stuart Hall describes three potential positions for the reader or viewer/consumer of mass culture. The negotiated reading is one in which consumers accept some aspects of the dominant reading and reject others. According to Hall, most readings are negotiated ones, in which viewers actively struggle with dominant meanings and modify them in numerous ways because of their own social status, beliefs, and values. See *Dominant-hegemonic reading, Oppositional reading.*

Neoliberalism The belief that market exchange and economic liberalism should be the ethical guides of human behavior, which is a key value system of global capitalism. Neoliberalism has spread since the 1970s, as national governments have privatized and deregulation of the media and business has been rampant throughout North America and Europe.

Noeme In photography, the quality of the image to indicate a "that has been" status, which means that the power of the image comes from the fact that it existed in copresence with the camera. *Noeme* is a term originally derived from phenomenology. See *Phenomenology.*

Objective/objectivity The state of being unbiased and based on facts, usually referring to scientific, rational ways of understanding the world that involve a mechanical process of measurement and judgment rather than empirical human sense perceptions alone. Debates about the inherent objectivity of photographs, for instance, have centered on whether a photographic image is objective because it was taken mechanically by a camera or is subjective because it was framed and shot by a human subject. See *Subjective.*

Oppositional reading In Stuart Hall's formulation of three potential positions for the viewer/consumer of mass culture, the oppositional reading is one in which consumers fully reject the dominant meaning of a cultural product. This can take the form not only of disagreeing with a message but also of deliberately ignoring or even appropriating and changing it. See *Dominant-hegemonic reading, Negotiated reading.*

Orientalism A term popularized by cultural theorist Edward Said that refers to the ways that Western cultures conceive of Eastern and Middle Eastern cultures as other and attribute to these cultures qualities such as exoticism and barbarism. Orientalism sees a binary opposition between the West (the Occident) and the East (the Orient) in which either negative or romanticized qualities are attributed to the latter. For Said, Orientalism is a practice found in cultural representations, education, social science, and political policy. For instance, the stereotype of Arab people as fanatic terrorists is an example of Orientalism. See *Binary oppositions, Other.*

Other, The A term used to refer to the category of subjectivity that is set up in binary opposition to the dominant subject category in a culture. The other refers to that which is understood as the symbolic opposite to the normative category. The slave is other to the master; the woman other to the man, the black person other to the white person; and so forth. The category of person marked as other is disempowered through this opposition. The concept of the other has been taken up by various theorists, including Edward Said, to describe the psychological dynamic of power that allows those who occupy a position of Western dominance to imagine a racial or ethnic other, against whom he or she may more clearly elaborate his or her own self. The function of the other, in Western thinking, is as a foil against which the dominant subject may know and understand himself better. In Freudian psychoanalytic theory, the mother is the original mirror-like other through whom the child comes to understand him- or herself as an autonomous individual. See *Binary oppositions, Marked/unmarked, Orientalism, Psychoanalysis.*

Overdetermination A term that in its usage in Marxist theory (most associated with French theorist Louis Althusser) indicates a case in which several different factors work together to make the meaning of a social situation undergo a substantive change or shift. For example, the popularity of the *Mona Lisa* is overdetermined both by artistic qualities within the painting and by mythologies surrounding the woman in the painting, as well as its meaning as one of the most famous paintings in the world. See *Marxist theory.*

Panopticism A concept used by French philosopher Michel Foucault to characterize the ways that modern social subjects regulate their own behavior, borrowing from nineteenth-century philosopher Jeremy Bentham's idea of a panoptic prison, in which the prisoner can always be observed by the guard tower yet not know when that gaze is directed on him and when it is not. The guard-observer might be looking elsewhere or on break, but the prisoner cannot see the observation place and so never can really know whether the guard is looking. Foucault suggested that in contemporary society we behave as if we are under a scrutinizing, panoptic gaze and that we internalize the rules and norms of the society as we imagine ourselves to be always potentially under a watchful eye that expects us to perform this way. See *Gaze.*

Parody Cultural productions that make fun of more serious works through humor and satire while maintaining some of their elements such as plot or character. Cultural theorists see parody (as opposed to the creation of new and original works) as one of the key strategies of postmodern style, though it is not exclusive to postmodernism. See *Postmodernism/postmodernity.*

Pastiche A style of plagiarizing, quoting, and borrowing from previous styles with no reference to history or a sense of rules. In architecture, a pastiche would be a mixing of classical motifs with modern elements in an aesthetic that does not reference the historical meanings of those styles. Pastiche is an aspect of postmodern style. See *Postmodernism/postmodernity.*

Perspective A technique of visualization that was popularized in Italy in the mid-fifteenth century that is emblematic of the Renaissance interest in the fusion of art and science. To use perspective to create a painting, a painter would use a geometric procedure to project space onto a two-dimensional plane. The central aspect of linear perspective is the designation of a vanishing point (or points), with all objects receding in size toward that point, creating a sense of depth and directing the eye of the viewer into that space. The introduction of perspective was enormously influential in realist painting styles, in part because it was understood as a scientific and rational way to organize visual space. Debates about the dominance of perspective have proliferated—impressionism presented an alternative, emphasizing light and color not line, and cubism played with the order and logic of conventional linear perspective. Central to the critique of perspective is its designation of the viewer as a single, unmoving spectator. See *Renaissance.*

Phallus/phallic In psychoanalytic terms, the symbol of the power that men have in patriarchal society. Psychoanalytic theorists including Jacques Lacan have debated the extent to which the phallus (the symbol) is equated with the penis (the real thing) as the specific object that awards power to men. Nonetheless, to call something phallic is to attribute to it both aspects of male power and the symbolism of the penis. The representation of a gun, for instance, is considered to be phallic because it is a powerful object associated with male culture that also physically evokes the shape of the penis. See *Lack, Psychoanalytic theory.*

Phenomenology A philosophical position that centers on the dimensions of subjective human experience in how we react bodily and emotionally, as well as intellectually, to the world around us. Phenomenology emphasizes the importance of the lived body in how we experience and make meaning of the world. Phenomenologists thus talk of being-in-the-world, meaning that we are rooted in the here and now of bodily experience. The mainstream of phenomenology does not see this experience as socially (or sexually or racially) determined. Instead, phenomenology talks about bracketing out the social context to imagine a direct encounter of people with the world around them. Philosophers and visual theorists such as Elizabeth Grosz and Vivian Sobchack have emphasized the specificity of bodily experience and the place of sexuality in embodied experience. Applications of phenomenology to visual media have focused primarily on the specific capacities of each medium that affect the experience of viewers. Phenomenology's founders were Edmund Husserl and Maurice Merleau-Ponty.

Photographic truth As images produced by a mechanical device designed to record reality, photographs are associated with truth and tend to be seen as unmediated copies of reality. The concept of photographic truth is a myth, in that photographs are not objective records of reality. Rather, they are the product of human choice, selective composition and manipulation no less than other forms of representation. The truth-value of photography and camera imaging is the subject of ongoing debate, one that has been heightened by the introduction of digital imaging techniques that make photographic images easy to manipulate.

Pixel Short for picture element, a pixel is the smallest unit, or point, in a digital image or on a digital screen. When pixels are visible in a digital image, they appear as squares. The greater the number of pixels per square inch, the higher the resolution of the image or screen. See *Digital.*

Polysemy The quality of having many potential meanings, sometimes all at once. A work of art whose meaning is ambiguous is polysemic because it can have many different meanings to one or different viewers.

Pop art An art movement in the late 1950s and 1960s that used the images and materials of popular or "low" culture for art. Pop artists took aspects of mass culture, such as television, cartoons, advertisements, and commodities, and reworked them as art objects and in paintings, sometimes using mass media forms such as the screen print to critique the strong association of art with cultivated taste and aesthetics and to mark and celebrate the everyday person's culture and taste. Pop art's primary proponents were Andy Warhol, Roy Lichtenstein, James Rosenquist, and Claes Oldenburg.

Pop surrealism A postmodern art movement of the 2000s that appropriates the politics and aesthetics of surrealist art of the early twentieth century, using a surrealist sensibility to appropriate and mix references from other styles and painting and design elements from the Dutch masters, the Pre-Raphaelites, mid-century graphic design, and 1960s-70s popular culture. Pop surrealists comment with ironic reverence or irreverence on the contemporary political and cultural imaginary and themes such as beauty and normality, life in technologically and scientifically advanced society, and notions of taste, high culture, and distinction. A strong influence on pop surrealism is the work of artists such as Takashi Murakami in Japan associated with the neo-pop aesthetic of the 1990s. Sometimes referred to as low brow art, pop surrealism is probably better understood as a distinct approach in that all of the work associated with it does not embrace the low-culture aesthetic. Artists associated with this style include Anthony Ausgang, Tim Biskup, Kalynn Campbell, Charles Krafft, Marion Peck, Isabel Samaras, and Shag. See *Postmodernism/postmodernity, Surrealism.*

Positivism A philosophical position that is strongly scientific in inspiration and that assumes that meanings exist out in the world, independent of our feelings, attitudes, or beliefs about them. Positivism assumes that the factual nature of things can be established by experimentation and that facts are free of the influence of language and representational systems. It believes that only scientific knowledge is genuine knowledge and that other ways of viewing the world are suspect. For example, the assumption that photography directly gives us the truth of the world is a positivist assumption.

Postcolonialism A term that refers to the cultural and social contexts of countries that were formerly defined through relationships of colonialism (both colonized and colonizer), and to the contemporary mix of cultures in former colonies, including neocolonialist practices, diasporic migrant cultures, and continuing colonial domination and cultural imperialism toward former colonies. The term *postcolonial* refers to the broad set of changes that have affected both former colonies and colonizers and in particular to the mix of identities, languages, and influences that have resulted from complex systems of dependence and independence. Most theorists of postcolonialism insist that the breakup of older colonial models is never complete and does not put an end to forms of domination between more and less powerful countries. See *Colonialism*.

Postindustrialization Economic contexts and relations that have followed industrialization and that are characterized less by industrial growth and more by the rise of a service economy, information economies, and global capitalism.

Postmodernism/postmodernity Postmodernity is a term used to capture life during a period marked by radical transformation of the social, economic, and political aspects of modernity, marked by the flows of migration and global travel, the flow of information through the Internet and new digital technologies, the dissolution of nation-states in their traditional sovereign form in the wake of the collapse of the Soviet Union and the demise of the Cold War, as well as the expansion of trade liberalization, and the increased divide between rich and poor. It describes a set of social, cultural, and economic formations that have occurred "post" or after the height of modernity and that have produced both a different worldview and different ways of being in the world than was the case in modernity. It has been referred to as a period of questioning of "metanarratives" by French philosopher Jean-François Lyotard and of the premise that unified accounts and theories could adequately capture the human condition. It has also been described by Fredric Jameson as a historical period that is the cultural outcome of the "logic of late capitalism."

Postmodernism has been characterized as a critique of modernist concepts such as universalism, the idea of presence, the traditional notion of the subject as unified and self-aware, and faith in progress. Postmodernism is often understood as existing in the detritus of modernity. The concept is also used to describe particular styles in art, literature, architecture, and popular culture that engage in parody, bricolage, appropriation, and ironic reflexivity, as if there is nothing truly new to say, no ultimate knowledge to reveal. In terms of its application to art and visual style, postmodernism is a set of trends in the art world in the late twentieth century that question, among other things, concepts of authenticity, authorship, and the idea of style progression. Postmodern works are thus highly reflexive, with a mix of styles. In popular culture and advertising, the term *postmodern* has been used to describe techniques that involve reflexivity, discontinuity, and pastiche and that speak to viewers as both jaded consumers and through self-knowing metacommunication.

See *Discontinuity, Hyperreal, Metacommunication, Modernism, Modernity, Parody, Pastiche, Pop surrealism, Reflexivity, Simulation/simulacrum, Surface.*

Poststructuralism A loosely used term that refers to a range of theories that followed and criticized structuralism. Poststructuralist theories examine those practices that are left out of a structuralist view of society, for example, desire, play and playfulness, and ambiguities of meaning, especially in the arts. Poststructuralism attempts to provide toolboxes for moving beyond the closed systems of structural logic, models, and methods. Its primary theorists are Roland Barthes (in his later work), Gilles Deleuze, Paul de Man, and Jacques Derrida. See *Structuralism.*

Power/knowledge A term used by Michel Foucault to describe the ways that power affects what counts as knowledge in a given social context and how, in turn, knowledge systems within that society are caught up in power relations. Foucault posited that power and knowledge are inseparable and that the concepts of truth are relative to the networks of power and knowledge systems (such as educational systems that award degrees and the designation of expertise) of a given society.

Practice An important concept in cultural studies that refers to the activities of cultural consumers and producers through which they interact with cultural products and make meaning from them. Thus one can speak of practices of looking as the activities undertaken by viewers of art, the media, and popular culture to interpret and make use of these images.

Presence The quality of immediate experience that has been traditionally contrasted with representation and with those aspects of the world that are the product of human mediation. The quality of being "present" has thus been understood historically to mean that one can be in the world in a way that is direct and experienced through the senses and unmediated by human belief, ideologies, language systems, or forms of representation. Postmodernism criticizes this concept of presence as the illusion that we can actually experience the world in a direct and complete way without the social baggage of language, ideology, and so forth.

Presumption of relevance In advertising, the manner of speaking that makes the presumption that the issues presented are of utmost importance. In the abstract world of advertisements, for instance, the statement that having shiny hair is the most important aspect of one's life does not register with viewers as absurd because of the presumption of this as relevant within the ad's message.

Propaganda A term with negative connotations that indicates the imparting of political messages through mass media or art with the intent of moving people in calculated ways to enlist them through their emotions in precise political beliefs. For example, in Nazi Germany the rousing film *Triumph of the Will* was intended to win over the masses for the Nazi cause in its depiction of Hitler as a charismatic leader of a proud, energetic, and beautiful populace.

Pseudoindividuality A term used in Marxist theory, primarily by the Frankfurt School, to describe the way that mass culture creates a false sense of individuality in cultural consumers. Pseudoindividuality refers to the effect of popular culture and advertising that addresses the viewer/consumer specifically as an individual, as in the case of advertising that actually claims that a product will enhance one's individuality, although it is speaking to many people at once. It is "pseudo" individuality if one attains it through mass culture because the message is predicated on the contradiction of many people receiving a message of individuality at the same time, suggesting not individuality but homogeneity. See *Culture industry, Frankfurt School, Marxist theory.*

Psychoanalytic theory A theory of how the mind works, derived originally from Austrian psychoanalyst Sigmund Freud (1856–1939), that emphasizes the role of the unconscious and desire in shaping a subject's actions, feelings, and motives. Freud's work emphasized bringing the repressed materials of the unconscious to the surface through what was called the talking cure. It focused on the construction of the self through various mechanisms and processes of the unconscious as laid out in Freud's writings and in accounts of his analyses. In its beginnings in the late nineteenth century, psychoanalysis was much maligned in the United States, where ego psychology held sway during Freud's heyday in Europe.

Psychoanalytic theory is the application of many of these ideas not as a therapeutic practice but to analyze systems of representation. French theorist Jacques Lacan updated many of Freud's ideas in the 1930s through the 1970s in relationship to language systems and inspired the use of psychoanalytic theory to interpret and analyze literature and film. See *Alienation, Exhibitionism, Fetish, Gaze, Lack, Mirror phase, Phallus/phallic, Repression, Scopophilia, Unconscious, Voyeurism.*

Public sphere A term that originated with German theorist Jürgen Habermas that defines a social space (which may be virtual) in which citizens come together to debate and discuss the pressing issues of their society. Habermas defined this as an ideal space in which well-informed citizens would discuss matters of common public not private interests. It is generally understood that Habermas's ideal public sphere has never been realized because of the integration of private interests into public life and because it did not take into account how dynamics of class, race, and gender make access to public space unequal. The term has been used more recently in the plural to refer to the multiple public spheres in which people debate contemporary issues.

Punctum A term used by Roland Barthes to indicate the aspect of a photograph that grabs our emotions or attention, and is felt to be uniquely personal by the individual viewer. Barthes wrote that the punctum "triggers" a shock or a prick to the viewer; it is the unintentional detail of the photograph from which we cannot turn away. For Barthes, punctum is distinct from *studium*, the common or banal quality of the image. See *Studium.*

Queer Originally a derogatory term for homosexuals, queer was appropriated as a positive term for sexual identities that do not fit within dominant heterosexual norms. The term *queer* is thus a good example of appropriation in action, in changing a negative term to a positive, even progressive, one. A queer reading of a cultural product or text reads against the grain of dominant sexual ideology to look for unacknowledged uses of representations to articulate gay, lesbian, or bisexual desire. Queer theory is an area of scholarship that examines assumptions about gender and sexual identity. See *Appropriation, Transcoding, Oppositional reading.*

Referent In semiotics, a term that refers to the object itself, as opposed to its representation. Semiotician Ferdinand de Saussure referred to the referent, in the example of a horse, as "what kicks you," meaning that whereas you could not be kicked in real life by the representation of a horse, you could be by a real horse. In semiotics, some theorists such as Roland Barthes use a two-part model to explain signification (signifier, signified), whereas others, such as Charles Peirce, use a three-part system (sign, interpretant, object), thus making a distinction between the representation (word/image) of an object and the object itself. The term *referent* is helpful in explaining the difference between representation (the re-presentation of real-world objects) and simulation (the copy that has no real equivalent or referent, and that might in fact kick you). See *Interpretant, Semiotics, Signified, Signifier, Simulation/simulacrum.*

Reflexivity The practice of making viewers aware of the material and technical means of production by featuring those aspects as the "content" of a cultural production. Reflexivity is both a part of the tradition of modernism, with its emphasis on form and structure, and of postmodernism, with its array of intertextual references and ironic marking of the frame of the image and its status as a cultural product. Reflexivity prevents viewers from being completely absorbed in the illusion of an experience of a film or image, distancing viewers from that experience. See *Modernism, Modernity, Postmodernism/postmodernity.*

Reification A term from Marxist theory that describes the process by which abstract ideas are rendered concrete. This means, in part, that material objects, such as commodities, are awarded the characteristics of human subjects, whereas the relations between human beings become more objectified. For instance, in an advertisement, a perfume may be given the human attributes of sexiness or femininity and described as "alive" or "vibrant." Marxist theorists use the term *reification* to refer to the alienation that is experienced by workers in their identification with the means and products of production, thus causing them to lose their sense of humanity while at the same time commodities are anthropomorphized.

Renaissance A term first coined in France in the nineteenth century to look back on a particular period of history that began in Italy in the early fourteenth century and reached its height throughout Europe in the early sixteenth century. Characterized by a resurgence of cultural, artistic, and scientific activity and a renewed interest in classical literature and art, the Renaissance is understood as marking a broad transition between medieval time—which was mischaracterized as a time period with little intellectual or artistic activity—and the modern era. The art of the Renaissance, which flourished in particular in Italy, emphasized both the technique of perspective and a fusion of science and art through such figures as Leonardo da Vinci, Sandro Botticelli, Michelangelo, and Raphael. See *Perspective.*

Replica A copy of an art work that was produced by the original artist or under his or her supervision. A replica of a painting, therefore, would be another painting that had been made to be as close to it as possible. Replicas differ from reproductions in that they are composed in the same medium and are not easily reproducible. A replica is thus not an exact copy or reproduction. This artistic tradition became less popular with the rise of techniques of mechanical reproduction. See *Reproduction.*

Representation The act of portraying, depicting, symbolizing, or presenting the likeness of something. Language, the visual arts such as painting and sculpture, and media such as photography, television, and film are systems of representation that function to depict and symbolize aspects of the real world. Representation is often seen as distinct from simulation in that a representation declares itself to be re-presenting some aspect of the real, whereas a simulation has no necessary referent in the real. See *Mimesis*, *Simulation/simulacrum*, *Social construction*.

Repression A term in psychoanalytic theory that refers to the process by which the individual relegates to and keeps within the unconscious those particular thoughts, feelings, memories, or desires that are too difficult or socially inappropriate to deal with. Freud postulated that we repress that which produces fear, anxiety, shame, or other negative emotions within us and that this repression is active and ongoing. He felt that it was only through this repression that we become functioning and normative members of a society. The "talking cure" of psychoanalysis is intended to help release that which is repressed in the neurotic person. Michel Foucault offered another approach, in which he argued against the idea that these desires are hidden and go unexpressed in everyday life. Foucault wrote that systems of control are indirectly productive rather than fully repressive. By this, he meant that social structures encourage such desires to be expressed, spoken, and rendered visible in indirect ways, thereby allowing them to be named, known, and regulated. For example, in a Foucaultian approach, talk shows in which people confess their bad behavior and secret wishes would be seen as a context in which desires can be witnessed, catalogued, and controlled. See *Power/knowledge*, *Psychoanalytic theory*, *Unconscious*.

Reproduction The act of making a copy or duplicating something. Reproduction of images refers to the means through which original works are rendered into multiple copies in the form of prints, posters, postcards, and other merchandise. German theorist Walter Benjamin wrote a famous essay in 1936 on the impact of "mechanical reproducibility" of art images. Benjamin emphasized the importance of the role of the copy in changing the meaning of the original image (in his case, a painting). See *Replica*.

Resistance In the context of popular culture, the term *resistance* refers to the techniques used by viewers/consumers to not participate in or to stand in opposition to the messages of dominant culture. Bricolage, or the strategies by which consumers transform the meanings of commodities from their intended meaning, is an example of a resistant consumer practice. See *Appropriation*, *Bricolage*, *Oppositional reading*, *Tactic*, *Textual poaching*.

Scientific revolution The time period covering the fifteenth to seventeenth centuries that was characterized by scientific development and a struggle for power between the Church and science. This time period includes the Renaissance, the great navigations of European countries to the New World, the Protestant Reformation, and the emergence of Spain as the first great world power. It was a time period of scientific discovery in astronomy (with Copernicus and Galileo), the development of perspective in art, the development of experimental method by Francis Bacon in the seventeenth century, the philosophy and mathematics of René Descartes, and the discovery of gravity by Isaac Newton. By the beginning of the eighteenth century, science had emerged as an unquestioned pursuit of human endeavor, with a separation of the moral world of the Church and the goals of science. See *Renaissance*.

Scopophilia In psychoanalytic terms, the drive to look and the general pleasure in looking. Freud saw voyeurism (the pleasure in looking without being seen) and exhibitionism (the pleasure in being looked at) as the active and passive forms of scopophilia. The concept of scopophilia has been important to psychoanalytic film theory in its emphasis on the relationship of pleasure and desire to the practice of looking. See *Exhibitionism, Psychoanalytic theory, Voyeurism*.

Semiotics A theory of signs, sometimes called semiology, concerned with the ways in which things (words, images, and objects) are vehicles for meaning. Semiotics is a tool for analyzing the signs of a particular culture and how meaning is produced within a particular cultural context. Just as languages communicate through words organized into sentences, other practices in a culture are treated by semiotic theory as languages made up of basic elements and the rules for combining them. For instance, wearing tennis shoes with a formal menswear suit (as comedian Ellen DeGeneres has done) communicates a different meaning for each element, tennis shoes and tuxedos, because of the expectations of the codes of fashion (which can be thought of as a language with its own forms of correct and incorrect grammar).

The two originators of semiotics are the Swiss linguist Ferdinand de Saussure at the beginning of the twentieth century and the American philosopher Charles Peirce in the nineteenth century. Contemporary applications of semiotics follow from the work of French theorists Roland Barthes and Christian Metz and Italian theorist Umberto Eco in the 1960s. Their work provides important tools for understanding cultural products (images, film, television, clothing, etc.) as signs that can be decoded. Roland Barthes used a system of signifier (word/ image/object) and signified (meaning) as the two elements of a sign. Charles Peirce used the term *interpretant* to designate the meaning that a sign produces in the mind of the person. Peirce also divided signs into several categories, including indexical, iconic, and symbolic signs.

Semiotics is central to understanding culture as a signifying practice that is the work of creating and interpreting meaning on a daily basis in a given culture. See *Iconic sign, Indexical sign, Interpretant, Myth, Referent, Sign, Signifier, Signified, Symbolic sign*.

Sign A semiotic term that describes the relationship between a vehicle of meaning, such as a word, image, or object, and its specific meaning in a particular context. In technical terms, this means the bringing together of signifier (word/image/object) and signified (mental concept of the referent) to make a sign (meaning). It is important in semiotics to note that signifiers have different meanings in different contexts. For example, in a classical Hollywood film, a cigarette might signify friendship or romance, but in an antismoking ad it would signify disease and death. See *Semiotics, Signified, Signifier*.

Signified In semiotic terms, the mental concept of the referent, which together with the signifier (object/image/word) makes the sign. For instance, the signified of a smiley face is happiness, which in combination with the image of a smiley face constitutes the sign smile equals happiness. See *Semiotics, Sign, Signifier.*

Signifier In semiotic terms, the word, image, or object within a sign that conveys meaning. For example, in an advertisement for sports shoes, an inner-city basketball court is a signifier of authenticity, skill, and coolness. The relationship of a signifier and a signified together forms a sign. Semiotic theory often refers to a free-floating signifier, by which it means a signifier whose sense is not fixed and that can vary a great deal from context to context. See *Semiotics, Sign, Signified.*

Simulation/simulacrum Terms most famously used by French theorist Jean Baudrillard that refer to a sign that does not clearly have a real-life counterpart, referent, or precedent. A simulacrum is not necessarily a representation of something else, and it may actually precede the thing it simulates in the real world. Baudrillard stated that to simulate a disease was to acquire its symptoms, thus making it difficult to distinguish between the simulation and the actual disease. For example, a casino or amusement park simulacrum of the city of Paris can be seen as a substitute for the actual city and can perhaps for some viewers seem to offer a more compelling experience of Paris than the city itself, which may be totally out of reach for the viewer. See *Postmodernism/postmodernity, Representation.*

Social construction A theory that gained primacy in the 1980s in a number of fields that, at its most general level, asserts that much of what has been taken as fact is socially constructed through conjunctures of ideological forces, language, economic relationships, and so forth. This approach understands the meaning of things to be relative to context and historical moment, and to derive from how things are constructed through systems of representation, such as images and language, rather than understanding meanings to be inherent in things, separate from human interpretation. Thus we can make meaning of the world around us only through systems of representation, and they, in effect, help to construct our experience of the material world for us. For example, in science studies, social constructionists examine the social factors (class, gender, ideology, work practice) that influence knowledge and the facts in laboratory experimentation.

Spectacle A term that generally refers to something that is striking or impressive in its visual display, if not awe inspiring. The term *spectacle* was used by French theorist Guy Debord in his book *Society of the Spectacle* to describe how representations dominate contemporary culture and how all social relations are mediated by and through images.

Spectator A term derived from psychoanalytic theory that refers to the viewer of visual arts such as cinema. In early versions of this theory, the term *spectator* did not refer to a specific individual or an actual member of the viewing audience but rather was imagined to be an ideal viewer, separate from all defining social, sexual, and racial aspects of viewer identity.

In contrast, film theory in the late 1980s and 1990s emphasized specific identity groups of spectators, such as female spectators, working-class spectators, queer spectators, or black spectators. This work shifted away from the abstraction of the category to include more specific aspects of identity and processes such as identification and pleasure that are shaped by specific embodied experience. In addition, film theory has increasingly emphasized how one need not occupy an identity group to identify within that group's spectator position. For example, in action films, one does not have to be male to take up in fantasy the position of the male spectator. See *Gaze, Identification, Psychoanalytic theory.*

Strategy A term used by French theorist Michel de Certeau to describe the practices by which dominant institutions seek to structure time, place, and actions of their social subjects. This is in contrast to the tactics by which those subjects seek to reclaim a space and time for themselves. For example, the television programming schedule is a strategy to make viewers watch programming in a particular order, whereas an individual's use of a remote control or a TiVo is a tactic to decide viewing in their own way. See *Tactic.*

Structuralism A set of theories that came into prominence in the 1960s that emphasized the laws, codes, rules, formulas, and conventions that structure human behavior and systems of meaning. It is based on the premise that cultural activity could be analyzed objectively as a science, and structuralists emphasize elements within a culture that created a unitary organization that could be understood through theory and interpreted through a closed method. This often takes the form of defining the binary oppositions that structure ways of viewing the world and cultural products as well. Structuralism is considered to have originated with the structural linguistics of Swiss theorist Ferdinand de Saussure in the early twentieth century and in the mid-1950s through the work of Russian linguist Roman Jakobson. It was explored in influential ways by French anthropologist Claude Lévi-Strauss, who applied it to studying various cultures.

In popular culture, structuralism has been used to identify the recurrent patterns and formulas in genres of film or literature. For example, Italian theorist Umberto Eco wrote a well-known structuralist analysis of the James Bond spy thriller novels of Ian Fleming, in which he argues that no matter how much the details change from story to story, the structure remains the same. Eco saw this structure organized around a limited set of binary oppositions, such as Bond/villain, good/evil, and so forth, that lead to a defined and limited set of plot elements that recur in each story. Analyzing these elements and pinpointing their regularity is a practice of structuralism. Much of the theory that followed structuralism, which is often called poststructuralism, criticized structuralism for emphasizing structure at the expense of other elements that do not fit into these formulas or conventions. See *Binary oppositions, Genre, Poststructuralism.*

Structures of feeling A term used by Raymond Williams to describe the intangibles of an era that explain the quality of life and distinct sense of native style. According to Williams, in any given time and context, structures of feeling emerge, often through the arts, that define the tone of a particular time.

Studium From Roland Barthes, a term that means the common banal meaning of the photographic image. This is distinct from the punctum, which grabs our emotions and is particular to individual viewers. See *Punctum.*

Subculture Distinct social groups within wider cultural formations that define themselves in opposition to mainstream culture. The term *subculture* has been used extensively in cultural studies to designate those social groups, usually youth groups, who use style to signify resistance to dominant culture. Subcultures, which might include punk rockers, followers of rave, or subgroups of hip-hop, use style in fashion, music, and lifestyle as signifying practices to convey resistance to norms. Bricolage, or the use of commodities in ways that change their meaning (such as wearing jackets backward or extra-large pants slung low) is a central practice of subcultures. Since the 2000s, subcultures have proliferated, but not always or necessarily in opposition to a central or dominant culture. Rather, we have seen the proliferation of distinct and varied subcultures. See *Bricolage*.

Subject A term, used in philosophy and psychoanalytic and cultural theory, that refers to the available ways of being for humans in a given time period or context. Historically, the subject is a concept that has shifted away from the notion of the unitary, autonomous self of liberal philosophy and the thinking, rational self that sits at the center of Cartesian philosophy. Rather, today we understand the subject to be more fragmented, less self-knowing, and understanding itself to be constituted through processes of splitting. To speak of individuals as subjects is to indicate that they are split between the conscious and unconscious, that they are produced as subjects not by being born alone and independent but through the structures of language and society, and that they are both active forces (subjects of history) but also dependent on others and acted on by (subjected to) all the social forces of their moment in time. See *Psychoanalytic theory*.

Subjective Something that is particular to the view of an individual, hence the opposite of objective. A subjective view is understood to be personal, specific, and imbued with the values and beliefs of a particular person, experienced through the body and the senses and not through the abstraction of rational, disembodied thought. See *Objective*.

Subject position A term used to describe the ways that images, whether as films, paintings, or other forms, designate a position for their intended spectators. For instance, it can be said that films offer to their viewers a particular subject position. There is an ideal spectator of the action film, regardless of how any particular viewer might make personal meaning of the film, and the subject position of a traditional landscape painting is that of a spectator who luxuriates in the fantasy of ownership of sublime and bountiful nature. As theorized by Michel Foucault, subject position is the place that a particular discourse asks a human subject to adopt within it. For example, the discourse of education offers a limited set of subject positions that individuals can occupy, in which some are authoritative figures of knowledge, such as teachers, and others are relegated the position of students, or recipients of that knowledge. See *Discourse*.

Sublime A term in aesthetic theory, specifically in the work of eighteenth-century theorist Edmund Burke, that sets out to evoke experiences so momentous that they inspire intense veneration in the viewer or listener. The history of traditional landscape painting, for instance, was about imaging the sublime in that it intended to create in viewers a deep awe of the limitless splendors of nature.

Surface The idea in postmodernism that objects have no depth or profound meaning but instead exist only at the level of surface. This is in contrast to the idea in modernism that the real meaning of something is below the surface and can be found through acts of interpretation. See *Modernism*, *Postmodernism/postmodernity*.

Surrealism A political movement of the early twentieth century that extended around the world and was expressed through literature, theater, and the visual arts, surrealism focused on the role of the unconscious in representation and in dismantling the opposition between the real and the imaginary. The surrealists were interested in unlocking the unconscious and working against logical and rational processes of making meaning. Their ideas were later associated with Freudian psychoanalysis, but Freud and the surrealists were not really in conversation. Surrealist practices included automatic writing and painting and the use of dreams to inspire writing and art-making. Freud suggested that the surrealists did not really represent the workings of the unconscious but rather brought unconscious feelings to the level of literal expression. The movement's primary proponents were André Breton, Salvador Dalí, Giorgio de Chirico, Max Ernst, and René Magritte. Surrealism continued into the late twentieth century as an artistic movement in some countries, including the former Czechoslovakia and the current Czech republic, where some of its proponents have included the animator Jan Svankmajer and the late painter and ceramicist Eva Svankmajerová. See *Pop surrealism*.

Surveillance The act of keeping watch over a person or place. Camera technologies such as photography, video, and film have been used for surveillance purposes. For French philosopher Michel Foucault, surveillance is one of the primary means through which a society enacts control over its subjects through its encouragement of self-regulation. See *Panopticism*.

Symbolic sign A term in semiotics used by Charles Peirce to indicate those signs in which there is no connection between the signifier (word/image) and the thing signified except that imposed by convention. Language systems are primarily symbolic systems. Peirce distinguished iconic, indexical, and symbolic signs. For example, the word *university* does not physically resemble any actual university (in other words, it is not iconic), nor does it have a physical connection to the university (so it is not indexical), hence it is a symbolic sign. See *Iconic sign*, *Indexical sign*, *Semiotics*.

Synergy A term used in industry to describe the ways that corporate conglomerates own aspects of cultural production, programming, and distribution across many media and into many geographic locales. Synergy thus refers to the capacity of corporations that own across many media, such as broadcast networks, cable television, movie studios, film distribution companies, and magazines and other publishing entities, to both vertically integrate across programming and distribution and horizontally market products globally.

Tactic A term used by French theorist Michel de Certeau to indicate those practices deployed by people who are not in positions of power to gain some control over the spaces of their daily lives. De Certeau defined tactics as the acts of the weak that do not have lasting effect. He contrasted this with the strategies of institutions. For example, sending a personal e-mail while at work might be a tactic to give oneself a small feeling of empowerment in the alienation of one's workplace, whereas a company's monitoring of employee e-mail usage is a strategy. See *Strategy*.

Taste In cultural theory, taste refers to the shared artistic and cultural values of a particular social community or individual. However, even when it seems most individually specific, taste is informed by experiences relating to one's class, cultural background, education, and other aspects of identity. Notions of good taste usually refer to middle-class or upper-class notions of what is tasteful, and bad taste is a term often associated with mass or low culture. Taste, in this understanding, is something that can be learned through contact with cultural institutions.

Technological determinism A position that sees technology as the most important determining factor in social change, positing technology as somehow separate from social and cultural influence. In this view of technology, people are merely observers and facilitators of technology's progress. Technological determinism has been largely discredited in favor of the view that technological change and advance is the result of social, economic, and cultural influences and cannot be seen as either autonomous or outside those influences.

Television flow A term used by cultural theorist Raymond Williams to describe the way that television incorporates interruption, such as television commercials and the break between programs, into a seemingly continuous flow so that everything on the TV screen is seen as part of one single entertainment experience. Williams coined this term in the mid-1970s in an earlier era dominated by network television, and he was influenced in his experience by looking at the commercial interruptions in U.S. network television.

Text A term extended by French theorist Roland Barthes to include visual media such as photography, film, television, or painting to suggest that they are constructed on the basis of codes in the same that way that written language is organized to make a coherent, thematically and formally unified work or text. Insofar as they are constructions, texts can be broken down into their component parts through the work of analysis. Barthes in particular distinguished texts from works, such as artworks, to indicate an active relationship between the writer and reader or artist/producer and viewer in the former term. This is because the constructed nature of the text implies that its meaning is produced in a contextual relationship rather than simply residing in the work itself. To treat an artwork as a text means that we read it through codes that we recognize as such rather than passively absorb or stand in awe of the work without noting the means of its construction.

Textual poaching A term used by French theorist Michel de Certeau to describe the ways that viewers can read and interpret cultural texts, such as film or television, to rework those texts in some way. This might involve rethinking the story of a particular film or, in the case of some fan cultures, writing one's own version of it. Textual poaching was referred to by de Certeau as a process analogous to "inhabiting a text like a rented apartment." In other words, viewers of popular culture can "inhabit" that text by renegotiating its meaning or by creating new cultural products in response to it.

Third World A term coined in the post-World War II period and used until the end of the twentieth century, Third World referred to the countries located in Africa,

Asia, and Latin America. It was coined in response to the concept in political theory of the world divided into West (First World) and East (Second World), with two major superpowers, the United States and the Soviet Union. These countries established themselves as a "Third World" rather than taking sides with Eastern or Western superpowers. With the decline of the Cold War, the decline of the autonomous nation-state, and the expansion of new technologies and global media and information systems in many Third World countries, the concept of a Third World lost currency but continues to hold important historical meaning. See *Developing countries, First World.*

Transcoding The practice of taking terms and meanings and appropriating them to create new meanings. For example, in the 1990s the gay and lesbian and Queer Nation Movements reappropriated the term *queer,* which had been used as a derogatory term for homosexuals, to give it a new meaning, both as a positive term for identity and as a theoretical term indicating a position through which the norm is questioned, or "queered." See *Queer.*

Unconscious A central concept in psychoanalytic theory that indicates the phenomena that are not within consciousness at any given moment. According to Sigmund Freud, the unconscious is a repository for desires, fantasies, and fears that act on and motivate us though we are not aware of them. Freud's idea of the unconscious was a radical departure from the traditional idea of the subject that could easily know the reasons for his or her actions. Because the unconscious and the conscious sides of a human being do not work in concert, psychoanalytic theory speaks of the human as a divided or split subject. Dreams and so-called Freudian slips of the tongue are evidence of the unconscious. The term subconscious was rejected because it suggests it sits below consciousness, when in fact the two levels are equally active, interconstituive, and not hierarchical. See *Psychoanalytic theory, Repression.*

Use value The practical function originally assigned to a commodity; in other words, what it does. This stands in contrast to its exchange value, which is what is paid for it. Marxist theory critiques the emphasis in capitalism on exchange over use value. For example, a luxury car and a less expensive compact car have the same use value of being means of transportation, but the luxury car has a much higher exchange value. See *Capitalism, Commodity/commodification, Commodity fetishism, Exchange value, Marxist theory.*

Virtual Because electronic technology can simulate realities, the term *virtual* has come to indicate phenomena that exist though in no tangible or physical way. A virtual version of something is capable of functioning in a number ways that simulate the experience of its actual physical or material counterpart. For example, in virtual reality, users wear gear that allows them the sensations of a particular reality, and they can respond as if they were in that physical space. Airline pilots use virtual reality systems to train on the ground as if they were flying through actual space. Virtual images have no referent in the real but can be both analog and digital. The term *virtual space* has been used broadly to refer to those spaces that are electronically constituted, such as space defined by the Internet, the Web, e-mail, or simulated worlds online, but that do not necessarily conform to the laws of physical, material, or Cartesian space. Many aspects of virtual space encourage us to think of these spaces as being similar to the physical spaces that we encounter in the real world (when virtual spaces are referred to as "rooms" for instance); however, virtual space does not obey the rules of physical space. See *Analog, Cartesian space, Digital, Web.*

Virtual reality See *Virtual.*

Visuality The quality or state of being visual. It is believed by some that visuality characterizes our age because so much of our media and everyday space is increasingly dominated by visual images. Some of the theorists who consider visuality emphasize the general condition and place of visuality in a culture or era, and not necessarily specific entities (such as photographs, for example) that are designed to be seen. Visuality can concern how we see everyday objects and people, not just visual texts.

Voyeurism In psychoanalytic terms, the erotic pleasure in watching without being seen. Voyeurism has historically been associated with the masculine spectator. Voyeurism is also used to describe the experience of the cinematic spectators who in the traditional viewing context of the movie theater can view the images on screen while themselves being hidden in darkness. See *Exhibitionism, Psychoanalytic theory, Scopophilia.*

Web Originally known as the World Wide Web, a system of interlinked hypertext documents accessed through the Internet, in a system introduced to the public in 1989. Developed by Tim Berners-Lee at CERN in Switzerland, the Web is the central communication and information network for a large sector of the populations of developed countries. Web 2.0 refers to the "second-generation" social networking sites on the Web that emerged in the early 2000s. See *Hypertext.*

picture credits

p. 10, Fig. 1.1 — Weegee, *The First Murder*, before 1945. Gelatin silver print. 10 1/8 × 11". The J. Paul Getty Museum, Los Angeles. © International Center for Photography. Photo: Courtesy The J. Paul Getty Museum, Los Angeles.

p. 11, Fig. 1.2 — Photographer unknown, Institute of Contemporary Photography/ Getty Images.

p. 12, Fig. 1.3 — Courtesy Chicago Defender. Used with permission.

p. 13, Fig. 1.4 — Henri-Horace Roland de la Porte, *Still Life*, c. 1765. Oil on canvas, 20 7/8 × 25 1/2". Norton Simon Art Foundation.

p. 14, Fig. 1.5 — Marion Peck, *Still Life with Dralas*, 2003. Oil on canvas, 16 × 20". Courtesy Sloan Fine Art.

p. 14, Fig. 1.6 — René Magritte, *The Treachery of Images (This is Not a Pipe)*, 1928–29. Oil on canvas, 60 × 80 cm. Los Angeles County Museum of Art, purchased with funds provided by the Mr. and Mrs. William Preston Harrison Collection (78.7). Photo © 2007 Museum Associates/Los Angeles County Museum of Art. Painting © C. Herscovici, London/ Artists Rights Society (ARS), New York.

p. 15, Fig. 1.7 — René Magritte, *Les Deux Mysteres (The Two Mysteries)*, 1966. Oil on canvas, 65 × 80 cm. Photo: © Photothèque R. Magritte-ADAGP / Art Resource, New York. Painting © C. Herscovici, London/Artists Rights Society (ARS), New York.

p. 19, Fig. 1.8 — Robert Frank, *Trolley—New Orleans*, 1955. © Robert Frank, from *The Americans*. Photo: Bowdoin College Museum of Art.

p. 22, Fig. 1.9 — Nancy Burson, *First Beauty Composite* and *Second Beauty Composite*, 1982. Courtesy of the artist and ClampArt.

p. 24, Fig. 1.10 — Carte de visite, Brady National Photographic Art Gallery, Washington, D.C. Black and white negative (LC-MSS-44297-33-179). James Wadsworth Family Papers, Library of Congress Manuscript Division, Washington, D.C. Image courtesy Library of Congress.

p. 25, Fig. 1.11 — © 1994, *Newsweek*, Inc., all rights reserved, reprinted by permission.

p. 28, Fig. 1.13 — Yue Minjun, *BUTTERFLY*, 39 ½ × 31 ¾ ". Courtesy of the artist and Max Protetch Gallery, New York.

p. 30, Fig. 1.14 — Courtesy of California Department of Health. Campaign by Asher & Partners, Los Angeles, 1997.

p. 31, Fig. 1.15 "The Veil" from *Persepolis: The Story of a Childhood* by Marjane Satrapi, translated by Mattias Ripa and Blake Ferris, translation © 2003 by L'Association, Paris. Used by permission of Pantheon Books, a division of Random House, Inc.

p. 33, Fig. 1.17 Vincent van Gogh, *Irises*, 1889. Oil on canvas, 28 × 36 5/8". Courtesy of The J. Paul Getty Museum, Los Angeles.

p. 37, Fig. 1.20 Photo: Jeff Widener/AP Photo.

p. 37, Fig. 1.21 Photo: Reagan Louie.

p. 38, Fig. 1.22 Raphael, *The Small Cowper Madonna*, c. 1505, oil on panel, 23 3/8 × 17 3/8", Widener Collection 1942.9.57. (653), Image courtesy of the Board of Trustees, National Gallery of Art, Washington.

p. 39, Fig. 1.23 Joos van Cleve, *Virgin and Child*, c. 1525. Oil on wood, 27 3/4 × 20 3/4". The Metropolitan Museum of Art, The Jack and Belle Linsky Collection (1982.60.47). Image © The Metropolitan Museum of Art.

p. 40, Fig. 1.24 Dorothea Lange, *Migrant Mother, Nipomo, California*, 1936. Gelatin silver print, 12½× 97/8". Library of Congress FSA/OWI Collection.

p. 41, Fig. 1.25 Andy Warhol, *Marilyn Diptych*, 1962. Synthetic polymer paint and silkscreen ink on canvas, 6'10" × 5'7". © 2008, Andy Warhol Foundation for the Visual Arts/Artists Rights Society, NewYork. Photo: Tate Gallery, London/Art Resource, NewYork.

p. 43, Fig. 1.27 Photo: Gill Allen/AP Photo.

p. 44, Fig. 1.28 Isabel Samaras, *Behold My Heart*, 2003. Oil on wood, 16 × 12". Courtesy of the artist.

p. 45, Fig. 1.29 Daniel Edwards, *Monument to Pro-Life: The Birth of Sean Preston*, 2006. Courtesy of the artist and Capla Kesting Fine Art.

p. 58, Fig.2.3 Photo: Andy Piatt/iStockphoto.

p. 59, Fig. 2.4 Komar and Melamid, *Italy's Most Wanted Painting* and *Italy's Most Unwanted Painting* (from *People's Choice* series), 1997. Courtesy of the artists and Ronald Feldman Fine Arts.

p. 61, Fig. 2.5 Obey Giant Logo, Courtesy of Shepard Fairey, obeygiant.com.

p. 63, Fig. 2.6 David Teniers the Younger, *Archduke Leopold Wilhelm in his Picture Gallery in Brussels*, c. 1650–51. Oil on copper. 106 × 129 cm. Museo del Prado, Madrid.

p. 64, Fig. 2.7 Reprinted by permission of the publisher from *The Predicament of Culture: Twentieth-Century Ethnography, Literature, and Art* by James Clifford, p. 224, Cambridge, Mass.: Harvard University Press, Copyright © 1988 by the President and Fellows of Harvard College.

p. 65, Fig. 2.8 Thomas Struth, *Hermitage I, St. Petersburg*, 2005. Courtesy of the artist and Marian Goodman Gallery.

p. 67, Fig. 2.9 Fred Wilson, *Mining the Museum: An Installation by Fred Wilson*, 1992—1993, The Maryland Historical Society and The Contemporary, Baltimore. © Fred Wilson, courtesy PaceWildenstein, New York.

p. 68, Fig. 2.10 Fred Wilson, *Guarded View*, 1991. Wood, paint, steel, and fabric, Dimensions variable. © Fred Wilson, courtesy PaceWildenstein, New York.

p. 71, Fig. 2.11 Barbara Kruger, *Untitled (Your manias become science)*, 1981. 37 × 50". Courtesy of Mary Boone Gallery, New York.

p. 73, Fig. 2.12 Photo: Tracey Nearmy/AAP Photo.

p. 77, Fig. 2.13 Photo: Eugene Robert Richee/John Kobal Foundation/Getty Images.

p. 79, Fig. 2.14 From *City Indians: Photographs of Western Tribal Fashion*, by Chris Wromblewski, Martin Knox and Nelly Gommez-Vaez, Frankfurt: Eichborn Verlag, 1983. AP Photo.

p. 80, Fig. 2.15 © Ted Soqui/Corbis.

p. 81, Fig. 2.16 Chiho Aoshima, *The Rebirth of a Snake-Woman*, 2001. Inkjet print on paper, 1000 × 1420 mm. Courtesy Blum & Poe, Los Angeles / Galerie Emmanuel Perrotin, Paris and Miami. © 2001 Chiho Aoshima / Kaikai Kiki Co., Ltd. All rights reserved.

p. 83, Fig. 2.17 Gordon Parks, *Ella Watson*, 1942. Courtesy of Library of Congress Prints and Photographs Division, Farm Security Administration, Office of War Information Photograph Collection (digital ID: ppmsc 00237).

p. 84, Fig. 2.18 Gran Fury, *Read My Lips (girls)*, 1988. Poster, offset lithography, 16½ × 10 1/8".

p. 85, Fig. 2.19 Poster by Copper Greene, 2004.

p. 97, Fig. 3.1 Photo: Harold Lloyd Trust/Getty Images.

p. 98, Fig. 3.2 Photo: Mansell/Time & Life Pictures/Getty Images.

p. 99, Fig. 3.3 Vladimir Tatlin next to *Monument to the Third International*, 1919. Courtesy David King Collection.

p. 104, Fig. 3.5 Diego Velázquez, *Las Meninas (The Maids of Honor)*, 1656. Museo del Prado, Madrid.

p. 107, Fig. 3.6 From *The Works of Jeremy Bentham*, Vol. IV, John Bowring edition of 1838–43, reprinted by Russell and Russell, Inc., New York, 1962.

p. 108, Fig. 3.7 Photo: Akira Suemori/AP Photo.

p. 109, Fig. 3.8 AP Photo/Metropolitan Police, HO.

p. 110, Fig. 3.9 © Bettman/Corbis.

p. 114, Fig. 3.12 Jean-Léon Gérôme, *The Bath*, ca. 1880–1885. Oil on canvas. 29 × 23 1/2". Fine Arts Museums of San Francisco, Museum purchase, Mildred Anna Williams Collection.

p. 115, Fig. 3.14 Jean-Auguste-Dominique Ingres, *La Grande Odalisque*, 1814. Oil on canvas, 91 × 1.62 cm, Louvre, Paris.

p. 117, Fig. 3.15 From Malek Alloula, *The Colonial Harem*, trans. Myrna Golzich and Wald Golzich, Minneapolis: University of Minnesota Press, 1986.

p. 119, Fig. 3.16 Guerrilla Girls, "Do women have to be naked to get into the Met. Museum?" © Guerrilla Girls, Inc. Courtesy the artists: www.guerrillagirls.com.

p. 123, Fig. 3.17 Lorenzo Lotto, *Venus and Cupid*, early 1500s, Oil on canvas, 36 3/8 × 43 7/8". The Metropolitan Museum of Art, Purchase, Mrs. Charles Wrightsman, Gift in honor of Marietta Tree, 1986 (1986.138). Image © The Metropolitan Museum of Art.

p. 124, Fig. 3.18 Titian, *Venus With a Mirror*, c. 1555. Andrew W. Mellon Collection, National Gallery of Art, Washington. Oil on canvas. 49 × 41 1/2" Image courtesy of the Board of Trustees, National Gallery of Art, Washington, D.C.

p. 127, Fig. 3.21 Sylvia Sleigh, *Philip Golub Reclining*, 1971. Courtesy of the artist.

p. 128, Fig. 3.22 Robert Mapplethorpe, *Arnold Schwarzenegger*, 1976, © The Robert Mapplethorpe Foundation. Courtesy Art + Commerce.

p. 129, Fig. 3.23 Ana Mendieta, *Silueta Works in Mexico*, 1973. 20 × 16". © The Estate of Ana Mendieta Collection. Courtesy Galerie Lelong.

p. 133, Fig. 3.25 Catherine Opie, *Self-Portrait/Cutting*, 1993. Chromogenic print, 40 × 30", edition of 8. Courtesy of Regen Projects, Los Angeles

p. 144, Fig. 4.1 Julia Margaret Cameron, *Pomona, Portrait of Alice Liddell*, 1872. Courtesy of the Royal Photographic Society/National Media Museum/ Science & Society Picture Library.

p. 146, Fig. 4.2 Vladimir and Georgii Stenberg, *Man With a Movie Camera* film poster, 1929, © Estate of Vladimir and Georgii Stenberg/RAO, Moscow/ VAGA, New York. Offset lithograph, 39 ½ × 27 ¼", Museum of Modern Art, Arthur Drexler Fund, Department Purchase. Courtesy of VAGA, New York.

p. 147, Fig. 4.3 Courtesy of Museum of Modern Art Film Stills Archive.

p. 148, Fig. 4.4 Serafima Ryangima, *Higher and Higher*, 1934. Collection Kiev Museum of Russian Art, Kiev, Ukraine.

p. 149, Fig. 4.5 Evgeny Rukhin, *Untitled*, 1972. Oil on canvas. 98 × 99 cm. Collection of Art4.RU Contemporary Art Museum, Moscow.

p. 150, Fig. 4.6 Papyrus from the Book of the Dead of Ani, 70 × 42.2 cm. Courtesy of British Museum, Gift of Sir E.A.T. Wallis Budge.

p. 154, Fig. 4.8 Sandro Botticelli, *The Cestello Annunciation*, 1489–90, tempera on wood panel, 150 × 156 cm. Uffizi Gallery, Florence.

p. 155, Fig. 4.9 Simone Martini, *The Annunciation*, 1333. Tempera and gold leaf on wood, Uffizi Gallery, Florence.

p. 156, Fig. 4.10 From the 1686 French edition of *Tractatus De Homine* (*Treatise of Man*, first published in 1662) by René Descartes. Image: Science Museum Library/Science & Society Picture Library.

p. 158, Fig. 4.11 Andrea Mantegna, *The Lamentation over the Dead Christ*, c. 1480. Tempera on canvas, 68 × 81 cm. Pinacoteca di Brera, Milan.

p. 159, Fig. 4.12 Photographic Collection, Warburg Institute, University of London.

p. 160, Fig. 4.13 Albrecht Dürer, *Adam and Eve*, 1504. Engraving, 9 7/8' × 7 7/8". The Metropolitan Museum of Art, Fletcher Fund, 1919. Image © The Metropolitan Museum of Art, New York.

p. 161, Fig. 4.14 Salvador Dalí, *Slave Market with the Disappearing Bust of Voltaire*, 1940. Oil on canvas, 18 1/4 × 25 3/8", collection of the Salvador Dalí Museum, Inc., St. Petersburg, Florida, 2006. © 2008 Salvador Dalí. Fundación Gala-Salvador Dalí/Artist Rights Society (ARS), New York.

p. 163, Fig. 4.16 Johannes Vermeer, *Lady at the Virginals with a Gentleman (The Music Lesson)*, 1662–1665. 74.6 × 64.1 cm. The Royal Collection, St. James' Palace, London. © 2008, Her Majesty Queen Elizabeth II.

p. 165, Fig. 4.17 Claude Monet, *La Gare Saint-Lazare*, 1877, oil on canvas, Musée d'Orsay, Paris. © domaine public. Photo: Herve Lewandowski/ Réunion des Musées Nationaux/Art Resource, New York.

p. 165, Fig. 4.18 Claude Monet, *Arrival of the Normandy Train, Gare Saint-Lazare*, 1877, oil on canvas, 59.6 cm. × 80.2 cm, Mr. and Mrs. Martin A. Ryerson Collection (1933.1158), The Art Institute of Chicago. Photo © The Art Institute of Chicago.

p. 166, Fig. 4.19 Georges Braque, *Woman with a Guitar*, 1913. Oil on canvas, 130 × 73 cm. Musée National d'Art Moderne, Centre Georges Pompidou, Paris. © 2008 Artist Rights Society (ARS), New York/ADAGP (Société des Auteurs dans les Arts Graphiques et Plastiques), Paris. Photo: Jacques Faujour. CNAC/MNAM/Dist. Réunion des Musées Nationaux / Art Resource, New York.

p. 167, Fig. 4.20 Pablo Picasso, *Les Demoiselles d'Avignon*, 1907. Oil on canvas, 8' × 7'8". © 2008 Estate of Pablo Picasso/Artist Rights Society (ARS), N.Y. Acquired through the Lille P. Bliss Bequest, Museum of Modern Art, New York (333.1939). Digital Image © The Museum of Modern Art/Licensed by SCALA/Art Resource, New York.

p. 168, Fig. 4.21 Photo of Mbuya (sickness) mask, Zaire, 1959, collection RMCA Tervuren, Photo: © R. Asselberghs, RMCA Tervuren.

p. 169, Fig. 4.22 Giorgio de Chirico, *Melancholy and Mystery of a Street*, 1914. Oil on canvas, 88 × 72 cm., private collection. © 2008 Artists Rights Society (ARS), New York / SIAE, Rome.

p. 170, Fig. 4.24 Jackson Pollock, *Number 1, 1948*. Oil and enamel on unprimed canvas, 68" × 8'8". Museum of Modern Art, NY. © 2008 The Pollock-Krasner Foundation/Artists Rights Society (ARS), New York. Digital Image © The Museum of Modern Art/Licensed by SCALA/Art Resource, New York.

p. 171, Fig. 4.25 Yves Klein, *Anthropometry of the Blue Period (ANT 82)*. 1960. Pure pigment and synthetic resin on paper laid down on canvas, 156.5 × 282.5 cm. Musée National d'Art Moderne, Centre Georges Pompidou, Paris, France. © 2008 Artists Rights Society (ARS), New York/ ADAGP, Paris. Photo: Adam Rzepka. CNAC/MNAM/Dist. Réunion des Musées Nationaux/Art Resource, New York.

p. 172, Fig. 4.26 David Hockney, *Pearblossom Hwy., 11–18th April 1986 (Second Version)*, 1986. Photographic Collage, 71 ½ × 107". © David Hockney. The J. Paul Getty Museum, Los Angeles.

p. 173, Fig. 4.27 Mark Tansey, *The Innocent Eye Test*, 1981. Oil on Canvas: 78 × 120". The Metropolitan Museum of Art, Partial and Promised Gift of Jan Cowles and Charles Cowles in honor of William S. Lieberman (1988.183). © Mark Tansey. Photo © 1984 The Metropolitan Museum of Art.

p. 174, Fig. 4.28 Sims 2, Freetime, Hobby: Cuisine, 2004, © Electronic Arts Inc. Used with Permission.

p. 176, Fig. 4.29 Jon Haddock, *Wang Weilen - Screenshot Series*, 2000. Chromogenic print from digital file created in photoshop. 22.5 × 30". Courtesy of Jon Haddock and Howard House Contemporary Art.

p. 178, Fig. 4.30 Courtesy of Richard A. Robb, Ph.D., Biomedical Imaging Resource, Mayo Clinic, Rochester, Minnesota.

p. 185, Fig. 5.1 Jacques Henri Lartigue, *Grand Prix of the Automobile Club of France*, 1912. © Ministère de la Culture – France/Association des Amis de Jacques Henri Lartigue.

p. 186, Fig. 5.2 *Woman, Kicking*, Plate 367 from *Animal Locomotion* (1887) by Eadweard Muybridge, collotype, 7 ½ × 20 1/4". © Museum of Modern Art, New York, gift of the Philadelphia Commercial Museum.

p. 187, Fig. 5.3 Zoetrope, 9 1/4" diameter. Collection George Eastman House.

p. 188, Fig. 5.4 E. Linde, *Leisure Time (Für Die Mussestunden)*, ca. 1870s. Albumen print, Gift of 3M Company: ex-collection Louis Walton Sipley. Collection George Eastman House.

p. 192, Fig. 5.5 Friedrich von Martens, *La Seine, la rive gauche et l'ile de la Cite (The Seine, The Left Bank and L'Île de la Cité)* ca. 1845, 10.6 × 37.6 cm. George Eastman House. Gift of Eastman Kodak Company: ex-collection Gabriel Cromer.

p. 198, Fig. 5.7 Marcel Duchamp, *L.H.O.O.Q.*, 1930. © 2008 Artists Rights Society (ARS), New York/ADAGP, Paris/Succession Marcel Duchamp. Photo: Cameraphoto Arte, Venice / Art Resource, New York.

p. 198, Fig. 5.8 Eric Harshbarger, *Mona Lego*, 2000. 6 × 8'. Courtesy of the artist.

p. 200, Fig. 5.9 John Heartfield, *Adolf as Superman: "He Swallows Gold and Spits Out Tin-Plate,"* 1932. © 2008 Artists Rights Society (ARS), New York/VG Bild-Kunst, Bonn.

p. 201, Fig. 5.10 Alfredo Rostgaard, OSPAAAL (Organization of Solidarity with the Peoples of Africa, Asia, and Latin America), *Portrait of Che*, 1969, 66 × 39.5 cm.

p. 201, Fig. 5.11 Rafael López Castro and Gabriela Rodríguez (Mexico), *Por la ruta del Che (On the Path of Che), March for Latin American Student Solidarity 29 June—26 July 1998*, SUM-Mexico, OCLAE, CEU, 85 × 55 cm.

p. 202, Fig. 5.12 Courtesy of David Kunzle and the Center for the Study of Political Graphics, Los Angeles.

p. 203, Fig. 5.15 Photo: Cristobal Herrera/AP Photo

p. 203, Fig. 5.16 *Silence = Death*, 1986, by Silence = Death Project, poster, offset lithography: 29 × 24". Courtesy of ACT UP.

p. 207, Fig. 5.17 © Fred Prouser/SIPA

p. 209, Fig. 5.18 Michael Mandiberg, Image and certificate of authenticity from AfterWalkerEvans.com and AfterSherrieLevine.com, 2001. Courtesy of the artist, AfterWalkerEvans.com.

p. 210, Fig. 5.19 Art Rogers, *Puppies*, 1980. Courtesy of Art Rogers.

p. 215, Fig. 5.21 H. P. Robinson, *Fading Away*, 1858, Albumen print, combination print from five negatives, 24.4 × 39.3 cm., Gift of Alden Scott Boyer, George Eastman House. Photo: George Eastman House.

p. 216, Fig. 5.22 Deborah Bright, *Untitled*, from *Dream Girls* series (1989–1990). Courtesy of the artist.

p. 218, Fig. 5.23 AP Photo/Bush-Cheney 2004.

p. 220, Fig. 5.24 Chuck Close, *Roy II*, 1994, Oil on canvas, 102 × 84". Hirshhorn Museum and Sculpture Garden, Smithsonian Institution, Smithsonian Collections Acquisition Program and the Joseph H. Hirshhorn Purchase Fund, 1995. Photograph by Lee Stalsworth. © Chuck Close, courtesy PaceWildenstein, New York.

p. 225, Fig. 6.1 London Express/Hulton Archive/Getty Images.

p. 227, Fig. 6.2 Robert Rauschenberg, *Retroactive I*, 1964, © Robert Rauschenberg/Licensed by VAGA, New York.

p. 228, Fig. 6.3 Courtesy of Shepard Fairey, obeygiant.com.

p. 229, Fig. 6.4 Ant Farm (Chip Lord, Doug Michels, Curtis Schreier)/T.R.Uthco (Diane Andrews Hall, Doug Hall, Jody Procter), *The Eternal Frame*, 1975. Photo: Diane Andrews Hall. Courtesy of the artists.

p. 231, Fig. 6.5 Courtesy Comedy Central.

p. 240, Fig. 6.7 Poster for exhibition "The Situationist International: 1957–1972," Institute of Contemporary Art Boston, October 1989-January 1990. Courtesy of ICA Boston.

p. 243, Fig. 6.8 Courtesy of Paper Tiger Television (PPTV)

p. 245, Fig. 6.9 Courtesy of Michael Shamberg.

p. 245, Fig. 6.10 Courtesy Electronic Arts Intermix (EAI), New York.

p. 248, Fig. 6.11 Photo © Roger Viollet/Getty Images.

p. 251, Fig. 6.12 Photo © George Rodger/Time Life Pictures/Getty Images.

p. 253, Fig. 6.13 Photo © Spencer Platt/Getty Images.

p. 254, Fig. 6.14 Photo © Ron Haviv/VII/AP Photos.

p. 256, Fig. 6.15 Photo reproduced from www.nsarchive.org with the permission of the National Security Archive.

p. 258, Fig. 6.16 Photo © AP Photo.

p. 259, Fig. 6.17 Photo © AP Photo.

p. 270, Fig. 7.4 Photo by Gustave Eugene Chauffourier © Allinari Archives/Corbis.

p. 273, Fig. 7.6 Photograph by Margaret Bourke-White © Time & Life Pictures/Getty Images.

p. 274, Fig. 7.7 © Robert Landau/Corbis.

p. 281, Fig. 7.12 © The New Yorker Collection, 1999, Roz Chast, from cartoonbank.com. All rights reserved.

p. 283, Fig. 7.15 © 1997 G. B. Trudeau. Reprinted with permission of Universal Press Syndicate. All rights reserved.

p. 283, Fig. 7.16 Photo © Liza McCorkle/iStockphoto.

p. 287, Fig. 7.18 *Lucky Strike*, Stuart Davis, 1921, Oil on canvas, 33 1/4 × 18". Gift of the American Tobacco Company, Inc. © Stuart Davis, licensed by VAGA, New York. Digital image © The Museum of Modern Art/ Licensed by SCALA/Art Resource, New York.

p. 288, Fig. 7.19 Andy Warhol, *Two Hundred Campbell's Soup Cans*, 1962. Synthetic polymer paint and silkscreen ink on canvas, 6' × 8'4". © 2008 The Andy Warhol Foundation for the Visual Arts/Artists Rights Society (ARS), New York. Trademarks registered by Campbell Soup Company. All rights reserved. Image: Art Resource, New York, The Andy Warhol Museum, Pittsburgh, Pennsylvania.

p. 288, Fig. 7.20 Roy Lichtenstein, *The Refrigerator*, 1962. © Estate of Roy Lichtenstein.

p. 292, Fig. 7.24 Hank Willis Thomas, *Branded Head*, 2003. Lambda photograph, 40 × 30". Courtesy of Jack Shainman Gallery.

p. 293, Fig. 7.25 Hank Willis Thomas, *Priceless*, 2004. Lambda photograph, 48 × 60" Courtesy of Jack Shainman Gallery.

p. 299, Fig. 7.30 © Paul Sakuma/AP Photo.

p. 300, Fig. 7.31 Hans Haacke, *The Right to Life*, 1979. © Artists Rights Society (ARS) New York/VG Bild-Kunst, Bonn. Photograph © Allen Memorial Art Museum, Oberlin College, R.T. Miller, Jr. Fund.

p. 301, Fig. 7.33 Courtesy of Billboard Liberation Front.

p. 302, Fig. 7.34 Courtesy of Adbusters.

p. 322, Fig. 8.5 Cindy Sherman, *Untitled*, 1978. Courtesy of the artist and Metro Pictures.

p. 325, Fig. 8.6 Nikki S. Lee, *The Hispanic Project* (25), 1998. Digital Fujiflex print. Courtesy Sikkema Jenkins & Co.

p. 327, Fig. 8.7 Orlan, *7th Operation*, 1993. © 2008 Artists Rights Society (ARS), New York/ADAGP, Paris. Photo: Sichov/SIPA.

p. 329, Fig. 8.8 Sherrie Levine, *After Edward Weston (#2)*, 1980, © S. Levine. Courtesy of the artist and the Paula Cooper Gallery. Black-and-white photograph, 10 × 8". © S. Levine.

p. 331, Fig. 8.10 Jeff Wall, *A Sudden Gust of Wind (after Hokusai)*, 1993. Transparency in lightbox, 229 × 377 cm. Courtesy of the artist and Marian Goodman Gallery

p. 332, Fig. 8.11 Katsushika Hokusai, *A High Wind on Yeijiri*, from *Thirty-six views of the Fuji*, c. 1831–33. Print, 26 × 37 cm.

p. 333, Fig. 8.12 Christian Boltanski, *Reserves: The Purim Holiday*, 1989. Black-and-white photographs, metal lamps, wire, second-hand clothing. Courtesy the artist and Marian Goodman Gallery.

p. 338, Fig. 8.13 Courtesy of Lag4Peace.

p. 339, Fig. 8.14 © Ethan Miller, Getty Images News.

p. 341, Fig. 8.15 Photo © David Shankbone.

p. 342, Fig. 8.16 Photo © Jean-Pierre Muller, AFP/Getty Images.

p. 343, Fig. 8.17 Courtesy Teddy Cruz.

p. 348, Fig. 9.1 Print by Alan Archibald Campbell Swinton. Photo: Royal Photographic Society/National Media Museum/Science & Society Picture Library.

p. 350, Fig. 9.2 Title woodcut from Dr. Pollich of Mellerstadt, *Anathomia Mundini Emendata*, Leipzig, ca. 1493.

p. 350, Fig. 9.3 Leonardo da Vinci, *Vitruvian Man*, c. 1487. Pen and ink with wash over metalpoint on paper (344 × 245 mm.).

p. 352, Fig. 9.5 Rembrandt van Rijn, *The Anatomy Lesson of Dr. Nicolaes Tulp*, 1632. Oil on canvas, 216.5 × 169.5 cm. Mauritshuis, The Hague.

p. 353, Fig. 9.6 Thomas Eakins, *Portrait of Dr. Samuel D. Gross (The Gross Clinic)*, 1875. Oil on canvas. 8' × 6'6". Gift of the Alumni Association to Jefferson Medical College in 1878 and purchased by the Pennsylvania Academy of the Fine Arts and the Philadelphia Museum of Art in 2007.

p. 359, Fig. 9.8 Color engraving by British artist John Emslie, *Principal Varieties of Mankind*, 1850. Photo: Royal Photographic Society/National Media Museum/Science & Society Picture Library.

p. 360, Fig. 9.9 From Sir Francis Galton, *Inquiries into Human Faculty and Its Development*, London: Macmillan, 1883.

p. 361, Fig. 9.11 Photo used by permission of Wellcome Library, London.

p. 362, Fig. 9.12 From G.-B. Duchenne de Boulogne, *Mecanisme de la physionomie humaine ou analyse electro-physiologique de l'expression des passions*, Paris: Jules Renouard, 1862.

p. 363, Fig. 9.13 Jean-Martin Charcot, *Oeuvres complètes*, Volume IX, 1886–93. Paris: Bureau du Progrès Mèdical.

p. 363, Fig. 9.14 Albumen print. Courtesy Pitt Rivers Museum, University of Oxford (PRM: 1945.5.97.3).

p. 367, Fig. 9.17 Photo: Lennart Nilsson. Used with permission.

p. 368, Fig. 9.18 Photo: Fritz Goro/Time & Life Pictures/Getty Images.

p. 371, Fig. 9.19 Photo: Lennart Nilsson. Used with permission.

p. 372, Fig. 9.20 Image: Mark Lythgoe and Chloe Hutton/Wellcome Images.

p. 373, Fig. 9.21 Courtesy National Institute of Drug Abuse (NIDA).

p. 376, Fig. 9.24 Photo: Janes Ades, National Human Genome Research Institute.

p. 377, Fig. 9.25 Photo: Darryl Leja, National Human Genome Research Institute (NHGRI).

p. 378, Fig. 9.26 Photo: Ted Thai, Time & Life Pictures/Getty Images.

p. 379, Fig. 9.27 Nancy Burson, *Human Race Machine*, 2000. Courtesy the artist and Creative Time.

p. 384, Fig. 9.32 ACT UP Outreach Committee, *It's Big Business*, 1989, subway advertising poster, offset lithography, 11 × 22". Courtesy of ACT UP.

p. 391, Fig. 10.1 Photo: NASA. www.nasa.gov.

p. 395, Fig. 10.4 Photo: Craig Mayhew and Robert Simmon, NASA Goddard Space Flight Center (GSFC), based on Defense Meteorological Satellite Program. Data courtesy Marc Imhoff of NASA GSFC and Christopher Elvidge of National Oceanic and Atmospheric Administration and National Geophysical Data Center.

p. 395, Fig. 10.5 Image by World Wind/NASA.

p. 399, Fig. 10.6 Betty La Fea, Getty Images Entertainment; Ugly Betty © Michael Desmond/ABC.

p. 410, Fig. 10.10 Photo: Cathy Pinnock/AP Photo.

p. 413, Fig. 10.12 Courtesy Inuit Broadcasting Corporation (IBC).

p. 416, Fig. 10.14 Photo Claudio Cruz/AP Photo.

p. 417, Fig. 10.15 Rafa Rivas/AFP/Getty Images.

p. 419, Fig. 10.16 Louvre pyramid structure, designed by I.M. Pei.

p. 424, Fig. 10.17 Natalie Jeremijenko, *Feral Robotic Dogs*, 2002. Courtesy of the artist.

index